Publications of the
Carnegie Endowment for International Peace
Division of International Law
Washington

DIPLOMATIC CORRESPONDENCE OF THE UNITED STATES

UNITED STATES

INTER-AMERICAN AFFAIRS

1831–1860

DIPLOMATIC CORRESPONDENCE OF THE UNITED STATES

INTER-AMERICAN AFFAIRS

1831–1860

SELECTED AND ARRANGED BY

WILLIAM R. MANNING, Ph.D.

Division of Latin American Affairs
Department of State

Editor of DIPLOMATIC CORRESPONDENCE OF THE UNITED
STATES CONCERNING THE INDEPENDENCE OF
THE LATIN AMERICAN NATIONS,
to which this is
a sequel

VOLUME VI
DOMINICAN REPUBLIC
ECUADOR
FRANCE

DOCUMENTS 2191–2671

WASHINGTON
CARNEGIE ENDOWMENT FOR INTERNATIONAL PEACE
700 JACKSON PLACE, N. W.
1935

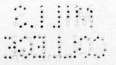

PRINTED IN THE UNITED STATES OF AMERICA
AT THE RUMFORD PRESS, CONCORD, N. H.

PREFACE

The Government of the United States, before the close of the period to which this publication is devoted, had not formally recognized the independence of the Dominican Republic, to whose correspondence parts one and two of this volume are devoted. A Dominican agent, sent to Washington for the purpose toward the end of 1844, announced that early in the same year his country had, by force of arms, won its independence from Haiti. He presented a formal application for recognition; and thereafter special agents were sent from time to time by the Secretary of State to investigate and report upon conditions in that country and on the fitness of its government to be recognized. Correspondence with these special agents and, in the interims between their visits, with the commercial agents of the United States at Santo Domingo, constitutes the bulk of the pertinent documents. Some of the same special agents also visited and reported upon Haiti; and since none were sent to Haiti, except in connection with the conflict between the two countries, and since, furthermore, the Government of Haiti was not recognized by the United States during this period, no separate part of the present publication is devoted to Haiti. Probably the most interesting documents in the Dominican portion of this volume relate to the use of the joint good offices of the United States, Great Britain, and France, in an effort to induce Haiti to cease its war against the Dominican Republic. The possibility that the United States or some European country would obtain a naval base in the Bay of Samaná looms large in the correspondence, as does also French and Spanish influence over the Dominican Government.

Parts three and four of the volume are devoted to Ecuador. No regular legation of the United States was established in that country until 1848, after which one was maintained there continuously through the period covered by this publication; but a chargé d'affaires accredited by the Government at Washington to the Peru-Bolivian Confederation was empowered in 1838 to stop en route and negotiate with the Government of Ecuador, which he did; and a special agent was sent in 1845 to negotiate concerning Ecuador's assumption of her share of the claims of the former ("Greater") Colombia. Ecuador had no regular diplomatic representative in the United States until 1853; and the one then appointed remained for less than a year. Communications concerning various apprehended or actual attempts of former President Flores to recover possession of Ecuador by force, and concerning the free navigation of the Ecuadoran branches of the Amazon River, occupy a considerable portion of the space devoted to this country.

The fifth and sixth parts of the volume are composed of documents which show the interest taken by France in the affairs of the Latin American na-

tions.   As indicated in the general preface in the first volume of this publication, these documents, as well as those containing correspondence with certain other European countries, have an important bearing on matters chiefly
dealt with in the volumes, or parts of volumes, containing the correspondence
with the various American countries.   For example, some of these French
documents are essential to a full understanding of the joint mediation of
Great Britain, France, and the United States, to induce Haiti to refrain from
attacking the Dominican Republic, a subject chiefly dealt with in the first
and second parts of this volume; and the French-British blockade of Argentine ports, chiefly dealt with in the first volume of the publication, is materially further illuminated by the French correspondence.   There will also
be found among these documents, usually as footnote material, several communications from Latin American diplomatic representatives at the French
court to United States representatives there, which reveal an inclination on
their part to look to the Government of the United States for aid against
European intervention in the affairs of their governments.   French interests
are revealed by these documents in Texan, Mexican, Central American, and
Cuban affairs.   Relatively few notes from the French legation in Washington have been included, since, in the period covered by this publication, they
dealt chiefly with claims of French citizens against the Government of the
United States.

WILLIAM R. MANNING

April, 1932.

CONTENTS

VOLUME VI

LIST OF DOCUMENTS IN VOLUME VI

Part I.—Communications to the Dominican Republic

PART II.—COMMUNICATIONS FROM THE DOMINICAN REPUBLIC

PART II.—COMMUNICATIONS FROM THE DOMINICAN REPUBLIC (*Continued*)

PART II.—COMMUNICATIONS FROM THE DOMINICAN REPUBLIC (*Continued*)

PART III.—COMMUNICATIONS TO ECUADOR

Doc. No.	From	To	Date	Page
2319	Edward Livingston, Sec. of State	Juan José Flores, President of Ecuador	June 4, 1832	223
2320	John C. Calhoun, Sec. of State	Delazon Smith, Special Agent of the U. S. to Ecuador	Jan. 7, 1845	223
2321	James Buchanan, Sec. of State	Vanbrugh Livingston, U. S. Chargé d'Affaires at Quito	May 13, 1848	224
2322	William L. Marcy, Sec. of State	Philo White, U. S. Chargé d'Affaires at Quito	Aug. 20, 1853	226
2323	Same	General José Villamil, Ecuadoran Chargé d'Affaires at Washington	Nov. 2, 1853	231
2324	Same	Same	Dec. 5, 1853	231
2325	Same	Same	Jan. 31, 1854	232
2326	Same	Philo White, U. S. Chargé d'Affaires at Quito	Aug. 14, 1854	232
2327	Same	Philo White, U. S. Minister Resident in Ecuador	Oct. 18, 1854	234
2328	Same	Same	Oct. 31, 1854	234
2329	Same	Same	July 11, 1855	235
2330	Same	Same	July 14, 1856	236
2331	Same	Same	Aug. 29, 1856	236

PART IV.—COMMUNICATIONS FROM ECUADOR

Doc. No.	From	To	Date	Page
2332	James C. Pickett, U. S. Chargé d'Affaires to the Peru-Bolivian Confederation	John Forsyth, Sec. of State	Jan. 30, 1839	239
2333	Same	Same	Feb. 27, 1839	240
2334	Luis de Saá, Minister of Foreign Affairs of Ecuador	James C. Pickett, U. S. Chargé d'Affaires to the Peru-Bolivian Confederation	March 8, 1839	240
2335	James C. Pickett, U. S. Chargé d'Affaires to the Peru-Bolivian Confederation	Luis de Saá, Minister of Foreign Affairs of Ecuador	March 15, 1839	241

PART IV.—COMMUNICATIONS FROM ECUADOR (*Continued*)

PART IV.—COMMUNICATIONS FROM ECUADOR (*Continued*)

PART IV.—COMMUNICATIONS FROM ECUADOR (*Continued*)

PART IV.—COMMUNICATIONS FROM ECUADOR (*Continued*)

PART V.—COMMUNICATIONS TO FRANCE (*Continued*)

Doc. No.	From	To	Date	Page
2481	Daniel Webster, Sec. of State	Sain de Boislecomte, French Minister to the U. S.	Aug. 24, 1850	457
2482	Same	Same	March 21, 1851	459
2483	John J. Crittenden, Acting Sec. of State	William C. Rives, U. S. Minister to France	Sept. 29, 1851	459
2484	Same	Count de Sartiges, French Minister to the U. S.	Oct. 22, 1851	460
2485	Daniel Webster, Sec. of State	Same	Nov. 18, 1851	464
2486	Same	Same	April 29, 1852	465
2487	Charles M. Conrad, Acting Sec. of State	William C. Rives, U. S. Minister to France	Oct. 14, 1852	466
2488	Edward Everett, Sec. of State	Count de Sartiges, French Minister to the U. S.	Dec. 1, 1852	466
2489	Same	William C. Rives, U. S. Minister to France	Dec. 17, 1852	476
2490	Same	Same	Feb. 23, 1853	478
2491	William L. Marcy, Sec. of State	John Y. Mason, U. S. Minister to France	Dec. 17, 1853	479
2492	Same	Same	Dec. 22, 1853	479
2493	Same	Same	March 17, 1854	479
2494	Same	Same	June 27, 1854	480
2495	Same	Same	Aug. 16, 1854	482
2496	Same	Same	Nov. 14, 1854	482
2497	Same	Same	Feb. 1, 1856	482
2498	Same	Count de Sartiges, French Minister to the U. S.	Feb. 26, 1857	484
2499	Lewis Cass, Sec. of State	John Y. Mason, U. S. Minister to France	May 16, 1857	490
2500	Same	Count de Sartiges, French Minister to France	Sept. 21, 1857	490
2501	Same	John Y. Mason, U. S. Minister to France	Nov. 23, 1857	490
2502	Same	Same	June 9, 1858	491
2503	Same	Same	Nov. 5, 1858	492
2504	Same	Same	Nov. 10, 1858	492
2505	Same	Same	Nov. 26, 1858	493
2506	Same	Count de Sartiges, French Minister to the U. S.	March 15, 1859	494
2507	Same	John Y. Mason, U. S. Minister to France	April 12, 1859	494
2508	Same	Same	April 12, 1859	497
2509	Same	Same	Sept. 19, 1859	498
2510	Same	Charles J. Faulkner, U. S. Minister to France	Aug. 31, 1860	499

PART VI.—COMMUNICATIONS FROM FRANCE

PART VI.—COMMUNICATIONS FROM FRANCE (*Continued*)

PART VI.—COMMUNICATIONS FROM FRANCE (*Continued*)

PART VI.—COMMUNICATIONS FROM FRANCE (*Continued*)

Doc. No.	From	To	Date	Page
2578	Jacob L. Martin, U. S. Chargé d'Affaires *ad interim* at Paris	James Buchanan, Sec. of State	Nov. 16, 1846	573
2579	Same	Same	Nov. 30, 1846	575
2580	Same	François Guizot, Minister of Foreign Affairs of France	Feb. 11, 1847	575
2581	François Guizot, Minister of Foreign Affairs of France	Jacob L. Martin, U. S. Chargé d'Affaires *ad interim* at Paris	Feb. 26, 1847	576
2582	Jacob L. Martin, U. S. Chargé d'Affaires *ad interim* at Paris	James Buchanan, Sec. of State	Feb. 28, 1847	577
2583	Alphonse Pageot, French Minister to the U. S.	Same	April 30, 1847	578
2584	Jacob L. Martin, U. S. Chargé d'Affaires *ad interim* at Paris	Same	May 15, 1847	579
2585	Same	Same	May 31, 1847	580
2586	Same	Same	June 16, 1847	581
2587	Richard Rush, U. S. Minister to France	Same	Dec. 10, 1847	582
2588	Same	Same	Jan. 14, 1848	583
2589	Same	Same	July 20, 1848	583
2590	Same	Same	July 29, 1848	590
2591	Jules Bastide, Minister of Foreign Affairs of France	Richard Rush, U. S. Minister to France	Aug. 28, 1848	592
2592	Richard Rush, U. S. Minister to France	James Buchanan, Sec. of State	Aug. 30, 1848	592
2593	Jules Bastide, Minister of Foreign Affairs of France	Richard Rush, U. S. Minister to France	Sept. 8, 1848	593
2594	Richard Rush, U. S. Minister to France	Jules Bastide, Minister of Foreign Affairs of France	Sept. 12, 1848	593
2595	Same	James Buchanan, Sec. of State	Sept. 14, 1848	594
2596	Drouyn de Lhuys, Minister of Foreign Affairs of France	Richard Rush, U. S. Minister to France	March 1, 1849	594
2597	Richard Rush, U. S. Minister to France	James Buchanan, Sec. of State	March 9, 1849	596
2598	Same	Drouyn de Lhuys, Minister of Foreign Affairs of France	April 21, 1849	598

PART VI.—COMMUNICATIONS FROM FRANCE (*Continued*)

PART VI.—COMMUNICATIONS FROM FRANCE (*Continued*)

Doc. No.	From	To	Date	Page
2616	William C. Rives, U. S. Minister to France	Daniel Webster, Sec. of State	Aug. 9, 1850	617
2617	Sain de Boislecomte, French Minister to the U. S.	Same	Aug. 20, 1850	618
2618	Same	Same	Dec. 21, 1850	619
2619	William C. Rives, U. S. Minister to France	Same	Sept. 10, 1851	619
2620	Same	Same	Sept. 18, 1851	620
2621	Same	Same	Oct. 2, 1851	623
2622	Same	John J. Crittenden, Acting Sec. of State	Oct. 23, 1851	625
2623	Count de Sartiges, French Minister to the U. S.	Same	Oct. 27, 1851	628
2624	William C. Rives, U. S. Minister to France	Daniel Webster, Sec. of State	Nov. 5, 1851	631
2625	Same	Same	Nov. 13, 1851	633
2626	Same	Same	April 3, 1852	634
2627	Count de Sartiges, French Minister to the U. S.	Same	April 22, 1852	636
2628	Same	Same	April 23, 1852	636
2629	Same	Same	April 29, 1852	638
2630	Same	Same	July 8, 1852	639
2631	William C. Rives, U. S. Minister to France	Edward Everett, Sec. of State	Jan. 6, 1853	642
2632	Same	Same	Jan. 13, 1853	643
2633	Same	Same	Jan. 20, 1853	646
2634	Same	Same	Feb. 2, 1853	649
2635	Same	Same	March 31, 1853	650
2636	John Y. Mason, U. S. Minister to France	William L. Marcy, Sec. of State	April 22, 1854	652
2637	Same	Same	July 20, 1854	652
2638	Same	Same	Oct. 5, 1854	658
2639	Same	Same	Oct. 25, 1854	659
2640	Same	Drouyn de Lhuys, Minister of Foreign Affairs of France	Oct. 27, 1854	661
2641	Same	William L. Marcy, Sec. of State	Oct. 30, 1854	662
2642	Drouyn de Lhuys, Minister of Foreign Affairs of France	John Y. Mason, U. S. Minister to France	Nov. 1, 1854	663
2643	John Y. Mason, U. S. Minister to France	William L. Marcy, Sec. of State	Nov. 11, 1854	665

PART VI.—COMMUNICATIONS FROM FRANCE (*Continued*)

Doc. No.	From	To	Date	Page
2644	John Y. Mason, U. S. Minister to France	William L. Marcy, Sec. of State	Feb. 13, 1856	666
2645	Same	Same	Feb. 18, 1856	666
2646	Same	Same	June 8, 1856	667
2647	Same	Same	June 9, 1856	668
2648	Same	Same	June 12, 1856	671
2649	Same	Lewis Cass, Sec. of State	June 8, 1857	673
2650	Same	Same	Dec. 12, 1857	674
2651	Same	Same	Dec. 12, 1857	675
2652	Same	Same	Dec. 24, 1857	678
2653	Same	Same	June 27, 1858	678
2654	Same	Same	July 10, 1858	681
2655	Same	Same	July 30, 1858	685
2656	Same	Same	Oct. 12, 1858	688
2657	Same	Same	Nov. 1, 1858	689
2658	Same	Same	Nov. 8, 1858	691
2659	Same	Same	Nov. 18, 1858	691
2660	Same	Same	Dec. 11, 1858	692
2661	Same	Count Walewski, Minister of Foreign Affairs of France	Dec. 12, 1858	694
2662	Count Walewski, Minister of Foreign Affairs of France	John Y. Mason, U. S. Minister to France	Dec. 12, 1858	695
2663	Minute of a conversation between John Y. Mason, U. S. Minister to France, and Count Walewski, Minister of Foreign Affairs of France		Dec. 16, 1858	695
2664	John Y. Mason, U. S. Minister to France	Lewis Cass, Sec. of State	Dec. 16, 1858	697
2665	Same	Same	Dec. 18, 1858	698
2666	Count de Sartiges, French Minister to the U. S.	Same	March 12, 1859	700
2667	John Y. Mason, U. S. Minister to France	Same	May 16, 1859	701
2668	W. R. Calhoun, U. S. Chargé d'Affaires *ad interim* at Paris	Same	Nov. 7, 1859	704
2669	Same	Same	Feb. 28, 1860	704
2670	Charles J. Faulkner, U. S. Minister to France	Same	May 28, 1860	705
2671	Same	Same	July 30, 1860	706

NOTE

The idiosyncrasies of spelling, punctua-
tion, capitalization and grammar of the
original manuscript stand uncorrected
in this print, except in case of manifest
and inadvertent error, where the correction could in nowise affect the ʾense.

PART I

COMMUNICATIONS TO THE DOMINICAN
REPUBLIC

COMMUNICATIONS TO THE DOMINICAN REPUBLIC

2191

*John C. Calhoun, Secretary of State of the United States, to José María
Caminero, Special Agent of the Dominican Republic to the United States* [1]

WASHINGTON, *February 21, 1845.*

SIR: The letter of the President of the Dominican Republic to the President of the United States [2] of which you were the bearer, with a copy of your credentials and also of the Constitution of your government and your memoir embracing a historical sketch of the events which led to the declaration of independence of the Dominican Republic and the establishment of a separate government have all been laid before the President and have received from him that deliberate consideration which their importance demands.

I am instructed by him to inform you that he has read your memoir with much interest and that he trusts that the people of the Dominican Republic will be able to maintain the independence they have declared and the government they have adopted; but that it has been the usage of this government before it recognizes the independence of one newly established to appoint a Commissioner to proceed to the country and to investigate and report his opinion on all the facts and circumstances on which it is deemed necessary to be informed before a decision is made. In conformity thereto, John Hogan, Esq[r] of New York has been appointed a Commissioner and instructed to proceed to the Dominican Republic and report with as little delay as practicable on all the points on which the government desires information to guide it in its decision in this case. On the receipt of his report a decision will be made which will be communicated to you.

M[r] Hogan has been instructed to take charge of any despatch to your government or communication which you may think proper to place in his custody.

I have the honor [etc.].

2192

*John C. Calhoun, Secretary of State of the United States, to John Hogan,
Special Agent of the United States to the Dominican Republic* [3]

WASHINGTON, *February 22, 1845.*

SIR: That part of the Island of St: Domingo which was formerly under the dominion of Spain; but which was subdued by Boyer in the year 1822,

[1] Special Missions, vol. 1.
[2] Below, this volume, pt. 11, December 5, 1844, doc. 2208. None of the enclosures mentioned are included in this publication.
[3] Special Missions, vol. 1.
John Hogan, of New York, special agent to the Dominican Republic, to whom this was addressed, was instructed on February 22, 1845, to examine into and report upon the re-

has recently shaken off the authority of his successors and established a government for itself under the title of the Dominican Republic. Dr J. M. Caminero has presented himself to our Government as its Envoy, with letters of credence from its supreme authority, and addressed a note to this Department, setting forth the events which led to the formation of the new Government, together with sundry statistical statements in reference to the population, resources and actual condition of the country, with a view to procure the recognition of its independence by the government of the United States. You will herewith receive a copy of these papers, [1] the originals of which have been laid before The President, who has examined their contents with a disposition favorable to the acknowledgement of the Republic.

Before deciding, however, on so important a step, it is deemed advisable to take the course heretofore adopted by the government in similar cases, by sending a Special Agent to examine into and make Report to the government of the power and resources of the Republic, and especially as to its ability to maintain its independence; and you have been selected by the President for the purpose.

The points to which you will more particularly direct your inquiries are:

First. The extent and limits of the territory over which the Dominican Government claims and exercises jurisdiction.

Second. The character and composition of its population; the degree of intelligence amongst the better portions of the people, and whether there is a general spirit of unanimity amongst all classes, and a determination to maintain their independence.

Third. The number, discipline and equipment of the troops, and what irregular or militia force may be brought into the field in an emergency.

Fourth. The aggregate population of the country and the proportions of European, African and mixed races; their mutual dispositions towards the existing authorities, and the names and characters of the principal persons in the Executive, judicial and legislative departments of the Government.

Fifth. The financial system and resources of the Republic, together with its foreign, coastwise and internal trade, and its connections, if any, with foreign Powers. In a word, your attention will be directed to all the points touched on in Mr. Caminero's memoir, and to such other subjects as may be connected with the main object of your mission.

You will be expected to communicate from time to time the progress of your inquiries and to return as speedily as possible to the United States,

---

sources of the country, and especially as to its ability to maintain its independence, as appears more fully in this document.

[1] See Caminero to the Secretary of State under dates of January 8 and January 25, 1845, below, this volume, pt. II, docs. 2209 and 2210.

when you will make your final report to this Department. In no event will you remain more than six months from the date of your departure from the United States, unless specially directed by the Department. In the meantime your compensation will be at the rate of eight dollars a day, exclusive of your necessary travelling expenses, of which you will keep a regular account, sustained by proper vouchers, in order that it may be submitted to the proper accounting officer of the Treasury.

I am, Sir, your obedient servant.

2193

John M. Clayton, Secretary of State of the United States, to Benjamin E. Green,
Special Agent of the United States to the Dominican Republic [1]

[EXTRACTS]

Confidential.   WASHINGTON, *June 13, 1849.*

SIR: It has been intimated to this Department by a person likely to be well informed, that the British Government has a Commissioner accredited to the Government of the Dominican Republic, who is charged to obtain by negotiation the cession to Great Britain of the Bay of Samana, that there is a draft of a Treaty by which England pledges herself to recognize the Government of that Republic, provided the cession adverted to be made to her, and that this condition is embodied in a secret article of the Treaty.

This information has been a motive for appointing you a special agent of the United States to the Dominican Republic. You will consequently proceed to the City of St. Domingo by the shortest and most expeditious route. As the success of your mission may in a great degree depend upon secrecy as to your public character, you will not divulge it to any one except in case of necessity. A letter introducing you to the Minister for Foreign Affairs of that Republic is herewith communicated to you. [2] You will request him not to disclose the fact that you are an agent of this Government to any persons who may not be entitled to know it. You will not, however even present my letter, if you can without it obtain the desired information respecting the Bay of Samana, and if, when obtained, you should find the Dominican Government to be unwilling to conclude a Treaty with the United States. As soon as may be convenient after you shall have arrived at the seat of government, you will endeavor to ascertain the truth of the reports relative to the cession of the Bay of Samana, and if you should find that the Dominican Government has gone too far to recede,

---

[1] Special Missions, vol. I.

Benjamin E. Green, of Kentucky, prior to his service as special agent to the Dominican Republic, was commissioned as secretary of legation to Mexico on May 24, 1843. He acted as chargé d'affaires *ad interim* from March 9 to September 1, 1844.

[2] Not included in this publication.

you will then communicate to the Department the terms of the cession and the purposes of Great Britain in acquiring it, so far as they may be within your reach. If the cession should not have been completed, you will endeavor to defeat it by strenuous yet respectful representations to the Minister for Foreign Affairs, the President, or other persons in high office in that Republic. If the Dominican Government is not unwary and unnecessarily eager, Great Britain will unconditionally acknowledge its independence. The leading object of the Foreign policy of that government being to provide new markets for British manufactures, if the Dominican government shall discreetly exercise its right of imposing restrictions or discriminations on the admission of those manufactures into the ports of that Republic, until its independence shall be recognized by the British government, that recognition will be sure speedily to follow. This would obviate the necessity of any such sacrifice as would result from the cession of the Bay of Samana and the country adjacent thereto. A grant of sovereign rights to Great Britain in that quarter, would be fraught with numberless and incurable ills to the Dominican Republic. To say nothing of the bickerings which could not fail to arise between the British inhabitants and the Dominicans residing in the country contiguous to the British settlement, however restricted in its limits that settlement might be by the Treaty, it would ultimately in practice be enlarged to suit the convenience or the cupidity of the grantee. In this respect the history of the British settlement at Belize, Honduras, affords an apposite and pregnant warning. That region having been discovered by Spain, was always claimed by her in virtue of the right thus acquired. Abounding, however, in mahogany and dye woods which were valuable in the English markets, adventurers from Jamacia, and British subjects from other quarters, at an early period resorted thither for the purpose of cutting those woods. This was connived at by Spain, whose government, however had the sagacity to perceive, that if the practice was not restricted to precise limits and the privilege strictly defined, her rights of sovereignty over that region would ultimately be impaired and endangered. Consequently, she never intended to allow settlements of axemen, tolerated for the purpose of carrying on their peculiar business, to afford a pretext for planting there a British Colony.

The result has shown the wisdom of her forecast. The lines within which by her Treaties with Great Britain she agreed to permit British subjects to cut woods and gather the natural fruits of the earth, have not been respected; it is understood that other branches of industry are now in successful progress at Belize and that the settlement has to all intents and purposes become a British Colony. If the Dominican Government were to allow Great Britain to obtain a foothold on the shores of the Bay of Samana, it is almost certain that the same consequences would ensue. These and other considerations which will occur to you, may be urged as dissuasives to any rash grant to Great Britain like that in question. You have read the reports of Mr. John Hogan to this Department [1] and of Lieutenant Porter to the navy Department upon the condition and prospects of the Dominican Republic. These contain our latest authentic information upon the subject. The Dominicans however have recently given to the world another signal proof of their ability to maintain their independence, in triumphantly repulsing a Haytien army sent for the purpose of attempting again to subjugate them. If your observations should confirm the statements of Messrs. Hogan and Porter in regard to their competency to discharge the duties of an independent state, the President would now be inclined to give a public acknowledgement of this on the part of this government. Endeavor, therefore, to ascertain whether or not the Spanish race has the ascendency in that government, is likely to maintain it, and whether in point of numbers that race bears as fair a proportion to the others as it does in the other Spanish American States. Direct your attention particularly to the administration of justice in both criminal and civil affairs, and inquire as to whether or not disputes either between our citizens there or between them and foreigners or the Dominican citizens or authorities are and will probably in future be correctly and impartially adjusted by the Courts. When a country is believed to be capable of repelling the attempts of another to conquer it which may claim jurisdiction over it, the capacity and disposition of its government to administer justice is the next thing to be considered in deciding as to the expediency of recognizing its independence.

If your inquiries and reflections upon these points should have a favorable issue, you will then sound the Dominican Minister for Foreign Affairs upon the subject of concluding a treaty with the United States. Should this overture be well received, you will request that a person or persons be authorized to negotiate with you. A full power from the President to act in behalf of the United States is herewith communicated to you.

. . .[2] After it shall have been signed, you will endeavor to ascertain the disposition of that government to grant to us a site on the coast of the Bay of Samana, suitable as a stopping place for the United States steamers and as a place of deposite for coal to be used by them. If this grant should not be refused, you will then ascertain upon what terms it may be obtained.

After, you shall have brought your business with the Dominican Government to a close, you will visit the Capital of the Republic of Hayti. With the territories of this Republic our merchants carry on an extensive and profitable trade, despite the impediments interposed by our omission formally to recognize its government. There is no intention materially to depart from this policy. As the interests of our citizens resorting thither,

[1] See below, this volume, pt. II, under the date of October 4, 1845, doc. 2213.
[2] The omitted portion, one page in length, relates to details concerning the proposed treaty, designed to be chiefly commercial in character. The treaty, of January 20, 1836, with Venezuela, was suggested as a model.

however, require more efficient protection than can be bestowed by the unrecognized commercial agents of the United States in Hayti, it is hoped that some compromise may be effected with that government, by means of which, without incurring any obligation to receive a diplomatic agent or Consul from them, we might obtain the substantial benefits of a full recognition of that government.   The recent case of the Schooner *Samuel Noyes* affords a strong illustration of the necessity for this course.   The master of that Vessel having bought from a government officer and taken on board a few logs of lignum vitæ to be used as fire wood on her return voyage to the United States, the shipment was complained of by the authorities at Gonaives [Gonaïves], the vessel was seized, adjudged to be confiscated, sold for the benefit of the Republic, and her master condemned to three months imprisonment and to a fine of twelve dollars and costs.   Mr Wilson the Commercial Agent of the United States at Cape Haytien, having attempted to enter into a correspondence upon the subject with the Minister for Foreign Affairs, was informed by him that the United States being without an official representative in Hayti, his request for information could not be granted compatibly with the dignity of the Haytien Government.   You will inquire particularly into this case and communicate the result to the Department.

From the copy of the House Document N° 36, 3d Sess: 27th Congress which is herewith communicated to you, you will perceive that citizens of the United States have other causes of complaint against the Haytian government to a considerable amount, and that abortive attempts have heretofore been made to bring about an adjustment of them.   Most of these claims have been long pending and are of undoubted merit.   The aggrieved parties, however can never hope for redress, without a resort to force, so long as this government may deem it expedient to adhere to the punctilio in regard to recognizing that of Hayti, which has hitherto been paramount in our councils.   It is believed, however, that the Haytien government would be satisfied with a partial recognition and that this might conduce to the adjustment and payment of the claims adverted to.   Without, therefore, in the outset allowing it to be known that you are an agent of this government, you will sound the Haytien authorities upon this subject.   Ask [whether], if the United States were to send an agent duly empowered to negotiate upon the subject of the claims of their citizens against the Haytien government, that government would receive him respectfully and would treat with him?   If you should get a satisfactory answer to this question, you may inform the Minister for Foreign Affairs that you have been appointed and authorized for that purpose as will appear from the power which is herewith communicated to you.   You may then at once propose the conclusion of a Convention for the settlement of the claims.   The best form for this would be for that Government to agree to pay a round sum in five annual instalments, in gold or silver money, to be distributed by this Government amongst the claimants. The Department has not the means of determining the exact amount of the claims, but from the information in our possession it is believed that we could not, in justice to the claimants accept less than three hundred thousand dollars in discharge of them. You may consequently agree to accept this sum if you cannot obtain more, but the instalments must draw interest from the date of the Convention until they are paid.

It is not unlikely, however, that, whatever, might be the course of that government if its finances were prosperous and the general condition of the country thriving, it may, under existing circumstances, be averse to entering into any stipulations for the recognition and payment of the claims of our citizens. If, therefore, you should find this to be the case, you will inquire whether or not if the United States were to commission Consuls to reside in Hayti, the Haytien government would wish for Consuls of that Republic to be received and recognized in this country. If they should insist upon reciprocity upon this point, the expediency of yielding it may then be held up for consideration, but nothing will be agreed to by you until the proposition shall have been submitted to this government and full time allowed to consider it.

The period of your absence from the United States must not exceed nine months.

You will from time to time communicate to the Department information as to your progress in the business with which you are charged, marking your despatches "private" on the envelope. Information of any kind which may tend to enable us to form an opinion in regard to the strength and character of the governments in St. Domingo and of the condition and resources of the country over which they bear sway, would at all times be acceptable. Your compensation will be at the rate of eight dollars a day from your departure from this City to proceed on your mission, of which you will advise me in writing, and you will also be allowed your necessary travelling expenses, of which you will keep a strict account which must be supported by vouchers whenever these can be obtained. The expenses consequent upon your abode in the cities of St. Domingo and Port au Prince or in any other place on your way thither or returning thence, are not to be considered as travel—ling expenses unless you shall there be detained by cases beyond your control. The sum of One thousand Dollars is now advanced to you on account of your expenses. You may also draw on this Department for any further sums which may be necessary and which may be due you at the date of your drafts.

I am, Sir, very respectfully [etc.].

2194

John M. Clayton, Secretary of State of the United States, to Benjamin E. Green,
Special Agent of the United States to the Dominican Republic [1]

WASHINGTON, *February 16, 1850.*

SIR: Your despatches to N° 4 [2] inclusive have been received. The information and suggestions which they contain are valuable. The facts which you mention, however, in regard to the application of the Dominican authorities for the protection of France, which must have been made from a dread of further invasions on the part of the Haytiens, would seem to indicate that the independence of the Republic is not established with such firmness as to warrant us in concluding a treaty with them. It is deemed advisable, therefore, that under existing circumstances you should make no overtures for this purpose. The period limited for the duration of your mission, will have expired by the time this communication reaches you. As soon thereafter as may be convenient, you will take leave of the members of the Executive Government of the Dominican Republic, but will be careful to assure them that we heartily sympathize in their efforts for independence, hope that they may be crowned with success and that a republican government may there be established adequate to the protection and development of the industrial pursuits of the inhabitants and to the repulse of the only foreign invaders whom they have occasion to dread.

The Department has requested the Secretary of the Navy to send a vessel of war to the City of St. Domingo for the purpose of receiving you on board and taking you to Port au Prince. On reaching there, your proceedings with reference to that part of your instructions which relates to Hayti, will be governed by circumstances and cannot in advance be prescribed more in detail. If, however, you should be unsuccessful in regard to the recognitions of Consuls of the United States, and the claims of our citizens against that Government, you will intimate to the Haytien authorities that this government will not view with indifference any further incursions on their part into the territories of the Dominican Republic for warlike or predatory purposes. You will endeavor to bring your correspondence to a speedy close in order that you may embark for the United States in the same vessel of war which will take you to Port au Prince.

I am, Sir, very respectfully [etc.].

[1] Special Missions, vol. I.   [2] Below, this volume, pt. II, January 4, 1850, doc. 2219.

2195

Daniel Webster, Secretary of State of the United States, to Robert M. Walsh, Special Agent of the United States to the Dominican Republic [1]

WASHINGTON, *January 18, 1851.*

SIR: In a Circular note to your predecessor Mr. B. E. Green, of the 22nd. of February last,[2] and to the British and French Consuls at the City of St. Domingo, the Minister for Foreign Affairs of the Dominican Republic solicited the mediation of the Governments of the United States, France and Great Britain, for the purpose of bringing about a peace between the Empire of Haiti and that Republic.

It is presumed that a copy of the Circular was forthwith communicated to their respective governments by the two last named functionaries, for in a note to the Department of the 11th. of May last, Sir Henry L. Bulwer, Her Britannic Majesty's Minister here,[3] stated that he had been instructed to represent that the French Government had expressed its willingness to coöperate with the governments of Great Britain and of the United States for the purpose adverted to and suggested a course to be pursued. Mr. Clayton replied under date the 20th of May,[4] that upon the return of Mr. Green to Washington, his correspondence would be submitted to the Senate with a nomination of a Chargé d'Affaires to the Dominican Republic, and that if the nomination should be confirmed, the President would be prepared to coöperate with the governments of England and France in the manner and for the purpose suggested. The short interval which elapsed between the return of Mr. Green and the decease of President Taylor combined with other circumstances, prevented the nomination referred to, and it has since, upon reconsideration, been deemed expedient to confide the business on the part of this government to a Special Agent. You have accordingly been selected to act in that character. You will herewith receive letters from Sir Henry L. Bulwer and M. Boislecompte,[5] introducing you to the Consuls of Great Britain and France respectively at Port au Prince and the City of St. Domingo. You will also receive a copy of the instructions which, pursuant to orders from his government Sir Henry proposes to address to Mr. Usher the British Consul at Port au Prince,[6] and I am assured by M. Boislecompte that his government will address instructions of a similar tenor to the Consul of France at the same place. The motives and objects of the intervening parties are so clearly and luminously set forth in these instructions that it is unnecessary for me to advert to them. I entirely concur in the views which they express and expect that you will be governed by them. On arriving at

[1] Special Missions, vol. I.
For a biographical sketch of Mr. Walsh, see above, vol. IV, doc. 1012, note I, p. 14.
[2] Below, this volume, pt. II, doc. 2225.
[3] See below, vol. VII, pt. II, doc. 2911.   [4] *Ibid.*, pt. I, doc. 2706.
[5] Not included in this publication. Their purport is adequately explained here.
[6] See below, vol. VII, pt. II, doc. 2938, note thereto.

Port au Prince you will accordingly seek a conference with Messrs. Usher and the Consul of France upon the subject of your mission, and particularly with a view of inducing the Emperor Soulouque to consent to a lengthened truce or a permanent peace with the Dominicans.   As in coöperating for this end, the three governments are actuated by philanthropic views to which they believe any material interests which all or either may have in the question are quite subordinate, you will endeavor, in all your communications, with your colleagues and with either the Dominican or the Haytien governments, to keep your mind free from any prejudice resulting from color or forms of government.   You will not deny justice to the Emperor Soulouque because he and his subjects are of African extraction and his government professes to be monarchical; and you will not be partial in your judgments in favor of the Dominican Government, because its officers are supposed to be for the most part of the Castilian race, and because it claims to be Republican in its form.

The material interests of the three countries, however, are largely involved in the restoration and preservation of peace between the contending parties in St. Domingo.   France is a creditor of the government of the Emperor Soulouque to a large amount.   She cannot hope for a discharge of her debt when the resources of his country, instead of being developed by pacific pursuits and in part, at least, applied to that purpose, are checked in their growth and wasted in a war with a conterminous State.   Great Britain and France are both interested in securing that great additional demand for their productions which must result from the impulse to be expected for industry in Haiti and the Dominican Republic from a termination of the war; and the United States have a similar interest both from the augmentation of their trade with the Island which would then ensue, and from the consideration that their commercial prosperity is intimately connected with that of both France and Great Britain.   When, therefore, you shall have held free and full conferences with your colleagues and shall have ascertained the reciprocal claims of the parties to the war, if the Emperor Soulouque shall insist upon maintaining a belligerent attitude until all his demands shall have been satisfied by the opposite party, you will unite with your colleagues in remonstrating against this course on his part.   If the remonstrance should prove to be unavailing, you will signify to the Emperor that you shall give immediate notice to your government that the President, with the concurrence of Congress, may adopt such measures in coöperation with the governments of England and France as may cause the intervention of the three powers to be respected, and you will lose no time in communicating the result to this Department.   The Emperor should be made properly aware of the dangers which he and his country may encounter, if he should be unfortunately advised to reject reasonable terms of pacification, but you will stop at remonstrance until further orders.

If, however, your joint and concurrent representations should induce the

Emperor Soulouque to make an abatement of his demands, which you and your colleagues may deem reasonable, you will, in concert with them, make this known to the Dominican Government and will recommend their adoption of a peace on that basis. You will, however, give a patient hearing to any objections which that government may advance, and, if you and your colleagues should deem those objections solid, you will communicate them to the Minister for Foreign Affairs of Haiti and will require from him an answer to them. If this answer should not be given within a reasonable time; or if when given it should not prove to be satisfactory, you will then conjointly with your colleagues require the Emperor to conclude a permanent peace with the Dominican government upon the basis which you may jointly prescribe to him, or to consent to a truce with that government of not less than ten years.

You will write to the Department as frequently as opportunities may permit, in order that, if further instructions should be necessary, they may, after consultation with the Ministers of Great Britain and France, be transmitted accordingly.

I am, Sir, very respectfully [etc.].

2196

Daniel Webster, Secretary of State of the United States, to Robert M. Walsh, Special Agent of the United States to the Dominican Republic [1]

Confidential. WASHINGTON, *January 18, 1851.*

SIR: Although in the letter of the Department of this date [2] you are directed to be governed in your proceedings in St. Domingo by the views expressed in the instructions of Sir Henry L. Bulwer to Mr. Usher,[3] yet as the latter may conceive those instructions to warrant him in demanding from the Dominican Republic in behalf of the Emperor Soulouque, concessions which, if yielded, would, it is believed, trench upon the just rights of that Republic, and would therefore render insecure any peace which may be established between the parties, it is deemed advisable to advert to those points, in order that you may endeavor to resist them so far as you can compatibly with the main object of your mission.

It is probable that Soulouque may require an extension of his dominions so as to include a part of the territory formerly belonging to the Spanish quarter of the Island, but now embraced within the territory of the Dominican Republic. This pretension will, it is presumed, be set up on the ground that the population of the French part of the Island is much more numerous than that of the Spanish part, and yet that the number of square miles em-

---

[1] Special Missions, vol. I.   [2] Above, this part, doc. 2195.
[3] See below, vol. VII, pt. II, doc. 2938, note thereto.

braced by the former is considerably less than that embraced by the latter. There might be some weight in this pretension if the difference between the areas of the territories of the parties respectively were greater than that which actually exists; if the boundaries between them were not naturally good; or if the population of Soulouque's dominions were inconveniently crowded or were likely to become so within any appreciable time.   As the reverse of all this, however, is believed to be the truth, you will object to any extension of Soulouque's territory.   If, however, a treaty of peace should be concluded between the parties, the boundary should therein be defined so as in future to leave no cause of dispute between them respecting it.

If, also, the Emperor Soulouque, should require from his adversary any concession of a humiliating character, such as the hoisting of his flag at the City of Domingo, even temporarily, you will oppose it as being incompatible with the actual state of the contending parties, and as being certain to leave a rancorous feeling in the bosoms of the Dominicans, dangerous to the perpetuity of peace.   They have shown much gallantry in expelling the Haitians in 1844 and in repulsing the subsequent attempts to resubjugate them. From the information in possession of the Department, it is believed that they desire peace, not so much through any consciousness of inability to maintain their independence, as from a wish to cultivate the arts of peace and thereby develope the vast and almost virgin resources of their part of the Island.   The mode of warfare adopted by the Haitians, impelled as they have on former occasions been, not by the lust of dominion only, but by their savage antipathy to a different race, is shocking to humanity, denounced by international law, and cannot claim any sympathy from civilized communities.

The Department understands that one of Soulouque's pretexts for bearing arms against the Dominicans is, that unless he can reestablish Haitian authority in their territory, he cannot, without the revenue which would then be collected in their ports, resume the payment of the Haitian debt to France.   There is some cause to apprehend that this pretext has not been without influence in the French councils adverse to the Dominicans.   It is difficult however to understand why it should there have made any impression, especially when it is considered that the Ordinance of Charles X. in 1825, by which the Independence of Haiti is recognized upon the condition of their paying 150,000000 francs to France, expressly confines that recognition to the French part of the Island.

I am, Sir, very respectfully [etc.].

2197

Daniel Webster, Secretary of State of the United States, to Robert M. Walsh,
Special Agent of the United States to the Dominican Republic [1]

WASHINGTON, *January 18, 1851.*

SIR: Mr. B. E. Green was instructed to propose to the Haitian government
an arrangement for the reciprocal recognition of United States Consuls in
Haiti and of Haitian Consuls in the United States.[2]   Any arrangement which
he might make for the purpose, however, was not to bind his own government until made known here for consideration.   Accordingly upon his application, the Commercial Agents of the United States in Haiti were recognized
as Consuls, and the Department has received a letter from the Minister for
Foreign Affairs of Haiti under date the 7th. of June last,[3] announcing the
appointment of Mr. B. C. Clark as Haitian Consul at Boston and requesting
his recognition in that character.   With this request we are not prepared to
comply, but we are willing that he or any other person not of African extraction should be appointed Commercial Agent of Haiti at Boston or any other
United States port where Haitian commerce may be supposed to require
such officers.   This is the class of officers which [the] United States now have
and for many years past have had residing in certain Haitian ports.   They
had experienced inconvenience in discharging their duties from the refusal
of the Haitian authorities to correspond with them in their official character.
This government, however, would have no objection to receive and consider
any communications which the Commercial Agents of Haiti in the United
States might address to it respecting the commercial or navigating interests
of that country, and will therefore expect that the Commercial Agents of the
United States in Haiti will receive similar treatment from that government.

You may inform the Haitian Minister for Foreign Affairs that there is
nothing in this arrangement which ought to offend any just pride in his government.   It is the course ordinarily adopted and assented to by governments who, for reasons of high expediency, may not think proper to commission or receive Consuls to reside at particular ports.   The United States
have a Commercial Agent at St. Thomas, because the Danish Government
declines to recognize a Consul there.

It is to be presumed, however, that, in process of time, and perhaps before
long, if the Haitian government shall abandon its ambitious projects of foreign conquest, shall devote its attention to the improvement of its own people
and shall succeed in that object so as to command the respect of dispassionate
and impartial men, no nation whose interests may dictate the measure, will
hesitate to send Consuls to their ports or to recognize Haitian Consuls in its
own ports.

I am, very respectfully [etc.].

[1] Special Missions, vol. I.
[2] See instruction to Green, above, this part, February 16, 1850, doc. 2194.
[3] Not included in this publication.   The content of the note is indicated here.

2198

William L. Marcy, Secretary of State of the United States, to William L. Cazneau, Special Agent of the United States to the Dominican Republic [1]

WASHINGTON, *November 2, 1853.*

SIR: The President desires to obtain full and accurate information of the present condition of the Dominican republic, particularly in regard to its relations with the Empire of Hayti, and for this purpose has concluded to send a Special Agent to that Republic. You have been selected to perform that duty, and are directed to proceed thither at as early a period as practicable and obtain, as far as you are able to do so, the desired information and report it to this Department.

The Emperor of Hayti, it is understood, still claims the Dominican State to be a part of his dominions. His efforts to reduce it to submission to his rule have for some time been intermitted in consequence of a long truce between the contending parties. A considerable part of the period for which it was to continue is yet unexpired.

It is important to ascertain the relative strength of the two States in order to form a correct judgement of the probable result of renewed hostilities, should they unfortunately be resumed before or at the end of the present armistice. Your attention will be particularly directed to the character of the government of the Dominican Republic, with special reference to its ability to sustain itself as an independent State. Has it the elements of durability? Is it a constitutional government? Has it resources to sustain and an organized force to defend itself against any attacks which the Emperor of Hayti is able to make upon it? Has its independence been recognized by any and what European nations? Have they or any of them established diplomatic relations with it? You will enquire into its foreign trade and the principal countries with which it is now carried on. The policy of the United States is to extend its commercial relations with all countries, and especially those on this side of the Atlantic.

All the West India Islands except Hayti are dependencies of European nations, and our commerce with them is regulated, not by the Islands themselves nor with reference to their own immediate interests, but according to the policy and interests of the countries to which they belong. A free commercial intercourse between the Dominican Republic and the United States, should that State be in the condition favorable to it, is the principal object this government has in view, and the result of your enquiries will aid

---

[1] Special Missions, vol. 3.
William L. Cazneau, to whom this instruction was addressed, was on November 2, 1853 instructed to proceed as special agent of the United States to the Dominican Republic. He returned to the United States the early part of the following year. On June 17, 1854 he was appointed a commissioner to that Republic. This mission was terminated the early part of June 1855. On April 7, 1859, he was again appointed as special agent to the Dominican Republic. The last despatch from him was dated June 28, 1861.

the President in deciding upon the policy of attempting to establish more intimate relations both commercial and political than now exist between the two countries.

It is desired that the information on the various points suggested should be presented in the most authentic shape practicable. Where it can, it should be sustained by documents. It may be necessary to present it or parts of it to Congress.

The duties assigned to you are special and temporary, indeed they are to a considerable extent confidential. The object of your visit should be kept secret, for in this way, it is believed, you will be better able to accomplish it than by making it known. It is not necessary nor is it desirable that it should be known that you visit the Dominican Republic as the agent of the United States. The government has no authority to employ an agent except for specified objects which can be accomplished in a short period.

It is presumed that the information which you are desired to collect can be obtained during a brief residence in the Dominican State. The President desires to be furnished with it by the first of February next, and your employment as Special Agent will not be extended beyond that time. Indeed it is desirable that it should terminate at an earlier period. Your compensation will be —— [1] dollars per day to commence when you enter on the duties after receiving official notice of your selection. You will be allowed your own travelling and personal expenses. Of these expenses you are required to keep an accurate and detailed account; and in order to get them allowed you will, so far as is practicable, present regular vouchers. You are instructed to communicate from time to time with this Department, and keep it advised of your movements and the progress you make in executing the duties herein assigned to you.

I scarcely need intimate to you that while in the employment of the government of the United States, it is expected that you will scrupulously avoid all interference with the political concerns of other countries, and abstain from engaging in any private enterprises in the slightest degree incompatible with the position you occupy as Special Agent of the United States, or their obligations to maintain entire neutrality in regard to all other nations with which they are on friendly terms.

I am, Sir, respectfully [etc.].

2199

William L. Marcy, Secretary of State of the United States, to William L. Cazneau, Commissioner of the United States to the Dominican Republic [2]

WASHINGTON, *June 17, 1854.*

SIR: You are appointed a commissioner to the Dominican Republic with the President's full authority herewith enclosed to make a treaty with that

[1] A blank space appeared in the file copy of this instruction.   [2] Special Missions, vol. 3.

State. You will also, herewith, receive the Draft of such a treaty as the United States propose to enter into with that Republic. There are no new or unusual provisions in it except that which I shall hereafter mention. To the several articles, excepting that which proposes a lease of a Coal Depôt &c it is not apprehended that there will be any objection on the part of the Dominican government. If it should be proposed to vary the form or language and by doing so the negotiation should be facilitated, you may yield to the wishes of that government in this respect, provided none of the essential features of the draft are altered and no new principle introduced. The stipulations in form and diction are such as are inserted in many other treaties, and there can be no object, that I can conceive, in departing from well established precedents.

The strongest inducement for recognizing the Dominican Republic and entering into a Treaty with her, is the acquirement of the advantages which the United States expect to derive from the possession and control of the tract of country on Samana Bay, for the limited purposes mentioned in Article XXVII. Should a more convenient place for the proposed objects than any one to be obtained on that Bay or Harbour be indicated, you will prefer it. The objects which such a possession is to subserve are indicated in that article, and the locality is to be selected with reference to these objects. As a coal depôt is one of the most important of these objects, regard will be had to the facility of conveying that article to it. The practicability and facility of approaching it with large ships must be especially regarded. Should an Engineer accompany you, as is proposed, his opinion as to the place, the quantity of land &c. will guide you in the selection. It is not proposed that the Territory to be leased be large—A mile square would probably afford all the conveniences which the United States seek to obtain.

It is deemed quite important you should obtain along with the grant of possession of the premises all the rights of authority and control over it proposed in the article relating to the subject. An essential curtailment of them would render the acquisition of such a place much less valuable—and without authority to protect persons and property there the possession would not be worth having.

Such a place in the occupancy of the United States, constantly resorted to by our Steamers and other vessels, could not fail to give stability to the Dominican Republic. You will suggest the various considerations—and they are many—which should make that Republic not only willing, but desirous that the United States should hold such a position on the Island for the purposes indicated, as is sought to be obtained by the proposed article.

It is desired that you should use all possible expedition in bringing the negotiation to a close. Should the Treaty be negotiated in the form proposed, you will at once return with it to the United States—if possible previously ratified by the Dominican government—so that it may be submitted to the Senate at its present session. I cannot authorize you to give any assurances to that government that a Treaty—without securing a Coal Depôt with such advantages—or nearly all of them, as are contained in the proposed article on that subject, will be approved by the Senate of the United States. Indeed, I am not authorized to say that the President would submit one without that article to the Senate for their advice.

The reservation of an annual rent is mainly to give a character to the grant. The sum to be inserted in the blank will consequently be small. It ought not to exceed two or three hundred dollars.

Your compensation, while employed in negotiating the proposed Treaty will be eight dollars a day, and your necessary personal travelling expenses which will not, however, include the expenses of your residence at the place of negotiation.   Of all your expenses you will keep an accurate account, supporting the same with vouchers in all cases where they can be obtained.

The President enjoins that the fact and object of your visit to Dominica, as well as the proposed provisions of the Treaty be kept a secret as long as practicable.

I am, Sir, respectfully [etc.].

2200

William L. Marcy, Secretary of State of the United States, to William L. Cazneau, Commissioner of the United States to the Dominican Republic [1]

WASHINGTON, *December 18, 1854.*

SIR: Your despatch of the 22ᵈ November [2] has been received.

It is to be regretted that you have failed to consummate the object of your mission to the Dominican Republic.

The President does not perceive any reason for believing that any satisfactory result will be attained by a prolongation of your visit.

He has directed me therefore to request you to terminate your official duties, and to return to the United States by the earliest conveyance which may present.

I am, Sir, respectfully [etc.].

2201

William L. Marcy, Secretary of State of the United States, to William L. Cazneau, Commissioner of the United States to the Dominican Republic [3]

WASHINGTON, *January 12, 1855.*

SIR: I wrote to you on the 18th. ultimo,[4] directing you to return to the United States, conceiving that no useful object was likely to be accom-

[1] Special Missions, vol. 3.
[2] No despatch of this date was found; but this apparently refers to that of November 23, below, this volume, pt. II, doc. 2269.   [3] Special Missions, vol. 3.   [4] Above, this part, doc. 2200.

plished by your remaining any longer in the Dominican Republic. Since that communication was sent, I have received several despatches from you [1] from which I infer that you do propose to continue some time longer in that country.

This government perceives no sufficient reason for such a course, and I am directed by the President to instruct you to return immediately. Indeed, I hope that my previous letter [2] has been received and that in compliance with the directions therein contained you are already on your way home.

I am, Sir, respectfully [etc.].

2202

William L. Marcy, Secretary of State of the United States, to William L. Cazneau, Commissioner of the United States to the Dominican Republic [3]

WASHINGTON, *February 3, 1855.*

SIR: Mr. Angulo A. Guride arrived here several days since with the despatches you committed to him.[4] They have been laid before the President and the subject to which they relate, fully considered. He sees no good cause for changing the views contained in my instructions of the 12th ultimo.[5] It is not perceived that any useful purpose is likely to be accomplished by your remaining longer in the Dominican Republic. I have only to repeat the instruction heretofore given for you to terminate your mission and return to the United States.

I am, Sir, [etc.].

2203

William L. Marcy, Secretary of State of the United States, to Jonathan Elliot, Special Agent of the United States to the Dominican Republic [6]

WASHINGTON, *October 5, 1855.*

SIR: You are aware that a treaty between the United States and the Dominican Republic was signed at St. Domingo City on the 5th. of October, last. This treaty is understood to have been laid before the Dominican Congress and to have been approved by that Body with amendments. Of

[1] See below, this volume, pt. II, November 23 and December 6, 1854, docs. 2269 and 2273.
[2] That of December 18, 1854, above, this part, doc. 2200.   [3] Special Missions, vol. 3.
[4] Probably the one of December 16, and possibly those of December 23 and December 26, 1854, with their accompanying papers, below, this volume, pt. II, docs. 2276, 2277, and 2278.
[5] Above, this part, doc. 2201.
[6] Special Missions, vol. 3.
In the headings for the despatches from Jonathan Elliot, below, this volume, pt. II, subsequent to the receipt of this instruction he is referred to as a special agent, since the full power sent to him on October 5, 1855, to negotiate a treaty made him more than a mere commercial agent, as he is designated in the headings to all previous communications. He had been commissioned on November 5, 1847, as commercial agent at Santo Domingo and continued to serve also in that capacity until the Dominican Government asked for his removal in September, 1860. For the reason see below, this volume, pt. II, p. 214, note 1. His successor was appointed, November 2, 1860.

these amendments this Department has never received a copy and, therefore, can form no opinion as to whether they would be likely to prove acceptable to the President and Senate of the United States. The Treaty, as
signed by the Plenipotentiaries, is similar to other Treaties between the
United States and foreign powers, and seems to be mutually just and advantageous in its stipulations and clear in its language. It is desired therefore, that, on your return to Santo Domingo, you will obtain and forward to
the Department a copy of the amendments referred to. You will at the
same time state whether from the best information which you may be able
to obtain, it is likely that the amendments will be insisted upon by that
government. If your opinion should be in the affirmative and the amendments should not be acceptable here, it will be necessary to relinquish for the
present, any expectation of concluding a treaty with that Republic. If,
however, you should be of the opinion that the Dominican government
would recede from those amendments and would conclude a new Treaty
substantially the same as that of the 5th of October last, you will make an
overture for the purpose. A power to enable you to carry it into effect
accompanies this letter.

An article, a copy of which you will also herewith receive,[1] was understood
to have been agreed to by the Dominican plenipotentiaries before the Treaty
was signed, but they were ultimately induced to omit it. This article proposed to grant certain privileges to the United States with reference to a
depôt for coal in the Bay of Samana for the use of United States Steamers.
The fact that the mail steamers between New York, Aspinwall, and San
Juan del Norte usually pass the eastern end of St. Domingo, shows how
desirable such an accommodation would be for us. If you could induce that
government to agree to such an article, you would render a material service.
There is reason to apprehend that the Dominicans were deterred from
acceding to our wishes on this subject, in part by unfounded apprehensions
that we purpose to become a territorial proprietor in that quarter, and that,
if allowed any such privileges as those desired, they would ultimately be
converted into right of sovereignty, contrary to the will of the Dominican
government. These apprehensions are quite unfounded. The stipulation
desired speaks for itself and, if granted, would clearly define and restrict the
limits of the privilege, which do not conflict with the rights of sovereignty of
that Republic.

If it should be found that such a place of deposite as is desired cannot be
obtained on the Samana Bay—the most desirable place known here—any
other place convenient for the purposes indicated, might be acceptable, but
we are not aware of any, and therefore could only agree to accept a site at
Samana. Should, however, the Government of the Dominican Republic
absolutely refuse to lease the place indicated and another be offered, this

[1] Not included in this publication.

Government might cause an examination to be made to ascertain its fitness for the purpose, but would not treat for it before that was done.

I am, Sir, very respectfully [etc.].

2204

William L. Marcy, Secretary of State of the United States, to Jonathan Elliot, Special Agent of the United States to the Dominican Republic [1]

WASHINGTON, *October 9, 1855.*

SIR: Although no full statement of the amendments proposed by the Dominican Congress to the Treaty of the 5th. October, last, has been received at this Department, one of them is incidentally mentioned in Mr. Cazneau's correspondence, respecting which it may be advisable to give you an instruction. I refer to the amendment to the third article, which proposed to place Dominicans in this country, of all complexions, on the same footing as citizens of the United States.

Of course, you will not even entertain an amendment of this tenor, for such a stipulation would certainly be contrary to the feelings of a large proportion of our citizens, which the government, in such a proceeding, is bound to respect. It is hoped, however, that you will be able to induce the Dominican government to recede from this amendment. I cannot perceive what practical interest they can have in insisting upon it. If it were to be relinquished, Dominican citizens would derive every substantial advantage from the Treaty. That government must be aware that few of those citizens of African extraction will ever desire or have occasion to resort to that part of this country where the social and political condition of that race is the same as it was in St. Domingo when that Island was a dependency of France.

The States of this Union where that condition is legalized, deem it necessary for their safety, peace and welfare to exclude foreigners of the same race. It is hoped that the Dominican government is enlightened enough to appreciate that necessity.

I am, Sir, very respectfully [etc.].

2205

John Appleton, Assistant Secretary of State of the United States, to Jonathan Elliot, Special Agent of the United States to the Dominican Republic [2]

WASHINGTON, *December 2, 1858.*

SIR: Your despatch N° 10 dated 21st of October last,[3] and the accompanying papers, which you entrusted to the care of Robert A. Parish Jr Esqr were delivered by him at this Department on the 30th ultimo.

[1] Special Missions, vol. 3.   [2] Despatches to Consuls, vol. 27.
[3] Below, this volume, pt. II, doc. 2305.

The information contained therein respecting the effort made by M⟨r⟩ Maxime Raybaud, Ex-Consul General of France at Hayti, to induce the Republic of St Domingo to unite with the Empire of Hayti, has been read with interest, and your recommendation of the present period, as offering a favorable opportunity for negotiating a Treaty with the said Republic, will receive due consideration.

I am, Sir, [etc.].

2206

Lewis Cass, Secretary of State of the United States, to William L. Cazneau, Special Agent of the United States to the Dominican Republic [1]

[EXTRACT]

WASHINGTON, *April 7, 1859.*

SIR: You have been appointed Special Agent of this Government to the Dominican Republic, and you will receive herewith a letter [2] to the Minister for Foreign Affairs of that Government, accrediting you in your official character, and an office copy of the same, together with a special passport.

Immediately on your arrival there, you will make yourself acquainted with the state of the Country and from time to time transmit all such useful information as you may collect to this Department. You are especially desired to report the situation and probable stability of the government, upon the prospects of the trade and productions of the Country, upon the security and protection of foreigners and particularly of American citizens, and whether there is any special subject which demands the interposition of this government. More explicit instructions will be sent to you, should they be rendered necessary on the receipt of your communications. . . .[3]

I am, Sir, your obedient servant.

2207

Lewis Cass, Secretary of State of the United States, to C. G. Kolff, designated Consul General of the Dominican Republic at Washington [4]

WASHINGTON, *December 17, 1859.*

SIR: In answer to your letter of the 14th. instant,[5] I have to inform you, that you are under a misapprehension in supposing that I made you a prom-

---

[1] Special Missions, vol. 3.   [2] Not within the scope of this publication.
[3] The omitted portion stated first, briefly, that it might possibly be found desirable for him to negotiate a commercial treaty with the Dominican Republic, and, if so, instructions regarding it would be subsequently given.   The rest of the instruction related to a claim against that government for losses in the case of the "Charles Hill," whose court proceedings, he was told, had constituted a denial of justice.
[4] Notes to Haiti, Hawaii, Dominican Republic, and Liberia, vol. 1.   [5] Not found.

ise that you should be recognized as "Consul General of the Dominican Republic."   I had no authority to make such a promise, the President alone possessing the power to act in cases of that nature.   Soon after my interview with you at this Department, I laid your application before him, and as he was not prepared to recognize you, no exequatur has yet been issued.

I am, Sir, your obedient servant.

PART II

COMMUNICATIONS FROM THE DOMINICAN REPUBLIC

COMMUNICATIONS FROM THE DOMINICAN REPUBLIC

2208

Pedro Santana, President of the Dominican Republic, to John Tyler, President of the United States [1]

[TRANSLATION]

SANTO DOMINGO, *December 5, 1844.*

MOST EXCELLENT SIR: The peoples of the former Spanish part of Santo Domingo, oppressed with the weight of the outrages and persecutions which they suffered for 22 years under the domination of the Haitians through one of the fatalities to which peoples are subject, on February 27 of this year resolved to claim their imprescriptible rights, and provide for their wellbeing and future happiness; Providence, propitious to their desires, favored them, and they have satisfactorily and completely attained their separation, constituting themselves a free, Sovereign and Independent State, on the basis of a liberal Government worthy of the esteem and consideration of cultured and philanthropic Nations.

Our envoy to Your Excellency, Doctor José Mª Caminero, who is invested with full powers, [2] will have the honor to present our fundamental Law to Your Excellency and to assure the Government over which Your Excellency worthily presides of the sentiments of peace, union and harmony which animate the Dominican Republic towards all Nations, and of its particular sympathy for the States of the Union, whose inhabitants will encounter a welcome reception, security and protection in their relations with the Republic.

We do not doubt that the Government of the United States will concede to this new political society all the consideration to be expected between individuals who govern and hold in view the great interests of their Nation and the welfare of humanity.

I take this occasion [etc.].

2209

José María Caminero, Special Agent of the Dominican Republic to the United States, to John C. Calhoun, Secretary of State of the United States [3]

[TRANSLATION—EXTRACT]

WASHINGTON, *January 8, 1845.*

SIR: In order to comply with the wishes of the Government of the United States for information on various points, connected with the actual condition

[1] Notes from the Dominican Republic, vol. 1.   No receipt date is on the original.
[2] His letter of credence, also dated December 5, 1844, conferring on him full powers as a public envoy, follows this note in the manuscript volume.
[3] Notes from the Dominican Republic, vol. 1.   No receipt date is on the original.

and organisation of the New Dominican Republic, as expressed in the first interview on the 6th inst, I have the honour to submit the following to your Consideration.

The former Spanish portion of the Island of St Domingo, remained under the dominion of Spain, until the beginning of 1822; when from one of those fatalities, to which nations are subject, in consequence of factions formed in times of political changes, and from having natural enemies as their neigh-bours, the country was united *de facto* to the Republic of Hayti, which then occupied the western part of the island formerly belonging to France; and this union, together with the abolition of slavery at the same time, occasioned a general unsettlement of habits, as well as of the principles of social life, to which the Spanish inhabitants had been originally subjected.

After enduring for twenty years, the heavy yoke of Haytian despotism, the white Dominicans, in order to put an end to their sufferings, by another act of a contrary nature, availed themselves of the opportunity offered by the revo-lution which led to the fall of Boyer; and on the night of the 27th of february 1844, they raised the cry of independence, to which all classes responded; and taking possession of the Capital of St Domingo, and of other fortified points in its vicinity, they succeeded on the following day, the 28th, in effecting the surrender, on capitulation, of the General commanding the district, and the Haytian forces, who a few days afterwards embarked for Port au Prince.

The new Dominican flag was then raised, and a provisional Government was formed in the capital, under the name of *Central Junta of Government*, composed of eleven individuals, from the various districts; whose authority was voluntarily recognised by the other cities and places, all rising, animated by the same enthusiasm and patriotism, and taking up arms, to defend the just and noble cause of their beloved country. . . .[1]

This is an exact and true sketch, so far as circumstances allow, of the or-ganisation and state of the New Dominican Republic, which considers itself entitled to take a place in the family of nations, in virtue of the recognition which it solicits, from the magnanimous and Christian Nation of the Con-federated States of the American Union, to which it has addressed itself, in preference as the founder of real liberty in the New World.

Upon the recognition of our country, as an independent State, and the establishment of relations of amity and commerce, the Dominican Republic, will be properly respected; for by this identification of its interests, the vigour of its forces and institutions will be increased, the confidence necessary to attract immigration will be established, and sciences arts and commerce will flourish.   Finally it will be thus soon placed in a condition to advance rapidly and to secure its stability.

---

[1] This omission, extending over about a dozen pages, gives the details of the victory over the Haitians and the organization of the new Dominican Government, and statistics concern-ing it.

The question of its recognition as an independent State, may be resolved affirmatively, and in its favour, the more easily, as it involves no responsibility whatever, like those of the other States which have hitherto presented themselves, for recognition in this hemisphere. For with respect to the Haytian Republic, neither has its political existence been ever recognised by the United States, nor has it nor could it ever, have had, legitimate dominion over the Spanish portion, the shameful occupation of which, was a real usurpation; and with regard to Spain, which held dominion over it, and of which the Dominicans were originally subjects, the indolence and indifference of that Nation, and her active abandonment of us, for twenty years, under the oppressions and vexations of the negroes of Hayti, shew and establish most positively, the right of the Dominicans, to reassume [Sp. *reasumir*] their own sovereignty, and to enjoy it in freedom, and to constitute themselves an independent State; it being unquestionable, that when protection on the part of the Sovereign ceases, with it also ceases the duty of obedience in the subject: and the inhabitants of the Spanish portion, should not be left in a worse condition than the other Republics of the South which have been recognised by Spain.—

I have the honour [etc.].

2210

José María Caminero, Special Agent of the Dominican Republic to the United States, to John C. Calhoun, Secretary of State of the United States [1]

[TRANSLATION]

WASHINGTON, *January 25, 1845.*

SIR: As an addition to my note of the 8th inst.,[2] and in order that the Government may well understand, that the union of the Spanish portion to the Republic of Hayti in 1822, was not a spontaneous and voluntary act, but was forcibly produced by circumstances, I have thought it necessary here more particularly to shew, the manner in which it was effected.

The Spanish portion of the Island of Santo Domingo, remained under the Government of Spain until the 30th of November 1821, on the night of which, the cry of independance was raised in the Capital City Santo Domingo, by Dr Don Jose Nuñez de Caseres, then Lieutenant Governor and Auditor of War, to whom the officers in charge, gave free entrance into the fortress, the arsenal, and the other forts in the vicinity, with the people of his party; and on the following morning, after the Governor and Captain General had been arrested, he published an act of Independance, assuming the title of President of the New State to which was given the name of Spanish Hayti, and hoisting the Colombian flag.

[1] Notes from the Dominican Republic, vol. 1. Received January 27.
[2] Above, this part, doc. 2209.

A few days afterwards, Brigadier General Don Pascual Real, the Governor and Captain General, together with the other head officers and garrison of the deposed Government embarked for Spain Porto Rico and Cuba.

The appellation of Spanish Hayti, coinciding with that of Republic of Hayti, which had been adopted by the negroes, and mulattoes occupying the French portion of the island, was a material error contributing to restrain the enthusiasm and prevent the co-operation of a part of the inhabitants. On the other hand the political change had not been previously communicated to that part of the population of each place, which was required to make up the public opinion and to restrain it from the moment of the declaration of independance; from which omission, it had not been unanimously received by the people, and in a few days a difference of views and opposition manifested itself in two or three places on the north side, which was fomented by some European Spaniards, inimical to American Liberty, hoisting the flag of the Republic of Hayti, at Monte Cristi, and Santiago de los Caballeros, and entering into relations with the chief of that Republic.

The new President Nuñez de Caseres in the month of December, officially communicated the Declaration of Independance to President Boyer, and made overtures to him for a treaty of alliance offensive and defensive, and the appointment of Commissioners to settle the proper stipulations to that effect: but Boyer being informed of the opposition declared by those places on the North side, which had raised the Haytian flag, and which already offered an opportunity for the breaking out of civil war among the Spaniards themselves, instead of acceding to the negotiation and recognising Nuñez as President, replied in January 1822, styling him simply Political Chief of the Spanish portion of the Republic of Hayti, inviting him to hoist the Haytian flag, with threats in case of his refusal, and manifesting all his views and plans for the immediate union of the two countries, and the dangers of an opposite determination.

This unexpected answer, demonstrated to Sr Nuñez, how far his ideas and hopes had been disappointed, and caused the utmost consternation in the public mind; particularly among that great mass of peaceable inhabitants, the heads of families, who took no part in the political change, and who foresaw the great and immediate peril, to which their lives and properties were exposed, as well from the preludes to a civil war, on account of difference of opinion as from the approaching and inevitable invasion by the Haytian negroes; the new Government under Nuñez being entirely without funds and arms necessary to resist it.—

In this deplorable state of things, all the civil and military authorities were convened in Council, at the Capital Santo Domingo, and having taken into consideration the threatening note of President Boyer, and reflected thereon, regarding it, as the only means of saving the people from the horrors of civil war, and from invasion on the part of the Haytian Republic, it was deter-

mined to submit to the unpropitious union, thus forced upon them. The
Haytian flag was accordingly raised and President Boyer made his entrance
into the city of Santo Domingo, on the 12th of February 1822, at the head of
more than ten thousand men: on the following day, he caused his constitution to be proclaimed, which had existed since 1816, for the French part only;
he abolished slavery, and on his departure left Haytian Laws, and institutions, entirely different in character and customs from those of the Spaniards;
for which reason, the two nations could never be united, as shewn by pos-
terior acts, and by the general spirit with which all classes have fought, for
the expulsion of the Haytians for ever, from the Dominican territory.

I avail myself of this opportunity to observe, that the portion of the people
of colour, that is mulattoes and samboes, free by birth are all natives of the
same Spanish Dominican soil, and not of the French part; that these have
always been in contact with the whites, and in the observance of the principles of religion and morality, to which they are accustomed from their in-
fancy, according to the old laws of Spain; and that in the course of the operations to throw off the yoke of the Haytians and in the actions and combats,
they have always taken the same resolution and displayed the same spirit
and interest to repel them. All the Republics of the South contain members
of this class.

I have the honor [etc.].

2211

*José María Caminero, Special Agent of the Dominican Republic to the United
States, to John C. Calhoun, Secretary of State of the United States* [1]

[TRANSLATION]

WASHINGTON, *February 22, 1845.*

SIR: I had the honour to receive your note of the 21st inst.[2] whereby among
other things you inform me of the appointment made by the President of Mr
John Hogan of New York as Commissioner to proceed to the city of St
Domingo with the object of investigating and obtaining information on the
points of which the Government desires to be informed in order to guide it in
its decision with regard to the recognition of the independance of the Dominican Republic; and allow me to avail myself of this opportunity to recommend
to you for the interest of the said Republic that so soon as Mr Hogan shall
have made his report the Government will deign to give its decision and to
make it known to me as you state in your said note; because the least delay
may occasion the greatest injury, on account of the arrest of the progress of
international and domestic affairs, supposing them to remain *in statu quo*
until that time.

[1] Notes from the Dominican Republic, vol. I. Received February 25.
[2] Above, this volume, pt. I, doc. 2191.

Permit me likewise to recommend to you Sir, to submit to the consideration of the Government, that if the Dominican Republic has directed itself in preference to the United States, it is because it desires to contribute to draw more closely, the bonds and interests of all America, and because it knows that in every point of America, the influence and controul of European Nations, should be kept off. This great and important question cannot have escaped your perspicacity; and it appears moreover that the Confederacy of the United States, of America, as the oldest Nation and the most powerful Nation from the force of its institutions, from its extensive means and resources, and even from the order of nature, appears to be called to be the support and safeguard of the West Indies.

Being persuaded that the Commissioner Mr Hogan, will find the accounts of the Dominican Republic given by me to this Government—exact, it is to be hoped that its independance will be promptly recognised; the more, as its firm establishment, must redound to the benefit of the greater security of the islands and possessions in its vicinity, where slavery exists, as it has freed itself from the Haytian Negroes, and has thus diminished the force of the bad example offered by those negroes, and restrained them from usurping the territory of others.

I have the honour [etc.].

2212

John Hogan, Special Agent of the United States to the Dominican Republic, to Tomás Bobadilla, Minister of Foreign Affairs of the Dominican Republic [1]

SANTO DOMINGO, *June 12, 1845.*

SIR: Having a deep desire to ascertain in behalf of the people of the United States, the political and social condition of the people of the Island of St. Domingo, and more particularly of that part of it known as the Dominican Republic, as assisting me to arrive at correct conclusions in the subject of my enquiry, I take the liberty of respectfully soliciting from you a map of the Island of San Domingo, and of asking you carefully to make on the map, the line which formerly divided this Island between France and Spain, and the line which now separates the Dominican from the Haitien Government.

Will the minister be also kind enough to make on the map, the political divisions of the present Dominican Republic; that is to say the boundaries of the Districts, Counties, provinces, parishes or of any other sub divisions, if there are any, into which the Republic may have been apportioned, with the name of each subdivision; also where each fort or military garrison on the frontier of Hayti is situated. Will he please also to designate the *Cities* and *ports* of *entry* within the Republic, together with the mines &^{c}, whether of copper, lead, coal, salt, sulphur &^{c} &^{c}.

[1] Special Agents, vol. 13; enclosure No. 1, with Hogan's report to the Secretary of State, undated, received October 4, 1845.

Will the minister be kind enough to furnish me with copies of any papers in his Department, if consistent with his duty, which will throw any additional light on the previous history of the Republic of St Domingo while under the French and Spanish authorities and while under the Government of Hayti.

Copies of stipulations, or any other documents which may have passed between President Boyer and the French and Spanish authorities, as to indemnities &ᶜ, or for any other purpose.   The nature of the agreement which was made between France on the one part, and the Haitien Government on the other, the amount which Hayti stipulated to pay to France &ᶜ &ᶜ.

Will the Minister likewise inform me at what time the Dominican Government was organized, and what lead to its establishment.   The number of harbors and Ports of entry within the limits of the Republic.   The number of square miles, the number of inhabitants, as near as may be known, which part of the Republic is best adapted for the growth of tobacco, which for Cotton, Coffee, and which for Sugar.   Whether the Republic is possessed of any lands, mines &ᶜ, and if it is, will he please state, to what extent.— Will he also state, what are the products of the different parts of the Republic, which are its navigable rivers, the extent of their navigation, and their adaptation to other purposes.

I would also, respectfully ask to be informed of the amount of the commerce of the Dominican Republic, and what was its amount during the time it was subject to the Haytiens?   Will the commerce of the Republic increase? and if it is your opinion that it will, be pleased to state the reasons for that opinion, and the sources from whence you suppose that increase will be derived?

How is the political power of the Republic distributed?   What are the names of the different Gentlemen, who compose the Executive, Administrative Departments of the Government?   How is the Judiciary organized? What is the principal system of the Govᵗ?   What is the probable amount of the annual revenues of the Republic, and from what sources are they derived?   Are there any commercial vessels belonging to citizens of the Republic?   What is the amount of the foreign and what of the coastwise trade?

May I also be permitted to inquire whether any connections exist between the Dominican Republic and any other nation? and if there does, with what nation, and what is the nature of that connection and to what extent?

What number of soldiers and men under arms, can the Republic muster, and at what points are they stationed?   What is the number of pieces of ordinance and where are they mounted or placed?   How many stand of arms are in the Republic, belonging to the Government?   What amount of powder and ball, and where are they deposited?   Will there be any more arms and amunition, imported into the Republic for the use of the Government?   From what Country have the munitions of war ordered by the Republic usually been procured?

What is the naval force of the Republic and how is it organized?

Are the Citizens and inhabitants of the Republic permitted to exercise their own choice as to their religion, and are all *sects held responsible only to their God* for the peculiarity of their views?

With assurances [etc.].

2213

John Hogan, Special Agent of the United States to the Dominican Republic, to James Buchanan, Secretary of State of the United States [1]

SANTO DOMINGO, *October 4, 1845.*

SIR: In conformity with the instructions from the State Department under date of the 21st February, 1845,[2] I proceeded as the special Agent and Commissioner of the United States to the Island of St. Domingo or Hayti.

The duties enjoined on me by my Government were particularly to inquire into, and report upon, the present condition, capacity and resources of the new Republic of Dominica, as preliminary to any decision being pronounced by the Executive upon the propositions submitted by the representative of that Republic for a recognition of its independence.   During my sojourn in the territories of the Republic, I occupied my time in investigating these important subjects, and availed myself of every opportunity personally to test the accuracy of the representations which I received from various sources, which I deemed authentic and entitled to credit, in my reference to them. The result of this examination I have now the honor of laying before you, for the consideration of the President.— It may be important before I proceed to state in detail the results of my inquiries upon the particular topics especially adverted to in my letter of instructions, to recall to your recollection some general views as preliminary to such more minute circumstances.

The Island known under the several names of Hispaniola, St Domingo and Hayti is, as is well known, in extent among the largest, and in fertility of soil, character, and quantity of its productions, one of the most important of the Islands of the West Indies.   The central position which it occupies in that Archipelago, separated from Cuba by a channel of only forty miles, intermediate between *Jama[i]ca* on the West and Porto Rico on the East, its vicinity to the commercial ports of the United States, the provinces of Honduras and Yucatan, and what has been long known as the Spanish Main of South America, confer upon it a political importance, second only to its commercial.   In the hands of a powerful & enterprising Nation its influence

---

[1] Special Agents, vol. 13.   Received October 4, 1845.   This report is undated except for the receipt date.   It is the only document from him and was probably written after he returned to the United States.

[2] His instructions, dated, however, February 22, 1845, are above, this volume, pt. I, doc. 2192.

would be felt in all the ramifications of human concerns.   This Island is again peculiar from the number and capacity of its harbors.   The entire coast is studded with deep and valuable ports and intersected with rivers penetrating far into the interior which render all its resources natural and industrial available in augmenting the power, and extending the commerce of the nation which might either acquire the power of sovereignty over it, or become connected with it in the relations of mutual independence.   A glance at the map, will exhibit at once to your eye the inestimable value of this Island, and its commanding position in a military and Commercial point of view.   Independently of its own internal resources, mineral and agricultural, its position renders this magnificent Island one of the most admirable positions which the world can exhibit for a Commercial emporium.   Its vast and secure Bays would afford shelter for the congregated navies of the world.   Its situation renders it accessible to the most important marts of this Continent.   All that is required to do more than restore it to more than its former grandure is that it should maintain its present independent character, preserve its free and republican character, continue to exercise the liberal principle upon which its institutions rest and be preserved from any preponderating and dominating foreign influence.   These points which the most intimate investigations into the subject enable me confidently to assert, as those most indissolubly connected with the prosperity of the new Republic of Dominica, are at the same time so exactly in accordance with the interest, and harmonise so entirely with the policy of the United States that I could not refrain from bringing them distinctly, though in general terms to the view of the Government which I have had the honor to represent.

The policy by which the United States have been governed in analogous circumstances has been distinctly exhibited and pursued without deviation, while the leading maritime nations of Europe have sought to enlarge their Commercial and political power by the establishment of Colonies in every part of the Globe, and by the subjugation to their authority of regions of vast extent, our institutions preclude the acquisition of such dominions we have therefore sought to enlarge the field of Commercial intercourse by establishing amiable connections throughout the world, by cherishing the growth of liberal principles wherever we see them beginning to germinate and by recognising the introduction of new communities among the nations of the Earth whenever we discover in them the disposition to liberate themselves from the yoke of Colonial subjection, and the capacity to maintain their political independence.   The one founds her greatness upon the enlargement of her foreign dominions by such means as are appropriate—the other by a liberal and generous participation with other communities.   In the mean while our enlargement of territory proceeds in our own immediate vicinity, not by subjecting by force of arms other Nations to submit to our yoke, but by the incorporation, by mutual consent, of so magnificent a region as Texas, upon the footing of perfect equality, into our happy and powerful union.

To return from this digression—my reception in Dominica was accompanied by every demonstration of personal & national respect. Every attention which Courtesy could dictate was exhibited towards me by the public functionaries and individual citizens.— Every facility was afforded me in prosecuting the object of my mission.— Every source of information was cheerfully laid open.— Every inquiry fully and promptly responded to, and every disposition manifested to lay open to me the subjects which I was desirous of examining, and furnishing me with the information which I was solicitous of obtaining.

In this manner I have procured the information which it is my present purpose to lay before you, in the Confidence that your experience in matters of State will enable you to appreciate the results of my labors and to deduce the important conclusions with which they appear to me to be pregnant.

The Island which has of late years resumed in the hands of the Blacks its original name of Haiti or Hayti, was usually known as St. Domingo by the English and French and as Hispaniola by the Spaniards. It lies about South East of the Island of Cuba from which it is separated by a Channel of about forty miles in width. Eastwardly from Jamaica, which is at the distance of one hundred miles—westwardly from Porto Rico, distant thirty miles.— It is directly South from the City of New York, which is about 1500 miles removed from Charleston & Savannah about 900 miles.— Within a few days sail of Nicaragua, Yucatan & Honduras, and equally convenient to Trinidad and the northern shores of the South American Continent. This commanding position in both a political & commercial point of view, is materially strengthened by the number and capacity of its harbors: The Bay of Sanmanae [Samaná?] on the Eastern extremity of the Islands trends into the interior for a depth of eight leagues; with a proportionate width and is capable of holding all the navies of the world. The character of the shores of this Bay and the noble timber which covers the adjacent Country furnish inexhaustible means for repairing or even building ships of every dimensions. This Island extends in its greatest length nearly from East to West, a distance of about three hundred miles, and from North to South its greatest breadth is about one hundred and fifty miles, with a superficial area of thirty thousand square miles. Its Indian name Hayti, meaning Mountainous, indicates the most striking feature in its physical conformation, the most elevated points rising to the hight of about 6000 feet above the surrounding ocean. The hilly region is however intersected with numerous valleys, where the fertile character of the soil and a genial climate produce an exhuberance of the most valuable and diversified vegitation. In other parts of the Island extensive natural meadows or savannahs appear which furnish an abundant provision for large quantities of cattle and horses. St Domingo is in general well watered by numerous rivers which penetrate into the interior and add to the productive capacities of a soil of unsurpassed fertility.— The irregular character of the surface, and the greater or less distance from the ocean occasion considerable diversities of climate, varying from the oppressive tropical heat which combined with a humid atmosphere renders some parts peculiarly obnoxious to the vomits or yellow fever, to the elevated mountain ridges, where the cold is sometimes found to be unpleasant to those habituated to the more enervating influences of the tropics. The excessive heat, which would otherwise be unsupportable, of the sea board, is however delightfully tempered by the sea breeze, which regularly at 10 o'clock A. M. lends its refreshing influences to the weary & exhausted sufferers.

Under such propitious circumstances, as may readily be supposed, the vegitable products of the Island are as abundant as they are diversified in character. Almost all the productions of the tropical and temperate Zones find a genial soil and climate, in some part of its various regions. The Sugar Cane, Cotton, Tobacco, Rice & Cocoa, are grown in great abundance, while the plantain, vanilla, potato and other minor articles are indigenous to the soil. The mountains are covered with valuable timber, among which are especially to be noticed the Mahogany Satin wood, live oak, and other useful descriptions of tree.

Nor are the mineral riches of this Island less important. It is well known that from the period of its discovery by the Spaniards, large quantities of gold have been extracted from the soil, chiefly however by washings from the hills. It is known that there also exist the most copious supplies of copper, coal, rock salt, Iron ore, nitre and other valuable minerals. These however, owing to the distracted state of the Country have been imperfectly developed.

This magnificent Island upon which nature has lavished her choicest treasures with a profuse hand, has, however been the victim of all the misery which man can inflict upon his brother man. It was occupied by the divided authority of France and Spain—the former possessing the Western portion and the latter the Eastern part of the Island, while the line of demarcation between them was [an] irregular one extending in a Northerly and Southwardly course across it. The part belonging to Spain extended over rather a greater extent of superficies than that which appertained to France.

About the year 1789 the Island had perhaps attained its highest condition of prosperity and its exports were then deemed more abundant and more valuable than those of Cuba—at that period broke out those devastating intestine commotions which spread horror and misery over this unfortunate region, marked by traits of ferocity and a depth of human suffering rarely equalled and never surpassed. The Black population of the French moiety of the Island rose in insurrection against their masters, a servile war raged with all its terrors, armies, the pride and boast of France, were annihilated by the combined influences of war and climate, the negroes established their ascendency and the independency of the Haytien Republic was finally recognized by the French Monarch in 1825 in consideration of a large pecuniary indemnity payable to the former proprietors of the soil.

It is however to be remarked, what cannot indeed be readily understood and has not been satisfactorily explained, so far as my information extends, that although the political authority of the Blacks has been extended, as early as 1821, over the Spanish portion of the Island, so that it was wholly subjugated to their sway, yet this recognition of independence by France is in terms restricted to the French part of the Island.

This extension of the Black authority continued without intermission until the opening of the year 1844 when the inhabitants of the Spanish portion of the Island raised the standard of revolt, threw off the ignominious yoke, which had been imposed by the authorities of Hayti, and declared their independence. The Republic of Dominica was then constituted— Since that period the war between the two parties has been continued but the new community has thus far successfully maintained its independence—has organized a regular form of Government, established a written fundamental constitution based upon republican principles and holds out the best founded prospects of triumphing in the contest even to the extent of extending its authority throughout the entire Island.

Such was the origin and in brief such the present position of the new Republic to which I have had the honor of being commissioned.

The territories of the Republic are those which formerly belonged to Spain and constitute about a moiety of the Island, whether we estimate the extent of the country, the character of the soil and generally the sources of wealth. The population consists of about two hundred and thirty thousand of whom forty thousand are Blacks and over One hundred thousand are whites.— During the preponderance of the Black government such was the animosity which prevailed on the part of those in authority against all who had a white complexion, exhibiting itself in frequent assassinations and other means of personal annoyance, in the exclusion of the latter from all participation in the Government that many of the whites unable longer to endure their position, so entirely subordinate to the negroes, emigrated from the Island and established themselves elsewhere. The effect of the policy which was pursued would ere long have resulted in either the expulsion of the whites from the Island, or their extermination upon it, and the reduction of the entire Island to the exclusive dominion of the Black race. The consequences might have been anticipated. Where that race had acquired the entire dominion & the exclusive possession of the soil every part of the Country had shewn the effect of its deleterious influences. The agricultural products, Coffee, Sugar &c had declined in quantity as well as quality, Nature was resuming her sway over what had been reclaimed from her dominion and extensive regions, once well cultivated & extremely productive, had relapsed into their pristine state. The negroes whether owing, as some imagine to an original and inherent inferiority of intellectual power, incapacitating them from the ability of self Government, or the entire ignorance of political science or the habits growing out of a long continued existence under the dominion of others, or possibly from the combined influence of all these causes, had diminished in numbers, deteriorated in character and exhibited every symptom of declension.   The form of governmental administration, was scarcely preserved to the eye, morals were disregarded or openly contemned, the innate aversion to labor, which characterises the race, having full scope for indulgence in the want, or irregular exercise, of authority, destitute of the stimulants to industry which a well organized and well administered Government furnishes, and superseded, by the natural capacity of the soil to supply all the necessaries of life, have been powerfully operative causes in producing these unhappy results.

As might have been anticipated, the watchful eyes of England and France have not been closed to the interesting events which have occurred in this region.   Their official and unofficial agents have been upon the spot, anxiously watching the course of events and industrious in turning them to the advantage of their respective nations.   Jealous of each other, but united in their jealousy of the United States, no means were left untried to annihilate in advance every hope on the part of this Country to participate in the advantages to be derived from the present circumstances in which the Republic of Dominica finds herself.

It is not easy to determine whether either of the nations, which have been named, have formed any definite system of operations or plan of policy in reference to this state of things, or if they have adopted such, to ascertain with certainty what their plans are.   It is beyond all doubt however that they are seeking to acquire to some extent, and in some way, an influence over the new Government and its concerns, and to accomplish these designs, for their own especial benefit to the exclusion, as far as possible, of any participation by us.

This position of things became obvious to me shortly after my arrival in the Island.   The information derived from intelligent American gentlemen on the spot was fully corroborated by my own observation.   It appeared to me, therefore, to be one of the most important objects to be accomplished to disabuse the minds, as well of the Government, as of the people, of the impressions, which had been industriously instilled into them, in regard to the policy and objects of the United States.

I availed myself, therefore, of every opportunity of giving fair representations of the views and designs of my government.   In particular I represented that we neither sought for, nor would we accept, any special or exclusive commercial privileges—that it was our anxious desire that whatever was granted to us should be offered to the other nations of the Commercial world —I explained fully to them that the United States did not wish, or ask for, any political influence in the administration of their own affairs, and that we should see with regret any such influence obtained by any other power—that our policy was to leave every Government entirely independent in its operations, and the people wholly free in pursuing its own views of policy—that the commercial arrangements which we made with foreign nations were based upon the principles of equal justice and equal participation in the benefits resulting from the intercourse.

I was highly gratified with the manner in which all such suggestions were received and the happy effect, which was obviously produced in awakening the kindest and most respectful feelings towards our Country—the most candid assent to, and concurrence in, the principles I anounced, and as I have every reason to believe a decided preference in all these particulars over the views and designs of the other foreign agents.   I entertain the most unhesitating confidence that if the Government of the United States will cultivate the amicable disposition, of which I have sown the seeds, no apprehension need be entertained but that our Country will enjoy a large proportion of the respect and good feelings of the Government and people of Dominica, and participate freely in every commercial privilege which may be granted to any other.

Accompanying this report, which has been prepared under all the disadvantages of a severe and enervating indisposition, you will find a Map of the Island of Hayti,[1] accompanied by such observations and explanations as will be eminently useful in exhibiting to you the subdivisions &c of the Island. You also have an official report from Mͬ Bobadilla, one of the most intelligent members of the administration, in reply to a communication which I addressed to him, soliciting information.   A tabular statement, with a report from the appropriate Department, of the Military strength of the Republic, both army and navy, shewing the number of troops at its disposal, as well regular as of the national guards—the number and calibre of the cannon, muskets, the quantity of powder, ball and all other munitions of war, the number & size of their public vessels &c &c &c also a Statement of the finances of the Republic, exhibiting its resources and expenditures, and indicating under the existing impediments, the full ability of the Country to meet with promptitude every demand upon its treasury.   In connexion with this branch of the subject I would take this opportunity of remarking, that

---

[1] The map is not in the manuscript volume with the report; but there is a document headed, "Translation of observations on Map," at the top of which is endorsed in pencil "Map missing."   Most, if not all, of the other documents mentioned in this and the next paragraph as enclosures are still with the report and constitute four or five times as many pages as the report.   Their more important contents are incorporated in the report with sufficient fullness, it is believed, to serve the purposes of this publication.   Most of them, and Hogan's report also, bear a rubber stamp impression reading: "41 Cong. 3 Sess. 1871, Senate Ex. Doc. 17."

the exigencies of the war which Dominica is now waging for her existence, oc-casioned her to incur a debt of somewhat over a million of dollars, which, with the exception of about $250,000, has already all been extinguished from the ordinary receipts of the treasury—while an offer made them by an Eng-lish agent to loan them a million sterling has been declined.— You have also a Statement of the number of American vessels engaged in the trade of the Republic. I also transmit other interesting documents for your perusal the one from the Roman Catholic Bishop, the other signed by a large number of persons belonging to the Methodist Episcopal Church, which will exhibit to you the views taken by these parties of the moral and religious character of the people.

It only remains for me to add that in reference to all these documents I have every reason to believe that they may be confidently relied upon as ac-curate—that I entertain no doubt that the Republic of Dominica, if not in-terfered with by foreign influence, has the entire capacity to maintain its independence, and even to extend its sovereignty, ere long, over the entire island, that the character of the population, and the form of its Government, hold out every reasonable prospect of internal happiness and prosperity, while the nature and amount of its mineral resources and agricultural prod-ucts will make it the theatre of an extensive and lucrative commerce with the United States.

I[n] conclusion I would repectfully invite the Special Attention of the Hon. Secretary of State to the useful and very intelligent reports, herewith submitted, of the Secretaries of State, Treasury, War and Navy of the Dominican Republic, and also, to those of Mess[rs] Burbank and Harrison, American Merchants of high repute, residing on the Island of St. Domingo, together with the letters of the Right Rev[d] Thomas De Portas, Roman Catho-lic Bishop and Rev[d] M[r] Stevenson Methodist Clergyman &c giving in detail the state of morals and religion on that Island, numbered from 1 to 6 inclu-sive.

With great Respect [etc.].

2214

Jonathan Elliot, Commercial Agent of the United States to the Dominican Republic, to John M. Clayton, Secretary of State of the United States [1]

No. 14   SANTO DOMINGO, *April 24, 1849.*

SIR: You will please receive accompanying, a copy of the Treaty made and concluded upon, between this Government and the Republic of France.[2]

The Treaty between this Government and England has not yet been signed there being some objection to it, on the part of this Government.

[1] Consular Letters, Santo Domingo, vol. 1. Received May 15.
[2] Not included in this publication, since it is almost exclusively commercial in character.

The Haytian Army are close to us. Almost all the extensive merchants, have packed up their goods and shipped them to the neighboring Islands, and [are] leaving with their families. This town is filled with women and children from the Country and famine is to be apprehended.

They have asked the protection of the French an answer to which will be here in about four days.

Captain Warren of Her Majesty's ship the Trincomalee, now in the Harbor has offered me any assistance I may require in case of need—large quantities of goods belonging to merchants in New York have been placed in my care.

The President has told me, that it is the intention, to set fire to the place in case they cannot hold out against the Haytians.— I have written to St. Thomas, Curacõa [Curaçao] and Jamaica for one of our men of war.

The merchants of Porto Plata have all shipped their goods and gone to Turks Island or St. Thomas. Mr. Edward Roth, Vice Commercial Agent appointed by me, remains there. I am hourly expecting to hear of the destruction of that town. Our commerce there is very small—not more than four or six vessels in a year. Our Commerce here, is greater, than all the other united. It equals near three vessels per month.

I have abstained from all participation in this war. I have not even expressed an opinion but I have been given to understand that Solouque who leads these men has a strong hatred to Americans, on the other hand these people afford us advantages and extend us privileges more than to other foreigners.

I have received no acknowledgement of the receipt of my communications since No. 8.[1]— Messrs Ayman & Co of New York will forward any you may please to send.

Would the Department favor me with a list of the Ministers, Consuls, &c &c.

I have the honor [etc.].

2215

Jonathan Elliot, Commercial Agent of the United States to the Dominican Republic, to John M. Clayton, Secretary of State of the United States[2]

No. 15   SANTO DOMINGO, *May 2, 1849.*

SIR: I have to inform you that since my last of April 24th,[3] the Haytian army under Solouque has been beaten and routed at all points.

I informed [you?] in communication No. 13[4] that this Government had asked the protection of France. On the application being made through the Consul here to the Consul General of all the Islands, who resides at Port Au

---

[1] No. 8 is not within the scope of this publication.
[2] Consular Letters, Santo Domingo, vol. 1. Received June 7.
[3] Above, this part, doc. 2214.
[4] This should have been his No. 14, above, this part, April 24, 1849, doc. 2214.

Prince, he referred them to France, promising in the mean time to bring fifteen hundred men here from Martinique, *if they could be had.* Also a special messenger, Monsieur Chedville [Chedeville?] was despatched by a French steamer from here to St. Thomas and from thence by the steamer of the 1st of May for France, bearing despatches, asking that Government to accept and confirm the protectorate. Meantime the English Consul here prepared despatches for Lord Palmerston, whose purport was, to oppose the aid to be given by the French and sent them by the English Corvette Trincomalee via, Norfolk, I will here add, that Sir Robert Schomburgk the English Consul also offered to obtain them the aid of England. He not being able to speak Spanish or the President here, English, I was requested to be Interpreter, hence I was let into all the secrets. The object of both parties is to get possession of the Bay of Samana one of the finest in the West Indies, possessing Coal, timber, &c and of fine resources for a naval depot, either in time of peace or war. Both the Consuls have the special power of their Governments to make or alter and sign Treaties with this Republic.

Lastly, the President requested a private interview with me, asking me for the protection of the United States and if I thought the United States would allow this Republic to annex themselves. I replied, that it was a matter in which I had no power whatsoever and upon which I could not even express myself. That I was only authorised to look after our Commercial interests in this quarter and no further. I think it probable that a delegation will be sent from here to Washington, whose object will be, to obtain the Recognition of their Independence by our Government. I have now been resident here two years and am well acquainted with the country and any information you may require, respecting it, I shall be happy to transmit.

I have the honor [etc.].

2216

Benjamin E. Green, Special Agent of the United States to the Dominican Republic, to John M. Clayton, Secretary of State of the United States [1]

No. 1—Private.   SANTO DOMINGO, *August 27, 1849.*

SIR: I reached here day before yesterday. Of course I have as yet been able to obtain but little reliable information as to the state of things in the Island. But as an American Brig sails this evening for New York, and may be the last opportunity of communicating with the United States until the Hurricane season is over, I avail myself of the opportunity to give you the crude impressions of 48 hours of observation:

On the flight of Jimenes, the late President, of which you will have heard before this reaches you, the administration of affairs was placed temporarily in the hands of Gen[1] Santana. An election was then had, and, Santana de-

[1] Special Agents, vol. 15. Received September 18.

clining to be a Candidate, Buenaventura Baez, late President of the Congress, was chosen President, and will be installed in a few days. The ceremony is only delayed for the arrival of Gen¹ Santana, who is at present in the interior.— I learn that Baez, the President-elect, was one of the Commissioners sent to France to obtain the recognition by that Government of this, and is supposed to be in the interest and under the control of the French Consul. This gentleman I have not seen, but learn that he is a man of considerable talent and captivating address, with a large salary and private fortune.— I learn further that with such facilities he has been able to form what is here called "the French party." This however is composed of a very few individuals, and is not likely to become a popular party, as many suspect, notwithstanding the French Consul's professions of friendship for this Govᵗ, that France would be pleased to see the Haytiens in possession of the whole Island, as at present they (the Haytiens) can not, and in such case might be able to, make some satisfactory arrangement of their indebtedness to France. I also learn that the Haytiens have applied to France to aid them, by an advance of money, to make a conquest of this part of the Island, whereby they might be better able to pay her claims.

There are not wanting those, who say, that the recent invasion by Souluque [Soulouque] was countenanced, if not instigated by the representatives of France.

The English Consul General, Sir Robᵗ Schomburgh, is a man of science & a gentleman of such pleasing manners as will qualify him to exercise a great influence over these people.

Gen¹ Santana and the Archbishop control everything here. The former is at present in the interior.— Notwithstanding a severe headache, I called yesterday morning upon the latter.— He is a venerable looking personage, with those bland and almost affectionate manners, characteristic of his order. He received me very kindly; but, as there were many persons with him, I made my visit very short, pleading fatigue & indisposition from recent exposure to the sun, which would have prevented my going out to call on any one but himself.

What these people desire above all things, and would make almost any sacrifice to obtain, is peace with Hayti and security from invasion. I learn from our Consul, Mʳ Elliott, from Sir Robᵗ Schomburgh [Schomburgk] & others that they are industrious (that is; for this climate, I suppose) and would soon be prosperous, if they could devote themselves to agriculture & labour, as they desire.— But exposed continually to invasion by the demi-savages of Hayti, they may plant their tobacco & other crops today, and tomorrow or next week are called to the frontiers, to repel a threatened or anticipated invasion, leaving their crops to rot ungathered; which they do with alacrity and without other pay than can be derived from a pure love of country, or the pleasure of fighting.

This has been the state of things now for several years, and has made them very poor.   They want peace that they may apply themselves to labour; and to obtain this, they will make almost any sacrifice.   Their sympathies and prepossessions are all with us.   They applied, first of all, to us for recognition. They have now been recognized by France and England, and such is their prepossession in favor of the United States that they fondly imagine that all that is necessary to secure to them peace and prosperity is recognition by the United States.

My impression now is that both England and France desire above all things to get possession of Semana [Samana]; and that this Government will not hesitate to grant it for a term of years or in perpetuity to whichever will negotiate and guaranty a Treaty of peace with Hayti, so as to enable them to go to work, and recover from the poverty, to which the long war has reduced them.   I have no doubt that they would prefer to make such an arrangement with the United States, and as little doubt that if we do not come forward to their aid, France or England will, and get possession of Semana, as the consideration for so doing.   You are already informed of the position and advantages of Semana.   I need therefore only say, that, in addition to its many other advantages, coal, said to be of a superior quality, has recently been discovered there, which discovery has doubtless whetted the English & French appetite, to get possession of it for a naval depot.

These are the hasty impressions, which a longer residence and further observation may in some measure modify.   But I think there can be no mistake in what I have said about the desire of England & France to get possession of Semana, and the willingness of this Government to cede it to any one, who will guaranty to them a few years of peace.

I have to request that you will inform me by the earliest opportunity how far our government would be willing to interfere between this government and Hayti, to bring about that result by negotiation or otherwise; and whether if offered to me, I may accept Semana as a consideration of our giving notice to the Haytiens that they must cease to molest these people.   As to their ever being able to conquer this part of the Island, without the effective and open assistance of France, it is impossible, as the uniform result of all their attempts has proved.

From all I can learn of the Haytiens, they are half savages, far below the Comanche Indians.   All the Mulattoes and Browns—all, who had any smattering of education, intelligence or civilization, have been driven out or shot by Souluque [Soulouque]; and their condition is such that there is no prospect of making any arrangements with them for the payment of the claims of our citizens.

The Hurricane season is considered as past by the 20 October, which on that account is held as a thanksgiving day throughout the West Indies.— The Sickly season will then be over also, and I would recommend that one of our vessels of war should be here by that time to convey whatever communications I may have to make.   But for the dangers of the Hurricanes & Sickly season, I would ask that one should be sent out at once.   At present however I could not advise it, as, in consequence of the long drought & present excessive rains, the fever is more than usually fatal.

Your ob[t] serv[t].

2217

Benjamin E. Green, Special Agent of the United States to the Dominican Republic, to John M. Clayton, Secretary of State of the United States [1]

No. 2   SANTO DOMINGO, *September 27, 1849.*

SIR: The Schooner *Lindsay* sails in a few days for Boston, being the first vessel since the date of my despatch of the 27 ulto, No. 1: and I avail myself of the opportunity to give you the more full & correct information, since obtained, as to the present condition of the Dominican Republic.

About a year since, Santana, then President, being confined by sickness during several months at his country residence at Seybo, Jimenes, then Minister of War, availed himself of the occasion to organize a conspiracy, the object of which was to force Santana to resign the Presidency in favor of the other.   With this view all the troops favorable to Santana were removed from the Capital, which was garrisoned by others, whom Jimines had found means to gain over to his interest.   On Santana's return to the Capital, he received the first intimation of what had been going on by a demand made upon him to resign.   This he did, rather than be the cause of a civil war, and Jimenes was thereupon elected President for which position, it would seem, he had neither the requisite abilities nor integrity.   His whole time was spent in cleaning, training and fighting cocks, it being frequently necessary to send acts of Congress and other official papers to the cockpit for his approval and signature.   Under such rule everything fell into confusion, which state of things was soon made known to Souluque [Soulouque] and incited him to the recent invasion.   He accordingly passed the frontiers with a force of from 8,000 to 10,000 men, the Dominican generals, either from cowardice or treachery, (I am not prepared to say which) retreating before him, until he had reached & passed Azua.   In the mean time Jimenes occupied with his favorite amusement of cockfighting, took no measures to repel the Haytiens, or even to fortify the Capitol, which was threatened.   The greatest consternation prevailed.   The Congress called upon Santana, who was then in retirement at Seybo, to come to the Capitol & take measures for the safety of the Country.   When he arrived and offerred to take command of the Army, or rather to lead those, who would volunteer to follow him against the

[1] Special Agents, vol. 15.   No receipt date is on the original.

Haytiens, (for in the retreat the Army was disbanded & had disappeared), Jimines [Jimenes?] refused at first to let him leave the City, but after a few days consented to let him go alone, but would give him no troops. Santana mounted his horse and almost unattended took the road to Azua. On the way he picked up from 350 to 500 men, with which small force he attacked & routed Souluque's army of 6000 men.

As soon as it was known that Santana had been called out by the Congress, the men, who were scattered over the country seeking their homes, turned to join him, so that in a short time, his name had brought together the dispersed army and he found himself at the head of 6000 men.

The Haytiens having been thus driven out, the provinces, dissatisfied with the mal-administration of Jimenes, called upon Santana to take charge of the Government. The latter marched to and having invested this City, remained before it twelve or fifteen days, waiting for the gates to be opened. The documents & correspondence forwarded by our Consul, Mr Elliott, have already fully informed you of the particular [sic] of the Convention negotiated by the Foreign Consuls.—

Jimenes having been thus deposed, Sr. Santiago Espaillat was elected President, but declined, when Buenaventura Baez was elected, to fill the vacancy, and installed on the 24th instant.—

On the 19 April last, when Souluque [Soulouque] was daily expected before the walls of this City, the Dominican Congress in secret session authorized the President to place the Republic under the protection of France, which resolution was the same day communicated to Mr. Place, the French Consul, & by him despatched, in charge of his Chancelier, to Paris. None of the proceedings have been made public, altho the fact of the application having been made was immediately known. I have obtained a copy of the letter of the Minister of Foreign Relations to the French Consul, which is hereto annexed marked N° 1.[1] It was the only correspondence that took place. This application, I also learn from unquestionable authority, was not made, until after consultation with Mr Place, and assurances received from him that the protection asked for would be granted, in consideration of the cession of the Bay of Semana [Samana].

The pressing necessity, which led to this application to France, passed by with the defeat and expulsion of the Haytiens. But the panic created by

[1] This enclosure follows:

José María Caminero, Minister of Foreign Affairs of the Dominican Republic, to M. Place, French Consul at Santo Domingo

No. 1.   SANTO DOMINGO, *April 19, 1849.*

SIR: I have the honor to make known &c "that the National Congress in its session of the 19 April, (at which the President of the Republic and the four ministers of State assisted) has resolved, as a speedy and first measure, (por pronta y primera medida) to solicit, and place the Dominican Republic under, the protection of the French Republic; leaving for another moment the arrangement of the conditions of the Protectorate."
I have the honor [etc.].

Souluque's early successes & near approach to the Capitol has determined them to place themselves on almost any terms under the protection of any foreign Government, that will afford them quiet & security from further invasions.   The most bigotted Catholic here would accept the protection of Jew, infidel or Turk rather than fall again into the power of the Haytiens, and all are anxiously looking for the return of the Chancelier, & the arrival of the French Protectorate.

Under these circumstances the arrival of a stranger in the midst of the hurricane and sickly season excited much speculation, and as no strangers venture here at this season on private business, it was immediately surmised that I came for the Government and in relation to the French Protectorate.   News of my arrival and that such was supposed to be my object, was immediately sent to the interior, and I have received several letters from Santiago & Port au Platte, asking whether, and expressing a hope that, we were going to acknowledge and annex them, and assuring me, that if the U States will aid them, they do not want to have anything to do with France.

When the ArchBishop returned my visit, which he did immediately, he asked me if it was true, as surmised, that I came in an official capacity to see about the French Protectorate, and offerred to give me any information on that subject.   To his direct questions, I thought best to answer that I had been sent by my government with powers to make a treaty of Friendship & Commerce; but that I had not come in consequence of the French Protectorate Affair, that not having been heard of by my Govt when I left home; that we had only heard of the rout of the Haytiens, whereby the Dominicans had given another proof of their ability to maintain their independence; that my Government sympathized with them in their gallant resistence to the Haytiens & was now disposed to recognize them by a commercial Treaty; but that I had been instructed, before presenting my credentials, to ascertain whether their government was conducted with such good order stability and fairness towards our citizens as to warrant that public recognition on our part; that for that reason I had come as a private individual in a merchant vessel, instead of a vessel of war, because, our government having already sent two agents to report upon the state of the Country without any result, I wished to remain unknown until I had satisfied myself of the propriety of making a Treaty with them, as I did not wish my coming again to excite on the part of the Dominicans hopes or expectations, which might not be realized; that the proposition for a French protectorate had embarrassed me; as my government might not be willing to recognize as independent an American republic seeking European protection, and that he must consider my communications to him as confidential until I could notify my government & learn whether, under the unexpected state of things, it was proper for me to enter upon the negotiation of a commercial Treaty.

The English Consul, Sir Robt Schomburck [Schomburgk], soon after my arrival, invited me to breakfast, when, being alone, he said that my visit to St^o Domingo was supposed to have been caused by the proposition for a French Protectorate. I answered that until I reached this city I had not heard a word on that subject. He spoke of the desire long entertained by France to get possession of Semana, to which I replied that, as his own government would doubtless wish to have possession of so important a position in the West Indies, it would take care to keep France out of it, until we should be ready to annex it some 20 or 30 years hence.—He answered that his Government did not so much desire to possess itself of Semana as to keep France out of it, and that, being satisfied that neither private business nor pleasure would have brought me here at this season, he had asked me to breakfast with him alone that he might have an opportunity of showing me Lord Palmerston's reply to the application of the Dominican Gov^t for English protection, and also the projet of a commercial Treaty, which had been offerred by H. M.'s Gov^t to this.

Lord Palmerston's reply to the application for protection was that the proposition was not fully understood; that if it was meant that H, M,'s Government should send troops &c to protect the Dominicans from Haytien invasion, British interests & commerce were not sufficiently involved to justify the expense. There was more in the despatch, and, as I thought, on the same subject, which was not read; seeing which I jocularly suggested that Semana would pay the expense. To this he replied that he could give me his word of honor that his government had no desire to get possession of Semana except with the view of preventing *the French* from getting hold of it. I have since seen much of him, and his word thus given can be fully relied upon. At the same time I have seen that he attaches very great importance to Semana, so much so as may hereafter cause his government to covet its possession, independent of a jealousy of France.

The 2^d Art of the projet of the English Commercial Treaty stipulates for *free* trade in favour of English Subjects, being in fact a provision against monopolies. The same projet was submitted to the Dominican Commissioners sent to London & Paris, & was disagreed to by them in consequence of this provision. It was again submitted to this Gov^t by Sir Robt Schomburck [Schomburgk], and again disagreed to by Sr. Baez, (President elect) also was the Dominican Plenipotentiary, having also been, as before stated, one of the Commissioners sent to Europe. Baez's opposition to this provision against monopolies is explained by his desire to establish a tobacco monopoly as the basis of a loan to be effected in France, on a plan, which is explained by the document annexed hereto, marked No 2,[1] and in which he is supposed to be personally interested. In consequence of his opposition, the English negotiations have been broken off, Lord Palmerston refusing to yeild

[1] Not included in this publication.

the question about monopolies.   The English Plenipotentiary declares that, having twice offerred them a commercial Treaty, he will not renew his propositions until they see proper to request it.   He starts on Monday next to explore the interior, under instructions from his government to do so.

With regard to the population, I have to report that if I should Judge by this city, the blacks and mulattoes would seem to be greatly in the majority. I am informed however that the proportion of blacks and mulattoes is much greater in this city than in other parts of the Island.   Baez, the newly elected President, is the son of an old Spaniard by a woman of color.   The whites however control the government and fill nearly all the civil offices.   Espaillat, who was elected President & declined, is a Spaniard of pure blood & high reputation for probity.   When he declined, there was great difficulty in deciding who should be elected, until Santana selected Baez, whose election, tho' in regular form, was mere form, the Congress being ready to proclaim any man whom Santana should name.   The reasons, which I have heard assigned for the selection, were 1st that he was supposed to be under the control of Santana, who would be President in fact; 2dly that it was thought necessary by the whites, anticipating another invasion by Souluque, to let the people of color see that they were not excluded from their full share of the Government —3d that Baez, having been well educated in France & some time abroad, was supposed to be better qualified & more manageable than any other, who would accept.   4th. It is said by some that Santana, being somewhat doubtful of the success of the French Protectorate projet, thought best to let Baez, who in conjunction with the French Consul at this port had originated that matter, take the responsibility, and incur the odium of disappointing the expectations, which it has excited.

I send herewith the inaugural discourse of the New President,[1] in which he refers to the necessity of a loan, and of accepting the protection of some foreign government on the best terms, which may be offerred.

I was informed this morning that as the Government was now formed, it was expected that I would in a few days present myself & make known the object of my visit.   I shall not however do so as yet.   Please inform me by the earliest opportunity whether, in view of the application for French protection, the election of Mr Baez and other facts above presented, I shall present my credentials and enter upon the negotiation of the Commercial Treaty.   In the mean time should the protectorate be accepted, with the cession of Semana as one of the conditions, I shall do all I can to prevent its consummation, and if necessary for that purpose, present my credentials, and protest officially against it.

Please also inform me more fully of the nature of the cession, which our government would accept, for a coal depot at Semana; the extent of territory

[1] Not included in this publication.

and Jurisdiction, which might be wanted, and the consideration, that would be given therefor.

With regard to the administration of justice, I have had no opportunity of Judging from personal observation; but from all I can learn, from others, these people would seem to compare favorably with Mexico, Cuba & other Spanish American countries, in that respect. Doubtless wrongs are committed, but I am inclined to believe that where such cases occur, they proceed rather from error of judgment than from wrongful intent of the Judges. When the Haytiens took possession of this point of the Island in 1822, they destroyed the flourishing university, which then existed in this city, and brought hither, for instruction, the youth of Cuba, Puerto Rico and the Spanish Main. During 22 years that they had possession, the Haytien Government waged a continual war against every species of knowledge and improvement; and as a necessary consequence, there are now here few, who are qualified to discharge the delicate and responsible duties of a judge. They are often, therefore, and for some time to come must be, compelled to select for such stations men, who with the best disposition to do right, may err for want of that extended information & study, which are essential to the Judicial character. At present (now that they are anxious to enlist the sympathies of foreign nations with them in their struggle with the Haytiens) there can be no doubt that the strongest disposition prevails in their courts and in every branch of the Government not only to render justice to, but to favor, foreigners in every way that may invite immigration. I am not prepared to say that this disposition would continue, were the motive for it removed. They seem, indeed, to be aware that, apart from the danger of Haytien invasion, they require immigration to populate the country & develope the resources of their rich and as yet almost virgin soil; but if once secure from further interruption by the Haytiens, the known jealousy of the Spanish character would perhaps show itself towards foreigners here, as in other parts of Spanish America.

Every inducement has been held out by this government to invite a white immigration, and it is intended to apply a large part of the proposed new loan to pay the expense of bringing out white settlers. At the same time the introduction of blacks from the United States has been prohibited— Could they succeed in obtaining the desired immigration, the permanent ascendancy of the white race would be secured; but if this Haytien war continues much longer, empoverishing the people and destroying their commerce by diverting so large a portion of their productive labour to guard against and repel invasion, it is not improbable that many of the white families now here will abandon the country.

I have to renew my request that you will place a man of war at my disposal as soon as possible.

I have the honor [etc.].

P. S. Oct 6ᵗʰ 1849.   The Schooner *Lindsay*, by which I expected to forward this despatch, has been detained by sickness of the crew, & may not get off for some days, as her mate and entire crew are down with the fever.   In the mean time, an American bark has come in from the Coast, and will sail direct to New York in a day or two.   I reopen this despatch to inform you of late occurrences here.

The new President, Baez, having with some difficulty and after considerable delay, formed his Cabinet, I availed myself of the first holiday (Sunday last) to pay a friendly visit to each member thereof.   On taking leave of Mr. Manuel del Monte, the Minister of foreign relations, I said that, having understood that my arrival had given rise to many surmises and that the government was anxious to know the object of my visit, it would give me pleasure to make it known to him at any time.   To this he replied that he would call on me at 4 o'clock the same evening.   When he came, I explained the object of my visit in the same terms, in which I had previously spoken to the ArchBishop, and concluded by saying that the application for the French protectorate had embarrassed me, & made it necessary to communicate with my government on the subject before presenting my credentials.   In reply, he said that the policy of the Haytien government was to exclude whites and shackle commerce; that of the Dominican Govᵗ to invite white immigration and to foster an intercourse with foreign nations, whereby they might regain what they had lost under the Haytien yoke, & keep up with the progress of the age; that their great desire was peace, because, tho' they might repel every invasion, the continuance of the war retarded the improvement of their social, political & commercial condition; that the application to France had been made when Souluque was within twenty miles of the Capital; that they still desired to place themselves under the protection of any civilized Government, which, by putting a stop to the invasions of the Haytiens, would give them leisure to emerge from their present depressed condition.   He said that no definite answer had yet been received from France, altho their last advices by the Catharina, which arrived from St. Thomas a few days since, gave them reason to believe that the Protectorate would be accepted by France.   I asked leave to give my opinion on that subject, not as an agent of the Govᵗ of the United States, but as a private individual, who had for some time felt a sincere interest in the success of their cause; and said, that, having visited Jamaica on my way hither I there saw the same evidences of decay as here: that the French W. I. Islands were fast falling into the same state of ruin & poverty; that if neither France nor England could do anything to ameliorate the condition of their present West Indian possessions, it could not be expected that the condition of the country would be improved by placing it under the control of either of those Govᵗˢ; and that I felt confident that France would not give the desired protection except on conditions, which this Govᵗ ought not to admit, & which perhaps might not be pleasing to the United States.   He then asked me, whether, in my opinion the government of the United States would take them under its protection, or (what they would prefer) annex them.   I replied that my government would prefer to see them maintain their independence; that such a protectorate on the part of our government was without precedent, and I could give no opinion on the subject; that annexation would be a subject for long discussion in our congress before it could take place, and that the best protectorate they could at present hope for would be a recognition (by Treaty) by the United States, and the sympathies of the American people, which would be excited by the publication of the Treaty.   On taking leave, Mr Del Monte asked whether he might give notice to his Gov^t of his conversation with me.   I answered that I desired him to do so, but that he would see that it was best for me still to maintain my private character, because should I make myself known, & afterwards go away without recognizing them, the effect would be to discourage his people, and give confidence to their enemies.

A few days after this interview, the President, on whom I had left my card, called to see me, and in the course of the conversation, took occasion to say that he had always been in the vanguard of those, who wished to place the country in the possession of France, not because he preferred that nation, but because he thought that France, having been more concerned in the affairs of the Island, would be more ready than any other to give them the aid they require.

Hereto annexed, No. 4, I send you a copy of a petition, addressed by the principal heads of families in the district of Santiago to Genl Santana, in favor of annexation to the United States.[1]   I understand that other similar

[1] This enclosure follows:

Dominican Citizens to General Pedro Santana, Former President of the Dominican Republic

No. 4.   SANTIAGO, *September 22, 1849.*

GENERAL: The undersigned persuaded of your desinterested affection to the Country, and convinced at the same time that the same love to our nationality (you have so well defended) would make you admit any thing, rather than see it destroyed by the barbarous Haytian, if the chances of war turn against us; knowing besides our poor resources and what is more the immense injuries this state of uncertainty brings upon the country; delaying its civilization and progress, interrupting its tranquility and exposing it to daily and heavy sacrifices; for these and other reasons we address you for the purpose of expressing in confidence and sincerity our opinion of the true interests of our country.

The object of the government of Washington in declaring the principle, that no European Power should interfere in the Affairs of America, has been to protect the interests of the new world, and undoubtedly it is the highest and most magnanimous act of a great and elevated policy.

The opportunity has arrived to put this principle into practice by reminding the Government of the United States, that we also belong to the grand American family and that not only by our common American character, but for the firmness with which we have maintained our independence, we are worthy of the advantages the 27 States of the Union enjoy.   It is superfluous to demonstrate the advantages of such an idea. The similitude of the Institutions, the proximity of both [the two] Countries, the intercourse of its Commerce, the migration they are able to promote and which would be the

petitions are being prepared here and in Port au Platte. Until this document was sent to me from Santiago by my old acquaintance, Don Nicolas Julia, I had no knowledge of the movement, (tho' it is doubtless one of the results of my arrival); nor have I given any countenance thereto. No. 5 is an anonymous letter, which was put under the front door of my house during the night.[1]

By the Sch[r] Catarina, we had an account of the Imperial Ceremonies at Port au Prince; also letters from the English Consul, & others at that port, stating that the Emperor was organizing his court and noblesse, and making arrangements to invade this part of the Island in November with the entire male population in Hayti. The Dominicans seem rather pleased at the news, hoping by one more blow to put an end to the war. The Gov[t] is actively preparing for the threatened invasion. They are much in want of arms & ammunitions. Money is not so necessary, for their troops fight without pay. Should Souluque come, as he threatens, the Dominicans will doubtless give him a warm reception, and perhaps draw him into the interior, with the view of cutting his army to pieces. Heretofore they have always manifested the most remarkable forbearance & magnanimity towards their invaders, when defeated. But their patience is now exhausted, and the next battle & pursuit will be one of extermination.

You have already been informed that we have three fourths of the trade of this part of the Island, which, tho' at present much crippled by the war, would under other circumstances be of considerable importance. You are also informed of the disposition manifested here to favor our merchants and traders; of the vexatious impositions, to which they are subjected in the ports of Hayti, and would be here, should the Haytiens get possession, and can readily see that it is a matter of much interest to our commerce that this war should end.

As to the Haytiens, I fear that there is no possibility of arranging for the payment of our claims upon them, nor of protecting our citizens, who venture there, from the piratical acts of that gov[t] & people for the future, until we shall have taken with them the same course as under similar circumstances was pursued with the Algerines.

Source of our wealth and prosperity; it is preferable a thousand times to be American than to be ruined by exposure to the chances of a war without end.

This is the only way to become respectable and maintain our independence, and form an independent State like those of the Union; because the name of American is the only one dwelling in the new world, which in the course of time will be the same Government and the same Nation.

Now we beseech you, General, to consider this as a proof of our patriotism, and that our principal object is the stability and progress of our Country, which we can only find in being connected with that great Nation.

We flatter ourselves, general, that if you are animated with the same sentiments you will favour our demand with our Government, with all the influence you possess in the affairs of this Country.

We have the honor [etc.].

[1] Not found.

2218

Benjamin E. Green, Special Agent of the United States to the Dominican Republic, to John M. Clayton, Secretary of State of the United States [1]

No. 3—Private.   SANTO DOMINGO, *October 24, 1849.*

SIR: For the last six years the Dominicans have sustained with great patience fortitude and courage a defensive war against four times their number. Their losses and sacrifices have been great, but cheerfully borne, in the hope that some one of the civilized nations of the world would ultimately interfere to put an end to a war, which has for its object the extermination of the white & mulatto population of this end of the Island. Having first applied to the United States for recognition without avail, they turned to France, and for some time past have been expecting from that quarter some aid, which, by enabling them to leave off fighting without pay for the common cause, would give them leisure for the improvement of their individual & national fortunes.

Last week it was rumored in the streets of this city that the French Protectorate had been refused, in consequence of a protest from the British Minister at Paris. In the same days there came several successive couriers from the north side of the Island, bringing news of preparations on foot at Guarico & other Haytien ports for a new invasion, and countermanding various commercial orders on that account.

Under these circumstances on saturday (the 20th inst) I called on the Minister of foreign relations, M[r] Manuel del Monte, and asked him if it was true that the Protectorate had been refused, and for the cause assigned. He replied that his information was that the British Government had interfered, not indeed by a protest, but by intimations, which had as much effect. I then said that the letters by the recent couriers manifested unnecessary alarm at the threatened invasion; that the failure of the application to France was calculated still further to dishearten his people; that something should be done to animate them to meet the invasion, should it come, with courage & confidence; and that if he thought my presenting myself publicly as the agent of the U. States would have that effect, I was willing, for that only purpose, to present my credentials without waiting for further instructions. He answered that all idea of the French Protectorate had been abandoned by his government, & that the presentation of my credentials would not fail to have a very favorable effect at this crisis of their affairs; whereupon I presented your letter.

At the same time I availed myself of the opportunity to say that, as a friend of the Dominican Republic, I was glad that the French protection project had failed. I referred him to Martinique & Guadalupe, where the same poverty & decay exists as here, & which by late advices were in a state of insurrection, to show that a connection with France would retard rather

---

[1] Special Agents, vol. 15.   Received December 13.

than promote the progress of his country; and to Jamaica, to show that there was as little to expect from a connection with England or any other European power.

On the 21st I learned that Mr Del Monte, immediately after this interview, had visited the French Consul, & remained closeted with him for several hours; and on the 22d it was intimated to me that the presentation of my credentials had been made the occasion of a new application to France.

I had been previously informed that Del Monte, and Baez, the President, are both the intimate friends of the French Consul; sought refuge in his house during the late commotions, look to him as their mentor and consult him on all occasions. They were the first projectors of a French protectorate, on which project they have staked their political reputation & consider its failure as fatal to their own importance & influence. With them the idea of making this country a colony of France was antecedent to the first movement for throwing off the Haytien yoke; they have clung to it for six years; & in a great degree owe to it their present position & will abandon it with great reluctance.

To ascertain how far this information was correct, I sought an interview with them on the 22d: told them that I had been informed that the Dominican Government had availed itself of the presentation of my credentials to make a new application to France, and wished to know whether that information was correct. They assured me that since the presentation of my credentials they had made no communication to the French Consul, in which I had been mentioned or referred to. This it seems was an equivocation, for I have obtained through a confidential person the annexed copy (marked A) of a letter from the Dominican Minister of Foreign Relations to the French Consul, which was written on the 21st, tho dated on the 18th, so as to make it appear to have been prior to the presentation of my credentials.[1]

A long conversation followed, in the course of which I discovered that their hopes of protection from France had very much revived since the 20th. The President, Baez, also spoke of the petitions addressed to Genl Santana

---

[1] The following is the text of his enclosure A:

A

Under date of the 18th Oct, but as I have reason to believe subsequent in fact to the 20 Oct, the Dominican Minister of Foreign Relations addressed the French Consul at Sto Domingo, as follows:—

"The Barbarous war of the Haytians, and the present condition of the country oblige me to request you, in the name of my govt, to urge (instar) the nation whom you so worthily represent, in order to obtain as soon as possible the definite solution of the so important question (of the Protectorate). If unfortunately the decision of France should be a negative one, let it at least have the merit of not being so late as to prevent us from applying to the Special Agent of the United States, who has just arrived in this capital, and to whom my government has until now not thought proper to make any proposition on that subject, in order to be consistent with the principles of frankness and good faith, which it has adopted as the rule of all its operations."

by the Provinces of Cibao, and particularly of that from La Vega (of which I send a copy hereto annexed marked B)[1] in a manner, which gave me clearly to understand that that movement (as he termed it) was displeasing to him. The reasons of his displeasure are 1st that the petitions are addressed to Gen[1] Santana; 2d, because the expression, "five years of useless & fruitless petitions to foreign nations", in the petition from La Vega, refers to the French Protectorate scheme, of which he has been and is the Corypheus; and 3dly, because all the petitions are anti French. To his remarks on the subject of these petitions, which he seemed to consider as intended to control him, I replied that I had no agency in promoting them, nor knew of them until copies were forwarded to me from Santiago; that nevertheless, as they were the spontaneous expression of the public feeling of the Cibao, on hearing of the arrival of a person supposed to be an agent of the U. States Govt, I was much gratified by the sentiments therein expressed, and the more so because I sincerely desired to see the Dominican Independence established, and thought these petitions calculated to excite sympathies in the United States, whence alone in my opinion they could reasonably hope for aid: that as to France, her sympathies and interests were both with the Haytiens, who speak her language and are largely her debtors; that in my opinion she would decline the protectorate, & would do so, not because of intimations from the British, but from the Haytien Minister; and that, if she interfered as a mediator it would be with a view to some arrangement, by which the Dominicans should assume a portion of the Haytien debt, or perhaps again submit to the Haytiens in the name of a reunion under a federal form of government. In fact this last, (which would be in effect to surrender all, for which the Dominicans have fought so bravely & suffered so much & would make it necessary for the whites & mulattoes to seek safety in flight) is being urged by the Haytien Agents in Paris, backed by the influence of the Institut d' afrique, and there is much reason to believe that the tendency of French diplomacy here is to that end & with that object.

I send hereto annexed marked C a copy of a letter from the French Consul at this Port to the Domn Minr of foreign relations, dated on, or a few days previous to, the 18th inst.[2] This letter seems to have been the foundation

[1] This petition, which covers four pages, in Spanish, is not included in this publication. Its character is reflected in Green's comments.

[2] The following is the text of his enclosure C:

C

The French Consul at Santo Domingo writes to the Dominican Minister of foreign relations, as follows:

"I this moment learn by a letter from the (french) Consul General at Port au Prince a fact, which seems to me to need explanation.

It seems that the English Consul in Hayti has been charged by his Minister to make known to the new Emperor that the Government of the Queen, having been called on to decide on a demand for protection addressed to it by the Dominican Government & transmitted by the English Consul at St° Domingo, had refused it, and had hastened to make known that refusal to France."

of the rumor that the British Gov[t] had interfered to prevent the acceptance of the Protectorate by France. I deem it of much importance, as another marked indication of the policy of the British Gov[t] in reference to this Island and of its desire to see established in the W. Indies a nation of pure blacks.

Hereto annexed, marked B[1], is a copy of a petition signed by all the most influential persons (civil, military & clergy) of La Vega, addressed to Gen[l] Santana, urging an application to the United States for protection and annexation. D is copy of a petition, to the same effect, from Santiago addressed to the President.[2] E is a copy of Gen[l] Santana's answer to the Santiago petition,[3] a copy of which was forwarded with my last despatch.

Your instructions contemplate as prerequisites to the recognition of this Gov[t] by ours, 1st the competency of these people to discharge the duties of an independent state; 2[dly] the ascendency of the Spanish race in the gov[t], and as fair a numerical proportion of that race to the others as in other Spanish American States.

The whites have always held the ascendancy in this government, and I believe will maintain it by reason of their superior intelligence, if not by force of numbers. But of the relative numerical proportion of the whites, mixed and blacks in the Republic I have no means of coming to an exact estimate. The greater number probably are of the mixed blood. Most of these, however, call themselves white; are received as such by those of pure blood, and by their adherence to the whites, rather than the blacks give to the former the preponderance. The cruelties of the Haytien rule have given such force and universality to the *white* feeling, not only among the mulattoes, but among the blacks of this end of the Island, that it is not uncommon to hear a very black negro, when taunted about his color, reply "soi negro, pero negro blanco", ("I am a negro, but a white negro") or

---

The Dominican Minister of F. Relations on receipt of the above, addressed the English Consul, Sir Rob[t] Schomburgk, as follows:

"It has reached the knowledge of the Dominican Government that the packet of the 15th of September carried to the English Consulate en Puerto Principe positive information that the Government of the Queen had under consideration an application for a protectorate addressed to it by the Dominicans in the time of the administration of the Ex President Jimenes, & transmitted by H. B. M's Consul in Santo Domingo.

The Government (Dominican), consistent with the principles of frankness and good faith, which it has adopted as the rule of all its operations, and desirous of knowing the engagements (compromisos) which may have been contracted in the name of the nation by former administrations, in order to give them (seal them with) the most strict fulfilment, immediately ordered an examination of the registers, which contain all its deliberations, and in them there does not appear the slightest trace of this act. With the same object, the former Minister of Foreign Relations until the fall of the above named President, has been interrogated and declares that he never signed any such act nor had any knowledge of its existence.

Wherefore, you being the only person capable of satisfying the just desires of my Gov[t], I apply to you to request that you will inform me of the facts in relation to this important subject."—

[1] See above, this part, p. 57, note 1.   [2] Not found.
[3] For the Santiago petition here referred to, see above, this part, p. 53, note 1. Santana's reply, dated October 6, 1849, is not included in this publication.

"Aunque tengo el cutis negro mi corazon es blanco", ("although I have a black skin, my heart is white"). If this end of the Island were once secured from Haytien invasion, and its independence established under the auspices of the United States, there can be no doubt that a large immigration of whites from the adjacent Islands & the Spanish Main, descendants of those who were driven out by the Haytiens, would speedily follow, and the Ascendancy of the white race be thus secured.

The application for the protection of France is in some measure an acknowledgment of the inability to maintain the character or discharge the duties of an independent State; and, together with the question of races, has led me to await your instructions before entering on any negotiations with them. After much reflection on the subject, I think that we should nevertheless not only recognize them, but, as far as possible, aid and support them, not only in view of our own Commercial interests, as explained in my last despatch, but because the real question at issue in their contest with the Haytiens is whether the white race shall be permitted to have any share in this Island. Nay, more. The object of the war is the establishment of a nation of pure blacks on this Island, to be the nucleus of a black empire, which, it is proposed, shall embrace the whole West Indies. By reference to the Haytien constitution of 27 Dec 1806, modified 2 June 1816, title 2, paragraphs 40, 41, you will see that the Haytiens then claimed the *whole* Island of Stº Domingo, with *the adjacent islands dependent thereon*, as the territory of their Republic. To this (the Spanish) part, which they thus claimed, they had no shadow of right, nor did they come into possession thereof until February 1822, when fraudulently entering as friends they kept possession as masters, until they were again driven out by force in 1844. Under the Spanish rule, the city of Stº Domingo was the Western Metropoli[s] of the Spanish Antilles, and the adjacent Islands, Cuba & Puerto Rico, were dependent on this, as the seat of the Colonial Government. As in 1822 Boyer was not content with the French part of the Island, to which alone the Haytiens had any right, so now the newly crowned emperor Souluque purposes the reconquest of this part of the Island, as the first step towards further extending his empire, by inciting the blacks of Cuba & Puerto Rico to rise and join him. However improbable this scheme may now appear, I have no doubt that it is seriously entertained by Souluque; and should he succeed, either by force of arms or of French intermediation, in reestablishing his power here, he or his successors may cause serious trouble not only in Cuba & Puerto Rico, but in our own Southern States.

Apart from these considerations, I would refer you to Wheaton's Law of Nations page 112, part 2, Section 10, where he speaks of the interference of the Christian powers of Europe in favor of the Greeks, and of the *right* to interfere "where the general interests of humanity are infringed by the excesses of a barbarous and despotic government." I consider his language as directly applicable to the position of affairs in this Island, and inasmuch as the Gov^t of the United States has repeatedly declared that it can not view with indifference the interference of European powers in the affairs of America, it would seem to have thereby incurred a duty not to be indifferent to the continuance of this war.

The rains and sickness still continue. I have been under the doctor for the last fortnight, am anxious to get away from here as soon as possible, and hope soon to receive your further instructions.

I am very respectfully [etc.].

2219

Benjamin E. Green, Special Agent of the United States to the Dominican Republic, to John M. Clayton, Secretary of State of the United States [1]

No. 4   SANTO DOMINGO, *January 4, 1849 [1850?]*.

SIR: Since the date of my last despatch, No 3,[2] I have been spending several weeks at Bani, for the benefit of its baths, and purer air, whilst awaiting your reply. This I hope will not be much longer delayed; for, in addition to my anxiety to reach home, I desire to escape as soon as possible from this ungenial climate, having, since my return from Bani, had fever & dissentery, & now an influenza, with which I can scarce see to write.

My last despatch, No 3, was forwarded via St. Thomas, to care of our commercial agent at that port. I now avail myself of an opportunity to send a duplicate by an American vessel to New York direct. To what is there said I have but little to add. To one fact, however, I would call your attention, as showing how our commerce suffers by the continuance of the predatory & incendiary warfare of the Haytiens. During the six months *previous* to their last invasion, the number of American vessels at this port amounted to 27, (a great falling off from former years); and for the six months *subsequent* to six only. This may be produced in part by the higher prices of mahogany, inducing shipments to Europe rather than to the United States; but the chief cause is the decrease of products in consequence of the abstraction of labor from industrial pursuits, to repel the Haytiens, who generally time their invasions at the season of harvest. The loss of their crops deprives them of the means of paying for our provisions &c, of which we formerly sent, and in peaceful times would again send, large cargoes.

---

[1] Special Agents, vol. 15. Received February 13.

The date, January 4, 1849, was clearly written on the date line of this despatch, in the hand and ink of the rest of the document. Above the year 1849, in red ink, followed by a question mark, is the date 1850, which is evidently the correct date, since Green's instructions to go to Santo Domingo were not written until June 13, 1849 (see above, this volume, pt. I, doc. 2193), and its serial number, 4, places it between his No. 3, of October 24, 1849, above, this part, doc. 2218, and his No. 5, of January 28, 1850, below, this part, doc. 2222.

[2] Above, this part, October 24, 1849, doc. 2218.

Whereas of the six American vessels, which have touched here in the last six months, not one brought cargo direct from the United States.

I send hereto annexed an extract from a letter of Messrs. Rothschild Coen & Co. of St. Thomas, to their house at this place;[1] from which it appears that Souluque [Soulouque] has been, through secret agents, tampering with the blacks of that Island for their aid in annexing it to his dominions. I write to our commercial agent at St. Thomas, requesting him to forward to you a correct and full account of the affair. I have no doubt however of the truth of the statements of the annexed extract, so far as it goes; and send it to you, as confirming what I had previously written of the magnificent intentions of the imperial court of Port au Prince.

Our information from the frontiers is that Souluque [Soulouque] is making great preparations for another invasion, which is looked for towards the middle of February.

I have already given my opinion in favor of making a commercial Treaty with the Dominicans. I would add that, if not deemed advisable to conclude a Treaty with them, notice should be given to Souluque, that, unless he desists from molesting them, we will interfere to put a stop to the war, which is desolating the finest & richest of the Antilles, and injuring our commerce to a corresponding extent. This alone would, I think, effect all that the Dominicans want—peace—and would involve the expense only of sending a man of war to give the notice, which might be well coupled with a demand for the payment of the claims of our citizens—In return for such assistance the U. S. may have whatever they may desire from the Dominicans. Should that notice not have the desired effect, and thereby involve us in the necessity of taking further steps for the pacification of the Island, I think our honor & interests alike require us to do so.

I am anxiously looking for a man of war with your further instructions, and do not think it advisable to present myself at Port au Prince, for the settlement of our claims, in any less imposing conveyance.

I have the honor [etc.].

2220

Manuel T. Delmonte, Minister of Foreign Affairs of the Dominican Republic, to Benjamin E. Green, Special Agent of the United States to the Dominican Republic [2]

A-1   SANTO DOMINGO, *January 24 [23?], 1850.*

HONORABLE SIR: I am charged by my government to communicate to you that, desirous of putting an end to the cruel war, which we have sustained

[1] Not included in this publication.
[2] Special Agents, vol. 15; enclosure A-1, with Green to the Secretary of State, January 28, 1850, below, this part, doc. 2222. In the translation, the date is January 24, but in the

against the Haytiens since the moment of our glorious separation, we would see with pleasure the intervention of the powerful Anglo-American nation, which you represent, to maintain [Note.   The word *obtener* is translated by Neuman 1. to *obtain;* 2, to preserve, maintain; which latter definition I have adopted, in the above translation, as the one, which best expresses the intention of the writer] peace, which is so necessary to the moral & physical progress of our country; it being well understood, preserving always our nationality and independence as a condition, *sine qua non*, of any agreement with our enemies.

With sentiments of the highest consideration [etc.].

2221

Benjamin E. Green, Special Agent of the United States to the Dominican Republic, to Manuel T. Delmonte, Minister of Foreign Affairs of the Dominican Republic [1]

A–2   SANTO DOMINGO, *January 24, 1850.*

SIR: I have the honor to acknowledge the receipt of your note of the 23ᵈ inst, informing me that the Dominican govᵗ, desirous of putting an end to the Haytian war, would be pleased to see the intervention of the Government of the United States for the restoration of peace, of which the maintenance of the nationality & independence of the Dominican Republic is mentioned as an indispensable condition.

By the earliest opportunity I will forward a copy of your communication to my government and request its prompt decision thereon.

I have the honor [etc.].

2222

Benjamin E. Green, Special Agent of the United States to the Dominican Republic, to John M. Clayton, Secretary of State of the United States [2]

No. 5   SANTO DOMINGO, *January 28, 1850.*

SIR: In my despatches, Noˢ 3 & 4,[3] I gave you concisely my views of the state of things in this Island, and the reasons why the Government of the United States should interfere to put a stop to the sanguinary & barbarous warfare, which is desolating this, the richest of the Antilles.   I have been

---

Spanish original it is *enero* 23; see reference to it, in the second paragraph of the transmitting despatch, No. 5, January 28, 1850, below, this part, doc. 2222.

[1] Special Agents, vol. 15; enclosure A-2, with Green to the Secretary of State, January 28, 1850, below, this part, doc. 2222.
[2] Special Agents, vol. 15.   Received February 28.
[3] Above, this part, October 24, 1849, and January 4, 1850, docs. 2218 and 2219.

anxiously waiting your reply and further instructions, having now been absent much longer than I expected & much, I fear, to the detriment of my affairs at home.

Mean while I have received a direct application for the intervention of the U. States, by a note from the Dominican Minister of foreign affairs, dated the 23ᵈ inst, of which I send a copy hereto annexed, with a translation and copy of my answer thereto, (A.)[1]

Since my first arrival here in August last, it has been the wish of the people of the northern provinces and also of a part of the Ministers, that such an application should be made to the U. States. Mʳ Delmonte, the minister of foreign relations, also, either despairing of assistance from France, or convinced by the arguments, which I have communicated to him through a mutual friend, that the true interest of the Dominicans is to remain independent & induce a white immigration from the U. S., some time since abandoned his French protection idea, and, as I am assured, now cordially unites with the other ministers in favor of independence, American alliance & white immigration from the United States.

Baez, the President, however, while he declares himself ready to accept the first combination, which may offer for the pacification of the Island, either has his own reasons for not entering into these, the present, wishes of his Cabinet, or still hopes that France will accept the protectorate, notwithstanding the return of Mʳ Chedeville, the french chancelier, who arrived here on the 20ᵗʰ inst, having been unable in 8 months to obtain any reply whatever from his government to the application, of which he was the bearer. I am told that in 1843, Baez, then a delegate to Port au Prince, there met as French Commissioner Mʳ Adolphe Barrot, a brother the Ferdinand Barrot of the new french ministry, who promised him the assistance of France, if this end of the island would separate from Hayti & hoist the french flag. The movement for separation was made before Baez's return from Port au Prince; instead of the French, the flag of independence was raised; Dʳ Caminero was despatched to obtain the recognition of our govᵗ, and the arrangement between Baez & Barrot thus failed. The failure of the application to the U. S. for recognition has contributed to place Baez where he now is, and those, who know him best, suppose that the advent of Ferdinand Barrot to the French Ministry has given him new hopes of ultimately carrying out the arrangement made with his brother. He himself assures me that he has no longer any such expectation, but those, who have been his best friends & supporters, begin to doubt his sincerity. Certain it is that it was only under the apprehension that a Spanish fleet, which had been off this harbor for several days, was Haytien, that he concurred in the application herewith submitted; a step which the ministers

[1] Both are above, this part, dated January 24, though the former should, doubtless, have been January 23, 1850, docs. 2220, and 2221.

have for some time desired to take, and which I have reason to believe he half regrets, now that his apprehension has passed by.

On the 21st inst the boy at the signal station announced a fleet of three sail in sight; on the 22^d they were again announced as Spanish men of war, but kept at so great distance from shore that their colors could not be distinctly made out. On the 23 they again appeared at a distance, & manœuvred in a manner to excite suspicion. It began to be rumored that they were the Haytien fleet. On observing their movements & size with a good glass I felt confident that the Haytiens could have no such vessels and was not without hope, in spite of their suspicious movements, that they might turn out to be Americans. In this hope I was preparing to send out pilots to meet & bring them in, when I met Genl Alfon [Alfau?], & from him learned that the Gov^t was about sending out a schooner to ascertain their true character & purpose. I told him that in my opinion they were not Haytiens; that on the contrary, I hoped they would prove to be the American fleet, & purposed to send our pilots or even to go myself to meet them.

The Gov^t, on learning this immediately offered me the schooner, which they were preparing, and two pilots. Being well satisfied that the vessels outside were either American or European, and if European, wishing to be the first to know their purpose, I at once determined to go out myself, & accepted their offer. Having done so, & while the schooner was completing her ballast, I called at the English Consul's, to learn what was going on. He, still ignorant of my intention to go out, told me that it was certainly the Haytien fleet, as the Capt of the Eng Man of War Persian had given him certain marks of the Haytien vessels, by which he could not fail to know them, & that his opinion was corroborated by an English Merchant Captain, which had just come in & passed near them. This was a further inducement for me to accompany the Pilots for the purpose of saying to the Commander (should it prove to be the Haytien fleet come to enforce the blockade declared some five years since but never made effective by the presence of a single armed vessel) that the American vessels now in this port and on the coast must not be molested or detained on pretext of that blockade.

I also prepared a letter, addressed to the Haytien Minister of foreign affairs, proposing a suspension of hostilities, until the views of my government in regard to the pacification of the Island could be known, & had it ready intending to be guided by circumstances as to the propriety of sending it.

On reaching the wharf I found that the opinion of the English Consul & Merchant Captain had got abroad, and very much alarmed the crew of the dutch Schooner, Anna, which was to take us out. The Captain insisted on having a clearance as usual for Curacoa; that given him having been made out (by my request), *at my disposal*, as special agent of the U. S, without naming any port of destination.

I would not consent to his taking a clearance for Curacoa [Curaçao], or any other paper, which could give a false character to the transaction; and having with much difficulty quieted his apprehensions, sailed out about midnight of the 23ᵈ & 24ᵗʰ.

At daylight we made the fleet several miles to windward. The Capt waked me for orders, when I directed him to steer straight for the frigate, which proved to be Spanish, the Isabel Segunda, commanded by Don Antonio de Arevalo, & accompanied by the Brigs, *Habanero* & *Patriota*, all recently from Havana.

On going on board the frigate, the Commander, looking first at a document, which I suppose were his instructions, asked me at once if I was Mʳ Green. On my answering affirmatively he gave me a very cordial welcome. He then asked me where I was going & on my answering "back to Stᵒ Domingo, whence I had only come out to speak with him", he put about to bring me back, the Schooner following to receive me when near the city. I told him that having seen him on & off the Port for several days, I desired, with that frankness & good faith, which characterize my govᵗ, & which Spain had so recently experienced, to know the purpose of his visit. He answered that he was on his ordinary cruise for the protection of Spanish Commerce, and also where occasion offered to protect that of the allies of Spain; that the Spanish Government fully appreciated the course of the Govᵗ of the U. S., in the recent Cuba invasion affair, and that if I required the assistance of himself or his fleet for the protection of American Commerce or for any other friendly office, during the absence of our own fleet, which had recently left Havana for Nicaragua, I had only to let him know wherein he could serve me.

Information of my arrival here was, I have reason to believe, immediately given to the Governor of Puerto Rico, accompanied with suggestions of my having much more extensive power than I really have, and within a few weeks after my landing here, the Turks Island Gazette announced that I had come fully *empower[ed]* to offer annexation.

It was evident that the Spanish Commander had some special instructions relative to this island, and also that my name and mission were mentioned in those instructions. He asked me many questions as to the military and naval force of the Dominicans & also of the Haytiens, and requested me, when I went ashore to send him one, or if possible, two pilots well acquainted with all the Coast & who could take him where he would find the Haytien fleet and into Port au Prince. When I told him that the Dominican Govᵗ. had found it necessary to call into service all their pilots, & that he could only get one by applying to the Govᵗ, he declined doing so, seeming unwilling to hold any communication with the Govᵗ or even to come to anchor. Seeing this I took occasion to intimate that the United States desired to see the Dominican Republic remain independent. He asked if the Dominicans had not applied for the protection of France, to which I replied that they were anxious for the intervention of any nation, which would pacificate the island, maintaining their independence.   He asked who were the aggressors in the war, and I told him that the Haytiens had always been till recently, and that the only object of the Dominicans is to force a peace by attacking their enemies at home.

On returning to the city, I made known to the Dominican Gov^t, verbally, his wish to obtain a pilot.   They immediately sent him two, with a note stating that they did so at my request, to which note he replied, returning his thanks.

He is to return here after passing to Port au Prince and round the Island. What his real purpose is I can not positively say; but think, that if it goes beyond the obtaining of information, it is hostile to the Haytiens, as he seemed very desirous of falling in with their fleet, and asked several times whether I thought the English would protect them.   It may also be to reassert the ancient rights of Spain to this end of the Island.

If your instructions in answer to my previous communications have not already anticipated the application, herewith sent, for the intervention of the U S, I trust that the answer thereto, whatever it may be, will be promptly given.

I have the honor [etc.].

2223

Benjamin E. Green, Special Agent of the United States to the Dominican Republic, to John M. Clayton, Secretary of State of the United States [1]

No. 6   Santo Domingo, *February 15, 1850.*

Sir: My father having written me, under date of the 25 Sept, that you promised to send a man of war to hasten my return, I have been anxiously awaiting its arrival with the further instructions asked for in mine, nos 3 4 & 5.[2]   I still hope to receive those instructions and to be on my way homeward before this reaches you.   If however more pressing matters have delayed your action on the questions involved in the state of things existing here, I beg for them your immediate attention; repeating at the same time the motives heretofore suggested for the Government of the U. States to sustain the Dominicans, and interfere to pacificate the island.   I ask your immediate action, not only because of my desire to reach home, but because the situation of these people, the exhaustion produced by the war; the facility of introducing among them spies, to produce disturbance and disaffection in their black population; the deplorable consequences of a single reverse of fortune; the shocking atrocities, which, judging by past experience, would certainly follow any success of their enemy; and, not least of all, the presence

[1] Special Agents, vol. 15.   No receipt date is on the original.
[2] Above, this part, October 24, 1849, January 4 and 28, 1850, docs. 2218, 2219, and 2222.

of active diplomatic agents of two European powers, France & England, both of which, there is great reason to believe, desire to see the Haytiens victorious & in possession of this end of the island—require a prompt solution of their difficulties and give them strong claims on the United States for sympathy and aid.

The Treaty made in Paris has not been ratified by France, and late advices announced that M. Place, the French Consul at this place, is to be removed in consequence of his being considered too favorable to the Dominican cause. I can only attribute the non ratification of the treaty to the protest of the Haytien Government, declaring that without the revenue of the ports of this end of the island, it can not continue to pay the French debt.

Of the English Consul (and plenipotentiary) who is a German recently entered into the diplomatic service of Great Britain, I have seen much. His official intercourse with the Dominican gov^t, his constant demands upon it, the news which he receives from Port au Prince and circulates here, his evident annoyance at whatever favors the Dominicans, the ill disguised pleasure, with which he receives news favorable to the Haytiens, and the tone of his private conversation, reflecting more and more, after every despatch received from Port au Prince or the foreign office, a decided partiality for the black emperor, leave no doubt on my mind that his instructions are dictated by a very strong bias in favor of the Haytiens.

Shortly after my arrival, he asked me, whether, as religious toleration is actually admitted here (there now being protestant churches in this city, at Puerto Plata & Semana) I would deem it advisable or necessary to introduce into a treaty an article securing the continuance of that toleration. I answered that, inasmuch as the Dominican Constitution makes the Catholic religion that of the State the continuance of the toleration as present existing ought to be secured by Treaty by all protestant countries recognizing the Republic.

Later he told me that he had received instructions, as the treaty offerred by Great Britain had been twice rejected, not to make another offer, and that in fact his Government did not wish to make any treaty with the Dominicans, because they were compelled to use British manufactures without a treaty, and the consumption would not be increased if there was one.

Recently however he has pressed for a renewal of negotiations, making a meditated scientific exploration of the provinces of Cibao the pretext for immediately entering on & concluding a treaty; and a plenipotentiary has, after some delay, been appointed to meet him; the conferences beginning this morning. I will forward by a vessel, which leaves day after tomorrow, a copy of the Treaty, which he proposes, if I can in the meantime obtain it.

The difficulty in the two former negotiations was in relation to the 2^d

Article, which provides that "the subjects of H. B. M. may buy & sell from & to whom they please, without being restrained by any monopoly, contract or exclusive privilege &c &c."

When in my former despatch, No 2, 26 Sep[1], I said that "Baez's opposition to this article was explained by his desire to establish a tobacco monopoly as the basis of a loan to be effected in France, in which he is supposed to be personally interested", I did so on English authority, and probably did the Dominican negotiator less than justice. His opposition to this Article was on the ground, as explained by himself, that the condition of the two countries was very different; that the Dominicans were struggling for existence in a war of life or death, and that pending the war they ought not, without an equivalent, to tie their hands. He admitted the impolicy of the monopoly system; that every monopoly was an evil; but that a time might arrive when it might be necessary to submit to a less evil to avoid a greater, to save life by the amputation of a limb. In this view of the subject, I think he was perfectly correct.

I do not believe that the present negotiations will result in the conclusion of a treaty—certainly not in one objectionable to the United States, without a change of ministry. On the contrary I suspect that the renewal of negotiations has no other object than to raise difficulties, which may apply to and prevent a treaty with the United States.

I send you herewith, No. 1, a copy of an opinion given by the Arch Bishop,[2] in reply to an interrogatory, addressed to him by the English Consul, (in anticipation of the renewal of negotiations) whether an article in a treaty, stipulating for religious toleration, would be acceptable to the Clergy.

Inasmuch as religious toleration actually exists in favor even of Dominican citizens; as the Arch Bishop has nothing to do with the negotiation of treaties, and no objection to such an article could be reasonably anticipated on the part of the Gov[t] or people, I can imagine no other motive for this departure from the usual course of diplomatic proceedings, unless to raise a question with the old ArchBishop, which might prove a difficulty to any negotiation with the U. S.

Notwithstanding the respect generally entertained for the ArchBishop, he is regarded as of a past age, and his opposition (should it be thus excited) to an article, securing the freedom of worship & burial to American citizens, would not be for a moment regarded by the Government. Nor would I deem it necessary to send you a copy of this paper, did I not believe it to be the product of an attempt to oppose obstacles to any negotiation, which I might propose favorable to the Dominicans.

[1] His No. 2 is above, this part, doc. 2217, but dated September 27, 1849. His No. 1, also above, this part, is dated August 27, 1849, doc. 2216.
[2] Not included in this publication.

No. 2 is a copy of a letter from Mᵣ Ridgway,[1] an American merchant in St. Thomas, to whom I wrote for full information in regard to the arrest at that place of the supposed Haytien Agent referred to in a former despatch.

I have the honor [etc.].

2224

Benjamin E. Green, Special Agent of the United States to the Dominican Republic, to John M. Clayton, Secretary of State of the United States [2]

No. 8   SANTO DOMINGO, *February 19, 1850.*

SIR: Since the date of the application of the Dominican government for the intervention of the United States, to pacificate this island (forwarded with my despatch No. 5) [3] the English Plenipotentiary, Sir Robᵗ Schomburck [Schomburgk] has been very urgent for the renewal of negotiations upon the Treaty, of which I sent you a copy with my last despatch, No. 7.[4] I have reasons to believe that one, if not the chief, object in renewing negotiations was to raise difficulties, which might apply to & prevent any negotiation with the United States.

It appears, however, that he seems very anxious to conclude the treaty immediately, and, as an inducement for this government to accept it in the terms he proposes, has intimated to, if not assured, the President that if the Treaty is signed and the mediation of England simultaneously asked for, it will effect the pacification they desire.

The Dominicans, however, have so long been accustomed to regard the English as the peculiar friends of the blacks, that they receive with great suspicion their offers of friendship & mediation. This call for mediation has been several times invited, but the Dominicans have hesitated to call for it, but they might thereby afford the English a pretext openly to take part in favor of the Haytiens. One of the members of the Cabinet, in speaking to me on the subject, said that to invite the mediation of the British Government, if it was not made a pretext openly to aid the Haytiens, would leave them (the Dominicans) in the condition of the horse, which, having invited the man to aid him in his battle with the other beasts, afterwards found a rider on his back, whom he could not get rid of. Such is the general sentiment, and so far from having to warn them against the encroaching spirit of the British Govᵗ, I have on various occasions sought to moderate their asperity towards that Government and its representative here.

[1] Not included in this publication.   [2] Special Agents, vol. 15. Received March 16.
[3] Above, this part, January 28, 1850, doc. 2222.
[4] Neither the text of the projected treaty nor the covering despatch is included in this publication. The treaty was commercial. In addition to mentioning the enclosed projet, the despatch discussed the presence, in the country, of negroes claiming United States and British nationality, and their desire to be relieved from military duty. He added that the English consul always insisted that any such ever having had, or even claiming, British nationality should be relieved, such relief having been conceded.

Yesterday morning, at the funeral of Commandant Fagalde, a french-man who commanded the Dominican fleet in their late cruises against the Haytiens, assassinated under circumstances, which have excited some suspicions that it may have been the work of Haytianism, the President requested an interview with me in the evening.   His purpose was—to tell me that he had positive information that the Haytiens were making great preparations for invading at an early day, & that, while the Gov^t felt confident of repelling them, as they have always heretofore done, it desired, if possible, to prevent the invasion and the additional exhaustion, bloodshed and misery which would ensue;—and to know what I could do.   I answered that of myself I could do nothing, until the arrival of the man of war with instructions, which I daily expected.   I could only say that I had urged my government to interfere, but could give no positive assurance as to what its decision would be.

He then told me that a Haytien Agent was expected to arrive here in a few days, ostensibly to propose conditions of peace; really, as he believed, to examine their strength, condition &c, previous to the invasion; that he had been and is now much pressed to call in the mediation of England, which he is unwilling to do, unless it should be conjointly with the United States and France; that the action of the United States on the application for intervention, if favorable, might be too dilatory to prevent the anticipated invasion; that as I could give no assurance as to what that action would be, he felt it to be his duty to omit no step, which might tend to peace & the benefit of his country, and was therefore inclined to invite the mediation of England, jointly with France & the U. S., if such a step would be acceptable to the latter.   He requested my opinion on the propriety of calling for such a joint mediation, which I declining to give on the moment, he asked me to consider the subject and give him another interview today.

This morning he sent for me to renew the conversasion.   I told him that there existed in the U. States a strong public opinion opposed to the interference of European powers in the affairs of America, which, together with the fact of our not having recognized Hayti, might prove an obstacle to our uniting in any such joint mediation; that nevertheless, if he had any reason to hope that the mediation proposed would be effective to produce peace & prevent the disasters of an invasion, I could not take the responsibility of advising him not to ask for it.   As he seemed apprehensive that such a step might not be well received by the Government of the United States and might weaken the sympathies of our people, which the Dominicans desire to cultivate, I could do no less than give my frank opinion, that, the action of the United States being uncertain, he owed it to the whites of this end of the Island and particularly to the frontier inhabitants to lose no possible chance of securing them against a repetition of the scenes of the last Haytien invasion.

He asked my opinion as to the best mode of making the application. I advised a circular to be sent to each of the diplomatic & consular representatives here, in the nature of a manifesto addressed to the whole civilized world. He seemed to think that too general to be effective, as what was addressed to all might be considered as requiring particular attention from no one, and desired to confine it to England, France and the United States, counting on the friendship of the two last to restrain the former, if disposed to make the call for mediation a pretext to sustain the Haytiens. In regarding France as their friend, the Dominicans are perhaps led astray by their confidence in the individual, who represents that country here; for the most probable explanation of the non-ratification of the Treaty & non-acceptance of the Protectorate is that the Haytien Gov^t declares its inability to pay the French debt, without the revenue of the ports of this end of the island; and it is to be expected that France may require as the condition of her mediation, having heretofore required as the condition of her recognition, that the Dominicans shall assume a part of the Haytien debt. On the other hand, as Great Britain desires to establish free trade and antimonopoly treaties, which the Dominicans are willing to enter into *in time of peace*, while new monopolies are being every day created by the Haytiens, it would seem natural that she should befriend the former, were it not for a fanatical fondness for the blacks, or a deeper political motive.

Lest they should be disappointed in counting on the unconditional friendship of France, I suggested that Spain, whose interests, from the position of Cuba & Puerto Rico, coincide with our own in requiring that the Haytiens should be kept within their legitimate bounds, should be included in the application.

For my own part I should prefer that the United States should alone meet the wishes of the Dominicans, & provide for the pacification of the island along with the settlement of our claims against Hayti. I believe this could be done without any expense beyond that of keeping a man of war always in these waters, which the commercial interests & personal safety of our citizens at all events & at all times imperatively demand.

Apart from considerations of interest—of the advantages, which the Dominicans would glady grant us in the Bays of Semana or Manzanillo, or both,—I hold it to be an action worthy of the United States to protect the whites of this island from those, whose uniform conduct, since the first massacre of their masters, has inseparably connected its name with the idea of blood and horror. In this work I should rejoice to see the United States foremost and alone. But in the uncertainty, (arising from the delay of the instructions asked for) whether the Government will adopt my view of the subject, I have, thus appealed to, felt it to be a paramount duty to give my consent to, & approval of, the proposed application for a joint mediation, which is not intended to modify the application heretofore made to the

United States for intervention, but is made in view of the possibility that they may decline, or too long delay, to interfere.

The draft of the circular will be submitted to my revision before being concluded on, & will be held back for the last moment to be in time to reach St Thomas for the European Steamer, in a Schooner, which the Dominican Gov[t] sends for the purpose.

In regard to our claims against Hayti, we may well demand that they shall be first settled and paid, before Soulouque [Soulouque] further exhausts his treasury by another invasion for conquest, which will only result in empoverishing still more both parties to the contest.

Feb. 22[d] The Captain of the American Schooner *Dacotah* has waited three days for me to obtain a copy of the circular, of which I send the original,[1] having no time to make a translation or copy. It will be sent to the English and French Consuls tomorrow or next day, & by them immediately forwarded to their respective governments by the Steamer of the 1st prox. I beg that you will write me immediately, and if possible send by a man of war, or revenue cutter, as no reliance can be placed on occasional merchant vessels, and I should regret if I did not receive an answer at least as soon as the English & French Consuls, whose governments are very prompt in answering communications from this place.

I have the honor [etc.].

P. S. Feb 23[d] After closing the above it was thought advisable to modify the language of the circular, and I had to detain the *Dacotah* until today, agreeing with the Captain, James Smith Jr., to pay him fifty dollars demurrage, which is but half what his Charter party would allow him for the time he has waited. I have given him a draft on the Department for that amount, which I hope will be approved of.

2225

Manuel T. Delmonte, Minister of Foreign Affairs of the Dominican Republic, to Benjamin E. Green, Special Agent of the United States to the Dominican Republic [2]

No. 10   SANTO DOMINGO, *February 22, 1850.*

HONORABLE SIR: It is now six years, since the Dominican People, shaking off the humiliating yoke which had bound them for the long period of twenty two years to Anarchical Haiti, swore to live independent within their own

[1] The text of the translation, evidently made in the Department of State, and which is found with the signed, rubricated original Spanish of the document in the manuscript volume, is below, this part, dated February 22, 1850, doc. 2225.

[2] Special Agents, vol. 15; enclosed with Green to the Secretary of State, No. 8, February 19, 1850, above, this part, doc. 2224. The accompanying despatch was not closed until February 23, hence this enclosure dated the 22d.

ancient and known boundaries, or be buried amid the ruins of their country. The proclamation of our Independence, dated the 16th of January, 1844, which was forwarded to your government in due season, contains a full and thorough exposition of the causes which impelled us to adopt a resolution, which was as necessary as it was heroic, as you will be able to Judge from the copy which I have the honor to enclose.[1]

The abiding principle of moderation, to which we have always adhered, during six years of protracted hostilities, throughout which, Victory has ever been on the side of our Just cause, is of itself, sufficient evidence, in the estimation of an impartial world, that we have religiously kept our promises, and also, that we have baptized in our own blood, the standard of rational liberty which we have hoisted.

Our rule of conduct, in all our operations, has been a profound sympathy with humanity; the rights of man and the usages of war have ever been the objects of our reverential respect; and the observance of plighted faith, our first duty.

Having banded together, in defense of our coasts and our frontier, we have calmly waited for the moment of aggression, in order to repel it with energy; showing, however, a proper regard for those laws and those principles which are universally recognized, and pursuing our onward march to victory, with as much moderation and forbearance, as our enemies have displayed of odious rancour and ferocity.

This conduct, Mr. Plenipotentiary, which is so noble and accords so well with those international laws that all civilized people respect, has been a source of very great annoyance to our enemies, who have invariably left a track of blood behind them, wherever their footsteps have been. Old and defenceless men, women and children, all have been made to succumb to their destructive rage; and while we return to them unhurt, hundreds of prisoners whom they compel to fight against us, again, in direct violation of the usages of war,—they shoot ours, destroy our domestic animals, when they cannot drag them along with them, and reduce to ashes our villages and towns.

The constancy of purpose manifested by the Dominican People, without distinction of classes, in bravely and cheerfully coming forward to repel the enemy whenever he has presented himself on our frontier, abandoning their domestic hearths and the culture of their fields,—the sympathy which our sacred cause has excited among all nations, and the repugnance, which the people of Haiti themselves have more than once evinced in regard to the prosecution of a war, which is unpopular and has not been provoked by us, are undoubtedly sufficient motives to have induced the ruling powers of Haiti to desist from their rash undertaking, and to have inclined them towards peace, which is so necessary to the happiness of both people. But

[1] Not found.

such has not been the case.   The man, who, trampling upon the semi-liberal institutions of his country, raised an imperial throne over the dead bodies of his own brethren, does not seem to relish the tranquillity of a country whose incessant turmoils have afforded him the means for decimating it, and to gratify his passions for luxury and power, without risk and without labor; accordingly, with this barbarous object in view, he is now making preparations for an extraordinary effort to carry out his favorite scheme of conquest and for driving upon our soil the entire mass of that population which he oppresses with monopolies of every kind and the most rampant despotism,— having publicly announced a war of extermination.

Under these circumstances, and with a view of sparing the world the horrid spectacle of two neighbouring people fighting hand to hand, and employing for their mutual destruction all the means that have been invented, and which are repugnant to the civilization of the present age,—a strife that can only end in the total extermination of one of the belligerent parties, or the ruin of both,—self-preservation being the paramount law,—and, being obliged, in case of a fresh invasion, to accept the alternative of war unto death without intermission or quarter,—a war that will be carried on with all the destructive enginries appertaining to such a struggle.—My Government, before rushing into this path of blood and horror, which the law of self-preservation has marked out for it, (for which it is sufficiently prepared beforehand) being desirous, while it is yet practicable, to show its respect for the principles, which it proclaimed in 1844, has resolved to implore, as by these presents I do implore, the mediation of the magnanimous nation which you represent, in order that by means of her assistance, conjointly with that of France and England, to whom we have also addressed ourselves, the government of Haiti may be compelled to sign a peace, honorable to both belligerent States, and guaranteed by the mediating powers.

Haiti would lose nothing by the results of such a peace, as she never took away any rights from our territory; while much would be gained by the other nations in thus contributing to the happiness of the Dominican Republic,— a happiness which would be participated in by all foreigners, to whom our liberal and comprehensive institutions extend proffers of equal rights and equal freedom—equal in every respects [sic] to the rights of native-born citizens.

The adopting this resolution, in advance, my government relies on the conviction of having done all that was incumbent upon it, to satisfy the calls of humanity, and to preserve the good name of the heroic people, whose destinies have been entrusted to its hands, from all stains of dishonor; it is now for your Government to complete the work; But, if unfortunately, (which we will not anticipate) our Just request, should be unheeded, from this moment, we disavow all responsibility for the horrors and disasters that may ensue in a contest like this, which is equally unjust and gratuitous;—

a real anacronism, discreditable to the enlightened policy of the Universe—and whatever may be the results or the harshness of the means we shall adopt, in order to preserve our nationality and the integrity of the territory, we shall be able to stand before the world, calm and serene, with the consciousness of having fulfilled a duty, rendered imperative by necessity.

I beg to inform you that a note of precisely the same character as this, has been addressed, under same date, to the respective consuls of her Britanic Majesty, and of the French Republic, near our Republic, for the purpose of securing concert of action in the matter.

With sentiments of the highest consideration [etc.].

2226

Benjamin E. Green, Special Agent of the United States to the Dominican Republic, to John M. Clayton, Secretary of State of the United States [1]

Private.   SANTO DOMINGO, *March 26, 1850.*

DEAR SIR: I have just learned that a vessel leaves in a few moments for the U. S., anticipating the time of her departure, on account of the Easter holidays.

I have been anxiously awaiting the instructions asked for in my despatches of Oct. 24, 49, of Jan. 24, 1850, and more especially a reply to my despatch, No. 5, of Jan. 28th. [2]

The only written communication, which I have received from the U. S. since I left, is a short letter from my father, dated 25 Sept. In it he says that you had promised to send one or more ships of war to hasten my negotiations & return.

Finding, on my arrival, the condition of things in this country to be as explained in my despatches, I thought best, before entering on any negotiations to have your views thereon; and daily expecting the promised ship of war, it seemed to me proper to await the instructions I had called for, and where possible to delay all action for their receipt.

In the mean time I have cultivated, & have the confidence of Gen[ls] Santana & Alfon [Alfau?], the men of most prestige in the country, and of others. With the President Baez, I have also sought to establish relations of confidence; but within the last few days I learn from a person, who was told by the English Consul, that he is my "enemy". My belief is that the English Consul, (perhaps assisted by another) has availed himself of his being of mixed blood to arouse his opposition to the U. S, and to acquire an unlimited control over him.

[1] Special Agents, vol. 15. Received April 29.
[2] All three are above, this part, docs. 2218, 2221, and 2222. The second reference, however, evidently should have been to his despatch of January 4, since he sent no despatch of January 24.

To this the delay of the instructions asked for has largely contributed.   I trust they will soon arrive.   The time has come when we must determine whether we will surrender to English control both parties on this island, and if speedy action is not taken, it will be too late.

My feelings have been so much enlisted for the whites of this end that, were I to speak as I feel, I might perhaps subject myself to the charge of enthusiasm.   But I believe, after calm consideration, that the U States are bound by every principle of humanity and every consideration of interest to take them under protection, and to promote the immigration and settlement here of a white population friendly to the United States, rather than permit one under the control of G. Britain.

The English Treaty has been signed, with some modifications which I suggested, to assimilate it as much as possible to the projet furnished me.   I will send a copy by first opportunity.

Commodore Parker was here a short time since.   I consulted him as to the course I should pursue in the absence of instructions.   He left orders for the Germantown, or Albany, which are both expected shortly, to give me a passage to Port au Prince.   I hope I will hear from you before the arrival of those vessels, as my detention here is not only a great injury to my interests at home, but the delay is also prejudicial to the interests of the U. States.

Yours truly.

2227

Benjamin E. Green, Special Agent of the United States to the Dominican Republic, to José María Medrano, Minister of Foreign Affairs of the Dominican Republic [1]

No. 1   SANTO DOMINGO, *April 11, 1850.*

SIR: I have the honor to inform you of my intention to leave this country within a few days in the U. S. Steamer *Vixen,* now in port, and to request that you will inform me of the time & place, when & where it will be convenient for H. E. the President of the Dominican Republic, to grant me an audience for the purpose of bidding him adieu.

I avail myself of the opportunity of renewing the assurances (contained in the letter of credence, which I had the honor some months since to present) of the interest, which my government takes in the prosperity of the Dominican Republic, and of its strong desire to cultivate and to deserve the friendship of the Dominicans.

In despatches recently received by the *Vixen,* I have been specially directed by my Government to assure the Dominicans that it heartily sympathizes in their efforts for independence, hopes that they may be crowned

[1] Special Agents, vol. 15; enclosed with Green to the Secretary of State, unnumbered, June 15, 1850, below, this part, doc. 2230.

with success and earnestly desires to see the Republican Gov^t established here prove adequate to the protection and development of the industrial pursuits of its citizens, and to the repulse of the only foreign invaders, whom they have any occasion to regard with uneasiness.[1]

I have also the honor to inform you that notwithstanding that the notes, addressed to me by the Dominican Minister of foreign affairs on the 23^d of January and 22^d of February last,[2] relative to the continuance of the Haytien War, had not reached my government at the date of my last advices, the subject had already been brought to its notice in my previous communications. The Government of the U. S. fully appreciates the disastrous results of that war, not only to both the parties thereto, but also to all other nations, having commercial relations with them; and has authorized me (in case it shall seem necessary & proper) to notify the Haytien authorities that it will not view with indifference any further incursions, on their part, into the territories of the Dominican Republic, for predatory or warlike purposes.

I have the honor [etc.].

2228

José María Medrano, Minister of Foreign Affairs of the Dominican Republic, to Benjamin E. Green, Special Agent of the United States to the Dominican Republic[3]

No. 2   SANTO DOMINGO, *April 13, 1850.*

HONORABLE SIR: I have received your note of the 11th inst,[4] in which you inform me of your intention to absent yourself from the country and desire that the President may give you an audience.

You likewise make known to me the interest, which your Government takes in the prosperity of our Republic, and the earnest desire, which it has, to cultivate and to merit the friendship of the Dominicans; & lastly that you have late instructions to make known to the Haytians that the Republic of the United States will view with displeasure every aggression on their part against us.

As to the leave taking and audience, which you ask of the President, he makes known through me that this will take place on tuesday, the 16th of the present, in the National palace, at half past twelve.

The Government believes that the illustrious government of Washington can not view with indifference the sufferings of a people so heroic as the

---

[1] This evidently refers to the instruction of February 16, 1850, above, this volume, pt. 1, doc. 2194.

[2] The former is not included in this publication; but the latter is above, this part, doc. 2225.

[3] Special Agents, vol. 15; enclosed with Green to the Secretary of State, unnumbered, June 15, 1850, below, this part, doc. 2230.

[4] Above, this part, doc. 2227.

Dominicans, who have given & give so many proofs of greatness & magnanimity.   As to the reciprocal friendship of the two people, we desire to strengthen it more & more, and in all time we will be constant in this principle.

As to the intimation, which may be made to our enemies, not to molest us, it is praiseworthy for a powerful people to incline to the support of a weak one, preventing also the evils, which might befall humanity by the disappearance of a young nation, which presents itself in the centre of the Antilles, dissipating the black cloud, which threatens (wishes) to obscure the lights of the present age in all of them, in order to sink them in the most horrible chaos.

God preserve you many years.

2229

Benjamin E. Green, Special Agent of the United States to the Dominican Republic, to John M. Clayton, Secretary of State of the United States [1]

PORT AU PRINCE, *May 9, 1850.*

SIR: The Haytien Government is making great preparations for an overwhelming attack upon the other end of the Island. I have just learned that Messrs. B. C. Clark & Co, of Boston, are preparing a vessel of war for the Haytiens, to aid in that attack; also that Messrs. Ropier & Co, of New York, are to send out a corvette; the armaments of both vessels to be sent out in a merchant vessel to meet them here.

These vessels seem to me to come under the same law as the Steamer "United States".—I beg to call your attention to the subject and hope that our neutrality laws will be put in force to prevent their departure, and that care will be taken to prevent any evasion of the law.

Very Respectfully [etc.].

2230

Benjamin E. Green, Special Agent of the United States to the Dominican Republic, to John M. Clayton, Secretary of State of the United States [2]

[EXTRACTS]

WASHINGTON, *June 15, 1850.*

SIR: The U. S. St^r Vixen, with your despatch of the 16 February last,[3] reached Santo Domingo on the 28 March.   On the receipt of that despatch, I should have left S^to Domingo at once; but at that time the Albany & Ger-

[1] Special Agents, vol. 15.   Received May 27.
[2] *Ibid.*   No receipt date is on the original.   [3] Above, this volume, pt. I, doc. 2194.

mantown sloops of war were daily expected and I had understood from Com. Parker that one of them was to proceed to Port au Prince. Believing that nothing could be done there,—that the Haytien Government would, as heretofore, refuse to hold any communication with me—unless accompanied by such a force as would imply that the Gov^t of the U. S. seriously intended to bring the long neglected claims of its citizens to a settlement, I determined to avail myself of the opportunity to arrive at Port au Prince in company with one of the sloops.

I have already explained to you that the French Consuls at both ends of the Island are labouring to bring about an arrangement, by which the Eastern part shall contribute towards the payment of the French claims on Hayti, for spoliations committed by the revolted blacks of the West end on the old French proprietors. This the Dominicans have heretofore resisted, contending that having had no part in the servile revolt of the West end they are not responsible for its excesses and are unwilling, by assuming a portion of the debt, to admit, even by implication, that they were participants or accomplices in the crimes & outrages, in which these French claims originated.

With France it seems to be purely a financial question. The English Agents at St° Domingo & Port au Prince, without having any such direct pecuniary interest, manifest still greater solicitude to effect the submission of the Dominicans and the extension of the Haitien Empire.

I knew that my departure, without giving any reply to their application for our intervention or mediation, would be a sore disappointment to the Dominicans and might give to the English and French Consuls an increased influence, whereby the Dominicans might be again (as in the application for French protection) placed in a false position and their subjugation, which the Haytiens have been unable to accomplish by arms, be brought about by diplomacy. I then anticipated some such fallacious propositions as were in fact soon after made through the British Consul, and altho the universal sentiment of the Dominicans is to abandon the Country, or die in the woods, rather than again submit to Haytien rule, I felt some apprehension lest a combined French and English influence might mislead the Government, disappointed and chagrined at my departure, into some step, tending to weaken the strength of their position and ultimately fatal to their independence, which I understood it to be the wish of our Gov^t to see maintained. I therefore deemed it important to manifest, by something more than verbal expressions of good will, that the Gov^t of the U. S. is not indifferent to their fate, & addressed to the Dominican Minister of foreign relations the note, of which No. 1 hereto annexed is a copy[1]   No. 2 is his reply,[2] the last paragraph of which I recommend particularly to your attention.

Having taken leave of the President and Cabinet on the 16th April, I

[1] Above, this part, April 11, 1850, doc. 2227.   [1] *Ibid.*, April 13, 1850, doc. 2228.

decided to wait no longer for the sloops, and embarked the next day. As we were getting under way the Albany hove in sight. I delivered to Capt. Randolph a sealed letter left with me for him by Com. Parker, at the same time stating my opinion that his presence at Port au Prince, if compatible with his orders and other interests of the service, would have a beneficial effect. He proposed to be there in a week, and I availed myself of the delay to visit the intermediate ports, Jacmel, Aux Cayes & Jeremie.

At Jacmel I met H. B. M.'s Brig Persian, waiting the arrival of Capt. Wyke, British Vice Consul at Port au Prince, who was expected the next day on his way to Stº Domingo. From an accidental remark of Mʳ Larke, U. S. Vice Commercial Agent (who is also British Vice Consul and son in law of the Duke of Tiburon, Haytien Minister of foreign affairs) I drew the inference that the object of his visit was to urge the acceptance of propositions from Souluque. Anticipating the nature of these propositions, and that their tendency and purpose were, by disarming the Dominicans, to facilitate their subjugation, I wrote by the Persian a private note to Genˡ Alfon [Alfau?], cautioning him against them. I regret that I kept no copy of this note; but deem it well to subjoin an extract from his reply[1] (No. 3) as I believe it expresses the common sentiment of the Dominicans.[2] . . .

On my arrival at Port au Prince I learned that the Haytien Govᵗ had chartered a vessel to go around to Jacmel, where it was waiting to convey the French Consul General to Stº Domingo, and that the object of his and the British Vice Consul's combined visit was to induce the Dominicans to hoist the Haitien flag, on the promise that, his authority being thus nominally recognised, Souluque [Soulouque] would leave them virtually independent. Learning at Jacmel that I was on my way to Port au Prince, Capt. Wyke sent despatches by the Persian to his colleague at Stº Domingo & returned to

---

[1] The following is the text of this enclosure:

Felipe Alfau to Benjamin E. Green, Special Agent of the United States to the Dominican Republic

No. 3   SANTO DOMINGO, *May 4, 1850.*

MY DEAR SIR & ESTEEMED FRIEND: With the greatest pleasure I have received your favor of the 19ᵗʰ ultº [Not found. For reason, see his despatch.—Ed.], appreciating highly the advices which it contains, and hoping that they may be repeated with more certainty after your arrival at that Capital.

As to the condition of the English mediation, of which we were already informed, rest assured that the Dominicans will see their country reduced to ashes before they will consent to any transaction with the Haitiens, which has not, for its basis, the formal recognition of their nationality and absolute independence. You already know that this is the sentiment of our present government, and I can assure you that it is also that of all Dominicans, who, altho they may differ in opinion on certain points, have never ceased to be of one accord to live eternally separated from the Haitians; there not being one, who, however much he may desire peace, would degrade himself so low as to accept it with the ignominious condition which is advanced—Our device is "Everything but Haitian and nothing which resembles that."

[2] This omitted portion tells of conversations with United States commercial agents and others, regarding claims against Haiti, and, also, discusses internal Haitian affairs.

his post.   The French Consul General, after delaying several days on account, as I suppose, of my arrival, proceeded on his mission.

Having obtained in the recognition of our Consuls all that could be effected
I availed myself of the delay agreed upon to return to St° Domingo, to ascertain there the precise nature of the propositions made by Souluque.

The Dominican President permitted me to read the communication of Sir
Rob, Schomburgh [Schomburgk], British Consul, containing them, but declined giving me a copy, as Sir Rob' had specially requested him, and he had
promised, not to do so.

The propositions were that the Dominicans acknowledge the authority of
the Emperor and hoist the Haitien flag; that in return Souluque would
promise to appoint none but Dominicans to office within their limits; would
confer titles of nobility on Santana & Baez, the President, the former of
whom might remain as Military, the other as Civil Governor of the Eastern
Departments; that he would likewise confer titles on such other Dominicans
as might be desired, and appoint several as members of the Senate at Port au
Prince; that he would station no troops within their limits and permit them
to maintain their army and navy in the same state of efficiency as at present.

This the Dominicans were urged to accept as a virtual independence and a
merely nominal submission.   You will readily perceive that by the acceptance of such terms, they would forfeit the sympathy, which their gallant
struggle (than which history records nothing more heroic) must excite wherever known, and would place them entirely at the mercy of Souluque [Sou-
louque].   Every sensible man on the Island knows that, having once lowered
their flag, they could not keep their army or navy together for six weeks.

Another most important result would follow.   It would arrest that white
immigration, which the Dominicans invite by liberal laws, granting to white
settlers bounty lands, and the expenses of their passage & maintenance until
established on their new possessions; and, along with the Dominican Republic, would fall one great barrier to the spread of Haitien Vandalism throughout the West Indies.

The reply of the Dominican Gov' was promptly given.   No. 14, hereto
annexed, is a copy.[1]

_____

[1] The text of this enclosure follows:

*José María Medrano, Minister of Foreign Affairs of the Dominican Republic, to Robert
Hermann Schomburgk, British Consul in Santo Domingo*

No. 14   SANTO DOMINGO, *April 30, 1850.*

MR CONSUL: The President, well informed of the contents of the official note, which
under date of the 28th instant you addressed to him, has commissioned me to give you
the due reply conformable to the sentiments, with which he is animated, with respect to
the subject of which it treats.

The President can not do less than make known to you how grateful it is to him to see
the interest, which the Government of H. Britannic Majesty manifests in putting an
end to the unjust and cruel war, which the Haytiens make upon us, without other right
than their pretended power, which however until now they have not been able to estab-

The President earnestly requested me to urge upon the Department the importance of an immediate reply to the application for the intervention or mediation of the Gov^t of the U. States—(See notes from the Dominican Minister of foreign relations, dated 23$^{\underline{d}}$ Jan and 22 Feb 1850,[1] forwarded with former despatches) I beg leave to call your attention specially to the subject.

Having obtained this information, I returned to Port au Prince, where my negotiations ended, as explained by process [procès] verbal hereto annexed (No. 13).[2]

No. 15 is copy of a note, which I addressed to the Haytien Minister of foreign relations, enclosing a list of the U. S. Commercial Agents in Hayti, and requesting him to give the necessary notice of their recognition to the local authorities.   No. 16 is his reply.[3]

---

lish. He, for his part, sustains this war, and will sustain it, by the obligation, which he contracted when he accepted the presidency, to maintain the Dominican nationality and consequently the independence of the Republic; after which he can accept such propositions for peace as may be consistent with such principles.

But as the Dominican Government has requested the mediation of three great powers, to wit, England, France, and the United States of America, no negotiation on this subject can be begun, before the certainty of the acceptance or denial of said request shall have been acquired.

In the mean time let it not seem strange to you to see us make the greatest preparations to repel our enemies, as we have heretofore done even when less able than now, if they still persist in invading our territory.

It is evident that this measure of defence is justified by the mere aggression, carrying with it also, as we hope, the conviction that the epoch of Haitien domination over our country has passed by, and that our government must be solemnly recognised as a condition sine qua non to the admission of any proposition to treat whatever.

This is all that the President can say to you, Mr Consul, in reply to the note, which you have thought well to address to him, repeating to you that he gives his most expressive thanks to the Government of Her Britannic Majesty, the Queen Victoria, for the good offices, which she employs, in the interest of humanity, to inclinar [sic] each party to come to a definitive arrangement for the consolidation of a perfect and lasting peace.

I have the honor [etc.].

[1] Both, above, this part, docs. 2220 and 2225; the first one, however, under date of January 24, although, doubtless, it should have been dated January 23.

[2] Not included in this publication. It recorded a categorical refusal of the Haitians to go into the matter of the claims of United States citizens against the Government of Haiti, at least until all available documentary evidence in support of them should be presented, an intimation being given that the Haitians thought many were not bona fide, and the rest were greatly exaggerated. It told also of arrangements made for recognition by Haiti of United States commercial agents.

[3] The texts of those two communications follow:

Benjamin E. Green, Special Agent of the United States to the Dominican Republic, to L. Dufresne, Duke de Tiburón, Minister of Foreign Affairs of Haiti

No. 15   PORT AU PRINCE, *May 9, 1850.*

SIR: It having been agreed between the Governments of the United States and of Hayti that the Consuls, Vice Consuls and Commercial Agents, appointed by the former for the ports of Hayti open to foreign trade, shall enjoy all the immunities & privileges conceded to the Consuls of other friendly nations; I have the honor to enclose herewith a list of the U. S. Commercial Agents for the different ports of Hayti, and request that Yr Grace will give the necessary notice to the authorities of the ports, to which they are respectively appointed.

With sentiments of high consideration [etc.].

N° 17 is copy of a note addressed to the same minister relative to the pacification of the Island. No. 18 is his reply—& No. 19 my rejoinder.[1]

When I left Port au Prince the French Steamer Crocodile was at Jacmel, waiting to convey the French Consul General to St° Domingo with new propo-

---

L. Dufresne, Duke de Tiburón, Minister of Foreign Affairs of Haiti, to Benjamin E. Green
Special Agent of the United States to the Dominican Republic

No. 16   PORT AU PRINCE, *May 24, 1850.*

SIR: I have had the honor to receive your despatch of the 9th instant, by which you transmit to me the list of the Commercial Agents & Vice Agents, who have been named to represent the Government of the United States in the following parts of the Empire, towit; Port au Prince, Cayes, Jacmel, Gonaives and Cape Haytien.

I have given to the authorities of those different places notice of these nominations, accompanied by the usual instructions.

Accept, Sir, [etc.].

[1] The three communications referred to follow:

Benjamin E. Green, Special Agent of the United States to the Dominican Republic, to L.
Dufresne, Duke de Tiburón, Minister of Foreign Affairs of Haiti

No. 17   PORT AU PRINCE, *May 8, 1850.*

SIR: The Government of the United States has instructed me to express its views in relation to the war of mutual destruction unhappily existing between the inhabitants of the old French and Spanish parts of this island; of which, though heretofore an inactive, it has not been an uninterested spectator.

It is hoped that the Haytien Government will desist from its views of conquest, seeing that the abstraction of labor from industrial pursuits and the large expense of maintaining fleets and armies, tend to demoralize and empoverish the people of Hayti, to destroy all confidence in the stability of its government and must ultimately exhaust and ruin both parties to the contest.

As to the revolting scenes necessarily incident to such a strife, the Government of the United States limits itself to an expression of its earnest desire—a desire common to the whole civilized & Christian world—that they may not be repeated.

The United States, however, have a direct interest in the termination of hostilities. Various citizens of the U. S. have large claims against Hayti, many of which are of long standing. The Government of Hayti is not now able, if disposed, to pay the full amount justly due, and each new military expedition or expenditure, by exhausting its resources, diminishes the security for some ultimate tardy reparation to the American claimants.

The continuance of the war by sea or land is moreover a source of annoyance and injury to American Commerce, placing in jeopardy the lives, no less than the property of American citizens, trading to this island or in the adjacent seas.

The Government of the United States has therefore instructed me to make known to the Haytien authorities its desire for the pacification of the island, and that it will not view with indifference any further incursions, on their part, into the territories of the Dominican Republic, for warlike or predatory purposes.

With sentiments of high consideration [etc.].

L. Dufresne, Duke de Tiburón, Minister of Foreign Affairs of Haiti, to Benjamin E. Green,
Special Agent of the United States to the Dominican Republic

[TRANSLATION]

No. 18   PORT AU PRINCE, *May 26, 1850.*

SIR: Your despatch of the 8th instant [Immediately above.—Ed.], which I had not the honor to receive until the 10th, makes known to me the instructions, which your government has given you relative to the difference, which exists between the Departments of the East and the rest of the Empire.

This difference no one deplores more than the Government of His Majesty: but it constitutes a question of internal polity, which ought to be decided in the family.   The

sitions from Souluque [Soulouque].   What they were I could not learn; but
am very confident that the Dominican Gov^t will not recede from the position
taken in the reply to the English Consul.

I have already informed you that Souluque is making great preparations
for an early & overwhelming attack on the Dominicans; and only awaits the
arrival of the Steamer and other armed vessels expected from England and
the United States.   One of them had arrived at Port au Prince before I left,
and another, as I hear, has already sailed from Boston.   I look with horror to
the possibility of his success.   I have official information that he has sworn
"*by the soul of his mother that he will not leave a chicken alive on the soil of the
Dominicans*", and he is one who will keep to the spirit of his words, if victorious.

I submit herewith copies of the Haytien Constitutions of 1816 and 1846.[1]
In the 1st you will observe, title 1, art. 5, this declaration.

"5.   The Republic of Haiti will never form any enterprise with the view of
making conquests, or of troubling the peace & internal government of foreign
states and islands."

Notwithstanding this declaration, they claimed (see title 2, arts. 40, 41,)

---

conviction of success and the consciousness of its right have alone led the Government
of His Majesty not to avail itself until now of the offers of mediation heretofore made at
different times by France and England with benevolent intentions.   And assuredly if
there be any Power, whose right, as creditor, could interest it in the question, that
would be France.

The constitutional law of the State formally consecrates the unity of the Empire,
the integrity of the territory of Haiti.   The imperative duty of the Emperor is to maintain them.   In the present case of a part of that territory, which attempts to detach
itself and to constitute a schism fatal to one national existence, the right of the Government of His Majesty to reestablish the indivisibility of Haitien territory by all means,
even by that of war, can not be doubted, and the exercise of that right can not be assim-
ilated to a conquest.

The reasons, Sir, which you allege, in favor of the pacification of Hayti, are those,
which militate in all cases against war; and if there were not cases, in which supreme
considerations of safety and national honor outweigh the security of labor and commerce, & the economy of public resources, no power, the strongest, the wisest, the most
civilized, would ever make war under any pretext.

These considerations, nevertheless, are of great weight in the resolutions of the
Government of H. M., since the constant aim of his policy is to effect the pacification
of the insurgent Department by all possible measures of conciliation.   I am happy to
repeat that he has the firm hope of success; he will only have recourse to war as an extremity, which is repugnant to him, but which he believes efficient and legitimate
definitely to extinguish insurrection and to preserve Haytien independence & nationality.

Accept, Sir, the assurance of my perfect consideration.

*Benjamin E. Green, Special Agent of the United States to the Dominican Republic, to L.
Dufresne, Duke de Tiburón, Minister of Foreign Affairs of Haiti*

No. 19   PORT AU PRINCE, *May 27, 1850.*

SIR: I have the honor to acknowledge the receipt of your note of yesterday, relative
to the war, which unfortunately disturbs the peace and prosperity of this Island.

Your note will be duly submitted to the Government of the United States by
Your ob^t serv^t.

[1] Not included in this publication.

"*The,* (whole) *island of Haiti (formerly called St° Domingo) and the adjacent islands dependent thereon*".

They were not then in possession of, and had no right to, the Eastern or Spanish part, which they afterwards conquered in 1822; and in the division of their territory, they left the Spanish part to be divided, when conquered, into Departments, the limits of which were to be fixed by a law.

In their later Constitutions (see that of 1846) they have had the consistency to omit the declaration against the conquest of the adjacent islands.

The miserable condition of Haiti is too well known to need that I should picture it. As, however, the religious teachers of any people furnish a criterion, by which to judge of their condition in other respects, it may be proper to remark that most, if not all, their priests have been excommunicated in other countries by the Church, which they profess to serve. I was informed by the Chief Priest at Port au Prince and by many others, in whose statements I have more confidence, that many of the Haitiens retain, or have returned to, their African superstitions and Fetishes, worshipping snakes and other idols.

In 1844, a few Dominicans driven to desperation, rose in the night at the City of St° Domingo, and seized the city gate, called conde. They had with them the sympathies of all the foreigners, some of whom, by exaggerating their number & strength, frightened the Haytien garrison into capitulation. The movement was sustained by the whole Dominican population, who at the first news flocked to the aid of those, who had begun the movement at St° Domingo. Without funds, or other arms than the machetes, or rough cutlasses, used in their agriculture they drove out the Haitiens & have since maintained their independence. It was a glorious struggle and against great odds.

Their magnanimity equalled their Courage. They gave free egress to all those, who desired to return to Hayti or leave the country, proclaiming equality of rights to those, who would aid in defending their cause. Their prisoners were treated with kindness; so much so that on one occasion, when, thro' the mediation of the French Consul, several hundred were released to be sent back to Hayti, they were unwilling to return, hid themselves in the woods, had to be arrested and forced to embark. They are a religious people, believing themselves invincible by the Haytiens, so long as they have the ArchBishop to pray, and Santana to fight, for them. They are much fewer in number than their aggressors, & being obliged to stand always at arms, they are poor and anxious for peace. They have nevertheless made considerable advances and amongst other things, the Gov^t, with its limited means, has undertaken to revive on a small scale the once so celebrated university of St Tomas de Aquinas, which the Haytiens destroyed, and of which the present Minister of the Interior, Caminero, was in Spanish times Doctor of Laws and Manuel Del Monte Minister of finance, Professor of Latin.

The President, who is a man of intelligence and was well educated in

France, was selected from motives of policy.   Notwithstanding that he is the son of an old Spaniard by a woman of color, the Dominican Republic must be considered as essentially a government of whites, with but little greater admixture of other blood than on the Spanish main.   It was impossible for me to ascertain with accuracy the number of inhabitants, or the exact proportion of races.   Perhaps the most correct estimate is 200,000 inhabitants, of whom a little more than one half are whites, three eights of mixed blood, light coloured, and the remainder dark brown & blacks.

These last are Spanish blacks, who have found the tyranny of the Haitiens far worse than the patriarchal rule of their old Spanish masters, and consequently side with the Dominicans, hating the French blacks even more bitterly than the whites do.   They constitute the chief part of the Dominican army & occupy the inferior military grades.

What forms the distinctive character of the Dominican and Haitien Governments is that while the latter declare (see their Constitution) that "no white man, of whatever nation shall place his foot on Haytien territory, with the title of owner or proprietor, nor acquire in future any immoveable property, nor the quality of Haitien", the former, prohibiting the immigration of blacks, invites the immigration of whites by grants of fifty acres of land & the rights of citizenship with special privileges, and by paying for their transportation and maintenance until established in their new homes.—   If then I be mistaken in estimating the proportion of blood other than white as not much greater than on the Spanish main & other parts of Spanish America, I have no doubt that, if the U. S. would lend the Dominicans that countenance, which humanity and their own safety require, the population would in a few years become almost purely white, that valuable island, with a climate, soil and mineral productions more than justifying the proud title of "the Prime of the Indies" (La primada de las Indias), if relieved from the pressure and uncertainty, into which Haitien aggression and the unaccountable neglect of other nations have plunged it, would immediately fill up with white immigrants from Cuba, Porto Rico, the adjacent islands, the Spanish Main, the United States and Europe.

In variety of climate, fertility of soil, in valuable woods and mineral productions, it surpasses the Island of Cuba, which it nearly equals in extent. It lies on the new high road, which recent events on the Pacific and in Central America are opening to Commerce; and the question presented to the Gov^t of the United States is whether, in the war of races, the blacks of Hayti shall be permitted to murder and drive out the whites of the East end and to monopolize its exclusive possession; whether under their desolating rule the whole shall remain a desert, an eye-sore, a spreading plague and a disgrace to the civilized world; or whether, under the more liberal principles of the Dominicans it shall be made by white men to blossom like the rose, adding by its vast productiveness to the commerce and happiness of mankind.

I therefore again beg leave to suggest that some steps should be immediately taken to stop this war, otherwise than by the sacrifice of Dominican independence as proposed by the English and French Consuls.[1] . . .

I have the honor [etc.].

2231

Jonathan Elliot, Commercial Agent of the United States to the Dominican Republic, to John M. Clayton, Secretary of State of the United States[2]

No. 23   SANTO DOMINGO, *July 13, 1850.*

HONORABLE SIR: Permit me to call your attention to the state of affairs in this Republic, for seven years they have been acting on the defensive and sustained themselves against the Haytians and honorably maintained their Independence without having involved themselves in debt.

The Treaty with the English (a copy of which I send you)[3] has lately been concluded and ratified, and has had the effect to entirely destroy our Commerce here. The feelings of the people here, their hopes and dependence rest entirely upon being noticed by the United States. These hopes have been raised by Agents sent out here.

I have learnt through Sir Robert Schomburgk the British Consul here, that the United States had agreed in conjunction with England and France to mediate between this Republic and the so called Empire of Hayti through their respective consuls. This added to Mr. Green's having been here eight months and it being well understood that he came here with powers to recognize this Republic and make a treaty and leaving here without entering into any negociation, has placed me in a disagreable position and destroyed the Confidence which this Government have heretofore had in me. I therefore beg as a favor to know, whether it is the intention of the United States to recognize or in any way notice this Republic, that I may at once dispel the doubts and hopes which the people here entertain of being recognized by the United States.

After both the Governments on this Island had applied and consented to the mediation of the three Powers, Emperor Soloupe [Soulouque] marched his men and comited depredations upon this people. The French and

[1] This omitted portion refers to a projected treaty between the Dominican Republic and Great Britain, recently signed, of which a copy was enclosed, and which was so unfavorable to the former that del Monte, who had been Foreign Minister, resigned in protest rather than sign it as it had been signed by Medrano. Most of the remainder of the omission discusses commercial or shipping matters; and, in conclusion, tells of "a magnificent altar piece of solid carved mahogany" which he had attempted to purchase to bring with him as an antique; but the Archbishop had refused to make an object of traffic what had been consecrated to the worship of God. However, it was presented to him by the Archbishop to be brought to Washington, to be placed in some Catholic Church of the capital; and, he added, he had bought it and attached copies of the correspondence concerning its acquisition.
[2] Consular Letters, Santo Domingo, vol. 1. Received July 30.
[3] Not within the scope of this publication.

English Consuls here, jointly made a protest against this movement.   Fully aware that the United States do not allow me any money that I may expend otherwise than that dictated by the Instructions, rather than permit the Consuls of France and England to stand forward in the cause of humanity and Republicanism more than myself, as the representative of the United States, I alone made a similar protest and shared with them the expense of sending the same to Hayti, which cost me eighty-four dollars and which I hope will be refunded me by my Government.

I have the honor [etc.].

2232

Jonathan Elliot, Commercial Agent of the United States to the Dominican Republic, to Daniel Webster, Secretary of State of the United States [1]

No. 24   SANTO DOMINGO, *September 16, 1850.*

SIR: I have the honor to acknowledge the receipt of the Circular announcing the death of President Taylor, for which sad event the Flags of the Forts Shipping and Consulates were half masted on the 7th of September.

Active preparations are being made by this Republic to defend themselves against the Haytians, whom it is expected will attack in the course of two or three months.   I have seen a letter from Lord Palmerston to Sir Robert Schomburgk, Her Majesty's Consul to this Republic, which stated that the United States had agreed in conjunction with England and France to mediate a peace between the Haytians and this Government, through their respective Consuls.   I have not as yet received any communication from the Department on the subject, but should be most happy to join my Colleagues here, in so humane an object.   I would respectfully suggest that if the United States intend that I should join the other Consuls to forward me notice so to do as soon as possible.

I have the honor [etc.].

2233

Jonathan Elliot, Commercial Agent of the United States to the Dominican Republic, to Daniel Webster, Secretary of State of the United States [2]

No. 25   SANTO DOMINGO, *September 28, 1850.*

SIR: I communicated to you the existing state of affairs in this Republic, in my last.[3]   Since then I have been officially informed by this Government, that the Emperor of Hayti, has made more attacks and aggressions, upon this Republic, although he agreed to an armistice, until the 30th of this

---

[1] Consular Letters, Santo Domingo, vol. I.   Received October 17.
[2] *Ibid.*   Received October 28.   [3] Above, this part, September 16, 1850, doc. 2232.

month, to allow steps to be taken by England, France and the United States, towards making a peace. I earnestly solicit you to send me speedily, some instructions and power to act in this, the same as the Consuls of the other two Powers.

I have always maintained the confidence and respect in the highest degree, of the Government and people here, and if another is sent on this mission, I shall lose much in their estimation, for they will naturally suppose, that my Government has but little confidence in me. I believe I am well known to you, through my Father who compiled the "Debates on the Adoption of the Constitution". I am much interested in the Country and shall esteem it an honor and a favor to be permitted to act in conjunction with my Colleagues to prevent the bloodshed and ruin, that must take place should this Haytian Emperor reach here. These people are all, American in their feelings and as Republicans look first to us for protection and aid.

Also please do me the favor to send me a list of the Ministers and Consuls and a copy of the Instructions to be retained in the office.

I have the honor [etc.].

2234

Jonathan Elliot, Commercial Agent of the United States to the Dominican Republic, to Daniel Webster, Secretary of State of the United States [1]

No. 26   SANTO DOMINGO, *September 29, 1850.*

SIR: You will please receive accompanying, a copy of the Treaty made between England and this Republic. The Treaty was ratified and concluded the 10th of this month.[2]

In my last communication [3] I urged the necessity of speedily sending me the power and instructions to mediate a peace between this Government and that of Hayti, as both the English and French Consuls here, have received their instructions to that effect. I hope the Government will favor me in this, since they have promised to join the other two Powers for that purpose.

All that these people ask for is peace with the Haytians. They have nobly sustained themselves for seven years as a Republic, without involving themselves in debt, they have fought well and bravely, have left their families to support themselves, while they, without pay—without medical attendance—without food and almost naked, have willingly marched and fought for the cause of liberty, while they hold the implement of Agriculture in one hand, to raise crops which it is doubtful they can reap, they are obliged to keep the sword in the other. To this I have been witness.

We had the principal part of the commerce of this Government heretofore,

[1] Consular Letters, Santo Domingo, vol. 1. Received October 19.
[2] Being a commercial treaty, it is not within the scope of this publication.
[3] Above, this part, September 28, 1850, doc. 2233.

but this English Treaty has effectually destroyed it. Our vessels have to pay *three* times the amount of tonnage and Port charges that English pay, and if England thinks it right and proper to recognize them as a Republic and make a Treaty with them, who had scarcely any commerce here, certainly it is a matter for the United States to take into consideration. The Emperor of Hayti is making his preparations to march—he has purchased vessels and arms from citizens of the United States, he threatens (and no doubt will do so) to put to death all the whites and confiscate their properties. His cruelties and oppressions are well known to the world. He openly marches as an *Emperor* to crush a *Republic* and this under our eyes and almost within sight of our shores.

I therefore beg you sir, to take some measures to prevent further bloodshed and suffering here. I presume I am too well known to you through my Father, Mr. Jonathan Elliot, to require further recommendation, to be entrusted with any negociation the United States may have to make in the affairs here.

I have the honor [etc.].

2235

Jonathan Elliot, Commercial Agent of the United States to the Dominican Republic, to Daniel Webster, Secretary of State of the United States [1]

No. 29   SANTO DOMINGO, *November 30, 1850.*

SIR: I have the honor to acknowlege the receipt of the Circular of September 1st 1850.[2]

In regard to the Mediation between this part of the Island and that of Hayti, I learn from authentic sources that England and France have determined to blockade the Ports of Hayti, in consequence of Solouque refusing to come to an armistice of ten years. The policy of the French is this, the Haytians owe to them a large sum of money which they never can pay, so long as they continue at war with these people. The policy of the English to sustain the negroes in the Antilles, is well known and the interference on their part, is more for the protection of Hayti, against certain supposed expeditions and to oblige them to work and improve their part of the Island.

I have understood that it is the intention of the U. S. Govt: to name a Commissioner for this part of the Island. I believe I am still in your recollection and base my claims upon my conduct in my office here, in protecting our citizens and commerce in the time of danger which has cost me a great deal of trouble and no small amount of money. The fees of my office do not exceed $300.$\frac{00}{100}$ per annum.

I have the honor [etc.].

[1] Consular Letters, Santo Domingo, vol. 1. Received December 26.
[2] Not included in this publication.

2236

Jonathan Elliot, Commercial Agent of the United States to the Dominican Republic, to Daniel Webster, Secretary of State of the United States [1]

No. 30   SANTO DOMINGO, *December 3, 1850.*

SIR: Enclosed you will please receive a receipt for sixty-six dollars and sixty-seven cents, for which I have given a draft on the Department and which I hope will be duly honored.

I informed you in my communication No. 23 July 13th [2] that I had been obliged to join the other two Consuls here in protesting against the aggressions of Solouque, having previously seen a letter from Lord Palmerston to the English Consul here, stating that the United States Government had agreed to join the English and French in mediating a peace between this Republic and Hayti. Believing that my government would fully sanction what I have done, to stand equal with other nations in the cause of justice and humanity, I contracted this expense jointly with my colleagues to send the Protests to Port au Prince.

I have the honor [etc.].

2237

Robert M. Walsh, Special Agent of the United States to the Dominican Republic, to Daniel Webster, Secretary of State of the United States [3]

No. 1   PORT AU PRINCE, *February 5, 1851.*

SIR: I embarked at Norfolk on the 25th of last month, the Saranac having been detained there until that date, and arrived here in the afternoon of the 2d inst, after a pleasant but not very rapid passage, of nearly eight days. The vessel, though an admirable one in many respects, does not seem to be remarkable for speed. From the Commodore officers I received every attention; and immediately on our arrival, Mr Usher, the Consular Agent of the United States, came on board and tendered me the hospitalities of his house, which I was glad to accept for the moment, the "warm welcome of an inn" being a luxury not to be had in this place.

The following day I announced my arrival to the Minister for Foreign Affairs, who is here addressed as "His Grace the Duke of Tiberon [Tiburón]", and requested an interview, which he gave me yesterday at nine o'clock in the morning. All business here is pretty much transacted before noon, when there is a general cessation of work for several hours on account of the heat. I was received by the Minister in full costume at his residence, which is sufficiently neat & well furnished, and put your letter in his hands. His gratifi-

[1] Consular Letters, Santo Domingo, vol. 1. Received December 26.
[2] Above, this part, doc. 2231.
[3] Special Agents, vol. 18. Received March 3.

cation at getting it was such that I think I may assert it made him one of the happiest & proudest of men.   Our conversation was of a general nature, as I did not wish to enter upon matters of business, not having been previously able to talk with the French and English Consuls, whom I had made unsuccessful efforts to see the day before.   The Minister agreeably surprised me by his appearance & manners & cultivated intelligence.   He is a tall light mulatto, with a pleasant face & very respectable grey locks, and all the tone of a man of education & good society.   On taking leave, I asked him to let me know when the Commodore & myself could pay our respects to the Emperor, and in the course of the day was informed by him that His Majesty would receive us this morning at nine.   We repaired accordingly to the Palace at that hour, accompanied by Mr Usher & a large number of officers from the Saranac, and were received with great parade.   The Court-yard was filled with troops, in rather motley attire, who saluted as we passed; and the hall of reception was crowded with Ministers & Generals & other dignitaries, who made quite a glittering show.   Soon after our entrance the Emperor made his appearance in a costume which though rich was not in bad taste, preceded by shouts of "Vive l' Empereur" from his Courtiers, and we were then presented in due form.   He seemed at first decidedly embarrassed, as if he did not know what to say or do, but after a while inquired how long the Commodore would remain, and on being told that the Saranac would leave in a day or two, manifested not the least chagrin.   The truth is the big ship in the harbour is not a pleasant spectacle to his eyes, and the sending such a one just now is a ceremony of which he would much prefer the breach to the observance.   It is a pity the Commodore Cannot protract his stay here, as the presence of the Steamer would materially assist our negotiations, the logic of force being the only kind which this Gov^t thoroughly comprehends, or, at least, is disposed to respect.   "Faustin the 1st" is stout & short & very black, with an unpleasant expression & a carriage that does not grace a throne.   He is ignorant in the extreme, but has begun to learn to read & write, and is said to exhibit Commendable diligence in his studies. Energy and decision are his most important traits, and no soft feelings are likely to interfere with their full display when occasion calls them forth, as it frequently does.   There has been considerable demand for them of late, in consequence of a formidable conspiracy which was discovered a short time since, the object of which was to restore the Republic.   Some prominent men were involved in it, and even his favorite aid de camp was arrested on a charge of being aware of its existence & concealing his knowledge.   The richest man of the Empire, a Mr Lafontant, was also brought into the city from his estates, the day before yesterday, & subjected to an examination, but nothing could be found against him & he was released.   People were much surprised at his escape, as it was supposed that the two hundred thousand dollars of which he is possessed, would be regarded as so many proofs of guilt.   There is no divinity that hedges his throne in the imaginations of his subjects, fond as they may be deemed of gewgaws & glitter.   His elevation was too hasty & unexpected, brought about, as it was, by the intrigues of a few, to produce any dazzling effect upon the mass, and the continuance of his power depends altogether upon the fidelity of his troops.   He is busy just now with preparations for his Coronation, which is to be celebrated with all the magnificence that his resources will permit; and it is stated that one of the chief causes of his intended expedition against the Dominican Republic, is his desire to be crowned in the city of S\u1d57 Domingo, the time-honored metropolis of the island.

I have made the acquaintance of the English & French Consuls, but it has not been possible as yet to converse with them on the subject of our mission, farther than to learn their impression that the decided stand taken by the three Governments Cannot fail to produce the desired effect.   No effort on my part shall be wanting to bring it about, and my colleagues seem to be actuated by the best dispositions.

This is a hasty scrawl, written against time, the vessel which is to carry it being on the point of departure, and with none but "the crude, unruminated ideas" incident to first impressions.   In my future despatches, I shall endeavour to give you all the information about the Country which you may wish; and I trust that it will soon be in my power to communicate the agreeable intelligence that the object of my coming here has been accomplished.

I have the honor [etc.].

2238

Robert M. Walsh, Special Agent of the United States to the Dominican Republic, to Daniel Webster, Secretary of State of the United States [1]

[EXTRACTS]

No. 2   PORT AU PRINCE, *February 14, 1851.*

SIR: The day after the date of my despatch N⁰ 1,[2] I had a full conversation with the French & English Agents, and was informed of all that had been done by them, in reference to the subject of our mission, up to the moment of my arrival.   In conjunction with M\u02b3 Usher, the Commercial Agent of the U. States, they had succeeded some time since, in obtaining a truce of two months with one month's notice of the renewal of hostilities, information of which, with the proper documents, was duly communicated by M\u02b3 Usher to the Department.   Since then they had continued to urge a definitive peace, but finding it impossible to achieve that result, they had at last, on the 19ᵗʰ of Decʳ, proposed a truce of ten years, in a note of which the en-

[1] Special Agents, vol. 18, but not in its proper chronological order.   Received March 17.
[2] Above, this part, February 5, 1851, doc. 2237.

closed, marked "A", is a copy.[1]   To that no answer had yet been given.
It was, therefore, deemed advisable that I should have an interview, alone,
with the Minister of Foreign Affairs, and talk to him in the plainest manner
my instructions would allow.   I called upon him, accordingly, the next day,
and spoke to him in substance, as follows:

> The Gov^t of the U. States, having determined to cooperate with the
> Gov^{ts} of England & France in bringing about the pacification of this is-
> land, had sent me as its agent for that purpose.   It believes that the
> only proper way to accomplish it, is for the Gov^t of Haiti to acknowledge
> the independence of the Republic of St Domingo, that independence
> having now been so long maintained as to prove the impossibility of its
> being overturned by the power of this Empire, and, in consequence, to
> establish its claim to general recognition.   Any farther prosecution,
> therefore, of the war, is abhorrent to the dictates of humanity and rea-
> son, and injurious to the interests of neutrals, rendering it their duty to
> use their best efforts to restore that tranquillity which is indispensable
> for the welfare of all.   The principle is now fully established that the
> actual possession of independence for a reasonable time, entitles a nation
> to be acknowledged as sovereign.   This is a principle which the Ameri-
> can world, especially, has consecrated & must ever uphold.   It is the
> sole foundation, in fact, of the independence of Haiti herself, and to at-
> tack it in any way is to strike at the very root of her own institutions.
> The best interests of the Empire demand the recognition of Dominican
> independence, which would give it a useful neighbour instead of a tur-
> bulent province or a determined foe.   Even if the Dominicans could be
> subjugated for a time, their efforts would be ceaseless to throw off a yoke
> which they detest, & thus the whole island would be kept in a state of
> constant distraction most injurious to its welfare.   When they suc-
> ceeded in those efforts, as they assuredly would,—for a people resolved
> upon freedom will always achieve it,—the Empire would find itself
> materially weakened, if not altogether exhausted, and would have for-
> feited all the sympathies of those now best inclined to regard it with a
> friendly eye.   In every point of view, therefore, the Gov^t of the U.
> States entertained the conviction that it was incumbent upon the Em-
> peror to recognize the independence of St Domingo, and I earnestly
> hoped that His Majesty would consent to do so without farther delay.

In reply, the Minister made a set speech, evidently prepared with care,
beginning with an elaborate geographical survey of the island & branching
off into various disquisitions connected with its history, which had very little
to do with the question, & manifested much more will than ability to make
out a justifiable case.   The sum total of his argument appeared to be simply
this—that Nature, in the first place, had designed the whole island to be
under one & the same Government; and, in the second place, that the Constitution of 1816 had proclaimed it to be one & indivisible, and this Constitution the Emperor was obliged to maintain—also, that the Dominicans

---

[1] Not included in this publication.   Its important contents are indicated here.

having voluntarily annexed themselves, had no right to withdraw from the connection.

It was difficult to reply gravely to such logic as this. Wishing, however, to show all possible respect, I set to work deliberately to prove that the "designs of nature," even when unmistakeable, were not necessarily good titles in law, and that the proclamation, as a fact, of what did not exist, by no means called it into being; for the Constitution of which the Minister spoke, was promulgated long before any junction of the different parts of the island had been effected. If, I said to him, the geographical reasons which he urged were admitted as sound, they would speedily change the map of the world. Most nations, especially the strong, would find conclusive arguments of the sort for appropriating the territory of their neighbours; and eventually it would, doubtless, be discovered that all the islands of the West Indies ought to be brought under the same control. This reasoning, moreover, would give the Dominicans as much right to claim dominion over Haiti, as it could give the latter to claim dominion over the Dominicans. Besides, the island had always, from the time of its discovery, been divided into separate states. When Columbus first landed upon it, there were five different tribes of aborigines governed by chiefs entirely independent; and it was long before the divisions were reduced to the two which now exist. The declaration of its indivisibility was thus belied in every way, and could devolve no obligation whatever upon the Emperor, such as was assumed. No rights or duties were either originated, revived or bequeathed by the assertions of the Constitution referred to; and all arguments, therefore, based upon them, were of no account.

As to the statement that the union of the two Countries had been brought about by the voluntary act of the Dominicans, so far from weakening their case, it gave it great additional strength. It corroborated the fact that Haiti had no original claim upon their territory, and proved that the dominion of the former was altogether incompatible with their well-being as a people, which it was their right & their duty to maintain. They had sought annexation in the hope that it would contribute to their happiness, but finding, on the contrary, that it resulted in oppression & suffering, they had no resource [sic] but to revert to their previous condition of separate nationality. The compact of union had been first broken by the Haitians when they perverted it into an instrument of intolerable despotism.

The Minister acknowledged that the Gov.ᵗ of Haiti had not always acted well towards the Dominicans, but said that the most satisfactory offers had been made to them for their future security, which they ought first to try before resorting to the extreme measures they had adopted. To this I replied that they were the best judges of what they might expect from the experience which they already possessed, and that the Gov.ᵗ of Haiti having given them ample reason to believe that submission to it was synonymous with misery & degradation, could not now complain of their want of confidence in its promises. I referred playfully to the English proverb about a burnt child dreading the fire, and, in the phrase of ancient Pistol, "discussed the same to him in French," which somewhat relaxed the severity of his ministerial brow.

I then went on to say that all this debate was about abstractions, and did not touch the real merits of the case. The only thing for foreign nations to consider was the simple fact that the Republic of St Domingo is positively independent and entitled to be treated as such, whatever may have been the original rights or pretensions of Haiti; and the only thing for the Imperial Gov^t to consider was, whether it would expose itself to the various evils likely to result from the pursuit of an unattainable object, instead of wisely acquiescing in a "fixed fact" and making the best of what could not be helped.

He persisted in declaring that the Emperor would never abandon his rights, and said that even if he should consent to do so, his people would not permit it. Seeing that all farther conversation was useless just then, I took my leave.[1] . . .

On leaving the Minister for F. Affairs I called at once upon my colleagues and had a consultation with them as to the best course to be pursued. It was unanimously decided to be worse than useless to waste any more time in discussion. The question had been presented to this Gov^t in every light, and abundant time had elapsed to enable it to come to a conclusion. We agreed, therefore, to send in at once the note, a copy of which is enclosed,[2]

[1] This omission discusses the complete subservience of officials of the Haitian Government to the Emperor, and the latter's determined will to continue the war.
[2] The following is the text of their joint note:

Special Agents of the United States, France, and Great Britain, to L. Dufresne, Duke de Tiburón, Minister of Foreign Affairs of Haiti

[TRANSLATION]

PORT AU PRINCE, *February 11, 1851.*

The Undersigned, Agents of the U. States, France & Great Britain, have already had the honor of explaining clearly to the Minister of Foreign Relations, the views of their respective Governments in regard to the aggressive hostilities of which the Dominican people have for so many years been the object. They now request from the Gov^t of His Imperial Majesty a categorical answer to the following proposition:
*A definitive treaty of peace or a truce of ten years between the Empire of Haiti & the Dominican Republic.**
The interests of both the belligerents, those of the commerce of neutrals, and those, especially, of humanity, admit, in the conviction of those high Powers, of no other solution. The Undersigned cannot doubt that the Gov^t of H. I. M. in the face of such a declaration, will decide at last upon the only course which it can adopt in order to avoid the consequences that may result from any longer persistence in its resolution to destroy the nationality of St Domingo.

(Signed)   WALSH   MAX. RAYBAUD   USHER
          Special Agent   Consul General   Consul of
       of the United States.   of France.   Great Britain.

* The agents of England & France having previously proposed the truce as an alternative, it was deemed necessary to repeat it in the present note.

marked "B". It was written in French, that being the language of one of the agents as well as of the Gov⁺. Great stress was laid by my colleagues on the fact that the cooperation of the U. States would have a more intimidating effect than any threats of theirs, and that it was particularly advisable to strike while the iron was hot. No answer has yet been returned, but if one be not soon given, we will call upon the Minister personally, and urge it as strenuously as policy will admit.

I regret to say, Sir, that I have not yet succeeded in finding a map of the Country such as you desired me to send you, though I have made every effort to obtain one.

With great respect [etc.].

2239

Robert M. Walsh, Special Agent of the United States to the Dominican Republic, to Daniel Webster, Secretary of State of the United States [1]

[EXTRACT]

No. 3   PORT AU PRINCE, *March 3, 1851.*

SIR: Our note of the 11th ult?[2] of which I sent a copy with my last despatch,[3] not having been noticed, my colleagues & myself called on the Minister for F. Affairs on the 18th, to ask him when we might expect a reply. He said that the matter was one which demanded the maturest Consideration, as it involved a breach of the Constitution, which proclaims the integrity of the island, so that the Emperor could not decide upon it without first consulting the Senate. He could not, therefore, give us hopes of a positive answer before the latter portion of the month of March, as the Senate is not now in session and must be especially convened; and he could not promise that we would certainly have it even then. We combated, of course, the preposterous idea of the Constitutional impediment, but all in vain, for as it is the least absurd reason which the Government can advance for its claim upon S⁺ Domingo, it is adhered to with the tenacity of desperation. Besides, it furnishes an apparent excuse for delay, and His Imperial Majesty cherishes, it is said, the hope of extricating himself from the grasp of the three Powers by a 'wise inactivity'. A few days since, his private Secretary was dining on board the French Steam Sloop of War now lying in the harbour, and becoming rather communicative under the influence of Champagne, very candidly informed the officers that his master would let the plenipotentiaries, as he styled them, amuse themselves for awhile with speeches and notes, but would eventually get rid of them without committing himself in the least—a piece of intelligence which the officers naturally conveyed to the French Consul General as calculated to interest both himself and

[1] Special Agents, vol. 18. Received March 24.   [2] Above, this part, p. 96, note 2.
[3] Above, this part, February 14, 1851, doc. 2238.

his colleagues.   The Emperor would fain believe that the *entente cordiale* between the three Powers cannot long endure, and builds confident expectations, particularly, upon "the scambling & unquiet time" in France.   On every arrival from that country, he inquires with great earnestness about the state of affairs there, and evinces infinite disgust when he ascertains that chaos has *not* come again.   Our duty, in consequence, is to urge a decision at the earliest possible moment, & make him clearly understand that our Governments are thoroughly in earnest and not inclined to be amused with rediculous excuses and evasions.   We accordingly protested against the intention intimated by the Minister, of what might be deemed an indefinite postponement of a question which the Govᵗ had already been given ample time to consider; telling him that even if the constitutional difficulty existed in regard to a definitive peace, it had nothing to do with a truce, which he could not deny the Emperor was empowered to make on his sole responsibility, without even the appearance of overstepping his prerogative.   It required some command of countenance upon the part of his Grace of Tiburon to insist upon the incompetency of the Emperor to conclude a peace, knowing as he well does, that the latter can do, and does do, whatever he pleases, & that scarcely a day goes by without his violating the sacred instrument invoked, for the nonce, to prevent him from performing an act to which he is averse. The Minister, however, had learnt his lesson and repeated it to the end— "His Majesty would do nothing without consulting the Senate, his first duty being to guard and preserve the Constitution."

I thought I might then try the effect of an argument, which I took care to represent as wholly unofficial & private, my Govᵗ having no knowledge of it whatever.   The day before I left Norfolk I was told by a friend that he had been offered a command in an expedition, which was contemplated, to go to Sᵗ Domingo and assist its inhabitants against the Haytians.   This fact I communicated to the Minister with all plausible emphasis, dwelling upon the perilous probability that should such an expedition ever land upon the island, all the miseries and horrors with which the Emperor was now threatening the Dominicans, would be brought to his own door—that the desperadoes composing it would never rest until they had exhausted every effort to overwhelm the Empire, and that even if they should fail in destroying it, the evils it would suffer would be almost equivalent to ruin.   The only sure way, I added, to arrest the danger, was to conclude a peace, and by thus depriving the expedition of the lawful motive of lending aid to a people whose independence was wrongfully assailed, it would become the duty of the United States to prevent it from leaving their shores.

The chord was one which seemed to vibrate more strongly than any other, for the Government has been in great dread of such an expedition ever since the attack upon Cuba.   I begged the Minister, therefore, to inform His Majesty of what I had said, in order that he might fully appreciate all the dangers of procrastination; and this he assured me he would do. My colleagues, however, rather doubted his having nerve enough to keep his word, though they agreed in the opinion that the expedition would be the most effective shape of terror which could be brought before the Imperial eyes. At all events, he promised, on our taking leave, that he would exert himself to cause an answer to be given at the earliest possible moment.

The next day but one we received a note of which a copy, marked "A", is enclosed, informing us that the Government had appointed four Commissioners to confer with us. The object of this appeared so plainly to be delay, that we deemed it indispensable to make the declaration contained in our reply—note "B". To this we received the rejoinder "C", and at the same time an informal intimation that the Commission would facilitate the action of the Government by, perhaps, rendering unnecessary the convocation of the Senate. This, whilst it showed how little real care was felt for the Counsels of that body, gave us some hope of benefit from meeting the Commissioners, and we expressed our willingness to do so, in the note marked "D". Note "E" is the Minister's answer.[1]

[1] The texts of the five communications, described in this paragraph (which should have accompanied this despatch, but actually came with his No. 4 of March 16, 1851, below, this part, doc. 2240), follow:

L. Dufresne, Duke de Tiburón, Minister of Foreign Affairs of Haiti, to Robert M. Walsh, Special Agent of the United States to the Dominican Republic

A   PORT AU PRINCE, *February 21, 1851.*

The Minister of Foreign Relations of Haiti has had the honor to receive your collective note dated the 11th inst., in which you request from the Gov! of His Majesty a categorical answer to the propositions made by you, in the name of your three Gov!s, in regard to the question of the Eastern part of the island.

The questions raised by this note are of the gravest nature, and the Gov! of H. M. believes that they ought to be maturely considered & seriously treated; and it has just appointed a commission composed of Mess!s A. La Rochel, D. Labonté et V. Plésance, Senators, and M! Laforestrie, in order to come to an understanding with you concerning the object of your communication.

The Undersigned [etc.].

The Special Agents of the United States, France, and Great Britain, to L. Dufresne, Duke de Tiburón, Minister of Foreign Affairs of Haiti

B   PORT AU PRINCE, *February 21, 1851.*

The Undersigned &c. have rec! the note of this date which the Minister of F. R. has addressed to them, announcing that the Gov! of H. M. has named a Commission of four members, for the purpose of coming to an understanding with them concerning the object of their note of the 11th inst.

The Undersigned will be happy to enter into immediate relations with the said Commission, if it be empowered to regulate, in concert with themselves, the basis of the peace or the conditions of the truce of ten years which the mediating Powers have determined upon as indispensable for securing the tranquillity of the island. But if its object be to discuss that determination, they deem it their duty to inform the Minister of F. R. that after the clear and precise notification of it which they have made to the Gov! itself, all that remains for them to do is to treat either of peace or a truce, or to communicate the refusal of the said Gov! to acquiesce in it.

The Undersigned [etc.].

R. M. WALSH	M. RAYBAUD	T. USSHER
Special Agent, U. S.	Consul Gen! of France	Consul of G! Britain

The Commissioners are to make a report to the Emperor which will, doubtless, be favorable or the reverse as he may direct.   It may be that his object in appointing them is to enable him to submit with a better grace, by giving his submission the air of yielding to advice; and this, as I have intimated, is the reason which has induced us to acquiesce in what we are well aware is a mere farce.   For my own part, however, I confess that I do not

---

L. Dufresne, Duke de Tiburón, Minister of Foreign Affairs of Haiti, to the Special Agents of the United States, France, and Great Britain

C   PORT AU PRINCE, *February 24, 1851.*

The Minister of F. R. of Haiti has had the honor to receive the note of the agents &c. &c. dated the 1st inst, in which they decline all discussion of the propositions which they have presented in the name of their Govts.

Those propositions raise too serious questions & those questions are too vital, not to give the Govt of H. M. at least the right of knowing the reason & the motives of them, and of having the satisfaction of not taking in regard to them any resolution whatever, unless with full comprehension & after mature deliberation.

The Govt of H. M. insists, therefore, that its Commission should confer with the agents of the three Powers concerning the object of their note of the 11th inst.

The Special Agents of the United States, France, and Great Britain, to L. Dufresne, Duke de Tiburón, Minister of Foreign Affairs of Haiti

D   PORT AU PRINCE, *February 27, 1851.*

The Undersigned Agents &c—have the honor to acknowledge the receipt of the note of the M. of F. R., dated 24th of this month.

His Excy insists that the Commission named the 21st, should confer with the said agents concerning the object of their note of the 11th.   The Haitian Govt requests to be informed, through the medium of that Commission, of the reason & the motives of the three Powers in wishing to secure the tranquility of the island by a treaty of peace, or at least by a truce of ten years.

Having already obeyed the orders of their Govts to acquaint the Haitian Govt itself with that reason & those motives, and the said Govt having been placed by them in possession of official documents sufficient for their appreciation, the Undersigned are painfully surprised at seeing themselves again called upon to communicate them to a Commission without powers to treat.

They must remind the Minister that their mission is not to discuss the resolution, but only the mode of executing the resolution, of the three high Powers, to put an end to the war waged so long & so uselessly against the nationality of the Dominicans.

Nevertheless, to comply as far as they can with the wish of the Haitian Govt to have a commission, which is doubtless consultative, directly informed by the Undersigned of the necessity of an immediate decision, they will present to the Commission a definitive exposition of the causes & the object of the resolution above mentioned of the three Powers—an exposition which shall be sufficiently clear & precise to admit of no doubt or misapprehension.

R. M. WALSH   M. RAYBAUD   T. USSHER
&c &c   &c &c &c   &c &c &c

L. Dufresne, Duke de Tiburón, Minister of Foreign Affairs of Haiti, to the Special Agents of the United States, France, and Great Britain

E   PORT AU PRINCE, *March 1, 1851.*

The Minister of F. R. has recd the note which the Agents &c &c &c have done him the honor to address him, under date of 27th of last month, in which they consent to confer with the Commission named by the Govt of H. M.

The Members of the said Commission have been apprized of it and directed to agree with the Representatives of the three Powers upon the day & hour of the conference.
&c &c &c

think he is yet sufficiently frightened, to abandon a project which he has sworn to accomplish, and in which his vanity & ambition are so deeply engaged.   Until he is thoroughly convinced of the definiteness & imminence of danger from refusing the proposition, his obstinacy will be almost invincible. At the same time, I do not believe that he has any idea of marching just now against the Dominicans, although he is actively employed in augmenting his forces.   The town of Gonaives, some sixty miles to the North, on the coast, was recently stripped of its male population, who, to the number of five hundred, were marched across the country to this place.   Many of them are mere boys and many are respectable men in business, whose families will be left wholly destitute.   The plight in which they arrived here was miserable in the extreme.   Some idea may be derived from this fact, of the extent & cruelty of the despotism exercised by this Constitutional Emperor, especially if the reason assigned for the peculiar severity with which the town in question was treated be the true one, which is hardly credible—that its inhabitants did not salute the Commandant lately sent there, with proper respect.   The Minister of Foreign Affairs, who is also Minister of War & Marine, has assured us that these enrolments are not designed for an expedition against St Domingo, but are only made for the purpose of keeping up the army to its requisite strength.[1] . . .

With great respect [etc.].

2240

Robert M. Walsh, Special Agent of the United States to the Dominican Republic, to Daniel Webster, Secretary of State of the United States[2]

[EXTRACT]

No. 4   PORT AU PRINCE, *March 16, 1851.*

SIR: I have the honor to transmit herewith translations of the documents which should have accompanied my last despatch.[3]

On the 6th of this month we held our first & only interview with the Commission, to whom we presented the note "F."[4]   This was all that we had

[1] This omission contains interesting but unimportant comment regarding the Emperor and his family, and the recent festivities in his honor.
[2] Special Agents, vol. 18.   Received April 28.
[3] Above, this part, March 3, 1851, doc. 2239, and for the documents which should have accompanied it, see note 1 thereto, pp. 99–100.
[4] Below is its text, followed by the texts of the other two documents, referred to in this paragraph, marked G and H:

The Special Agents of the United States, France, and Great Britain, to L. Dufresne, Duke de Tiburón, Minister of Foreign Affairs of Haiti

F   PORT AU PRINCE, *March 4, 1851.*

The Undersigned Agents &c. &c. &c. proceed, in compliance with the promise made by them in their note of the 27th ult? [Document "D", in footnote above,

promised to do, but the Commissioners appeared so desirous of talking, that we entered into a long Conversation with them, in which we gave them every explanation they could wish & listened to all the objections they could urge.   It would be useless to record the Conversation, as it was a mere

this part, p. 100.—Ed.] to the Minister of F. Affairs, to explain to the Commission named on the 24th, the motives which have induced their three Gov[ts] to demand a cessation of hostilities against the Dominican people.

Before, however, they make this explanation, which they will do as briefly as possible, of the manner in which the said Gov[ts] regard this question of humanity & general interest, they must repeat their inability to enter into any discussion of those motives, or to *confer* with the Commission except in reference to the conclusion of a peace or the accomplishment of a truce, as proposed long since, without success, to the Gov[t] of H. I. M.

In the eyes of the three Powers the independence of the Dominicans, reposes upon a right as sacred, a fundamental compact as respectable, a fact as consummate, as those which secure the independence of Haiti itself.   In their eyes, that people is in legitimate possession of all the titles which constitute nationalities the most incontestable: a regular administration, a legislation protecting equally the persons & property of all, a military organization both on land & sea, a flag enjoying the honors due to that of a free country, international relations through accredited agents, & even a solemn treaty of recognition & commerce with one of the chief nations of the earth.

Reduced to the alternative of renouncing those advantages, or of perpetually fighting to retain them, the Dominicans have been compelled to request the intervention of the Powers with whom they are connected by the aforesaid international relations, in order to free themselves from a position so deplorable.

That intervention they justly obtained, because a few words inserted in the often modified Constitution of Haiti, are by no means sufficient to create for that country a right of perpetual possession of the territory of its neighbour—a possession entirely fictitious at the time when that Constitution was formed, continuing so during eighteen subsequent years, & again becoming so after the lapse of seven, and of which the temporary existence only demonstrated the radical impossibility of blending two races of different origin, customs, manners and language.

The Minister of F. Affairs said to the Undersigned in his note of the 24th February [Document "C", in footnote above, this part, p. 100.—Ed.], that their proposition of a peace based upon a separation of those races, or even of a truce, constitutes a vital question for this Country.   This is to say, in effect, that the Haitian State cannot live if it does not annihilate the nationality of a people determined to perish rather than give it up; if it does not, therefore, annihilate that people itself.   The step taken by the three Powers shows how much they reprobate such a doctrine.   Far from perceiving in the termination of the war a dangerous question for the Haitian State, they regard it as necessary for the consolidation & prosperity of that State, causing as it will, a cessation of ruinous sacrifices for an object vainly pursued during seven years & which has now become unattainable.

The Undersigned have thus set forth the views of their Governments.   They abundantly answer the only two objections presented by the Haitian cabinet to the making of a peace or a truce with the Dominican nation.   They hope, therefore, that the Gov[t] of H. I. M., assured of the sentiments of genuine interest by which the three Powers are animated in regard to it, will no longer delay a categorical answer to their proposition.

The Undersigned being directly accredited near the said Gov[t], must declare, before concluding, that they cannot commune with it through the medium of third parties; at the same time they will be happy to discuss with the Commissioners the means best calculated to accomplish the object of a pacification such as has been proposed, if it be deemed proper to invest them with the requisite powers.

<table>
<tr><td>R. M. WALSH
&c &c &c</td><td>M. RAYBAUD
&c &c &c</td><td>T. USSHER
&c &c &c</td></tr>
</table>

L. Dufresne, Duke de Tiburón, Minister of Foreign Affairs of Haiti, to the Special Agents of the United States, France, and Great Britain

G   PORT AU PRINCE, *March 11, 1851.*

In their exposé of the 4th ins[t] [Immediately above.—Ed.], the Representatives of the three Powers persisting in their refusal of a discussion upon the bases of the proposition

repetition of the conferences with the Minister of Foreign Affairs which I have already detailed. Having thus, as we fancied, deprived the Government of all pretext for further delay, as far as we were concerned, our surprise was not small at receiving the note marked G. in which it is attempted to make us responsible for the necessity of convoking the Chambers—a necessity which the Minister had previously assured us was created by the Constitution. Our reply is marked H. It has been our effort throughout, to make the Gov.ᵗ clearly understand that, as we have no authority to enter into any arrangement not based either upon a peace or a truce of ten years, all discussion in regard to aught else would be perfectly futile. This it seemed determined not to understand, its object being to bring on a discussion of the whole matter, ab initio, in order to gain time in the hope that something might eventually turn up to relieve it from the necessity of a decision. Had we assented to its wish, there would have been no

---

presented by them in the name of their Govᵗˢ to that of H. M., & insisting again upon a categorical answer to that proposition, the Undersigned has the honor to transmit them the following resolution of H.'M.'s Govᵗ.

In regard to questions so grave as those raised by the proposition, the Govᵗ of H. M. has determined to consult the opinion of the country through its legitimate organs. The Chambers will be immediately convoked, & the proposition made collectively by France, England & the U. States relative to the difficulty which divides the Departments of the East from the rest of the Empire, will be submitted to them.

The Govᵗ of H. M. will hasten, as soon after the convocation as the care of its responsibility will permit, to communicate to the three Powers its definitive resolution.

&c &c &c

The Special Agents of the United States, France, and Great Britain, to L. Dufresne, Duke de Tiburón, Minister of Foreign Affairs of Haiti

H   PORT AU PRINCE, *March 13, 1851.*

The Undersigned, Agents &c. &c. &c. have had the honor to receive the note of His Excʸ the Minister of F. Affairs, of the 11ᵗʰ insᵗ [Immediately above.—Ed.], in which he announces to them that the Chambers are to be convoked forthwith, to take cognizance of the proposition concerning a peace or a truce which has been several times made to the Haitian Govᵗ in the name of the three Powers.

Any determination on its part, which may put an end to the difficulties that have hitherto impeded the accomplishment of their pacific mission, can only be agreeable to the Undersigned; for those difficulties, if protracted, must result in affecting injuriously the friendly feelings of the three Powers towards the said Govᵗ.

But as His Excʸ begins his note by asserting that the convocation of the Chambers is necessitated by the continued refusal of the Undersigned "to admit a discussion of the bases of the proposition" which they have transmitted to him, they are again compelled to remind him that the only discussion which they have refused, is that of the reasons which actuate their respective Govᵗˢ in their wish to bring to a close the hostilities which have been waged against the Dominican people.

Their duty was to communicate those reasons to the Govᵗ of the Emperor & not to discuss them. They have frequently done so both in writing & in conversation, as clearly & fully as possible, & far from rejecting a discussion of the *bases of the proposition* of the three Powers, whether the bases of a peace or of a truce, they have never ceased, on the contrary, to court it & to see it declined. Neither the seriousness of the question, nor the interest taken in it by their Governments, is compatible with the continuance of this misunderstanding.

The Undersigned [etc.].

R. M. WALSH	M. RAYBAUD	T. USSHER
&c &c &c	&c &c &c	&c &c &c

hope of obtaining a definitive answer within the period to which my connection with the mission is limited.   The Chambers have been regularly
summoned for the 25th of this month.   No one doubts that they will do
exactly what the Emperor tells them; but I begin to have hope that he will
tell them to counsel him to yield.   From what I now learn, he is becoming
impressed with the idea that the three Powers are positively in earnest,
and that it is better to have their friendship than their enmity.   If such be
the fact, we may expect an answer of a favorable description in a few days
after the meeting of the Chambers.   The hope, however, is still a faint one,
as everything depends upon the degree of apprehension under which he may
be laboring at the moment.[1] . . .

   With great respect [etc.].

2241

Robert M. Walsh, Special Agent of the United States to the Dominican Republic,
to Daniel Webster, Secretary of State of the United States[2]

[EXTRACTS]

No. 5   PORT AU PRINCE, *March 31, 1851.*

   SIR: Enclosed are copies of a recent correspondence with the Minister of
Foreign Affairs.[3] . . . You will perceive that in my note of the 24th,[4] I
made a last effort to bring the Gov.ᵗ to its senses upon the Dominican question, as the Chambers were on the eve of meeting.   If the language which
I have used is stronger than perhaps my instructions would altogether war-

   [1] This omission comments on minor officials and unimportant matters.
   [2] Special Agents, vol. 18.   Received April 28.
   [3] This omission reports that the Haitians had taken great umbrage at the phrase "not of
African extraction," which he had copied into his first note from the Secretary of State's
instruction to him.
   [4] Omitting a brief paragraph about a Haitian consul at Boston, the pertinent portion of
this document, and the pertinent portion of the response to it, follow:

   Robert M. Walsh, Special Agent of the United States to the Dominican Republic, to L.
   Dufresne, Duke de Tiburón, Minister of Foreign Affairs of Haiti

[EXTRACT]

                                              PORT AU PRINCE, *March 24, 1851.*

   The U, will avail himself of the opportunity to say also to the Minister, that as the
period to which his mission is limited is drawing to a close, he trusts that the Haytian
Gov.ᵗ will use all possible expedition in giving an answer to the proposition of the three
Powers in regard to the pacification of the island, and that it will be such as they desire
to receive.   He would warn the Gov.ᵗ for the last time, in the most earnest and emphatic manner, against any attack upon the Dominican Republic.   It may be assured
that any attempt of the kind will only result in disaster to itself.   He cannot, however,
permit himself to suppose that it will be so insensible to the commonest dictates of
prudence & reason, as to sacrifice, in pursuit of a wholly unjustifiable & unattainable
object, the respect & friendship of the three nations whose good-will is so essential for the
welfare of the Haytian Empire & people.
   The U. &c &c

rant, it is because the only possible chance of success consists in intimidation. My colleagues, moreover, before my arrival, had menaced coercive action; and if I had allowed it to be suspected that there was not a perfect agreement between their Gov^ts & that of the U. States in regard to ulterior measures, all hope of a favorable result would have been crushed. I have taken care, however, to say nothing which can commit my Gov^t in any way to anything more than an acquiescence in the employment of force by England & France, which is authorized by the instructions of Sir Henry Bulwer. It is the intention of the English & French Consuls to announce to this Gov^t an immediate blockade of its ports, in case of a refusal to make either a peace or a truce. All that I shall do will be to remonstrate, as directed, but in such a mode as to indicate that no opposition will be made by the U. States to the enforcement of the blockade.

The Chambers were opened on the 27th, a delay of two days having been occasioned by the want of a quorum. The speech of the Emperor is enclosed.[1] It is pacific enough in its tone, but nothing is known of his intentions; and opinions seem to be equally divided as to the result.[2] . . .

I have the honor [etc.].

2242

Robert M. Walsh, Special Agent of the United States to the Dominican Republic, to Daniel Webster, Secretary of State of the United States[3]

[EXTRACTS]

No. 6   PORT AU PRINCE, *April 8, 1851*.

SIR: In my last I announced the opening of the Chambers, and enclosed a copy of the Emperor's speech.[4] . . .

In the enclosed Journal there is a report of the doings of the Legislature

---

L. Dufresne, Duke de Tiburón, Minister of Foreign Affairs of Haiti, to Robert M. Walsh, Special Agent of the United States to the Dominican Republic

[TRANSLATION—EXTRACT]

PORT AU PRINCE, *March 26, 1851*.

SIR: . . . As to the considerations with which you terminate your last note, I can only say that I have taken note of them. I do not wish, in any way, to anticipate the judgment of the country, which will doubtless manifest itself by the organ of its representatives.

&c &c &c

[1] Not included in this publication. It is printed in French in the issue for March 29, 1851, of *Le Moniteur Haïtien*.
[2] This omission reports the execution of several Haitians and comments on minor matters.
[3] Special Agents, vol. 18. Received May 1.
[4] His last despatch, No. 5, of March 31, 1851, is above, this part, doc. 2241; but the Emperor's speech is not included in this publication.
This omission refers to the gorgeous clothing worn by the Emperor and his suite at a recent ceremonial, and discusses the dangers surrounding him.

up to the 1ˢᵗ of this month.   From the apparent earnestness of the proceedings, it might be inferred that the members are fully impressed with the
nature of the duty they are called upon to perform; and were it not so perfectly understood that the whole is a solemn farce, & that their decision
upon "the grave question of national interest" communicated to them by
the Emperor, will also be communicated to them by the same august personage, there would be good reason for predicting that their voices will not be
for war.   If His Majesty should intimate the expediency of peace, he will
unquestionably receive the most willing & conscientious advice to that effect
from his faithful Senators & Deputies; but we are still in a state of uncertainty as to his intentions.   They will be revealed, however, before the end
of this week.

You will see by the Journal the correspondence which has taken place
between the Minister of F. Affairs & the Chambers in regard to a request
made by my colleagues & myself to be present at the discussion of the
Dominican question.   It seems to have embarrassed the Legislators; and
at last they determined to sit with closed doors, so that we can obtain no
satisfactory intelligence of their proceedings.

With great respect [etc.].

2243

*Robert M. Walsh, Special Agent of the United States to the Dominican Republic,
to Daniel Webster, Secretary of State of the United States*[1]

[EXTRACTS]

No. 7   PORT AU PRINCE, *April 10, 1851.*

SIR: I am informed that the Chambers have appointed a joint Committee
to make a report upon the Dominican question; and that the Emperor had
added to it six Generals, in order that the army may be represented in the
business.   The town is now full of military personages, all the principal
officers of the Empire having been summoned here, to the number of nearly
five hundred Generals & twice as many Colonels, for the double purpose of
ascertaining their views concerning the war, and of giving them the decorations just arrived from France of the order of Sᵗ Faustin—an order instituted by the Emperor.[2] . . .

With great respect [etc.].

[P. S.]   *April 13, 1851.*

SIR: I learnt this morning from a reliable source, that in the report of the
Committee, which will be given in tomorrow, there is a recommendation

---

[1] Special Agents, vol. 18.   Received May 15.
[2] This omission describes the origin, character, and decorations of this order, and tells of
other orders and the prevalence of such decorations.   He then discusses at length the end-
less succession of absurdly ridiculous circumstances followed by sickening bloody tragedies.

that the Gov.ᵗ shall send agents to London, Paris & Washington, to open negotiations of its own for the settlement of the question—a step which would not only be absurd but, under the circumstances, might be deemed offensive.   I thought it my duty, therefore, to put a stop at once to any design of the sort, and sent an intimation to the Minister of F. Affairs that an answer of such a description would be regarded not only as a refusal of the propositions, but as a disrespectful refusal.   The message was received by him in such a way as to induce a confident hope that it will accomplish its object, as well as to prove that my information had been perfectly correct.[1] . . .

2244

Robert M. Walsh, Special Agent of the United States to the Dominican Republic, to Daniel Webster, Secretary of State of the United States[2]

No. 8   PORT AU PRINCE, *April 23, 1851*.

SIR: On the 19th we received the definitive answer of the Haytian Gov.ᵗ to the propositions of a peace or a truce of ten years with the Republic of S.ᵗ Domingo.   You will perceive by the enclosed translation of it,[3] that both

[1] This omission tells of the outbreak of a rebellion in the northern part of the country.
[2] Special Agents, vol. 18.   Received May 15.
[3] Below is the text of the Haitian answer, followed by that of the rejoinder of the representatives of the three powers:

L. Dufresne, Duke de Tiburón, Minister of Foreign Affairs of Haiti, to the Special Agents of the United States, France, and Great Britain

PORT AU PRINCE, *April 19, 1851*.

The Undersigned has the honor to transmit to the Agents &c. &c. &c. the definitive reply of the Gov.ᵗ of H. M. to the propositions which they have presented to it in the name of their Govt.ˢ.

This reply contains the resolution of H. M.'s Gov.ᵗ in accordance with that of the Legislative Body.

The Constitution does not permit the Haitian Gov.ᵗ to subscribe to the first proposition of the three Powers, because, by so doing, it would violate articles 1, 4, & 116 of that Constitution, and consent to the alienation of a part of the territory of the Empire.

The second proposition, which tends, in effect, to the same result, cannot, either, be accepted by the Haitian Gov.ᵗ, for the aforesaid reasons.

Nevertheless, deeming it a matter of urgency to give a solution to the question of the East, & to arrive, by some means compatible with the rights, the interests & the dignity of the nation, at a definitive pacification of that part of the island, the Haitian Gov.ᵗ, actuated by the principles of humanity in the name of which the three Powers have interfered in the dispute, proposes that all the points of difference be regulated & settled by deputies named for the purpose by the two parties, in equal number on both sides, and that the decision be effected under the mediation & guarantee of the representatives of the three Powers.

The Gov.ᵗ of H. M. takes upon itself, besides, the engagement, from the present moment, of continuing the truce which exists in fact since the commencement of the negotiations to this day.   In testimony of its desire of peace & conciliation, it further proposes to the inhabitants of the East, that relations of commerce & friendship should be immediately reestablished between them & the rest of the Empire.

The desire of a pacific solution so clearly manifested by the Haitian Gov.ᵗ, the importance of the commercial relations & of the interests of the three Powers with Haiti,

propositions are positively rejected. The proposal of another mode of arrangement which is contained in the note is, of course, inadmissible, as it involves the recognition by the Dominicans of the sovereignty of Haiti, as a sine quâ non. There being a promise, however, of abstaining from hostilities until the three Gov^{ts} are informed of what has been done, the English & French Consuls did not think themselves fully authorized to menace a blockade; and we therefore sent a reply, which we could all sign, a translation of which is enclosed. There is little doubt that the Emperor is pretty well satisfied of the impossibility of ever getting possession of "the Eastern part of the island," and that he will scarcely make another attempt to conquer it. So far, therefore, our mission has been productive of good— of great good, I may say—for it would be a consummation most deeply to be deplored, if the Dominicans were to be brought again under the dominion of this wretched Gov^{t}, which would only drag them along with it to inevitable perdition. But he will never acquiesce in any such arrangement as has been proposed until he sees a squadron in the harbour; and then he will yield at once. In the meanwhile he will assume all the airs of a hero setting at defiance the world in arms, to the infinite admiration of the mass of his subjects; and will have a plausible excuse for keeping up the immense army in which he beholds his glory & his strength. His hatred, also, of the Dominicans will be gratified, by keeping them in a state of uncertainty & disquietude, which will prevent their devoting themselves to those peaceful pursuits which are indispensable for their welfare.

It is matter of satisfaction that the idea of sending agents to the three Gov^{ts}, to which I adverted in my last despatch,[1] is not broached in the note

---

the kindly intercourse of constant friendship between the latter & the Gov^{ts} represented by the three Agents, the principles of the strictest justice & of the impartiality of mediators who, in an arrangement between two parties to be reconciled, cannot exact from one of them exclusively sacrifices incompatible with its existence, all give to the Gov^{t} of H. M. the hope that the Agents of the three Gov^{ts} will second its desire of pacifying definitively the East—but on equitable conditions.

The U. &c &c

The Special Agents of the United States, France, and Great Britain, to L. Dufresne, Duke de Tiburón, Minister of Foreign Affairs of Haiti

PORT AU PRINCE, *April 19, 1851.*

The Undersigned, Agents &c. &c. &c., have the honor to acknowledge the receipt of the note of His Enc^{y}.   &c. of this day's date [Immediately above.—Ed.], by which—in answer to the propositions of a definitive peace, or a truce of ten years, between the Empire of Haiti & the Dominican Republic, which they made in the name of their respective Governments—he informs them of the positive rejection of those two propositions.

In consequence, they will communicate to their Gov^{ts} this unfortunate issue of the negotiations which they were directed to pursue, and will act in conformity with the instructions that have been given to them for such a contingency.

The U. &c &c &c

R. M. WALSH   M. RAYBAUD   T. USSHER

[1] Dated April 10, 1851, above, this part, doc. 2243.

of the Minister of F. Affairs.   It is certain, however, that it was suggested in the report of the Chambers.

I need not call your attention to the absurdity of the reasons assigned for the refusal of the propositions, as they are the same that have always been given by the Gov.ᵗ for its action.   They are more especially absurd, however, as coming from the Legislative Body, under the circumstances of its convocation, the pretense for which was that it possessed the power that it now declares it is not competent to exercise.

If the Water Witch should not arrive before the end of this month, I will leave for S.ᵗ Domingo in the French Steamer, "the Crocodile," & there await your orders.

With great respect [etc.].

2245

Robert M. Walsh, Special Agent of the United States to the Dominican Republic, to Daniel Webster, Secretary of State of the United States[1]

SANTO DOMINGO, *May 6, 1851.*

SIR: There being no news of the Water Witch & nothing more for me to do at Port au Prince, I came here, with the French Consul General, in the French war steamer the Crocodile.   Soon after our arrival we called upon the President & the Minister of F. Affairs, to the latter of whom I delivered your letter.[2]   They were disappointed, of course, at learning that the Emperor of Haiti would not consent to make peace, but gratified to hear that he had promised not to make war—though they expressed the utmost confidence in their ability to repel an invasion should it be attempted.   It is not the dread of being subjugated, but the necessity of remaining under arms which causes them, they say, to be so anxious for the pacification of the island. We gave them all the assurance in our power of the desire & intention of the three Powers to accomplish that object & relieve them from their painful suspense, for which they begged us to convey their grateful acknowledgments.

As the four months to which my mission is limited, have nearly expired, I shall proceed without delay to the island of S.ᵗ Thomas & embark there in the English steamer for New York, where I shall probably arrive before the first of next month.[3]

I have the honor [etc.].

[1] Special Agents, vol. 18.   Received May 31.
[2] Not included in this publication, since it was merely a letter introducing Mr. Walsh to the Dominican Government.
[3] He reached Washington on or just before June 10, 1851, and signed there, on that date, what he referred to as "a brief report of my mission to the island of St. Domingo, from which I have just returned," which report is not included in this publication, since it contained little pertinent information not embodied in his reports sent from Port au Prince and Santo Domingo, above, this part, *passim.*

2246

Jonathan Elliot, Commercial Agent of the United States to the Dominican Republic, to Daniel Webster, Secretary of State of the United States [1]

No. 34   SANTO DOMINGO, *June 14, 1851.*

SIR: You will please receive accompanying, a communication directed by this Government, to the Consuls here, stating that the Haytians have again commenced hostilities.[2]   The Government and people are anxiously expecting some interference, or assistance.

I have the honor [etc.].

[1] Consular Letters, Santo Domingo, vol. I.   Received July 7.
[2] The following is a translation of this communication:

José Mariá Medrano, Minister of Foreign Affairs of the Dominican Republic, to the Special Agents of the United States, France, and Great Britain

[TRANSLATION]

No. 34   SANTO DOMINGO, *June 6, 1851.*

GENTLEMEN: The undersigned has the honor to inform you that on the 29th and 30th ultimo, we were again attacked by the Haitians.   As always, with the assistance of Providence, which favors the justice of our cause, we were fortunate enough to conquer them and they have been severely punished for their temerity on the field of Postrerrio. According to official advices the number of their dead is more than fourteen.

The Dominican Government and People were resting in the confidence that the truce which was concluded de facto through the generous mediation of England, France, and the United States of America for both belligerents would be respected.   Our army, observing this solemn engagement, ceased to make inroads in the camp of the enemy and to watch his movements, in order to avoid every reason for suspicion.   Protected by this frank and straightforward conduct, the Haitians assembled their forces and beat back some of our advanced lines, extending their line of operations to the point where they were defeated, about sixteen leagues to the rear of our advanced lines.

It is a demonstrated fact that the Haitians have no respect for the sake of honor itself, without coercive measures, for agreements with other nations; and that therefore our safety rests only on judicious use of force.

On this occasion, we regret the invasion more on account of the offense which it gave to intervening Powers, who showed their interest in peace by so humanitarian and noble a proposal, than on account of the injury to ourselves, as the Dominican arms have sustained their honor and punished the insult; but it is the duty of the Government to denounce this offense, this lack of faith on the part of the constant enemy of the Dominican people, which proves the premeditated character of this intentional act.   From another standpoint, it is incumbent on the mediating Powers to qualify the audacious act performed in spite of the measures taken by them.

The military importance of the point of Neiba, the number of troops by which it was threatened, the distance traversed despite the resistance of the intermediate guards, everything proves the intention of forcibly taking possession of the place, in order to extend the line of invasion.   The concerted manner in which troops appeared at the same time at other frontier points, drawing attention either by displaying forces or by admonitions of peace, clearly show that this attack was the result of a combination of superior strength and not merely the excesses of some one of the corps which covered the frontier.

At the same time that they carried out the invasion, the troops disseminated a seditious proclamation of the Emperor Soulouque, addressed not to the Government, but to the people, an act which was insidious and improper, at a time when, under the mediation of friendly nations, an attempt was being made to conclude peace between the two governments.   Copies of the proclamation accompany the original.

The evidence appears from that moment of the plan to take possession of a few important points, defeating our troops by surprise and extraordinary cunning in order to propose to us amid general consternation, free from the beneficent influence of the

2247

Juan E. Aybar, Minister of Foreign Affairs of the Dominican Republic, to Jonathan Elliot, Commercial Agent of the United States to the Dominican Republic [1]

[TRANSLATION]

No. 71   SANTO DOMINGO, *December 31, 1851.*

MR. AGENT: It was with considerable surprise that the Dominican Government saw the part of the message of His Excellency the President of the United States, with regard to Santo Domingo, which you set forth in your note of the 27th instant,[2] to which it replied with the frank and succinct statement of the facts which you request of me, and which show the true status of the matter in question.

The three great Powers, in accepting the task of mediation, established as bases for the pacification of this Island, "definitive peace or a truce for ten years," as the only means capable of holding in check the unjust plan of conquest on the part of the Haitians and the bloody scenes of war, in conformity with international law and in the interest of humanity.

The Dominican Government manifested then and will manifest in all its acts, its full consent to the said bases, and its willingness to enter into negotiations with the sanguinary Haitian enemy, through the three mediating Powers, with regard to either of the two. This is not the case, however, with the Haitian Government, which, from the first notification until the present time, has not given a reply in favor of acceptance or chosen one of the two bases, but, on the contrary, has used and is using all means to avoid them, to evade mediation and to plan new aggressions in secret, in contempt of the agents.

In proof of this assertion, I shall point out to you what it did on the 29th and 30th of May of this year on the frontiers of Neyba, on the pretext of bringing a printed letter addressed to the inhabitants of the East, for which purpose an army was not needed, and the contents of which [letter], far from being a proposal of peace, represented a base fraud and a vexatious insult to the Dominican Government and the people of the Republic.

---

mediating Powers, instead of the peace in which they take such interest, a humiliating submission.

Everything therefore indicates that, in spite of our generous sentiments and the esteemed intervention of the great Powers who have considered this measure useful and necessary, the Haitian emperor desires war, desires devastation, and desires the shedding of blood. We Dominicans will not imitate their perfidious acts, but are resolved to repel the aggression with force.

In the meantime, the Haitians must be held responsible to the world for the blood which is being shed and for all the excesses which in the fury of a war of races disgrace humanity.

I take this opportunity [etc.].

[1] Consular Letters, Santo Domingo, vol. 1; enclosed with Elliot to the Secretary of State, No. 38, January 10, 1852, below, this part, doc. 2248.   [2] Not found.

It should be noted that at that time there was in fact a truce agreed upon by the contending parties through the agents of the three Powers, for although the period had expired, it was a condition of the truce that a notice of its cessation should be given one month in advance, which was never done. Consequently, the truce continued in full force and vigor, and the Neyba attack must necessarily be considered a lack of good faith.

I shall also point out to you what is a notorious fact, that on the pretext of visiting the Department of the North of Haiti, Soulouque left the capital with a numerous army and with all the war vessels of his flotilla, aboard which he had secretly placed arms, projectiles, and as great a quantity of subsistence and war supplies as was necessary to invade the territory of the Republic by way of the frontiers of the North, in the vicinity of which he camped his army at Juana Mendes.

The Dominican Government, convinced of the suspicious character and the machinations of the Haitian enemy, reinforced its frontiers of Cibao in the Canton of Guayubin with a sufficient number of troops, and placed itself in a defensive position such as to repel the enemy successfully if he had put his plan into execution; and this imposing attitude in our ranks and the notice which was given to Soulouque by the agents of Great Britain and France, to refrain from any attack on Dominican territory or [attack] by sea with his vessels, as in case it should be carried out, his ports would be blockaded, caused the enemy to desist from any attack.

Frustrated in his plans, Soulouque returned to the capital of Haiti where he was to make a definitive reply to the notifications given by the agents of the three Powers, but instead of that, he declared by a letter from his Minister of Foreign Relations, dated October 16th, that he consented and pledged himself to a truce of twelve months, not with the desired object of negotiating peace between the two nations, but in the delusive hope that the Dominican Republic would again submit itself to the Haitian flag and yoke.

The note of the Haitian minister was brought to this capital by Her Britannic Majesty's warship, Inflexible, Commander Dyke, and transmitted to my Government October 22–23, and as the President of the Republic was absent in Cibao, it could only be answered by this Ministry on November 20.

By the copies which I have the honor to enclose, both of the note of the Haitian Minister and the reply of my Government, it will be seen that the twelve months' truce proposed, was not for the purpose of concluding the definitive peace or the Truce of Ten years, the bases established by the three mediating Powers, but a deviation therefrom, and an evasive stratagem on the part of the Haitian Government for the purpose of extending the statuquo.

This is corroborated by the fact that the Haitian Minister speaks only of peacefully terminating domestic differences, referring to previous proposals published in Haiti to invite the Dominicans to a fusion and to sacrifice their nationality by submitting themselves to that Government, and that moreover, it was understood that during the truce of these twelve months, affairs on both sides would remain in their present state; and from this standpoint, the Dominican Government, which does not wish to deviate by a single point from the bases of mediation established by the three Powers, could not do otherwise than declare its non-acceptance, unless the purpose of the truce was to enter into negotiations for peace or for a truce of ten years, and declaring its willingness to proceed to the appointment of the respective agents. Up to the present, there has been no other incident or communication, and one wonders how the communication as to the twelve months' truce which was not accepted, could have been interpreted as a concluded peace.

In order to give you further proof of the duplicity and artifices of the Haitian Government for the purpose of maintaining the *Statu quo* and evading mediation and the bases thereof, the following consideration will suffice. The chief object of the Dominican Republic, in soliciting the mediation of the Three Powers was to escape from the *statu quo* of uncertainty with its continual threats, in which the Haitian enemy keeps it, obliging it to make the greatest sacrifices and incur the greatest expenses, to take its citizens away from their agricultural occupations in order to hold themselves in the proper state of defense, and by the lack of confidence caused by war, hampering the advance of the liberal institutions which it has proclaimed and the progress which it is on the alert to secure, in order to enhance and conserve the rank which it occupies among civilized nations. The Haitian Government, on the other hand, maintains a standing army which it has to pay in war or in peace, in order to maintain the chief and the rulers of the disgraceful empire erected in Haiti, and cooperate in the maintenance of the reactionary principles of exclusion, interdictions, and arbitrary acts.

I believe that I have fully answered your note above mentioned, and, in conclusion, I shall assure you that my Government is inclined to peace, but on the bases and with the intervention of the mediating Powers, which are the only means by which to succeed in pacifying this Island.

I avail myself of this opportunity [etc.].

2248

Jonathan Elliot, Commercial Agent of the United States to the Dominican Republic, to Daniel Webster, Secretary of State of the United States [1]

No. 38   SANTO DOMINGO, *January 10, 1852.*

SIR: Having read in the Message of President Fillmore,[2] "that peace had been concluded between the contending parties on this Island and knowing the same to be a mistake, I addressed a letter to this Government,[3] to know how the case really was.   Accompanying you have the answer [4] and copies of all the correspondence that has taken place in regard to the mediation since our Special Agent, Mr. Walsh left for the United States.[5]

[1] Consular Letters, Santo Domingo, vol. 1.   Received February 4.
[2] There are no corresponding closing quotation marks in the original.
[3] Not found.
[4] Above, this part, December 31, 1851, doc. 2247.
[5] The following are translations of the other two documents, found with this despatch:

L. Dufresne, Duke de Tiburón, Minister of Foreign Affairs of Haiti, to Robert H. Schomburgk, and Eugéne Lamuessens, British and French Special Agents, respectively, at Port au Prince

[TRANSLATION]

PORT AU PRINCE, *October 16, 1851.*

The Minister of Foreign Relations, in conformity with the promise which he made in his note, dated at Gonaïves on the 3d instant [Not found.—Ed.], to the agents of the mediating Powers, has the honor to transmit them the reply of the Haitian Government to their note of the 24th of July last.   [See below, in the volume and part containing Communications from Great Britain, as a footnote to British Minister Crampton's note to the Secretary of State, dated August 21, 1851.—Ed.]
The Minister of Foreign Relations renews to the agents of Great Britain and France, the assurance of the pacific intentions of His Majesty the Emperor, constantly expressed in the negotiations and the despatches of the Haitian Government, relative to the affair of the East, and so many times proclaimed in public acts, especially in the address of His Majesty to the inhabitants of the East, under date of the 14th of May last.
His Majesty approves and promises to extend for twelve months the truce authorized by the latter act, which was to last throughout the negotiations, which His Majesty proposed to the Eastern Provinces, for the purpose of peaceably terminating our domestic difficulties, which amounts, in fact, to the same thing, as the last proposal of the agents of France and Great Britain, but the truce in this form is in consonance with the duties, the dignity, and the honor of the Government of His Majesty and the Haitian nation.
It is understood that during the period of this truce, things will remain on both sides in their present status.
His Majesty, while deferring to the desire of the mediating Powers, is happy to give this new proof of his ardent and sincere desire for peace.
The undersigned begs the agents of Great Britain and France to accept the assurance of his highest consideration.

José Mariá Caminero, Minister of Foreign Affairs of the Dominican Republic, to the British and French Special Agents

[TRANSLATION]

No. 61   SANTO DOMINGO, *November 20, 1851.*

The Minister of Foreign Relations, in conformity with the offer which he made in his note of the 24th of October last, No. 58 [Not found.—Ed.], has the honor to transmit the reply [Presumably in the following paragraph.—Ed.] of the President of the Dominican Republic to the official communication of the agents of Great Britain and France

The uncertainty in which the people of this part of the Island now are, owing to the pending mediation, being unable to make a peace, or permitted to carry on the war, is bringing on them certain ruin.   The United States is blamed for having entered into this mediation and not taking the part that England and France have.

I beg seriously to call your attention to this, that the Government may take some action and escape further censure.

I have the honor [etc.].

2249

Jonathan Elliot, Commercial Agent of the United States to the Dominican Republic, to William L. Marcy, Secretary of State of the United States [1]

No. 48   SANTO DOMINGO, *March 7, 1853*.

SIR: I have to inform you that the inauguration of General Pedro Santana, as President of this Republic, took place on the 15th of February.

On the 27th being the tenth anniversary of their Independence, at a review of the troops, he made a short address, a copy [2] of which you will find in the accompanying newspaper.

The object of Marianna Torrente who recently came here in the Spanish Steamer, "Isabella la Segunda", was to form an alliance with this Government.   He offered to land here a Spanish force of five thousand men, in case difficulties should arise with the United States, and the proposition has been favorably received.   He also went to Hayti, to make the same propositions.

The French are also intriguing for favor here.   They are building a Steamer for this Government, and are completely to man, equip and furnish everything except the hull, for which, this Government have paid them forty-

---

of the 23d of the same month of October [Not found.—Ed.], concerning the new truce of twelve months proposed by the Haitian Government.

The Dominican Government has observed that in the Minister's note of October 16th [Above, this footnote.—Ed.], it is intimated that the extension of the truce for twelve months is in harmony with the vexatious language and proposals, issued out of order, in the Emperor's printed letter of May 14th [Not found.—Ed.] to the inhabitants of the East, and in this sense, the new truce is not only absolutely unacceptable, but would, moreover, be in conflict with the principles laid down by the great mediating Powers for establishing peace between the two states, which have as a basis *a truce for ten years or a definitive peace, with recognition of the Dominican Republic.*   If the object then of the truce of twelve months is to negotiate a definitive peace, as between state and state, the President of the Republic, will be willing to appoint at the same time as the Emperor, his respective agents or representatives to begin conferences within a month thereafter and enter into negotiations, the place of meeting to be agreed upon.

This inclination of the President toward peace should make manifest to the agents of Great Britain and France, the peaceful intentions with which the Government is animated in favor of humanity.

The Minister of Foreign Relations takes this occasion [etc.].

[1] Consular Letters, Santo Domingo, vol. 1.   Received April 4.
[2] Not within the scope of this publication.

five thousand dollars.   The French Consul General, M. Raybaud is shortly expected here, and I believe one of his principal objects is to make a secret Treaty of Alliance with this Government, as it is well known here that they have requested a military force from France, the greater part of which is to be placed at Samana.

According to Article 210. of the Dominican Constitution, the President has absolute power to do as he chooses, without consulting Congress, consequently he need not make public his acts.   I shall use my utmost endeavors to obtain copies of all this secret business, for the use of the Department.

To day Mr. Juan Abril, embarked for Havana, via St. Thomas, to negotiate with the Governor General of Cuba in regard to the propositions made to this Government.   It is very probable he will come to Washington to make propositions.   His departure and mission has been kept very secret. Should this Gentleman arrive in Washington to propose a Treaty and should the Government be disposed to enter into negotiations, it would be well to make me acquainted with the same, as I have some suggestions to make, which will be of great importance to the Government.

I earnestly request that the President, will not send any more Special Agents here, it has done no good, but to the contrary a great deal of injury to our interests.   To treat with these people it is necessary to have a thorough knowledge of them.   Our Agents who have been here, have so flattered and promised, without ever fulfilling, that they view us with great distrust. Something should be done, and that promptly, or this Island will be made a rendevous [rendez-vous], and garrisoned by European troops, if difficulties should occur, between the United States and Europe.

I have the honor [etc.].

2250

Jonathan Elliot, Commercial Agent of the United States to the Dominican Republic, to William L. Marcy, Secretary of State of the United States [1]

No. 52   SANTO DOMINGO, *May 3, 1853.*

SIR: I informed you in my previous despatches [2] of the visit of the Spanish Steamer, "Isabella the 2nd," to this City.   On Monday the 25th of April, also arrived here the Spanish Brig of War, "Scipion," of twelve guns.— The Commander was very much occupied with this Government for four days, when he sailed direct for Havana.   His business has been kept very secret, but I believe that Spain is making some alliance with this Government, to protect them against the Haytians and more particularly to prevent any large emigration to this part of the Island from the United States.   I

---

[1] Consular Letters, Santo Domingo, vol. 1.   Received May 25.
[2] Above, this part, *passim.*

shall keep you as well informed as I possibly can on this business. The French Treaty has been ratified and concluded.   I hope to send you a copy by next opportunity.   The President (Gen! Santana) told me, in conversation, that he intended to send a mission to Washington, to obtain the recognition of this Republic and make a Treaty.   He asked me "when I thought would be the most favorable time."   I replied, "that he had better defer it some months, as the United States Government having recently changed its Officers, were very much occupied at the present time."   My object was that more time should elapse because if it is true, that Spain is to give protection here, it will materially alter the course of affairs.   The Country at present is in such a wretched state and no disposition in the people to work, under any circumstances, that unless a large emigration come here, it is impossible for this Republic to sustain itself.   At present the climate is very fatal to Europeans, so much so, that I believe, that if thirty thousand were landed on the eastern part of this Island, the probability is, that there would not be five thousand alive, at the end of twelve months, but this will be ameliorated by clearing and draining the land.

If the Government wish full information in regard to this Republic, I am perfectly willing and ready at any moment to embark for Washington.

I have the honor [etc.].

2251

Jonathan Elliot, Commercial Agent of the United States to the Dominican Republic, to William L. Marcy, Secretary of State of the United States [1]

No. 63   SANTO DOMINGO, *November 27, 1853.*

SIR: I beg to inform you that great excitement has existed in this city, for the last three or four days, on account of difficulties between the French and this Government.

Two French subjects arrived here from Hayti, and this Government suspecting them to be spies, or suspicious persons, obliged them to leave the Country, for this, the Government have been forced by the French Consul and a French Steamer of War, to pay two thousand eight hundred dollars. Not content with this, the French Consul required of the President to expel from office the Secretary of the Treasury the Governor of this City and the Comptroller of the Custom House giving as reason that one Col. Mendes, who has been receiving the sum of two thousand dollars per annum, to drill the troops, had been grossly offended.   This the Government has refused to do.   The Secretary of State has been despatched to France, as well as the Secretary of the French Consul to settle the difficulty there, also despatches have been sent to the French Consul General in Hayti.   I have good reason

[1] Consular Letters, Santo Domingo, vol. I.   Received December 22.

to believe that the intention of the French, is to overthrow the present President of this Republic General Santana, a man of liberal principles and place Ex President Baez again in power, a mulatto who most cordially hates Americans and all that is American and is purely a Frenchman in his heart. It would be well to send immediately a vessel of war to this Port, by which time I shall have authentic information of what I have stated. I have also understood that Mariana Torrente of Cuba, is now in Europe, assisting this movement of the French, to govern this Island. I had an interview with President Santana this morning, he seemed very down hearted and expressed his regret that the United States would not recognize this Republic, the same as other nations had. He requested me, to ask you, if you would receive a Special Plenipotentiary to negotiate a Treaty. We ought to notice these people in some way and if the President of the United States is so disposed I am ready to give him every information that he may desire.

I have the honor [etc.].

2252

Jonathan Elliot, Commercial Agent of the United States to the Dominican Republic, to William L. Marcy, Secretary of State of the United States[1]

No. 64   SANTO DOMINGO, *November 30, 1853.*

SIR: I beg to call your attention to my previous despatches No. 59,[2] with the English protest against this Government, and also No. 63.[3] The French are using all their endeavors to overthrow or destroy this little Republic. The head quarters of their operations is at St. Thomas. I am keeping a good watch on them and you may rely upon having all authentic information very soon. Meanwhile any instructions that you may be pleased to send me I shall be happy to receive.

I would respectfully suggest that a vessel of war be despatched for this Port, to reach here in the begining of January. I beg that in this case the Government will trust entirely to *me*, because if any person was specially sent out here, it would prove of little benefit.

I have the honor [etc.].

[1] Consular Letters, Santo Domingo, vol. 1.   Received January 13.
[2] Not included in this publication. It contains two brief paragraphs. The first one refers to the recent erection of a lighthouse. The second one refers to an enclosed copy of a note from the British Consul to the Dominican Minister of Foreign Affairs, regarding the arbitrary expulsion of foreigners from the Republic. It refers, also, to an earlier joint note by the British, French, and United States consuls protesting against the arbitrary expulsion of a Venezuelan citizen. In this separate note, the British consul said he had been recently instructed by the British Secretary for Foreign Affairs "to protest in the name of his Government against a Foreigner being ordered to quit the Dominican Republic without Trial or Enquiry or without being informed of what offence he is accused."
[3] Above, this part, November 27, 1853, doc. 2251.

2253

Jonathan Elliot, Commercial Agent of the United States to the Dominican Republic, to William L. Marcy, Secretary of State of the United States[1]

No. 65   SANTO DOMINGO, *December 13, 1853*.

SIR: Since my last[2] I have learned that the French Consul General of Hayti, is to arrive here, on or about the 25th of December, his coming, bodes no good for this Republic.   Yesterday another messenger was despatched by this Government to Porto Rico, to ask Spanish protection.   In my former despatch I mentioned, that one had been sent to Madrid.   I think it proper, now to mention, that if these applications to Spain fail, (which I have every reason to believe will) this Government and people will solicit the protection of the United States.   In such an event, I shall act with every prudence and caution keeping you correctly and promptly informed of all that may occur. I neither spare trouble or expense to get every information of what is going on here and I shall shortly give another proof to the many—that the European Powers, are no friends to Republics.

I have the honor [etc.].

2254

William L. Cazneau, Special Agent of the United States to the Dominican Republic, to William L. Marcy, Secretary of State of the United States[3]

OCOA, DOMINICAN REPUBLIC, *January 23, 1854*.

SIR: In compliance with your instructions[4] I have the honor to lay before the Department the result of my inquiries into the condition and prospects of the Dominican Republic.

The meeting of Congress for the revision of the Constitution has called together the leading men from the various sections of this Republic.—   This circumstance not only aids our insight into the probable policy of Dominica but opens to the United States a favorable crisis for giving it a more American direction and making the young republic, in fact as well as name, an independent American power.

The actual situation of Dominica is peculiar and embarrassing.

With a limited population of less than three hundred thousand souls it is compelled to draw heavily on its industrial forces to be in readiness to defend itself against the attacks of its irreconcilable neighbor Hayti who has nearly treble its numerical strength.

None of the American powers have given this sister republic the just and

[1] Consular Letters, Santo Domingo, vol. I.   Received January 5.
[2] Above, this part, November 30, 1853, doc. 2252.
[3] Special Agents, vol. 19.   Received March 10.
[4] Above, this volume, pt. I, November 2, 1853, doc. 2198.

politic support of a friendly recognition, which leaves it dependent upon the good will of France and England for even the temporary relief of the existing truce with Hayti.— Ignored by America, while it is recognized and—as the Dominican people are constantly and ostentatiously informed—*protected* by Europe, Dominica has had no choice but to submit to the requirements of European policy.— It is to be regretted that it has not suited this policy to end as it could do at will—the terrible war of races which has scourged this Island for half a century and place this republic on a solid basis of prosperity.

Aside from this harassing war with Hayti Dominica possesses within itself encouraging elements of durability.— It is a compact state, seperated by the sea from entangling neighbors on every side but that of Hayti, about equal in extent to Denmark, and considerably larger than either Switzerland, Holland, or Belgium. It is advantagiously situated for commerce and is pre-eminently gifted with such productions as must invite trade to her ports.— Perhaps no other country in the world can exhibit within itself such a full and varied list of mineral and agricultural productions. It may be remarked that among these are coffee, cocoa, mahogany dye-stuffs and other articles that are not produced in the United States, though largely consumed there; and for which our flour, provisions, fabrics &c., are required in return. Dominica revolted from the domination of the blacks of Hayti and established her independence without the aid of any foreign power and after victoriously sustaining this unequal struggle for upwards of nine years wholly upon her own domestic resources, she is still entirely free from debt.— She has also created a small navy, of seven vessels and about fifty guns, for Coast and Mail service, besides maintaining the force necessary to preserve internal tranquillity.— The people have borne cheerfully the burden of the revolution and seem every where contented with and obedient to, their exist- ing institutions. They have evinced courage and constancy in their defence and have unbounded confidence in the patriotism and capacity of their leader in the War of independence, Genl Pedro Santana, now for the second time their constitutional President.

The constitution of the Dominican Republic is liberal, democratic and representative, though central.— It is moreover a practical reality; it is recognized, respected and acted upon as the supreme law by the government as well as the people.— The Executive, Legislative and Judicial powers are clearly defined and freedom of election is secured to the people and their representatives, I will transmit a copy of the revised constitution as soon as it shall be completed.— This revision has now proceeded so far that I can say with confidence that the amended constitution will not be less liberal and democratic than the old one, and I have reason to believe it will contain some new provisions likely to prove of great utility to American interests in the future.— Security of person and property and perfect freedom of con- science is guaranteed to all, whether citizen or stranger, both by the law and the practice of the republic.   There is a protestant congregation at Samana, two at puerto plata and another at the city of Santo Domingo, and in each of them are persons who hold office under the government.

Foreigners are permitted to hold and transfer real estate but the laws regulating landed property seem crude and defective.— I am assured however that these will receive some important and benificial amendments during the extra session of the regular Congress which meets on the fifteenth of February.

Children born of Dominican parents in a foreign land may, at their option, remain citizens of the country in which they were born or claim, and thereupon receive, full citizenship in Dominica.   With the same liberality the children born of foreign residents in Dominica have the right to record themselves Dominican citizens or, if they desire to retain their Nationality, they may register themselves under the flag of their parents.

There are two societies in Santo Domingo—one religious, the other a benevolent mutual aid society of about seventy members—composed entirely of emigrants from the United States and their children.— These emigrants were invited over and portions of land assigned them when Hayti governed the whole Island, yet at the end of thirty years they are still strongly attached to their Nationality.— They call themselves Americans, teach their children to speak English, and conduct their Church and society in that language.— There are five hundred persons of this class in the republic and they are generally esteemed as industrious intelligent and orderly Citizens.

The main reliance of Dominica against the attacks of Hayti is in her regularly organized and drilled Militia.   Once a week the whole available population is mustered for drill throughout the republic.   From them are drafted in rotation a certain proportion for Military duty.   Eight thousand men are always in arms for immediate service without any perceptible burden on the revinue, although a small allowance is made them for rations.   There are about two thousand veteran troops in the regular army—and in the arsenals of Santo Domingo and Puerto plata there is a sufficient supply of arms and ammunition for any emergency.

Since the establishment of the republic in 1844, it has purchased in the United States its Military supplies, including artillery and thirty thousand stand of arms.— It is creditable to those who managed her affairs that all this, with her navy, were paid for out of her infant resources without involving herself in debt or receiving aid from any foreign power.

The independence of this republic has been acknowledged by England, France, Denmark and the Netherlands and formal treaties have been entered into with them all—that with the Netherlands being in the course of ratification.

It is of interest to the United States to know that vessels belon[g]ing to Nations recognizing and in treaty with Dominica pay but half tonnage—or fifty cents per ton—while the vessels of the United States and all others not recognizing her pay one dollar per ton.—

When this republic first seperated from Hayti she reduced the duties on the products of the United States but the Dominicans complain that all their efforts to obtain the friendship and sympathy of the great republic of the North were altogether fruitless.

In speaking of the Diplomatic relations of this country it becomes my duty to refer to some delicate and embarrassing points in the position of this republic as an independent American power which I find it difficult to approach, but which cannot be passed over in silence.—

That portion of the island which was a French colony originally, and is now comprised in the Empire of Hayti, engaged to pay France a large sum to indemnify the Colonists who were despoiled of their property and driven from the country by the blacks.— Dominica does not admit that she is bound to pay any part of this debt as her portion of the island had no share in the wrong-doing or in the compensation.— France thinks otherwise and the members of this government do not hesitate to express the opinion that but for the determination publicly avowed by the United States not to permit foreign powers to create new Colonies on this side of the Ocean France would take possession of so much of the territory of Dominica as would satisfy this demand.—

The moral influence of this American position will be sufficient to protect Dominica from being reduced to a European colony but while it is not recognized and treated as an American power, by the United States, it will not have the self-confidence to resist many severe exactions.— In the absence of this recognition by the other American powers and entirely surrounded, as it is by European Colonies—which with the single exception of this Island wholly occupy and enclose the Mexican and Carribbean seas it must continue to feel something of the dependence of a European Colony.

If Dominica could refer their disputes with more powerful Nations to the arbitration of a neutral power it would relieve her from many difficulties, and have a salutary effect on her domestic as well as foreign relations.— The successful establishment of her independence proves that she is competent to maintain her government and sustain herself against Hayti if left free from undue foreign pressure.

Whether this dangerous conflict of races is fomented by other parties and how far it is made use of to excite prejudices against the people of the United States, will be made the subject of another communication but some points touch so forcibly on the future destiny of this republic that it would be wrong to pass them without notice.

Hayti is exclusively a nation of blacks.— It will not grant citizenship to whites, nor will it permit white settlers to take up its waste lands or develope its untouched mines.— In Dominica on the contrary the whites are essentially the governing class—though the constitution makes no distinction respecting race or color—and public sentiment is now teeming in favor of emigration.   The whites begin to realize that it is the best means to increase their ratio of strength and capital and enable them to force Hayti into peace. —The Emperor of Hayti however will not easily consent to recede from his pretensions to the sovereignty of the whole Island and the right to hold the whites in a lower scale of subjugation than his colored subjects.—   Between these parties foreign diplomacy manages to obtain for itself the balance of power.—   If either State is refractory it has but to threaton to cast its weight into the opposite scale to insure conditions which it would not venture to propose under other circumstances.

A settled peace would greatly increase the agricultural and commercial resources of the republic by returning to their regular occupations the seventh part of the male working population which it is computed is now diverted from regular employment to military service.—   This scarcity of hands is much felt in the mahogony cuttings and must influence the price of that wood in our markets.—

The ports nearest Hayti are now closed to commerce, to the serious inconvenience of our vessels, particularly those engaged in the mahogany trade.—   In lieu of going directly to and from their places for loading they are compelled to go to one of the open ports there take their permits and pilots and proceed to a distant point to load, and then return to their port of entry to clear for their final destination.—   These additional trips consumed about as much time as would carry them to one of our Atlantic ports.—

If closer relations should arrise between the United States and this republic this difficulty could be immediately obviated.—   In such an event I am confident Dominica could be induced to declare a frontier port neutral of war and open to the commerce of all nations on favored terms—the flag of each country protecting its own vessels.—   It would be premature to enter more fully into this subject at present but I hope to communicate to the Department some further particulars at an early day and also to forward some statistical details which I have not yet been able to collect and present in an authentic shape.

I have the honor [etc.].

2255

William L. Cazneau, Special Agent of the United States to the Dominican Republic, to William L. Marcy, Secretary of State of the United States[1]

SANTO DOMINGO, *February 12, 1854.*

SIR: I have the honor of transmitting to your Department the within copies of the treaties entered into by the Dominican Republic with various foreign powers [2] and I would most respectfully beg leave to call your attention to some clauses in them which perhaps may be found worthy of consideration.

You will observe that in Article 6th of the Treaty with France the right of holding and inheriting real estate is mutually guaranteed by each party to the citizen of the other nation.— My attention was called to this clause as it presents a satisfactory precedent to Americans who desire to purchase the rich yet exceedingly cheap lands of this republic. The law as it stands permits foreigners to acquire and transfer real estate without impairing their rights of Nationality but efforts are being made to have this provision more distinctly and permanently engrafted in the revised constitution.— This will greatly increase the productions and resources of Dominica by effectually opening this tropical garden to the enterprising industry of our Citizens.

Articles 18th and 19th of the same Treaty define on the most liberal American basis the rights of Flag and provide against undue latitude of search on the high seas.

If this is a precedent from a European power it is not an unimportant item in case of a general European war which would make our vessels neutral carriers in those waters to an incalculable extent.

In Article 9th however of the Treaty with Great Britain this government concedes in certain cases the discretionary privilige of search to British cruisers, but in the same article the right to withdraw this priviledge on a years notice is expressly reserved by Dominica.

Perfect religious freedom is already enjoyed by all persons in the Dominican Republic but it is also guaranteed by treaty, and placed beyond the caprice of government, to the citizens of any power that chooses to require this additional pledge.

In my letter of January 23d I had the honor of calling the attention of the Department to the 100 pr. ct. additional tonnage duty charged on vessels belonging to nations which have not recognized this republic.— For example one of our vessels of 500 tons can make about six voyages from a United States port to Dominica in a year paying one dollar pr ton each trip, in all

---

[1] Special Agents, vol. 19.   Received April 1.
[2] Not included in this publication.   They are printed in Spanish, each in a separate pamphlet.   They were with the Netherlands, France, and Great Britain, and related to peace, friendship, commerce and navigation.

three thousand dollars, while under a recognizing flag she would only pay the same as a Dominican vessel—or fifty cents pr ton—making a difference of fifteen hundred dollars in her duties for the year; and the European vessel of the same value and burthen, could make but three trips out and back in the year paying only seven hundred and fifty dollars to the Dominican revenue.—

If closer relations were established and this class of distinctions removed from our vessels trading to this Republic, the United States from their proximity to this Island should control the chief supply of its markets and have nearly the monopoly of its carrying trade. At present American fabrics are rarely used or understood in this country.— Europe supplies almost the entire consumption although we manufacture the goods best adapted to their wants and can compete with Europe in prices. Even much of the lumber, flour, salted and other provisions, which can only be supplied by the United States come here by the way of the free port of St. Thomas and in European vessels.

I think it proper here to advert to the deep feeling constantly expressed by members of this government with regard to the amity of the United States. President Santana is aware that from its geographical situation and the character of its institutions the correct policy of this constitutional republic is to take position as an American power and soon after his first election to office he dispatched Don Jose [José] Maria [María] Caminero (who did not succeed in his mission however) to obtain recognition and arrange a treaty with the United States.

The successors of President Santana in office were men who had no sympathies with our people and were more disposed to fraternize with Hayti, or ally themselves with Europe, than to enter earnestly into a system of independent American policy. President Baez did not conceal his repugnance to the introduction of American settlers nor his predilections for Europe, where he received his Education.—

The re-election of Gen! Pedro Santana, and the return to power of some of the ablest men of the progressive party, have brought into action more liberal views and I cannot in justice avoid stating my convictions that the present is a most propitious time for establishing mutually advantagious relations between our own and the Dominican people.

Gen! Mella was dispatched a few months since on a secret mission to Spain, and the European party here affect to believe that it is to negociate the return of this country to its old allegiance to Spain under the subdued title of a protectorate—but the ruling policy of the present administration is to make the republic an independent American power and only in the extremity of a choice between subjection to Hayti or a dependence on Europe would it submit to the latter alternative.

I have the honor [etc.].

2256

A. Alfau, Minister of Foreign Affairs of the Dominican Republic, to Jonathan Elliot, Commercial Agent of the United States to the Dominican Republic[1]

[TRANSLATION]

SANTO DOMINGO, *April 24, 1854.*

MR. AGENT: Reliable intelligence has been received from San Tomas, stating, as a positive fact, that preparations are being made, on the part of the Haitian government, with a view of attempting an invasion of the Dominican Republic, renewing the hostilities which had been suspended until now by the generous intervention of the mediating nations.

My government, Mr. agent, has the satisfaction to know, that it has always maintained a purely defensive attitude, and that it has not provoked this new war; therefore it will be under the necessity of adopting all the measures which the defense and the preservation of the Republic require, without being responsible before your government, or before the world, for the results of such war, which may be fraught with fatal consequences.

As the representative of one of the mediating nations, I have the honor of making this circumstance known to you, begging that you will be pleased to communicate the same to your government, to be dealt with as it may be thought proper.

I avail myself of this occasion [etc.].

2257

Jonathan Elliot, Commercial Agent of the United States to the Dominican Republic, to William L. Marcy, Secretary of State of the United States[2]

No. 70   SANTO DOMINGO, *April 27, 1854.*

SIR: Accompanying you will please receive a copy, of an official letter, that I received from this Government,[3] informing me that the Haytians were about to commence hostilities and requesting me to make it known to you.

I have the honor [etc.].

[1] Consular Letters, Santo Domingo, vol. 1; enclosed with Elliot to the Secretary of State, No. 70, April 27, 1854, below, this part, doc. 2257.
[2] Consular Letters, Santo Domingo, vol. 1.   Received May 16.
[3] Above, this part, April 24, 1854, doc. 2256.

2258

Jonathan Elliot, Commercial Agent of the United States to the Dominican Republic, to William L. Marcy, Secretary of State of the United States [1]

[EXTRACT]

No. 71   SANTO DOMINGO, *May 16, 1854.*

SIR: . . . The French and English have prevented Emperor Solouque [Soulouque] from marching against this Republic.

I have the honor [etc.].

2259

William L. Cazneau, Commissioner of the United States to the Dominican Republic, to William L. Marcy, Secretary of State of the United States [2]

SANTO DOMINGO, *July 24, 1854.*

SIR: I have the honor to inform you that the Columbia arrived at her anchorage off Santo Domingo the 17th Inst and that I landed in this City the next morning.— I immediately presented my credentitials to the Minister of Foreign Relations Don Nepomaceno Tejera who I may observe *en passant* is a man of American ideas and not unfavorably disposed. President Santana is absent on his Estate in the provincia of Seybo, but a courier was promptly dispatched at my instance to request his presence here and he is now hourly expected.

In the interviews which I have since had with the other members of the government it became evident to me that the only possible obstacle to the early and complete success of my mission [3] was a vague dread of the real intention of the United States.—

Foreign influence has been very powerful in this feeble and hitherto neglected American Republic and Europeans here labor incessantly to instill into the Dominicans a belief that their domain will be seized, the native whites set aside, and the blacks enslaved if the Americans gain a foot-hold on their Island.— President Santana and the enlightened members of his government may have different opinions, but if the masses actively take up such a prejudice no Cabinet can resist it. On this account I was anxious that no marked step should be taken in the direction of Samana Bay until negociations were fairly and favorably commenced and the consent of the Executive politely asked and received.—

Cap[t] M[c]Clellen of the Eng[s], who is naturally and properly desirous not to

[1] Consular Letters, Santo Domingo, vol. 1.   Received June 7.
The omission, at the beginning, acknowledges the receipt of the routine circular of general consular instructions.
[2] Special Agents, vol. 19.   Received August 18.
[3] See his instruction dated June 17, 1854, above, this volume, pt. 1, doc. 2199.

lose time at this bad season of the year, wrote me from on board the Flagship Columbia the 19th Inst suggesting the propriety of proceeding to make the reconnaissance of Samana without waiting the permission of this government.— I answered him at once that such an act would at this moment be highly impolitic and strongly recommended a few days delay.—

On the 20th Comde Newton wrote informing me of his intention to proceed immediately to Samana as he considered this roadstead unsafe, but I communicated to him my reasons for desiring him not to go in that direction just at this moment—and I had before intimated that it would be better for the public interest if he selected the equally safe, and much nearer, Bay of Ocoa for a weeks anchorage. Comde Newton did not reply before he sailed but I trust he will not, under the circumstances, go to Samana; or if he does that Capt McClellen will be cautious in his operations.—

Mr Elliott the U. S. Commercial Agent, had prepared to go to Samana on this trip, but I objected decidedly to this additional eclat to a step that, is, I regret to say, already a subject of street talk and he obligingly yielded the point.

After the Columbia left, the National Schooner Buenaventura was dispatched to Puerto Rico to bring home Genl Mella, late Minister to Spain from this Republic, and probably to inform the Spanish authorities of all the surmises afloat as to the objects of the Columbia in these waters.

On the arrival of President Santana I hope to have the honor of transmitting to you a more satisfactory account of the progress of my mission—

I have the honor [etc.].

2260

William L. Cazneau, Commissioner of the United States to the Dominican Republic, to William L. Marcy, Secretary of State of the United States[1]

SANTO DOMINGO, *August 8, 1854.*

SIR: Since I had the honor of addressing you on the 24th July,[2] President Santana has returned, to the Capital.— On the 1st: inst: he named to treat on the part of this Republic Don Juan Nepomaceno Tejera, Minister of Foreign Relations, and Genl Juan Franco Luis Bido, member of the Dominican Senate from the Santiago District, both men of liberal principles.— The indisposition of Señor Tejera has unfortunately retarded negociations, altho' I labor incessantly to forward them, as I am exceedingly anxious to render an account of my mission at the earliest possible day.— Capt McClellan wrote me on the 3d inst. informing me:—"The position selected for a coal depot &c will require at least two square miles of land and perhaps somewhat more; it will be necessary to obtain the use & control of the Levan-

1 Special Agents, vol. 19. Received September 23. 2 Above, this part, doc. 2259.

tados bays at the entrance of the Bay. There are five of these bays, two large (the largest containing about 64 acres) and three very small ones."

"The place selected for a depot is the harbor of Carenero Chico."

In persuance of instructions I will endeavor to obtain these concessions; which I notice in comparing reports, the Spanish, French and British surveys concur in representing as excellent positions.

Our most reliable friends here regret with me this premature demonstration in Samana Bay, as the report reached here immediately over-land and the Anti-American party raised the absurd cry that the United States intended to take the country, and that Gen[l] Santana was conspiring to betray the colored population into slavery.

It was desirable to prepare the way before any movement was made by us which could in any manner be perverted to excite popular opposition, nevertheless I continue of opinion that I shall effect in the main, the just views of my government.

The determination formally announced by France and England of compelling Hayti to enter into a long truce or permanent peace with the Dominican Republic, renders the recognition of the United States of less importance to this people now than it was some months back; still there is too much intelligence and American feeling here not to appreciate its value.—

With the greatest respect [etc.].

2261

William L. Cazneau, Commissioner of the United States to the Dominican Republic, to William L. Marcy, Secretary of State of the United States [1]

SANTO DOMINGO, *August 19, 1854.*

SIR: In my former communications to the Department of State I have expressed my convictions—amounting to a moral certainty—that the Consuls of England and France were opposing an active, though secret, influence to the good understanding which the United States is disposed to enter into with the Dominican Republic.—

This opinion is now confirmed by the Official action of H. B. M. Consul Sir Robert Schomburgh.— He yesterday made an official call on the President and Cabinet and in the name of his government protested against any stipulations or agreement which would give to the United States a coal depot—misrepresenting the object of my mission as an attempt to create a permanent establishment within the Dominican Territory.— A member of the Dominican Cabinet notified me officially—but confidentially—of this fact, intimating that in the critical position of the Dominico-Haitien question such a procedure was equivilant to a serious threat and might prove

[1] Special Agents, vol. 19. Received September 23.

embarrassing to this young and comparatively defenceless Republic.—
The European party no doubt fear that the recognition of the United States
will make this Republic too independent of their dictation and are evidently
disposed to make common cause with the blacks and force a re-union with
Hayti.   Some of the most eminent members of the Dominican government
concur with me in beleiving this peace with Hayti is only intended as a
preliminary to that result and this is the true meaning of the vehement
opposition of the British diplomatic Agent to any treaty with the United
States.

Several members of the Dominican Congress, now in Session had before
this assured me that the Consul of H. B. M. was remonstrating with them
in strong terms against treating with the United States and that the Hon[1]
T. S. Heneken—an Englishman by birth and residing with the British Consul, but a naturalized citizen and member of the Dominican Congress—was
endeavoring to organize a party in that body to defeat any treaty which
should concede to the United States a Coal Depot or even a hospital site.—

But for this obstinate and unwarrantable interference, there is no doubt
that before this day I would have concluded with this Republic a treaty
mutually benificial to both countries and highly advantagious to the general
interests of commerce.—

Every point but one is definitely agreed upon and notwithstanding this
opposition I hope to report by the end of this month the ratification of a
satisfactory treaty by the Dominican Congress.

I have the honor [etc.].

2262

*William L. Cazneau, Commissioner of the United States to the Dominican
Republic, to William L. Marcy, Secretary of State of the United States*[1]

[EXTRACTS]

SANTO DOMINGO, *September 23, 1854.*

SIR: I have the honor to inform you that after much delay and hesitation
I am about concluding a treaty of friendship, commerce and extradition with
the Dominican Republic.

The peculiar circumstances of this Government compelled me to vary
somewhat the form and phraseology of the *projet* I received, but—with one
exception—no important feature is changed, while in some points much has
been gained for American interests.[2] . . .

I have been obliged to defer the objects of Art. 27 of the original *projet* for
future action.—   This is to me a painful necessity, and the more painful

---

[1] Special Agents, vol. 19.   Received October 20.
[2] This omitted portion reviews certain stipulations, mostly commercial, of the proposed treaty.

because I am forced to admit this postponement has been caused in a great measure by the unadvised precipitation of our own Officers.

All the unfavorable consequences to which I alluded in my notes of 24th July and 8th and 19th of August [1] as likely to follow the premature visit of the Columbia to the Bay of Samana, and its reconnaisance by the United States Engineers before negociations were properly commenced, have been unfortunately realized to the most serious detriment of my Mission.—

On the arrival of President Santana at the Capital to meet me, he found the report current that the U. S. Frigate Columbia was at Samana Bay with engineers on board making surveys, and that the Albany and a Steamer were ordered to join her there. Sir Robert Schomburgh, H. B. M. Consul and Diplomatic Agent here, had also sent an express for a war steamer (as in effect the Devastation did come) to watch the movements of the Americans.

I had hoped to overcome these obstacles to a just understanding by patient and persevering explanations, and at one time every thing—a naval depot included—was agreed upon, but meanwhile the Devastation arrived for the second time and the British Consul declared the Dominican Republic could have no peace with Hayti if a depot of any kind should be allowed to the United States.

Under these circumstances the Dominican government, feeling itself at the mercy of European policy, was forced to recede in this particular for the present—but it is only a postponement, not a final rejection—for the Dominicans are now convinced of the benifits which will accrue to the Republic from a closer intercourse with the United States.

The Dominican Congress adjourned before the terms of the treaty could be adjusted, but that body will be re-convened for the purpose, as soon as it is ready to be submitted for ratification—upon which I shall return with it for the consideration of my Government.

I have the honor [etc.].

2263

Juan N. Tejera, Minister of Foreign Affairs of the Dominican Republic, to William L. Cazneau, Commissioner of the United States to the Dominican Republic [2]

[TRANSLATION]

Private and confidential. SANTO DOMINGO, *September 28, 1854.*

ESTEEMED SIR: Complying with the wish which you expressed to me more than once, I am taking up my pen to inform you of the true causes of the unexpected delay which you have noticed with respect to the conclusion of the treaty we have been negotiating.

[1] All three are above, this part, docs. 2259, 2260, and 2261.
[2] Special Agents, vol. 19; enclosed with Cazneau to the Secretary of State, December 23, 1854, below, this part, doc. 2277.

It is quite true, General, that on the seventh day of this month I called on you with my colleague, the Honorable Bidó, as you say in an official communication dated the thirteenth of this month, [1] and that at that interview we said to you that President Santana finally accepted slight changes in Article 28 of the treaty relative to the grant of an appropriate site for the Government of the United States to establish in the Bay of Samaná a coaling station for the mail steamers, etc.   It is also true that we agreed that on the following day we would draw up that Article and have it copied for submission to the Congress for its approval; and unfortunately it is no less true that the Consuls of England and France, and especially that of the first-named nation, were the cause of the President's change of mind about Article 28.

Indeed, Mr. Schombourgk called on the President at 7 a.m. the day after that interview and returned with Mr. Darasse, the French Consul at 1 p.m. I have already told you by word of mouth and I now repeat it that the object of those interviews was a declaration by those gentlemen against the granting of the said Article 28.   They did so in such terms that Mr. Schombourgk went so far as to say that France and England would protest against any grant of that kind made to the United States *even though it were for only one inch of land*.   I was present at the time of the interview as also were the other Ministers and may assure you that President Santana handled the question with all the needful tact, never admitting that the incident had for its object anything but a private matter without any official character.   The protest, however, never was made in writing.

You will no doubt wonder why President Santana has changed his mind with regard to Article 28 as neither France nor England has any right over the Dominican Republic, and what is more, no communication has been made to the Government of the Republic of that intended protest.   I will explain it to you in a few words.

The political situation of the Dominican Republic is somewhat exceptional in that it has to keep an eye on its unfair and bold enemy, Haiti, and also with regard to that same enemy has to maintain perfect harmony with the mediating powers, England and France; to which may be added the diversity of the elements in its social make-up.   Therefore, its conduct has always to be based on systematic watchfulness, which places it in an awkward and trying situation, and yet is necessary because on that system largely depends the political balance, since while it is strong and big enough to prevent Solouque from stepping over the boundary line of the two States, it is too small and weak to jeopardize its existence with either of the European nations to which I have reference; and on the other hand it wishes to avoid any displacement of its domestic ties.

President Santana understands this awkward situation full well and as

[1] Not found.

his honesty and patriotism will not allow any impairment of the tranquillity, independence and honor of the nation even in the slightest degree, he
rightfully feared, that any assent at this time to the stipulation in Article 28
might give rise to serious difficulties, which at least would have caused bloodshed, involved the State in great expense and in every way thrown the country backward, and wished to avoid it; and he had all the more cause for fearing this as those very Consuls of England and France mentioned in the said
interview that the Consuls of the other nations in Haiti had sent them copies
of an official note from the Minister of Foreign Relations of that Empire in
which they were told that Solouque [Soulouque] would refuse to agree to any
armistice in favor of this Republic if it should conclude the Treaty of Friendship, etc. with the United States.   But it is to be noted that neither was that
warning officially made known to my Government, in spite of the fact that
the British and also the French Consuls were asked to communicate it in
that way.

These, and no others, have been the causes of the sluggishness of our
friendly diplomatic negotiations.   I ought not to refrain from reminding you
of the character of this communication.   I have written it in confidence, and
I know you are a gentleman.

I remain your most affectionate friend and servant.

2264

*William L. Cazneau, Commissioner of the United States to the Dominican
Republic, to William L. Marcy, Secretary of State of the United States*[1]

SAN CARLOS, DOMINICAN REPUBLIC, *October 9, 1854.*

SIR: I have the honor to inform you that the convention of Friendship,
Commerce and Extradition between the United States and the Dominican
Republic was signed the 5th instant, on the basis indicated in my letter of
Sept. 23^d [2]—a duplicate copy of which I herewith enclose.[3]

[1] Special Agents, vol. 19.   Received November 6.
[2] Above, this part, doc. 2262.
[3] The following is the text of the treaty, copied from Unperfected Treaties, R:

TREATY OF FRIENDSHIP, COMMERCE AND NAVIGATION BETWEEN THE UNITED STATES OF
AMERICA AND THE DOMINICAN REPUBLIC

[SANTO DOMINGO, *October 5, 1854*]

The United States of America and the Dominican Republic alike animated with the
desire of maintaining the cordial relations and good understanding which subsist between their respective States and territories, and of augmenting with all the means at
their disposal commercial and social intercourse between them, have come to the
determination to enter into negociations for the conclusion of a general convention of
friendship, navigation and commerce and for the surrender of fugitive criminals: and at
the same time to make formal recognition on the part of the United States of the

Footnote 3, p. 133—*Continued*

independence of the Dominican Republic. For which purpose the President of the United States has conferred full powers on William L. Cazneau a citizen thereof, and the President of the Dominican Republic on his part has conferred like powers on Juan Nepomuceno Tejera, Minister of State in the Department of Justice, Public Instruction and Foreign Relations &ᶜ and Juan Luis Franco Bidó member of the Senate. And the said Plenipotentiaries after an exchange of their full powers found in due form have [concluded] and signed the following articles.

Article I

It is agreed by the contracting parties that there shall be a firm, inviolable and universal peace, and a true and sincere friendship between the United States of America and the Dominican Republic and between their respective territories and people without exception of persons and places. If unfortunately a war should occur between the two nations the term of six months after the declaration thereof shall be allowed to the merchants and other citizens and inhabitants respectively on one side and on the other to withdraw themselves with their effects and movables which they shall have the right to carry with them, send away, or sell at their will, without the least obstruction, nor shall their effects, much less their persons, be seized during such term of six months; and also passports which shall be valid for a term necessary, for their return to their own country shall be given to them for their vessels and the effects which they may wish to send away or carry with them, and such passports shall be a safe-conduct against all the insults and prizes which privateers may attempt against their persons and effects. And the money, debts, shares in the public funds or in the banks or any other property, personal or real, belonging to the citizens of the one party in the territories of the other, shall not be confiscated or sequestered.

Article II

The citizens of one of the two contracting parties residing or established within the territory of the other, shall be free from personal military duty; but they shall be liable to the pecuniary or material contributions usually imposed on residents not citizens of the country, but such contributions shall not in any case exceed those required of the citizens thereof.

Article III

The citizens of the contracting parties shall be permitted to enter, sojourn, domiciliate and reside in all parts whatsoever of the said territories, and to have and occupy warehouses provided they submit to the laws, as well general as special, relative to the rights of residing and travelling. While [they] conform to the laws and regulations in force, they shall be at liberty to manage their own business subject to the jurisdiction of the country as well in respect to the consignment and sale of their goods by wholesale or retail, as with respect to loading, unloading and sending off their ships or employing such agents or brokers as they may deem proper, and shall be treated as the citizens of the country in which they reside.

They shall have free access to the tribunals of justice for prosecuting their claims and enforcing their rights of persons and property on the same terms which are granted by the laws and usage of the country to their own citizens, for which purpose they may employ in defense of their interests and rights such advocates, attorneys and other agents as they may think proper and are permitted by the local laws.

Article IV

The citizens of each of the contracting parties residing in the other shall enjoy the most perfect security of conscience. They shall be subjected to no inconveniences whatever on account of their religious belief. Nor shall they in any manner be annoyed or disturbed in the exercise of their religious worship in private houses or in the chapels and places which they may select for that purpose, provided that in so doing they observe the respect and decorum due to the laws, usages and customs of the country.

It is likewise agreed that the citizens of either country who may die in the territory of the other country may be interred in it and in the cemeteries which the citizens of each of the two Republics may freely establish and maintain for this purpose, which shall be protected against molestation, as well as the funeral processions going to or returning from the same.

Footnote 3, p. 133—*Continued*

Article V

The contracting parties hereby agree that whatever kind of produce, manufacture or merchandise of any foreign country, can be lawfully imported into the United States in their own vessels may be imported in the vessels of the Dominican Republic and no higher or other duties upon the tonnage or cargo of the vessels shall be levied or collected, whether the importation, be made in a vessel protected by the flag of the United-States or in a vessel protected by the flag of the Dominican Republic. And reciprocally whatever kind of produce, manufactures or merchandise of any foreign country, can be from time to time lawfully imported into the Dominican Republic in her own vessels, may also be imported in vessels of the United-States,—and no higher tonnage upon the vessels or duties upon the cargo, shall be levied or collected whether the importation be made in a vessel protected by the flag of the Dominican Republic or in a vessel protected by the flag of the United States.

Whatever can be lawfully exported by one party in its own vessels, to any foreign country, may in like manner be exported or re-exported in the vessels of the other, and the same duties, bounties and drawbacks shall be collected and allowed, whether such exportation or re-exportation be made in vessels of the one or the other party. Nor shall higher or other charges of any kind be imposed in the ports of one party on vessels of the other than are or shall be payable in the same ports by its own vessels.

This article is not applicable to the coasting trade and navigation of the contracting powers which are respectively reserved by each exclusively for its own citizens.

Article VI

Those vessels which are declared by the laws of the Dominican Republic to be Dominican and which carry the papers necessary to establish that fact, shall be considered Dominican by the United-States, and reciprocally the same principle shall be applied to the vessels of the United-States by the Dominican Republic.

Article VII

No higher or other duties shall be imposed on the importation into the United-States of any article the natural product or manufacture of the Dominican Republic, and no higher or other duties shall be imposed on the importation into the Dominican Republic of any article the natural product or manufacture of the United-States than are or shall be payable on the like article the natural product or manufacture of any foreign country.

No higher duties and charges shall be imposed in the United-States on the exportation of any article to the Dominican Republic or on the exportation of any article to the United States, than such as are or shall be payable on the exportation of the like article to any other foreign country.

No prohibition shall be imposed on the importation or exportation of any article the natural product or manufacture of the United-States or the Dominican Republic from or to the ports of the United States or the Dominican Republic which shall not equally extend to every other foreign country. If however either party shall hereafter grant to any other nation any particular favor in navigation or commerce, it shall immediately become common to the other party, freely where it is freely granted to such other nation or on yielding the same compensation when the grant is conditional.

Article VIII

The contracting parties do not recognize the barbarous rights anciently claimed to wrecks of the sea. On the contrary, not only in time of peace, but in time of war (if unfortunately it should arise) vessels belonging to either nation which may be wrecked, stranded or suffer damage on the coasts or in the waters of the other shall receive (unless they carry troops, munitions or other evidence of hostile intention) the same aid and protection for their persons, ships and goods as if they were citizens of the nation in which the accident occurs—being subject like them to pay the costs and dues of salvage which are of usage in such cases.

If the operations of repair shall require that the whole or any part of the cargo be unloaded, they shall pay no duties of custom, charges or fees on the part which they shall reload and carry away, except such as are payable in the like case by the vessels of the nation in which the unloading is made. It is nevertheless understood that if while the vessel is under repair the cargo shall be landed and kept in a place of deposit destined to receive goods, the duties on which have not been paid, the cargo shall be liable to the charges and fees lawfully due for storage.

Footnote 3, p. 133—*Continued*

Article IX

The citizens of either of the contracting parties may sail with their ships and merchandise (contraband goods always excepted) from any port whatever to any port or place of those who are or may be enemies of the other, with perfect security and liberty without regard to who may be the owners of the goods on board.   And they may equally sail their ships and trade with their merchandise with the same freedom not only directly from the places and ports of the enemy aforementioned without any opposition or disturbance whatever to neutral ports and places, but also from one place belonging to an enemy to an other place belonging to an enemy of the other contracting party, whether they be or be not under the jurisdiction of the same power unless such ports or places shall be effectively blockaded, beseiged or invested.   And whereas it frequently happens that vessels sail for a port or place belonging to an enemy without knowing that the same is either beseiged, blockaded or invested, it is agreed that every vessel so circumstanced may be turned away from such port or place, but she shall not be detained, nor any part of her cargo, if not contraband, be confiscated unless after notice of such blockade or investment she shall attempt to enter,—but she shall be permitted to go to any other port or place she shall think proper, provided the same be not blockaded, beseiged or invested.   Nor shall any vessel of either that may have entered into such port or place before the same was actually beseiged, blockaded or invested by the other, be restrained from quitting such place with her cargo, nor if found therein after the reduction and surrender of such place shall such vessel or her cargo be liable to confiscation, but they shall be restored to the owners thereof.

Article X

In order to regulate what shall be deemed contraband of war, there shall be comprised under that denomination,—gunpowder, salt-petre, petards, mach [mechas], ball, bombs, grenades, carcases [carcasas], pikes, halberts, swords, belts, pistols, holsters, cavalry saddles, and fornitures [sic], cannon, mortars, their carriages and beds, and generally all kinds of arms, ammunition of war and instruments fit for the use of troops; all the above articles, whenever they are destined to the port of an enemy, are hereby declared to be contraband and just objects of confiscation, but the vessel in which they are loaded and the residue of the cargo shall be considered free, and not in any manner infected by the prohibited goods whether belonging to the same or a different owner.

Article XI

It is admitted as a principle that the flag covers the goods, and that every thing shall be deemed to be free, exempt and of lawful commerce which shall be found on board the ships belonging to the citizens of either of the contracting parties although the whole lading or any part thereof should appertain to the enemies of either, contraband goods always excepted.   It is also agreed in like manner that the same liberty be extended to persons who are on board a free ship—with this effect,—that although they be enemies to either party, they are not to be taken out of that free ship, unless [they] are soldiers and in actual service of the enemy.

Article XII

In time of war the merchant ships belonging to the Citizens of either of the contracting parties which shall be bound to a port of the enemy of one of the parties, and concerning whose voyage and the articles of her cargo there shall be just grounds of suspicion, shall be obliged to exhibit, as well upon the high seas as in the ports or roads, not only their passports but likewise their certificates showing that their goods are not of the quality of those which are specified to be contraband in the articles of the present convention.

Article XIII

And that captures on light suspicions may be avoided, and injuries thence arising prevented, it is agreed that when one party shall be engaged in war and the other party be neuter [sic], the ships of the neutral party shall be furnished with passports that it may appear thereby that the ships really belong to the citizens of the neutral party; they shall be valid for any number of voyages, but shall be renewed every year, that is if the ship happens to return home in the space of a year.   If the ships are laden, they shall be provided not only with passports above mentioned, but also with certificates given by the competent officers so that it may be known whether they carry any contraband goods.   No other papers shall be required,—any usage or ordinance to the contrary

Footnote 3, p. 133—*Continued*

notwithstanding.   And if it shall not appear from the said certificates that there are contraband goods on board, the ships shall be permitted to proceed on their voyage.   If it appears from the certificates,—that there are contraband goods on board any such ship, and the commander of the same shall offer to deliver them up, the offer shall be accepted,—and the ship be at liberty to pursue its voyage, unless the quantity of the contraband goods be greater than can conveniently be received on board the ship of war or privateer, in which case the ship may be carried into port for the delivery of the same.

If any ship shall not be furnished with such passport or certificates as are above required for the same, such case may be examined by a proper judge or tribunal,—and if it shall appear from the other documents or proofs, admissible by the usage of nations, that the ship belongs to the Citizens of the neutral party,—it shall not be confiscated, but shall be released with her cargo (contraband goods excepted) and be permitted to procede on the voyage.

If the master of a ship named in the passport should happen to die, or be removed by any other cause and another put in his place, the ship and cargo shall nevertheless be equally secure and the passport remain in full force.

Article XIV

In all cases where vessels shall be captured or detained under pretence of carrying to the enemy contraband goods, the captor shall give a receipt for such of the papers of the vessel as he shall retain, which receipt shall be anexed to a descriptive list of the said papers: and it shall be unlawful to break up or open the hatches, chests, trunks, casks, bales or vessels found on board, or remove the smallest part of the goods, unless the lading be brought on shore in presence of the competent officers, and an inventory be made by them of the said goods.   Nor shall it be lawful to sell exchange or alienate the same in any manner unless there shall have been lawful process, and the competent judge or judges shall have pron[o]unced against such goods sentence of confiscation.

Article XV

And that proper case [care] may be taken of the vessel and cargo, and embezzlement prevented, it is agreed that it shall not be lawful to remove the master, commander or super cargo of any captured ship from on board thereof, during the time the ship may be at sea after her capture, or pending the proceedings against her or her cargo, or any thing relative thereto.   And in all cases where a vessel of the citizens of either party shall be captured, or seized and held for adjudication, her officers passengers and crew shall be hospitably treated.   They shall not be imprisoned or deprived of any part of their wearing apparel, nor of the possession and use of their money, not exceeding for the captain, supercargo and mate five hundred dollars each, and for the sailors and passangers one hundred dollars each.

Article XVI

It is further agreed that in all cases, the established courts for prize causes, in the country to which the prizes may be conducted, shall alone take cognizance of them.

And whenever such tribunal of either of the parties shall pronounce jud[g]ment against any vessel, or goods, or property claimed by the citizens of the other party, the sentence or decree shall mention the reasons or motives on which the same shall have been founded, and an authenticated copy of the sentence or decree and of all the proceedings in the case, shall, if demanded, be delivered to the commander or agent of the said vessel without any delay, he paying the legal fees for the same.

Article XVII

It shall not be lawful for any foreign privateers who have commissions from any Prince or State in enmity with either of the contracting parties to fit their ships in the ports of the other nation, to sell their prizes, or in any manner to exchange them; neither shall they be allowed to purchase provisions except such as shall be necessary to their going to the next port of that Prince or State from which they have received their commissions.

Article XVIII

No citizen of the Dominican Republic shall apply for or take any Commission, or letters of Marque for arming any ship to act as privateers against the said United States or any of them or against the property, people or inhabitants of the United States or any of them or against the property of any of the inhabitants of any of them from any Prince or State with which the said United-States shall be at war, nor shall any Citizens or

Footnote 3, p. 133—*Continued*

inhabitant of the United-States or any of them apply for or take any Comission or letter of Marque for arming any ship or ships to act as privateers against the Dominican Republic, or against the persons or property of its citizens or inhabitants or any of them, from any Prince or State with which the said Republic shall be at war, and if any person of either nation shall take such Comission or letters of Marque he shall be punished according to their respective laws.

Article XIX

The two contracting parties reciprocally grant to each other the liberty of having each in the ports and other commercial places of the other Consuls, Viceconsuls and Commercial Agents of their own appointment who shall enjoy the same privileges, powers and exemptions as those of the most favored nations.   But if any such Consuls shall exercise commerce, they shall be subjected to the same laws and usages to which private individuals of their nation, or subjects or Citizens of the most favored nation are subject in the same places in respect to their commercial transactions.

It is also agreed that each of the contracting parties is nevertheless at liberty to except those ports and places in which the admission and residence of Consuls, Vice-Consuls and Commercial Agents shall not be deemed convenient.

Article XX

It is understood that whenever either of the two contracting parties shall select for a Consular Agent to reside in any port or commercial place of the other party, a citizen of this last, such Consul or Agente shall continue to be regarded nothwithstanding his quality of a foreign Consul as a Citizen of the nation to which he belongs, and consequently shall be submitted to the laws and regulations to which natives are subjected in this place of residence.   This obligation, however, shall in no respect embarrass the exercise of his consular functions or affect the inviolability of the consular archives.

Article XXI

The said Consuls, Vice-Consuls and Commercial Agents are authorised to require the assistence of the local authorities for the search, arrest, detention and imprisonment of the deserters from the ships of war and merchant vessels of their country.   For this purpose they shall apply to the competent tribunals, judges and officers and shall in writing demand said deserters proving by the exhibition of the registers of the vessels, the rols of the crews or by other official documents, that such individuals formed part of the crews, and this reclamation thus substantiated, the surrender shall not be refused. Such deserters when arrested, shall be placed at the disposal of the said Consuls, Vice-Consuls or Commercial Agents, and may be confined in the public prisons at the request and cost of those who shall claim them, in order to be detained until the time when they shall be restored to the vessel to which they belonged, or sent back to their own country by a vessel of the same nation, or any other vessel whatsoever.   But if not sent back within three months from the day of their arrest, they shall be set at liberty and shall not again be arrested for the same cause.   If however the deserter should be found to have committed any crime or offence, his surrender may be delayed until the tribunal before which his case should be depending shall have pron[o]unced its sentence and such se[n]tence shall have been carried into execution.

Article XXII

The citizens of each of the contracting parties shall enjoy in the territories of the other all the power to obtain, occupy, purchase, rent, inherit, dispose of, or bequeath, all the goods and property of whatever class which is now, or shall be hereafter allowed by law or treaty to the citizens of the most favored nations, said goods and property being governed in its possession, distribution and succession by the laws of the country in which it is situated, having the same protection and subject only to the same taxes and dues as the inhabitants of the country pay in like cases.

Article XXIII

The United-States of America and the Dominican Republic on requisitions made in their name through the medium of their respective diplomatic and consular agents shal[l] deliver up to justice persons who being charged with the crimes enumerated in the following article committed within the jurisdiction of the requiring party, shall seek asylum or shall be found within the territories of the other.   Provided, that this shall be done only when the fact of the commission of the crime shall be so established as to

Footnote 3, p. 133—*Continued*

justify their apprehension and commitment for trial if this crime had been commited in the country where the persons so accused shall be found.

Article XXIV

Persons shall be delivered up according to the provisions of this convention who shall be charged with any of the following crimes, to wit:

Murder (including assassination, parricide, infanticide, and poisoning:) attempt to commit murder: rape, counterfeiting, forgery or the emission of forged papers, arson, robbery, burglary, embezzlement by public officers or by persons hired or salaried to the detriment of their employers, when these crimes are subject to infamous punishment.

Article XXV

On the part of each country the surrender shall be made only by the authority of the Executive thereof. The expences of detention and delivery effected in virtue of the preceding articles, shall be at the cost of the party making the demand.

Article XXVI

The provisions of the aforegoing articles relating to the surrender of fugitive criminals shall not apply to offences committed before the ratification thereof or to those of a political character.

Article XXVII

Ships of war—and steam vessels of the United-States which may be employed by the government in carrying the public mails of the United-States, shall have free access to the ports of the Dominican Republic, to refit, to refresh, to land passengers and their baggage, and for the transaction of any business pertaining to the public mail service of the United States, and shall be subject in such ports to no other or greater delays, duties, or charges, than are imposed on the vessels of war of the Dominican Republic.

Article XXVIII

If any of the citizens or inhabitants of either party shall infringe any article contained in the present treaty, the said citizens or inhabitants shall be personally responsible, and the harmony and good understanding of the two nations shall not be interrupted thereby; and each solemnly pledges itself in no manner to sanction such violation, or protect the offender under pain of rendering itself responsible for the consequences.

Should unfortunately any of its conditions be violated in any other manner whatever, it is expressly agreed that neither of the contracting parties shall order or authorise any act of reprisal, nor make war against the other on complaint of injuries resulting therefrom until the party considering itself aggrieved shall first have presented to the other a statement or representation of such injuries or damages verified by competent proofs and demanded redress, and the same shall have been either refused or unreasonably delayed.

Article XXIX

The present treaty shall remain in force for the term of ten years from the day of the exchange of ratifications and if one year before the expiration of this period neither of this [*sic*] contracting parties shall have announced to the other by an official notification its intention to arrest the operation of the said convention it shall remain obligatory one year beyond that time, and so on until the expiration of the twelve months, which will follow a similar notification whatever is the time at which it may take place.

It is understood and agreed by both parties that even when the stipulations of commerce, navigation and extradition shall have ceased, the obligations of peace and friendship shall remain in full force and be perpetual with both parties.

Article XXX

The present Treaty of Peace, Friendship, Commerce, Navigation and Extradition shall be ratified and the ratifications exchanged at the city of Santo Domingo within ten months from the date of the signature thereof, or sooner if possible.

In faith whereof the Plenipotentiaries of the contracting parties have signed the present Convention and thereto affixed their respective seals.

Done at the city of Santo-Domingo, in the Dominican Republic this fifth day of October in the year of our Lord one thousand eight hundred and fifty four.

WILLIAM L CAZNEAU.
J. NEPOMUCENO TEJERA
J. LUIS F. BIDÓ

The Dominican Congress is summond to meet in extra session the first of November, when the Treaty will be ratified and I shall proceed with it immediately to Washington.

I have the honor [etc.].

2265

William L. Cazneau, Commissioner of the United States to the Dominican Republic, to Juan N. Tejera, Minister of Foreign Affairs of the Dominican Republic [1]

[TRANSLATION]

A   SANTO DOMINGO, *November 16, 1854.*

SIR: It is now six weeks since the Plenipotentiaries of the United States of America and the Dominican Republic definitely agreed upon and finally affixed their signatures to the treaty of Friendship, Commerce &ᶜ between the two Republics.

The articles of this Convention had been maturely considered and approved by the Executive Power before they were signed.— Some of them were introduced, and others modified, at the special request of His Excellency President Santana, and the undersigned was therefore not only certain of the entire concurrence of the Executive Power in the terms and spirit of the convention but had besides the personal assurance of the President that the treaty would be sent to Congress for ratification so soon as there should be a quorum.—

The Congress of the Republic has now been some days in full session and I feel constrained to enquire when it is proposed to submit the treaty for ratification.—

I am far from supposing that the Dominican government intends any discourtesy to that of the United States, and much less can I believe it capable of refusing the sincere and disinterested friendship of the sister republic:— Neither am I willing to believe the display of a strong naval force before the walls of your Capital will in any manner impede the free action of an independent American Government.— Although I am perfectly aware that certain European agents have ventured an arrogant interference in affairs pertaining exclusively to this Republic and the United States—but as inconveniences may arise from continued delays—I must request of Your Excellency to inform me when I may reasonably expect the conclusion by the Dominican Republic of the act which we hope will forever bind our respective nations in firm friendship and inviolable peace.

Permit me to renew to you Sir [etc.].

[1] Special Agents, vol. 19; enclosed with Cazneau to the Secretary of State, November 23, 1854, below, this part, doc. 2269.

2266

Juan N. Tejera, Minister of Foreign Affairs of the Dominican Republic, to William L. Cazneau, Commissioner of the United States to the Dominican Republic [1]

[TRANSLATION]

No. 2   SANTO DOMINGO, *November 17, 1854.*

SIR: I am receipt of Y. E.'s note, dated the 16th instant;[2] and after having communicated it to the government of the Republic, I proceed to reply to it, according to the instructions I have received from the same.

The Executive has seen with regret that Y. E. is uneasy concerning the involuntary delay, which you notice, has taken place in transmitting to the National Congress of the Republic, the treaty of friendship, commerce, and navigation, etc, concluded between the latter and the United States; Although, on the other side, it sees with satisfaction that Y. E. is far from supposing that any discourtesy is intended to the nation which you so worthily represent. The causes, Sir, of the delay of which we are speaking, have their origin in high reasons of policy of the Republic, as Y. E. may perceive from the accompanying printed copy of the last message of President Santana to the Chambers of the Nation, urging them to enter upon the task of revising the constitution promulgated in last February. It has been, therefore, indispensable to wait until Congress has come to a decision upon a matter of so much importance to the general progress of public affairs; Y. E. however, may firmly rely that on the 27th of this month, the treaty of friendship etc, will be sent to the Legislature, in order that, without loss of time, it may proceed to ratify the same, in accordance with the 11th paragraph of the 68th article of the fundamental law.

Allow me, Sir, [etc.].

2267

Juan N. Tejera, Minister of Foreign Affairs of the Dominican Republic, to William L. Marcy, Secretary of State of the United States [3]

[TRANSLATION]

SANTO DOMINGO, *November 17, 1854.*

SIR: I had the honor to receive, in due time, the note which Your Excellency was pleased to address me, under date of the 17th of last June,[4] presenting to me Mr. William L. Cazneau, as Commissioner of the United States near

[1] Notes from Dominican Republic, vol. 1; enclosed with Dominican Minister of Foreign Affairs to the Secretary of State, December 13, 1854, below, this part, doc. 2275.
[2] Above, this part, doc. 2265.
[3] Notes from Dominican Republic, vol. 1. Received January 25.
[4] Not within the scope of this publication, for reasons explained in the preface to the first volume.

this government, to which I did not make a reply before, because I was desirous that Mr. Cazneau himself should be the bearer of it.

He exhibited his credentials, and during the negotiations which he opened with this government, he conducted himself in a manner so satisfactory to the Republic, that there has been concluded, between our respective countries, a Treaty of Friendship, Commerce, Navigation, and Extradition, equally advantageous to both, without any thing occurring, during the protracted conferences which have been held with His Excellency Mr. Cazneau, on the subject, except what was justly calculated to make us look upon him as a faithful interpreter of the good wishes which, as Your Excellency tells me, animate the American Government as well as Your Excellency in favor of our Republic, to which, the Dominican Executive has not failed properly to respond.— And, for my own part, Sir, I must assure you, that I am ready to do whatever lies in my power, in order to preserve in the best harmony the bonds which, from this day, will unite in a firm and sincere friendship our respective countries.

Allow me, Sir, to avail myself of this occasion [etc.].

2268

William L. Cazneau, Commissioner of the United States to the Dominican Republic, to Juan N. Tejera, Minister of Foreign Affairs of the Dominican Republic [1]

SAN CARLOS, *November 18, 1854.*

SIR: In reply to the note which I had the honor to receive yesterday from your Excellency [2] I can only say that the ratification of the treaty at the period alluded to, will be a gratifying evidence that the Dominican Republic sincerely responds to the true and loyal friendship of the United States.—

I enclose a copy of the protest I deemed it necessary to address to the Consuls of France and England [3] which will explain the present position of our relations.

I beg leave [etc.].

[1] Notes from Dominican Republic, vol. 1; enclosed with Dominican Minister of Foreign Affairs to the Secretary of State, December 13, 1854, below, this part, doc. 2275.
[2] Above, this part, dated November 17, 1854, doc. 2266.
[3] The text of this protest follows:

William L. Cazneau, Commissioner of the United States to the Dominican Republic, to the British and French Consuls in Santo Domingo

B   SANTO DOMINGO, *November 17, 1854.*

SIR: The undersigned Commissioner Plenipotentiary of the United States of America near this Government having good reason to know that the Agents of France and England have by various means—aided by the menacing display of an armed force before this Capital—over-awed and controlled the free action of the Dominican Republic in its

2269

William L. Cazneau, Commissioner of the United States to the Dominican Republic, to William L. Marcy, Secretary of State of the United States[1]

SANTO DOMINGO, *November 23, 1854.*

SIR: It is my unpleasant duty to inform you that the Dominican government has been coerced by the Agents of the French and English governments to evade the ratification of the Convention of Amity, Commerce &ᶜ which it had invited from the United States, and which was negociated and signed by its plenipotentiar[i]es under the special direction of the Dominican Executive.

The whole course of negociations will prove that the Dominican government, when acting upon its own freewill, desires to pursue an independent and American line of policy.

On the 7ᵗʰ of Sepᵗ last all the articles of the treaty were agreed upon, as I had the honor to inform you, on the basis of the original *projet*—including a coal depot &ᶜ for our vessels—with the entire concurrence of President Santana. The next morning—the 8ᵗʰ—was named for the final signing of the treaty by the Plenipotentiaries, which was to be transmitted to Congress —then in session—for immediate ratification. But meantime H. B. M. Steamer Devastation arrived and the British Consul had forced an interview with President Santana at 7 in the morning.—This Executive interview was followed by another with both the French and English Consuls at noon in full Cabinet in which this government was informed the Emperor Faustin would

---

relations with the United States, hereby protests in the name of his Country, against this breach of honorable faith towards his Government and against this unwarrantable encroachment upon the sovereign rights of an independent American power.

Every enlightened government in amity with the United States is perfectly informed of their determined purpose, as a nation to oppose whatever measure may be intended to subject the independent nationality of an American people to the arbitrary will of a foreign power, or make its action—and even existence—dependent on the dicta of a foreign policy and none of those nations have taken exception to this immutable principle of the American Systim.

The United States makes no difference in the application of this rule between the strong and the weak of their Sister republics and they have a just right to expect the powerful and magnanimous nations of Europe will follow their example.

These facts being so well understood I must call your particular attention Sir—to this inconsiderate violation of the relations of Amity and Commerce now subsisting between our respective countries in the trust that you, as the responsible representitive of your government at this Capital, will use the necessary precautions to guard those relations from further disturbance.

If this due care should be omitted, the government and people of the United States may conceive they have just cause to distrust the sincerity and good faith of any government whose Agents in these waters are thus permitted to interfere in affairs and negociations belonging entirely and exclusively to the interests of the United States and the Dominican Republic—I am confident that you Sir—would regret equally with myself the consequences which might result from this unauthorised inter-meddling with the sanctity and freedom of inter-American relations.

Yours Respectfully

[1] Special Agents, vol. 19. Received December 27.

not consent to a peace if the treaty with the United States was carried into effect and that France and England would also withdraw their protection and leave the Dominican territory and people at the mercy of Hayti.—Thus constrained by the Three Powers—for Hayti alone would not be feared by Dominica—President Santana was induced to stay the Treaty.—

The next day—Sepr 9th—I had an important conference with the President in which after alluding to the embarrassing position of the republic with regard to the Three Powers he expressed an earnest desire to perfect the treaty in all its parts—provided the Dominican Republic could be assured of the protection of the United States.

After the Devastation left Santo Domingo this government made some explanations and negociations were resumed, but with a manifest anxiety on the part of all the leading Dominicans that the treaty should be concluded and the ratifications returned from the United States before England and France should have time to ripen their measures and endanger the existence of the republic.—In view of the critical situation of this young American State I consented so to modify the treaty as to take from the European powers every possible pretext for executing their to me evident plan of subjecting the Dominican Republic to Hayti.

On the fifth of October this modified treaty was signed by the Dominican plenipotentiaries, but in the meantime the Congress had closed its regular session.— It had however been summoned to meet on the first of November when I was positively assured by this government—and I have not the slightest doubt in absolute good faith—the treaty would at once be ratified.

Octr 27 M. Raybaud, the French Chargé d'Affaires at Port au Prince, arrived from Hayti and the rumour instantly became current that a large squadron was on its way to Santo Domingo to put an end to the treaty with the United States.

H. B. M. Steamer Buzzard had preceded him some days and on the 28th—the day after M. Raybaud's arrival—the British Consul formally notified the Dominican government that he was instructed by Lord Clarendon to inform it of the disapprobation with which Her Majesty's government learned that *"notwithstanding the advice"* offered by France and England President Santana had thought proper *"to negociate a treaty with the United States by which the safety and welfare of the Republic would be greatly and immediately endangered"* and he adds—always in the name of Lord Clarendon.— Such arrangements should not have been made without their knowledge and sanction *"particularly with a power which has hitherto refused to acknowledge the independence of the Dominican Republic, and the suddeness and perremtory character of whose procedings must cause well-founded suspicions of its ulterior object"*.

Novr 7th, I visited Vice President Regla Mota, who in the temporary absence of the President held the Executive power, and called his attention to the general belief that M. Raybaud on the part of France and Hayti, and Sir R. H. Schomburgh on the part of England, were taking threatening ground against the ratification of the Treaty.   He admitted in effect the interference of the Three Powers but implied the Dominican Government would not be intimidated by their menaces from completing its engagements with the United States. He also expressed much annoyance at an insult publicly offered by M. Raybaud to a member of the Dominican Cabinet, on a subject nearly touching the domestic peace and independence of the Republic.

Nov.ʳ 9ᵗʰ Accompanied by Mʳ Elliott the United States Commercial Agent, I called on President Santana, who had just returned to the Capital, and he repeated his promise to send in the treaty for ratification as soon as there should be a quorum—and then but one Senator was wanting—expressing no manner of doubt or hesitation as to the benifits which would accrue to his country from closer relations with the United States.

Nov.ʳ 10th—A French Steamer anchored in front of the town and the approach of a French squadron was immediately announced.

Nov.ʳ 12ᵗʰ The President of the Dominican Senate, Don Benigno de Rojas, called and informed me that Congress had obtained a quorum.—In discussing the ratification of the treaty he did not deny the interference of the Agents of France and England—for being the intimate and confidential friend of the British Consul he could not but know the fact—but he implied his belief, though by no means a firm certainty, that they would fail in their object.

Nov.ʳ 13ᵗʰ A French Frigate and Sloop of War joined the Steamer at anchor in front of the City and it was reported a large aditional force was ordered to unite with them before Santo Domingo.

Nov.ʳ 16ᵗʰ I had sure intelligents that the Dominican government was so much intimidated by the attitude of the Three Powers that neither the Cabinet nor Congress would venture to act upon the treaty in defiance of Lord Clarendon's letter and the verbal protests of M. Raybaud who—whether accredited or not—is positively the acting envoy of France and Hayti to this Republic.—Upon this I addressed a letter to the Dominican government (copy enclosed herewith marked A)[1] enquiring when it was proposed to send the treaty to Congress for ratification.—Congress adjourned the same afternoon.

Nov.ʳ 17ᵗʰ I addressed a note to the Consuls of France and England (copy enclosed marked B)[2] protesting against this interference in affairs and negociations pertaining exclusively to the United States and the Dominican Republic.—This may seem a decided step, but I shall exhibit proofs that I was forced to adopt this course in justice to my Country.

On the same day the Dominican government replied to my note of the

[1] Above, this part, doc. 2265.   [2] *Ibid.*, November 17, 1854, p. 142, note 3.

16th [1] by a positive promise that the treaty should be sent in for ratification on the 27th of Nov[r] when Congress would be re-convened;—which however I am confident will not be done—or be done only in the mode and intent dictated by the French and English agents if the eighty four guns of the French squadron continue to command the Dominican Capital.

Nov[r] 18th I answered [2] the note of the Dominican government in reply to mine of the 16th (enclosed Marked C).—On the same day I received brief notes from the Consuls of France and England,[3] denying nothing and admitting nothing, but informing me they would transmit my note of the 17th to their respective governments.

This, Sir—is an exact account of our present relations with this republic and if it were a stronger power my course of duty would be very obvious: But in this case it seems more just to await with forbearance the final action of the Dominican Government as I feel an extreme reluctance to abandon this post at a crisis which must decide whether the Dominican Republic is, or is not, to exist as an independent American State.

I have the honor [etc.].

2270

William L. Cazneau, Commissioner of the United States to the Dominican Republic, to Juan N. Tejera, Minister of Foreign Affairs of the Dominican Republic [4]

SANTO DOMINGO, *November 23, 1854.*

SIR: Having decided to inform my government in detail of the remarkable course persued by the Dominican Executive with regard to the United States—I am constrained to notify your Excellency that I withdraw for the present the Convention of Recognition, Friendship &[c] now pending between our respective nations, from the farther action of the Dominican Government.

Under circumstances which have recently come to my Knowledge this Convention must remain in abeyance until the government of the United States can demand certain explanations and decide whether it is consistent with American Principles to submit it for ratification.

I avail myself of this occasion [etc.].

[1] Both his note and the Dominican Government's reply are above, this part, docs. 2265, and 2266.   The latter note came also, as an enclosure, with the Dominican Minister of Foreign Affairs' note to the Secretary of State, dated December 13, 1854, from which it was transcribed.
[2] Above, this part, doc. 2268.   It came also, as an enclosure, with the Dominican Minister of Foreign Affairs' note to the Secretary of State, of December 13, 1854, from which it was transcribed.
[3] Neither one was found.   Their purport is sufficiently indicated.
[4] Notes from the Dominican Republic, vol. 1; enclosed with the note of the Dominican Minister of Foreign Affairs to the Secretary of State, December 13, 1854, below, this part, doc. 2275.

2271

Juan N. Tejera, Minister of Foreign Affairs of the Dominican Republic, to William L. Cazneau, United States Commissioner to the Dominican Republic[1]

[TRANSLATION]

SANTO DOMINGO, *November 27, 1854.*

SIR: I have received the communication which Y. E. has done me the honor to address me, under date of the 23[d] instant,[2] in which you apprise me of your determination to inform Your Government, etc, etc.

My government, Most Excellent Sir, has seen with marked astonishment, this unexpected determination on the part of Y. E. precisely at the time, when, according to the promise made to Y. E., in my note of the 17th instant,[3] the treaty signed on the 5th of last October by the plenipotentiaries of our respective nations, whose mission terminate[s] with the sealing and approval of this act, was, this day, to have been submitted, for ratification, to the National Congress, the only power to which exclusively belongs the right of approving or rejecting the same.

My aforesaid note of the 17th instant, and the intention of my government to submit the above mentioned treaty to the National Congress for ratification, explains very clearly the direction which the Dominican Executive was bound to give to this act, and this conduct, on its part, is not susceptible of a contrary interpretation.

Nevertheless, Most Excellent Sir, my government wishes to know, whether, agreeably to Y. E.'s note aforesaid of the 23[d] instant, it is Y. E.'s intentions to withdraw the treaty altogether, because, otherwise, there is no principle of international law, which can dispense with its presentation to the national Congress.

I avail myself of this occasion [etc.].

2272

William L. Cazneau, United States Commissioner to the Dominican Republic, to Juan N. Tejera, Minister of Foreign Affairs of the Dominican Republic[4]

SANTO DOMINGO, *December 4, 1854.*

SIR: I am under the painful necessity of announcing to Your Excellency that the extraordinary indignity which President Santana has been induced

[1] Notes from the Dominican Republic, vol. 1; enclosed with the note of the Dominican Minister of Foreign Affairs to the Secretary of State, December 13, 1854, below, this part, doc. 2275.   [2] Above, this part, doc. 2270.   [3] *Ibid.*, doc. 2266.
[4] Special Agents, vol. 19; enclosed with Cazneau to the Secretary of State, December 6, 1854, below, this part, doc. 2273.

by foreign dictation—aided by domestic treason—to offer to my government, compels me to withdraw entirely from the farther consideration and control of the Dominican Executive the treaty of recognition and friendship which was negociated—but in no form completed—on the part of our respective Countries.

I must also inform Your Excellency that my instructions and powers were not to cease until I had placed the treaty ratified by the Dominican Republic in the possession of my government, and had thus declared on the faith of my official appointment that this was in fact and in truth an independent American State.—No longer believing this to be true, and having besides but too many evidences of an intention to subject the Dominican people to the despotism of Hayti—severely against their will—to which if this were a recognized American power in amity with our country the American people would never consent—I am constrained to declare to your Excellency in the name of my government that no treaty of recognition exists, or can exist with the Dominican Repbᶜ under the present circumstances.

I must be permitted to remind Your Excellency that my country has the right by the laws of nations to inforce by all the means in its power the satisfaction and redress which the United States is now forced to demand for the singular equivocations and repeated injustice practiced towards our Citizens and Government by the Dominican Executive.

I have the honor [etc.].

2273

William L. Cazneau, United States Commissioner to the Dominican Republic, to William L. Marcy, Secretary of State of the United States[1]

SAN CARLOS, *December 6, 1854.*

SIR: Under date of Novʳ 23ᵈ I had the honor to transmit a statement[2] of the unfortunate check imposed by the Diplomatic Agents of France and England upon the ratification of the treaty I had negociated and signed on the part of the United States with the Dominican Republic.

I then informed my government, upon sure data and my own knowledge, that from the period in which the interference and protests of those agents were sustained by the presence of a strong naval force, the Dominican government has been in *duress*, and all its action with regard to the United States has been shaped under the dictation of M. Raybaud, the joint representative of France and Hayti at this Capital: endorsed and assisted to the best of his capacity by H. B. M. Consular Agent.

This treaty was negociated with the Dominican government alone, but the undue intervention of France and England in its conclusion has so

---

[1] Special Agents, vol. 19.   Received January 9.   [2] Above, this part, doc. 2269.

changed its conditions and guarenties that the contract became vitiated, if not void, and to continue action upon it in the name of the Dominican Republic as if it were a free and uncontrolled power, would be a fraud upon my government.

When these facts were confirmed to me beyond the possibility of doubt, and when several members of the Dominican Congress gave me proofs that this foreign dictation would be as absolute over that body as it had been over the Executive, I felt it was due to the honor of my country not to submit its negociations to such unwarrantable action.

I therefore notified the Minister of Foreign Relations Novr 24th [1] that

> I withdraw for the present from the further action of the Dominican Government the Convention of Recognition, Friendship &^{c} now pending between our respective Nations.
>
> Under circumstances which have recently come to my knowledge this Convention must remain in abeyance until the government of the United States can demand certain explanations and decide whether it is consistent with American principles to submit it for ratification.

Novr 27th the Dominican government replied [2] by enquiring whether I intended withdrawing the treaty altogether as in any other case it had the right by international law to submit it to Congress. Not wishing to put on written record the whole harsh, offensive truth of the subjugation of the Dominican Executive, I explained verbally to the Minister of Foreign Relations my perfect knowledge of the facts and also of the circumstances that this very reply of Novr 27th was written under the direction of M. Raybaud and the fear of the five Men of War now before the Capital, and therefore the United States must cease to recognize or negociate with the Dominican Government while it continued under this duress.

I wished to leave the treaty in abeyance and refer the case to my government for advisement.

Notwithstanding this it was in a few day's publicly known and declared in the streets of Santo Domingo that the French and English agents had resolved the treaty should be presented to Congress in defiance of my protests; and the form and substance of the offensive mutilations and additions which that body was ordered to make were written upon the margin of printed copies of the treaty and circulated a week beforehand from the French and British Consulates. Still until Decr 3^d I had no official notice that this government would lend itself to the purposes of the Diplomatic agents of France and England, in a form to screen them from responsibility and draw upon itself the just resentment of the United States for its evasions and duplicity. On that day I was informed the treaty had been actually

---

[1] The note, from which this quotation is taken, is found above, this part, doc. 2270, but is dated November 23, 1854. The 24th may have been the date on which he delivered it.
[2] Above, this part, doc. 2271.

presented to Congress.   The next morning I addressed a note (copy herewith enclosed) [1] to the Dominican government to which I have not yet received any reply: The day following, Dec[r] 5, Congress passed a mutilated caricature of the treaty so opposite to the spirit and intent of the original Convention that it could not under any possible circumstances be entertained by my government.

Trusting that the measures forced upon me by the intricate and embarrassing situation in which I found myself, may meet the approbation of my government I shall remain and await further orders.   If I were to retire now many of the best men of the country who have taken an active part in favor of the American treaty would be immediately sacrificed.   The *Porvenir*, a moderate and irreproachable paper was suppressed at the command of M. Raybaud for publishing only a few sentences advocating the American treaty, and the editor narrowly escaped imprisonment.

A number of respectable white families are preparing to leave the island if it is abandoned by the United States, for no intelligent person here doubts that the object of this persevering European interference is to subject the Dominican Republic to the Empire of Hayti.

With great respect [etc.].

2274

Juan N. Tejera, Minister of Foreign Affairs of the Dominican Republic, to William L. Cazneau, United States Commissioner to the Dominican Republic[2]

[TRANSLATION]

Santo Domingo, *December 7, 1854.*

Sir: The communication which Y. E. was pleased to address me on the 4th instant,[3] has been submitted by me to the Executive, who has read the same, reserving himself to reply to it, at a better opportunity: Accept, Y. E. [etc.].

---

[1] Above, this part, December 4, 1854, doc. 2272.
[2] Notes from the Dominican Republic, vol. 1; enclosed with the note of the Dominican Minister of Foreign Affairs to the Secretary of State, December 13, 1854, below, this part, doc. 2275.   [3] Above, this part, doc. 2272.

2275

Juan N. Tejera, Minister of Foreign Affairs of the Dominican Republic, to William L. Marcy, Secretary of State of the United States[1]

[TRANSLATION]

SANTO DOMINGO, *December 13, 1854.*

MOST EXCELLENT SIR: The undersigned, Secretary of State of the Dominican Republic, charged with the direction of foreign affairs, has the honor to make known to Y. E., in the name of his government, the conduct of Mr. William L. Cazneau, Minister Plenipotentiary of the United States, towards the Dominican executive.

The government of this Republic, M. E. Sir, saw with pleasure the arrival, at this place, of Mr. Cazneau; it gave him the most favorable possible reception, and prepared to conclude with him a treaty of freindship, commerce and navigation, naming its respective plenipotentiary for that purpose. This act having been accomplished, Mr. Cazneau begged that it might be submitted to the National Congress, in order to obtain its sanction, and, notwithstanding that this government was quite ready to do so, at the first opportunity, he showed himself uneasy on account of its not having been submitted at the first opening of Congress, and addressed a note to this department on the subject, of which, and of the latter's reply to the same, I transmit copies to Y. E., marked N° 1. and 2.[2]

When the government of the Undersigned, in fulfilment of the promise made to Mr. Cazneau, was about to submit the treaty to the National Congress, for its discussion and sanction, it received another note, by which Mr. Cazneau withdrew the treaty from the further action of the Dominican government, until it had been decided by the U. S. government, whether this step was consistent with American principles.—note of November 23ᵈ N° 3.[3]

The Dominican Government, Most Excellent Sir, thought that a treaty concluded by a plenipotentiary ceased to be under his control, and that it belonged to the authority of the respective legislatures, whose province it was to approve or reject the same.   Such was the reply which was given to him on the 27th of November, N° 4,[4] and, consequently, this act was submitted to the National Congress.

The Dominican government thought that it had not only complied with the promise made to Mr. Cazneau, but that it had acted in a just and proper manner; and yet it had received a third communication dated the 4th instant, which I enclose, marked N° 5;[5]— a note, the purport of which is disrespectful

[1] Notes from the Dominican Republic, vol. 1.   Received January 16.
[2] Above, this part, dated, respectively, November 16 and 17, 1854, docs. 2265 and 2266. The former note came also, as enclosure, with Cazneau's despatch to the Secretary of State, dated November 23, 1854, above, this part, doc. 2269, from which it was transcribed.
[3] Above, this part, doc. 2270.   [4] *Ibid.*, doc. 2271.
[5] *Ibid.*, doc. 2272.   It came also as an enclosure with Cazneau to the Secretary of State, December 6, 1854, from which it was transcribed.

towards this government, and most especially, to the President of the Republic, and which concludes with sundry threats on account of imaginary insults and repeated acts of injustice on the part of the Dominican government, committed against citizens of the U. S., adding moreover, that there are many indications of a desire to subject the Dominican people, against their will, to the despotism of Haiti.

In view of these circumstances, of the late conduct of Mr. Cazneau, and his insulting and improper language, the government of the undersigned has thought it its duty to appeal to Y. E., not only with a view of laying before you, the decorum, decency, and good faith with which it has proceeded in this case, but to express its regrets at the acts of Mr. Cazneau, trusting that the government of Y. E. will deem it proper to restrain and disapprove the same, for it cannot believe, and does not believe, that he has been authorized to act in this manner.

The treaty has pursued its proper legal course, and notwithstanding some modifications introduced into it by Congress, of which the undersigned sends herewith a copy to Y. E. marked N° 6,[1] the Republic as an independent State, has a right to treat with another nation, in a manner suitable to her interests and with perfect reciprocity, and this government, Most Excellent Sir, is ready to remodel the treaty with the same, or any new plenipotentiaries the government of the United States may think proper to name for the purpose, in as much as it is the most fervent wish of the former to draw closer its relations of friendship and of commerce with the civilized nations of both the old and the new world.

The undersigned renews to Y. E. [etc.].

[1] The following is a translation of the document referred to:

[TRANSLATION]

No. 6   SANTO DOMINGO, *December 6, 1854.*

Remarks made by the National Congress of the Dominican Republic, on the Treaty of Peace, Commerce, Navigation and Extradition, concluded in the City of San[to] Domingo, on the 5th of October 1854, between the respective Plenipotentiaries of the Dominican Republic and the United States of America

1st   That in article 3d of the treaty, Dominicans must submit to the special laws which are in force in the several States of the Union, and these laws being so much at variance in different States, it is necessary, in order that there may be perfect reciprocity, that said article should be conceived in these terms:—that all Dominicans, without any distinction of race or color, shall enjoy, in all the States of the American Union, the same and equal rights and prerogatives, that the citizens of those states enjoy in the Dominican Republic.

Among other reasons which Congress has for this amendment, one is, that there are states in the American Union where all men are equal before the law and enjoy the same rights, but that there are also other States, where they are not only not equal, but where there is a race and branches of the same, which are entirely excepted.

2dly   In the 9th article, there should be inserted after these words, 'from any port whatever' the following,—*open to foreign commerce.*

3dly   The 16th article is not sufficiently explicit, and therefore requires greater clearness, to prevent interpretations which may be burthensome to the Republic.

4thly   The 17th article requires likewise some explanation or modification.

2276

William L. Cazneau, United States Commissioner to the Dominican Republic, to William L. Marcy, Secretary of State of the United States [1]

Private.   SAN CARLOS, *December 16, 1854.*

SIR: I am just informed the Dominican Government is Sending by an English vessel bound to the United States, copies of my correspondence &ᶜ— and perhaps a copy of the treaty of Octʳ 5th as it came from Congress under the direction and with the amendments of M. Raybaud.   I avail myself of the same conveyance to write privately that I am preparing to send on my

---

It says:—"that it shall not be allowed to any foreign privateer, having letters of marque from any prince or state at War, to fit up vessels in the ports of the other nation, nor to sell her prizes or in any manner to barter the same, nor to purchase provisions, except what are necessary for her voyage to the nearest port of the Prince from whom said privateer has received letters of marque.

That a vessel of war of an enemy should not be allowed to fit up in the port of the nation which is not at war; that she should not be allowed to sell her prizes, nor barter the same, appears just; but that she should be prevented from purchasing provisions, repair damages, and remain in the neutral port as long as she may desire, does not seem right; because, in the same manner as it is stipulated in articles 1ˢᵗ, 8ᵗʰ and 13ᵗʰ, that in case of war, the citizens of both nations shall be at liberty to leave, with their persons and property, free from insult and capture, without their property being liable to confiscation;—that in case of shipwreck in time of war, the individuals thus shipwrecked shall receive, for themselves personally, their vessels, and their property the same assistance and protection which they would receive, if they were persons belonging to the same nation where the accident has occurred,—as it is said that when one party is engaged in war, and the other keeps neutral, the vessels of the neutral party shall be provided with passports or permits, in order that it may be seen that they belong to the neutral party, for the purpose of preventing captures, etc, etc,—so it seems that similar considerations ought to prevail with regard to the vessels of war mentioned in the 8ᵗʰ article already quoted.   That they should not be allowed to fit out their vessels, procure letters of marque, sell or barter their prizes, seems right; but to limit the purchase of provisions for their use, to prevent them from repairing damages, and to compel them to sail straight for the port of the Prince from whom the privateer has received letters of marque, does not appear just; because then, it would be to be wanting [sería faltar] in that hospitality and friendship which the neutral power is obliged to observe between itself and the United States.

5ᵗʰˡʸ   The 19ᵗʰ article requires the following addition to the last paragraph—"that, what has been agreed upon cannot be carried into effect, whenever in said port or place, there is a consul or commercial agent of any other Nation.

6ᵗʰˡʸ   The 27ᵗʰ article also requires some amendment; it says—that vessels of war and steamers of the United States employed in carrying the mails, shall have free access to the ports of the Republic, for the purpose of repairing, reinforcing, landing passengers and their baggage, and for any other business appertaining to the public service of the United States.

It is thought that this provision can only be carried into effect in the ports of entry of the Republic and the word to reinforce the vessels of war and steamers of the United States requires some explanation; because to reinforce might mean to increase the forces of vessels by means of cannons, armaments and people, with a view, it may be, to wage hostilities against a nation friendly to the Dominican Republic, and this would be to compromise the latter, whereas the policy of this government must be, to live in peace and good understanding with all nations, and not to grant to one advantages or privileges over the other, without observing and meeting out equality of rights, friendship and considerations.

                                            True Copy.
(Signed)   BOBADILLA   The Minister of Foreign Relations
                                                TEJERA

---

[1] Special Agents, vol. 19.   No receipt date is on the original.

official report—sustained by the fullest and most incontestable proofs of foreign interference, even to the point of forcing a spurious ratification of the treaty through Congress.

These proofs are drawn from the highest sources but I cannot endanger the lives of the most valuable men in this Republic—who have thus compromised themselves out of a zealous desire to serve American interests—by intrusting them to any but undoubted and trustworthy hands.   On this account I have selected Mr A. Angulo to proceed with them to the United States in the American brig Reindeer which sails in a few days.   Besides being an honorable and intelligent gentleman, Mr Angulo is intimately acquainted with Dominican affairs and can give much timely and desirable information.

Among the documents I shall have the honor to transmit by him, I will only allude now to one (No. 6.) from authority second to none in this Republic, which explains the incapacity of the present Congress to act upon the treaty as it was convened on the 27th ult: in the special capacity of a Convention to revise the Constitution and as such was divested of its Legislative and co-executive powers—[1]

This ratification was a deceit, as well as a discourtisy towards the United States and the weak equivocating course of the Dominican Executive deserves the severest reprehension.

I will add no more as the whole mass of facts and evidence will be in your hands almost—perhaps quite—as soon as this can reach Washington.

I have the honor [etc.].

2277

William L. Cazneau, United States Commissioner to the Dominican Republic, to William L. Marcy, Secretary of State of the United States [2]

SANTO DOMINGO, *December 23, 1854.*

SIR: I would respectfully beg leave to call your attention to the documents herewith enclosed [3] as they present a full and connected chain of evidence, from the most eminent and indisputable witnesses, that the interruption of the friendly relations between the United States and Dominican Republic, was entirely effected by the menaces and intrigues of the Diplomatic Agents of France and England in their active hostility to the interest of the United States.

France and England assume here under the title of the "Mediating Powers," a dictatorial supervision altogether incompatible with the independence

---

[1] Not included in this publication.   This enclosure, No. 6, is a brief letter to Cazneau, dated December 14, 1854, from del Monte, which is labeled in Cazneau's hand, "Opinion of the President of the Supreme Court of the Dominican Republic."

[2] Special Agents, vol. 19.   No receipt date appears on the original.

[3] See detailed reference further on in the despatch.

of the Dominican Republic.   They claim this authority to control an American State partly on the plea that they were the first to recognize it as a Nation, and partly as they say, because they have been engaged for several years in mediating a peace for it with Hayti.   It must be noted however this peace —to obtain which the Dominicans have been forced into so many humiliating concessions—is not yet established, though the position of Hayti with regard to those great nations would seem to imply that nothing is required to complete it but a firm and distinct expression of their will.

The Dominican people did not receive their independent nationality in gift from any foreign power.

Unknown and unaided they rescued their soil and liberties from the usurpation of Hayti by their own brave efforts, and the most important result which the Dominican Republic has experienced from the presence and interference of the "mediating powers" is the harassing fear that at last some trick of policy may induce them to cast their weight exclusively and fatally on the side of Hayti.

The counter-check to this dread was the hope that the recognition and amity of the United States would give stability and protection to their Young republic; but it did not suit the views of those powers to allow this hope to be realized.

The papers I now remit contain the statements and declarations of the most honorable and distinguished men in the Dominican Republic (made from their own personal knowledge and intrusted to me at the peril of life and fortune) explanatory of the manner in which the Agents of those powers commanded and enforced the annihilation of the American treaty.

The confidential letter "No 1." dated Santo Domingo Sept: 28th[1] details under the hand and signature of the highest and most competent authority the officious and peremptory (yet at first wholly irresponsible) measures taken by the French and British Consuls to suppress and set aside the first *projet* of the treaty.   This document corroborates, point by point, my official reports that the entire convention—including Art: 28. and the concession of a coal depot at a point of immense value to the commerce of both republics—would have been signed on the 8th of September and immediately submitted to Congress, then in session, for ratification, but for the vehement opposition, and even menaces, of the representatives of France and England.

The threatening manner in which the power of those governments was used to sustain the arrogant pretensions of Soulouque in case "a single inch of ground" was permmitted to the Americans, could not be resisted by a feeble and irresolute government.   As this writer truly observes "it was placed in a bitter and violent, but unavoidable condition" and was driven by the law of self preservation into breaking its engagements with the United States.   "It is sufficiently strong and great" he adds "to keep Sou-

[1] Above, this part, doc. 2263.

loque [Soulouque] from passing the dividing line of the two states but too small and weak to venture its existence against either of the European nations to which I have alluded".

From this and other not less conclusive evidence that the Dominican Government was constrained by an unfortunate combination of circumstances to yeild temporarily to this foreign pressure, I passed as lightly as possible over the occurrences of September and renewed negociations on a modified basis.

Understanding it to be the policy and desire of my government to respect the integrity and strengthen the independence of this young republic, I consented to avoid giving to the "mediating Powers" any pretext at this juncture for attacking its existence—taking precautions however to place any future interference of their agents with the free course of United States negociations, in a tangible and undeniable form.

"No. 2."—The protest of H. B. M. Consul, Sir R. H. Schomburgk[1] is one result of this precaution. This document in effect prohibits the negociation of treaties by the Dominican Republic without the knowledge and sanction of France and England, particularly with such a dangerous and suspicious power as the United States, and it expressly states that this pretension to supervise and control our inter-American relations emanates directly from Lord Clarendon and the British Cabinet, who claim it as the joint right of the French and English governments.

M. Raybaud presented himself about this time as the common envoy of France and Hayti, charged to assume the general direction of the measures to be taken by the three powers to annihilate, in every form, the friendly relations about being established between this republic and the United States. —As he was sustained by a sufficient naval force his visits, advice and protests were intruded on the Executive at all hours, and their effects immedi-

---

[1] The text of this enclosure follows:

Robert H. Schomburgk, British Consul in Santo Domingo, to Juan Nepomuceno Tejera, Minister of Foreign Affairs of the Dominican Republic

SANTO DOMINGO, *October 28, 1854.*

SEÑOR MINISTER: I am instructed by the Earl of Clarendon Her Majesty's Secretary of State of Foreign Affairs, to inform the Dominican Government that Her Majesty's Government learn with surprise that notwithstanding the advice offered by the Representatives of the Mediating Powers, which could have no other object than to promote the safety and welfare of the Dominican Republic, the President has thought proper to negociate a Treaty with the United States by which both the safety and welfare of the Republic will be greatly and immediately endangered.

England and France have on more than one occasion interfered to uphold the independence of the Dominican Republic, when that independence was threatened by a neighbouring Power and they had a right to expect that the arrangements contemplated by this treaty should not have been made without their knowledge and sanction, particularly with a power which has hitherto refused to acknowledge the independence of the Dominican Republic and the suddeness and peremptory character of whose present proceedings must cause well-founded suspicions of its ulterior object.

The undersigned [etc.].

ately became visible in the wavering, intimidated and wholly anti-American policy of this government.

We have the explicit testimony of M.ʳ Elliot, the United States Commercial Agent, on this point. He wrote me Nov.ʳ 16.ᵗʰ ("No. 3.")[1] that he was assured by members of the Cabinet that M. Raybaud's opposition had ["] prevented President Santana from presenting the American treaty to Congress *or making any Treaty* with our government".—"From what I learn from the ministers of this government, the President is afraid to do any act contrary to the wishes of M. Raybaud on account of the French force now at anchor in this harbor". This note also states that several influential Members of the Dominican Congress had declared to him that "no Congress exested since the day before yesterday" (the day of the arrival of the French squadron) "as they had been threatened with force and could not act under the circumstances".

All this was confirmed to me in almost the same terms by many leading members of this government and it was time to make the representatives of France and England accept the responsibility on the part of their governments, or cease this interference in United States affairs.—It was also due my government to learn whether the Dominican Republic was an independent power or a semi-colony under European tutelage, and I addressed to them respectively my notes of Nov.ʳ 16.ᵗʰ and 17.ᵗʰ [2]—heretofore remitted.

[1] The text of Elliot's letter follows:

Jonathan Elliot, Commercial Agent of the United States to the Dominican Republic, to William L. Cazneau, United States Commissioner to the Dominican Republic

SANTO DOMINGO, *November 16, 1854.*

SIR: I am informed this day at 2 O'clock, by my Father in Law, the Minister of the Interior and J. N. Tejera the Secretary of State of this Dominican Republic, that Maxime Ribaud, Consul General of France to Hayti, has prevented the President Santana from presenting the American Treaty to Congress, *or, making any Treaty with our Government.* This Mr. Ribaud has always, for the six years that I have resided here, been interfereing in and governing the actions of this Government and from what I learn from the Ministers of this Government, the President is afraid to do any act, contrary to the wishes of Mr Ribaud on account of the French force now at anchor in this harbour.

Both the Ministers above referred to, were deeply mortified at the result of this business and stated "that they were ashamed to look Gen! Cazneau in the face. I would moreover state that yesterday at 2 O'clock in the evening I met Mr. Mateo Perdomo an influential member in the Dominican Congress and in conversation he remarked "that no Congress existed since day before yesterday (the day of the arrival of the French Squadron) as they had been threatened with force and could not act under the circumstances, this was in reply to my asking him, "when the Congress would act on the American Treaty. In conclusion I would add that I have conversed with three other Representatives of the Dominican Congress and they have answered me almost in the same manner and certainly with the same signification.

I have the honor [etc.].

[2] His note of November 16, 1854, is above, this part, doc. 2265; but no note from him of the 17th was found. The Dominican reply, dated the 17th, to Cazneau's of the preceding day is found above, this part, doc. 2266, as is, also, the latter's response of November 18, doc. 2268, to the former's of the previous day.

As neither the European Consuls nor the Dominican Government attempted to deny this controlling interference, I had no choice but to withdraw the treaty I had negociated from the action of these unexpected third parties in my notes of 18th and 24th Nov[r] [1] also remitted.

It was one of those cases in which extraordinary circumstances become their own fountain of law and make their own precedent.

"No. 4": is a minute and accurate summary of the whole course of foreign interference by a gentleman whose position made him intimately acquainted with the parties, times and methods employed by the European Consuls to operate against, first the accepted project of September, and afterwards to nullify the signed treaty.—He is in the confidence of this government and knew well its original sentiments in favor of the United States, and how it was forced into its contradictory action by the arts and menaces of foreign diplomacy.[2]

"No. 5": contains the same facts by an equally reliable witness who, like the writer of "No. 4," has intimate personal relations with the highest members of this government.—It will be observed he gives the names of the distinguished gentlemen to whom M. Raybaud declared he had come from Hayti to "break up the American treaty, *even by force, if necessary*".

This document (like No. 4) gives in detail—with important names and dates—the manner in which the Convention of October 5th was first withheld from the Congress to which it should rightfully have been presented for ratification, and afterwards wrongfully sent to an incompetent body where it received a pretended but spurious ratification under the direction of M. Raybaud.—When the President of the Constituent Congress wished to soften some offensive expressions in the "amendments" prepared by M. Raybaud, for that body to pass with its pretended ratification, M. Raybaud "*made him*", to use his own words, take the most objectionable phase, and boasted of having done so in a conversation he had with Senator De Rojas on the subject.

With regard to the validity of this enforced ratification I remit the legal opinion ("No 6.") [3] of the highest authority on Constitutional subjects in this Republic that it "is unconstitutional and void" even if other circumstances had not annulled the Convention.

---

[1] Such notes from him of those dates were not found; but his notes of November 23 and December 4, 1854, above, this part, docs. 2270 and 2272, appear to meet this description. A footnote reference to the date "24th" reads: "The original was dated Nov[r] 23[d] by mistake; it should have been Nov[r] 24th." There is a note above, of November 18, 1854, but it says nothing about withdrawing the treaty.

[2] Neither this No. 4 nor the No. 5, mentioned in the next paragraph, is included in this publication. The former, extending over seven pages, and labeled by Cazneau "Statement of the Secretary of the Dominican Plenipotentiaries," named J. Debrin, is briefly reviewed in the despatch, and the latter, covering eight pages, which Cazneau says, "contains the same facts," and which covers eight pages, is signed by Alejandro Angulo Guridi. Concerning the latter, see reference to Mr. Angulo, doubtless the same person, above, this part, December 16, 1854, doc. 2276.

[3] This is the document referred to in footnote 1, above, this part, p. 154.

It was submitted to the Constituent Congress which was summoned to meet in "extraordinary session" in the form prescribed by law for the sole and exclusive object of Revising the Constitution and could not in its especial capacity of a Convention of Revision perform any legislative or co-executive acts.

The Executive had—as directed by the Constitution, expressed the object of the extraordinary session in the decree of convocation and it could not present to this body treaties or other executive business "for," as this eminent authority goes on to say, "the Executive power has its limits and ceased from the moment in which the Congress entered upon the business for which it was convened." "Neither can it be pretended" continiues the same authority refering to the Congress "that this body is supremely sovereign and can act *ad libitum* on all occasions."

In brief the Constituent Congress of Nov.ʳ 27.ᵗʰ having been called and organized for one determined object, all that it has been made to do outside of that object "bears the seal of unconstitutionality and is therefore null and of no effect". Some leading members of the Constituent Congress, declared to me they were of the same opinion but in the present critical state of the Country "that body was unable to resist the will of France and England as represented by M. Raybaud".

I could multiply a hundred fold these proofs of the constraint imposed by the Agents of France and England on the free action of the Dominican Government in its relations with the United States but I have selected from the mass in my possession only the testimony which seemed essential to present distinctly and consecutively the important features of the case; and those witnesses whose position and character would give the most incontestable weight to their statements. I can vouch with life and honor for the facts and the men, but I must urgently request that these papers may be used with extreme caution *so far as they involve Dominican names*. A neglect of this precaution, while the Dominican Republic is under this foreign dictatorship, would lead to the immediate sacrifice of some of the best men of this unfortunate country. On this account I have refrained from using many names and circumstances of weight, in this and other reports, and now only remit them under the seal of sacred confidence in order to show how thourough and conclusive are the evidences of this unwarrantable foreign domination.

With the greatest respect [etc.].

2278

*William L. Cazneau, United States Commissioner to the Dominican Republic,
to William L. Marcy, Secretary of State of the United States* [1]

SAN CARLOS, *December 26, 1854.*

SIR: After closing the report which I had the honor to direct to you of
Dec.ᵣ 23ᵈ [2] I succeded in obtaining the enclosed copy of the conjoint ultimatum of the Consular and Diplomatic Agents of France and England. [3]—The
obvious intent of its stipulations is to exclude our citizens and commerce
from any share in the natural wealth and superior harbors of this central and
favored island and to retain this republic in its present forced dependence on
European will and policy.

This note is the last and conclusive link in the chain of evidence I have laid
before the government in support of my statements respecting the dictatorial
interference of the French and British Agents in our inter-American relations; and of its results in seriously disturbing the friendly relations which
the United States were disposed to establish with the Dominican Repbᶜ.

[1] Special Agents, vol. 19.   No receipt date is on the original.
[2] Above, this part, doc. 2277.
[3] The following is the text of this document:

*P. Darasse, French Consul, and Robert H. Schomburgk, British Consul in Santo Domingo,
to General Pedro Santana, President of the Dominican Republic*

[TRANSLATION]

Confidential.   SANTO DOMINGO, *December 14, 1854.*

MR. PRESIDENT: The undersigned Consuls of England and France, intending to smooth
away the last difficulties that might stand in the way of a long term truce between the
two parts of the Island, wish to know whether the Dominican Government would agree
to give the following pledges to the two mediating powers should the Emperor of Haiti
put the said pledges as a condition to his accepting such a truce under the guarantee of
the same said powers:
    1. Not to alienate, lease, mortgage or transfer or donate either permanently or tem-
porarily any part of the Dominican territory, particularly on the Samaná Bay, to
any Government whatsoever;
    2. Not to enter into any financial contract with any foreign State, either to accept
any subsidy from it, or to pledge or mortgage to it any part of the revenues of the
Dominican State;
    3. Not to concede in its favor any alienation of the sovereign national jurisdiction;
    4. Not to permit any Government whatsoever to establish or occupy on the Domini-
can territory any maritime or other institutions, factories, or stations whatsoever;
    5. Not to tolerate on any part of the same territory the landing of any troop of ad-
venturers whether in arms or not;
    6. Not to conclude any treaties granting to any power whatsoever anything beyond
what has already been granted to others by previous conventions, and above all, no
treaty which would not guarantee at the hands of that power the same treatment, the
same rights, the same advantages, the same privileges to all Dominicans, regardless of
origin or color.
    The undersigned Consuls considering the urgency of the case beg Your Excellency
to let them have your answer to this as promptly as possible.
    They avail themselves of this opportunity, [etc.]
    I have seen the *originals* of both this and the British Consul's note of Oct 28ᵗʰ [Above,
this part, p. 156, note 1.—Ed.] and know the copies I remit to be accurate.
                                                                    W. L. C.

Their pertinacious intervention has far exceeded the bounds of candid and honorable diplomacy—sustained as it is by indirect menaces and the significant permanence of a strong naval force in front of this Capital—while their governments were making public professions of friendship to the United States and drawing infinite advantages from their honorable faith and strict neutrality in the European war.

It has been declared in writing—and much more strongly and frequently in words—that these agents have the instructions and authority of their governments for these covert and unprovoked attacks on American interests. Under whatever direction the proof is positive, that—taking unfair advantage of its situation at a dangerous crisis—they have by threats and intimidation forced a young and friendless American State to sacrifice its best hopes and its national honor, as well as the valuable friendship of the United States by the violation of its solemn and voluntary engagements.

The Dominican Government informed me in September that European Consuls based their chief objections on Art: 28 of the first convention because it opened to our shipping a peculiarly convenient depot in the Bay of Samana. —This bay is by nature one of the best commercial points in the American seas, not only by its excellent resources in wood, water, provisions &ᶜ but by its secure, central and commodious harbour for all classes of vessels, and its extensive beds of coal for the supply of our inestimable and always increasing steam marine in these waters.

I yielded with extreme regret, even temporarily, conditions so desirable for our commerce and so favorable to the progress and prosperity of the Dominican people, but when I became certain that in the event of this concession France and England were determined to aid Hayti in reducing this Republic to the last extremity, I waived it for the present and the stipulations of Art: 28. were omitted in the convention of October. This forbearance deprived those powers of their alleged motive for injuring this republic and I had hoped that more distinct relations with the United States and a settled peace with Hayti would place the independence of the Republic on such a basis that it would henceforth be enabled to make its treaties without the fear of European intervention.

The patience and equity of the United States has only increased the exactions of the representatives of France and England, and they now demand of the Dominican Government to bind itself *never* to make any treaty whatever with any nation except within such narrow and suffocating restrictions as must be fatal to the independence and prosperity of this republic.

I am not able to say what answer the Dominican Government has given to the European ultimatum but I strongly suspect it is one which will be destructive to the prosperity of the republic without imposing any corresponding obligation on France and England to aid or protect it. Thus far those powers have exacted a colonial submission, while they endeavor to evade all share in the responsibility of the offensive action they compel it to adopt towards the United States.

I have the certainty that within a few days *important secret concessions* have been wrung from President Santana and M. Raybaud left last evening with the documents.   I have not learned their exact nature but it is my impression they relate to the occupation of the Bay and Peninsula of Samana by a French imitation of the British East India Company.   The European governments may avoid coming in direct conflict with the American principle of anti-European colonization but a private company may do the work and monopolize its advantages while American enterprise is effectually excluded by the terms of this ultimatum from the ports and territory of the republic.

In conclusion I beg leave to state my fixed conviction that the Dominican Government only requires to be releived from the pressure of this foreign encroachment and to be assured that the Government of the United States will firmly protect the fredom and integrity of its negociations with this Republic to gladly accept and punctually fulfil all the clauses and stipulations of the original Convention of September.

There is much said in the Cabinet circles of a "triple protection to be established by France Spain and England over the Antilles," and the Spanish Plenipotentiary—known to be on his way here to treat with the Dominican Republic—is supposed to be the bearer of some propositions of that nature. I give this rumor for what it is worth, but I have no doubt that in some form a strong and combined—though probably secret and indirect—effort is in preparation by those powers to efface the only American Nationality in the West Indias.   This is the only territory under American government in this whole circle of islands, with their three and a half millions of population and near one hundred thousand square miles of territory.   All the other islands are European Colonies and if this republic is constrained to accept the conditions of the within note of the European agents, its position, in every point of American policy, will have all the inconveniences of Colonial subjection, without any of its counterbalancing advantages.

I have the honor [etc.].

2279

William L. Cazneau, United States Commissioner to the Dominican Republic, to William L. Marcy, Secretary of State of the United States [1]

SANTO DOMINGO, *March 22, 1855.*

SIR: I had the honor to receive yesterday by M![r] A. Angulo Guridi your note of Feb![y] 3![d] [2] and shall immediately proceed to comply with the instructions.

[1] Special Agents, vol. 19.   Received April 30.   [2] Above, this volume, pt. I, doc. 2202.

I regret to say the communication of 12th Jan.y[1] alluded to, has never come to hand.

With the greatest respect [etc.].

2280

Jonathan Elliot, Commercial Agent of the United States to the Dominican Republic, to William L. Marcy, Secretary of State of the United States [2]

No. 82   SANTO DOMINGO, *May 5, 1855.*

SIR: The revolution to overthrow this Government has been entirely suppressed. Five who were condemned to be shot were pardoned. In a recent interview with President Santana, he expressed a hope that the negotiations for a Treaty with the United States would still be pending. The United States can have all they desire here.

The Spanish Treaty has been concluded. I have not yet got a copy.— The principal item is, "that they are not to permit strangers to hold any part of this Territory."

I have the honor [etc.].

2281

William L. Cazneau, United States Commissioner to the Dominican Republic, to William L. Marcy, Secretary of State of the United States [3]

WASHINGTON, *June 9, 1855.*

SIR: In announcing the unsuccessful termination of my mission to the Dominican Republic I can only reiterate what I have had the honor to state in my former reports,[4] that the failure to establish friendly and mutually beneficial relations with that republic is wholly attributable to the dictatorial intervention of the Agents of France & England who would not permit the Dominican Government to enter upon any treaty with the United States except upon the terms set forth by European policy.

I have detailed in my former communications—and transmitted with them the corresponding proofs—of the manner in which they coerced the Dominican Government into annulling the Convention its plenipotentiaries signed with me Oct.r 5th 1854 although that treaty was eminently in accordance with its own wishes and interests. In the remarkable notes of which I obtained and forwarded faithful copies—their right to supervise and control our inter-American negociations is claimed for France and England and the purpose of excluding our Citizens from their natural share in the commerce and advantages of that rich and central territory is distinctly laid down,

---

[1] Above, this volume, pt. I, doc. 2201.
[2] Consular Letters, Santo Domingo, vol. 2.   Received June 1.
[3] Special Agents, vol. 19.   Received June 11.   [4] Above, this part, *passim.*

though in a form to screen the European powers from expence or responsibility. The Dominican Republic is always placed in the front to meet alone whatever dangers and losses may arise from the course of action forced upon it by the combined will of France & England. When they had compelled this weak government to vitiate the Convention of Oct 5th they sheltered themselves from accountabillity by inducing an incompetent body to assume their acts and proffer to the Government of the United States their European substitute instead of the original treaty which was the true and voluntary act of the Dominican Government.

After this experience of the unfortunate condition of the Dominican Government I would have demanded my passport and left the country in Dec[r] but for certain considerations to which I alluded at the time in my communications to the Department of State. One was the probability that the reformed Administration, which was about to come into power, would have the firmness to emancipate their country from this European dictation. Some of its most leading members assured me they had determined to do so and intreated me to assist their effort to assume an independent and American line of action by remaining a short time longer to give them the moral support of the presence of a representative of the United States.

England & France are undoubtedly co-operating with Hayti and the negro party headed by Baez to extinguish the Dominican Republic and convert the whole island into an African dependency. It is the avowed and leading object of those powers to check the advance of American principles and restrict the scope of American enterprise in the Antilles. To this end their Agents in St. Domingo gave every possible aid to the party of "Baez and the Blacks." There were limits however which could not be conveniently passed while a Commissioner appointed by the Government of the United States to recognize and treat with it as a sovereign American State was actually in the country, and they did not conceal their anxiety for my early departure. As I remained much longer than they had been led to expect by advices from their Ministers at Washington there were several postponements of the time fixed upon for the outbreak and every postponement was a loss to the conspirators and a gain to the cause of law and order.

When at last the revolution was attempted and suppressed the rebel leaders went directly to the European Consulates for protection and were received and entertained in defiance of the request of the Dominican authorities that they should be surrendered for trial. Even those who were taken and condemned to death had their sentence remitted at the demand of the European Consuls—sustained as usual by an imposing naval force—and none of the negro leaders have been allowed to pay the penalty of their treason, except five who were taken by President Santana in the interior and executed under sentence of a military court before the Consuls had time to rescue them.

Whatever may be the ultimate fate of the Dominican Rep[l] it cannot be considered competent to make treaties and fulfill them with other nations while the European powers continue to rule its most important domestic and foreign relations and in the conviction that this European dictatorship would not cease immediately I had no choice but to inform the Dom[n] Gov[t] of the termination of my mission. Your instructions Sir—to that effect only reached me March 21st and your notes of 18th Dec[r] 1854 and Jan[y] 12th 1855[l] were not received until Ap[l] 25th a few days previous to my departure.

The semi-colonial and irresponsible position of the Dominican Republic makes it impossible for the United States to rely upon its treaty engagements, yet the absence of such engagements is operating severely to the detriment of our trade and citizens. Our people do not enjoy the same privileges and security of person and property which France & England exact in favor of their subjects and justice will never be conceded to us until the Dom[n] Gov[t] is made to understand the necessity of placing the United States on an equal footing with the most favored nations.

I have the honor [etc.].

2282

Jonathan Elliot, Special Agent of the United States to the Dominican Republic, to William L. Marcy, Secretary of State of the United States [2]

No. 1   SANTO DOMINGO, *January 16, 1856.*

SIR: I arrived here the beginning of November, and as this Government agreed that they would recede from their proposed amendments to the Treaty,[3] I made overtures to them on the 3[d] of December to negotiate the same. At this time a sudden invasion of the Haytians stopped all the business of the Government.

I have this day received word from President Santana (who has been all the time with the Army) that he will be here in a few days, when the Treaty shall be immediately attended to and concluded as soon as possible.

As many of the Senators are with the Army, I do not expect to get through before the end of February. The Treaty will pass substantially the same as that proposed by W. L. Cazneau.

They desire to make a separate convention in regard to Samana, when the Country is more tranquil. The Haytians publicly accuse Santana of wishing to give this Island to the Americans. Also Mr. Segovia Chargé d'Affaires and Consul General of Spain, has arrived, to join the English and French

[1] Both are above, this volume, pt. I, docs. 2200 and 2201.
[2] Consular Letters, Santo Domingo, vol. 2. Received February 21.
[3] See his instructions, dated October 5, and October 9, 1855, above, this volume, pt. I, docs. 2203 and 2204.

Consuls in opposition to our having a Naval Station here, but I believe that I shall succeed in all that you have desired me to do.

I have the honor [etc.].

2283

Jonathan Elliot, Special Agent of the United States to the Dominican Republic, to William L. Marcy, Secretary of State of the United States [1]

No. 4   SANTO DOMINGO, *March 22, 1856.*

SIR: I send you by the Bearer of this, Mr. William Read, the Treaty as made and concluded between the Plenipotentiaries of the United States and the Dominican Republic. As there will be no direct communication from here under a month, I have told him to proceed via St Thomas, by the most expeditious route. Please pay him the highest sum allowed for such service.

I have the honor [etc.].

2284

Jonathan Elliot, Special Agent of the United States to the Dominican Republic, to William L. Marcy, Secretary of State of the United States [2]

Private.   SANTO DOMINGO, *March 22, 1856.*

DEAR SIR: It is impossible at the present time to do anything relative to Samana. The opposition of the European Consuls, particularly of Spain has been very strong. The President of this Republic is at swords points with them and a little later will cede us the Depot or Naval Station and would now if the United States will protect the Republic, from the consequences. Santana is disposed to have a difficulty with Spain and would were it not for England and France. There is no doubt, that before long, you will hear of serious difficulties here.

I have the honor [etc.].

[1] Consular Letters, Santo Domingo, vol. 2. Received May 2.
The treaty referred to here, which was signed on March 8, 1856, by Jonathan Elliot, Jacinto de Castro and Tomás Bobadilla, is filed in Unperfected Treaties, Series S. It is not included in this publication; but for the text of that signed by Cazneau on October 5, 1854, as to which Elliot said in his No. 1 of January 16, 1856 (above, this part, doc. 2282) that this treaty would be "substantially the same as," see above, this part, p. 133, note 3. There is no No. 3 of this series of despatches from Elliot in the manuscrpt volume; and his No. 2, dated January 16, 1856, merely gave, in accordance with an instruction, the dates of the despatches written in 1855, during his previous residence in the Dominican Republic.
[2] Special Agents, vol. 19. Received June 7.
Why this should be bound in this volume with Cazneau's despatches while Elliot's of January 16, 1856, above, this part, doc. 2282, and several others, below, this part, *passim*, should be bound with consular letters from Santo Domingo, is not evident.

2285

*Jonathan Elliot, Special Agent of the United States to the Dominican Republic,
to William L. Marcy, Secretary of State of the United States* [1]

No. 5   SANTO DOMINGO, *March 22, 1856.*

SIR: I send you accompanying two copies of the Treaty as ratified
between this Dominican Republic and Spain.   You will perceive by Articles
6 and 7 that Spain is seeking to again govern this part of the Island and
numbers are now claiming Spanish protection under said Treaty.

I also send you two copies of the new Commercial Laws of this Republic.
You will perceive that Article 8 of Chapter 2 is very important for our
Commerce.

I have the honor [etc.].

2286

*Jonathan Elliot, Special Agent of the United States to the Dominican Republic,
to William L. Marcy, Secretary of State of the United States* [2]

No. 12   SANTO DOMINGO, *July 5, 1856.*

SIR: In despatch No. 5,[3] I called your attention to Art: 7 of the Treaty
between Spain and this Republic.   A difficulty arose as to the meaning of
said article, and it was agreed to wait the decision from Spain, but all at
once the Spanish War Steamer "Blasco de Garay" and Brig of War "Gra-
vina" anchor off this port and the Spanish Consul begins issuing Certificates
of Citizenship to all who choose to ask them and in this way will make a
large number of Dominicans, mostly blacks, Spaniards, as they are glad to
get out of Dominican Service.   The Haytians can then easily enter, but I
trust that something will turn up to save this Republic.

The Spanish Consul did all he could to stop our making a Treaty,[4] and it
is very evident that this calamity has fallen on this Republic, by reason of
that Treaty and the object is to crush the Republic and have it under the
Haytians who do not permit foreigners to hold property, or do business in
their own name.

It is very probable that the mediation of the United States will be asked
on this question.

I am, Sir, [etc.].

[1] Consular Letters, Santo Domingo, vol. 2.   Received May 2.
   Instead of two copies of one treaty with Spain there is, with the file copy of this despatch,
one copy (filling a pamphlet of twenty-three pages, in Spanish) of a treaty of Recognition,
Peace, Friendship, Commerce, Navigation, and Extradition, signed February 18, 1855,
and ratifications exchanged August 19, 1856, and a copy of a pamphlet of the same size
containing the text of a law of Maritime Commerce of the Dominican Government, dated
June 30, 1855.   [2] Consular Letters, Santo Domingo, vol. 2.   Received August 14.
   [3] Above, this part, March 22, 1856, doc. 2285.
   [4] See Elliot's private letter to the Secretary of State, above, this part, March 22, 1856,
doc. 2284.

2287

Jonathan Elliot, Special Agent of the United States to the Dominican Republic, to William L. Marcy, Secretary of State of the United States [1]

No. 14   SANTO DOMINGO, *July 19, 1856.*

SIR: The following information in regard to matters here, has been furnished me by a person on whom I can rely and who holds one of the highest positions in this Republic.

Mr. Antonio M. Segovia Spanish Chargé and Consul General arrived here about the end of December last, and from the very day of his arrival, he began speaking to all the members of this Government of the extreme injury the American Treaty, if made, would cause to Spain, and advised the Executive in all his interviews, to reject the same, resolutely and at all peril.   He then desired that the making of the treaty should be delayed sometime, so as to give him a chance to go to Port Au Prince and notify Solouque [Soulouque] that he should vacate that portion of the Dominican territory that he then occupied and compel him to peace, offering at the same time a Spanish loan and to create the means of forming *a purely Spanish emigration*, but this was not done, because President Santana was determined and would not listen to him.

After the treaty was signed he proposed to this Government, that they should withdraw it, or refuse to ratify its exchange and in order to accomplish this, he offered a Spanish protectorate—a quantity of troops and a good Navy, besides he would answer for all the consequences that might occur in making opposition to the United States—this was also refused—he then declared that the Spanish Government would infinitely prefer securing this for the Haytians, than for it to be under any American influence.—Incensed at his failure he has determined to destroy the present Administration, or in other words wage an open war against the Country, and in particular towards those individuals, who have supported at all peril the American treaty.   He is now endeavoring to undermine the Republic by matriculating in direct opposition to the 7th Article of the Spanish treaty with this Republic, not only matriculating Dominican Citizens, born here after Spain abandoned this in 1821 to the butchery of the Negroes, but also Dutch, Americans, and French who have become Naturalized Citizens. He has Agents traveling the Country assuring the people, that there is no longer necessity for them to defend their Country in case of Haytian invasion —that their new Nationality will secure them from all danger, and free them from the Military service, which they are now obliged to perform and that the gold and silver of Spain will abound in place of the Dominican paper currency and that this is the only way that they can be free from the despotism of Santana and his Government (*note* who are all white persons).   The

[1] Consular Letters, Santo Domingo, vol. 2.   Received August 25.

result of these reports is that the Government are reduced to a small number, almost insufficient to defeat the plans of revolution of the partizans of Baez (a mulatto who hates Americans and has pledged himself that there shall be no American treaty) who openly declare their intention to have a Negro Government, by destroying the liberal Citizen in a fratricidal war.

This Government has sent a Minister to the Court of Madrid, to settle the true interpretation of Art. 7, which is according to the treaty and the right of Nations, and it was agreed to suspend the Matriculation, until the question was settled; The violation of this rule of Civilized Nations reveals a formal plan to destroy this Republic, as also all American interests here and this is known to all. On the 17th Inst: he obliged them to hoist the Spanish flag and salute his vessels of War in Port, after returning the salute, he obliged them again to fire twenty-one guns and the Secretary of State personally to apologize to him and his officers "for not treating Spain with more respect.[1]

He is also about to establish a Newspaper here to be called "Isabella Segunda" for the purpose of advocating and maintaining the interests of Spain.

This, Sir, is the actual State of the Republic chiefly owing to their friendship for the United States, and their wishing to make it more firm by the treaty and certain destruction awaits this Republic if the United States do not immediately and energetically interfere, as this Government are paying very high prices and spending all their means to keep their troops under arms.

I can assure you that now the United States can make any Convention that they desire with this Government. We can have Naval Stations where we choose on our own terms and in case of necessity depend on assistance from these people—if we only take some interest in them. By sending two or three vessels of war here, the whole can be arranged without any difficulty occurring between the United States and any other power.

Should the United States determine to have a Naval Station here and open the immense wealth of this Island to its Citizens, as well as to make secure the independence of this Republic—no time is to be lost, for the moment this Government are overthrown, the Republic is lost and the United States will have a strong enemy so situated as to prove very destructive to her Commerce and interests in general.

I have the honor [etc.].

[1] The corresponding closing quotation marks are lacking.

2288

Jacob Pereira, Acting Commercial Agent of the United States to the Dominican Republic, to William L. Marcy, Secretary of State of the United States [1]

No. 15   SANTO DOMINGO, *August 7, 1856.*

SIR: Mr. Jonathan Elliot left this on the 2nd inst for the United States by the British Steamer of War Falcon Via Jamaica on very important business, and having empowered me to act during his absence, I take the liberty of addressing you in order to acquaint you of the state of affairs here.—

Mr. Elliot will no doubt have informed you that proposals were made to Ex President Santana to reconcile with Mr. Buenaventura Baez who was expatriated by him in 1852. Yesterday his reply was received, stating that if the Goverment thought, the return of Baez was really indispensable in the Country, and that his supposed influence, would not only reconcile the present local disturbances, but also cause the Spanish Consul to cease his hostile intentions towards his unhappy and unprotected Country, he would agree to the return of Mr. Baez, but whilst yielding to the determination of the Spanish Consul, to whom he attributes this exigent proposal, he tendered his resignation as Commander and Chief of the Dominican Army.— His resignation was read in the Senate, and it created a most extraordinary sensation, as it is supposed, that his withdrawal, indicates how much he disapproves of the step.—

Santana said after reading the official despatch received from the Government; this is what I am reduced to for having signed the American Treaty, and what have I gained with the friendship of the United States? not even a vessel of War to investigate matters; and Baez once here, adieu to all American projects or Convention.

It is supposed that all negotiations for the admittance of Baez in the Republic will be suspended until the result of Mr. Elliot's mission is known.

The Vice President and his Brother who is a member of the Senate, told me last night, write to the United States Government, that if they will furnish Mr. Elliot with the same Carte-blanche that Mr. Segobia [Segovia] has, to do and undo, with at least four powerful Vessels of War, and a good Steamer, we will enter into any negotiations with them, but that we are resolved, not to have any further engagements with the United States, unless they are accompanied by the means of defence, say more, that the Dominicans know their duty as a Nation, but are not sufficiently strong to repel Spain, whose Consul is the cause of our having written for the treaty, insisting at same time, that the Letter should be handed to him to be forwarded, so much did he doubt that the Government would not accomplish this unprecedented step.—If the United States Government intends securing its interest in this Country, there is no time to be lost, as it is a common

[1] Consular Letters, Santo Domingo, vol. 2. Received August 29.

report, since Mr. Elliot's departure, that the Spanish Government will land an armed force here to meet the Americans.—Mr. Segobia [Segovia] says that a War between the United States and Spain is indispensable this Year, and it will better suit Spain, to meet the Americans here as the field of battle, instead of Cuba.—I do really think that much can be done and obtained by the United States, if its action is prompt, and with sufficient force.—Mr. Segobia ought by all means to be removed by request of the United States Government, as his influence in a certain class, will at all times tend to injure American rights,—in fact the whole Gover^t would be happy to see him recalled.—

I am, Sir, [etc.].

2289

Jacob Pereira, Acting Commercial Agent of the United States to the Dominican Republic, to William L. Marcy, Secretary of State of the United States [1]

No. 16   SANTO DOMINGO, *August 14, 1856.*

SIR: I wrote to you on the 7th inst[2] via St. Thomas, and as I then stated that it was supposed, all negotiations with regard to the admission of Ex President Baez in the Country, would be suspended until the result of Mr. Elliot's mission was known, I hasten to inform you, that it met with so much opposition, on the part of the Spanish Consul, and he became so exigent, as to compel the Government to carry out at once his plan, as such, a letter was written to Mr. Baez, who is now at St Thomas, and has been there since 1852, awaiting a favorable opportunity to return here, acquainting him that Santana was disposed to reconcile matters with him, provided he would agree, to return to the Country, as a private Citizen, respect its laws, and promese, not to put himself at the head of any party, or otherwise contribute in conspiring against its lawful Government, furnishing at same time the English French and Spanish Consuls as guarantee for this solem engagement—his answer is not yet known, but as the Spanish Consul has all along, evinced a deep interest in imposing Mr. Baez in the Country, there is no doubt in my opinion, that Mr. Baez will readily submit to the most humiliating conditions, particularly; as he is aware, that the Spanish Consul, has already paved the way for him to reach the Presidency—this naturally will be effected by means of a revolution to overthrow the present Administration, as the Spanish Consul is determined to have one like Baez at the head of Affairs, (who is a mortal hater of Americans) that will mar the progress of American projects, until he can destroy effectually the Dominican Nationality, and which seems to me will be brought about in the following manner. —A short time since a treaty of Peace was proposed by the Emperor of

[1] Consular Letters, Santo Domingo, vol. 2.   Received September 9.
[2] Above, this part, doc. 2288.

Hayti, who suggested at the time, that he would send here Mr. Lloyed (an Englishman) as special Minister, for the purpose of communicating to this Government, his conditions.—

Today a Danish Schooner is despatched by the three Consuls for Hayti by which conveyance, I now address you, informing the Emperor, that this Government is disposed to listen to his Conditions.—Now, I am morally convinced before hand, that a treaty between these two Governments is almost impracticable, and on this being well proved, the Haytians will be entitled to invade the Republic again, by which time the Dominican Army will be so reduced by the Spanish Matriculation, of which you have already been informed, that the defence of the Dominicans will be reduced to a very small number of Men, that must naturally yield to superior force, in which case, the Dominican Nationality will disappear and the Haytian flag and laws again govern here; this is very clear to me, as the intention of the Spanish Goverment, and I know it must eventually prove highly injurious to our interest.—I think that the United States Government can counteract this infamous Act, by extending her protection and aid to this Sister Republic, whose Sons are in heart and Soul Americans, but whilst entertaining that noble principle, they are compelled to conceal it, for want of support from the United States.—I have been thus particular in explaining all that is going on, as well as what is likely to occur, because I presume it will prove interesting to our Government, at a moment when we are about recognizing the free independance of the Dominican Republic.—

I am, Sir, Most Respectfully [etc.].

2290

Jonathan Elliot, Special Agent of the United States to the Dominican Republic, to William L. Marcy, Secretary of State of the United States [1]

WASHINGTON, *September 10, 1856.*

SIR: You will please receive accompanying, the official confirmation and ratification of the United States Treaty with the Dominican Republic,[2] by that Government, as also an English translation.

Spain, through her Chargé Señor Antonio Segovia, is doing all in her power to prevent our having any friendly intercourse with the Dominican Republic. She as well as England, France and other European Powers have their Treaties with this Republic.

[1] Consular Letters, Santo Domingo, vol. 2.   Received September 11.
[2] See reference to this treaty, above, this part, p. 166, note 1.

The Spanish text, printed in the issue, for April 8, 1856, of the *Gaceta de Gobierno*, and an English translation of the Dominican Senate's ratification, dated March 19, 1856, followed by President Santana's proclamation, dated March 27, 1856, are filed with the original of this.

On the 18ᵗʰ of this last July the Consuls of Spain England and France held a secret interview with the Dominican Cabinet, the object of which was, to oblige the withdrawal of the American Treaty, threat[e]ning them in case of refusal to put in execution, threats already made,—declaring "that it never would be permitted for the people of the United States, to have a foot hold in the Dominican Republic."

(I must here remark that the English Consul stated, that his Government would not consent to his taking part in such a project and that he has written to his Government condemning the conduct of Mr. Segovia.)

On the 19ᵗʰ Mr. Segovia penned a letter to you, asking to withdraw the Treaty and this letter was signed by the Secretary of State, M. Lavistida [Lavastida], and forwarded by Mr. Segovia, and this was done without the knowledge of any other member of that Government— All of them have assured me that they were ignorant of any such letter being sent and I have since learned that the Senate have called Mr. Lavistida to account.

I informed you in Despatch No. 14,[1] of the manner in which Segovia is converting all the Dominicans into Spanish subjects.

On the 30ᵗʰ of July he had another interview with the Dominican Government, wherein he was obliging them to receive back, an ambitious negro, called Baez (then in St. Thomas)—with the party he has created and with his Naval force, he intends placing this man at the head of the Government and a Spanish protectorate is to be given, consequently nothing can be done without the consent of Spain.—The majority of the people, particularly the whites, are to suffer the loss of all they have and probably their lives,— This is all about to happen for their making a Treaty with the United States.

If you will look at the Havana correspondence with our Consul, of the end of last November you will see that he has written you about the acts of this same Segovia against the United States when at Havana, on his way to St. Domingo.   He is the author of the article referred to.

The Dominicans, liberal in the extreme to all foreigners and adopting our mode and principles of Government, look to us to give them some countenance.   They hope that the United States Government, on behalf of her own honor and interests, will make known at Madrid, the conduct of Mr. Segovia and with the justice we have to do so, require his removal from the Dominican Republic.   I learn that since my departure Mr. Segovia expects nothing short of this and I was so informed by the French Consul who was passenger with me to Jamaica.

The Dominican Government (who are all whites) will stand firm until my arrival and I beg that the Executive will take some steps in this matter, if only so far as regards the interference of Spain in our own affairs, for there is very just cause to ask the removal of Mr. Segovia, and this alone will lift a heavy burthen from the Dominicans.

¹ Above, this part, July 19, 1856, doc. 2287.

If no action is taken the United States will be blamed and censured for having caused the destruction of the Dominican Republic.

I have the honor [etc.].

2291

Jonathan Elliot, Special Agent of the United States to the Dominican Republic, to William L. Marcy, Secretary of State of the United States [1]

Confidential.   WASHINGTON, *September 10, 1856.*

SIR: I have to inform you that the object of Jose [José] M. A. Segovia, Chargé de Affaires of Spain to the Dominican Republic, is, by a false interpretation of Art: 7 of the Spanish Treaty, to convert all the Negroes into Spanish Subjects—to place Baez, a Negro, at the head of the Government—make them join with the Haytians and crush the present white Republic of St Domingo, placing it entirely in the hands of the Negroes.

The whites are few in number, but they govern and the Spanish Negroes are fully aware that they are happier and more prosperous under a white government.

If the American Treaty should be confirmed, our own Citizens will flock there and at once make the whites the most numerous class.   This Island, which lies between Porto Rico and Cuba, is more fertile than either.   The Negroes are poor and ignorant and willing to work for a small pittance and by the Treaty our Capitalists will go in and a formidal [sic] rival, to all the other Islands, in West India productions, will immediately spring up.

I am authorized to offer to the United States Government, not only any location in the Bay of Samana, for their purposes, but the coal mines in that harbor, and any other commercial advantages they require—but on the condition that the United States will guard them against any of the consequences thereof.

The Dominican Republic is acknowledged by Treaties, as a free and independent nation by all Europe.   Her giving us a Naval Station, is not an unprecedented act—we have them all over the world.   They also ask that one of our vessels of War, shall frequently visit the Island, but having a Naval Station there we must in a short time naturally always have vessels of war there.

I beg you will call from the Navy Department, Commodore Newtons' report on the Bay of Samana.   It is the finest, most beautiful, healthy and commodious in the world, furnishing every material necessary for the repair and building of vessels.

Give me powers—let Commodore Paulding go with me, with two vessels of War, and at this moment I can accomplish all that may be desired.—

[1] Consular Letters, Santo Domingo, vol. 2.   Received September 11.

Spain England and France, may object, they have the same right as ourselves, but not the necessity, as they have their Cuba, Jamaica, and Martinique, for Naval Stations,—there is nothing unusual, or improper in our having a Station in this fine bay some objections will probably be raised, but would end in nothing.—I am firmly convinced that the business once concluded, the European powers would plainly see that they have no right to interfere with us in this case.

Therefore if you think proper to commission me, let me offer as liberal a sum as you can (for the Republic has spent all its means, although not as yet in debt,) and the business is concluded—Samana is worth millions to us, and if it is not secured immediately, incalculable advantages to the Government and people of the United States are lost forever.

I will act with all discretion and assure you that it shall not involve the United States in any difficulties whatsoever.

I have the honor [etc.].

2292

Jacob Pereira, Acting Commercial Agent of the United States to the Dominican Republic, to William L. Marcy, Secretary of State of the United States [1]

No. 17   SANTO DOMINGO, *October 30, 1856.*

SIR: My last despatches were N° 15 and 16,[2] since when I have not received a single line from you.—

As I informed you in N° 15 Mr. Elliot left this on the 2nd of August for the United States and were it not for the public papers, I should not have known of his arrival at Washington.—

I have now to inform You, that owing to Mr Elliot's delay, and in the absence of any sort of information as to the effect his mission would likely create, President Santana was compelled to yield to circumstances and contrary to his real sentiments he has reconciled with Mr. Baez, who without loss of time returned here, and he was immediately brought to the Presidency by Mr Segovia's intrigues.—

With just reason I now apprehend some trouble when the moment arrives to ratify the exchange of our treaty, which I think might have been avoided if the United States had thought proper to take timely measures.—

The Country is just now appearantly quiet, although the Marticula [Matricula.—Ed.] is yet in full vigor—notwithstanding the disapproval of the English and French Governments, who have informed their Agents here, that they are in Active Correspondence with the Spanish Government on the subject.—

The French Government has seriously disapproved of the Conference held

[1] Consular Letters, Santo Domingo, vol. 2.   Received December 15.
[2] Above, this part, August 7 and 14, 1856, docs. 2288 and 2289.

by their Agent relative to the withdrawal of the American treaty, stating, that such acts were Calculated to Create unnecessary difficulties: that the Dominican Government was free to treat with any friendly nation.—

Owing to an article that appeared in the New York Herald of the 1st September, stating that the Spanish Consul General had caused the American Schooner *Elliot* to be searched, Mr Segovia addressed me a letter requesting that I should refute the report, which I declined, because, I have too many proofs of that Gentleman being inimical to our Goverment, and most unfriendly to our Citizens: I send you under cover a copy of the letter addressed to me and my Answer which I trust will meet Your approbation. I must beg leave to observe to you that no such attempt was ever made by Mr. Segovia or any other party to search the Schooner Elliot, and under other circumstances, I should not have hesitated a moment in answering Mr. Segovia's letter to the point; but I thought no satisfaction was due to him from this Agency, at a moment when he obliged this unfortunate Government to withdraw our treaty, and besides declaring on the fourth of July, that his flag was hoisted for his own vessels of War and not in honor of the day, in the face of every other Consul showing the respect due to the day by hoisting their flag.—Another circumstance that shows the ill breeding and bad feelings of Mr. Segovia.—On the arrival of the Spanish Steamer of War here, Don Juan de Austria, as customary on the arrival of a vessel of War of a friendly Nation, every Consul hoists his flag, I performed the same Act of Civility: Mr. Segovia thanked all his Colleagues except the American. If I hoisted my flag for the Spanish Steamer of War, it was losing entirely sight of Mr. Segovia, and complementing the flag and Vessel of Her Catholic Majesty.—Please state whether I was right, and if this course of conduct ought to be continued, supposing the Case of Mr. Segovia's not paying the respect of hoisting flag on the arrival of any of our Vessels.— On the Birth day of Her Catholic Majesty, Mr. Segovia desired by Note to the different Agents which I saw, the favor of hoisting their flag for the occasion and the American Agent was omitted.— Now, was it to be expected in the face of such unprecedented conduct, that the American Agent would have come forward to refute an article in a public paper against Mr. Segovia? Such slights are of no consequence, in reality, particularly when it is well known that the Spanish Government would not have ventured to show that of the United States a slight or attempt any indecorous conduct;—but from one Agent to another, and when the intention is known to the public, such behavior is wounding to say the least of it.—On the 28th inst Mr Segovia appeared at this Agency with a declaration Signed by a number of residents requesting that I should *legalize the Signatures* which I did free of charge as per enclosed Copy, that document was refuting the article in the Herald, which strange to say, has affected Mr Segovia to the degree of moving his soliciting every Signature that could be procured in town.—

On the Night of the 11th inst a Mob assembled before this Agency for the purpose of pulling down the flag staff and National Sign,—but was not at the end carried into effect, the next morning I complained Officially to the Government, who answered in a very suitable manner, assuring me that every measure would be taken to guard against such disorder, accordingly the Commandant of Arms offered me a guard to place before the House which I declined stating that the American Agency of itself Commanded all necessary respect without the assistance of a guard.—No further cause for complaint has since arisen.—The correspondance on the subject is not of sufficient consequence to send you a copy.—

The treaty of peace between this [sic] and Hayti was proposed, but proved a complete failure.

I have the honor [etc.].

2293

Jacob Pereira, Acting Commercial Agent of the United States to the Dominican Republic, to William L. Marcy, Secretary of State of the United States [1]

No. 18   SANTO DOMINGO, *November 6, 1856.*

SIR: My last despatch was Nº 17.[2]— I am yet deprived of any communications from you.—

I have to inform you that it is a common report in town that the United States Commercial Agency is to be stormed tonight by the Spanish or Matriculated party.—As soon as it reached the knowledge of Captain Dunlop of H. B. M. Steam Frigate Tartar, he kindly tendered me, first in person and next through the British Consul any number of men from on board his Vessel to protect our flag and Office, which I have declined, with the object of granting free action to the mob created by Mr. Segovia, Spanish Consul General, and placing the authorities of the Country under the necessity of doing their duty, besides, I am actuated by this idea—if I accept, of a foreign armed force in this instance it will always become indispensable, and the day none is to be had, our Office will be left destitute of protection, whereas, as it is, I am resolved to stand the brunt and Maintain my own rights, although I am aware that my person and family, as Americans are in danger—I walk the streets with danger of my life.—

As a precautionary measure I have determined to withdraw all our Books and papers from the Agency and place them in safety.—

The whole Republic is in a dredful state of disorder, and I have just cause to dread its extending to bloodshed, which is up to this unknown here, but if the shedding of blood is once practiced, I do not hesitate in saying that there will be horrid slaughter and waste of life,—particularly among our

[1] Consular Letters, Santo Domingo, vol. 2.   Received December 19.
[2] Above, this part, October 30, 1856, doc. 2292.

Citizens.—You are now aware Sir of the situation of every American Citizen in this Country, and I thus leave it to your better judgement as to what ought to be done.—

I am, Sir, [etc.].

2294

Jacob Pereira, Acting Commercial Agent of the United States to the Dominican Republic, to William L. Marcy, Secretary of State of the United States [1]

No. 19   SANTO DOMINGO, *November 6, 1856.*

SIR: Since closing despatch N° 18,[2] I deem it proper to acquaint you of an observation made by Mr. Segovia to me, whilst soliciting the favor of my refuting officially the Article in the New York Herald, which I made mention of in despatch N° 17.[3]   I told Mr. Segovia in very candid language, that I ventured to assure him, that his conduct relative to our Treaty would be reproved, so soon as our respective Governments could understand the case properly.—To which he replied, that he had done his duty, besides that the treaty was Null in consequence of its having been Signed by President Santana, when he was not invested with the Executive.—Mr Segovia is in error, and Supposes that the American Agents are easily handled—The case is this—The Dominican constitution reads thus—In case of the Presidents death, resignation, or absence from the Capitol, the Vice President remains empowered with the Executive— Now, President Santana was absent whilst the treaty was being made, but returned just about the time it was to be presented to the Senate, during which process, and the Signing of the treaty, the vice President went to Bani—consequently Santana could not otherwise than re-assume that which he had conferred on the Vice-President. —It is well Sir, that you should be aware that this is the snare Mr Segovia and President Baez are to extend for destroying our treaty, should it be ratified by our Congress—They seem determined to entangle our politics in this Country.—

The arrival of the Packet from St Thomas with European Correspondance, brings the news of the Spanish Government having presented the former french Consul Mr. Darasse, and his Secretary of this place, each, with a splendid Cross, for the deep interest they took in the withdrawal of the American treaty.—   Of what interest it is to Spain to prevent our relations with this Republic I cannot imagine.—

I am, Sir, [etc.].

[1] Consular Letters, Santo Domingo, vol. 2.   Received December 19.
[2] Above, this part, dated also November 6, 1856, doc. 2293.
[3] *Ibid.,* October 30, 1856, doc. 2292.

2295

Jacob Pereira, Acting Commercial Agent of the United States to the Dominican Republic, to William L. Marcy, Secretary of State of the United States [1]

No. 20   SANTO DOMINGO, *November 6, 1856.*

SIR: After having sealed and delivered my despatches N° 18 and 19 of the above date,[2] and at the very moment of closing my office, a Gentleman worthy of credit and deserving of belief gave me the following information— that orders had been given by the Excutive to fortify every fortification of this City, and that similar instructions were already transmitted to the Commandant of Arms at Samana.—Now, I had a tinkling [*sic*] of this measure some three weeks passed, and concluded it was mere kitchen talk, but I have just returned from the nearest fortification, where I repaired as soon as I received the information for the purpose of convincing myself, and I can now attest that my informant was right, with this new feature, that the President assures, by the end of this month, Santo Domingo shall be reputed equal in every respect to Sebastapol.—

The motive alleged by President Baez for this strange measure, is, that information has, reached him, that a number of American Vessels of War, of the home Squadron are to arrive here very shortly for the purpose of exchanging the treaty and in the event of receiving a negative answer, they were to bombard the City.—

Returning to the question of our Treaty the same party has in a great measure made me penetrate the object of Spain in destroying our treaty.— It is well known, that the country formerly belonged to Spain—The English & French recognized its independance before the Gov^t had relinquished by its present treaty all claim and title:—but our Treaty was made after that of Spain, and consequently we recognized the Dominican Republic when she was a free and independent Nation.

The object now before Spain is evidently to Colonize this by means of the Matricula, but the American treaty if ratified at Washington and Exchanged here, becomes in the eyes of the Spanish Gov^t a stumbling block, because it is apprehended, that the United States, might step forward, and oppose it on the ground, that the Dominican Republic was recognized by her, when she was a free and independent Nation, and at liberty to treat as such, thereby demanding that her Nationality shall be respected by every Government and in particular by that of Spain, who wishes by the unfounded interpretation of the 7th Article of her treaty, to usurp its rights.—

I have elucidated the question as well as the hurry of the moment would admit but trust you will understand the true spirit.

I am, Sir, [etc.].

[1] Consular Letters, Santo Domingo, vol. 2.   Received December 19.
[2] Above, this part, docs. 2293 and 2294.

2296

Jacob Pereira, Acting Commercial Agent of the United States to the Dominican Republic, to William L. Marcy, Secretary of State of the United States [1]

No. 21   SANTO DOMINGO, *November 22, 1856.*

SIR: I wrote to you on the 6th inst [2] by the way of St. Thomas, since when, I have not received any communications from you.—I have now to inform you that Captain Dunlop of H. B. Majestys Steamer of War Tartar, unknown to me, called on President Baez on the 6th inst at 4 O'clock P M and told him of his being informed, that the rabble was determined that very night to Storm the United States Consulate, and that he was resolved, as a friendly Nation, to tender me officially, any number of Men from on board of his Vessel, to protect the said Consulate and Agent; if the President did not adopt such measures, as would insure the safety of American interest: In reply to which the President said, that he would do all in his power to guard against so disagreeable an event.—Accordingly he issued that very afternoon a proclamation, which I now enclose,[3] and beg to call your particular attention to the words dashed by me, they show a most evident connection with my despatch N° 20 [4] I am morrally convinced, that, if Captain Dunlop had not of his own free will and accord, intimidated the Authorities in the manner he did, every member of Mr. Elliot's family, as well as my own, would have fallen—victims that night to the rabbel, as such, I considered it my bounden duty, to address Captain Dunlop a letter of thanks in the name of the United States Gov^t, copy of which, I now enclose,[5] and trust, it will meet your approbation—With due respect, I would say, if it be not assuming too much on my part, that our Govern^t ought to thank Captain Dunlop through his Govern^t.—I also enclose a paper just published, "La Acusacion." [6]— On reading it, you will perceive the possitive down fall of Santana predicted— The object is, to prepare the people, for the purpose of reducing Santana to a state of accusation, for he is, in that paper, wrongfully charged with crimes, such, as he never committed— I will thank you to read with attention the following, page No. 2, Marked ☐ the Commission despatched alludes to Mr Elliot's departure, the next is page No. 3 Marked X directly addressed to our affairs, and the individual therein mentioned Mr. Thomas Chapoto, is Thomas Bobadilla, who signed the American Treaty.— I have good reason to consider, not only American Citizens in eminent danger, but likewise those Dominicans

---

[1] Consular Letters, Santo Domingo, vol. 2.   Received December 16.
[2] Above, this part, are three despatches from him, of that date, docs. 2293, 2294, and 2295.
[3] Not included in this publication.   [4] Above, this part, November 6, 1856, doc. 2295.
[5] Not included in this publication.
[6] It is designated as No. 1, of a weekly political newspaper, dated November 20, 1856, and contains only four octavo size pages.   Frequent use of the term "filibusters," in the portions cited, indicates that the writers intended to insinuate that citizens and friends of the United States were identical with filibusters.

who have sustained the American cause, for instance, Don Domingo de la
Rocha, the Father in Law of Mr. Elliot, who was the very first man, that
voted in the Senate for the American Treaty, has been trampled upon, and
where *ought he* to hope for relief? from the U. S. Gov^t, which, if unfortunately
denied, will beyond a doubt, be the means of crushing not only him, but the
best men to be found in the Dominican Republic.—Santana's down fall, can
only be attributed to the American Treaty, and will the U. S. abandone
him in particular?—I pray not, for he is deserving of its protection, I feel it
my duty to dwell somewhat on a subject, that ought to be noticed by the
U. S. Gov^t as early as possible, otherwise, Santana will be a lost man—he
who has shown himself to be a true Republican, and friend to the U.S.:   I am
yet of opinion, that Santana will rise with a large body of men against Baez,
and I think that he will conquer, but to gain the victory, it will be at the
cost of a great many lives—   He is a Man difficult to be roused, but on[c]e
moved, is resolved to conquer or to die.—   Now, in conclusion, I must
reiterate, that the Country is in a most deplorable state—a dreadful revolution may break out from one moment to the other—I therefore, in the name
of humanity, beg of the U. S. Gov^t to send here a vessel of War, merely to
guard our Citizens and Consulate, both being today, at the mercy of foreign
flags for Protection.—   I will now call your attention to a very simple
occurrence, but at the same time one that will serve to prove to you, how
much our Nation is slighted and destested by the President of the Republic—
Enclosed you will find an invitation served to me as Acting Comm^l Agent,
to assist at a Dinner given by President Baez.—   The health of the Emperor
of France—Queen Victoria—and Isabela Segunda were drunk by the
President himself, and not even through the Minister of Foreign Affairs, was
a Compliment paid to the President of the U. S.—This simple want of
attention, shows how inimical Mr Baez is to our Gov^t and people.—My
situation at the moment, was a very unpleasant one, which was considerably
increased the following day, by the common town talk, that Baez would not
drink to the President of the Filibusters, all these circumstances, are calculated to render the situation of the U. S. Agent a very painful and unhappy
one, such as would be very difficult to describe, without entering into such
details as would appear at first sight incredible to one absent from the scene
of disorder, for instance, almost every night, the common town Cry, is, down
with the Yankee's, down with the Eagle, and the American flag is trampled
upon in the streets, to all which, the President says he cannot interfere, and
I am obliged to endure the violence, and abuse, offered to my person, and
flag, by a set of wanton men, for the want of protection from the U. S.—
It is reported that the Constitution is to be revised for the third time in 14
Years of the dominican Independance.—   Mr Baez's object is too clear, and
evident—He intends by a Coup d'etat to have himself elected President for
life—but this, I do not think will be brought about, until Mr Baez has

succeeded, in removing the powerful obstacle he has in Santana.—In this question, Spain is to play a very active part, in proof of, Mr. Joaquin Ginebra, has been sent to Madrid with despatches from Mr. Segovia, on the subject.—I see the affairs of this unhappy Republic in a wretched state.—I likewise foresee, a large amount of trouble for the U. S. when the moment arrives to exchange our treaty.   The Spanish party with Mr Segovia at the head is resolved at all hazards to prevent our having the most distant relations with the Dominican Republic—and as matters stand, it would be impossible to say accurately, whether the present Administration, would not infinitely prefer, seeing the whole Country Crushed, rather than grant the Americans by means of a Treaty a foot hold here.—

Allow me Sir to observe, that I have written to you several despatches of the greatest importance, without the satisfaction of knowing whether they have reached you.—will you therefore be pleased, if nothing else, to acknowledge their receipt.

Most Respectfully [etc.].

2297

Jacob Pereira, Acting Commercial Agent of the United States to the Dominican Republic, to William L. Marcy, Secretary of State of the United States [1]

No. 22   SANTO DOMINGO, *November 29, 1856.*

SIR: The critical situation of matters here, induces me to address you so shortly after my last despatch of the 22nd instant.[2]

I have strange forebodings regarding the security of ex President Santana's person.—The second number of "La Acusacion," which I now enclose,[3] will serve to prove to you, how shamefully he is handled.—Permit me to call your attention to the said paper, and in particular, to that portion dashed by me.—You will perceive that the "Popular Assembly" invoke the protection of Spain, France, and England, in case the Republic should be threatened with any aggression, be it of whatever nature it may.—Next to know whether the existance of General Santana, is convenient or inconvenient to the security of the Republic.—

The Accusation is got up and supported by Mr. Segovia and his clique.—The object of the first question is, to impress on the public mind, that the liberty of the people, and the safety of the Republic, will be endangered ere long by an invasion of Filibusters, clandestinely supported by the United States Government, in favor of General Santana, it therefore becomes requisite to spread the necessity of soliciting foreign protection to guard against our Government, and gradually lead the ignorant people to rise "En Masse"

---

[1] Consular Letters, Santo Domingo, vol. 2.   Received February 18.
[2] Above, this part, doc. 2296.
[3] It is the same size as No. 1, and is dated one week later; see p. 180, note 6, above, this part.

and ask for their former birth right from Spain, or demand a spanish "Protectorate".—

The second question is concerning Santana, it is to bring the populace
together and sign a petetion addressed to the senate, demanding in the name
of the people, that Santana should be impeached, in which case, I am sure he
will be condemned by the criminal Court to Capital punishment, which
sentence may be commuted, by the Executive, to expatriation for life.—
This is the essence and definition of the two questions propounded by Mr.
Segovia through the "Accusation," such as it was confided to me by a member of the "Popular Assembly" in the strictest confidance.—

I should never have expected to read such questions in public print, regarding Santana in his own Country.—He who was honored with the title of
"Liberator" in 1849, because he was the first to give the cry of independance
for the Dominicans.—He who threw off the Haytian Yoke.—He who repelled
the Haytians in every case of invasion.—He who aspires to a white population.—And finally he who was the only man that would have dared to cause
a treaty with the U. S. to pass the Senate, is today crushed, by the Anti
American party, by the party of Mr. Baez—and why? because he supported
the treaty and the American Cause.

Can the U. S. Government view with indifference the Complete down fall
of General Santana?   No, I should blush as an American Citizen to suppose
it even within the bounds of possibility.—If it does not suit the views of the
U. S. Govᵗ to support General Santana in his own Country, it is then in
honor bound to offer him a "Home" in the bosom of the American Nation
where he will breath[e] the free air of Liberty, and enjoy those feelings of Republicanism so congenial with his own soul.—

I cannot refrain from expatiating on this very important question, a
question that is vital for General Santana, and were I a man of means, I
should not hesitate in performing my share of national gratitude, towards
one who owes his misfortune to the American Cause, as it is too well authenticated, that had he opposed the American treaty, with the same fervor
he supported it, he would have been Crowned with Laurels by the European
Governments, and in particular by that of Spain.—All this corroborates my
former despatches, leaving little doubt on my mind now, of the horrid end
that good man will have in this unhappy Country, if he allows himself to be
Accused.—Santana is yet on his farm, where he awaits quietly the result of
his forced reconciliation with President Baez.—I do not think that Santana
will submit himself to trial, particularly, when it is well known, that the
charges brought against him, are false, thus proving, that the only object of
the Govᵗ and Mʳ Segovia, is to extend a snare for him.—Once trapped, he
will be destroyed, for he is the only man in the whole Republic, possessing
the requisite influence with the lower class, to bring about any change in
favor of the U. States.—

I reiterate that I do not think Santana will submit to Baez, and in so saying, I confirm my last opinion, that he will rise against the Government, at the risk of being called a faction, and if he does, he will triumph, but that victory will be at the sacrifice of a great many lives.— In the event of so dreadful a revolution, you can easily imagine the great degree of danger for every advocate of the American cause, as well as for our own Citizens.— Let me therefore implore of you Sir, not to abandone our people, all ask for protection from the U. S., and I cannot doubt, but that you will send here, a couple of vessels of War, merely to look on, and see that no injustice is committed against our Citizens or their property.— I cannot refrain from repeating that this Country is in an awful state, of political disturbance, and that its present unhappy state is owing to the unprecedented neglect of the U. S. towards its welfare.— I fear the lamentable result of our affairs in this Country and if the treaty does pass in the U. S.—our Gover[t] must be well prepared for the difficulties that will attend its exchange here.—If the U. S. Gov[t] is determined to maintain its rights, by compelling M[r] Baez to the exchange of the treaty, the determination must be accompanied with very superior force, as I too plainly perceive, all the coming troubles that will offer at the last moment, not only on the part of the Dominican Government, but likewise from European Powers.— Since Mr. Elliot's departure, there are always three or four vessels of War anchored on the roads, and a Steamer in the River, ready at a moments notice to proceed for more vessels if requisite.— Do not I beg of you, Sir, suppose that I am unfounded in my apprehentions.— I am well aware of all that is going on, and I communicate it to you in time, in order that our Government may not be defeated for the want of Accurate information.— I close expressing in the warmest possible terms, the urgent and important necessity of our having at least two Vessels of War for some time before the City, for the personal safety of our own Citizens.—

With due Respect [etc.].

2298

Jacob Pereira, Acting Commercial Agent of the United States to the Dominican Republic, to William L. Marcy, Secretary of State of the United States [1]

No. 25 SAN DOMINGO, *December 5, 1856.*

SIR: A very important conversation having transpired between the President of the Dominican Republic and my self, not a half hour since, relative to the manner he views the question of our treaty, I hasten to inform you of it.— The President told me that he intended if the treaty passed at Washington, to propose to the U. S. Government, the modification of two or three Articles, which he hoped would be acceeded to—but if our Gov[t] de-

[1] Consular Letters, Santo Domingo, vol. 2. Received April 6.

clined, he would then only exchange the treaty, with the guarantee of England France and Spain.— This unprecedented proposal has been cooked at Madrid I am sure— I mention this in time, in order that the U. S. Gov^t, may, if it suits, communicate with the three Governments requesting their Non-intervention.—

The above was communicated to me by His Excellency in the strictest confidence.

With due Respect [etc.].

2299

Jonathan Elliot, Special Agent of the United States to the Dominican Republic, to William L. Marcy, Secretary of State of the United States[1]

[EXTRACT]

No. 7   SANTO DOMINGO, *March 9, 1857.*

SIR: . . . Some steps should immediately be taken by the Govt:, for since they see, that no notice has been taken of the gross insults offered to our flag—the Consulate and Citizens of the United States (for which I refer you to former correspondence,) they become more emboldened and there is no safety or security here for either our Citizens, or, their property.—

Neither the Dominican Government, or, any of its Citizens can assign any reason whatever for their conduct and my family are in constant alarm for my personal safety.

I have the honor [etc.].

2300

Jonathan Elliot, Special Agent of the United States to the Dominican Republic, to Lewis Cass, Secretary of State of the United States[2]

No. 11   SANTO DOMINGO, *April 27, 1857.*

SIR: I informed you in despatches No. 7 and 8[3] of the difficulties that were likely to occur to the American Schooner "Charles Hill," owing to an accidental collision she had with a Dominican Schooner. You will see by the accompanying correspondence[4] that I have had with this Government, that the Captain has been obliged to abandon his vessel, and is also sen-

[1] Consular Letters, Santo Domingo, vol. 2.   Received April 7.
Although this despatch of March 9th was addressed to Marcy as Secretary of State, he had been succeeded by Lewis Cass on March 6, 1857.
The omitted portion, at the beginning, tells of a collision between a United States merchant vessel and a Dominican vessel, which he thought was accidental, but for which the commander of the former is held responsible.   He makes drastic comment regarding the unfairness and corruption of Dominican courts.
[2] Consular Letters, Santo Domingo, vol. 2.   Received May 25.
[3] See an extract from the former, above, this part, under the date of March 9, 1857, doc. 2299; and for comment regarding the omitted portion, see footnote 1, above.   His No. 8 is not included in this publication.   [4] Not included in this publication.

tenced to twenty-four months imprisonment, or, until the sum of three thousand, two hundred dollars, is paid.

There is no justice here, for a foreigner and whenever they can get a pretext, they will fleece him of all they can.

To my surprise the English Consul here, has been taking some evidence of English Sailors, who were on board of the Dominican Vessel at the time and has sent the same to his Government, with what object, or, reason, I know not—he read the same to me, the whole purport of which is, that *in their opinion*, the American Captain was to blame. By the Court here the Captain has been sentenced for intentionally trying to run down the Dominican Schooner of War and also with his men attacking the vessel and crew— this is highly absurd, for how would a Captain of an empty Schooner in the dark, attack another vessel on the high sea, not knowing her nation, her size, and he without a single arm on board— Such has been published here to excite these people against Americans, a copy of which I also enclose and it no doubt, is written by the Secretary of State here, as nearly the same arguments and words are used, as in the last official letter to this Agency.[1] (See No. 8).

I can assure you, Sir, neither this Government, or the few persons, who at present sustain it, have ever had any cause to dislike the Government, or Citizens of the United States.

This present Government is entirely under the control of Spain, England, and France, they do not wish that our Citizens shall have any interests here and are now plotting with Hayti at the West end to the same effect. They wish to make these people believe, that they can prevent the United States from calling them to account for their mis-deeds, and if the English are allowed to meddle in the present affair of the Schooner, "Charles Hill" it will be published here to our great detriment. This Government ought to be able to explain its conduct and be made to know that European Powers will not protect them in unjust acts towards our Citizens.

I have the honor [etc.].

---

[1] Not included in this publication.

2301

Jonathan Elliot, Special Agent of the United States to the Dominican Republic, to Lewis Cass, Secretary of State of the United States [1]

[EXTRACT]

No. 14   SANTO DOMINGO, *July 11, 1857.*

SIR: . . . News reached here yesterday, that on Monday the 7th inst: the province of Santiago, the most populous and industrious of this Republic had revolted against the present Government and no doubt they will succeed in its overthrow, as the affair is headed by very skilful men and seems to be a populace move.   Meanwhile our citizens here are in the greatest danger, as this president Baez has an implacable hatred to all that is American and is vested with despotic powers, numbers have been arrested on the most false testimony and neither he, or his Ministers, show the least regard to justice or truth in their doings.

I beg the Government will pay some attention to this, and send our Commodore to investigate and learn the truth of the ill-treatment and insults our Citizens have to submit to and have power to act accordingly.

I have the honor [etc.].

2302

Jonathan Elliot, Special Agent of the United States to the Dominican Republic, to Lewis Cass, Secretary of State of the United States [2]

No. 16   SANTO DOMINGO, *August 22, 1857.*

SIR: I informed you in despatch No. 14[th][3] that a revolution had broken out here.   At this date the whole Republic has pronounced against the Government, who only hold this City with about 600 men, which is besieged on all sides.   There is a constant firing of cannon and small arms, night and day.   Up to this time, counting both sides about five hundred have been killed.   This City is so well fortified that it can hold out for a long time and the arrival of four hundred Frenchmen is daily looked for, who are to assist Baez.   Two Agents of the French Government have just arrived and the whole emmigration from France consists of four thousand persons who have committed crimes, and all are to be landed in this part of the Island before the first of January next.   One idea is to found a City in the bay of Samana at Punta Coroso, to be called "Buenaventura" in compliment to Baez.

[1] Consular Letters, Santo Domingo, vol. 2.   Received August 4.
The omitted portion tells of the revolution which broke out nine months earlier, by which the existing government obtained control, and of its insults to his family, to the agency, and to United States interests.
[2] Consular Letters, Santo Domingo, vol. 2.   Received October 2.
[3] Above, this part, July 11, 1857, doc. 2301.

The greatest suffering now exists in this City for the want of fresh provisions.

Mr. M. T. Hood, formerly English Consul at Montevideo, has arrived and entered on his duties as Consul here.

On the 10th inst. my flagstaff was struck by lightning and entirely destroyed, I was within six feet of it at the time—was a little stunned, but not hurt.

I have the honor [etc.].

2303

Jonathan Elliot, Special Agent of the United States to the Dominican Republic,
to Lewis Cass, Secretary of State of the United States [1]

No. 3   SANTO DOMINGO, *April 21, 1858.*

SIR: This City has now been besieged nine months and it may probably last some weeks longer.   All that Baez now holds, is this City, with between three and four hundred men.   The opposition party, who hold all the Republic, have elected and installed a President—Vice President, with a Cabinet and Congress, last month.   For some motive, the party outside do not attempt to capture this City—There is neither police, or security of person here. On Sunday night a Mr. Frederic Leyba, who has been a constant visitor at the British Consulate, was shot while coming out of Mr. Hood's house, and now lies in a dangerous state, I was at Mr. Hood's, at the time of the occurrence.   A few nights previous, one of their chief officers pointed his carabine at my wife, who was in the balcony and but for her quick retreat would have shot her; I went to the house of the Minister of Justice, Delmonte, to tell him of it, but received such a tirade of abuse from his wife and some other female, that I was glad to retreat.

Numbers have died and are now dying of starvation and it seems to me impossible, that such a state of things can last much longer.   The Spanish and French have taken an active part to sustain Baez, but his case is hopeless.   The walls of this City, have been manned and the Artillery managed principally by Spanish and French, against the Natives.   I am happy to state that no Americans have taken any part, on either side, in this affair.

I have the honor [etc.].

[1] Consular Letters, Santo Domingo, vol. 3.   Received June 8.

2304

Jonathan Elliot, Special Agent of the United States to the Dominican Republic, to Lewis Cass, Secretary of State of the United States [1]

SANTO DOMINGO, *June 11, 1858.*

SIR: The flag ship "Colorado" Commodore J. M. M°Intosh arrived here on the 24th Ult° finding us in all the dangers that belong to civil war, with no prospect of a termination of the same. He entered into negotiations with President Baez (who only held this City) and had some Communication with Santana, which has had the happy result of terminating this disastrous affair and thereby gained the friendship of all parties for our Government and Citizens and of all which he will give a full account to our Government.

I have the honor [etc.].

2305

Jonathan Elliot, Special Agent of the United States to the Dominican Republic, to Lewis Cass, Secretary of State of the United States [2]

No. 10   SANTO DOMINGO, *October 21, 1858.*

SIR: I have the honor to send you accompanying a Copy of a letter written by Maxime Raybaud, Ex Consul General of France to Hayti, directed to General Santana the President of this Republic, marked *No. 1.* By this you will see that said Raybaud, (who is now secretly employed by Hayti;) supposing this Republic to be in a very dependant and weak state, from the revolutions it has just passed through, (to maintain their independense against the intrigues of Europe,) advises them to unite with the Empire of Hayti, as the only means of salvation; in answer to which General Santana replied, by sending him his passport; to immediately leave the Country, which Mr. Raybaud did, in a vessel bound to Hayti. Please also notice the false calumnies he has directed against the United States Government and its Citizens.[3] This Mr. Raybaud at the head of the European Consuls to

[1] Consular Letters, Santo Domingo, vol. 3. Received June 28.
[2] *Ibid.* Received November 30.
[3] The text of this enclosure follows:

Jean François Maxime Raybaud, French Consul in Santo Domingo, to General Pedro Santana, President of the Dominican Republic

[TRANSLATION]

No. 1   SANTO DOMINGO, *October 2, 1858.*

Do we sing to the deaf?
Having voluntarily returned to private life, the keen sympathy which I have constantly felt for the Dominican cause, and which was manifested from 1847 to 1855 for the acts most prejudicial to the good relations which, as Consul General of France, it was my duty to maintain with the Government near which I was accredited, has alone inspired me with the desire to come, after four years' absence, to judge for myself

this Republic, has prevented our having a treaty and excited feelings against us, as well as creating civil war here, the whole object of which, was, to place this part of the Island under the Haytians, to be more secure in the large debt that Hayti owes to France.

---

of the degree of social misery to which you are considered in Europe as definitively fallen.

In truth, there is nothing lacking in this misery. I see it, and I hear it admitted, with grieving all around me.

Nothing . . .

Neither the ruin of public and private fortune.

Nor the more annoying fact of a daily increasing debt whose irregularity defies all investigation.

Nor the destruction of the means of defense.

Nor the abandonment of your ports.

Nor the inefficacy of your customs collections.

Nor the scarcity, at least at present, of the products of your soil.

Nor the discords, destructive to nationalities.

Nor the incurable hatreds which survive them.

Nor the absence of foreign consideration which results therefrom.

Nor the mourning caused by the proscriptions.

Nor the most culpable disregard on the part of the Government of the need for understanding.

Nor the undervaluation of the highest public offices, converted for lack of special men into secondary occupation of the merchants.

Nor the abandonment of the Dominican name, announcing the downfall of your social edifice.

Nor the lassitude of the two interceding European Powers, feeling the expenses of their armaments, their officers and crews decimated by the fever in order to procure for you more than twelve years of tranquillity, misspent in battles of influence, in dark intrigues for the advancement of a third who will not agree to one of them gathering the fruit of his sacrifices.

There is nothing lacking in your misery, I say.

Neither the future full of international claims, armed and threatening.

Nor the ignorance of the danger, this time more serious than ever, of a supreme invasion.

Nor the probability of the excesses which would avenge the humiliation of many defeats upon a population innocent of the country's ills.

Nor the absence, finally, of the slightest sign of a possible return of vitality because of the fatal lack of men uniting the valor to defend the nation with the personal consideration and inspiration indispensable to its direction and prosperity.

May you not lose sight of these liabilities.

The day has finally arrived to establish your balance with that clarity and conciseness which is equally opposed to the idle recriminations and patriotic phraseology on which they have been fed here for so many years.

Then, what is the use of discussing the causes of the evil? It is enough to sound its depth and find the remedy, if this remedy exists.

These are your assets.

1. The desire for a prolongation of the truce with Haiti.

2. The conviction of being able to contract a loan in Europe.

3. The hope of obtaining a new advantage over the Haitians.

Let us add, the concern among many of the neighboring nationality, which ten years of tranquillity, wellbeing and progress make an object of comparison necessarily worthy of envy, for whom these benefits do not now exist; finally, the thought among others of putting the country at the mercy of a people of a different faith, for whom the slightest contact with a man even suspected of African blood is considered a stigma; a people who do not suffer or wish to touch his hand, or sit at the same table, or sleep under the same roof, or travel with him, or pray at the same altars, or rest under the same earth.

Thus, then, your assets consist of two illusions, an uncertain hope, a concern justified in some, an aspiration shameful in others.

I am going to explain.

In some interviews which I have recently had with President Santana, he has expressed a strong desire, to make as close as possible the friendly relations between this Republic and the United States, by Treaty and all reasonable advantages that can be extended to us, and if the United States desire such, now is the time.

If the Emperor Faustinus, profiting by his former reverses, hoping always to blot out their memory, as there is no reason to doubt; if, as is certain, he has collected all his forces to that end; if he does not, consequently lack munitions, provisions, or money; if accurate arms have been procured; if his soldiers, better disciplined, more confident, have learned their use by means of European instructors; if he now has under his direction hundreds of deserters and Dominican outlaws, seeking to guide him across the difficulties of your soil; if he is, above all, master of the sea, as it appears that you forget,—what object is there in obtaining from him the prolongation of the truce? Is it perhaps that you have treated [greater?] need for it than ever today, or the respect that you manifest for it since your easy triumph over your brothers, of Cibao, provoking and directing insults and threats against it in your Official Gazette, your proclamations, and by your priests in the churches, a war whose indignity yields only to ridicule.

As to the loan, the facility with which you see its execution, is scarcely pardonable in one who does not know of Europe's financial situation and present preoccupations; in one who does not suspect the discredit that you yourselves suffer for the reasons set forth in the beginning of this note; in one who forgets, finally, the weakness of the thread on which your political existence hangs.

Let the miracle be fulfilled, however, paying for it with the proceeds of your customs, the sole income of the country, and by introducing into your midst an administration of foreign agitators; if you see therein a remedy for all your ills, a safeguard against all your dangers; others, in the light of a number of similar precedents, see only an apple of discord which would lead the over-stimulation of covetousness to the point of an outburst, for whom the mere thought of such an expedient already produces among you another risk for your nationality.

This nationality, consider it well, has never been of any political interest to anyone: especially to the United States, which, accepting it only as an inevitable transition to its advantage, has done nothing to strengthen it, if, perhaps it has not been an obstacle to mediation.

For France and Great Britain, who alone, definitively and with no underlying motive, interposed their armament between it and its enemies, it was in the beginning only a question of humanity, which, unfortunately for you, has been complicated, apropos of the Bay of Samana, by a menace to the good relations between the three mediating Powers. Moreover, this question is reduced in itself to the lowest proportions, since a careful examination has resulted in the political sentiment which only today absolves the sovereign of Haiti from the projects of atrocious revenge which public partiality in your favor has attributed to him for the past eight years: I will say more; this sentiment has ended in winning for him in Europe the sympathy and respect of many important persons, who approve of his not compromising with his duty, with the duty of preserving this island, asylum of his race and of those who share it, from the dangerous introduction of men boasting of the hatred and most brutal contempt which they profess for it. Do you believe that you will yet overthrow the Haitians? It may be, but, moreover, what will that success amount to if it is as undecisive as formerly, if their resources are not diminished thereby, if, finally, it only results, for you, in aggravating this precarious and miserable existence in which your people cannot, nor do they now wish to live?

Every situation which becomes too tense comes to an end sooner or later. If you absolutely reject the supposition that yours can be set to rights by a catastrophe, I have nothing to add.

In the contrary case, it is already time to firmly calculate its consequences, and to ask yourselves whether there is more true patriotism in encountering them, than in preserving the people from them by the means still offered in a state of affairs which is on the eve of becoming desperate.

But these means are today limited.

In less critical times, in spite of an almost general recognition of your nationality and of the encouragements of your friends, you already proclaimed your inability to

A Contract was signed by this Government, with a company composed of English and French, ceding to them the right to work *all the mines* of this Republic, under the following conditions, on the 14th of this month, viz:

One million of Francs to be paid on account, within three months from date of contract, or, the same to be void.

---

exist without a European protector, which was successively refused you by three Powers for political reasons which it is not given to me to appreciate.

You offered also, with no greater success, the sacrifice of that nationality, resigning yourselves to accept the modest rank of colony. Placed, then, between the necessity and the confessed impossibility of remaining Dominicans in fact and in name, is it not worth more to you to be so at least in name or fact, if your peace and tranquillity depend thereon, and since nothing better, nothing more, presents itself between those two alternatives.

The question of your future thus established, is reduced, therefore, to the two following propositions.

Taking into account the color of the Dominican people (color which is all too forgotten here and not known in Europe), would it be of advantage to be dependent, even if it were only by way of obligation, upon a people who consider as an insult the sending of Consuls of mixed blood to their ports, upon a people who in their treatment relegate such blood among the lowest white people and slaves; among that class which they indiscriminately insult with the nickname of inferior races, where instruction, virtue, fortune and even the laws protect none against the abuses of every white rascal?

At such a price you could still remain Dominicans in name. The supposition that it might be desired also to renounce this name in order to enjoy more directly such advantages, not being admissible, I have no reason to discuss it.

The second proposition imposes upon anyone whose duty it is, or who wishes to engage in finding a solution for the serious circumstances confronting the country, an imperative and conclusive obligation, that of asking his conscience whether, finally, it would not be preferable for you not to return to be vassals of the Power whose anarchy and arbitrariness you deserted in 1844; but to participate as privileged citizens in all the advantages already realized by a nation which has steadily progressed in prosperity for the past eight years, which requires no sacrifice in your return to it, whose credit and wealth are ten times greater than yours, it may be because of the enormous difference which exists between the comparative value of your currency; by a nation which is assured an honored post for the extension and security of its transactions; and whose chief, finally, although illiterate, at least encourages public instruction, loyally discharges burdensome obligations, whose heritage he has not wished to repudiate, and who maintains with an energy, a solicitude, to which even his enemies are bound to render homage, the respect of his authority and the faith of his word.

I have spoken of privileges. Since, are by no means unworthy the attention of any impartial man, those which it would probably still be possible for you to obtain from him under the conditional guaranty of the Mediator Powers, and from the position in which you would perhaps have already fallen were it not for that truce granted at the request of the agents of France and England; a truce, whose provisions, you well know, left you sufficient latitude to take advantage of your latest dissensions in the interest of your policy.

And if in restitution of the triple unity of flag, power and legislation, administrative, military and judicial isolation should be conceded to you, the official use of your language, the inviolability of property, even of that confiscated from the Haitians, the power to maintain the positions, acquired, the amortization of your national debt, and the application of the revenue of the country to its development and prosperity; would this not be a highly satisfactory and perfect conquest, in view of the condition in which you find yourselves? Would it not mean remaining free and Dominicans in fact, without seeing yourselves deprived of the means to preserve this status?

Such is my personal opinion as to the preferable solution of the Dominican problem. But I earnestly desire to make it clear that I have not studied it from the point of view of those who, after having gone through the terrible catastrophe of a decisive invasion because of their obstinacy, would avoid its consequences, pretending to make their flight from the country acceptable as a last act of patriotism.

Certainly not: I have done it from the much more important and perfectly distinct point of view of this unhappy people whose sufferings they find themselves powerless to

To commence operations within three years—the Dominican Government to receive ten per cent upon the gross products of the mines. This only refers to the mines that may exist on the lands, now actually belonging to the Government. All the mines, of whatever class they may be, on *private* property can only be worked by consent of this Government and these are now open to the enterprise and labor of any Citizens of the United States, who may choose to avail themselves of the same. In my opinion very few mines that are valuable exist on the public lands and if we had a simple Treaty with this Republic, it would *secure* our Citizens in any investments they might make, Agreements or, Contracts can also be made for valuable timber (for shipbuilding and other purposes,) that abounds in this Island.

Also please receive accompanying a document which is very scarce, entitled "An idea of the value of the Spanish part of the Island of St Domingo"—[1]

No. 2. This pamphlet contains very correct information and I would call your particular attention to the same, particularly to Chapters 6–26 and 27.

The instructions given me by Secretary Marcy on October the 5th 1855 [2] in regard to making a Treaty with this Republic, stated "that I could render a very material service to the U. S. Government if I could obtain them a Naval and Coal Depot in the Bay of Samana.[3]—I am told by this Government that it is impossible for them to cede exclusive jurisdiction to any Power over any part of their territory *but* that if they (the U. S. Govt) can contract with any private persons, or companies, who are owners, or who may legally become such, for a piece of land for such purposes as the United States desire, that this Government will afford all the facilities in their power, to secure the U. S. Govt: in the secure and peac[e]able possession of the same for any period of time desired.

Therefore, any American can purchase land here and lease the same to the United States, under a guarrantee from this Govt: that there shall be no

---

relieve, and whom, satisfied with having exhausted the resistance, they would abandon without scruple to all the disasters and all the violence of that catastrophe. I have studied it, above all, from the point of view of those gallant soldiers, whose rags inspire more admiration than pity, and whose heroic sacrifice for an idea, which they can not make prevail, merits as a recompense at least the preservation intact of the honor of their past successes.

I find myself of this true and just conviction after having spent a month in rendering myself as exact an account as possible of the dangers of your situation, and of the real value of the hopes that remain to you. Independent today, as much as a man can desire, indifferent now to gratitude as well as to ingratitude, I freely lay it before you, with the right acquired by seven years of forgotten sacrifices for this cause, compromised since 1852, which finally succumbs a victim of the rivalry of those whose mission it was to make it triumph. However, far from pretending to impose it upon anybody, I am ready, on the contrary, to bow before any other solution of a nature to free this unfortunate country from its present difficulties, to free it in a manner at the same time more advantageous and less irrevocable, if it does not find its happiness therein; but it is time to establish without declamation or useless words, the logical demonstration of its possibility and of the preference which it may merit.

[1] This is a pamphlet of ninety-five pages, printed in Spanish, at Santo Domingo in 1853.
[2] Above, this volume, pt. I, doc. 2203.   [3] There are no closing quotation marks.

interference on the part of the Authorities or, other persons, in the occupation and use of the same for commercial purposes, or any others that do not jeopadize or conflict with the sovereignty of the Republic.

I have the honor [etc.].

2306

Jonathan Elliot, Special Agent of the United States to the Dominican Republic, to Lewis Cass, Secretary of State of the United States [1]

No. 12   SANTO DOMINGO, *October 22, 1858.*

SIR: In accordance with Chap: 15 of "Consular Regulations", I make known to you, that owing to a revolution that began the 7th of July, 1857, and lasted until the 12th of June, 1858, (nearly one year) all trade and commerce with this Republic ceased.   During the whole year up to September 30th 1858, only two American vessels arrived here, one of which sailed for the U. S. the other was sold to this Government, and only two foreign schooners (Danish) left here for the United States,   During the year 1857, Seventeen American Schooners arrived at Porto Plata, their tonnage amounting in all to 2500 tons, their inward cargoes provisions, and outward, tobacco, hides, and Mahogony.—A second revolution broke out which lasted until the 2nd of September, and as there has been no communication with Porto [Puerto] Plata, I have not received the Returns for the first two quarters of 1858.

A contract has recently been entered into, between this Government and a company composed of English and French; to work all the mines of every description, that exist on public lands, the Government is to receive ten per cent on the gross amount of the products.   There is said to be large quantities of coal in Samana bay, but these are mostly on private property and from the impossibility of obtaining labor in this country, owing to the indolence of its people, its climate being so fatal to foreigners, and its continued unsettled state, the mines cannot be made profitable.

This Government has also despatched an Agent to Europe to obtain a loan; I am not aware, what are the terms they propose, but do not believe they will meet with success, as their neighbors the Haytians are about to make another attack and should they prove successful will immediately put their laws in force, which do not permit foreigners to possess property, speculate, or trade in the country.   The first step towards foreigners having any security for their investments here, must be the recognition of this Republic by Hayti, as the latter still claim this as their territory.

This Republic is in a very distressed state,—no commerce, no credit and a currency depreciated to a nominal value, their people worn out and ruined

[1] Consular Letters, Santo Domingo, vol. 3.   Received November 22.

by the fourteen months revolution they have just passed through; renders them an easy conquest for their enemies the Haytians; who, if they succeed, will trample on and oppress the whites and mulattoes of this part.

The Dominicans, are certainly a superior race to the Haytians their laws are liberal, in the extreme for foreigners, they occupy three fourths of the Island, the richest in land, timber, and minerals, of all the West Indies, but they have never had a moments peace, or, a chance to develope its resources and this has principally been owing to European intrigues.

The only productive part, has been a small portion called the Cibao, yielding from sixty to seventy thousand quintals of tobacco annually.— Its exports, on a very limited scale, are mahogony, tobacco, hides, wax and some sugar to the United States and Europe, nearly all the European vessels come here in ballast,   The principal import trade has been with the Island of St. Thomas and some provisions from the United States,   In fine some very great change must take place, before this beautiful Island can give forth its riches to the world and occupy the position in commerce to which it is entitled.

This is all the information that I can now communicate.

I have the honor [etc.].

2307

Jonathan Elliot, Special Agent of the United States to the Dominican Republic, to Lewis Cass, Secretary of State of the United States [1]

No. 4   SANTO DOMINGO, *March 21, 1859.*

SIR: Your despatch of the 2nd of December last,[2] was received here the 2nd of March, in reference to a Treaty with this Republic.

It is advisable for the U. S. Government, not to send any Agent here for such purpose, as it leads the ignorant to suppose that we wish to possess their country. The following circumstances will oblige this Government to send an Agent to Washington—Viz:

In my despatch No. 10, Oct: 21, 1858,[3] I informed you of a contract they had with an English and French company, to work the mines here. They have also attempted to get a loan of five million of dollars in Europe— both projects have failed. Their tobacco and other crops here have failed— finally it is likely that the Danes will shortly blockade their ports, on account of a claim that this Government have refused to listen to, these added to the great misery produced by the revolution obliges them to open their country to us as a last hope. The time has arrived when we can have a good station for our Navy and depots for our steamers in these waters. Samana is very

---

[1] Consular Letters, Santo Domingo, vol. 3.   Received April 18.
[2] Above, this volume, pt. 1, doc. 2205.   [3] Above, this part, doc. 2305.

beautiful; but presents two grand obtstacles; Viz: sailing vessels are sometimes days before they can get out and it is very sickly and fatal to foreigners.
In January last, I went to the bay of Ocoa, situated about sixty miles west
of this City, it is one of the finest I have ever seen in my life, it has most
excellent drinking water and a whole fleet may anchor in safety.   I spent
two days examining this port, one on the water the other on land and obtained a good deal of information.—At the Salt works, (or Salinas) a vessel
can anchor close to shore in five fathoms of water and have from 18 to 20
fathoms at her stern.   The bay of "Calderas," adjoining is the finest port
on this side of the Island and ranges from 3 to 15 fathoms—joining to the
west is the Ocoa—you can anchor close on either side of the river—vessels
seek shelter here from the hurricanes, all these Ports are united, surrounded
by mountains, which abound in all kinds of timber, quantities of game of
all kinds the bay abounds in fish, lobsters, oysters &c. &c. and on account
of its dry climate and excellent water a healthier place does not exist.   Our
Sick Sailors would soon regain their health there.   If the Government will
send a small Steamer and some intelligent officer I will go there in her and aid
him to obtain all information.   We can go there under plea of getting fresh
water, we can take soundings and go on shore, concealing the object of the
visit, so that when this Government make their offers, to grant the U. S.
facilities to their commerce and Marine, (which I will urge them on to) that
the desired spot shall already be secured, at a very small cost, which I can
accomplish for the Government, by purchasing in my name and renting it
99 years at a nominal sum, or cede, or sell it to the U. S. as may be desired.
   I have the honor [etc.].

2308

*William L. Cazneau, Special Agent of the United States to the Dominican
Republic, to Lewis Cass, Secretary of State of the United States* [1]

[EXTRACTS]

No. 1   SANTO DOMINGO, *June 19, 1859.*

   SIR: Immediately on receiving my instructions [2] I proceeded to New York
to seek the most speedy and direct conveyance to the city of Santo Domingo
the capital of the Dominican Republic.—
   After diligent enquiry for a direct passage I learned from those formally
engaged in the trade that they had abandoned it altogether.
   This, among other causes, is in consequence of the heavy discrimination
in favor of those nations who have treaties with the Dominican government

---

[1] Special Agents, vol. 19.   Received December 20.
[2] Presumably those contained in the letter dated April 7, 1859, above, this volume, pt. 1,
doc. 2206.

—for these distinctions are made to operate to the exclusion of American traders.[1] . . .

The largest of these plateaus—the great plain of La Vega—is a leading feature in this capability for a splendid system of internal communication, but it also opens a dangerous inlet of invasion from the side of Hayti. While Hayti remains the stronger power and nourishes the idea of reconquering the Dominican Republic the eastern section of the island can never enjoy an assured tranquillity.

This plain undulates westward in easy waves to the Bay of Mancenelle, which is commanded by Hayti and is the key of La Vega. Hayti has the western shore of this fine bay and from it a hostile force may penetrate the heart of the Dominican territory by the navigable river Yaqui and by the Santiago roads, which can easily be made passable for heavy artillery.— A very fair road track of eighty miles leads from Monte Christi—the most western port of this republic and situated on the verge of Mancenille Bay— to Santiago and thence on; thirty farther east, to the central town of Conception where a conquering army would be completely the master of its position.—From that centre a competent general could forage the country and dictate terms to the helpless, disjointed fragments of the white republic.

The Emperor Faustin [Soulouque] made more than one attempt to avail himself of these topographical features for the subjugation of the Dominican Republic but the people under the lead of Gen[l] Santana always rushed in mass to meet him at the frontier, and thus far they have never failed to drive the Haytiens back within their own limits.

These repeated invasions have laid desolate, from sea to sea, a broad belt of the Dominican frontier.—It is a valuable strip of country forty or fifty miles in width; rising inland in lofty mountain ridges, rich in ores and abounding in mahogany and other precious woods, and descending on each side—North and South to the coast in fine, fertile slopes well suited to the culture of coffee, cacao indigo & sugar—There are good harbors at both ends of this depopulated border land, but one of them demands special attention as being that Bay of Mancenille of which I have already spoken as the key of La Vega and a standing menace to Dominican independence.

Commercially and politically it would be an excellent site for a free & neutral port if Hayti, and her European allies, would consent to such an arrangement.—It is one of the most secure and central harbors in the West Indias and is much better situated for a coaling and distributing depot than St. Thomas for our trade in the Caribbean Sea—particularly in the direction of the Isthmus routes.—It is capacious and well sheltered from the winds most to be feared in these latitudes. It opens to the east and is protected by a cluster of islands which—taken with the favorable curve of the land—

---

[1] This omission, extending over ten pages, tells of the trade and resources of Puerto Plata, the port on the north coast where he landed, and the region around it and Santiago.

gives for the space of four miles a choice of excellent anchorage close in shore, with from ten to fourteen fathoms water.—

From the Haytien shore the Bay receives Dajabon river and some smaller streams: but the place for a good sea port is on the Dominican side of Mancenelle.—

In a confidential interview with the President the exposed and utterly defenceless condition of the Haytion line of frontier was brought forward and I frankly advised that the government should declare the depopulated strip of country neutral territory and invite colonists to it from every part of the world by the offer of free homesteads and permanent exemption from the costs and penalties of war; opening the port of Mancenelle at the same time to general commerce somewhat on the plan of St. Thomas.

By this formal declaration of free trade and strict neutrality, this frontier port and territory would be placed under the protection of all the maritime powers, Those citizens would naturally turn to such a safe and convenient locality for commercial settlement and thus raise an efficacious barrier to invasion—Hayti would not venture to disturb so many foreign interests by crossing this neutral belt with a hostile force and she is not likely to be very soon in a condition to equip a navy and attack the Dominican territory by sea.

This suggestion of a neutral line of frontier, was made—so to speak—on invitation, and simply in my private capacity as the personal friend of Gen¹ Santana.—It is quite probable however that it would be accepted and acted upon, should our government see proper to have it officially recommended as a common necessity both to Hayti and this Republic.   It would be to us the gain of a free commercial enterpot [entrepôt] at the gates of the Gulf of Mexico and Caribbean Sea, and might be the means of saving the harassed remnant of the white race on this island from impending destruction. It would certainly give this young State its best chance to lay down its arms and cultivate its neglected resources.

The representatives of France, England & Spain may oppose the establishment of a free port and neutral territory on the Haytien frontier, on the same grounds that they have hitherto interdicted the important Bay of Samana to our trade—because it would be too favorable to American progress.   To open either Samana or Mancenelle would create a perfectly independent stronghold for American commerce—where it is much needed—and where none now exists—at the cross roads of our West Indian & Central American trade.

All the great maritime powers of Europe have colonies of their own in our seas and enjoy all they require in the way of harbors for the shelter, supply and repair of their shipping, in peace or war, and they have no desire to see central and commanding situations like Samana—and Mancenille ripen into great commercial entrepots under an independent American flag and wholly beyond their dictation. It was avowedly because Samana would be so convenient and valuable to our inter-American trade, that the Dominican Government was in 1854–55 so sternly commanded by England, France and Spain not to open it to our commerce—Hayti has always been made a partner in these acts of prohibition because Hayti always claims for the negroes the dominion of the whole island and the agents of all these powers favor the pretensions of Hayti.

These observations on the position and necessities of the Dominican Republic are the result of attentive personal investigation and I am irrisistably led to the conclusion that this young state must change its whole line of policy, or it will very soon cease to exist as an independent republic and lapse into a negro protectorate on the "Mosquito Kingdom" pattern.

The terrible insurrection of the negroes, with their wholesale massacres of the whites and half a century of anarchy, mutual slaughter and confiscation, explain for themselves the decadence and bankruptcy which despite the lavish gifts of nature rule the aspect of this Island. Yet the Dominican Republic, would it but take its stand as a really American nationality, has within itself the most encouraging elements of prosperity. It has a compact territory; is admirably situated at the intersection of the new pathways of trade with which steam and free interchange are revolutionizing commerce; is richly endowed in natural resources and except on the side of Hayti—is protected by sea from entangling and disorderly neighbors—while but for the question of races is [it] has a pre-eminently docile and easily governed population.

In extent, population, general capabilities and political responsibility it compares favorably with most of the Central American States and perhaps no one measure would go so far towards securing an independent and hopeful future for this isolated republic as an honorable recognition by the United States.

I have only to add that after many delays I arrived in this city on the 14th inst: and thus closed a long and close tour of inspection across the country.

On the 15th I presented my credentials to Don Miguel Lavastida, the Minister of Foreign Relations, who immediately arranged a confidential interview with President Santana.— This conference embraced the leading points of common interests to both republics and was extremely suggestive, but I regret to say it decidedly confirmed what I have herein stated of the difficult position and gloomy prospects of the Dominican Republic.

I have the honor [etc.].

2309

William L. Cazneau, Special Agent of the United States to the Dominican Republic, to Lewis Cass, Secretary of State of the United States [1]

[EXTRACTS]

No. 2   SANTO DOMINGO, *July 2, 1859.*

SIR: Since I had the honor to address you on the 19th ultimo.[2] I have had an interview by special appointment with Don Miguel Lavastida on the subject of indemnifying the owners of the Schooner "Charles Hill" for her unjust confiscation by order of ex-President Baez.— The Minister admits in effect the wrongful seizure of the Chas Hill but pleads that it was not the act of the present governm^t and that the United States ship of war Colorado was on the ground in time (June 1858) to have forced the perpetrators of the wrong, who were still in possession of the government, to make restitution.[3]
. . .

The Baez party, which aims at placing the Supreme Power in the hands of the Negroes, was defeated and driven from the City in July 1858, after sustaining a seige of eleven months, but it is far from extinct.— Its leaders rely on the sympathy of England, France and Spain, because the agents of those powers have invariably lent their counsels and countenance to the negro party.— The chiefs of this party are undoubtedly planning an insurrection in favor of Baez, and should they succeed, there is an end to the rule of the whites in the Dominican Republic. The white race will be despoiled of property and citizenship if not life.

At present the Cabinet, Congress and high courts are filled by white men— to an extent unparalleled in most of the Spanish American States—but the restoration of Baez, or the annexation to Hayti so strongly but secretly urged by France & England, would sweep them out in mass, to be replaced by blacks selected from the class most bitterly opposed to American interests.

Baez was negotiating with France and Spain for the return of the Dominican Territory to European vassalage at the time he was expelled the country, and every overture he made in that direction was accompanied by the most atrocious insults to the American flag.[4] . . .

After Baez had exhausted his financial game and it was evident that he must make a speedy escape from Santo Domingo—within whose walls Gen! Santana had caged him—the European Consuls intervened in a body to procure his safe retreat by capitulation— In advance of this capitulation

---

[1] Special Agents, vol. 19. Received December 20.   [2] Above, this part, doc. 2308.

[3] The omitted portion showed the falsity of the position here taken; it indicated also that the existing revolution prevented serious attention to the case, making financial settlement impossible, and intimated that favorable consideration would probably be given later.

[4] This omission merely refers to the seizure of the schooner *Charles Hill* as one of the troublesome legacies which the Baez régime left, but states that it was insignificant beside the difficulties resulting from the unlimited issuance of unsecured paper currency which quickly depreciated.

however—so the government affirms—some of these consuls collected large quantities of this Baez paper at unknown prices, but the public rate of exchange at the time ranged from $40.000 to $50.000 "papeletes" the doubloon.

On the re-establishment of President Santana as constitutional President, it became one of the first cares of the government to dispose of this flood of equivocal papeletes.—   The large army of holders naturally desired to have it placed on a par with the earlier issues of national currency, which all parties recognized as legitimate, and the heavy speculators in it were of course the most clamorous of all.

It was finally decided by act of the Legislative power, May 5th 1859, that it should be redeemed and cancelled at the rate of 32.000 "papeletes" the doubloon—   This was an advance of 20, or, 30 pr. ct. on the rates at which Baez left it.—   But this did not satisfy the wholesale dealers in the Baez issues, although this vast addition to the paper circulation reduced its value from the old Santana standard of 60 or 70 papeletes to the dollar to two hundred.

The Consuls of Spain, France & England protested against this act of the Dominican Legislature and officially notified the Minister of Foreign Affairs that they "would consider it null and void so far as it concerned the Citizens of their nations."   M. Lavastida, the Dominican Secretary of State returned their note as a document which he could not lay before the Executive because of its "deficiency in the moderate tone which civilized nations are accustomed to use in their international relations" and also on account of the "inconceivable want of knowledge of National Rights" displayed by the consuls in assuming to "exercise a veto power over the acts of the Dominican Legislature."—   The consuls persisted in their demands to have the currency endorsed in full by the government, and finally struck their flags and left the country because it was not conceded.

This correspondence is signed by Santandre the Consul for France, who also brought in Denmark and Sardinia by implication, as he was acting for those governments in the absence of their consuls; by Martin I. Hood the English Consul; by David Leon his vice and by T. Faraldo Consul for Spain & Holland, but there is no evidence that any private citizen of the countries they respectively represented held much of the Baez money.

The British consul and vice consul are reported to have extensive dealings in it, but the course of the French and Spanish—who had no personal interest involved must have been actuated by purely political motives.

The three consuls Santandre of France, Hood of England, and Feraldo of Spain are supposed to have acted strenuously—though secretly—together to effect the annexation of the Dominican Republic to Hayti and this Santana and his party will oppose to the last gasp—with reason, for incorporation with Hayti would be a death warrant to their hopes of creating a free and prosperous republic on this island.—   If the governments of France,

England and Spain are really determined on the suppression of the Dominican Repub° as many members of this government fear the measure would
be suitably initiated by a formal suspension of friendly relations.

Although this government has signed a truce with Hayti it has an over-
powering dread that this movement of European displeasure will find vent
in that direction—or in the forcible restoration of Baez—and I am reliably
informed it is secretly supplicating the return of the consuls.—Should they
come back strongly supported in their demands by their governments, I do
not see how the Republic can maintain its independence.

It is on account of its unfortunate bearing on the future destiny of this
island that I have given so much space to the "papelete" question.—   No
representative of the United States can look on with entire indifference while
the immediate death or renovated existence of the only State in the West
Indias Islands covered by an American flag, is a problem at the point of
solution.—

It is painful to see this government so completely subjugated by its fears
of a European coalition with Hayti.   It feels the need of closer relations
with the United States; it deserves the stimulus of a more extended trade
and is perfectly aware that good ports would be of the greatest possible
benefit to its own people, but it is afraid to act lest it should seem like making
concessions to American interests.—

Nevertheless the Dominican Executive has come to the resolution to open
the port of Samana in the course of a month or two.—   I am promised that
this shall be done in any event, though this government would be glad to
have the step preceded or followed by a treaty similar to those made by the
United States with all the other Spanish American Republics.

The Bay of Samana is naturally one of the best positions for inter-
American trade to be found in our seas.—   It may be discribed as a
choice series of landlocked harbors congregated in a bay thirty miles deep
from east to west, by eight wide from north to south.   This bay opens to
the Mona passage with Porto Rico on the opposite side of the strait, distant
about sixty miles from the eastern point of this island.   It lies well to the
windward of Cuba, Jamaica, the Gulf of Mexico and most of the Isthmus
crossings.   The largest fleets may ride in safety in this capacious bay and
find in it every facility for repairs and supply.—   The high and fertile
peninsular of Samana abounds in wood, water and provisions.   It is
distinguished for the excellence of its ship timber, and much of it is very
convenient to points which competent Spanish, French English & American
officers have reported as eminently advantagious sites for naval purposes.

The river Yuna, which might be navigated by light draft steamers perhaps
fifty miles, falls into the western end of Samana Bay after draining one of the
most fertile districts of the island.   It is now but thinly peopled and the
land mostly given up to pasturage, but under more favorable cercumstances

it would contribute large quantities of Sugar, Coffee, Cacao, Tobacco &c for exportation. Most of this will be carried in American Ships to be exchanged in our markets for flour, salt provisions, cotton fabrics, farming implements and other productions of American industry. This trade must fall to our shipping whenever it has an equal chance in the race with European vessels.

I hope to induce the Dominican government to place American merchantmen on a par with those of the most favored nations when—or at least very soon after the port of Samana shall be declared open to commerce—

With great respect [etc.].

2310

William L. Cazneau, Special Agent of the United States to the Dominican Republic, to Lewis Cass, Secretary of State of the United States [1]

[EXTRACTS]

No. 5   SANTO DOMINGO, *July 30, 1859.*

SIR: It would be impossible to convey to my government a correct idia of the present situation of the claims of our Citizens against this government unless at the same time the extraordinary fact is taken into consideration that the very existence of the Dominican Republic, as an independent Nationality, may at any moment be exposed to an abrupt termination.

I have before detailed in Dispatches Nos 1. and 2.—June 19th and July 2[d] [2] the embarassments attending President Santana's return to power and now, after two months close personal observation, my doubts as to the possibility of his maintaining the independence of the republic, should any additional burden of unpopularity be suddenly forced upon him, are decidedly confirmed.

The treasury is utterly bankrupt—there is no coined money of any kind to be seen in circulation and the whole country is overwhelmed with a paper currency which in its intrinsic worthlessness and rapid depreciation can only be compared to the "continental money" of our own revolutionary days.

All the European Consulates still remain closed for the alledged reason that their respective citizens were wronged by the repudiation of the Baez currency as I explained in Despatch No. 2.

Many members of this government regard the simultaneous abandonment of the Dominican territory by the corps of European Consuls as something like a combined declaration of outlawry against the Dominican Republic in

---

[1] Special Agents, vol. 19. Received August 29.
His No. 3, of July 14, and No. 4, of July 23, deal with two claims of United States citizens against the Dominican Government, one for the seizure of the schooner *Charles Hill*, and the other for the seizure of a quantity of Dominican coins belonging to a Mr. William A. Read.
[2] Both above, this part, docs. 2308 and 2309.

consequence of its refusal to incorporate with Hayti on European recommendation.

Whether these circumstances should have any influence on the time and manner of enforcing the just claims of our despoiled citizens is for the wisdom of my government to determine at the suitable moment.[1] . . .

The presence of the U. S. Frigate Sabine has been of much advantage here; inasmuch as it is a proof that our government is watching over the welfare of its Citizens abroad; but it is an inconceivable drawback to the peace and safety of American interests in these waters, that our Naval Officers have not as much power to enforce summary redress when our people are outraged by these revolutionary and irresponsible semblances of government, as the Officers of France and England invariably employ, in conjunction with their civil representatives, whenever French and British subjects are despoiled in like manner.—

The knowledge that our Officers have no power to redress such wrongs— while the wrong-doer is yet in a position to answer for his acts is the short and simple explanation of nine-tenths of the lawless atrocities which the feeble anarchies about us, have for years past been in the habit of inflicting upon the citizens of the United States.

I have the honor [etc.].

2311

William L. Cazneau, Special Agent of the United States to the Dominican Republic, to Lewis Cass, Secretary of State of the United States [2]

[EXTRACTS]

SANTO DOMINGO, *October 17, 1859.*

SIR: Since I had the honor to address the Department, of the date of July 28th, (No 5) [3] the Dominican Republic has narrowly escaped a fatal

---

[1] This omission discusses briefly the status of the *Charles Hill* and the Read claims.
[2] Special Agents, vol. 19. Received November 14.
The following letter of the same date, to President Buchanan from Mrs. Cazneau, the original of which is filed in the same volume of manuscripts, is of sufficient interest to include. On the back of what appears to have been the folded sheet of paper within which this reached the Department, is endorsed, "18 Nov: 59. Referred to the State Department. J. B."

Mrs. W. L. Cazneau to James Buchanan, President of the United States

SANTO DOMINGO, *October 17, 1859.*

MY DEAR MR. BUCHANAN: Our residence here has been little better than an incessant round of sickness and privation yet for worlds I would not have failed to come and learn what we have learned. We see and I believe the whole Union will soon fully comprehend the change which the firm yet considerate policy of your administration is working in the whole Spanish American sentiment. Unquestionably your present action is working out the social and political salvation of the Dominican Republic. It was posi-

[3] For his No. 5, dated July 30, 1859, however, see above, this part, doc. 2310.

revolution. The Baez party, which is seeking annexation to Hayti, as a means of excluding the white race from the Island, had concerted a general revolt to take place in all the districts simultaneously, in which the negro element largely predominates.[1] . . .

Yet in the face of these troublesome considerations, and with the volcano of a half extinguished revolution under his feet, President Santana has had the courage to open the central and splendid port of Samana to our commerce. The European Agents have always insisted that Samana should remain closed to commerce, as the leading Powers of Europe had no use for it with so many ports of their own on our coast and were not willing that one so strictly American in its character and so pre-eminent in natural advantages as Samana should arise in the very centre of the Caribbean sea, to compete with theirs, and to become the centre of a vast inter-American trade.

---

tively at its last gasp as an independent state in which white men had a right to live in freedom & security.   One party was soliciting the return of their old European masters, another intriguing for annexation to Hayti and even the small minority capable of understanding the real wants of the country had given up the hope of satisfactory relations with the United States.   President Santana and his possible successor José Valverde of Santiago are of the party of "Independence and Progress" and they have been much strengthened by the presence of an American agent during the severe crisis the Republic is now undergoing.

General Cazneau landed on the north coast at Puerto Plata and traversed the country from side to side through the troubled districts and thus had an opportunity to disabuse them of the idea that the United States want to annex this island.   This is [the] black phantom of the colored races and is always paraded when their chiefs plan a revolt. American vessels, American land holders and American sympathies had almost vanished from the sight and thoughts of the Dominicans when your agent presented himself.

There was no time lost in renewing old friendships with members of the Cabinet and standing Senate (Senado Consultor) and in awakening better ideas than that of submission to Hayti.

Befor[e] leaving New York my husband made thorough inquiry of leading merchants as to the condition prospects and capabilities of the trade with St. Domingo.   He found there was no difficulty in making it a respectable feature in American progress could it but be relieved from the doubts and restrictions which have gradually suffocated it.   He made it his business therefore to convince this cabinet of the necessity of abandoning its suicidal course and he has perfectly succeeded as will be evident to all the world in another month or two.

Our merchants wanted the free use of the safe and commodious harbor of Samana and Samana is open to them now.   Our citizens wanted access to the mines for this is another California, and this concession will be made whenever you authorize a treaty with the Dominican Republic.   When the question of a full act of recognition by formal treaty is brought forward the answer has been that with such questions as the Charles Hill and Wm A. Read claims unadjusted no discussion can be thought of on more remote points.

These claims will be soon settled and I entreat you in justice to your own fame and in behalf of this isolated young state not to leave the Dominican Republic much longer out of the pale of United States recognition.

Up to this time there has been no day in which I have not been on a sick bed myself or waiting and watching at the side of fever stricken members of my family but with the approach of the dry season our health and hopes take new life.   But in all times and under whatever circumstances the ruling thought is to accomplish well the duties before us whatever they may be.

Very Respectfully,

[1] This omission, covering four pages, tells at length of the recent frustrated revolutionary attempt.

The Bay of Samana is an unrivalled harbor combining within itself every advantage for the supply of vessels, abounding in wood, water, coal and provisions; and its commanding position on the Mona Passage makes it the natural entrepot of an immense trade between the United States and all the countries on and around the Caribbean sea.

In addition to this decided measure the Dominican government has given me the most unequivocal pledges to reduce the tonnage duties on American vessels and to place our trade in that and all other respects on the footing of the most favored nations without waiting for a formal treaty to that effect.—

I should also have stated that I have removed one obstacle by inducing the "Senado Consultor" to recommend an immediate and liberal adjustment of the "Charles Hill" claim altho it was urged in the debates that the claim was rather exorbitant.

I have the honor [etc.].

2312

William L. Cazneau, Special Agent of the United States to the Dominican Republic, to Lewis Cass, Secretary of State of the United States [1]

No. 7   SANTO DOMINGO, *December 13, 1859.*

I had the honor to lay before you in former communications the peculiar circumstances in which the Consuls of England, France and Spain, closed in a body their official relations with the Dominican government and left the country.

I have now to add in continuation that on the 30th ult: three vessels of war—two French and one English—arrived here with their respective Consuls, and immediately afterwards they were joined by a Spanish war Steamer having on board the Spanish Consul. Before any of them landed this government was notified by the French and British Consuls of the conditions on which friendly relations were to be re-established.—

After a warm discussion on the question of salutes—during which Don Miguel Lavastida resigned the portfolio of Foreign Relations rather than yield to their demands, the Consuls obtained all they required.— The main subject, the payment of the Baez "papeletes" followed & the conditions proposed by the Consuls were substantially accepted.—

The Dominican government legalizes and assumes the payment of the entire issue of Baez papeletes at eight thousand to the doubloon, instead of thirty two thousand, as fixed by act of Congress.— Bonds drawing six per cent interest are issued to the holders—The interest to be paid semi annually in cash or through the Customs.— Besides this, on all government dues payable in gold or silver, six per cent of the amount may be paid in these bonds in lieu of specie.

[1] Special Agents, vol. 19. Received January 14.

As this arrangement contravenes a law of Congress and creates a lien on the public revenue, it will have to be submitted to the legislative body for ratification—but this is a mere form.

The Dominican government has struggled hard to avoid a public debt, except that which exists in the form of a domestic paper currency, but the precedent is now established and the reclamations of our Citizens may be adjusted in the same way if it would be satisfactory.— Unless instructed I do not however [sic] to do so, I do not feel authorized to admit for example the settlement of the "Charles Hill" case in any other way than the full payment in cash of the amount demanded.

The simultanious appearance of the French, English and Spanish Consuls with this demonstration of force, created no small excitement in official circles, where it is taken as the prelude to some very decided attack upon the independence of the Republic.

The leading members of the Cabinet and Senate are very anxious to obtain a treaty recognition from the United States and President Santana would now propose it in form, but for his morbid dread of a failure, which he firmly believes would precipitate the downfall of the Republic.

I have already stated what the President and Minister of Foreign Relations say on the subject of American interests and of their desire to enter upon a more liberal policy towards our Citizens if it can be done without imperilling the existence of the Republic.

At this juncture they would make a Treaty which would hold all the resources of the Dominican territory invitingly open to American enterprise —Without straining its stipulations beyond what is already conceded by the laws, or has been heretofore granted to other nations; the vast natural capabilities of this country could be made almost as free to our people as if it were their own soil.

In adverting to this subject, and to the circumstances which are now bringing it so prominently forward in the Dominican Cabinet, I presume it is unnecessary for me to say that I have avoided the most remote participation in any discussion outside of my ligitimate business here.

I have the honor [etc.].

2313

William L. Cazneau, Special Agent of the United States to the Dominican Republic, to Lewis Cass, Secretary of State of the United States [1]

[EXTRACTS]

No. 8   SANTO DOMINGO, *January 30, 1860.*

SIR: I have the honor to inform you that the Dominican Government has this day settled in full the claim of William A. Read for $275.000 Domin-

[1] Special Agents, vol. 19.   Received February 23.

ican currency, seized by the authorities of Puerto Plata in November 1857.[1] . . .

I am pressing vigorously for immediate indemnity for the owners of the Charles Hill and if not done sooner I hope the Dominican Congress, which assembles the 27th February will provide for it.

There is a visible growth of good-will and confidence towards our country in every direction, and I cannot but believe that my government will confirm and perpetuate this sentiment by a speedy treaty recognition— Those who are unfriendly to American predomirance in the Antilles are opposed to every measure which would make this people and their interests tributary to our commercial systim, but all the friends of progress desire it with an earnestness difficult to express.

I should be remiss in my duty were I to omit stating my firm conviction that the future of the Dominican Republic is, under divine providence, at the disposal of our government.— Should it decide to admit this state to the same treaty relations which it holds with the other Spanish American states of equal claims, our citizens would come here with their capital, and thus enterprise machinery and habits of combined action, would create a new life in this long suffering country.

If this is refused, the Dominican Republic must sink into a negro province under the Haytien constitution. It is reported that Chevalier Maxime Raybaud, late Charge d'Affairs of France at the court of Soluque [Soulouque], will return here very soon to urge the old Anglo-French plan of re-uniting this republic to Hayti. The cabinet seems divided in opinion whether he is to come back as the Consul General of France, or simply as the secret agent of the Emperor under cover of a diplomatic mission from the Haytien government. I am certain that secret propositions for a treaty with Hayti— looking at ultimate annexation—are now before the Cabinet and is giving no small anxiety to the leading members of government.

I ventured to suggest in a private conversation—simply in my individual capacity as a personal friend—that the Dominican government might easily place itself right before the world and silence officious dictation by agreeing to a treaty *provided* Hayti would renounce her barbarous restrictions against the white race. Her laws, as they stand, would exclude a large portion of the Dominican population from the benefits of any general treaty with Hayti and until this is amended none ought to be made.

President Santana is now at his estate in Seybo and the Vice President, Gen[l] Antonio Abad Alfau, is in the exercise of the "Executive Powers."— He is a brave soldier and a well-tried patriot, but he is nevertheless an unpractised and therefore an irresolute and wavering Statesman. He has moreover from his youth upward, lived and been educated under European influences to the exclusion of sound American ideas. Thus with the best

---

[1] This omission discusses the details of the manner of payment.

intentions for his country he might at any time sacrifice its highest interests to European counsels from inability to break from his old habits of thought and enter with decision on an independent line of policy.   While our government is duly represented here and its just and friendly sentiments kept before the Cabinet and country there is less danger of this government compromising its position as an independent American State, but I consider it in the highest degree advisable that this propitious time should [be?] seized to make a treaty which will open this fine country to the mining, agrecultural and commercial enterprise of our citizens.

I have the honor [etc.].

2314

William L. Cazneau, Special Agent of the United States to the Dominican Republic, to Lewis Cass, Secretary of State of the United States [1]

No. 10   SANTO DOMINGO, *March 4, 1860.*

SIR: I have the honor to inform you that this government has received notice from Gen! Felipe Alfau—its Envoy at Madrid—that the Spanish Ministry is disposed to accede to the plan of a protectorate for the Dominican Republic.—   This Dominican Envoy is the brother of the Acting Executive, Vice President Abad Antonio Alfau, who has very decided predilictions for whatever is French or Spanish and would not hesitate to make his country a direct appanage of either crown if it could be done with safety.

My information is confidential—so far as it concerns the public here— but it comes from a source so high and authentic that there can be no doubt of the forward state of the negociations for a European protectorate.

It is fully expected by its movers here that it will cover and sustain a general revolution in the industrial condition of the island.

It is the opinion of a member of the Cabinet, who professes however to be opposed to the whole scheme, that Indian apprentices and Asiatic coolies will be brought in under the French, Spanish and English flags and that the same Anglo-French pressure which creates a protectorate here will give force and significance to the measure by a corresponding modification of the slave systim in Cuba & Porto Rico.   I cannot ascertain on what basis the hope rests but they have an idea that this group of islands will soon be provided with a "non hereditary system of servitude" on something like a common principle—equally suitable to the French, English and Spanish colonies, and highly profitable to all—yet wholly out of the reach of rival American planters.

[1] Special Agents, vol. 19.   Received April 3.
His No. 9, of February 22, 1860, tells of the opening of the Bay of Samaná to foreign commerce, prospective investments of United States capital there and elsewhere in the Republic, and of the change since his arrival, during the preceding summer, in the sense of security felt by citizens of the United States in the Dominican Republic.

I have the most positive knowledge that plans for the importation of coolies, and of Indians from Yucatan and Honduras, in large numbers, has been earnestly—though privately—discussed in government circles, and that these arguments have mingled in the discussion.—

Vice President Alfau is the leader of this movement and I am inclined to beleive that it will be so conducted as not to meet any dangerous amount of opposition from the masses.

The project is warmly encouraged by the small but powerful clique interested in pressing the European protectorate.— They regard it as part and parcel of the accepted Anglo-French system of servitude, and therefore a natural object of European favor.— They also consider it much cheaper and far more accessible than our form of African slavery, and they beleive the rice and sugar growers of the United States would be unable to compete with them in economy of production.   The ruling thought however of this party is that it would create and confirm a social order in the Antilles which must forever preclude the annexation of any of these islands to the American Union.

I submit these circumstances for what they may be worth, well knowing that my government will be able to detirmine much better than I can their probable value.

With regard to the domestic prospects of the country it remains to all appearance in a hopeful state of repose.— Some public improvements are contemplated and others are proposed by various American Companies, but I have reason to beleive that the most important of them are held in abeyance—like the treaty with Hayti—until Spain shall have decided on the protectorate question.—

It seems hardly worth stating, yet it might be wrong to altogether omit mentioning; that among those of our citizens who are soliciting mining concessions; colonization grants and other priviliges, from the Dominican government there are one or two persons here who are suspected of being the agents of a very questionable "Emigrant Association" from the vicinity of Chesapeake Bay.

I have no evidence of wrong intentions beyond their own statements—as reported to me by respectable parties—that they are the representatives of a strong "order" lately organized with reference to an extensive occupation in St Domingo and counting quite as much upon the rifle as the plough for effecting its views.

All this may have very little solid foundation, but it is unfortunate language as it chills the disposition of this government to open the country freely to our citizens—and the more unfortunate that it has been held at the house of the U. S. Commercial Agent and in the presence of persons already opposed to the spread of American influence in the Dominican Republic.

I have the honor [etc.]

2315

William L. Cazneau, Special Agent of the United States to the Dominican Republic, to Lewis Cass, Secretary of State of the United States [1]

[EXTRACTS]

No. 11   SANTO DOMINGO, *May 12, 1860.*

SIR: In the first dispatches which I had the honor to address to the Department of State, after coming to a frank understanding with this government, I mentioned the extreme depression in which I found our trade in the Dominican ports.

Our merchants could not contend with the double tonnage duties and port charges, in addition to an unfavorable tariff, and they were consequently abandoning the trade altogether to the subjects of France, England, Holland and Denmark, to whom preponderating advantages were secured by formal treaties.

I have labored assiduously to convince the Dominican Government of the incalculable benifits which would enure to its own people from a free and active intercourse with the United States. It could not but see that ours is the only country which can supply them with the men, money and machinery indispensable for the developement of their rich natural resources, and this developement is the only rational reliance of the government for its means of permanent maintenance.—

There were many anti-American fears and prejudices to overcome, but as they were removed I received assurances that in all respects, our people, our productions, and our commerce, should have every immunity and advantage conceded to the most favored nations. This engagement is now honorably redeemed by various concessions to American enterprise which I have heretofore mentioned and finally by the passage of a general law placing the vessels of all nations on an equal footing—a copy and translation of which I herewith enclose.[2]—

The Dominican government has treaties with all the commercial powers of any importance except the United States, and therefore our people are in fact the only parties interested in, and benifited by, this law—and it is so understood by its framers.

Preliminary to this decree of May 9th the commodious harbor of Samana was declared a port of entry and may—if at any time our government choose to negociate for it—be obtained for a coal depot and mail or naval station; and none better can be found in the Antilles.

Macoris, on the south coast—a port of secondery consequence however—is also open to general commerce, and the more important Bay of

[1] Special Agents, vol. 19. Received July 3.
[2] Not included in this publication. It is clipped from a Spanish language newspaper. It is dated May 9, 1860.

Mancenille will probably under certain circumstances be made a free and neutral port and the whole border district between the Haytien and Dominican settlements thrown open to colonists from Europe and the United States.

This extention of port facilities, and the complete establishment of American commerce on an equal basis with that of the most favored nations, must result in throwing the great mass of Dominican commerce in the hands of our citizens.[1] . . .

This government has serious anxieties concerning the Haytien frontier. It seems to be the focus of intrigues and conspiricies of the Baez party and their European as well as Haytien abettors.   Santana has been notified of these disorders and is hourly expected here to take measures for the reinforcement of the border posts.

I have the honor [etc.].

2316

William L. Cazneau, Special Agent of the United States to the Dominican Republic, to Lewis Cass, Secretary of State of the United States [2]

No. 12   SANTO DOMINGO, *July 31, 1860.*

SIR: The *projet* of a Spanish Protectorate of which I had the honor to advise you under date of March 4th (Despatch No. 10) [3]—a duplicate of which I herewith enclose—appears now to be in active process of realization.—

It no longer admits of a doubt that the Spanish and Dominican governments have entered into an understanding to garrison this republic with Ten thousand Spanish Subjects and to place its standing army under the "instructions" of Spanish officials selected and furlowed for this particular duty.

About fifteen hundred persons have already arrived and three vessels more are under government contract and will be due here in the course of the next two weeks, exclusively loaded with Spanish subjects who are to be permanently settled in the Dominican territory.   All of these emigrants are to remain under the protection of the Spanish flag but the entire public domain of the republic is surrendered to their use and occupation.   The whole movement is conducted in a quiet systimatic manner which of itself proves a careful prearrangement.—   Many were at once distributed to lands recently obtained by various members of the government where they are settling down, sober, willing and industrious laborers.

Some years back there was a large emigration from the Canary Islands to Venezuela but not finding that country a safe residence the majority became

[1] This omission relates to claims cases.
[2] Special Agents, vol. 19.   Received September 3.   [3] Above, this part, doc. 2314.

discontented and the Spanish and Dominican governments proposed to give them a more tranquil home in this republic.

On the 28th inst. a Spanish War Steamer arrived direct from Cadiz with nearly a hundred persons to whom the Spanish government had given free passage to Santo Domingo, being—as a member of the government informs me—"citizens of the better class—engineers, teachers and professional men competent to take influential positions among the Dominican people".— The Steamer also landed some arms and munitions, together with a portion of the military men selected to re-organize and instruct the army. Another Spanish Man of War is to follow immediately with a party of three hundred more of these "instructors" for the Dominican people who are to be put in the way of social and military education free of cost by the provident care of the mother country.

The policy of transferring such a large portion of the Dominican soil to Spanish occupants has zealous, though cautious, opponents, for it is feared that the grand ulterior object is the introduction of the coolie systim of servitude, on the basis already established by France, England and Spain in the neiboring colonies.— They foresee that collisions must inevitably arise between the Spanish coolie-masters and the native authorities, which would give occasion for Spain to employ the strongest measures in behalf of her subjects.— It is also feared that this position of supreme yet wholly irresponsible domination accorded to Spain may not only destroy the national independence of the Dominican Republic but seriously impede those close relations with the United States on which the liberals found their main hope for the regeneration of their country.—

On the other hand the advocates of Spanish domination contend that isolated as this republic is from the notice and sympathy of all the other American states, she has no alternative but to throw herself without reserve into the protecting embrace of the mother country who they assert cannot fail to deal generously with them, inasmuch as this island may by adopting the coolie systim become a strong link of security between Cuba and Porto Rico and serve to keep all three out of the grasp of the United States.

They contend that in view of the gealousy of races the only safe and profitable systim of labor which capitalists can depend upon is to be found in the introduction and employment of coolies by European subjects under the guaranties of their respective flags.

A full and steady supply of coolies would as they suppose keep up the industrial prosperity of the Antilles while it would introduce a balancing element between the white and black races.

These are in brief the arguments of those members of the government who are desirous of uniting Cuba St. Domingo & Porto Rico in a common destiny, founded on the three principles of perpetual European domination, the equality of races and a labor-systim in which the United States can take no part—and in consiquence can have no inducement to acquire either of these islands.

President Santana has not yet returned from the Haytien frontier—where he has established perfect order—and it is uncertain how far his judgement will carry him towards the complete subjection of his country to Spanish rule. My own conviction is that he would make even at this late hour a strong effort to maintain the republican independence of the Dominicans were he fortified by a timely recognition and some public demonstration of kindly interest on the part of the United States.

I have the honor [etc.].

2317

William L. Cazneau, Special Agent of the United States to the Dominican Republic, to Lewis Cass, Secretary of State of the United States[1]

No. 14   SANTO DOMINGO, *October 13, 1860.*

SIR: The Spanish guardianship over the Dominican Republic—the progress of which I have had the honor to lay before the Department of State as it advanced [2]—has now become an admitted fact, and is beginning to operate seriously on American interests.

About the 3ᵈ inst. the Dominican government received information that a party of Americans were actively engaged in shipping guano from the rocky islet of Altavela, near the south coast of the Dominican Territory.

This barren little spot, has never been occupied, and in fact was considered uninhabitable, until the American discoverers of the guano deposits made an establishment there, and they were at work for some months before the Dominican authorities heard or thought of such a possibility.

The first intimation came from a Dominican in New York, who heard there of the arrival of valuable guano cargoes from Altavela, and advised this government to claim some advantage out of its contiguity to this republic.

An agent was therefore dispatched to inquire into the case and he returns with the report that he found a small body of American laborors in full possession of Altavela. They were ordered to haul down the flag of the United States and abandon their works. The Americans refused to do either, asserting that they were pursuing a lawful business, under the guaranties of an act of Congress, in utilizing for the general benefit of man-

---

[1] Special Agents, vol. 19. Received November 28.

His No. 13, dated September 10, 1860, is devoted exclusively to reporting that Mr. Jonathan Elliot, United States commercial agent, had become such a hopeless drunkard and had indulged in such excesses and violence when intoxicated, that the Dominican Government had reluctantly, and with apologies, asked his removal. All other citizens of the United States in the Dominican Republic were also asking his removal.

[2] Above, this part, *passim.*

kind a desert sand-spit, which the whole world had previously neglected as utterly valueless, and which no government had deemed worthy of notice until the money and industry of the Citizens of the United States had developed in it an unexpected capacity to yield profits.—The employment of the capital, and the labor, necessary to make Altavela of value, has undoubtedly been the sole work of the parties now in possession.

In opposition to this American position, the Dominican Secretary of State insists that Altavela, though never occupied or used in any manner by this people, has always been considered an appanage of the republic. It is admitted to be more than three leagues from the main coast, but they say it is not that distance from Beata—another and somewhat larger desert island, which intervenes between Altavela and the main shore.

The Dominican Executive has received a full explanation of the scope of the act of Congress respecting the discovery and *exploiting* of guano islands by our citizens, and of the reserved right of our Government to terminate such occupation, at any time that the just representations of a friendly power, or the intrinsic circumstances of the case, may make it proper to take this course.

Upon this explanation the Dominican Cabinet manifested a more amicable disposition, but I regret to say, these friendly assurances were immediately followed by counter-indications from the Spanish officers deputed from Madrid to govern this government.

President Santana is reposing awhile at his estate in the interior, and the Acting Executive, Vice President Alfau, with a portion of the Cabinet, attended Don Mariano Alvarez and Gen¹ Pelaez—the civil and military representatives of Spain—on an official visit to him at Seybo, having regard to this and other matters pertaining to the "protectorate".

On their return yesterday, I obtained a half reluctant admission from the Minister of Foreign Affairs, that while there might be some postponement in the action of the government, it would bind itself to nothing with respect to the American intruders at Altavela.—

The Minister of Hacienda leaves tomorrow, or next day, in the Spanish War Steamer, Don Juan de Austria, to confer with the Captain General, and to negotiate a loan of half a Million of dollars which is promised in Cuba, under the presumed guaranties of Spain.

On the completion of this loan depends the future independence of the Dominican Republic, and with it the safety, or spoliation, of Americans interests in this quarter.

Up to the month of September, the preservation of the Dominican Nationality seemed to turn upon the full and friendly recognition of the United States, but now three fourths of the Cabinet and Senate have become zealous partizans of Spanish rule.

The masses do not concur in this sentiment and the white population of

Santiago and the Vega, murmur ominously of secession, but the Spanish party count upon a sufficiently strong military force from Cuba to suppress any attempt of that kind.

Among all these complications there is imminent danger that American interests may be suddenly distroyed and I have taken the responsibility of calling the attention of the United States Consul General at Havana, to the state of affairs in this direction, and to the propriety of sending a national vessel to Altavela—(copy herewith enclosed) [1] trusting that under the pressure of existing circumstances this course will meet the approval of my government.

I have the honor [etc.].

2318

William L. Cazneau, Special Agent of the United States to the Dominican Republic, to Lewis Cass, Secretary of State of the United States [2]

No. 15   Santo Domingo, *November 17, 1860.*

Sir: The Dominican government after some vacillation has finally decided to accept in full the policy dictated by its Spanish Protectors.

In order to carry out this understanding General Santana is formally invested with a temporary Dictatorship. The promise of military support from Spain, with immediate pecuniary aid, in the form of a loan of half a million of dollars, decided his course as well as that of the "Senate in Council" in its sanction of his assumption of extraordinary powers.

Should this loan happen not to be forthcoming, or should Spain take the alarm and recede from her liberal engagements, or finally should the bitter and wide-spread discontent of the masses, at the re-introduction of their old Spanish masters, break forth in a revolution, there will be an instant change of programme.

In that event the Dominican Republic will once more implore the friendly recognition of the United States, and it will again proffer a free port at Samana or Mancenelle as an inducement to our government to enter into treaty relations.

Unless one or the other of these contingencies should arise to put a new face on affairs, the Dominican Republic—now the avowed ward of the Spanish Crown—will tranquilly subside into a coolie colony under the absolute government of the Mother Country, with possibly an after thought of ultimate cession to France.

[1] Not included in this publication, since it adds nothing of importance to what is embodied in this despatch, excepting possibly, the following sentence: "As this government partly affects to consider them outlaws, they are liable to be arrested and brought to this capital for punishment like common felons."

[2] Special Agents, vol. 19.   Received December 22.

This new policy is likely to be openly proclaimed at an early day, for the leading Spanish Officers not only privately assure the Dominican Cabinet that the United States will soon be forced to abandon the Monroe Doctrin[e], but ostentatiously assert in their social circles that their government is "seeking an opportunity to repress American pretentions in the sea of the Antilles".

Immediately on the return of the Spanish representatives from the late decisive conference with Santana, the Dominican War Schooner La Merced, was ordered to proceed forthwith to Altavela, and a merchant vessel, the Degalo, was pressed to take down a detachment of soldiers.

The expedition found twelve persons at Altavela getting out guano, as they stated, for the firm of Paterson & Murguiondo of Baltimore.

They were ordered to collect their property and quit the island in twenty four hours.—The Dominican officer was informed that the manager, Capt R. S. Kimbal, was absent with the Schooner Alice Mowe, and they had no way of leaving the island until his return.

The commander answered that his instructions were peremptory, but in the absence of other conveyance he would give them passage.

Permission was then asked for one man to remain at Altavela in charge of the property until Capt Kimbal should arrive with the Alice Mowe, that he might learn what had happened and make arrangements for the relief of the party carried to Santo Domingo.

This was also refused and the whole party embarked in the Dominican vessel with as much of their property as could be taken on board. They reached Santo Domingo Oct 27th and were turned over, with their effects, to the United States Commercial Agent, without further proceedings against them.

With the consent of the Dominican commander, a letter to Capt. Kimbal was left where he was likely to meet it on his return to Altavela, informing him of these events, and that he would find his ejected laborers at the City of Santo Domingo.

On the 15th inst Capt Kimbal appeared before this port in the Schooner Alice Mowe, to ask the advice and protection of the United States Commercial agent. He anchored outside and sent in a note to Mr Elliot to that effect. Mr Elliot replied by a verbal direction to come inside; which was accordingly done; though I fear this step may lead to disagreeable results, as the Spanish members of the Dominican Cabinet are inclined to confiscate his vessel.

When the intelligence of the American works at Altavela reached this government, it was thought that the President of the United States—knowing it to be a barren, outlying key, off the desolated coast in dispute between the Dominican Republic and Hayti—had sanctioned its temporary occupation under the corresponding act of Congress.

Hence my anxiety to prevent the entanglements incident to the operators there being carried off by force. Up to this period the Executive has not yielded to those members of the Cabinet who urge severe measures, and I hope the whole affair will be amicably adjusted.

Capt: Kimbal's explanations are to this effect.—He was one of the earliest explorers for guano islands in the Caribbean Sea, and had frequently visited Altavela between the years 1842 and 1860, in which he finally entered upon its occupation. In all these visits, and during his seven months occupation, neither he nor his people had ever met, to the best of his knowledge and belief, a single Dominican in that vicinity, except on one occasion and that one one of no significance, until the period of their expulsion. He generally found Haytiens on the island of Beata (between Altavela and the main land) and always saw them in unmolested possession. The Haytien authorities once sent an Officer to enquire into the business of the Americans at Altavela, but learning they were engaged in a purely industrial pursuit, no objection was made to their stay.

Knowing that Hayti does not admit that the nearest adjacent coast belongs to the Dominican Republic, and seeing that whatever there was of occupation and jurisdiction, was to all appearance fully and exclusively exercised by Haytien Citizens and officials, he contends that he had a right to suppose that he was—at the worst—a tenant by sufferance of the *de facto* sovereign of Altavela, if that island really belonged to any government at all.—

He also asserts that no resistance was ever offered to the Dominican Officers, and that the report of some of the persons sent down in the first instance, that his employees refused to haul down the American flag and evacuate the island, is wholly unfounded.—That was simply an official visit of inquiry, and the occupants gave their answers and explanations in all frankness and respect.—

According to this showing, the case dwindles down to an involuntary trespass on the Dominican soil, and ought to be settled on the spot without much difficulty.

This government considers Altavela an appanage of the province of Azua, but the portion of its territory opposite this island and Beata, is included in the depopulated district foraged by the Haytiens. It is claimed by this republic because it is within the lines of the old Spanish Colony.—Hayti insists that those lines were effaced forever by the fusion of the ancient French and Spanish divisions in one nation.

The dividing line between Hayti and the Dominican Republic is therefore at present an open question, but it is feared here that it will soon be settled on terms terribly adverse to the Dominicans. I am confidentially informed that this government has been notified that France *positively insists* on an immediate treaty with Hayti, and that a naval force may be expected here in a short time to enforce this demand.   That this is the prelude to a compulsory annexation to Hayti, no one in the secret doubts, but what part Spain has taken, or will take, in the affair, is evidently a question of anxious and bewildering uncertainty with every member of this government.[1]

I have the honor [etc.].

[1] Cazneau's next despatch was dated January 11, 1861, which places it outside of the chronological limits of this publication.   It began: "The arrangements for a Spanish protectorate—or more strictly speaking for a military dictatorship—over the Dominican Republic . . . are to be carried into immediate effect."

PART III
COMMUNICATIONS TO ECUADOR

COMMUNICATIONS TO ECUADOR

2319

Edward Livingston, Secretary of State of the United States, to Juan José Flores, President of Ecuador [1]

WASHINGTON, *June 4, 1832.*

SIR: I am directed by the President to say that he has received with great pleasure your letter of the 13th Jany. last[2] by which you announce that you are at the head of the Government of the State of the Equator. Gratified as he is by the terms in which you are pleased to speak of him personally, he is much more so by the assurance you give that the Citizens of the United States enjoy in the State of Equator, all the advantages which are assured to them by the treaty with Colombia, of which your State formed a part, and the consideration, which as citizens of a free State, they ought to enjoy from those of another.

I am also instructed to express the President's hope that a speedy reunion of the several States lately composing the republic of Colombia, may secure the blessings of peace at home and consideration abroad to all its political members, under a free Government wisely administered. No where are the advantages of a Representative Government more highly prized, more ardently desired, for all our sister Republics. No where, are the dissentions, that have afflicted some of them, more deeply deplored than in the United States and by no Government would a friendly intervention to prevent or heal them be more cordially offered to obtain so desirable an end.

I have the Honor [etc.].

2320

John C. Calhoun, Secretary of State of the United States, to Delazon Smith, Special Agent of the United States to Ecuador [3]

[EXTRACTS]

WASHINGTON, *January 7, 1845.*

SIR: The President having appointed you Special Agent of the United States to the Republic of Ecuador, you will herewith receive a sealed letter to the Minister for Foreign Affairs of that Republic, introducing you in your

[1] Notes to Foreign Legations, vol. 5.
[2] Not included in this publication. The purport of the letter is given within this note.
[3] Special Missions, vol. 1.
Delazon Smith, of Ohio, to whom this instruction was addressed, was empowered on December 28, 1844, as special agent to Ecuador, to negotiate concerning claims against Ecuador and the late Republic of Colombia.

official character, and an open copy of the same.[1]   As soon as may be convenient after your arrival at Quito, you will address a note to the Minister, informing him thereof, and requesting him to appoint a time for you to present your letter of introduction.   You will embrace the opportunity which will thereby be afforded you to assure him of the anxious desire of the President to maintain the most friendly relations with the Republic of Ecuador, and that to promote this end is one of the objects of your mission.

The state of our relations and the commerce between the two countries, do not, it is considered, warrant either the establishment, on our part, of a formal mission at Quito or the employment there of a formal diplomatic agent of any grade.   It is believed that the objects contemplated in your mission may be as well accomplished by means of a Special Agent as by a Chargé d'Affaires; and in expressing a desire on the part of our government to cultivate the most friendly relations, you will endeavor, by proper explanations, to allay any dissatisfaction which may be entertained on account of the informal character of your appointment.

Ecuador was one of the three States which composed the Republic of Colombia, and is consequently bound by the liabilities contracted by that Confederacy previous to its dissolution in 1830.   On the 23d of December, 1834, a Convention between those States was signed and subsequently duly ratified, which provided for the adjustment of all the debts of Colombia. By this Convention, New Granada assumed fifty per cent of the debts, Venezuela twenty eight and a half and Ecuador, twenty one and a half per cent. . . .[2]

It will be your duty from time to time to transmit to the department an account of your proceedings.   Accurate information respecting the public affairs and the condition of that country and books and documents illustrative thereof, would be particularly acceptable. . . .[3]

With high respect [etc.].

2321

James Buchanan, Secretary of State of the United States, to Vanbrugh Livingston, United States Chargé d'Affaires at Quito [4]

[EXTRACT]

WASHINGTON, *May 13, 1848.*

SIR: You are the first Diplomatic agent which this government has appointed to reside at the Capital of Ecuador.   The importance of your mis-

[1] Not included in this publication.
[2] The omitted portion refers to claims of citizens of the United States against Ecuador.
[3] The omitted portion contains further reference to claims and mentions other routine matters.
[4] Instructions, Ecuador, vol. I.
Vanbrugh Livingston, of New York, to whom this instruction was addressed, was commissioned as chargé d'affaires to Ecuador on April 10, 1848.   He left on November 12, 1849.

sion is enhanced by this circumstance.   The impression which your personal
conduct and character may make upon the authorities of that government,
will have great influence, not only upon the result of your official proceedings,
but upon the reputation of your country.   You will omit no proper opportunity to declare that our delay in establishing a regular mission at Quito, ought
not to be imputed to any want of interest in the welfare of Ecuador as an independent American Republic.   On the contrary, we have always felt the
liveliest sympathy with her fortunes as well as with those of our other Sister
Republics of this hemisphere, and have expressed this sentiment and acted in
accordance with it, upon every suitable occasion.

The military and naval expedition which General Flores, formerly President of Ecuador, organised a year or two since in Europe for the supposed
purpose of recovering his authority, connived at as it was believed to have
been by some of the monarchical governments of that quarter, created
great alarm, not only in Ecuador itself but in the neighboring Republics,
from the apprehension that its ulterior were more extensive and important
than its ostensible designs.   It was fortunately arrested however, before its
departure, Señor Don Manuel Bustamente, the Minister for Foreign Affairs
of Ecuador, addressed to this Department an interesting communication
upon the subject under date the 26th November 1846,[1] which was received
about the same time that intelligence of the failure of the expedition reached
this City.   Owing to this circumstance, the note was not formally answered,
as any proceedings of this government with reference to the expedition were
rendered unnecessary.   General Castilla, the President of Peru, also made an
informal application in regard to it to Mr Prevost, the Consul of the United
States at Lima.   The accompanying extract from a letter of this Department
to Mr Prevost,[2] embodies the views of the President relative to the expedition, and you may at a proper time communicate the same to the Ecuadorian Minister for Foreign Affairs.   You will also assure him that the intervention or dictation, direct or indirect of European governments in the
affairs of the Independent States of the American Hemisphere, will never be
viewed with indifference by the government of the United States.   On the
contrary, all the moral means, at least, within their power, shall upon every
occasion be employed to discourage and arrest such interference.

The commercial relations between the United States and Ecuador are regulated by the Treaty signed at Quito on the 13th of June 1839.   The operation
of this Treaty is believed to have been mutually advantageous. . . .[3]

I am sir, respectfully [etc.].

[1] Below, this volume, pt. IV, doc. 2342.
[2] The extract referred to was probably taken from a letter from the Secretary of State to
Prevost at Lima, under date, March 24, 1847, for which, see below, volume and part containing Communications to Peru.
[3] The omitted portion relates to pending claims.

2322

William L. Marcy, Secretary of State of the United States, to Philo White,
United States Chargé d'Affaires at Quito [1]

No. 2   WASHINGTON, *August 20, 1853.*

SIR: In assuming the duties devolved upon you by the President, you will
find that our relations with Ecuador are of the most cordial and friendly
character. A large proportion of the just claims held by citizens of the
United States against that government has been placed in a condition of
speedy liquidation, and no doubt is entertained as to the final and satisfactory settlement of any others remaining unadjusted.

The most important question which will probably demand your attention,
and that in which the mutual interests of both countries are intimately involved, is the navigation of the Amazon and its tributaries from Ecuador to
the Atlantic.[2] You are acquainted with the policy Brazil has seen proper to

[1] Instructions, Ecuador, vol. 1.
Philo White, of Wisconsin, to whom this instruction was addressed, was commissioned as
chargé d'affaires to Ecuador on July 18, 1853. He was commissioned as minister resident
on June 29, 1854, and presented his credentials as such on September 2, 1854. He took
leave on September 14, 1858.
[2] The following interesting document bearing on this subject, from the Ecuadoran Chargé
d'Affaires to his home government, the original of which was not found, was transcribed from
Ecuador, Notes, vol. 1. This translation was undoubtedly made in the Department of State,
and presumably the original was personally left by the Ecuadoran Chargé d'Affaires with the
Secretary of State, and subsequently returned to him, since there was nothing in the manuscript volume to indicate that it was sent as an enclosure in any note from him.

José Villamil, Ecuadoran Chargé d'Affaires at Washington, to Teodoro Gómez de la
Torre, Minister of Foreign Affairs of Ecuador

[TRANSLATION]

WASHINGTON, *June 7, 1853.*

SEÑOR MINISTRO: I arrived at this Capital on the 3d instant. On the following day I
called at the Department of State, to inform the Secretary of State that I would not
solicit my official reception as yet, in consequence of my suffering greatly from pain in
the breast. I did not find him at his office. On the 5th our Consul General called to inform him that I was confined to my bed. I still continue sick.
It would have been unworthy of me, Señor Ministro, to have accepted a mission to
my native land [He was born in the United States but lived many years in Ecuador.—
Ed.] if I had not contemplated to further the interests of the country of my children. I
keep that object in view. In my travels from New Orleans to this capital, having
traversed several of the Southern and Western States of the Union, and come in contact
with many of the most influential men in those States, I had an opportunity to find out
the predominant feeling of the day. This feeling points towards the "Amazons."
Since my arrival, notwithstanding my sickness, I have conversed with many prominent men, and there is not the slightest doubt that a great Commercial and colonization
movement is preparing in South America. The late measures adopted by the governments of Peru and of Bolivia, would have convinced me on that point, if I had entertained any doubt.
In this state of things, I ought to introduce the interests of Ecuador in the question
which will very soon create a commotion in Venezuela, New Granada, Peru, Bolivia,
Buenos Ayres, and Brazil, but having glanced over my instructions, I find, with extreme
regret, that I am not authorized to take any part in this great question. I do not believe, therefore, that I can do anything without new instructions. I abstain from asking
for any; but my love for Ecuador would render it a crime on my part, were I to omit sub-

adopt in reference to the exclusion of Foreign Commerce from all access to
the Pacific Republics through the waters of this South American inland highway,—a policy which this government considers alike unjust and unwise.
The Republics of Venezuela, New Granada, Ecuador, Peru and Bolivia are

---

mitting some remarks to you, on the subject, for the information of the President of the
Republic.   I beg that you will give me all your attention.

The excitement in this country, in regard to the free navigation of the "Amazon,"
and the establishment of Commercial Relations with those Republics whose eastern
waters fall into that river, amounts to enthusiasm: it borders upon delirium.

At the present moment, the people of all the States, in the Mississippi Valley, and of
all those along the coast, South of Maryland, are assembled in convention in the city
of Memphis, State of Tenessee; and one of the objects of this convention, as it may be
seen from the language of the address, calling for the same, is to take into consideration
the question of the "Amazon" as it has been presented by Lieutenant Maury in his
writings.

The late decrees of Peru and Bolivia, establishing free ports in those branches of the
"Amazon" belonging to them, have been well received here, although the most thinking
men in the country, do not consider them sufficiently liberal to accomplish the object
which those governments have in view.   In these decrees, emigrants are promised small
grants of land, seeds, and instruments for cultivation.   An exemption from taxation
etc, for a certain number of years is likewise promised to them.   These offers are not, in
fact, sufficient to stimulate capitalists, nor to induce farmers to venture upon unknown
lands.   It is necessary, at first, fully to survey this land, and produce evidence of its advantages.

Moreover, Brazil keeps the entrance to the "Amazons" closed, and the small amount
of trade which at the present time, is carried on with those republics that are in possession of the upper part of that river, will never stimulate anybody to go in search of the
advantages, that said portion of the river may present.   Hence it is that the decrees of
Bolivia and Peru have failed to induce capitalists to venture to operate in that direction;
and hence it is also, that in this country, where the most enterprising men in the world
are to be found, no one has been known as yet, to talk, even, of taking advantage of the
privileges granted by those governments.

From what I have been able to gather, this is now the true state of the question concerning the "free navigation of the Amazons" and it is this very state of indecision
which impels Ecuador to take a part, in regard to those immense regions which she
possesses eastward of the eastern branch of the "Cordillera" whose waters flow into the
"Amazon."

The government must, therefore, give an impulse to those luxuriant regions; this impulse should be properly directed, and for that purpose, it must do more than Peru and
Bolivia have done; it must tear asunder the veil which conceals our Eastern provinces
from the eyes of the world, in order to enlist the powerful influence of this colossal
republic and to enable the latter, by this means, to obtain from Brazil, the free navigation of the river Amazon; and in order to be able to aid the spirit of enterprise and the
energy of the capitalists of this country, who are indispensable to us, for developing the
resources which the eastern part of our Republic offers to the world.   Let us to work
then, tearing asunder the veil, in the manner which I shall point out hereafter.

It is generally believed here that President Pierce wishes to signalize his administration by means of the free navigation of the "Amazons."   Should he succeed in this
nothing would equal his popularity and his éclat in this country; and, as the time for
opening negotiations with Brazil, on this important question, has not as yet arrived, he
has no decent pretext whatever for requiring any thing from Brazil, in this respect.   It
is certain that Bolivia and Peru have invited the whole world to the enterprise; but
whether it be on account of the country not being yet known, or whether it be owing to
reasons which have already been explained, the short of it is, that no Capitalist in the
United States seems disposed to accept of the invitation, nor to ask his government to
open to him the way to the "Amazons."

I am however inclined to believe that this government would, without any hesitation,
embrace any plausible pretext for taking the initiative with Brazil, in regard to the
question of "free navigation of the Amazons"; and therefore I should wish that our
government would not allow the opportunity to escape, for calling the attention of this
government to the immense amount of commercial treasures which lay hidden among

all interested in procuring the removal of the restrictions which now, practically, deprive them in a considerable degree of the advantages and resources of that portion of their respective territories which would be thereby opened to an extensive and profitable foreign commerce. Possessing an area

---

the resources that are as yet undeveloped in the eastern section of Ecuador and to ask the United States to send two of their war steamers to explore the *Napo*, the *Pastasa* and the other branches of the Amazon as far as their head sources: This is the way of making the world know the value of our eastern regions.

It is generally believed that the Cabinet of General Pierce would receive a request of this kind from our government with enthusiasm. At least several members of the Cabinet have given assurances to that effect. They assert, moreover, that with this request of Ecuador in one hand, they could say to Brazil, "here we have an invitation given us to send an expedition to explore the Ecuadorial head sources of the 'Amazon' for the purpose of facilitating discoveries and the acquisition of knowledge; for the benefit, not of Ecuador, nor of the United States, but for the benefit of commerce in general, —of the whole world."

What would be the results of such a step on the part of Ecuador and of the United States? Brazil is a country too much advanced in civilization to offer any opposition, at the present period of the world, to the progress of knowledge and to the march of the age; and she cannot be so blind, and so utterly destitute of that spirit of enterprise and of liberality which, at this day, characterizes all the nations of the world, with few exceptions, which is even a cause of shame to them, as to refuse a transit by the "Amazon" to this mission of peace and of good will.

This expedition although undertaken at the invitation,—at the instance of Ecuador, its expenses would be defrayed by the United States without the least responsibility on our part; as soon as it had attained the end which it would encompass, it would prove to be precisely one of those enterprises, by which Ecuador can gain much, without running the slightest risk of losing any thing.

If Brazil should refuse to grant a free passage to the exploring vessels, she would derive no other advantage than to excite more and more the prejudices of the world, concerning her exclusive policy, in regard to the "Amazons" and in relation to her uniform conduct towards those nations, who are in possession of the other branches of this river and who can do nothing by themselves, as to the exploration of their own rivers.

If she should allow transit to these vessels because they are vessels of war, and out of deference to the mission, keeping the entrance closed against merchant vessels, the expedition being, as it would be, commanded by well-experienced and scientific officers of the American navy would reveal to us, at all events, the value of our treasures which are as yet concealed in the heart of our eastern regions. The progress of the expedition would attract the attention of all the world, and, on the opening of the navigation (which soon or late will happen) people would pour into our eastern regions, which they would convert from horrid deserts, as they are now, into smiling gardens.

Let us suppose, on the other side, that the negotiations (which must necessarily be set on foot before long) should terminate in the free navigation of the "Amazon," towards which the contemplated expedition could not fail to contribute materially, Ecuador would still derive the first advantage from this stupendous event, and the greater glory would be hers.

A considerable amount of money has been devoted by Peru to the exploration of the head-waters of the "Amazon" which run through her territory. There is at this moment here an individual lately arrived from Lima, with whom the Peruvian Government has contracted for two steamers, one of fifty tons and the other eighty, for the sum of seventy five thousand dollars, and I am credibly informed that the two steamers will not cost one fourth of the amount above mentioned.

Let us suppose that Brazil allows these vessels to ascend the "Amazon," as belonging to one of the republics which possess unquestionably rights to the navigation of that river, what will be the result? Perú has no men experienced in the management of river steamers, and it may be predicted, without hazarding much, that this Peruvian expedition will, for some cause or other, run aground somewhere. A river steamer cannot be managed with the same facility as a steamship on the high seas, without dearly bought experience.

Let us avail ourselves of the errors (?) the experience, and the unconquerable perseverance of the North Americans. Before the government or the citizens of Ecuador, under-

somewhat greater in the aggregate than two-thirds of the territory of Brazil, these countries, lacking the power which unity of purpose and effort exerts, are compelled to submit to the exactions of their more powerful neighbor.

Bolivia and Peru have already taken steps for testing the extent to which the pretensions of Brazil may be maintained;—they have opened free ports

take at their own expense, to navigate their branches of the "Amazon" by steam, let us smooth away the road by means of the skill and the experience of the United States in this species of navigation.   The North American people, owing to the number and extent of their rivers are infinitely more skilful than any other, in all that relates to the management of river steamers.   I have acquired this conviction during a journey of 2000 miles which I have just made from New Orleans to Wheeling.   I was lost in wonder and admiration, in beholding a palace three stories high, resting upon a body measuring more than one hundred yards in length, six inches above water, and less than five feet draught, managed with the same facility as a Peruvian tamer of horses, manages his horse.

I entertain but very little doubt of the success of the measure which I propose, and of the exploration under the management of this government, if I, (or any other person) were authorized to propose the fitting out of the expedition, to be commanded by officers of the American Navy: Above all, there is nothing to be lost in proposing the matter; and when I suggest such a proposition, it must be supposed that I do not venture upon such a step without reflection.

This question which engrosses my mind in so positive a manner, is of vast importance; and the amount of interests which Ecuador has, depending upon it, both in regard to the free navigation of the "Amazon" and the improvement of her uncultivated eastern lands, is of two much magnitude for us to hesitate as to the means to be adopted for accomplishing the object.   We not only want the immediate exploration of our branches of the Amazon, and the free navigation of that river, but we want to introduce river steamers there, trade, and settlers; and while we ought to encourage the latter by every available means it is our interest, and it should be our cardinal & unvarying principle of action, to grant no monopolies, unless it be but for a very short time.   We should stimulate commerce and the spirit of enterprise throughout the world without allowing any one the right of monopolizing any branch of industry.

I would therefore propose, that "Assumption" on the banks of the Putumayo; "San Miguel" on the banks of the Napo; "Pinchez" on the banks of the "Pastasa," or any other ports on the banks of these rivers, be declared "free ports" and that the vessels of all friendly nations be invited to frequent them, with the assurance, that neither the vessels aforesaid nor their cargoes, shall be subjected to the payment of any duty, until new provisions be made, which will not be enforced before the expiration of two years after the publication of the corresponding announcement.

I would likewise propose that American Capitalists be stimulated to introduce, from this moment, steamers and emigrants upon our branches of the "Amazon."   I say, "American Capitalists" not only on account of the eminent skill of the Americans, in the construction and the management of river steamers, but also on account of the solicitude with which the government of the United States watches over the commercial interests of its citizens.   Let them be encouraged to come over with their vessels, and they will become our most powerful auxiliaries in this enterprise, for they will never cease urging upon their government the necessity of opening negotiations with Brazil, in order to obtain the great result which the world is waiting with impatience—"The free navigation of the Amazons."

Such, Señor Ministro, are the suggestions which I deem it my duty to submit to you, for the information of H.E. the President of the Republic.

You will moreover allow me to remind you, that in consequence of the imprudent dismemberment of Columbia, Ecuador has had to struggle with a considerable debt; a debt which worries and exhausts all the resources of her inhabitants; a debt which never will be paid unless we have recourse to extraordinary measures; a debt which increases daily; a debt, in short, which will become the consuming cancer of Ecuador, if it be not cut off and the wound healed up.   This debt intimidates the nation and depresses the government, because they both believe the payment to be extremely difficult.   It is a mistake.   Nothing is more easy to Ecuador than the payment of this debt.   Let Ecuador strain all her nerves; let her bring into action that energy which is the distinguishing characteristic of the present age; let her turn her immense, known resources to advan-

and established local government thereat:—they have offered every facility and many inducements to traders and settlers;—and this government has every reason to believe that Ecuador is in no respect behind these countries in liberality of spirit and enterprise.   With her Southern boundary washed by the main branch of the Amazon, there are advantages offered to her by her direct communication with the ocean, which none of the smaller States mentioned can so preëminently enjoy.   Besides, she is now governed by an enlightened and liberal administration, which you will, doubtless, find ready and anxious to coöperate with the United States, and with her nearer sister Republics, in a just effort to secure the freedom of the Amazon.   To this end, it would be well for you, at a proper time, to present to the government the advantages that would accrue to Ecuador, in following the example of Bolivia and Peru.   For, when all of the five States, whose fertile regions are watered by the Amazon and its tributaries, shall have thrown open their rivers and ports to foreign commerce, it is thought that Brazil will not be able long to withstand the moral power which will thus be arrayed against her selfish and restrictive policy.   And I speak thus confidently as to the probable course of Ecuador, when this subject shall be directly presented to her attention, because Mr. Clay, our present Minister at Lima, has already addressed the Ecuadorian Minister in Peru, upon this subject, and has received from him every encouragement to believe that the project is viewed not unfavorably by his Government.[1]

For your information in regard to the policy of the United States, I enclose, herewith, a copy of the instructions given to Mr. Trousdale, our recently appointed Envoy to Brazil.[2]   Concert of action among the several representatives of the United States, residing in those countries directly interested in the subject presented in this instruction, cannot fail to contribute materially to a successful result.

I am, Sir, respectfully [etc.].

---

tage; and, above all, let her propose, at once, the exploration of her branches of the Amazon, and the debt will be paid.

You will observe that the trade which will immediately spring up, by way of the Pacific, is destined to eclipse the trade which has been carried on in every part of the world, until now.   Behold the whole of the Eastern Coast of Asia shaking hands with the Western Coast of both Americas!   Behold Europe and Africa wending their way towards the Darien! and mark you, what will happen.   Men disappear from the scene of action; nations are immortal!   Ecuador is a nation; she possesses innumerable elements of prosperity.   Why should we allow ourselves to be crushed by a debt which we can pay by means of the treasures hidden in the lap of our Eastern possessions?   Moreover, Señor Ministro, God has created the Torrid Zone to be the abode of man.   All the varied climates of the earth are to be found there; the future of Ecuador is unbounded; let the Ecuadorian people only wish to be great and happy, and they will be *great* and *happy*.

With sentiments of perfect consideration,
I have the honor [etc.].

[1] See note from Moncayo, the Ecuadoran minister to Peru, to Clay, dated March 14, 1853, in a footnote to Clay's No. 135 of March 25, 1853, to the Secretary of State, below, in the volume and part containing Communications from Peru.

[2] Above, vol. II, August 8, 1853, doc. 484.

2323

William L. Marcy, Secretary of State of the United States, to General José Villamil, Ecuadoran Chargé d'Affaires at Washington [1]

WASHINGTON, *November 2, 1853.*

The undersigned, Secretary of State of the United States, has the honor to acknowledge the receipt of the Note of General Villamil, Chargé d'Affaires of the Republic of Ecuador, of yesterday,[2] representing that another hostile expedition against that Republic has been organized in part, in upper California, and requesting that orders may be given to the authorities in that State with a view to its suppression.   In reply, the Undersigned has the honor to acquaint General Villamil, that, standing orders on this subject had previously been given to those authorities, and there is reason to believe that they are vigilant in carrying them into effect.   In compliance with General Villamil's request, however, those orders have been repeated.

The undersigned [etc.].

2324

William L. Marcy, Secretary of State of the United States, to General José Villamil, Ecuadoran Chargé d'Affaires at Washington [3]

WASHINGTON, *December 5, 1853.*

The undersigned, Secretary of State of the United States, has the honor to acknowledge the receipt of the Note of General Villamil, Chargé d'Affaires of the Republic of Ecuador, of the 1st instant,[4] upon the subject of a publication in the San Francisco Commercial Advertiser, of the 29th of October last, entitled "Movements in South America."

In reply, the undersigned has the honor to state, that the freedom which, as General Villamil is aware, is the privilege and the characteristic of the press of this country, usually leads to an expression, on its part, of various opinions and, not unfrequently, to the indulgence of extravagant speculations, especially in regard to the foreign policy of the Government of the United States.   That policy, however, so far at least, as it may relate to the independent countries of the American hemisphere is well known, has long been established, and, so far as the Undersigned is aware, no change therein is either probable or contemplated.

[1] Notes to Bolivia and Ecuador, vol. 1.
José Villamil, to whom this note was addressed, presented his credentials as chargé d'affaires of Ecuador to the United States on June 10, 1853.   He took leave on April 13, 1854. He was born in the United States, but lived many years in Ecuador.
[2] Below, this volume, pt. IV, doc. 2384.
[3] Notes to Bolivia and Ecuador, vol. 1.
The date of this note was originally written in the file copy as 1855, but the last 5 was cancelled, and the figure 3 written in pencil above it.   The correct date is evidently 1853.
[4] Below, this volume, pt. IV, doc. 2386.

Under these circumstances, the Undersigned trusts that General Villamil will find no occasion for his sensibility to be excited by unauthorized and irresponsible newspaper publications.

The undersigned [etc.].

2325

William L. Marcy, Secretary of State of the United States, to General José Villamil, Ecuadoran Chargé d'Affaires at Washington [1]

WASHINGTON, *January 31, 1854.*

The Undersigned, Secretary of State of the United States, referring to his letter of the 2ᵈ November, last,[2] has now the honor to enclose to General Villamil, Chargé d'Affaires of the Republic of Ecuador, a copy of a letter just received from the District Attorney of the United States, for the Northern District of California, dated the 23ᵈ December, last,[3] from which General Villamil will learn that no apprehensions are entertained by that officer of any violation of the territory of Ecuador by expeditions sailing from California, and that, should any hostile demonstrations against the peace of a friendly nation be made, the laws of the United States, applicable to such cases, will be promptly executed.

The undersigned [etc.].

2326

William L. Marcy, Secretary of State of the United States, to Philo White, United States Chargé d'Affaires at Quito [4]

[EXTRACTS]

No. 14   WASHINGTON, *August 14, 1854.*

SIR: You are aware, I presume, of the importance of Guano to the agricultural interests of the United States. Hitherto the country has been for the most part dependent on Peru for this valuable manure. The principal source of supply being on the Peruvian Islands, that Government is able to control in the article the markets of this country, and to make it a fruitful source of revenue. Our citizens resorting to the guano Islands are obliged to pay an exorbitant price for it, and are subjected to much delay and expense in procuring cargoes. The Government of Peru itself is connected with some houses here and share in the proceeds of the business. The effect of these arrangements is that guano can only be obtained at a very high price, and the supply at any rate is inadequate to the demand. The Government of the

¹ Notes to Bolivia and Ecuador, vol. 1.   ² Above, this part, doc. 2323.
³ Not included in this publication, since its content is indicated within this instruction.
⁴ Instructions, Ecuador, vol. 1.

United States has failed in its endeavors to make any arrangement with that of Peru whereby our citizens would be able to get a full supply at a fair price. . . .[1]

If you should find it impossible to secure an exclusive right for this country, you will contract for a full participation by our citizens in a common right freely to resort to the Galapagos Islands for guano, paying therefor a specified rate per ton with an express stipulation, that other nations shall be charged a price at least equal to that agreed to be paid by our citizens, and that the latter are at all times to be supplied with it on as favorable terms as may be granted to others.

Perhaps the Ecuadorian Government would prefer to grant, for a fair consideration, to the United States, the right to exclusive possession of its islands, for a long term of years, or in perpetuity with an unrestricted right to take away the guano found thereon.

Without more knowledge than we possess here at this time, it is impossible to form an opinion of what such a grant would be worth. Should it be ascertained that there was on these Islands, an inexhaustible supply of guano of a good quality, the United States would very readily give a liberal sum for such a grant, unencumbered with any private rights. I can conceive the quality and quantity to be such as this government might consent to pay two or three millions for the islands, or the unrestricted and exclusive right, in perpetuity, or for a long term of years to resort to them for that article. The supply may be so limited, and the article of such a character, that the grant would be a bad bargain, at a far less sum,—perhaps indeed, worth but very little. Should you make an arrangement of this kind you will take pains to collect all the information you can gather on the subject, and transmit it to this government, that it may be enabled to determine the question of accepting or rejecting it. Whatever arrangement you may make, it must, necessarily, be laid before the Senate for its concurrence therein, and it will naturally be expected that the government will be able to furnish the members of that body with information in relation to the benefits to be derived from the proposed contract.

Should your efforts to make any arrangement on the subject fail altogether our citizens might derive considerble advantage, if there be a rich deposite of guano on the Galapagos islands, in obtaining the recognition of Mr. De Brissot's rights as a discoverer. If these rights are as extensive as he believes them to be, and if they were recognized in an explicit manner, and under circumstances which would warrant this Government to interpose to protect them in case they were invaded, our citizens might, by arrangement with him, derive advantages important to our agricultural interest and

[1] The omitted portion directs White to support the efforts of De Brissot, a citizen of the United States, to obtain a favorable concession, exclusive, if possible, for removing the guano of which he claimed to be the discoverer, and encloses to him a full power from the President to enter into a convention with Ecuador on the subject.

general prosperity.   You will therefore do what you can, in case you fail to
make any of the arrangements above suggested, to get his claim as discoverer
recognized in its fullest extent and obtain in behalf of your Government, a
guarantee from that of Ecuador, that his right shall be respected and made
available in his hands, or in those of his assignees.

It may be advisable, though I can hardly conceive it will be, to get De
Brissot's rights recognized, defined and secured, preparatory to entering on
the negotiation for a convention with the United States.   If, in your judgment, this should be so, it is not intended by the foregoing remarks to prevent
you from aiding in such an arrangement, but in case you do, you will take
care to have inserted in any arrangement between him and the Government
of Ecuador a limit to the sum which he shall be allowed to charge to the
citizens of the United States, and bring down that sum as low as possible
consistently with a fair and reasonable reward to him for his discovery.

It is so entirely uncertain what will be the character of the agreement you
will be able to make, that it is not possible to furnish you with any form of a
convention for a guide.   You will adopt with the modifications which circumstances may require the usual Introduction to ordinary Treaties between
the United States and other powers.   The stipulations which will follow will
be in the nature of an agreement or contract.   The articles of any Treaty
will furnish you with the formal expression proper to be used on the occasion.

You will communicate freely and frequently with this Department on the
foregoing, as well as other subjects of a public interest.

I am, Sir, respectfully [etc.].

2327

William L. Marcy, Secretary of State of the United States, to Philo White,
United States Minister Resident in Ecuador

No. 16   WASHINGTON, *October 18, 1854.*

SIR: [Same as instruction No. 8, of this date, to John W. Dana, U. S.
Minister to Bolivia, concerning maritime law.] [1]

2328

William L. Marcy, Secretary of State of the United States, to Philo White,
United States Minister Resident in Ecuador [2]

No. 17   WASHINGTON, *October 31, 1854.*

SIR: It is apprehended that the suggestion contained in your Nº 28[3] in
regard to articles upon the subject of the navigation of the Amazon, in the

---

[1] Above, vol. II, doc. 391.   [2] Instructions, Ecuador, vol. I.
[3] See below, this volume, pt. IV, August 22, 1854, doc. 2397.

form you mention, might be construed by Peru, if not as a guarantee to Ecuador of ports and places on the river which she claims, yet as an uncourteous disregard on our part of her claim to those ports and places. Under these circumstances, it is deemed advisable and more in accordance with the well settled policy of the United States, to wait until the boundary between Ecuador and Peru shall have been adjusted, before we conclude a treaty with either party which may contain a stipulation relating to territory which may be claimed by the other.

I am, Sir, respectfully [etc.].

2329

William L. Marcy, Secretary of State of the United States, to Philo White, United States Minister Resident in Ecuador [1]

No. 23   WASHINGTON, *July 11, 1855.*

SIR: Your despatches to No. 55,[2] inclusive, have been received.

In that numbered 55, you translate a paragraph of General Flores' recent Manifesto, to the following effect:—

> And if fortune shall some day place me in a situation to vindicate my rights, acknowledged by the representatives of England, France, Spain, the United States and Chile, (who recognize the quarrel between myself and the violators of the public faith in Ecuador as a domestic affair) the people of Peru and their noble chief shall receive my unfeigned acknowledgments and gratitude for their kind hospitality.

You state that this declaration had excited much concern; that enquiries had been addressed to you for the purpose of ascertaining its truth; and that both in behalf of this Government, of yourself, and of your Colleagues in South America, you had expressed your disbelief that any such statement was warranted by facts; and you desire an explicit expression of opinion upon the subject.

After the assurances so recently given to General Villamil, the diplomatic representative of Ecuador in the United States,—assurances which were confirmed by the active exertions of the officers of this Government to maintain the integrity of the neutrality laws, when there was reason to apprehend their violation by General Flores,[3]—it is somewhat to be wondered at, that the Government of Ecuador should attach the slightest consequence to the vague intimations of General Flores, when alluding, in his manifesto, to the acknowledgment of his rights by the representatives of the United States. Of itself, and with reference to its citizens, this Government will maintain the

---

[1] Instructions, Ecuador, vol. I.
[2] For No. 55, see below, this volume, pt. IV, May 23, 1855, doc. 2411.
[3] See the notes from the Secretary of State to Villamil, above, this part, November 2, 1853, and January 31, 1854, docs. 2323 and 2325.

strictest neutrality towards the contending parties of other countries, recognizing the Government established by the popular will, and scrupulously repressing any known attempt on the part of its citizens to interfere with the tranquility of other nations.

The Department cannot of course, know to what extent the private expression of opinion by the Diplomatic Agents of the United States, in South America, may have given color to the statement of General Flores; but it has that confidence in their discretion which warrants the belief that they would not, either officially, or otherwise, afford the slightest encouragement to any individual or party, contemplating an invasion of a country at peace with the United States. On the contrary it is well understood that some of these Agents are using all proper influence to induce the Governments to which they are accredited to discountenance and discourage the hostile movements, which, it is feared, General Flores is endeavoring to organize against the present administration in Ecuador.

I am, Sir, respectfully [etc.].

2330

*William L. Marcy, Secretary of State of the United States, to Philo White,
United States Minister Resident in Ecuador*

No. 32   WASHINGTON, *July 14, 1856.*

SIR: [Same as instruction No. 20, of this date, to James A. Peden, U. S. Minister to Argentina, concerning maritime law.][1]

2331

*William L. Marcy, Secretary of State of the United States, to Philo White,
United States Minister Resident in Ecuador*

No. 33   WASHINGTON, *August 29, 1856.*

SIR: [Same as instruction No. 24, of this date, to James A. Peden, U. S. Minister to Argentina, concerning maritime law.][2]

[1] Above, vol. I, doc. 32.   [2] *Ibid.*, doc. 34.

PART IV

COMMUNICATIONS FROM ECUADOR

COMMUNICATIONS FROM ECUADOR

2332

James C. Pickett, United States Chargé d'Affaires to the Peru-Bolivian Confederation, to John Forsyth, Secretary of State of the United States [1]

[EXTRACT]

No. 3   QUITO, *January 30, 1839.*

SIR: . . . The latest accounts from Peru, represent that country as being still in a very unsettled state. It is the general impression in Quito, that although Gen[1] Santa Cruz may succeed in driving the Chilians out of Peru, yet that the experiment of the Peru-Bolivian Confederation is a failure, and that it must be abandoned. It is unpopular in Ecuador, and in all South America, I believe. It is believed (right or wrong) to have originated in the ambition of Santa Cruz, and that he has more at heart, his own personal aggrandizement than the welfare and prosperity of the states, of which he is the Chief. The title too, of Protector, which he has assumed, has given much offence. Those who find fault with it, say, that it is arrogant and presumptuous in any man, to style himself the Protector of countries, claiming to be free and independent, and which ought to be able to protect themselves.

There is but little room to hope, that I shall be successful in settling the claims of the citizens of the United States, on my arrival at Lima; and although in my last communication, I said, that it was rather early, either to despair or to despond, yet in truth, there is but little to encourage me. Señor Vidaurre, who is the Peruvian Commissioner for settling those claims, is now in Quito, in the capacity of a Minister Plenipotentiary from the Peru-Bolivian Confederation, and it is altogether uncertain, when he will return to Peru. There is also a Chargé d'Affaires commissioned by Gen[1] Gamarra, when he was in possession of Lima. The President has received them both, the rule here, being to receive all the diplomatic agents that are sent; it being left to the Gov'ts sending them to decide which is the rightful representative.

I think I will leave Quito for Lima, as soon as I conclude a treaty, without

---

[1] Despatches, Peru, vol. 5. Received June 8.

This and subsequent despatches relating to Ecuador were probably bound in the above volume because Mr. Pickett, the writer, had been commissioned chargé d'affaires to the Peru-Bolivian Confederation and had been empowered to negotiate a treaty with Ecuador before proceeding to his post in Peru. See the biographical sketch of him, vol. v, p. 479, note 1.

The two omitted portions of this despatch relate chiefly to his efforts and the prospects of success in negotiating a treaty of commerce and navigation.

waiting for the action of the Congress, which may not take place, until the month of May. . . .

I have the honor [etc.].

2333

James C. Pickett, United States Chargé d'Affaires to the Peru-Bolivian Confederation, to John Forsyth, Secretary of State of the United States [1]

[EXTRACT]

No. 5   QUITO, *February 27, 1839.*

SIR: . . . I received a letter a few days since, from the U. S. Consul at Lima, in which he says, that Gen[l]. Santa Cruz has been entirely defeated, in a battle fought with the Chilians, on the 20th of January last, ninety leagues from Lima, having lost, in killed, wounded &[c] 4050 men. He considers the Peru-Bolivian Confederation at an end, and advises me, if accredited to that Government only, to apply for new credentials, to be addressed to the Gov't of Peru or North Peru. He adds, that he wrote to this effect to the Department of State, on the 26th of November last. I think his suggestion a good one, for if the Confederation is not at an end already, it soon will be, no doubt, & so will be my mission to Lima, without other credentials. . . .

I have the honor [etc.].

2334

Luis de Saá, Minister of Foreign Affairs of Ecuador, to James C. Pickett, United States Chargé d'Affaires to the Peru-Bolivian Confederation [2]

[EXTRACT]

QUITO, *March 8, 1839.*

The Undersigned has examined the *projet* of a treaty of peace, friendship, navigation and commerce, between the United States of America and the republic of Ecuador, which Sr. J. C. Pickett, Minister Plenipotentiary of said states, has been pleased to present, and he makes the following observations:

1st. That a law of the 21st of March 1837, having granted some particular privileges to vessels built in the dock yards of Ecuador, the encourage-

---

[1] Despatches, Peru, vol. 5. Received June 8.

The omitted portions at the beginning and end of this despatch, report that he has made no progress with a treaty of commerce and navigation, but that he no longer fears the French influence in Ecuador against his making one.

[2] Despatches, Peru, vol. 5; enclosed with Pickett to the Secretary of State, No. 7, May 1, 1839, below, this part, doc. 2338.

The omitted portion at the end of this despatch relates to observations on the seventh, tenth and twelfth articles of the treaty, which concern real estate and other matters, not pertinent to this publication.

ment of which is absolutely necessary, for the prosperity to which its ports ought to aspire, it is essential, that in the second article of the *projet* presented, there should be an exception made in favor of those vessels, which are not now comprehended in it.

2nd.   That the aforesaid second article shall not prevent any conventions whatever, that Ecuador may think proper to conclude with Spain and the new republics of South America, more advantageous for them; and shall not be regarded as authorising any claim for extending them to the United States; since the relations that exist between Ecuador, the Peninsula, and the new republics of South America, may, by their peculiarity, require stipulations, not usual, and confined to them alone. . . .

very obedient Servant.

2335

James C. Pickett, United States Chargé d'Affaires to the Peru-Bolivian Confederation, to Luis de Saá, Minister of Foreign Affairs of Ecuador [1]

[EXTRACT]

QUITO, *March 15, 1839.*

The Undersigned, Plenipotentiary of the United States, has had the honor to receive the note of His Excellency the Minister of Foreign Relations &ᶜ dated the 8th instant,[2] and containing observations upon the *projet* of a treaty between the U. S. and Ecuador, submitted by him on the 4th of January last; and upon these observations, he begs leave to make the following remarks:

To the first observation of His Excellency, he replies; that the privilege granted by a law of Ecuador, of March 21st 1837, to vessels built in the dockyards of this country, may be secured to them, by a clause to be inserted in the second article of the treaty, or in any other article that may be more suitable.

Upon the second observation, the Undersigned has to remark, that to subject the provisions of a treaty between the U. S. and Ecuador, to be controlled, modified or annulled by treaties to be made hereafter, between Ecuador, Spain and the Republics of South America, would be attended, probably, with so many inconveniences, that a treaty, formed upon a basis so contingent and uncertain, does not seem, to the Undersigned, to be, either desirable or expedient.   There are treaties now subsisting, between the United States and the following Hispano-American states; Mexico, Central America, Venezuela, Chile and the Peru-Bolivian Confederation. In none of them can be found, a provision similar to the one proposed; and the Undersigned is well satisfied, that no such proposition was made on the part

[1] Despatches, Peru, vol. 5; enclosed with Pickett to the Secretary of State, No. 7, May 1, 1839, below, this part, doc. 2338.   [2] Above, this part, doc. 2334.

of those states; or if made, the final result shews, that it was abandoned. And it may be added, that the treaty between the U. S. and the Republic of Colombia, which was in force twelve years in Ecuador, and until the year 1837, contained no article of the kind.

If the treaties between Ecuador and Spain and the states of South America, now contemplated, were already made and in force, the position of the United States towards Ecuador, would then be very different. In that case, the latter might insist, with great propriety, that they should be respected, and that a treaty with the United States must conform to their provisions.

The basis, upon which the United States have always negotiated treaties, is, *equal favors & reciprocity*. Upon these principles, the first treaties they formed, after becoming an independent nation, were based; and they have been maintained, in all subsequent negotiations. This is now, the settled policy of the United States, and experience has shewn it to be sound and safe, as well as liberal & enlightened. To it, is to be attributed, in a great degree, the unparalleled commercial prosperity of those states; and, if adopted and pursued by Ecuador, why might it not be followed by the same results, in this country?

It is known to His Excellency, that the late Executive Chief of Ecuador (Sor. Rocafuerte) invited the Government of the United States, to send an agent to Quito, for the express purpose of negotiating a treaty with this Govt. The President of the United States lost no time in complying with the invitation, and almost three years ago, the Chargé d'Affaires of the U. S. at Bogotá, was instructed to proceed to this capital, to negotiate a treaty; but unfortunately, the instructions were lost at sea, with the vessel in which the bearer of them, had taken his passage, (as this Govt. has been informed.) But the Govt. of the U. S. always desirous of cultivating the most friendly relations with the republics of the South, despatched, as soon as it could be conveniently done, another agent (the Undersigned) to Ecuador, not doubting that he would find the Govt. at Quito, disposed to treat upon equal and liberal terms; and indeed, the invitation and the assurances of friendly feelings which accompanied it, admitted of no other inference. But that the terms proposed by this Government, of being at liberty to grant to seven or eight other states, privileges and favors to be withheld from the United States, are not equal, requires no argument to prove. And if a treaty should be made upon the basis proposed by His Excellency, the consequence would be, probably, ill feeling, altercations and collisions, between the United States and those South American States, with which they now have treaties.[1] . . .

The Undersigned has the honor [etc.].

---

[1] The omitted portion comments upon the seventh, tenth and twelfth articles of the treaty, which concern real estate and other matters, not pertinent to this publication.

2336

Luis de Saá, Minister of Foreign Affairs of Ecuador, to James C. Pickett, United States Chargé d'Affaires to the Peru-Bolivian Confederation [1]

[TRANSLATION]

QUITO, *March 22, 1839.*

SIR: On the 18th instant, the Undersigned transmitted to the Honorable Chamber of the Senate, the following communication:

I have the honor of transmitting to your Honorable body, a copy of a communication of the Plenipotentiary of the United States,[2] confined exclusively to the point of the treaty of friendship, commerce and navigation, upon which he has dissented, upon coming to an understanding. (*al estarse ajustando.*) The Executive believes, that the particular privileges which may be conceded to Spain and the republics of South America, ought to be extended to those of the North; because, with respect to them, there are equal motives and perhaps greater, for, referring to Mexico only, it is evident, that an active commerce is maintained with her, whilst Paraguay and Buenos Ayres are remote. His Excellency believes also, that the United States ought to be included in the immunity; (*esencion*) on account of the sympathies which exist towards that nation, and the readiness with which she became a party (*se prestó*) to the Congress of Panamá or Tocabaya, which was intended to secure the preservation and prosperity of the new American states, is a decisive proof of her determination to make common cause with them, upon their greatest interests.

The Undersigned has the honor [etc.].

2337

James C. Pickett, United States Chargé d'Affaires to the Peru-Bolivian Confederation, to John Forsyth, Secretary of State of the United States [3]

No. 6   QUITO, *March 27, 1839.*

SIR: Since I had last the honor of addressing you, (on the 27th ultimo.) [4] I have made some progress with the negotiation of a treaty with the Government at Quito, but have not yet concluded any thing. The Minister of Foreign Relations (Dr. Saa) has proposed various additions to the *projet* which I had presented; to some of which I assented, as being of no great importance, and some of which have been abandoned by this Gov't. The only question, now under discussion, (which is one of great magnitude however,)

[1] Despatches, Peru, vol. 5; enclosed with Pickett to the Secretary of State, No. 7, May 1, 1839, below, this part, doc. 2338.
[2] Evidently the one dated March 15, 1839, above, this part, doc. 2335.
[3] Despatches, Peru, vol. 5.   Received June 8.   [4] Above, this part, doc. 2333.

is, whether Ecuador will make a treaty with any foreign power, without providing, that it may be controlled by any treaties that may be hereafter made, with Spain, or with the South American states formerly her colonies; this Govt. claiming the privilege of inserting a clause to that effect. This, to me, was altogether new and unexpected. I, of course, have said that the Gov't of the United States could not make a treaty with such a condition annexed to it, and had the Minister persisted, the negotiation would have been at an end. But after giving my views at some length, in a note,[1] the proposition was abandoned, and the Minister sent my communication to the Senate, accompanied by one from himself,[2] recommending that the United States should be placed upon a footing with the S. American States. I am informed that the matter was referred to the Senate, because the objection originated, in part, in that body; so that it acts upon the treaty, before it is concluded, instead of acting upon it afterwards. This is rather anomalous, even here, where anomalies in legislation, are not unfrequent; but if I make the treaty, and it is sanctioned by the Congress, it is not very material, I suppose, what the forms may be. But whether it will be sanctioned or not, I still regard as very uncertain.

Much to my surprise, a feeling decidedly friendly to Spain, and not friendly to other European nations, has manifested itself, to a great extent, in this country; and there is a strong party in favor of making any concessions almost, that may be demanded, for the sake of establishing friendly relations with that power, and of securing a recognition of the independence of Ecuador. The same party is opposed to making treaties with all other foreign powers, unless with the states, formerly Spanish colonies; and if there should be an exception in favor of the United States, it will be, because they are regarded as belonging to the American family, and as being more friendly to the South American states, than the European Powers are. They talk much here, of a general South American Congress, of a S. American System, and of a S. American Code of International Law: which, I suppose, will all come to nothing. The Peru-Bolivian Confederation is certainly at an end, and General Santa-Cruz, the *Protector* of it, is now in Guayaquil. Instead of finding support and cooperation in the South, as he expected, and of returning to Lima, in three or four months, with eight or nine thousand troops, as he said he could do, when he left it, he found every where, revolutionary movements against himself, and was fortunate to be able to escape from Arequipa, (which he did with difficulty) to the port of Islay, where a British vessel of war received him and eight or ten officers on board, and brought them to Ecuador. In Bolivia, also, there has been a revolution fatal to his authority and influence, and in that state, Gen[l]. Ballivian, his enemy, is now at the head of affairs.— Among the Gazettes of Quito, a packet of which I

[1] Evidently the one dated March 15, 1839, above, this part, doc. 2335.
[2] The accompanying note is quoted in the Ecuadoran Minister's note to Pickett, above, this part, March 22, 1839, doc. 2336.

forward, will be found (in N? 279) an account of these transactions.— I forward also, three Reports of the Ministers of Ecuador, to the Congress.[1]

I took the liberty of suggesting, in my last communication, that it would be well to forward to me, other credentials; for Peru, or North Peru; that is, provided the President thinks proper to continue the Legation at Lima, and to re-commission me, as Chargé d'Affaires.

All my communications to the State Department, from my arrival at Quito, to the 27th ultimo, were forwarded from Guayaquil to Panamá, on the 10th instant.

I have the honor [etc.].

2338

James C. Pickett, United States Chargé d'Affaires to the Peru-Bolivian Con-federation, to John Forsyth, Secretary of State of the United States [2]

[EXTRACTS]

No. 7   QUITO, *May 1, 1839.*

SIR: I have the honor to transmit herewith, a correspondence with the Minister of Foreign Relations, and other documents relating to the negotia-tion of a treaty with Ecuador; numbered from one, to fifteen, inclusive.[3] N? 9 (translation N? 15.) is the *basis* adopted by the Congress, for a guide to the Executive in all future negotiations; and to which, all treaties, hereafter

[1] None of these was found.   [2] Despatches, Peru, vol. 5. Received July 15.
[3] For those included in this publication, see above, this part, March 8, 15 and 22, 1839, docs. 2334, 2335, and 2336, excepting No. 15 which follows:

No. 15
The Senate and Chamber of Representatives of Ecuador, in Congress assembled,
Having attentively examined the note of the Minister Secretary of State, in the De-partment of Foreign Relations [See above, this part, March 22, 1839, doc. 2336, for the content of this communication.—Ed.], in which it is recommended, that the favors and privileges conceded to the Hispano-American States, shall be extended to the United States of the North, as their Plenipotentiary, Sr. Pickett has proposed,
DECLARE,
Article 1. That all the Hispano-American Republics shall be entitled, in their public treaties, with Ecuador, to greater favors and privileges, than the nations of Europe.
Article 2. That the United States of the North, ought to be considered as a sister Republic, and entitled to the same favors and privileges, as the Hispano-American States.
Article 3. That the convenience of the State, shall be the measure of those favors.
Article 4. That to no nation, shall be conceded, privileges, as to the *most favored nation.*
Article 5. That therefore, those words should be excluded from every public treaty.

Done in Quito, the 13th of April 1839.—The President of the Senate, *Pedro José Arteta.*—The President of the Chamber of Representatives, *Antonio Bustamante.*—The Secretary of the Senate & Senator, *Antonio Martines [Martinez] Pallares.*—The Deputy & Secretary of the Chamber of Representatives, *Manuel Ignacio Pareja.*
Palace of the Government in Quito, April 20. 1839. *Juan José Flores.*
By H. E. Minister of Finance acting in the Dep! of the Interior, *Luis de Saa.*
Es copia—*Salazar.*

made, are to conform.   It was adopted, only the day before the Congress adjourned, not to meet again until the 15th of January 1841.   Thus, the whole session passed away, before the President could say, upon what terms he could conclude a treaty; in consequence of his having referred the subject, rather unnecessarily, I think, to the legislative body; for should a treaty be made, it must be again submitted to that body, for its sanction, which cannot be given, in much less than two years.

You will perceive, that according to the *basis*, the United States are to be placed upon an equal footing, with the Hispano-American Republics, and are to be entitled to greater favors and privileges than the nations of Europe; with an implied understanding, however, that Spain may be made an exception.   The object of the Resolution, though not expressed on the face of it, is understood to be, in part, to enable the Executive to make such concessions to Spain, as may be deemed expedient, as an equivalent for a recognition, on her part, of the independence of Ecuador; should it be recognized, formally, as it has been, virtually; for friendly and commercial relations are already established between the two countries: Ecuador has a diplomatic agent & consuls, in Spain, and Spanish vessels come, like those of a friendly nation, into the ports of Ecuador.

Another object of the Resolution, in excluding the words, '*most favored nation*' from all treaties, is, to avoid any onerous or entangling arrangements, with the European Powers; of whose views and pretensions, they are jealous in Ecuador, and with whom, they do not seem desirous of maintaining any very intimate commercial relations.   A different feeling appears to prevail, at present, towards the United States; and it is very emphatically announced in the Resolution, the phraseology of which, is remarkably laconic and unequivocal.

The President and the Minister of Foreign Relations both assure me, that a treaty shall be concluded with the United States, in conformity with the basis indicated by the Congress, and without delay; and I presume it will be, though there are many influential persons here, opposed to any treaty between Ecuador and the nations, which are considered powerful, & the U. S. being regarded as a powerful nation, that feeling has to be combatted; but I am inclined to think that it will manifest itself, more distinctly, and in a more formidable shape, when the treaty shall be referred to the next Congress, for approval; should it be referred.

A day or two before adjourning, the Congress approved, or sanctioned (as they say here) the treaties with Mexico & Venezuela, and rejected the treaty with France, although it had been already ratified by the King of the French. The principle cause of this rejection, is, very probably, the recent proceedings of the French Government, towards Mexico and Buenos Ayres.   The British treaty, with the republic of Colombia, has been recognized, though rather obscurely and equivocally, as I understand it; and the Government at Quito, insists upon making a new one, to be limited in its duration, and in which, shall be inserted various articles, more favorable to Ecuador than those of the existing treaty. . . .[1]

I forward five numbers of the Govt. Gazette. (the only newspaper printed in Quito.) They contain nothing that has a reference to the interests of the United States, except an extract from President Van Buren's last message, to Congress, (in Nº 281) upon the subject of our relations with Mexico; the publication of which, had a good effect, as the sympathies of the Ecuatorians are, and have been, decidedly with Mexico, in her present and recent difficulties, with foreign powers.

I have the honor [etc.].

2339

James C. Pickett, United States Chargé d'Affaires to the Peru-Bolivian Con-federation, to John Forsyth, Secretary of State of the United States [2]

[EXTRACTS]

No. 8 GUAYAQUIL, *July 3, 1839.*

SIR: I have the honor to inform you that I arrived at this place, the 30th ultimo, bringing with me, a treaty between the United States and Ecuador, which was signed on the 13th of June; and I transmit herewith, two original copies of it; one in English, the other in Spanish.[3] . . .

The 34th article of the treaty is an additional one, and is inserted in conse-quence of the Resolution of the Congress of Ecuador, approved by the President of the 20th of April last, a duplicate copy and translation of which are now enclosed.[4] (Nºˢ 7 & 8 of the accompanying documents.) As the Resolution declares, that "to no nation shall be conceded privileges, as to the most favored nation," it became necessary to insert an article shewing precisely, upon what footing the United States would be placed, in Ecuador, which will be that upon which Spain, Mexico and the other Hispano-American states will be placed; and as these will undoubtedly be the most favored nations, in Ecuador, this article, taken with the third and fourth articles, appears to me, to secure all that can be expected; and as much, as though the United States were placed explicitly & in so many words, upon a footing with the most favored nation.

From some cause or other, (inadvertence probably) Spain is omitted in the Resolution, and if it were literally construed, she would be classed with

---

[1] The omitted portion tells of the title of "Minister" and "Excellency" being applied to him in spite of his protests, and also states that he expects to leave Quito before the middle of June. [2] Despatches, Peru, vol. 5. Received September 10.

[3] For the text of this treaty, see Malloy, *Treaties, Conventions, etc., between the United States and Other Powers,* vol. 1, p. 421.

The omitted portion states that the treaty between the United States and Venezuela was adopted as the basis for the present one, and also comments upon some of the articles of the treaty. [4] For this resolution see above, this part, p. 245, note 3.

the other European nations: But it is well understood, and is notorious, that it was the intention originally, to grant commercial privileges to her, not to be granted to any other nation; provided she would acknowledge the independence of Ecuador.   But the Gov't. at Quito determined finally to have but two classes of treaties; those with Spain and the American states (including the United States) to form the first, and all others to form the second.   This determination was adopted in consequence of the Resolution of the Congress transmitted by the Minister of Foreign Relations to me, in his note of the 8th of May last:[1] (copy and translation Nᵒˢ 1 & 2 of the enclosed documents.)   The Decree of the 13th of April 1837, referred to in the Resolution, places the subjects, merchandises and vessels of France, upon a footing with those of the most favored nation, until a new treaty should be concluded.

The enclosed decree (Nᵒ 5 of the documents) of the last Congress,[2] concerning the vessels and productions of Spain, shews conclusively, that a very friendly feeling now prevails in Ecuador, towards that nation, which will be much strengthened, no doubt, should she recognise, formally, the independence of this country, as she has already done, virtually, by receiving diplomatic and consular agents from Ecuador, and by establishing commercial relations with her.

I inserted Mexico specially, in the 34th article, because a treaty between Ecuador and that state has been approved by the Congress of the former, and will, I have no doubt, be ratified and carried into effect.   This treaty (which has not yet been published) is a copy, to a great extent, of the one between the United States and Mexico.   Even the words, '*the most favored nation*,' are used and will be retained, the late decree prohibiting them, not being intended, I apprehend, to have a retrospective effect.

I informed you in my communication of the 1st of May last,[3] that the treaty between Ecuador and Venezuela had been sanctioned by the Congress of the former.   This was a mistake on the part of my informant.   It was not approved, nor was it rejected: there being some objection to one of the articles, it was left among the unfinished business, there not being time to act upon it, finally.[4] . . .

President Flores is desirous that a diplomatic agent should be sent from the United States to Quito, as soon as may be convenient, and he informed me that a communication would be despatched to Washington, on the subject; and it is now, I believe, on the way.   The presence of such an agent

---

[1] Not included in this publication.   In this resolution the Legislature resolved briefly, that, after considering the treaty between France and Ecuador lately presented for ratification, it would not consider "any nation as the most favored" excepting "the privileges to be conceded to Spain and to the American States," and that, in the meantime, France was to be considered as any other European state not having special treaties with Ecuador.

[2] Not included in this publication.   [3] Above, this part, doc. 2338.

[4] The omitted portion continues a discussion on this treaty, and also relates to claims of citizens of the United States against Ecuador.

would have a good effect.   He could maintain a friendly understanding between the two countries, & might do something towards liquidating and collecting the claims of our citizens against Ecuador.   His presence might en-
sure also, the sanction of the treaty just concluded, for I cannot but regard
its fate before the Congress, as uncertain.   Some of the members will be opposed to it; others will be indifferent and careless, and its real and efficient
friends will be but few.   The President says, however, that it will certainly
be sanctioned.

S. Sweetser Esq. Consul of the United States at this place, bears the treaty
to Washington.   Its approval by the President is made a condition precedent
to his receiving any compensation, as you will perceive from my instructions
to him.   (Nº 14.)   I have taken this course, because objections may be
made, possibly, to the form of the treaty, (which is certainly a very unusual
one,) although the substance is, I think, effectually secured: And as Mr.
Sweetser returns to the United States on private business, he was very willing
to bear it, on the terms stipulated.

I expect to sail for Lima, in the U. S. Sloop of War Lexington, now here, on
the 5th instant.

I have the honor [etc.].

2340

*James H. Causten, Ecuadoran Consul in Washington, to Daniel Webster,
Secretary of State of the United States* [1]

WASHINGTON, *October 7, 1842.*

SIR: The Minister of Foreign Affairs of the Republic of Ecuador, under
date of the 19th of March 1842, has addressed to me a communication,[2] an-

[1] Notes from Ecuador, vol. I.   Received October 7.
James H. Causten, the writer of this document, was commissioned consul for the District
of Columbia by the Republic of Ecuador, and applied to the Secretary of State for an
exequatur on September 23, 1842.   Again, on April 19, 1847, he applied for an *exequatur* to
occupy the same position.   It was not until 1853 that Ecuador had an accredited diplomatic
representative in the United States.
[2] This note follows:

*F. Marcos, Minister of Foreign Affairs of Ecuador, to James H. Causten, Ecuadoran
Consul in Washington*

[TRANSLATION]

QUITO, *March 19, 1842.*

SIR: Official evidence of the actual exchange of ratifications of the treaty of Peace and
Friendship, which was concluded and signed at Madrid on the 16th day of February
1840, has been received at this Department; and although the document establishing
that fact has not come accompanied with the original ratification of her Catholic
Majesty—so that the treaty might be promulgated as a law of the Republic—yet the
President considers that the exchange of ratifications being complete (as is evident) the
treaty has acquired full force and validity, and has therefore become obligatory on the
respective parties to it.   To this conclusion, from which neither party can withdraw,
may be added a further confirmation in the circumstance, that the Spanish Government

nouncing, that a Treaty of Peace and Friendship between the Republic and the Government of Spain, had been concluded at Madrid, on the 16th of February 1840, and that the ratifications thereof had been exchanged.

I hasten to submit to you, as I have the honor to do herewith, a copy and translation of said document (though not specially instructed so to do, but under the impression that such was intended,) in the belief that it will afford pleasure to the Government of the United States to learn that its benevolent intercession, long and earnestly exerted, towards effecting the recognition by Spain of the Independence of the South American Governments, has been so far crowned with success.

And I respectfully submit to your consideration, the propriety of giving publicity to said communication, through your Department, in order to notify the Merchants of the United States of the increased security they may now enjoy in their commerce with the Republic, from the happy termination of the afflicting state of war which has long existed against it on the part of the Spanish Monarchy.

I have the honor [etc.].

2341

Delazon Smith, Special Agent of the United States to Ecuador, to John C. Calhoun, Secretary of State of the United States [1]

QUITO, *August 10, 1845.*

SIR: I have the Honor to inform you, that I arrived here (at this Capital) the 16th ultimo, in fifty seven days from Lima, and fifty one from Payta, the port at which I disembark'd, and from which I proceeded into the interior on my way to this City, via Loxa, Cuenca, Rio Bamba, &ᶜᵉ The time usually employed in the Journey from Payta to Quito is from thirty to thirty five days, the extra time consumed by me was caused by the existence of a civil revolucion in this republic, and the consequent difficulty of procuring beasts (horses and mules) to ride and tra[n]sport my baggage, there being no other mode of conveyance in this country.

---

immediately put into execution all the stipulations contained in said treaty; and still further, to evince its benevolence to the Republic, it declared that an Ecuadorian vessel and her cargo then in one of her ports from Guayaquil, should enjoy the benefit of the priveleges agreed upon in the 16th article thereof, altho' her arrival at Cadiz took place some days before said exchange was effected.

In consideration whereof, and after mature reflection, the President of the Republic has declared that the treaty of Peace and Friendship concluded with the Spanish Monarchy is obligatory upon her; and I am extremely happy to inform you thereof, for ulterior purposes.

I have the honor [etc.].

[1] Special Agents, vol. 13. Received January 2, 1846.

Although this despatch of August 10 was addressed to Calhoun, he had resigned on July 22 and had been succeeded as Secretary of State by Webster.

Before leaving Lima, I had the Honor of informing the Department in a note dated the 10ᵗʰ of May, of my arrival in that City in Eighty five days from Norfolk, having employed but Seventy of these in sailing, by far the most speedy passage on record.

I also informed the Honorable Secretary, in the same note, that as Comodore Sloat had ordered the "Portsmouth" (in which I sailed) back to Valparaiso to carry the Honorable Mᵣ Crump, Chargé D'affair[e]s to Chile, I was obliged to remain in Lima one month, in order to obtain a passage in the "Warren" which had been ordered to the East Indies, I further acquainted the Department with the facts which I gathered in Peru in relation to the Republic of Ecuador, to wit, that the whole country was in a state of civil revolution, that the Government was, for the time being, in a most unstable condition, and that the yellow fever was raging most fearfully in the City of Guayaquil, the only seaport town belonging to the Ecuador &ᶜ &ᶜ. Notwithstanding these facts, I notified the Department that I still deemed it my duty to visit the Capital to which I had been directed by the Government.

When in Lima I saw and conferred with Mᵣ Rocafuerte, formerly President of the Republic of Ecuador, I found that he was deeply and warmly engaged in the then existing revolution. He bitterly denounced Genˡ Flores, the late President, as a foreigner, a ursurper, a tyrant, a mulatto, a thief &ᶜ &ᶜ

He was confidently of the opinion that Flores, who was then at the head of such Government Troops as he could induce into his service, would be defeated, and either executed or driven out of the country within three months at farthest. He knew that his Nephew, Mᵣ Sweetser, United States Consul for Guayaquil, was in Quito and that he had been in communication with the Government, but what he had accomplished he knew not. He assured me, voluntarily, that "the true Patriots" the revolutionary or "liberal party" were not only very anxious to cultivate the most friendly relations with the North American States but that, *as soon as they possessed the means*, they would pay the debts due the Citizens of the United States. Believing that the war would speedily terminate, the Government be fully restored and tranquility and prosperity follow, he advised me either to remain in Lima, two or three months or go directly to the Capital and there await the formation of a new Government. Fearing that his desires for self-agrandizement (for he confidently expects to succeed General Flores) might have biassed his Judgement and render'd him too sanguine, I concluded to proceed to Quito, with as little delay as possible.

I determined upon this course the more readily, as many Gentlemen were decidedly of the opinion that General Flores would promptly destroy his enemies and sustain himself at the head of the Government. These, therefore, believed it a most propituos period for me to present myself at the seat of Government, let who might be at its head, as the party in power would, probably, be disposed to make concessions and concede to terms in the hope of securing either aid or countenance in their troubles, which they would refuse and reject in time of peace.

On my journey from Payta to Quito, soon after entering the territory of the Ecuador from Peru, I met General Stagg, the son-in-law of General Flores, with Mʳ Malo, the late Secretary of Foreign Affairs of this Republic, on their way to Lima, with (it was said) thirty or forty thousand dollars in cash, besides a large quantity of Jewellery, diamonds &c. &c. Their, reported, intention was to purchase in the Bay of Callao, a vessel of War with which to blockade the port of Guayaquil, as the inhabitants of that city and province were the first to move in the revolution, and the last in exciting the populace to rebellion. But ere I left the town in which I first met them, they were seized by a company of the opposing party and deprived of a portion of their money, escaping but with their lives, and a part of their treasures. Following close after General Stagg, was twenty one cargoes of Silver bars, or about fifty hundred pounds. This was designed for the same purpose, but this also fell into the hands of the revolutionary party.

I was informed, by General Stagg, that, though Mʳ Malo, was leaving the Country, and General Flores was in the field with his troops, their places had been supplied in the Government, and that I would, therefore, find legitimate representatives of the Republic at the Capital.

About this period I learned that Geneˡ Flores had been defeated in the successive engagements with what is termed "the Guayaquil party." On arriving in Cuenca the Governor of that Province (acting under an appointment from the new government of Guayaquil) addressed me a note (see document marked A.A.)¹ enquiring whether I travelled through the country in an official or private capacity. This note I replied to verbally, and in person. After having been made acquainted with the character in which I journed, and that it was my intention to go to Quito, he positively refused me a passport or permission to proceed, whereupon I declared myself his prisoner, and notified him, that, in the event of my not receiving a passport before ten o'clock the following day, I should acquaint the United States Commodore, commanding in the Pacific, of the facts, and call upon him to redress my grievances. The Governor and his Councillors desired the time given for deliberation. At nine O'clock on the succeeding day, I received a passporte (marked C.C.) accompanied by a letter (marked BB) in which the Governor protests on two points."

1ˢᵗ my personal safety would, in his judgement, be jeopardized, in consequence of the aggitated state of the country, and in the event of molestation or injury, *his* Government (that of Guayaquil) would hold itself guiltless. 2ⁿᵈ That whatever treaty I might form with the Government of

¹ Neither this, nor any of the subsequent notes mentioned herein, between the Governor and Smith, have been included in this publication, since their contents are adequately reviewed within this despatch.

Quito or of General Flores, would be treated as null and void, by the newly organized Government.

To this letter I replied, without alluding to his protestations, (see letter marked D.D). This correspondence, the Governor of Cuenca transmitted to the Secretary General of Guayaquil, who approved his course, and published his approval together with copies of the letters addressed by the Governor to me, above referred to, (marked E.E).

On reaching Quito, I learned that G.¹ Flores had capitulated with the Guayaquilenans, He, surrendering both his arms and the Precidency; they paying him "twenty thousand dollars" as a *bonus*, sending him as Minister to France for two years, recognizing him as the Commander-in-Chief of the Army of the Republic and paying to his family, three thousand dollars per annum during his absense &.° &.°

I forego the specification of particulars inasmuch as the accompanying documents exhibits a full and minute history of the revolution—its rise, progress, and finale.

Since the cessation of hostilities, the Guayaquil Government have called a National Convention, to assemble in the City of Cuenca some time in October next, to revise the present Constitution and to reorganize the Gov.ᵗ

This movement gives great umbrage to the Citizens at the Capital, who are indignant, because the Convention was not summoned to assemble in Quito.

A settled spirit of animosity and rivalship, has always existed between the Citizens of Guayaquil and those of Quito.— And now as the former were the first to move in the late revolution, and as they have "borne the heat and burthen of the day" only joined by the Quitonians "at the eleventh hour" they claim the right to dictate and to determine. Hence they have called the proposed convention at a place of close proximity to theirs and remote from the Capital. This, it is generally believed, will cause a fresh revolution between the Citizens of Guayaquil and those of Quito. Should, however, the convention result harmoniously, three months will transpire, from the time of holding the convention, before the people will have elected a new Congress; two additional months will pass, ere that congress will assemble, and every reason exists to induce the conviction that such congress will have adjourned before any foreign Agent can tax the attention or obtain the response of any newly appointed Minister for Foreign Affairs, and should he, contrary to every legitimate expectation now, obtain an hearing and an answer at that, a prior or much subsequent period, the answer would, beyond every possible contingency be, "however just the claims of the Citizens of the United States, (or other government) upon the Government of Ecuado they cannot be now liquidated, nor for many months or perhaps, years to come, as the recent revolution has drained the Coffers of the Republic of every dollar, and exhausted the last farthing of the former credit of its people!"

On arriving at the Capital, I, in obedience to instructions, called upon Seth Sweetser Esqʳᵉ and delivered the letter addressed to him by the Honorable Secretary of State, After perusing it, he replied to me, that he intended "to deal very plainly with me" that the Government of the United States, asked him to communicate to me important information which had cost him much labour, time, and money, and still refused to pay his draft for the paltry sum of "five hundred dollars," and therefore, "he should do no such thing."

The day following this interview I addressed to him the accompanying note, (marked 0.0.) To which I received a reply, (marked 1.1.)[1]

Perceiving that he had changed his mind, I called upon him again and had "a full and free conversation with him" in regard to the claims of our Citizens, and the progress he had made in adjusting them.

He subsequently handed me for my perusal and examination, a file of his correspondence with the Government here in relation to these claims, accompanied with a letter of explanation (marked 2.2) all of which I now transmit to the Secretary of State.

During the period of this correspondence, I had frequent interviews with Mʳ Sweetser, and also with many of the late Officers of Govᵗ here, and several of the Diplomatic Agents from foreign States, all of which has comspired to satisfy me that I shall best answer to the letter and spirit of my instructions from the Department of State, and more wisely consult the interests of my Government and its Citizens,—Creditors of this,—by returning immediately to the United States, than by remaining here for an indefinite number of months in waiting upon an ignorant, a selfish, a pennyless, and a rebellious people for the formation of a Government which I can properly address;—a people whose presumption display's a constant burlesque upon the very name of republican, and a Government which, day, by day, belies the labels upon its text books. For at present there is neither legitimate Government or money adequate for the days wants in the Republic of Ecuador.

In travelling nearly five hundred miles on the territory of this republic, I witnessed little else than ignorance, indolence, wretchedness, dishonesty, and misery, on the part of the great mass of the people, and selfishness, low-cunning, sordid ambition, avarice, and blood-thirsty revenge on that of those who either lead or force the unconcious, unthinking multitude. The country too, is nearly as miserable as those who inhabit it.—Nineteen-twentieths of the surface of the earth is insusseptible of cultivation, and forty nine-fiftieths of its inhabitants cannot read, whilst they support a Government expending more than a million of dollars yearly, with an income not to exceed Six, or Seven hundred thousand dollars per annum; a people too, stared at on every hand by the Sable Cowl of an ignorant, illiberal, indolent,

---

[1] Not included in this publication.   Sweetser was the United States consul for the port of Guayaquil.

and licentious priesthood, whose name is Legion! a people almost constantly harrassed by civil discord and violent revolutions; and yet even so weak and defenceless, that three thousand well disiplined soldiers from the United States would march through their Republic, conquering, taking, and possessing, every Town, City, and Province.

Every department of the Government is, if not deteriorating, at a perfect stand still. Some idea can be formed of the *rapidity* (!) with which intelligence is conveyed through the Country when I state the fact that I brought to the Capital of Ecuador the *latest* intelligence from the United States, having been six months in reaching here after leaving Norfolk!

The latest news received here from the United States before my arrival was that, Congress had convened, on the first of December, and President Tyler's message had been received!

The *last* information received, acquaints us with the adjournment of Congress and the inauguration of President Polk, at present, however, the roads are closed on account of the revolution, but when open and free, the mails are carried only about eight leagues in twenty four hours!

The Capital of the Ecuador participates in the general retrograde movement of the country, Her public buildings are fast falling to decay, Her population is less than it was forty years ago, whilst those who remain are quite, as ignorant and intolerant—equally joined to their idols, Of the seventy thousand souls which the City now boasts, I am the only person, save my servant, born in the United States, and the only one, five excepted, who speak the English language; These are detained here, for the time being, from the force of a concatenation of personal circumstances, or from their official relations. The English Consul, with Special powers, is one of the number, who is waiting patiently, the restoration of a Government, some Six, Nine, or twelve months, hence, that he may urge the payment of at least a *part* of the *interest* upon *thirteen millions* of dollars, that being the amount which his Government claims of this.

There is but one paper (and that a very small and indifferent one) published in this City, and but three (of the same class,) printed in the entire republic, copies of these I forward you; No works, upon either philosophy, Science, Government or the arts, have been published here for many years.

Mr Sweetser, in obedience to instructions has returned to his Consulate at Guayaquil, I deem it unjustifiable in me, in view of the existing state of this Republic, to address the Department of State in Washington and await here its renewed instructions, as, to accomplish this, would require from ten to twelve months,—an amount of time far exceeding that allotted me by the Government.

I leave here for the United States on Monday next, the 12th ins^t To return to Payta would require from one to two months time, besides leading me in the opposite direction from the United States. The port of Guayaquil is not approachable on account of the yellow fever, which rages constantly, having destroyed one half of her former citizens within the three years last past. Foreigners are its favorite and especial victims.   No way of egress, therefore, remains for me but through Pasto, Popayan, to Bogotá, and from thence to Carthagena, whence I hope to arrive some time in October, which will enable me, probably, to reach Washington about the first of December.

I have the honor [etc.].

2342

Manuel Bustamante, Minister of Foreign Affairs of Ecuador, to James Buchanan, Secretary of State of the United States [1]

[TRANSLATION]

QUITO, *November 26, 1846.*

SIR: The Undersigned, Minister of Foreign Relations of the Republic of Ecuador, has the honor to address his Excellency the Minister of the like department in the United States of America, for the purpose of informing him of an important affair, intimately connected with the preservation of the independance, liberty, and honor of the American Continent.

Before entering upon the principal subject of his communication, the Undersigned will take the liberty to recall to the most excellent minister, some circumstances in the history of Ecuador, since the commencement of its political existance, indispensable to form a clear idea of the most material points, to which the present note relates.   His Excellency, the Minister is no doubt aware, that upon the dissolution of the former republic of Colombia, the remains of the army which fought in Peru, in aid of that country, in the war of independence, were in this part of the said republic.   That the ex-General Juan Jose Flores, a native of Venezuela, then holding the military command of these provinces, availed himself of those forces, to effect their seperation; that he thenceforth ruled the country, according to his own will, without respect for the republican principles established in the constitution, which the people of Ecuador adopted; that after three years of his despotic rule, the greater part of the Nation arose in mass, to throw off his yoke and at the expense of blood, he succeeded in repressing for some time, the wish of the Nation and dictated another fundamental code, conformable with his will, but this not being sufficient to realize his plans of perpetual dominion, he eight years afterwards, caused another constitution to be drawn up, setting forth maxims, anti-republican and essentially despotic.—   Contrary to the constitutional principles, which form in a certain degree, part of the public right of all the American Nations, he likewise caused himself to be re-elected President, though wanting the qualification of being a native of

[1] Notes from Ecuador, vol. 1.   Received February 9.

Ecuador, as well as others, no less necessary, according to the laws of the country; and by such acts, and with the support of those foreign forces, he ruled this republic during fifteen consecutive years, until divine providence brought his illegal and tyrannical power to an end.

The Ecuadorian Nation neither could nor would longer bear a usurped and ignominious authority; it rose at once in arms on the sixth of March 1845, to throw off that authority; and under the auspices of the valor inspired by a just cause it succeeded, obliging General Flores to capitulate, as he did, at the Hacienda of La Virginia.   In this capitulation, the provisional Government of the Republic generously granted to its enemy, the sum of twenty thousand dollars, in order that he might leave the country, although he was and is responsible for immense sums, which he had embezzled during his administration, and he might have been tried for various crimes, subjecting him to the severest punishment.

This capitulation, which he unjustly and maliciously called a treaty, was submitted, as was necessary, to the national convention; afterwards assembled, which disapproved it as contrary to the independance and security of the Nation and as it might form a basis for the anarchical operations commenced by General Flores from the moment when he saw himself obliged to evacuate the territory and to the plans of future agression which he had already premeditated.

Flores immediately on leaving Ecuador accompanied by one of his foreign officers who had been the instruments of his power traveled through Europe assuming the title of President of this republic and employing the money bestowed on him for his support by the munificence of this government in obtaining audience in European courts with the object of deceiving by impostures and false titles of legitimacy those who knew him only by his former political position.

The Government of Ecuador in full justice to the governments of the Atlantic could never believe that Flores without rights or under any pretext should be considered in any other character than as a private individual; and it therefore from self respect did not judge it necessary to give any intimations to the Nations with which it was in amicable relations.

The Government of the undersigned thus continued, without any other idea than that of consolidating the peace of the country, and securing advantages to the people, until the month of August of the present year; when information was received through the newspapers of Madrid, and afterwards through those of France and England, that Flores was enlisting troops and officers in the Peninsula for the invasion of this republic.   The Government of the Undersigned and all thinking men, natives as well as foreigners at first doubted, the truth of this news; but on its repetition through official as well as private channels, the fact can no longer be doubted; and though it should not be invested with all the circumstances mentioned respecting the project of a monarchy, it is sufficient to arrest the attention of all the governments of the New World.

Can a man give himself the title, which is assigned to him in Europe, or entertain a project menacing the political existance of a part of the American territory, and enter it with impunity, to put in operation the nefarious plans which he has conceived? Can the inhabitants of Europe be assembled in a small or a great number, to assail us by force, and as if they were associated for a hunting party in forests and deserts? It is under this point of view, that the Government of the Undersigned regards this enterprise; and it invites the attention of the Government of the United States, as it has invited that of all the South American Republics; for although this attack might not be carried into effect against the powerful states of the Union, as it is offensive to the independance of the new continent, it ought to be considered as deeply injurious to the honor of the American Governments, however feeble may be the part which is injured.

The solem protests which have been at all times, and most particularly at the present, made by the Cabinet of Washington, against all European intervention in the political affairs of America, afford a guarantee to the government of the Undersigned; it is moreover intimately convinced, that the most Excellent Minister now addressed, will never allow this agression to be committed under any pretext; in defiance of the enlightened views of the age. If it were the exclusive work of the ambition of Flores, Ecuador and the adjoining republics would be sufficient to defeat it, even though at the cost of immense sacrifices; but if it is in support of the secret pretentions of any European power, and especially of Spain, which can never regard with indifference the independant progress of these countries, the Government of Ecuador hopes for the effective co-operation and aid of the illustrious Republic of the United States, which will doubtless defend with all its power, the democratic principles, established in the American continent, and the independance and liberty of these nations.

Whether Flores be acting as the instrument of a foreign power, or he come on his own account, under any title, to invade this republic, the Government of the undersigned hopes, that proper orders will be given by that of the United States, to its ships of war stationed in the Pacific, to investigate the legality of the flag and the titles, under which the said expedition sails.

With sentiments of high consideration and esteem [etc.].

2343

James H. Causten, Ecuadoran Consul in Washington, to James Buchanan
Secretary of State of the United States [1]

WASHINGTON, *March 8, 1847.*

SIR: The Secretary of State of the Republic of Ecuador having communicated to this Consulate, under date of 29th December 1846, the adoption of a
decree, made in conjunction with the Governments of Chile and Peru,
affecting the relations between the Governments of Ecuador and Spain—
and required of the undersigned to make the same known to the Government
of the United States; I have, in pursuance thereof, the honor to submit,
herewith, a copy of said communication.[2]

I have the honor [etc.].

[1] Notes from Ecuador, vol. 1.
[2] This communication follows:

Manuel Gómez de la Torre, Minister of Foreign Affairs of Ecuador, to James H. Causten,
Ecuadoran Consul in Washington

[TRANSLATION]

QUITO, *December 29, 1846.*

The Government of Ecuador, in conjunction with the Governments of Peru and
Chile, has deemed it proper to decree as follows:
"The expedition which Don Juan José Flores is now preparing in the territory of
Spain, with the knowledge and under the protection of the Spanish Government, an expedition which is not only being organized with Spanish civilians but likewise with
experienced leaders, officers and soldiers who are enlisted in the service of the army of
the same nation, has put the Republic in a state of alarm, and in danger of maintaining a
defensive war against those forces, which are directed against the South American coasts,
and with special designs against those of Ecuador. In such a conflict my Government
is imperatively obliged to provide for the defense of the State; and in the exercise of this
defense, to adopt beforehand the measures which may lead to its salvation. Consequent upon these principles, and upon the communication addressed December 2 last
by my Ministry to his Excellency the Minister of Foreign Affairs of Her Catholic
Majesty, declaring that should the Government of Spain show itself indifferent to the
recruiting of soldiers and other preparations for the departure of the expedition, the
Government of Ecuador will consider as not subsisting the treaties of peace and friendship which at present exist between the two nations; the government has resolved as
follows.
    1. Not to admit to the ports of the Republic any Spanish vessel, merchandise or
invoice, of any class whatsoever, all that may arrive being subject to sequestration.
    2. That Spanish persons or subjects who may come from the Peninsula or any other
place shall not be admitted into Ecuador, and those who touch upon its shores shall be
treated as enemies and all that belongs to them shall be confiscated.
    3. That the persons and property of Spaniards resident in Ecuador remain under the
protection of its laws, provided they observe good conduct and remain passive.
    4. That the above rule does not include the property of Spaniards residing on the
Peninsula, or of those who at the time may be encountered navigating to the Republic
or in its territory, since such shall be immediately considered as enemy property.
    5. That no document or contract executed by Ecuadoreans living nearby or residing
in Ecuador in favor of Spanish subjects, shall have force or effect, nor shall any civil
action arise therefrom in the territory of the Republic.
    6. As these measures are founded on the duty of the Government to make war on its
enemies, or on those who are preparing with the forces or elements of war, they will be
effective from this date if the preparations for the expedition continue, or if this should
be realized; since they will be void only in case it should be learned that all the prepara-

2344

General Juan José Flores, former President of Ecuador, to James Buchanan,
Secretary of State of the United States [1]

WASHINGTON, *September 29, 1847.*

General Flores late President of the Republic of Equator, presents his
best compliments to the Honb^le the Minister for foreign Affairs of the
United States, and being desirous of paying his respects to His Excell^y the
President, before leaving Washington, he begs the Minister for foreign Affairs
will be so good as to inform him when he can have that honor.

2345

Vanbrugh Livingston, United States Chargé d'Affaires at Quito, to James
Buchanan, Secretary of State of the United States [2]

No. 2   QUITO, *August 14, 1848.*

SIR: I have the honor to apprize the Department of my arrival at this
capital on the 6th Inst.

On the 10th I addressed a communication to the Minister for Foreign
Affairs of this Government informing him of my arrival in the character of
Chargé d'Affaires of the United States to this Republic, and requesting him
to inform me of the time and place at which I might be admitted to present
my letter of credence.

I transmit accompanied herewith a copy of the same.[3]

A reply was received on the following day, a copy of which is also transmitted herewith.

By this it will be perceived that my reception was appointed to take place
on the 12th at which time I had the honor of presenting my letter of credence
to the Minister for Foreign Affairs, and of being introduced by him to his
Excellency El Señor Roca, President of the Republic.

In my interview with the Minister, I embraced the occasion of stating,
that the delay on the part of the United States in establishing a regular
mission at Quito ought not to be imputed to any want of interest in the welfare of Ecuador as an independent American republic, but that our Govern-

---

tions of war against Ecuador or against any other of the Republics of South America
should not have proven to be true."

I communicate the above to you for your information and timely use.

God and Liberty.

[1] Notes from Ecuador, vol. I.

No response was found to this note, and this was the only communication in the volume
from General Flores.   [2] Despatches, Ecuador, vol. I.   Received November 11.

[3] Neither this, nor the reply mentioned in the next paragraph, is included in this publication.

ment, on the contrary, had always felt the liveliest sympathy with her fortunes as well as with those of our other sister republics of this continent.

I also stated that I had been instructed by my Government to say that I could not better obtain its approbation than by using my best endeavors to confirm the friendly relations and good understanding which happily subsisted between the two Republics.

The Minister, after expressing the great pleasure which this opportunity afforded to his Government of opening diplomatic relations with the United States, remarked that the former had, for some time, entertained the design of sending a diplomatic agent to reside at Washington, but that circumstances had hitherto prevented its execution.

He further expressed the very great respect he had towards the United States, and said he hoped that the friendship which subsisted between the two countries would be strengthened by the diplomatic intercourse which had now been commenced.

As there appears to be a good deal of excitement, at the present time, in regard to an apprehended invasion of the country on the part of Gen! Flores and his followers, I have deemed it expedient to delay the period of inviting the attention of the Government to the claims of our citizens upon it, to a more favorable opportunity.

In the mean time, I shall lose no opportunity of endeavoring to improve the present friendly relations between the two Governments. By these means it is expected that the way will be prepared for a better introduction of the matter of the claims adverted to.

I further transmit herewith the duplicate of a letter addressed to the Department from Guayaquil on the 13th Ult.[1]

I have the honor [etc.].

2346

Vanbrugh Livingston, United States Chargé d'Affaires at Quito, to Manuel Gómez de la Torre, Minister of Foreign Affairs of Ecuador [2]

QUITO, *August 22, 1848.*

SIR: In my interview with your Excellency of the 12th you will recollect that I had the honor of stating to you that I had been instructed by my Government to say to you that the United States had always felt the liveliest sympathy with the fortunes of Ecuador, as well as with those of our other Sister Republics of this hemisphere. And that they had, moreover, expressed this sentiment and acted in accordance with it upon every suitable occasion.

[1] Not included in this publication, since it relates to his salary account.
[2] Despatches, Ecuador, vol. 1; enclosed with Livingston to the Secretary of State, No. 3, September 8, 1848, below, this part, doc. 2348.

Agreeably to these feelings I embrace with much pleasure the present opportunity of communicating to you the views of the President of the United States, in relation to the military and naval expedition on the part of General Flores formerly President of Ecuador. This, as is understood, was organized, a year or two since in Europe, for the supposed purpose of recovering his authority, and connived at, as it was beleived to have been, by some of the monarchical Governments of that quarter. The attempt, moreover, was also understood to have created great alarm, not only in Ecuador itself, but in the neighboring republics, partly from an apprehension that its ulterior, were more extensive and important than its ostensible, designs. It was fortunately arrested, however, before its departure.

An interesting communication upon the above subject was addressed to the Department of State at Washington, by Señor Don Manuel Bustamente the Minister for Foreign Affairs of Ecuador under date of the 26th November. 1846.[1] It was received about the same time that intelligence of the failure of the expedition reached the above named capital.

Owing to this circumstance the note was not formally answered, as any proceedings of the Government of the United States, with reference to the expedition were rendered unnecessary.

General Castilla the President of Peru, also made an informal application in regard to it, to Mr Prevost the Consul of the United States at Lima.[2] And I now take much pleasure in sending you, accompanied herewith, an extract from a letter of the Department of State at Washington to Mr. Prevost,[3] as embodying the views of the President of the United States relative to this expedition.

I here take the opportunity, at the same time, of assuring you that the intervention or dictation, direct or indirect, of European Governments in the affairs of the Independent States of the American Hemisphere, will never be viewed with indifference by the Government of the United States. On the contrary all the moral means, at least, within their power, shall upon every occasion be employed to discourage and arrest such interference.

With sentiments of distinguished consideration [etc.].

[1] Above, this part, doc. 2342.
[2] See below, in the volume and part containing Communications from Peru, Prevost's note to the Secretary of State, under date of December 9, 1846.
[3] The extract was not found, but for the letter in full, see below, in the volume and part containing Communications to Perú, under date of March 24, 1847.

2347

*Manuel Gómez de la Torre, Minister of Foreign Affairs of Ecuador, to Vanbrugh
Livingston, United States Chargé d'Affaires at Quito* [1]

[TRANSLATION]

QUITO, *August 31, 1848.*

SIR: I had the honor to receive the very estimable communication of
Your Lordship dated the 22d instant,[2] the contents of which clearly manifest
the fair views entertained by the enlightened Government at Washington
when General Juan José Flores, betraying the standard of American independence, prepared on the Spanish coasts an expedition ostensibly directed
against the sovereignty of Ecuador, but concealing the real designs of that
attempt, which appeared to embrace a vast plan conceived by the ambition
of European monarchs. With this same motive, Your Honorable Lordship
was good enough to recall a communication which the Government of
Ecuador had the honor to address to the Department of State at Washington,[3]
with the object of arousing the sympathies and powerful influence of the
fraternal Government of the American Union in favor of the sovereignty
of this Republic and in opposition to the European snares and designs which
apparently were to be developed in a great sphere of action; a dispatch
which, not having been answered at the time by the worthy American
Government, Your Lordship has now been so good as to acknowledge,
completely satisfying the wishes of the Government of Ecuador which so
greatly desired to know the tendencies of the American policy with regard
to the grave matters submitted to the attention of the Minister of Foreign
Affairs at Washington in the said correspondence.

Referring to this same interesting subject, Your Honorable Lordship has
had the goodness to include an extract from the official letter addressed
by the Department of State at Washington to Mr. Prevost, Consul of the
United States at Lima,[4] which document contains a frank and explicit declaration on the part of the American Government respecting the conduct it would
observe should the European Powers attempt to intervene in the independence of any of the Nations of this Continent; the said communication particularly expressing the noble interest which animates the Supreme Government of the Union for the prosperity and happiness of Ecuador.

The President of the Republic of Ecuador, well informed of all the points
brought out in the interesting communication of Your Honorable Lordship,
has directed me to reply to Your Lordship in terms deeply significant of its
sentiments of gratitude toward the Government of the United States of

---

[1] Despatches, Ecuador, vol. 1; enclosed with Livingston to the Secretary of State, No. 3,
September 8, 1848, below, this part, doc. 2348.

[2] Above, this part, doc. 2346.   [3] *Ibid.,* November 26, 1846, doc. 2342.

[4] The extract was not found, but for the letter in full, see below, in the volume and part
containing Communications to Peru, under date of March 24, 1847.

North America for the assurances of fraternal goodwill which it was so kind as to offer the Government of Ecuador at a time when threats of an unjust and aggressive war obliged it to seek the support and moral protection of a Nation which is a Friend and sister of all those which form and compose the New World.

Kindly accept, therefore, Your Honorable Lordship, these assurances of such sincere and just gratitude, and transmit them to the illustrious American Government, for whose glory and aggrandizement the Ecuadorean Government and people fervently and constantly hope.

It is a pleasure for me to assure Your Honorable Lordship of the esteem and deference with which I have the honor to subscribe myself [etc.].

2348

Vanbrugh Livingston, United States Chargé d'Affaires at Quito, to James Buchanan, Secretary of State of the United States [1]

[EXTRACT]

No. 3   QUITO, *September 8, 1848.*

SIR: I have the honor to transmit herewith a copy of a communication which I addressed to this Government on the 22nd Ult. together with that of the answer thereto.[2]

The recent attempt on the part of the adherents of Genl Flores, to revolutionize the country, & to which I adverted in my last despatch,[3] has been frustrated, and public affairs are now returning to a state of comparative tranquility. . . .[4]

I have the honor [etc.].

2349

John Trumbull Van Alen, United States Chargé d'Affaires at Quito, to John M. Clayton, Secretary of State of the United States [5]

No. 27   QUITO, *February 1, 1850.*

DEAR SIR: I have the honor to inform you, that no further disturbances of a threatening political character, have occurred at Guayaquil.   The moral

---

[1] Despatches, Ecuador, vol. 1.   Received November 11.
[2] For these two notes, see above, this part, August 22 and 31, 1848, docs. 2346 and 2347.
[3] Above, this part, August 14, 1848, doc. 2345.
[4] The omitted portion relates to claims.
[5] Despatches, Ecuador, vol. 1.   Received April 8.
The writer of this despatch, John T. Van Alen, of New York, was commissioned chargé d'affaires of the United States to Ecuador, on June 5, 1849.   No record of when he actually left Ecuador was found.   The last despatch received from him was dated July 18, 1850, from Guayaquil, where he had repaired after the dissolution of the government at Quito and

power of the citizens has proved superior to military unfaithfulness. The revolters became, apparently, soon conscious, that they had raised a spirit, which threatened to overmaster them, and, accordingly they were fain to unite with others, to repress it. Nevertheless, I cannot regard the state of that province as entirely satisfactory. The recent mortifying defeat of the disturbing party was owing, greatly, to the want of a leader able, prompt and equal to the emergency. It is by some suspected, that the disaffected are looking about for a leader, who shall summon together their subdued forces, and make them effectual in a more determined and better organized outbreak. They may have cast their eyes upon Gen Flores, now poor, pining and discontented in exile. Indeed, a Peruvian journal, in commenting upon the recent movement in Guayaquil, speaks of it as made by the partisans of Gen Flores. This is not strictly the case, yet the friends of the banished Ex-president may be in secret contriving another demonstration hostile to the present Government.

About two years ago, the adherents of Gen. Flores attempted a revolution in his favor, but it failed for want of concert in action, and many of the leaders of the movement were banished by the late President Roca, who acted, on such occasions with considerable coolness, decision and intrepidity.

This affinity of disaffected persons, should it take place, would be the less surprising from another consideration. There has occurred at Costa Rica, where Gen. Flores has been recently residing, a revolution, in which the party friendly to him, has been defeated. He has, consequently, retired from that place. Information has been received, that he has just been chosen Commander In Chief of the forces of Guatemala, for the purpose of resisting the Indians of that country, who under the command of an Indian, Carrera, have made a formidable insurrection.

Since more prominence is now given to this individual, who, with the exception of Mr. Rocafuerte, is the only man, ever connected with the Government of the Ecuador, deserving particular notice, and, as his present position may lead to his reassumption of authority in this Republic, I have thought it worth while briefly to sketch his career, as far as I have been able to learn it from sources worthy of credit.

Juan José Flores was of humble, Indian origin. When very young, he was a servant in the employment of a Spanish Officer, who was engaged at the time, in the protracted resistance against the struggles of Spanish America for independence. His master was taken prisoner in an action,

the establishment, in Guayaquil, of the government of the revolutionary party. A letter from him, dated "New York, Aug. 8, 1850," explained that his ill health had compelled him to return home and that he "had permission to do so from the late President." From a letter from the Secretary of State to him, dated August 27, 1850, he apparently resigned on the 24th of that month.

He apparently continued the serial numbers of the despatches of his predecessor, as despatch No. 25 was the first received from him. It is not included, however, since it deals with a claims case.

and young Flores, after some time, was found a private soldier in the ranks of the army of the Patriots. His courage, ambition and perseverance were marked by his successive stages of advancement, until he received from Bolivar a General's commission. He was, then, appointed Intendant of the province of Quito. But, he was of a restless, unquiet spirit, and soon began to betray uneasiness in this subordinate sphere, and, at length, he boldly aspired to independent authority, though at the risk of breaking up the Republic of Colombia. His ardent ambition was impeded by no diffi-culties, and any sacrifice which it required, he was not merely willing, but eager to make. His measures were generally chosen with an astonishing degree of ingenuity and skill, and he had a profound knowledge of men and of motives. His persuasion was almost irresistible, and the fascination of his presence and manners was great. He brought over the army to his designs, and, thus strengthened and emboldened, declared the independence of the province of Quito. In this emergency, Gen Sucre was dispatched by Bolivar to supersede him in his Government, but on the way thither, he was assassi-nated, and some hesitate not to ascribe the deed to the instigation of Flores himself. Bolivar was about to send a force to Quito, to reduce it to quiet and subordination, but, before the necessary arrangements were completed, he died, and Flores, being thus unembarassed by the only man, whom he had occasion really to fear, found himself comparatively secure, whatever might be his plans. His great purpose of the division of the Republic, he now fully accomplished, in conjunction with Gen. Paez, of Venezuela, and he was elected the first President of the new Republic of the Ecuador, whilst his coadjutor likewise became the President of Venezuela.

The division of Colombia took place in 1830, when Gen Flores was elected President for four years. At the expiration of that period, he was elected for two years more, shortly before the end of which, a commotion took place, and he resigned the chief authority into the hands of Rocafuerte, who was elected to succeed him for four years. This man earnestly desired the welfare of his country, and governed it with enlightened prudence and en-ergy. He had spent some years in Europe and in the United States, and had improved the opportunities afforded by acquaintance with distinguished men, and by the study of history and general politics. He returned to the Ecuador, pre-eminently qualified to govern, and to advance all its interests. He set about great reforms, necessary to secure to the country its due position among civilized states. His thoughts were always occupied about the progress of the nation, and his hand was ever ready to accomplish what his mind decided to be requisite. He failed to receive that sincere and hearty cooperation, which he deserved and needed for full success. He was before his time, and was eventually banished and died in Peru.

Subsequently, Flores was elected for two years, and, when they had passed, Congress not having become organized, owing to disputed seats, he held office, in violation of the Constitution, for two years longer. When the next Congress met, the Constitution was amended, and Gen. Flores was elected for eight years, two only of which elapsed, when a revolution of a violent character broke out, against the President, and he capitulated. By the terms of the treaty, it was agreed, that there should be paid to him, annually, the sum of twenty thousand dollars, and that his private fortune should be secured to his family, provided that he would retire from the country, He did so, but these conditions have never been fulfilled on the part of the Ecuador, and hence have arisen the attempts of Gen Flores to regain his position, since he has never by word or deed, renounced his constitutional right to the Presidency, but only the practical exercise of the office.

After thus finding the party in power faithless to their expressed stipulations, Gen. Flores repaired to Europe, with a determination to promote his interest in some way. Such were his skill and address, that he succeeded in procuring from Queen Cristina, of Spain, a loan of two millions of dollars, to further his designs. It is regarded as in the highest degree marvellous, that Cristina, well known as exeedingly penurious, should have aided so largely a design, about the accomplishment of which there must have been very much uncertainty. It is stated, on good authority, that Cristina entered into the plans of Gen. Flores, for the sake of providing for her children by Munoz [Muñoz], to whom it was proposed to give, at length, three crowns, those of New Granada, Ecuador and Peru. Flores collected together 6,000 men, with whom he intended making the endeavor to reestablish his authority. Only two hundred of this number were soldiers. The rest were mostly artisans. An agent of his was engaged in fitting out several vessels in the port of London, when the agent of this country in England became aware of the undertaking, and complained respecting it to the Government of England, and the vessels were seized. The expedition being thus defeated, Gen Flores left Europe, and retired to Costa Rica, where he has, until very recently, resided. I think that he has been, for some time concerting measures with the disaffected in this country, for a renewed endeavor to regain his authority. His recent elevation to a high post in Guatemala will materially assist his purposes; it will tend to increase the devotion of his friends, and to incline the hesitating favorably towards him. From what I have learned, he governed the Republic with great skill and energy. He made many valuable improvements. He courted the members of the old established families, and drew them, generally, to his support. His well nigh irresistible persuasion often changed an enemy into a fast and valuable friend. That, in a country, exposed to constant political convulsions, he, for so long a time, held the reins of power, is owing, as much as to any single cause, to his winning and captivating address. His success in Europe may be attributed to the same cause. His reverses have, undoubtedly, much disciplined and enlarged his mind, and his greater acquaintance with men and with the world has, unquestionably, given him a deeper insight into the theory and practice of Government. His mind is one of surprising acuteness and readiness of apprehension. He is a constant observer and quick thinker. He would, probably, now, be the best Governor of a State, in South America, It should be added that he has not the reputation of a sanguinary man, which fact is, in these countries, a singularity. He has always preferred to gain men over to his side by flattery and artful policy, than to inflict on them summary vengeance. His attempt upon the Republic was not, as has been represented, an effort to usurp dominion or to continue in office longer than his allotted period, but, primarily at least, to secure the prerogatives which he had been lawfully chosen to exercise, and which he was forced, temporarily, to suspend, not by the people, generally, but by an interested and jealous faction.

Had he succeeded in bringing into the country nearly 6000 workmen, he would have conferred upon it an incalculable benefit. The great want here is of men guided by intelligent industry. The artisans are imitative, and ready to adopt improvements, but seeing few, they walk in the same steps as their forerunners in the various trades. But a small portion of the soil, which is as fine as any in the world, is cultivated, and that poorly. The Ecuador contains in itself the climates of all the zones, and her productions are of corresponding variety. Consequently, were her soil under the culture of men of intelligence and skill, she would be, for most of the articles of common necessity and comfort, more independent than most nations on the Globe. The difficulties in the way of her national progress, I am persuaded that General Flores has seen more clearly than any other man, and he has endeavored to remove them. His present position attaches much interest to him, and, if he be successful in repelling the inroads of the Indians, he will, perhaps, assume a higher position, and attract more general notice than at any previous part of his career. He is at present, notwithstanding his many and various experiences, but about fifty years of age.

I have the honor [etc.].

2350

*Courtland Cushing, United States Chargé d'Affaires at Quito, to Daniel
Webster, Secretary of State of the United States* [1]

[EXTRACTS]

No. 1   QUITO, *June 3, 1851.*

SIR: I have the honor to inform you that I arrived in Quito on the 30th
ultimo, . . .

The opinion is universal in Quito that war between New Granada and
Ecuador is now inevitable.—I have not enough information yet to form
reliable opinions as to the causes or the probable consequences of this war.—
It is however certain that the Government of Ecuador has encouraged
certain revolutionary tendencies and movements in the adjacent Province
of Pasto.—Much anxiety and alarm is felt here under the impression that
Ecuador is not able to check the New Granadian troops now on the march to
invade this Country.

In view of this war the Diplomatic Agents of Spain, France and Peru now
residing here, have written to their respective Governments for special
instructions.—If you think it advisable to instruct me in reference to it
I shall be pleased.

I have the honor [etc.].

2351

*José Villamil, Minister of Foreign Affairs of Ecuador, to Courtland Cushing,
United States Chargé d'Affaires in Ecuador* [2]

[TRANSLATION]

[C]   GUAYAQUIL, *February 26, 1852.*

Information received by the last steamer from Lima through persons of
whose veracity the Government can entertain no doubt, confirms that
previously received, to the effect that ex-General Juan José Flores was organizing an expedition of vandals to invade Ecuador, and that this invasion
was very soon to take place, this City being indicated, as the point probably
to be attacked.

In consequence, the undersigned Minister of Foreign Relations has received orders from his Government to transmit this information to the
Honorable Chargé d'Affaires of the United States, and to declare to His

[1] Despatches, Ecuador, vol. 2.   Received July 8.
   The writer of this despatch, Courtland Cushing, of Indiana, was commissioned chargé
d'affaires to Ecuador on September 28, 1850.   He left on October 31, 1853.
   The omitted portion relates to his journey from Guayaquil to Quito, and also to the presentation of his credentials.
[2] Despatches, Ecuador, vol. 2; enclosed with Cushing to the Secretary of State, No. 14,
March 13, 1852, below, this part, doc. 2353.

Lordship that, being bound by the laws of nature and of the State, the national will, and its own convictions, to save the independence, the nationality and the very existence of the Country from the destruction which threatens them, it is resolved to repel vandalism with law and war with war, even though it should be necessary to have recourse to more violent measures to accomplish it. But since this is not a war between nations, since the invaders do not belong to any recognized nation; nor is it a civil war, since they are neither Ecuadoreans nor can they rightfully invoke any principle, the Government will adopt such measures with them as natural justice and the Law of Nations authorize against enemies of this class, which must be and are considered as pirates, as was evidenced by the conduct observed by Great Britain and the Republic of France with respect to the expedition which invaded the Island of Cuba.

The Government of the undersigned being likewise informed that the vessels bringing the expedition to the coasts of Ecuador are flying the Ecuadorean flag, and as these vessels may very well cause serious injury to those of other nations, the Government is obliged to declare, as it solemnly does declare, that the vessels composing the said expedition have no right to use the flag of Ecuador, and that if any one of them used it heretofore with legitimate title, it loses its right to do so from the moment it becomes associated with a piratical expedition; being, therefore, subject to capture by the ships of any nation whatsoever. The Government of Ecuador likewise declares that since it is impossible for any nation to authorize with its flag undertakings of a piratical nature such as the present, neither will it recognize as legitimate any other flag of which, with equal abuse, the expeditionary forces may make use to invade the territory of Ecuador.

The undersigned will not conclude this note without calling the attention of the Honorable Chargé d'Affaires of the United States to the grave injuries which the threatened invasion will inevitably cause national and foreign Commerce, and the unforeseen disasters to which the property and even the lives of all the inhabitants of this City will be exposed by the hostilities of the invaders; but whatever may be the circumstances in which this City may find itself, even in case it should be converted into a Field of battle, the Government of the undersigned will lend every support and protection to neutrals who may be in the city and to their interests.

The undersigned takes this opportunity [etc.].

2352

*Courtland Cushing, United States Chargé d'Affaires in Ecuador, to José
Villamil, Minister of Foreign Affairs of Ecuador* [1]

[D]   GUAYAQUIL, *February 28, 1852.*

SIR: The undersigned Chargé d'Affaires of the United States has the
honor to acknowledge the receipt of your interesting letter of the 26th
instant [2] informing him that the Government had received reliable information by the late Steamer from Lima that Ex General John J. Flores is
organizing an expedition to invade Ecuador.—That the invasion is soon to
be made and this City is indicated as the point of attack.—That the Government of Ecuador being bound by the laws of nature and of the State, by the
National will and its own convictions, to save the independence and sovereignty of the Country from the destruction which threatens them, is resolved
to repel the invaders and to adopt such measures for the purpose as natural
justice and the law of nations authorize against enemies of that class &c.

The undersigned will avail himself of the first opportunity to communicate
this important information to the Government of the United States—In
the meantime, being satisfied that this expedition is a sequel to the one
projected by General Flores in 1846 and which was checked by the timely
interposition of the Government of Great Britain, the undersigned feels
fully authorized to say that the Government of the United States cannot
view with indifference such an attempt to interfere with the independence
and sovereignty of this Republic.

The undersigned [etc.].

2353

*Courtland Cushing, United States Chargé d'Affaires in Ecuador, to Daniel
Webster, Secretary of State of the United States* [3]

No. 14   GUAYAQUIL, *March 13, 1852.*

SIR: I have the honor to transmit herewith a copy (A) of a letter from
Mr Clay Chargé d'Affaires of the United States ["to Peru"?—Ed.],[4]

[1] Despatches, Ecuador, vol. 2; enclosed with Cushing to the Secretary of State, No. 14,
March 13, 1852, below, this part, doc. 2353.
[2] Above, this part, doc. 2351.
[3] Despatches, Ecuador, vol. 2.   Received April 8.
[4] This letter, dated February 8, 1852, follows:

*John Randolph Clay, United States Chargé d'Affaires in Peru, to Courtland Cushing,
United States Chargé d'Affaires in Ecuador*

A. Confidential.   LIMA, *February 8, 1852.*

SIR: I have marked this letter "confidential" because I do not wish to be cited as
authority for the intelligence it conveys, although I think it to the interest of the United
States that the Government of Ecuador should be acquainted with what is going on

on the subject of a projected invasion of Ecuador by General Flores, and respectfully commend to your attention the concluding paragraph.—That Mʳ Adams British Chargé d'Affaires at Lima is giving countenance to the movement is more than probable—Mʳ Macguire a young merchant of Baltimore who recently came here from Lima informs me that an acquaintance of his a Young Irishman had received an appointment a few weeks ago from General Flores as Adjutant General upon the recommendation of Mʳ Adams.—(B) is a copy of my reply to Mʳ Clay [1] and correctly represents

here.—Possibly, its agents in Lima may have advised the Minister of Foreign Affairs and led him to expect a movement from this quarter.—

It appears that the partisans of General Flores are busily engaged in organizing an expedition against the Ecuador.—I am informed by a person on whose word I can rely that two vessels have been chartered in Callao to convey the persons who have enlisted to some point on the coast of that Republic.—They are said to number about 600, which is "all they want".—I use their own words,—General Flores has been ill with the dysentery and is still confined to the house, although somewhat better, so that it is uncertain when the expedition will sail.

It seems almost impossible that the Peruvian Government should be ignorant of what is going on, notwithstanding that the Minister of War assured me that there was nothing on foot, and that the present Administration were in favor of General Urbina—for how could a secret be kept by six hundred men from a Government that makes use of spies on occasion.—

I give you the information as I received it and leave it to your option, to communicate it to the Ecuador Government; only I should not wish to have my name mixed up in the matter.

With regard to the difficulty between the Ecuador Government and the Spanish Consul, I think that the latter acted most unjustifiably and should be reprimanded by his own Ministry when he arrives in Spain.—

Two American vessels have been taken possession of, by the convicts at the Chillian settlement in the straits of Magellan. One of them had a quantity of gold dust on board from California.—I understood that the British Admiral had dispatched two armed Steamers to the Straits in pursuit of them.—Comodore McCauley left Callao in the Raritan on the 22ᵈ ultimo in search of the Marauders.—I addressed a note to the Peruvian Minister of Foreign Affairs on the subject and requested that orders might be issued to the authorities to arrest the said vessels in case they should appear in any port of the Republic—orders to that effect have been accordingly sent forward. I think however that the vessels have been directed to Buenos Ayres or Montevideo as they would have the wind and currents in their favor from the Straits.—

I omitted to mention that I am under the impression that the British Government, although it might not openly assist Gen! Flores in any expedition against the Ecuador would be pleased to see him restored to power; as Lord Palmerston instructed both the Chargé d'Affaires of Central America and at Lima to show General Flores particular attention upon his arrival in either of those Countries.—It would seem therefore that the British Government was at least aware of his intended movements.

I remain [etc.].

[1] Cushing's reply, dated February 29, 1852, follows:

Courtland Cushing, United States Chargé d'Affaires in Ecuador, to John Randolph Clay, United States Chargé d'Affaires in Peru

GUAYAQUIL, *February 29, 1852.*

SIR: On the 13ᵗʰ instant I received your interesting letter of the 8ᵗʰ [See footnote immediately above.—Ed.]. The information relative to General Flores appeared to me so important that I immediately called upon the Secretary of Foreign Affairs and communicated it to him.—The Government received corresponding information on the same day by letters from private individuals, though its agent in Lima seems to be under the impression that Flores is not moving.—The Government however relies

Footnote 1, p. 272—*Continued*

upon the information communicated and is actively engaged in preparing to repel the invasion.—

My predecessor Col. Van Alen regarded General Flores with favor and entertained the opinion that his return would be advantageous to Ecuador; Under the influence of Col. Van Alen's opinions I came to this Country with prepossessions favorable to the General; but having learned much of his public and private history since my arrival I am compelled to think that he has been and continues to be a curse upon Ecuador and that his return and restoration to power would be one of the greatest calamities that could befal the Country.—I am fully persuaded that nine tenths of the people who think upon the subject at all are utterly opposed to him and not one in a hundred ever intimates a desire for his return.

The statement of a few facts will suffice to show that the general opposition to him in this Country is founded on good reasons.

He is a native of Venezuela of humble origin.—His public carreer began very early in life and he was continually in the public service in either military or civil stations until he left the country in 1845.—He conspired against his friend and patron General Bolivar and was mainly instrumental in dissolving the Colombian Confederacy. —The division took place in 1830 and from that time until he left the Country he was continually President of Ecuador either by election or usurpation, with the exception of four years—the presidential term of Rocafuerte.—During all this time he did nothing for the Country but used the public revenues for the benefit of himself and his favorites. —He has not left a single monument of his patriotism.—Nothing to show that he cared for the general welfare.—He erected for himself a splendid mansion in Quito at an expense of about eighty thousand dollars in which his family still resides.—He gave another house worth some seven or eight thousand dollars to a strolling actress.— He owns three estates between Guayaquil and Quito either of which is equal in extent to one of our largest Counties and would be considered princely under a stable Government.—He also owns valuable gold mines.—None of this property came to him by descent or marriage; he acquired the whole of it while in the public service upon salaries not sufficent to support a man of his expensive habits.—After the expiration of Rocafuerte's term, Gen! Flores was reelected President for two years—then held the office two years longer in violation of the Constitution—and then to mitigate the odium which rested upon him at home and abroad in consequence of this bold and palpable usurpation, he constituted a Junta at Quito which he denominated a Convention; consisting of members virtually chosen by himself.—This Junta adopted a new constitution dictated by him and then elected him President for a term of eight years—The proceedings of this Junta did not pacify the disaffected citizens of Ecuador but rather increased the opposition to General Flores.—A revolution and civil war ensued which resulted in his capitulation upon terms agreed to between him and the provisional Government constituted by the leaders of the revolution.—He agreed to submit and leave the country for two years on condition that they would pay him twenty thousand dollars in money to support him during his absence—continue to pay him an annual salary equal to that of Commander in Chief of the Army—pay the Military Officers who served under him regular pensions according to their rank—protect his private property &c.   The twenty thousand dollars were paid to him and he went to Europe.—Before the two years expired, in concert with the Queen of Spain he was fitting out an expedition to invade and subjugate this Country.—This project was frustrated by the Government of Great Britain.—The agreement in respect to his salary has not been complied with, and I believe the opinion is general in Ecuador that a nation cannot be bound by any such agreement with a usurper and traitor.—

What plausible pretext can he have for the expedition which he is now organizing in Peru to invade this Country?   There is no corresponding movement here.—This Government is at peace with all nations and there are no indications of a serious opposition at home.   Such an expedition cannot easily be carried on without interfering with the commerce and citizens of other nations—Can such interference be tolerated? I regard this expedition as indefensible as that of Lopez against Cuba.   If the Government of Peru permits it to be organized within its territories without an effort to put it down, it ought to be held responsible for the consequences so far as our Commerce and citizens may be injuriously affected.—But if the expedition be organized and carried on in despite of the efforts of Peru to put it down, then to what nation are we to look for redress for any injuries that may be done to our citizens by the invaders?—The right to make war is a prerogative which belongs only to independent nations who can be held responsible for all violation of neutral rights which may be occasioned thereby.—In a

the public opinion of this Country in regard to General Flores,—(C) is a letter from the Secretary of Foreign Affaires on the subject of the expected invasion and (D) is my reply.[1]—On the night of the 9th instant a Bark which had been despatched for that purpose by the Ecuadorean Charge d'Affaires at Lima, brought intelligence that a part of the expedition had sailed from the Port of Callao.—Since the receipt of this information the people of this City have been in a state of intense anxiety.—A determination to repel the invasion seems to pervade the whole community.—I do not believe he will attempt an invasion at this point.—He must know the people of this City too well to rely upon any cooperation here, and according to the information we have his force is too small to succeed without.

The attention of the Government has been so occupied by General Flores for two or three months past that I have not been able to fix it properly on the claim of John D. Danels [Daniels?].

I have the honor [etc.].

2354

Courtland Cushing, United States Chargé d'Affaires in Ecuador, to Daniel Webster, Secretary of State of the United States [2]

No. 15   GUAYAQUIL, *March 14, 1852.*

SIR: The British Mail Steamer has just arrived from Lima bringing most alarming intelligence in respect to the Flores expedition.—As the Steamer will leave in the course of half an hour I have only time to say that I have a long communication from Mr Clay [3] on the subject in which he says that an agent of Genl Flores had called upon him recently and said that I had publickly declared in the streets of Guayaquil that I had received intelligence in respect to the expedition from Mr Clay and had also declared that the Government of the United States would regard the expedition as piratical

---

civil war the unfortunate Country in which it exists is responsible for the acts of both parties.—In a war between nations one or the other is always responsible for any consequent violations of the rights of neutrals.—But here is an expedition organized in a foreign land to make a hostile invasion of Ecuador which cannot be efficiently carried on without injury to citizens of other nations.—An expedition that is not openly sustained by any nation,—That has no national indorser.—In my judgment it is the common duty as well as right of all nations whose commerce or citizens are likely to be injured by this lawless expedition, to put it down by force.—

One of my motives for writing to you so much on this subject is to induce you to unite with me in urgently requesting Comodore McCauley to send a vessel of war to this port as soon as possible to watch the current of events and if need be afford protection to our commerce and citizens.—By the Steamer which carries this I will send a few lines on the subject to our Minister in Chili.

I am very respectfully [etc.].

[1] For these two notes, see above, this part, February 26 and 28, 1852, docs. 2351 and 2352.
[2] Despatches, Ecuador, vol. 2.   Received April 1.   [3] Not found.

and authorize the vessels of war of the U. States to capture any of the ships engaged in it &c.—

I beg you to rest assured that I have not committed any such folly.— What I communicated to the Government from Mr Clay was in strict confidence.—I have made neither threats nor promises in behalf of the United States touching this expedition.

I have the honor [etc.].

2355

Courtland Cushing, United States Chargé d'Affaires in Ecuador, to Daniel Webster, Secretary of State of the United States [1]

EXTRACT]

No. 16   GUAYAQUIL, *March 27, 1852.*

SIR: . . . The Expedition of General Flores consisting of from 700 to 1000 men, one steamer, one brig and two barks, is now lying off the Island of Lobos—His vessels carry the flag of the late Colombian Government.— I have no doubt of the ability and determination of the Government of Ecuador to put down the Expedition without aid from any quarter.—But if the Captain of the Sweedish Frigate comes across armed vessels upon the ocean without some flag to indicate their nationality I shall not be surprised to hear of his treating them as lawless adventurers.

I have the honor [etc.].

2356

José Villamil, Minister of Foreign Affairs of Ecuador, to Courtland Cushing, United States Chargé d'Affaires in Ecuador [2]

[TRANSLATION]

[J]. Confidental.   GUAYAQUIL, *April 6, 1852.*

The undersigned, Minister of Foreign Relations of Ecuador, has the honor to address himself to the Honorable Chargé d'Affaires of the United States by direction of his Government, in order to call the attention of His Honorable Lordship to certain facts of the greatest gravity, the tendencies of

[1] Despatches, Ecuador, vol. 2.   Received April 23.
The omitted portion relates to Cushing's letter of thanks to the captain of a Swedish frigate for securing the capture and return of a United States whale ship, which had been forcibly seized by a band of pirates, two or three weeks before.   It relates, also, to the surrender of a former British mail steamer which had been sold to General Flores, and which tried to enter the harbor at Guayaquil.
[2] Despatches, Ecuador, vol. 2; enclosed with Cushing to the Secretary of State, No. 17, April 13, 1852, below, this part, doc. 2358.

which would be disastrous to the Republican order adopted as a form of Government by the nations of the South American Continent.

The Honorable Mr. Cushing is perfectly informed as to the character of the expedition formed in the ports of Peru by the expatriated American Juan José Flores, to invade this Republic, and as to the circumstances which have contributed to its formation; and he must be convinced that such an expedition is not an isolated act with the sole object of restoring Flores to the power which he lost in Ecuador by the sovereign will of all the people composing it. The Government has reason to believe that this criminal enterprise is the continuation of that projected by Flores in Europe in 1846, with the wicked design of making monarchies of the independent republics which were formerly Spanish colonies, and is gratified to see that the Honorable Mr. Cushing shares this opinion, as is evidenced by the note of February 28 which he addressed to this Ministry in reply to that of the undersigned of the 26th of the same month.[1]

They are not mere suspicious or uncertain calculations that lead the Government of Ecuador to believe in the existence of a secret plan of monarchization which is developing under the appearance of an isolated attempt of Flores against Ecuador; the facts which reveal and prove it are positive and well known, and I shall cite the most notable of these facts to His Honorable Lordship.

Too well known were the origin and tendencies of the expedition formed by Flores in 1846, and the persons who furnished its resources and protection, for there to be any doubt respecting the course it was then desired to give to the plan to monarchize the republics of America, a plan contrived in Europe long ago, whose principal seat of action is in Spain, and in the interest of which some attempts had made their appearance in America at various periods, as in those of General San Martin, General Bolivar and others. These attacks of the monarchical principle against the Republican; this struggle between dominator and dominated, from the time that America proclaimed her independence, have been the cause of continued upheavals and an obstacle to the progress and consolidation of the growing Republic.

Although this plan was frustrated by the dissolution of the fleet of Flores in England, its authors did not therefore abandon it; and seeing in the war which Flores waged against Ecuador, a means to continue it and a powerful instrument for its realization, they have always protested the designs of that leader.

The expedition with which Flores has departed from Peru to invade us, is evident proof of that protection; since it is no secret that Flores, an outlaw, abandoned to his own resources and to those of his personal followers, outlaws like himself, would not have been able to pay even his own passage to Ecuador, much less to arm an expedition costing more than half a million

---

[1] For these two notes, see above, this part, docs. 2351 and 2352.

dollars (*pesos*).   It is in Peru, then, that Flores has found the resources he lacks and the protection he needs; and I wish to call the attention of the Honorable Mr. Cushing to the fact that Peru is the only one of the nations of America in which monarchical ideas are welcomed, with the notable circumstance that the individuals who compose the present Cabinet of that Republic and who have accorded to Flores such a good reception and so marked a protection, have long been known as decided partisans of the establishment of Monarchies in America.

If Flores were not therefore charged with carrying out such a plan, would it be credible that they would have given him those resources and that protection in a foreign country, being, as he is, an outlaw, solely to serve him?   Is not the tolerance with which it has seen that expedition arm itself and depart, and the acts of sovereignty exercised by Flores in its territory, shooting four of the men he had enlisted in his service, a proof that the Government of Peru is resolved to protect in every way the expedition of Flores?   And does not the apparent indifference, with which the Agents of the States of Europe in Peru and in this republic have viewed the consummation of an act so outrageous and so contrary to the laws of their own countries, give grounds for the belief that a combination exists which guarantees the success of the Flores enterprize?

But what concerns my Government even more are the publications which are now being issued by all the newspapers of the Peninsula and the Antilles, while Flores is invading Ecuador; publications which, after plainly discrediting the republican principle, and characterizing the policy of the United States as that of invader and destroyer of all nationalities, proposes, as a remedy for the evils which America deplores, and as a barrier to the supposed pretensions of the Republic of the North, an offensive and defensive league between all the Spanish-American republics and the Spanish nation, and that the latter *should lead* in the combat.   These publications clearly reveal the existence of a plan to monarchize the republics, poorly disguised under the idea of that alliance; since it is not possible to explain in any other way this sudden concern on the part of a nation, situated on a continent so far from ours, and without sufficient naval forces to enforce its action, for the nationality of peoples who, although of the same origin, profess such different principles, and whose interests are so diverse.

These circumstances have justly alarmed the Government of the undersigned, which, after having notified the other American States of the shameful fact of the Flores expedition and its tendencies, believes it its duty to call the attention of His Honorable Lordship to all these points; and intends to indicate to the Convention which is to meet next July the necessity of a treaty of guaranty between this Republic and the model Republic of North America to uphold the principles common to both against the grave dangers which encompass them; and there is no doubt that such a project has the approval of the National Assembly and the assent of the Government of the Union.   But as nothing could be so agreeable or have greater influence on the counsels of the National Assembly than the previous and explicit knowledge of the sentiments entertained by the Government of Your Honorable Lordship on this important matter, the undersigned has been especially charged by His Excellency the Supreme Chief to signify to Your Honorable Lordship the necessity and desirability of obtaining this knowledge in due time.

With this end in view, the undersigned [etc.].

2357

Courtland Cushing, United States Chargé d'Affaires in Ecuador, to José Villamil, Minister of Foreign Affairs of Ecuador [1]

K   GUAYAQUIL, *April 12, 1852.*

SIR: The undersigned Chargé d'Affaires of the United States has the honor to acknowledge the receipt of your very interesting communication of the 6th instant,[2] showing that the Government of Ecuador has reasons for believing that the present Criminal Enterprize of General Flores is a continuation of that projected by him in Europe in 1846, with the wicked dezign of making monarchies of the Independent Republics which were formerly Spanish Colonies—That the Government in view of the circumstances intends to indicate to the convention which is to assemble in July next the necessity of a treaty of guarrantee between this Republic and that of the United States for the purpose of sustaining the principles common to both; and that in the meantime nothing could be more agreeable or have greater influence on the counsels of the National Assembly than to be explicitly apprized of a corresponding disposition on the part of the United States.

The undersigned will avail himself of the first opportunity to communicate this important information and commend it to the particular attention of his Government.—

Hitherto the Government of the United States has never entered into any such treaty as the one suggested—having adopted the maxim of "Friendly relations with all, but entangling alliances with none."   But the Government of the United States cannot be an idle spectator at any attempt on the part of Foreign Powers to interfere with the Soveregnty and independence of any of the American Republics.—

The Undersigned avails himself [etc.].

[1] Despatches, Ecuador, vol. 2; enclosed with Cushing to the Secretary of State, No. 17, April 13, 1852, below, this part, doc. 2358.   [2] Above, this part, doc. 2356.

2358

Courtland Cushing, United States Chargé d'Affaires in Ecuador, to Daniel Webster, Secretary of State of the United States [1]

[EXTRACT]

No. 17   GUAYAQUIL, *April 13, 1852.*

SIR: . . . The course of Captain Virgin[2] in relation to the Expedition is regarded as rather singular. It is evident from his own statements and those of his first Lieutenant, that he left Callo [Callao] with the intention of putting it down by force if necessary. The day after his arrival at Guayaquil however, M⟨r⟩ Montholon, Chargé d'Affaires of France called upon [*sic*] at the house of the Supreme Chief and cautioned him in the most earnest manner not to take hostile measures against the Expedition. Told him that the first Expedition of Flores (1846) was encouraged or supported by the Governments of Spain France and England. That the latter in consequence of some disatisfaction with the Government of Spain put a stop to it. That the present Expedition was doubtless a sequel of that. Alluded to the contemplated matrimonial alliance between Louis Bonaparte and a Swedish princess and suggested that a hostile interference on his part might offend his Sovereign. I am credibly informed and believe that M⟨r⟩ Montholon talked thus to the Captain. He used the same arguments to prevent me from advising a resort to hostile measures. Several days afterwards, however, Captain Virgin wrote to the Minister of Foreign Affairs from Puna where his frigate was then at anchor, that he was going to drop down a little to take a better position and the Government might rest assured that he would remain there until an American vessel of war arrived.—That he would not only prevent a bombardment of the City but also prevent the Expedition from disembarking within the river.—Within forty eight hours of the date of this letter the frigate had disappeared and the Expedition was at Puna, where it has remained ever since—some ten days—evidently too weak to make an attack upon the City—but maintai[ni]ng a sort of blockade.—Some three days ago a regularly documented merchant vessel of the United States was boarded by order of General Flores and detained at Puna some twenty four hours—then compelled to go out to sea, altho' the Captain having lost an anchor, wished for that cause to return to Guayaquil.

G & H are copies of letters from M⟨r⟩ Clay United States Chargé d'Affaires at Lima in relation to the Expedition, "I" is my reply.[3]

In consequence of this Expedition there has been little or no commerce for

[1] Despatches, Eucador, vol. 2. Received May 4.
The omitted portion relates chiefly to correspondence between the Ecuadoran Minister of Foreign Relations and Cushing, relative to United States seamen.
[2] He was the captain of the Swedish frigate *Eugénie.*
[3] Enclosure G was not found, and I is not included in this publication, since it merely acknowledges receipt of Clay's letter (enclosure H) which follows:

a month past.—Two American merchant vessels the "Homer" of Boston and the "Nancy" of Baltimore had to leave here without cargoes and will probably sustain losses to the amount of ten or twelve thousand dollars in consequence.—

Since General Flores left this country in 1845 there has never been any public manifestation in favour of him.—Yet in defiance of the popular will he seems determined by force or fraud to get possession of the Government—Directly and indirectly he has been the cause of every revolution that has taken place in Ecuador since the War of Independence.—

Letter J is an important confidential communication from the Government to which I particularly invite your attention.—K is my reply.[1]—This communication is indicative of a prevailing disposition among the people of this province to place Ecuador under the protection of the United States.—I therefore most respectfully but earnestly commend the subject to your attention.

On the 6th ultimo the Government issued a proclamation calling a Convention to assemble on the 17th of July next in Guayaquil for the purpose of forming a Constitution.

The American brig "Silas Marine"[2] Captain Long, from Baltimore has just arrived in this port.— The Captain states that the "Admiralte Blanco"

John Randolph Clay, United States Chargé d'Affaires in Peru, to Courtland Cushing, United States Chargé d'Affaires in Ecuador

LIMA, *March 22, 1852.*

SIR: Enclosed you will find copies of a note adressed to me by General Elizalde, the Chargé of the Ecuador on the 8th instant [See below, in the volume and part containing Communications from Peru.—Ed.], transmitting the decree of the 27th February by which his government has declared Flores and his Expedition to be pirates, as soon as they shall sail from the port where it has been organized; and of my answer to the same dated the 9th of this month [See below, in the volume and part containing Communications from Peru.—Ed.]—I also send a copy of the correspondence which has taken place between Gen! Elizalde and the Peruvian Minister of Foreign Affairs [Not found in the manuscript volume with this letter.—Ed.], which the former has published in the Comercio, edited in this capital.   As he did not consult the Minister before publishing the notes, it has the appearance of a direct appeal to the Peruvian nation, against one of its cabinet, which is altogether unusual and undiplomatic.   The notes signed by Elizalde are supposed to have been written by Mr Arosemena, the Chargé d'Affaires of New Granada, who has made himself conspicuous in the matter of the Expedition.

Mr Arosemena adressed a note to me on the 12th of May requesting that I should induce the commander of any U. S. ship of war, arriving at Callao, to interfere and prevent the Expedition of Flores from landing at Choco in N. Grenada, which I refused as you will see by my answer to him [Not found.—Ed.].—Flores is said to be still lying off Callao in his Steamer the "Chile" receiving men and provisions from his agents on shore.—He left Lima at 11 at night on the 11th instant.   Elizalde, as you will see by his note of the 20th has asked for his passport which has been sent him.   Between ourselves, he has been outwitted by the Peruvians.—I have not time to add more or even to keep a copy of this despatch.

Very Respectfully [etc.].

[1] For these two notes, see above, this part, April 6 and 12, 1852, docs. 2356 and 2357.
[2] Various spellings of the name of this brig appeared in the manuscript volume.

one of Flores' armed vessels fired on her six times, but having a pilot on board and a stiff breeze she did not come to,

I have the honor [etc.].

2359

Courtland Cushing, United States Chargé d'Affaires in Ecuador, to Daniel Webster, Secretary of State of the United States [1]

[EXTRACTS]

No. 18   GUAYAQUIL, *May 1, 1852.*

SIR: I have the honor to inform you that the Flores Expedition is still laying at Puna—getting weaker and weaker every day.—About two hundred and fifty Chillaneans have left it.—Eighty six of them arrived in this City yesterday.—All the Chillaneans 380 in number, were enticed from their homes by the assurance that they were taken directly to the mines of California. They were brought from Chile to Puna in a United States merchant vessel called the Lyons—F. O. Davis ostensible owner. It sailed as far as Tumbes under the United States flag and then hoisted the Ecuatorian flag under which it is now laying at Puna. The American crew of that vessel arrived here on the 29th ultimo in the United States Sloop of War Portsmouth, having come for the purpose of obtaining their wages through the intervention of the United States consul at his place. . . .[2]

The United States frigate Raritan arrived at Puna about the 16th ultimo. As soon as it was known here by the arrival of Lieutenant Dulaney in a boat from the frigate that Commodore McCauley was on board of her, the Government of Ecuador by a note of which (B) is a copy politely tendered me the use of its steamer to enable me to pay my respects to him.[3] Accordingly on the 21st ultimo I visited the Commodore and remained with him about five hours, during which time I communicated to him verbally as fully as I could my information and views in respect to the Expedition and also handed him a written communication of which C is a copy.[4] . . .

I have the honor [etc.].

[1] Despatches, Ecuador, vol. 2. There was no receipt date on this despatch, but on an enclosure with it there appeared at the top of the page, "Recd 7. June."
[2] This omitted portion relates to the case of a United States seaman who was denied a passport by the Ecuadoran authorities because it was known that he was a volunteer member of the Flores expedition; and the omitted portion, at the close of this despatch, relates to the affidavits of the captains of the two merchant vessels, mentioned in the first letter of footnote 4, below.   [3] Not included in this publication.
[4] This letter, and also another, from Cushing to McCauley, follow:

Courtland Cushing, United States Chargé d'Affaires in Ecuador, to Commodore Charles S. McCauley, United States Navy

GUAYAQUIL, *April 19, 1852.*

SIR: It is notorious that an Expedition was lately organized in Peru by General Flores, for the purpose of invading Ecuador.—This Expedition consisting of a steamer and

Footnote 4, p. 281—*Continued*

several other armed vessels and some six hundred armed men, is as you know lying at Puna about forty miles from this City.—The men engaged in it are nearly all foreigners of different nations and languages and having no interests or ties in this Country.—If General Flores has any supporters in Ecuador it must have been known by them for several months past that he was engaged in organizing the Expedition, yet there has been no corresponding movement whatever in any part of the Republic.— Not the slightest public manifestation in his favor.—Indeed since he left the Country in 1845 there has never been a public movement or manifestation in favor of him in any part of the Republic.—On the contrary in every Province, City and village of Ecuador, there have been during that time repeated and unequivocal manifestations of the popular will against him.—

The aniversary of the 6th of March 1845.—The first day of the Revolution which resulted in his expulsion from the Country is "the 4th of July" of Ecuador.—It has ever since been observed as a day of general rejoicing throughout the Republic; and all official papers issued from the Government since his Expulsion, show that it is the Epoch of liberty to Ecuador.—

The Government of Ecuador by a public proclamation and decree has declared the Expedition piratical. And the Government of Peru upon whose soil it was organized has issued a proclamation against it similar to that issued by the President of the United States against the late Expedition of Lopez. In these circumstances it must be regarded as a lawless Expedition by the whole civilized world. An Expedition impudently exercising national prerogatives without national responsibility.

I know of several instances in which this lawless Expedition will cause heavy pecuniary losses to citizens of the United [States?] and which in my judgment would justify you in putting it down by force. But you will see from the affidavits certificates &c which I herewith enclose [Not included in this publication.—Ed.] that the Expedition has to answer for something more than consequential damages.

It appears from these that on the night of the 8th instant the "Charran" a merchant vessel of the United States was boarded taken possession of and detained twenty four hours by order of Genl. Flores and then compelled to go to sea although the Captain having lost an anchor desired for that reason to return to Guayaquil.

It also appears that on the 9th instant the "Silas Marrean" another merchant vessel of the United States was fired on five times by one of the vessels pertaining to the Expedition. They were both regularly documented merchant vessels of the United States and under our national flag when thus assailed. It is therefore obvious that the outrage cannot be overlooked—

In conclusion I respectfully suggest that the most effectual method of protecting our commerce against similar outrages is to make a public example by putting an immediate end to the lawless Enterprise.

&c. &c. &c.

Courtland Cushing, United States Chargé d'Affaires in Ecuador, to Commodore Charles S. McCauley, United States Navy

GUAYAQUIL, *April 23, 1852.*

SIR: The United States merchant vessel "Charran" returned to this port this morning. M. P. Game Esqr United States consul at Guayaquil has taken sworn declarations from the Captain Henry Collins and the mate William Gurney which I herewith enclose [Not included in this publication.—Ed.] and from which you will see that General Flores has attempted to deceive you in regard to the detention of that vessel.

I have already informed you that the Government of Ecuador has declared the Expedition of General Flores piratical and that, the Government of Peru has by a public proclamation warned the citizens of Peru that they would forfeit all right to the protection of their Government by engaging in it. The accompanying copy of the late message of the President of New Grenada [Not found.—Ed.] shows that he also regards it as a lawless Expedition and will aid Ecuador if necessary in putting it down.

Having previously informed you that our commerce has been seriously injured and our flag grossly insulted by this lawless Expedition, I have nothing further to add but the assurance that I am [etc.].

2360

Courtland Cushing, United States Chargé d'Affaires in Ecuador, to Daniel Webster, Secretary of State of the United States [1]

[EXTRACT]

No. 19   GUAYAQUIL, *June 1, 1852.*

SIR: The Flores Expedition still exists at Puna. The United States Sloop of War "Portsmouth" is at anchor in front of my house and the United States Frigate "Raritan" is laying at Payta. General Flores made explanations or apologies to Comodore McCauley and to Captain Dornin in relation to his detention of the United States merchant vessel "Charran" and his firing upon the United States merchant vessel "Silas Marean" [Marine?] I am not fully informed in regard to these explanations or apologies and therefore refrain from any comments on the subject.

In previous despatches including copies of my letters on the subject to J. Randolph Clay Esqr, United States Chargé d'Affaires at Lima—to Captain Virgin of the Swedish frigate "Eugenie" and to Comodore McCauley my views in regard to this lawless Expedition are distinctly expressed.[2]

It is notorious in this region that the Expedition is "not under the acknowledged authority or deriving protection from the flag or commision of any Government." Without any such authority or protection it was permitted to sail from Callao and has been allowed to obstruct commerce and insult national flags with impunity.

The Government of Ecuador having purchased four or five vessels for the purpose is actively engaged in fitting them out to go down and attack the Expedition. This little fleet will be commanded by General Illingworth an English Gentlemen of much intelligence and excellent character who was a very distinguished officer of the Colombian navy during the War of Independence.—

About a week ago the Peruvian War Steamer "Rimac" arrived at this Port having left a Peruvian brig of war at Puna. The object of the visit was to tender the mediation of the Peruvian Government between the Government of Ecuador and General Flores. The proposition, however, was not distinctly made owing to the fact that the first intimation on the subject from the Peruvian Chargé d'Affaires was promptly met by a declaration from the Supreme Chief that he could make no terms with a man who had been declared a pirate by the Government and was so regarded by the people of Ecuador. The steamer having made a very short stay returned with the brig to Callao.

[1] Despatches, Ecuador, vol. 2. Received July 3.
The omitted portion at the end of this despatch relates to internal politics, to an enclosed affidavit in regard to the two merchant vessels, mentioned in the first paragraph of this despatch, and to Cushing's salary account.
[2] See above, this part, p. 272, note 1, his letter to Clay, and in the same part, p. 281, note 4, his letters to McCauley. Those to Captain Virgin are not included in this publication.

You are doubtless apprized of the movements of the Government of New Grenada [Granada] in respect to the Expedition and of its declared intention to aid Ecuador in putting it down. The people of Ecuador are utterly opposed to the return of General Flores and I think there is no reasonable probability of his success unless he is sustained by some Government more powerful than that of Peru. . . .

I have the honor [etc.].

2361

José Villamil, Minister of Foreign Affairs of Ecuador, to Courtland Cushing, United States Chargé d'Affaires in Ecuador [1]

[TRANSLATION]

GUAYAQUIL, *June 7, 1852.*

SIR: The Undersigned, Minister of Foreign Relations of the Republic of Ecuador, has been instructed by his government to address himself to the Chargé d'Affaires of the United States, and to inform him that a steamer has arrived at Puna with forty citizens of the United States, brought here for the purpose of imparting greater activity to the work of destruction begun by the bandit Flores. The statement, an authentic copy of which accompanies this,[2] reveals this fact, with regard to a very substantial part of it, and although the deponent has not had an opportunity of learning the name of the vessel, nor to ascertain what flag she has hoisted, every thing tends to the conviction that it is the American Steamer "Quickstep," whose arrival from California, as an auxiliary of Flores, was daily expected, as it has been shewn to the Chargé d'Affaires of the United States; this then is the second time that Flores has had the audacity of making the glorious spangled banner subservient to his criminal designs.

It is not the arrival of this vessel, nor the reinforcement she brings, that have been the cause of the instructions which the Undersigned has received, to address himself to the Chargé d'Affaires of the United States: No; ten times the number of the forces and auxiliaries that Flores has brought with him, would not be that which could intimidate men who have had the courage to bury themselves under the ruins of their habitations, rather than consent to their disgrace. A worthier motive than the presence of these men, is what has called forth the present note. Before explaining this motive, the Undersigned will take a brief survey, although nobody stands in need of it, of the origin of the nefarious expedition which threatens the political existence of a free and independent Republic, and the lives of all its inhabitants.

This expedition, the shame and the scandal of the 19th century, was armed

[1] Despatches, Ecuador, vol. 2; enclosed with Cushing to the Secretary of State, No. 20, July 1, 1852, below, this part, doc. 2362.   [2] Not found.

in the ports of Peru and Chili, to the knowledge of the governments of those Republics; and its work of destruction was commenced and carried on in sight of the various ships of war of different nations, that had penetrated as far as the mouth of these waters. Ecuador had no reason to be surprised, because she knows the tendencies of this horrid expedition, and of its abettors.

But the Undersigned is impelled by an irresistible impulse to ask the Chargé d'Affaires of the United States, whether Ecuador could ever have had cause to fear that a part of this expedition, protected by the American flag and composed of Americans, so zealous in their own country for the preservation of their political rights, and their liberty, would have sailed from a port of the United States, for the purpose of coming to enslave, to plunder, and to annihilate a sister republic, the friend and ally of the former, on account of identity of principles and the irresistible affinity of causes;—a Republic, where a Chargé of the United States resides, and where the flag of the United States is displayed on board a vessel of war, in the port which has been attacked? Sir, it is necessary to see this, as we are seeing it, in order to believe it; and without attributing any other but a legitimate meaning to what the undersigned is about to utter, he would say, that this unjustifiable aggression against a free people, by citizens of the country of Washington, which until now has been held up as the model of Republics, is the only one, out of the whole series of such dark events, which has succeeded in depressing the spirits of the people of Ecuador.

The foregoing remarks embrace the substance of what the Undersigned has been instructed to say to the Chargé d'Affaires of the United States; he will not conclude this note, however, without assuring the latter, that if a party of heartless Ecuadorians, (the hypothesis can neither be assumed nor admitted) were to attempt a similar aggression, against the most insignificant village in the United States, the act would not be consummated in sight of the flag of Ecuador, floating on board a man of war, whatever might be its calibre. The honor of the flag would teach such vessel her duty, which no human consideration could prevent her from performing.

The Undersigned being persuaded, from an abundance of proof repeatedly given, that Mr. Cushing is penetrated with a sense of the justice and forcible causes, which militate in favor of Ecuador, in this contest of extermination; being convinced, moreover, that he is seriously grieved on account of the complicated evils which threaten this Republic, he has the honor [etc.].

2362

Courtland Cushing, United States Chargé d'Affaires in Ecuador, to Daniel Webster, Secretary of State of the United States [1]

[EXTRACT]

No. 20   GUAYAQUIL, *July 1, 1852.*

SIR: The Flores expedition is still in the river Guayaquil. For nearly three months it has been within forty miles of this city plundering farms & vessels belonging to Ecuadorean citizens. In the perpetration of these acts it has lost more than a hundred men who have been encountered & killed or captured by the Government troops. In every encounter the expeditionists have been completely routed. By desertion, death, and capture, the expedition has lost not less than three hundred and fifty men, and although it has received some accessions from Peru and Panama, it is weaker than when it first arrived at Puna. Some five days ago the vessels of the expedition came up and anchored about six miles from this city where they are still lying.

Nothing of note has since occurred except that a few of the expedition who were sent ashore to take cattle have deserted, others have been killed and two or three captured.

When the vessels first arrived so near the city the little government steamer "Guayas" went immediately down and fired a few shots at them by way of defiance. These were responded to by the steamer "Chili." After exchanging a few shots in full view of the city, both retired. The Captain and other officers of the "Portsmouth" think that the "Guayas" behaved very gallantly on the occasion.

The French frigate "Penelope" with the Commodore on board arrived in the harbor about two weeks ago. The French sloop "Prudente" is also here. While at Puna the Commodore declined the offer of a visit from General Flores.

On the 7th ultimo I received a letter from the Minister of Foreign Affairs, of which "A" is a copy [2]—"B" is a copy of my reply. [3]

On the 8th ultimo I communicated to Captain Dornin a copy of the Minister's letter with a note of which "C" is a copy. [4] Captain Dornin's arrange-

---

[1] Despatches, Ecuador, vol. 2. Received August 2.
[2] Above, this part, doc. 2361.
[3] Not included in this publication, since it merely acknowledges receipt of the Ecuadoran Minister's letter, and states that he will transmit its contents to Captain Thomas A. Dornin, of the United States sloop of war *Portsmouth.*
[4] It follows:

Courtland Cushing, United States Chargé d'Affaires in Ecuador, to Captain Thomas A. Dornin, United States Sloop of War Portsmouth

GUAYAQUIL, *June 8, 1852.*

SIR: I herewith transmit to you a copy of an official communication from the Government of Ecuador [Above, this part, June 7, 1852, doc. 2361.—Ed.] informing me that a steamer has arrived at Puna with forty citizens of the United States, for the purpose of

ments were made to proceed to Panama, but he promptly assured me that if after arriving at Puna he should think there was danger of the city being attacked by the expedition he would immediately return.   When about twelve miles above Puna, Captain Dornin was surprised at seeing the whole fleet of General Flores coming up in good order.   Capt. Dornin immediately ordered all hands to their posts—got the "Portsmouth" ready for action, and started back to Guayaquil.   The wind being unfavorable for a time and Gen¹ Flores having a steamer to tow his other vessels, the fleet passed the "Portsmouth." In passing the steamer lowered its flag, but Captain Dornin very properly declined to notice the salutation.   The wind having become favorable the Portsmouth passed the fleet and despatched a boat to inform me of Gen¹ Flores approach, and in a short time came to anchor again in front of my house.   Captain Dornin's deportment gave great satisfaction to the government and citizens here.   The fleet came to anchor about nine miles below and after remaining there two or three days returned to Puna. . . .¹

I have the honor [etc.].

2363

Courtland Cushing, United States Chargé d'Affaires in Ecuador, to Daniel Webster, Secretary of State of the United States ²

[EXTRACTS]

No. 21   GUAYAQUIL, *August 1, 1852.*

SIR: I have the honor to inform you that the wretched Expedition of Gen¹ Flores is broken up and dispersed.   Though secretly encouraged and aided by the Government of Peru; though favored here and in Lima by the diplomatic representatives of some of the most powerful Governments of Europe —though tolerated as a lawful belligerent by all the Squadrons in the Pacific, in despite of the most conclusive proof that it was "not under the acknowledged authority, or deriving protection from the flag or commission of any

---

giving greater activity to the work of destruction begun by the bandit Flores.   In submitting this communication to your consideration I cannot but express my deep regret that you are about to forsake us at this critical time.   When I consider the lawless character of the Flores expedition—the atrocious acts of man-stealing, robbery and plunder which have attended its organization and progress—the injury it has done to commerce, and the manner in which it has prostituted and insulted our national flag, I am fully convinced that the United States Naval force now in this vicinity ought to be exerted to put an end to the lawless enterprise.   But if the Commodore and yourself viewing the subject in a different light, should suffer it to exist still longer, I trust that you will not withdraw the restraining influence of your presence.

Most respectfully [etc.].

¹ The omitted portion refers to correspondence between Captain Dornin and the Chilean Consul at Guayaquil, which is not included in this publication, and relates, also, to Cushing's salary account.
² Despatches, Ecuador, vol. 2.   Received September 14.

Government"; and that it was organized and conducted in flagrant violation of the rules of civilized warfare. Yet the curse of an overruling Providence rested upon it.

In the night of the 1st of July, one of the vessels of the Expedition *named "Providence"*, was blown up and fifty two men, including some fifteen or twenty citizens of the United States, instantly perished by the explosion.— The same vessel some two months previously, after bringing supplies from Tumbez to the Expedition, came to this port under the flag of the United States, and after lying a day or two between my house and the Portsmouth, without having any commercial business whatever, and without any cargo but some fowls and pigs, returned and joined the Expedition at Puna.

The 4th of July was observed here in a most signal and gratifying manner.—. . .[1] About fifteen minutes before 11 oclock at night, when many of the principal officers, lulled by the festivities of the day, had no apprehensions of an attack, the whole City was aroused by the report of two guns in quick succession from the lower battery, which were immediately responded to by the Steamer "Chili" and the "Almirante Blanco". The invaders having taken advantage of the occasion and of the darkness of the night, in the most clandestine and assasin-like manner to attack the City. A brisk firing of cannon and musketry was kept up on both sides for some thirty minutes, when the vessels retired.—In the beginning of the attack the lower battery was for a moment silenced, but by the timely arrival of Gen¹ Villamil, Secretary of Foreign Affairs, who rushed to the spot with a company of infantry amidst a shower of cannon balls and grape shot—the firing from the battery was vigorously resumed and the invaders compelled to retire. But three persons in the City were killed and only five or six wounded.

Two 18 pound balls passed through several rooms of my house one of them after killing my nearest neighbor Mr Reina on his balcony, passed through my bedroom and parlor and lodged in an adjoi[ni]ng room. During the next night the City was again aroused by information that the whole fleet was approaching. The next morning all the vessels six in number were lying in full view of the City. The Steamer, being within gun shot, was compelled by one [or?] two shots from the lower battery to retire to a more secure position. The naval force of this Government was in a state of preparation but not ready for action. Hence the fleet was suffered to lie there two or three days in security—when all the vessels raised anchor and went down about sixty miles where Gen¹ Flores landed with from three hundred and fifty to four hundred men and took possession of the village of Machala where he remained pillaging and plundering as usual until the 17th ultimo. During the time however the armed peasantry encountered his men by night and by day with the utmost fury and with terrible effect.—

On the 17th ultimo the National Assembly was installed in this City and

[1] The omitted portion relates to the events of the day.

Gen¹ Urbina elected President ad interim.—I send herewith a paper containing an account of the proceedings.¹

On the 18th ultimo while the President and his Cabinet—the Diplomatic Corps—the members of the Assembly—officers of the army and others were partaking of a banquet in the Hall of the Assembly—it was announced that the little steamer "Guayas" which had gone down that morning with troops for Machala, was returning and in sight. The President at once said something of importance must have occured and immediately ordered all officers to their posts. He had scarcely given the order when the Steamer Chili appeared in full view about 5 P. M. with four white flags flying. The little "Guayas" behaved so coquettishly and the faithless character of Gen¹ Flores was so well known here, that at first some treachery was apprehended —but all doubts were soon dispelled by the cheering information that about one hundred and twenty men with the Chili had abandoned the Expedition. The Steamer was immediately taken possession of by the Government. After this defection the other vessels dispersed leaving Flores at Machala, from whence he was soon driven into the adjoi[ni]ng Province of Peru with about one hundred and fifty men the miserable remnant of his Expedition. There they were met and disarmed by the Governor of Tumbez—

A is the copy of a letter from Mʳ Clay United States Chargé d'Affaires. B is a copy of my reply—²

¹ Not included in this publication.
² These two letters, dated July 23 and 30, 1852, follow:

John Randolph Clay, United States Chargé d'Affaires in Peru, to Courtland Cushing, United States Chargé d'Affaires in Ecuador

LIMA, *July 23, 1852.*

SIR: It has been some time since I had the pleasure to hear from you and consequently I am in doubt respecting the actual state of Affairs in the Capital of the Ecuador.— I presume, however, from a letter I received from Commander Dornin of the Portsmouth and from the report of two Ship Masters, who have returned from Puna to Lima that the Expedition of Gen¹ Flores has proved to be a failure, as the President of Ecuador has sufficient resources to defend the Country against any attack from that quarter.—It is to be hoped that such will be the end of the untoward affair and indeed peace may yet be preserved along the coast should the army of New Granada not enter the territories of the Ecuador; for Peru would then have no margin upon which to ground any complaint against the latter. Should however the New Granadians go into the Ecuador, it may happen that the Peruvian Government will act upon the offensive and endeavor to take possession of the Port of Guayaquil, to check what many here believe to be the designs of New Granada against this Country.—And there are some of the friends of General Echenique, who are decidedly in favor of aggressive steps, in anticipation of any on the part of New Granada.—In my opinion it will be necessary for the President of Peru to adopt some decided course with regard to the Ecuador— either for or against it—to avoid disturbances in this Republic—Which should they begin might easily end in the overthrow of his Administration.—People here and elsewhere in Peru are dissatisfied.—And from discontentment to open revolt there is unfortunately but a short step in these bastard Republics.

The consequences of a war between the Ecuador and New Granada and Peru would be disastrous to all those nations but more particularly to the Ecuador the weakest and poorest of the three, and its effects upon the commercial interests of neutral powers would be for the moment ruinous.—It behoves every Government interested in the affairs of the Pacific to use its efforts for the preservation of peace and so well am

The Government of Chile has offered its mediation between Ecuador and Peru, but for the reason stated in my reply to Mr Clay, it will be declined by the former.   But although Commodore McCauley has treated the Expedition as a lawful belligerent and the President of Ecuador is somewhat mortified that no notice has hitherto been taken of the confidential letter which I

I convinced that it should be maintained at almost any price, that I have expressed the opinion in my despatches to the Secretary of State "that the United States ought to interfere and *force* these nations to be quit".—I can scarcely hope that our Government will consent to do so, for most of our statesmen have not yet become perfectly convinced that the principle of non intervention in the affairs of other nations, laid down by our fore fathers, should not be modified.   And yet it is very certain that in this age of progress, a great nation—*the* great Republic—cannot avoid th[r]owing its mighty weight in the international balance.

Sooner or later we shall all of us be convinced of this at least in so far, that there will arise cases in which the United States must act as mediator either amicably or forcibly.— With respect to these nations a positive expression of opinion by the United States would generally suffice to keep them in order and at peace.—Their wars are in general not wars of principle, but struggles between the partisans of military chiefs, commiting without scruple, unconstitutional acts while invoking the constitution in aid of their respective causes.—Such should be restrained by the strong hand of a great civilized nation, and the sooner the better.

Trusting that you have recovered your usual health, I remain [etc.].

Courtland Cushing, United States Chargé d'Affaires in Ecuador, to John Randolph Clay, United States Chargé d'Affaires in Peru

GUAYAQUIL, *July 30, 1852.*

SIR: In reply to your letter of the 23^d instant [See document, above, in this footnote. —Ed.], I must for the want of time, be as brief as possible.—The Expedition of General Flores is at an end.—It was a more villanous Enterprise than that of Lopez against Cuba.—One of the objects of the latter was to advance republican principles.— While on the contrary one of the main objects of the former was to check the republican progress which now prevails in New Granada and Ecuador.—It was for this that the Echinique [Echenique] Administration permitted it to be organized at Callao and secretly aided and encouraged it, while perfidiously professing friendship to the Government of Ecuador and giving the most positive assurances that the Expedition would not be tolerated by the Government of Peru.—It was for this that the British and French Chargés in Lima, and the French, Spanish and Peruvian Chargés in Ecuador, secretly encouraged the lawless Enterprise by every means in their power.—It was for this that the Commanders of the British and French Squadrons in the Pacific, treated it as a lawful belligerent—as a party to a civil war, without a particle of evidence that any such war existed.—Why the Commander of the United States Squadron permitted it to interupt Commerce and prostitute and insult our National flag with impunity, I have not been able to understand—especially as it is perfectly plain to me that the tendency of his course in this respect, was to give Genl Flores an opportunity to put down a Government particularly friendly to the people and institutions of the United States, and substitute one that would certainly be European and anti republican in its tendencies.—

Genl Urbina the President of Ecuador is a Gentleman of very fine capacity and I believe a true patriot.—The revolution which placed him at the head of affairs was a political necessity—the only means of avoiding an unjust and desolating war with New Granada and preventing the return of Gen! Flores—the worst enemy of Ecuador.— Genl Urbina conducted the provisional Government with remarkable forbearance, prudence and firmness and has been triumphantly and enthusiastically sustained by the people as well as by the National Assembly which is now in session in this City.—This Assembly is composed of Gentlemen selected from the most enlightened and best Citizens of the Republic and is strongly imbued with the Spirit of Republican progress.— From what I know of its leading members as well as of Gen! Urbina and his cabinet, I feel quite confident that there will be no war between Peru and Ecuador if it can be honorably avoided by the latter.—At the same time it is to be borne in mind that

had the honor to communicate to the Department with my despatch No. 17 of the 13th of April,[1] I am very confident that the mediation of the Government of the United States would be promptly accepted by Ecuador.

Within a few months past several changes have occured in the Diplomatic corps at this place.   In compliance with the request of this Government Mr Bourman late Chargé d'Affaires of Spain was promptly recalled by his Government.   Mr Prado, Secretary of Legation, is acting as Chargé *ad interim.*—Mr Morreyra late Chargé d'Affaires of Peru has also been recalled by request of this Government.   Mr Anceisar [Ancízar] is Chargé d'Affaires of New Grenada [Granada] in place of Dr Sanchos resigned on account of bad health.

I have the honor [etc.].

2364

*José Villamil, Minister of Foreign Affairs of Ecuador, to Daniel Webster,
Secretary of State of the United States* [2]

[TRANSLATION]

GUAYAQUIL, *August 31, 1852.*

MOST EXCELLENT SIR: My government, feeling highly grateful to the protective policy of the American principle, which the Government of the United States has always followed, has directed me, to acquaint the latter,

---

the Government of Peru is clearly responsible for the expenses and damages which have resulted to Ecuador from the Expedition.—The indignation of the people of Ecuador against the Echinique [Echenique] Administration is so strong and universal that the chances of an amicable settlement would be very much increased by a change of Administration.—I believe that every peaceful remedy will be exhausted by the Government of Ecuador before resorting to war.

Having declared the Expedition piratical by a solemn decree, it cannot accept the mediation of any Government that has subsequently recognized it as a lawful belligerent; and therefore the proferred mediation of Chile will be declined.

If after exhausting every peaceful remedy, the Government of Ecuador should be compelled to seek redress by resorting to war, the Government of the United States could not prevent it by force from attempting to assert its just rights in this way, without a total and most impolitic abandonment of its neutral policy.   If war should unfortunately take place between Ecuador and New Granada on one side and Peru on the other, I predict that Peru will suffer much more than Ecuador.   It is true that the former has greatly the advantage in moneyed resources, but the latter will have the advantage of a just cause, a united people and a well disciplined and brave army.

Wishing health to yourself and family I am [etc.].
P. S.
Gen[l] Flore's [Flores'] wearing apparel including his uniform and his badges of distinctions confered upon him by European Goverments—Also a great number of letters from his correspondents were brought up with the Steamer and delivered to the Goverment.—Some interesting developments will probably be made before long.

[1] Both the confidential letter, dated April 6, 1852, from the Ecuadoran Minister of Foreign Affairs, and the despatch in which it was enclosed, are to be found above, this part, docs. 2356 and 2358.
[2] Notes from Ecuador, vol. 1.   Received October 6.

through your Excellency's respected channel, with some events, which might produce results affecting the whole continent, and which, for that reason, ought to be watched and suppressed from their origin.

Your Excellency will no doubt have been informed of the scandalous proceedings, which have engaged the attention of all the South American Republics, within the last few months,—viz,—the appearance of Ex-General Flores, at the head of a body of men, collected at the different points, where, the monarchical principle, defended by Flores, had found partizans, and he will likewise have learnt, how this expedition has terminated.

Both before and since the contest with Flores, the conduct of the Diplomatic Agent of France, became so strange, that it admits of no explanation, and has given rise to much suspicion, in regard to the future prospects of these Republics.

During the time, that this agent served in the name of the French Republic, he conducted himself in a friendly and upright manner, towards the government of Ecuador; but as soon as a political change had taken place in France, there was also observed an astonishing difference in the Deportment of M. de Montholon, and a very remarkable change in the manner in which, he carried on his diplomatic relations with my government; but the strangest thing was, that, on the appearance of Flores, he declared himself the protector of the partizans of the latter, and harbored in the house appertaining to the French Legation, those persons whom Flores had selected, for the purpose of seducing the national troops, and to effect their demoralization by the most infamous means; my government made friendly and polite representations against these proceedings, which were replied to, in a negative manner, and with a degree of harshness, unbecoming the diplomatic character, with which he was invested. The French vessels anchored in the waters of Ecuador, took a position which interfered with the defence of this place; and a request having been made, that, said vessels might take a position, so as to leave the action of the National forces unincumbered, a refusal was the reply; new remonstrances were made, and then, the answer was, that my government could carry on its defense freely, even though his national vessels should be injured; by this measure, our defense was obstructed in two ways. 1st by placing his vessels in front of our batteries, when he was well persuaded that no orders would be given to fire in that direction, in as much as my government is not accustomed to inflict injuries of any kind, either upon the persons, or upon the property of a friendly nation, although the agents of the latter may allow such things to be done; 2dly because, even if my government had resolved to defend itself, without taking into consideration the injurious consequences, that might befall to those French vessels aforesaid, the ships of Flores could take such a position, as to find in the French vessels, thus intervening, a perfect screen of safety. The invasion was thus favored, and the neutrality broken, on the part of M. de Montholon. Since these occurrences, hostile under every aspect, and after the prudence and reserve, my government had used, in deference to the interests of peace, this Department received, not without much astonishment, a note from M. de Montholon, asking his passport, for himself and for his suite, under the pretext, that a Newspaper published in this city, had contained language, offensive to his nation, and to himself personally. My government offered, in vain, to give him full satisfaction, by directing the official gazette, to refute the assertions of the newspaper aforesaid, and by calling upon the authorities, to hold the author to a strict account; notwithstanding that the newspaper in question, was not of a responsible character, and was entirely disavowed by the enlightened portion of society. All this was of no avail; for M. de Montholon replied, that it was not on account of the newspaper article alone, but in view of other facts, which he did not condescend to particularize, that he insisted upon demanding his passports. My government forwarded the passport, after having courteously withheld it, and endeavored to calm the violence of feeling, which had characterized the action of the Chargé d'Affaires.

But this was not all: the rancor which M. de Montholon had shown against my government, and against the Ecuadorian Nation, had been evinced in a still higher degree, by the commander of the French Squadron in the Pacific; this rancor was shown in a note, which the aforesaid commander, addressed to this Department, wanting even in those formalities of politeness and delicacy, which are customarily used, even, among private individuals: this note was of a threatening character, and displayed a degree of rage, but poorly disguised.

All these transactions have been communicated to the French Government accompanied by corroborative evidence; and my government waits for a reply, in order to determine with certainty, whether these occurrences, have merely been an aberration on the part of the Chargé d'Affaires, & of the commander of the Naval forces, or whether the protection extended to the Monarchist Flores, proceeds directly from the monarchies, or semi-monarchies of Europe. It may be that this last conjecture is groundless; but as there is some foundation for supposing the fact to be such, my government has deemed it incumbent upon itself, to communicate all the circumstances to the Government of Your Excellency, because Your Excellency's government, is, in itself, a guaranty for the stability of the Republican principle, throughout this continent.

What I have just stated, is at least of sufficient importance, to induce all American Nations, to inform their agents in Europe, what have been M. de Montholon's tendencies in Ecuador, and to take especial care, in discovering the policy of the governments of Europe, in regard to our Republics; and nobody could fulfil this important mission, with more advantage, than the agent of Your Excellency's government; seeing that, he might not only observe, but also thwart, in time any injurious measure that might be adopted against the independence of the American Republics.

The Undersigned thinks, that this timely warning will suffice, to enable the perspicuous government of Your Excellency, to discover and remedy, whatever may directly or indirectly, interfere with the democratic usages which we have adopted and which inspire those who pursue a selfish policy, with so much Jealosy. My government hopes that the government of France will not refuse so just a request, as that asking for reparation for the injuries occasioned by its agent, or that said government shall at least disapprove of the conduct of the latter, in Ecuador, and if this should not be granted, it is to be expected that these abuses will be repeated towards all the American Nations, and then we will have no other alternative, than to limit our intercourse with the nations of Europe, to simply private commercial relations; and towards the adoption of this measure, my government thinks it has a right to expect much from all the Republics of America, in as much as they have the same political interests, and are exposed to the same risks.

I think it not improper to remark to Your Excellency, that this note is of a confidential and private character, since it has no other object than to forestal the European tendencies, and to induce the adoption of cautious measures, in order to prevent evils, before they have grown up into importance.

As soon as I shall have received the reply of the French Government, I will do myself the honor of communicating the results to Your Excellency; and I shall then be able to transmit likewise, the documents, in substantiation of what I have asserted.

My government which sees in that of Your Excellency, a powerful upholder of the American principle, feels a very great interest, in drawing closer, its relations of friendship, and reciprocal confidence.

I have the honor [etc.].

2365

Courtland Cushing, United States Chargé d'Affaires in Ecuador, to Daniel Webster, Secretary of State of the United States [1]

No. 23   GUAYAQUIL, *September 1, 1852.*

SIR: I have the honor to transmit herewith a printed copy of the general Message of the Supreme Chief of the late Provisional Government to the National Assembly of Ecuador, and respectfully commend it to your atten-

[1] Despatches, Ecuador, vol. 2.   The receipt date was not indicated.
None of the enclosures mentioned in this despatch are included in this publication, except the one marked B, from the French Commodore to the Ecuadoran Minister of Foreign Affairs, which follows:

tion not only on account of its truly American and republican character, but because it gives the fullest and most accurate account that has been published of the internal condition and foreign relations of this Republic—

This Message you will observe refers to some disagreeable incidents with the Legation of France. That Mr Montholon tried in various ways to depreciate and thwart the Provisional Government in its efforts to repel the lawless Expedition of General Flores, was evident for several months not only to the Government but to the citizens of Guayaquil generally—As soon as the Expedition failed he exhibited his chagrin by trying to pick a quarrel with the Government on account of some offensive remarks that were published about him—the French Corvette "Prudente" then here—and the Prince President, in one of the Newspapers of this City. The Goverment expressed its right at these remarks—but as the paper was independent— having no connection whatever with the Goverment—declined proceeding against it arbitrarily. Mr Montholon thereupon asked his passports and received them. Some four weeks previously however the Government of Ecuador had complained to the Government of France of Mr Montholon's conduct, of which he was duly informed as soon as the complaint was

---

Commodore Alphonse Pellion, Commander in Chief of the French Naval Station, to José Villamil, Minister of Foreign Affairs of Ecuador

[TRANSLATION]

STATION OF THE WESTERN COASTS OF AMERICA.

No. 104. The Frigate *Penelope*, at GUAYAQUIL, *August 17, 1852.*

GENERAL: An infant and weak state has doubtless the same political rights as a great power, but it should never lose sight of the fact that it is a product of civilization, and could not give rise, with respect to it, to the prerogative of using toward others forms of behaviour unknown among civilized nations. In spite of the moderation and sincerity of the accredited representative of France, the impassive attitude of the Naval Station and the prudent reserve of the French established at Guayaquil, the Ecuadoran Republic has not feared to heap insults upon a generous nation of which she called herself a friend, and to cap the climax, she has rendered impossible the continuance of these friendly and conservative relations which it is the particular mission of diplomacy to cultivate and maintain. These relations being broken off between our two cabinets, General, it is my place to protest in my turn, as I hereby formally do protest, against the conduct which the Government of Ecuador has had directly towards the French Legation and the naval forces which I command in the circumstances through which we have just passed. Being charged by my Government with causing my country's flag to be respected and protecting efficaciously the persons and property of my compatriots, throughout these seas; freed, thank God, from the obligation to act through *notes* which do not always lead to frank explanations, I declare to you, once and for all, General, in order that you may make such use of it as may be suitable, that I will not suffer from anyone whomsoever, henceforth, the slightest neglect of the regards due to France and the French, and I am determined to demand and obtain, in a proper case, by all means in my power, prompt and full reparation for any act of this sort, whoever the authors thereof may be. I am going to retire from this inhospitable region, General, but I know the road to the Guayas. I shall always have a watchful eye on what may happen there; and you would see me hasten in from the far reaches of the Pacific, if it were necessary, and energetically keep my promises. I like to think that the Ecuadoran Government, better advised, if not by a return to sentiments of justice, at least by its own interest, will not force me.

Accept, I beg you, General, the assurance of my high consideration.

made.—The accompanying copy of a letter addressed by the Minister to
Mʳ Montholon marked (A) exhibits some of the grounds of complaint
against him.—

On the 17ᵗʰ ultimo the French frigate Penelope sailed from this Port with
Mʳ Montholon, his attachés and his family. At the moment of sailing
the French Comodore sent a letter to the Minister of Foreign Affairs of
which B is a copy and also left a copy of it in the hands of a French druggist
of this City which he exhibited to various persons the same day.—The
frigate proceeded to Puna where it met the French sloop Brilliant.—After
remaining there together four or five days, the latter came to this port in the
night time and anchored opposite to the lower battery.—The following
morning She came up and anchored in front of the Custom house—Whereupon a company of Artillery appeared in full view of the vessel prepared to
respond to the Customary Salute.—But no salute has yet been given by the
vessel except to the Spanish Chargé ad interim with whom the archives of
the French Legation were left.—For what purpose the Brilliant came here is
not certainly known by the Goverment, but it is generally believed that she
was sent by the French Comodore to provoke a quarrel with this feeble
Republic.—

One of the officers informed me last evening that the vessel would sail
from this Port in three or four days.

C is a copy of a note from the Minister informing me that the President
ad interim was about to proceed to Daule (a neighboring village) for the
purpose of improving his health. With the exception of three or four days
he has been absent ever since, but is expected to return to-morrow for the
purpose of being inaugurated as President having been elected by the
Assembly on the 30ᵗʰ ultimo.—

For two months past my own health has not been very[1] but it is better now.
I have the honor [etc.].

2366

*Aaron H. Palmer, Consul General of Ecuador for the United States, to Charles
M. Conrad, Acting Secretary of State of the United States* [2]

Private and Confidential.   WASHINGTON, *October 8, 1852.*

The undersigned consul General of the Republic of Ecuador for the
United States has the honor to represent to Hon. John [Charles] M. Conrad,
Acting Secretary of State,—that from information just received at this
consulate General, it appears certain American citizens who have received
Military Commissions from General Flores, and were engaged in his late
unsuccessful Military and Naval Expedition against Guayaquil, have

[1] Evidently the word "good" has been inadvertently omitted here.
[2] Notes from Ecuador, vol. I.

recently returned to the United States for the express purpose of raising recruits on the Atlantic and Pacific seaboard, for a new filibustering and marauding expedition to be again commanded by Flores for the invasion of the territory of the Republic of Ecuador and deposition of its present President H. E. José María Urbina,—constitutionally re-elected to the Executive Office by a large majority of the votes of the National Constituent Assembly of that Republic, on the 17th July last.

In view of these facts, and of the amicable relations now so happily subsisting between the two sister Republics,—the Undersigned trusts the Government of the United States, in the exercise of its national comity, will take early and efficient measures for the arrest and punishment of all persons whomsoever, citizens or aliens, who may be found enlisting men, procuring arms, or munitions of war, or in fitting out any armed party or expedition from its territory, for the object above mentioned.

The undersigned avails of this occasion [etc.].

2367

Courtland Cushing, United States Chargé d'Affaires in Ecuador, to Daniel Webster, Secretary of State of the United States [1]

[EXTRACT]

No. 25   GUAYAQUIL, *November 1, 1852.*

SIR: . . . I herewith send a number of the Official paper 6th of March containing a copy of an Act passed in secret session by the National Assembly [2]—reciting that the participation of the Government of Peru in the piratical Expedition of the traitor Juan José Flores is fully proved by documents produced by the Executive, and investing him with authority to declare and make war against Peru, if after exhausting all peaceful remedies he fails to obtain satisfactory reparation. Mr Montcayo [Moncayo] President of the late National Assembly was sent to Peru for the purpose of demanding satisfaction and has been received by the Government of Peru with great consideration and respect.—It is not improbable that the Government of the United States will be requested to act as umpire between the parties . . .

I have the Honor [etc.].

[1] Despatches, Ecuador, vol. 2.   Received December 13.
Although this despatch of November 1 was addressed to Daniel Webster, the writer could not have possibly learned at this date of his death on October 24.
The omitted portions, at the beginning and end of this despatch, relate to correspondence announcing two appointments, in less than a month, for the office of Secretary of State *ad interim* for the Departments of Interior, Foreign Relations and Hacienda, and also relate to the appointment of a Dr. Marcos to treat with Cushing on the subject of claims.
[2] Not included in this publication; its content is sufficiently revealed within this despatch.

2368

Courtland Cushing, United States Chargé d'Affaires in Ecuador, to Charles M. Conrad, Acting Secretary of State of the United States[1]

GUAYAQUIL, *December 2, 1852.*

SIR: By the Mail which left early this morning I had the honor to acknowledge the receipt of your letter of the 25th of October communicating the melancholy intelligence of the death of Mr Webster.—I have since received very important information from Mr Ancisar [Ancízar] Chargé d'Affaires of New Granada and as a vessel is on the point of sailing from this Port to Panama I embrace the opportunity to communicate the intelligence to you. Mr Ancisar received a despatch from his Goverment on the 30th ultimo thirty days from Bogota, informing him that a treaty had just been signed by the Minister Plenipotentiary of Peru at Bogota and the Minister of Foreign Relations of New Grenada by which it is agreed that Peru will pay what is called her Colombian debt amounting to between nine and ten millions, being for expenses incurred by the late Colombian Confederacy in achieving the independence of Peru and for which she is to issue her bonds bearing six per cent interest.—

That the Goverment of Peru will satisfy the Goverment of Ecuador for the support given by the former to the late Flores Expedition—will deliver to Ecuador all the vessels of that Expedition which were seized by authority of Peru, or pay the value of them in money. That Peru will never allow another Expedition of the sort to be organized within her territories, nor give asylum to Gen[l] Flores.—The question whether Peru shall pay the expenses incurred by Ecuador in its defence against the Expedition is to be submitted for decision to a disinterested Goverment. The provision relative to the payment of the Colombian debt is subject to be ratified or rejected by the next Peruvian Congress. The other provisions relative to the Flores Expedition are to be submitted to the President of Peru who by virtue of extraordinary authority conferred upon him by the late Congress, has power to confirm or reject those provisions. A Commissioner from New Grenada who brought this intelligence to M[r] Ancisar is now on the way to Lima with a copy of the treaty and with instructions from his Goverment to insist upon a prompt confirmation of the provisions relative to the Expedition— In the matters embraced in this treaty New Grenada, Ecuador and Venezuela make common cause. The latter has an army of three thousand men on the New Grenadian frontiers waiting the action of Peru & ready to unite with the forces of New Grenada and Ecuador in an invasion of Peru. There are two other provisions in the treaty as follows—that Peru shall immediately liberate all slaves within her territory that were born in New Grenada; and dis-

[1] Despatches, Ecuador, vol. 2. Received January 4.

miss from service Gen.¹ Dustua, Admiral of the Peruvian Navy, who acted a leading and disgraceful part in aiding the Flores Expedition.—

I have no time to take a copy of this hurried letter and will be obliged if you will send me one.—

I am Sir, very respectfully [etc.].

2369

Courtland Cushing, United States Chargé d'Affaires in Ecuador, to Edward Everett, Secretary of State of the United States ¹

[EXTRACT]

No. 26   GUAYAQUIL, *January 1, 1853.*

SIR: . . . In my letter to the Department dated 2ᵈ of December last ² I had the honor to communicate some information which I had then just received relative to a treaty recently agreed to at Bogota between the Government of New Grenada and Mʳ Tavara Representative of the Government of Peru. The latter Government promptly disavowed the treaty and recalled Mʳ Tavara, and thereupon Major Landoval the Agent of the New Granadian Government by whom a knowledge of the treaty was communicated to the Peruvian Government, immediately returned to Bogota. It is difficult to form an opinion whether this State of affairs will result in a rupture or not. During the time that I have resided in this Country, the conduct of the Peruvian Government has been so eccentrick and deceptive especially towards Ecuador and New Grenada that I cannot judge of its future by its past course. There are some circumstances however to justify the opinion that the difficulty will be settled without war. The democratic or liberal party in Peru is very much dissatisfied with the present Administration of the Government and anxious to imitate the example of New Grenada by establishing a practical Republic founded upon the liberal principles by which the Constitution of the Government of New Grenada is eminently distinguished; And as revolutions have hitherto been the customary remedies for existing political evils the Government of Peru is in constant apprehension, I may say danger, of such a movement. The Government of Bolivia has also assumed a threatning attitude towards Peru and is said to have an army of two thousand men on the Peruvian frontier. It is understood that the Government of the United States will not allow the Port of Panama to be blockaded, this being true, there is no point on the Pacific where New Grenada can be seriously injured by the boasted Navy of Peru, the whole of which would not

¹ Despatches, Ecuador, vol. 2.   Received February 19.
   The omitted portion relates chiefly to the receipt of a despatch from the Hon. Mr. Everett announcing his appointment as Secretary of State.   ² Above, this part, doc. 2368.

be a match for one of our first class Steamers.—The independence of
Peru was in a great measure achieved by New Grenadian Soldiers. The
Peruvians have no military renown, while the New Grenadians have always
been distinguished by their prowess since the beginning of their struggle for
independence, and are nowhere more respected or dreaded than in Peru.
The rank and file of the New Grenadian army are chiefly negroes and
mullatos. Many of them liberated slaves. An invasion by such an army
with a proclamation of freedom to the forty thousand Slaves of Peru would
soon result in the downfall of the present Government. In view of all these
circumstances I am led to believe that Peru will yet settle with New Grenada
substantially upon the terms agreed to by her representative at Bogota.

Mr Saves recently accredited as Minister Plenipotentiary by the Government of Peru to the Government of Ecuador, arrived here on the 29th
ultimo.—

I herewith transmit a copy, marked A, of a note from Mr Cevallos late
Minister ad interim [1] announcing the termination of his office and the appointment of his successor Dr Marcos Espinel as Minister of the Interior
and Foreign Relations.

I have the honor [etc.].

2370

*Courtland Cushing, United States Chargé d'Affaires in Ecuador, to Edward
Everett, Secretary of State of the United States* [2]

No. 27   GUAYAQUIL, *January 6, 1853.*

SIR: I have just been informed by General Illingworth the ablest and most
confidential adviser of President Urbina, that a brig of war will be despatched
to Panama this evening with a bearer of despatches from the Goverment
of Ecuador to the Government of France; And have the honor by this opportunity to inform you that the object of these despatches is to counteract
the efforts which Mr Montholon late Charge d'Affaires of France in Ecuador,
is now making in Paris to induce the Government of France to exact indemnity for insults which he alleges that he received from the authorities
and people of Ecuador.   In my despatches N°s 17 and 23 [3] Mr Montholon's
hostility to this Government is distinctly indicated.

I had scarcely presented my credentials to the Government of Ecuador
when Mr Montholon exhibited to me the copy of a long letter written by M^r
Morreyra then Chargé d'Affaires of Peru in Ecuador to his Government the
object of which was to impress upon that Government the necessity of checking the alarming progress of what he was pleased to term red repu[b]licanism,

---

[1] Not included in this publication.
[2] Despatches, Ecuador, vol. 2.   Received February 19.
[3] Both of these despatches are above, this part, respectively, April 13 and September 1,
1852, docs. 2358 and 2365.

in New Grenada [Granada]—At the same time Mr Montholon informed me that Mr Bourman then Chargé d'Affaires of Spain in Ecuador, had written a letter of the same purport to his Government.   The evident object of Mr Montholon was to impress me with the same views, but I told him frankly that the progress of New Grenada as I understood it, was entitled to my warmest sympathies.   At this period the Goverment of Ecuador was pursuing a policy in accordance with the views and wishes of these diplomatists, but manifestly in opposition to the popular will.   This state of things produced a revolution which soon resulted in a change of Administration and of policy, to the evident disappointment and chagrin of these Gentlemen, who became odious to the people by opposing the Government and favoring the Expedition of Genl Flores.   Mr Montholon especially was vindictive in his opposition to the Government and his unceasing and disreputable efforts in favor of the Expedition are subjects of general notoriety in Ecuador.   Soon after the failure of the Expedition he took advantage of some trifling manifestations of the popular feeling which his own misconduct had excited against him, to quarrel with the Government and ask his passports.—The accounts lately published in the Paris newspapers relative to the matter and which are supposed to correspond with Mr Montholon's representations to his Government are grossly untrue.

I have the honor [etc.].

2371

Courtland Cushing, United States Chargé d'Affaires in Ecuador, to Edward Everett, Secretary of State of the United States [1]

No. 31   GUAYAQUIL, *March 1, 1853.*

SIR: I have the honor to acknowledge the recipt of your despatch numbered 10 [2] with the copy of a letter addressed to the Department by Matthew Howland, Esqr on behalf of the owners of the Ship "George Howland," showing that a claim is set up against the Government of Ecuador, for the capture of that vessel by the convicts upon Charles Island, one of the Gallapagos [Galápagos] group, on or about the 2^d of March 1852.   In obedience to your instructions I will avail myself of an early opportunity to present the claim to the Government of Ecuador.   The fact and circumstances of the Capture are known by this Government and upon that point no proof is needed, but inasmuch as Mr Howland states the damages only in general terms at forty thousand dollars, I respectfully suggest that he may be requested to furnish a statement of the particulars which constitute this sum, supported by affidavits or other sufficient evidence.

The Government of Ecuador is too helpless to take care of the Gallapagos Islands, and as they yield no revenue, might be disposed to cede them to the

[1] Despatches, Ecuador, vol. 2.   Received April 11.   [2] Not included in this publication.

United States upon reasonable terms. If such an acquisition is desirable the presentation and prosecution of this claim would furnish a fit opportunity to sound the Goverment on the subject. I have seen private letters recently, stating that guano has been discovered on one of the islands.

In compliance with your instructions Consul Game will immediately transmit the bond which he holds against the owners of the "George Howland."

I have this day drawn on the Department in favor of M. P. Game Esqr for the sum of Seven hundred and fifty dollars on account of my Salary.

I have the honor [etc.].

2372

Courtland Cushing, United States Chargé d'Affaires in Ecuador, to Edward Everett, Secretary of State of the United States [1]

No. 32   GUAYAQUIL, *March 2, 1853.*

SIR: I have the honor to inform you that W. Cope Esqr British Consul and diplomatic agent in Ecuador has just shown me a letter from his Government of the 15th of December last informing him that the French Government had communicated to the British Goverment a copy of *the letter* addressed by the Commander of the French frigate Penelope to the Government of Ecuador (a copy of which was transmitted with my despatch numbered 23 [2]) That the British Government thereupon asked what it meant and the French Government replied that it was written in consequence of a refusal by the Government of Ecuador to render satisfaction for injuries to a French citizen and for insults to Count Montholon late Chargé d'Affaires in Ecuador.—That a Commodore of the French Navy had been ordered to proceed to Guayaquil and obtain satisfaction by force if necessary.—That an expression of regret by the Government of Ecuador and a reasonable compensation in money would be satisfactory.—

In connexion with this subject I deem it proper to say that there are two great political parties in the South American Republics struggling for ascendency, the liberals or democrats and the Conservatives.—The liberals regard the Government and institutions of the United States as their model and their sympathies are with us. The Conservatives are opposed to Republican progress and regard the Government and institutions of the United States with dislike—Numerically physically and intellectualy the liberals have greatly the advantage but they are constantly impeded insulted and oppressed by European Governments and diplomatic agents—At the present time the liberals are in power in Venezuela, New Grenada [Granada], Ecuador, and Bolivia.—The Conservatives in Peru and Chili.

[1] Despatches, Ecuador, vol. 2. Received April 11.
[2] For the despatch, see above, this part, September 1, 1852, doc. 2365, and note 1 thereto, p. 294, for the enclosure with it.

For some information relative to the difficulty with France I respectfully refer you to my despatches numbered 23 and 27.[1]

The message of General Urbina late Supreme Chief and now President of the Republic, to the National Assembly, of which I herewith transmit a copy,[2] reflects the republican sentiments and American feeling of the liberal party and I respectfully commend to your particular attention that portion of it which relates to the foreign relations of Ecuador.—

I have the honor [etc.].

2373

Courtland Cushing, United States Chargé d'Affaires in Ecuador, to William L. Marcy, Secretary of State of the United States[3]

No. 35   GUAYAQUIL, *May 1, 1853*.

SIR: I have the honor to acknowledge the receipt of despatch numbered twelve informing me that the President has appointed you Secretary of State of the United States and that you have entered upon the duties of that office.—Also of despatch numbered eleven, but the box therein mentioned has not been received.[4]

A French squadron under the comma[n]d of Vice Admiral Fevier des Points arrived here on the 24th ultimo and is now laying in front of the City. It consi[s]ts of the Frigate, "Fort" 60 guns Steamer "Le Prone" 5 guns Sloop "Prudente" 12 guns Brig "L' Obligado" 16 guns with about eight hundred and fifty sailors and marines.

It is understood that the object of this Expedition is to obtain satisfaction from Ecuador for an alleged insult to Carlos de Montholon late Chargé d'Affaires near this Government and for injuries to a French Citizen named Landron.—I am informed that the person complained of was long since tried for the alleged insult and acquited.—And that although Mr Montholon informally spoke to the President, then Supreme Chief of the Provisional Government, of the alleged injuries to Landron resulting from the arbitrary conduct of a Provincial Govenor, no demand for reparation was ever made.

Soon after the Admiral arrived he transmitted to the Govenor of the Province of Guayaquil a sealed letter directed to the Minister of Foreign Relations together with a message that he required an answer in twelve days—The letter was despatched the same evening to Ambato where the President and the Minister are now sojourning on their way to establish the Government in Quito, and will doubtless be answered within the time limited.—The Admiral has not disclosed to any one the contents of this letter,

[1] Above, this part, September 1, 1852, and January 6, 1853, docs. 2365 and 2370.
[2] Not included in this publication.   [3] Despatches, Ecuador, vol. 2.   Received June 9.
[4] Neither of these despatches is included in this publication.

but the impression is universal that the difficulty will be amicably settled in a
few days.—He is about sixty five years of age and all who have visited him
concur in opinion that he is a very prudent and good natured Gentleman.

I have this day drawn on the Department in favor of Cox Game & co for
five hundred dollars

I have the honor [etc.].

2374

*Courtland Cushing, United States Chargé d'Affaires in Ecuador, to William L.
Marcy, Secretary of State of the United States* [1]

No. 36   GUAYAQUIL, *May 11, 1853.*

SIR: I have the honor to transmit herewith a copy marked A of a despatch
from the Honorable J. Randolph Clay, Envoy Extraordinary and Minister
Plenipotentiary of the United States, in Lima, relative to the French Squadron which is the subject of my despatch numbered thirty five.   Also a copy
marked B of my reply.[2]

The satisfaction demanded by the French Admiral has been rendered and
the business is settled.   The Government of Ecuador has saluted the French
flag and expressed its regret for the alleged insult to Mr Montholon late
Chargé d'Affaires and Consul General of France; and has agreed to pay eight
thousand dollars for supposed injuries to the French Citizen Landron.
It is worthy of note that the authorities of Ecuador, under duress and with
evident reluctance, raised and saluted the French flag, today, upon the same
spot where on the 4th of July last they voluntarilly and with great enthusiasm raised and saluted the flag of the United States.—

M[r] Thomaso acting French Consul at this Port is a man of intelligence and
integrity and although a citizen of Spain entertains liberal views in respect
to Civil and religous liberty.   He informed me this morning that the Admiral came here with orders to obtain prompt satisfaction.—   That three
thousand soldiers who have served in Africa are now in France waiting the
result of this Expedition, and in the event of a refusal by the Government of
Ecuador to comply with the Admirals demands, were to be sent here with
orders to take possession of the Country and not leave it until full satisfaction
should be obtained and all expenses of the Expedition paid.

C and D are copies of notes from the Minister of Foreign Relations and E
is a copy of my reply [3] relative to the fact that two French vessels of war and

[1] Despatches, Ecuador, vol. 2.   Received June 9.
[2] Neither is deemed of sufficient importance to include in this publication.   The information given in Clay's letter is practically identical with that reported in Cushing's No. 35,
to the Secretary of State, above, this part, May 1, 1853, doc. 2373.   Clay regarded the French
claim as a rather unjust one and thought the United States should interpose in behalf of
Ecuador.   Cushing replied that he thought there would be no occasion for so doing, since
he felt satisfied that there would be an amicable settlement of the affair.
[3] None of these are included in this publication, since their subjects are sufficiently indicated within this despatch.

the United States Sloop "Portsmouth" were then occupying positions which prevented the Government from the free use of its batteries. This information ought to have been communicated with my despatch of the 1ˢᵗ of August 1852 numbered twenty one,[1] but my attention was then wholly occupied by more exciting facts. Mʳ Montholon the French Chargé d'Affaires excused himself for not complying with his promise to prevent the City from being cannonaded, upon the ground that the firing commenced from the batteries of the City! And notwithstanding the barbarous attack described in my said despatch—and the fact that the vessels of the Flores Expedition remained in sight for several days thereafter—the French vessels of war, being so situated as to prevent the free use of more than half of the batteries of the City, continued to occupy their positions in utter disregard of the wishes of the Government.

F is a copy of a despatch from Mʳ Clay on the subject of the Amazon and Rio de la Plata and their tributaries, G is my reply.[2]

I have the honor [etc.].

[1] Above, this part, doc. 2363.
[2] These two letters follow:

John Randolph Clay, United States Chargé d'Affaires in Peru, to Courtland Cushing, United States Chargé d'Affaires in Ecuador

LIMA, *March 22, 1853.*

SIR: You will probably have seen by the newspapers that the President of Bolivia issued, on the 27ᵗʰ of January last, a decree declaring the rivers of that Republic, confluents of the Amazon and Rio de la Plata, open to the navigation and commerce of all nations and establishing free ports at certain places on the said confluents or tributaries of those rivers. That decree, therefore, is of immense importance as the first which the nations, possessing the navigable sources of the principal rivers of South America, have issued inviting foreign nations to carry on commerce with the interior of this continent—the vast treasures of which are but very partially known to the civilized world. Indeed a glance at the map will show that nearly two thirds of South America are unexplored and I cannot doubt, after a careful investigation of the subject for the last four years, that the natural products and other resources of the Interior are unrivalled by any country of the Globe. The whole of East Peru, Bolivia, parts of the Ecuador, New Grenada [Granada] & Venezuela, together with the districts or Provinces of Brazil adjacent thereto, might be converted into a garden spot. They are rank with the exuberance of nature, and when once opened to the enterprising spirit of our fellow countrymen, no accurate calculation of the amount of produce which will be shipped therefrom or of the benefit to mankind can be made.

The free navigation of the River Amazon has been my aim and that of Lieutenant Maury, Superintendant of the National Observatory at Washington, since 1849. In 1851 Lieutenant Herndon U. S. N. and Passed Midshipman Gibbon left Lima to descend the Amazon to Para. After going as far as Tasma and Jauja they separated. Lieut Herndon went [to?] Huanuco embarked on the Huallaga and descended that river to the Amazon, went up the Ucayali to Sarayaco and then returning to the Amazon continued his voyage to Para and thence to the United States. Mʳ Gibbon after leaving his companion went to Hauncavelica [Huancavelica?], Ayacucho, Cuzco, Puno, La Paz and then to Cochabamba in Bolivia, where he passed the winter.

Whilst there, he was instructed by me to endeavor to prevent the Brazilian Minister to Bolivia from succeeding in obtaining a treaty with that Government, similar to the one he had concluded with Peru, by which he hoped to deprive the citizens of the United States from participating in the navigation and trade of the Interior of South America. We were fortunate enough to counteract his plans and he left Bolivia in disgust. Mʳ Gibbon embarked on the river Mamoré descended it to its junction with

Footnote 2, p. 305—*Continued*

the Itenez, which latter he ascended to Puerto de Principe de Beira and after obtaining a new boat and some soldiers descended the Rio Madera [Madeira?] to the Amazon and this last to Para, where he had safely arrived at the last dates and is ere this I doubt not at home.

The voyages and observations of these officers, added to those made by the French traveller, Castelnan will doubtless throw great light upon the interesting countries through which they passed, but after all, comparatively speaking, little will be really known of the extent of territory lying between the river Amazon and the Beni and Madera [Madeira?]

Notwithstanding the treaty between Peru and Brazil—in the second article of which it is said that the Navigation of the Amazon should belong *exclusively* to the states possessing the territory lying upon it and its tributaries, I have induced the Peruvian Minister of Foreign Affairs, to consent to issue a decree declaring the port of Nauta on the river Amazon, within the boundary of Peru open to the commerce of all nations. The decree will probably be published next week.

I also addressed letters to the Envoy Extraordinary of New Grenada to this Republic and to D. Pedro Montcayo [Moncayo] the Envoy Extraordinary of the Ecuador at this place (dated February 22d and March 14) enclosing a copy of the Decree of the President of Bolivia, above referred to, and requesting them to urge upon their Governments the propriety of issuing similar decrees. Bot[h] Mr Arosemena and Colonel Montcayo have promised to use their influence with their respective cabinets, to obtain a declaration opening the navigable confluents of the Amazon within the dominions of N. Grenada [Granada] and the Ecuador.

My object, therefore, in addressing this despatch to you is to obtain your aid in carrying out the proposed plan. Your standing and influence with the Government of Ecuador are such, that I doubt not you will easily induence [*sic*] President Urbina to issue a decree for that Republic, in the same liberal spirit as characterises that of President Belzu—a copy of which Mr Montcayo informed me, he had transmitted to Guayaquil.

You are well acquainted with the geography and natural resources of the State to which you are accredited and it is not therefore necessary for me to enter into any explanation on the subject, or to attempt to prove the great advantages which must result to the Eastern Provinces of all these Republics by the opening to foreign commerce and foreign navigation of the main channel of the Amazon.—

The difficulties between Peru & the Ecuador arising out of the Flores Expedition have I understand been satisfactorily arranged between Mr Tirado and Col. Moncayo. The details you will most probably learn from General Urbina himself.

I have received a private letter from Mr Everett informing me that the President sent in my name to the Senate of the United States, on the 11th ultimo as Envoy Extraordinary to this Government. The Senate however had not acted upon it at the last advices.

I am Sir very respectfully [etc.].

Courtland Cushing, United States Chargé d'Affaires in Ecuador, to John Randolph Clay, United States Chargé d'Affaires in Peru

GUAYAQUIL, *April 1, 1853.*

SIR: I have read your interesting despatch of the 22d ultimo in regard to the Amazon an[d] Rio de la Plata [Above, in this footnote.—Ed.] with much satisfaction—And am pleased to inform you that the subject has engaged my attention for some time past. President Urbina is fully informed of the views and wishes of Lieut Maury relative to the tributaries of the Amazon and has expressed his intention to treat with me on the subject, but his attention has been so engrossed hitherto by difficulties arising out of the Flores Expedition that he has had no leisure to think of any thing else.

It is said that a French Admiral is now on the way to exact satisfaction from this feeble Republic for alleged injuries to a French citizen and insults to Count Montholon late Chargé d'Affaires in Ecuador. The Deportment of Montholon and of the comma[n]ders of the French war vessels "Penelope" and "Prudente" towards this Government during the time they were here was exceedingly offensive, such as no Government capable of asserting its rights would tolerate. A consciousness of this improper deportment, and their chagrin at the signal marks of respect that were paid to our national flag by Government authorities here in celebrating the 4th of July, added to their disappointment at the failure of the Flores Expedition are in my opinion the real motives which induced Montholon to demand his passports.—

2375

Courtland Cushing, United States Chargé d'Affaires in Ecuador, to William L. Marcy, Secretary of State of the United States [1]

No. 39   GUAYAQUIL, *August 11, 1853.*

SIR: I have the honor to inform you that President Urbina arrived in this City about ten days ago.— Today he sent an officer to inform me that he was anxious to see me, but was too unwell to go out and would be obliged if I would do him the favor to call at his house.— I therefore called upon him without delay.— His object in sending for me was to say that he has satisfactory information that General Flores and his agents abroad are preparing another piratical expedition against Ecuador.— That a vessel had recently sailed from Valparaiso for Sanfrancisco with a good supply of ordenance in the hold, under the Command of a Frenchman who commanded the "Almirante Blanco" in the late Flores Expedition.— That the vessel had touched somewhere on the coast and received a son of Gen[l] Flores on board and is now on the way to California where the Expedition is to be organized.— That he is apprehensive of trouble from that quarter, but that a Proclamation by the President of the United States forbiding that or any other piratical or lawless Expedition against Ecuador or any of the other South American Republics, would avert all danger and give great satisfaction to the friends of progress in South America. That he has written to the Government at Quito to address to me an official letter on the subject, but fearing the consequences of delay he requested me to communicate this intelligence to the Department at once and expressed a hope that the Government of the United States would promptly take the necessary steps to prevent the organization of such an Expedition in California.— I herewith enclose a newspaper entitled "La Democracia" containing an article on the subject [2] to which I respectfully invite your attention.— A substantial history of the late Expedition and my views on the subject may be found in my despatches from N° 17 to N° 21 both inclusive [3]—and in my letters to Commodore M°Cauley and Captain Dornin of which I transmitted copies [4] with those despatches.— Flores has scarcely the shadow of a party in Ecuador and if he were not encouraged and sustained by European interference and

---

President Urbina and the citizens of Guayaquil generally, I believe are satisfied with the terms of the treaty with Peru.

I cordially congratulate you upon your nomination as Minister Plenipotentiary and am

Very respectfully [etc.].

[1] Despatches, Ecuador, vol. 2.   Received September 12.
[2] Not included in this publication.
[3] See above, this part, April 13, May 1, June 1, July 1, and August 1, 1852, docs. 2358, 2359, 2360, 2362, and 2363.
[4] See above, this part, p. 281, note 4 and p. 286, note 4.

the enemies of free institutions in South America, this Republic would have nothing to fear from him.

As his late Expedition was allowed to insult and prostitute our national flag and fire into my house with impunity and in insolent defiance of our vessels of war then in this vicinity, and as no notice has been taken of the confidential communication from the Government of Ecuador which I had the honor to transmit with my despatch N° 17— I think some public expression by the Government of the United States of its determination not to tolerate similar Expeditions would be exceedingly well on this occasion and have a good political and commercial effect in this region.

I have the honor [etc.].

2376

Marcos Espinel, Minister of Foreign Affairs of Ecuador, to Courtland Cushing, United States Chargé d'Affaires in Ecuador[1]

[TRANSLATION]

QUITO, *August 17, 1853.*

SIR: I have the honor to address Your Honorable Lordship by order of my Government, with the object of calling your attention to a matter of the greatest importance to the peace of Ecuador, which can not be disregarded by the enlightened and liberal Government of the United States.

For some time the newspapers of Panamá and other points have been speaking of the new project conceived by ex-General Juan José Flores of organizing a new expedition against this Republic with men obtained in California.

Later the Government was more directly advised that the project of Flores is advancing and in proof thereof is assured that a son of this ex-General has started for this point in a ship of War commanded by the same Captain who came in the *"Almirante Blanco"* when the last invasion took place: other advices received by my Government are of the same tenor. I do not believe it necessary to take the time to lay before Your Honorable Lordship the special circumstances of the present state of affairs which tend to prove the truth of the repeated reports I have mentioned, as Your Honorable Lordship is informed of them all; and I shall confine myself to stating that it being in accordance with the institutions of the Republic of the United States and the will of its enlightened Government to secure the peace and tranquillity of the Republics of South America, as it has manifested on very solemn occasions, there will be no obstacle to guarding against the evils which might befall Ecuador if ex-General Flores, with his characteristic cunning,

---

[1] Despatches, Ecuador, vol. 2; enclosed with Cushing to the Secretary of State, No. 40, August 30, 1853, below, this part, doc. 2378.

should succeed in flouting the vigilance of the authorities of California, and obtaining the men and other elements necessary to organize his expedition. My Government believes that to prevent the enlistment, it would suffice if the Government of Your Honorable Lordship should issue a decree imposing the penalties of the law upon those who attempt to obtain men, munitions &c. from San Francisco and other points in California, extending said penalties to subordinate authorities who may not be sufficiently careful in the fulfillment of their duties, and to citizens who may have agreed or may agree to serve under the orders of Flores and his agents, and if it should declare that in the event that the expedition should be formed with men who are under the jurisdiction of the Government of the United States, it would be pursued by the North American fleet and the forces of the expedition severely punished.

My Government desires therefore that Your Honorable Lordship may be so good as to inform His Excellency the President of the United States of the present probability that the peace of Ecuador may be disturbed, and may indicate to him the easy way of remedying this evil in the manner which I have had the honor to describe; and it is for this purpose that it has fallen to my pleasure to address Your Honorable Lordship.

I seize this opportunity [etc.].

2377

Courtland Cushing, United States Chargé d'Affaires in Ecuador, to Marcos Espinel, Minister of Foreign Affairs of Ecuador [1]

GUAYAQUIL, *August 24, 1853.*

SIR: I have the honor to acknowledge the receipt of your very interesting letter of the 17th instant,[2] informing me of the probabilities that ex-General Flores is about to organize another Expedition against this Republic, with men and munitions to be obtained in California.— Suggesting a measure by which it may be prevented and requesting me to indicate to the Government of the United States the probabilities and the remedy. I will comply with the request by the first opportunity and in the meantime Your Excellency may rest assured that the Government of the United States will do whatever may be necessary and proper to prevent the Expedition.

I have the honor [etc.].

¹ Despatches, Ecuador, vol. 2; enclosed with Cushing to the Secretary of State, No. 40, August 30, 1853, below, this part, doc. 2378.   ² Above, this part, doc. 2376.

2378

*Courtland Cushing, United States Chargé d'Affaires in Ecuador, to William L.
Marcy, Secretary of State of the United States*[1]

No. 40   GUAYAQUIL, *August 30, 1853.*

SIR: I have the honor to transmit herewith a copy of a letter from the
Minister of Foreign Relations, relative to an apprehended Expedition by
General Flores against this Republic; also a copy of my reply thereto.—[2]
And respectfully refer you to my despatch N° 39[3] on the same subject.

I have the honor [etc.].

2379

*Courtland Cushing, United States Chargé d'Affaires in Ecuador, to General José
María Urbina, President of Ecuador*[4]

[TRANSLATION]

E   GUAYAQUIL, *October 5, 1853.*

MY DEAR FRIEND: I have already recounted to you a conversation between Señor Lisboa and a Merchant of New York with a view to showing you
the opinion of the Minister that *there is a possibility* that Ecuador may
develop its Amazon regions *within fifty or one hundred* years.   On the following day the Merchant questioned the Minister astutely on the policy of Brazil with respect to the Amazon.   They met at Bogotá and struck up a friendship there; but at the time the Merchant did not think much about the
navigation of the Amazon.   After conversing with me he began to manifest
an interest in the subject and a desire to learn the designs and policy of Brazil.   And the Minister frankly told him that the object of his mission to the
Amazonian Republics is to negotiate treaties with them concerning the
navigation of the Amazon, and the boundaries between them and Brazil.—
That having already satisfactorily negotiated with Peru, Venezuela, and New
Granada, he was going to treat with Ecuador in the same way.—   That all
four had claims to one and the same portion of the territory contiguous to the
territory of Brazil.—   That in negotiating, he recognizes the title of neither
one nor the other, leaving the question of the title to be settled between
themselves.—   But that he has already fixed the boundaries between Brazil
and Peru, Venezuela and New Granada, provided that the disputed portion
belongs to one or the other, and has granted to them the right to navigate the
Amazon in their own ships and under their own flags, on condition that they

---

[1] Despatches, Ecuador, vol. 2.   Received October 6.
[2] These two notes are above, this part, August 17 and 24, 1853, docs. 2376 and 2377.
[3] Above, this part, August 11, 1853, doc. 2375.
[4] Despatches, Ecuador, vol. 2; enclosed with Cushing to the Secretary of State, unnumbered, October 31, 1853, below, this part, doc. 2383.

will not concede or transfer the privilege to the flags of other nations.—
That Brazil will never concede the free navigation of the Amazon because it
fears the English and the Yankees. It fears that the effect of admitting the
flags of the United States and Great Britain will be to change the religion and
political institutions of Brazil, &c. Brazil is right if she desires to impede
the progress of tolerance and democracy.— But the Republic of Ecuador,
with "the invincible zeal of its sons for the guaranty and diffusion of the
democratic principle", has nothing to fear, but, on the contrary, everything
to hope for, from close commerce with the Yankees.— The Yankees are
not revolutionists.— They always respect the constitution and free institutions of their country.— And no Government which desires to be free,
liberal, and independent, should avoid commerce with such men.

Brazil has already bound with fetters the hands of Peru, New Granada,
and Venezuela, and it now hopes to do the same with Ecuador. Take the
advice of a faithful and true friend and remain free.— In the present circumstances, Ecuador, poor and without resources, must not treat with its
neighbors regarding the question of boundaries.— On this question I have
already offered you some suggestions in previous letters.— And what does
it matter to Ecuador whether or not Brazil recognizes its right to navigate
the Amazon under its own flag? Nothing—absolutely nothing.— When
can Ecuador open its Amazon tributaries and regions to steam navigation, to
agriculture, and to Commerce solely by the use of its own flag? Our grand-
sons will not live to see the day.— It is necessary—indispensable—to begin
this great enterprise under the flag of one or more of the great maritime
nations.

The development of the resources of her Amazonian regions is the only
hope that Ecuador can have of paying her English debt, and it is necessary
to adopt the most effective plan of accomplishing this object. I have already
in previous letters fully explained to you the plan which appears to me to be
the most certain and effective. But inasmuch as the question is of the greatest importance, you must take no step without reflecting.— A false step
is always worse than none.— Its true policy may be to establish some ports
of entrance on the Amazonian tributaries of Ecuador, and assign the duties
to its English creditors.— And at the same time to offer special inducements to enterprizing and industrious men of all nations to settle in the
Amazonian region as citizens of Ecuador.— And to permit the ships and
flags of the large maritime nations to participate in the trade of those rivers
equally with the ships of Ecuador during a period of some fifteen or twenty
years, on condition that in the meantime one or more of these nations will
guarantee the nationality and independence of Ecuador.— At the end of
which period Ecuador can continue the navigation of her rivers and maintain her nationality and independence without the aid of any nation.—
The false steps of the other Republics with respect to the Amazon have im-

proved the relative condition of Ecuador.— You must avoid negotiating with Sr. Lisboa and the Congress of Plenipotentiaries of the Amazonian Nations which he desires shall meet at Lima.— Those projects are full of danger to the liberal party of South America.— You must not trust the promises and preparations of Brazil concerning the Amazon.— It wishes to gain its object—the exclusion of the Yankees—nothing more.

By today's post I am sending a California Gazette to Colonel Lannigan, hoping that he will read you a few paragraphs from it.— He knows nothing of our correspondence.

With a sincere desire for the progress of Ecuador, and the success of your Administration, I remain, as ever [etc.].

2380

General José María Urbina, President of Ecuador, to Courtland Cushing, United States Chargé d'Affaires at Quito [1]

[TRANSLATION—EXTRACT]

F   QUITO, *October 5, 1853.*

MY DEAR FRIEND: Being unable up to the present to write to you with my own hand as I desire, and reserving the privilege of doing so when I am better, I have today the pleasure of replying to your esteemed letter of the 28th of last month. [2]

You are familiar with my fixed ideas regarding the Amazon; nothing contrary to them nor to the suggestions you have given me will be done.

I hope that the Minister of Brazil may arrive here in order that I may judge of his intentions, and I am grateful to you for the information you have been so good as to give me concerning this matter. * * *

2381

General José María Urbina, President of Ecuador, to Courtland Cushing, United States Chargé d'Affaires at Quito [3]

[TRANSLATION—EXTRACT]

F   QUITO, *October 12, 1853.*

MY VERY DEAR FRIEND: * * * Your reflections upon the designs of the Representative of Brazil and their possible consequences to the navigation of

[1] Despatches, Ecuador, vol. 2; enclosed with Cushing to the Secretary of State, unnumbered, October 31, 1853, below, this part, doc. 2383. The asterisks indicate an omission in the original manuscript.
[2] Not found. Cushing states in his despatch, below, this part, October 31, 1853, doc. 2383, that "Of my first letter on the subject I did not keep a copy."
[3] Despatches, Ecuador, vol. 2; enclosed with Cushing to the Secretary of State, unnumbered, October 31, 1853, below, this part, doc. 2383. The asterisks indicate omissions in the original manuscript.

the Amazon appear very prudent to me.[1]   I shall bear them in mind when the
occasion arises, and in the meantime please accept my gratitude for your
solicitous interest in favor of those of my country. * * *

2382

*General José María Urbina, President of Ecuador, to Courtland Cushing,
United States Chargé d'Affaires at Quito*[2]

[TRANSLATION—EXTRACT]

F   QUITO, *October 21, 1853.*

MY VERY DEAR FRIEND: * * * I am sending you a copy of the *Periodico
Oficial* in which you will find the Speech addressed to me by the Minister of
Brazil on the day of his official reception, and my reply.[3]   As the ideas rela-

[1] See Cushing's note to him, dated October 5, 1853, above, this part, doc. 2379.
[2] Despatches, Ecuador, vol. 2; enclosed with Cushing to the Secretary of State, unnumbered, October 31, 1853, below, this part, doc. 2383.   The asterisks indicate omissions in the
original manuscript.
[3] These two documents, translated from the above-mentioned newspaper, follow:

*Speech of Miguel María Lisboa, Brazilian Minister to Ecuador, to General José María
Urbina, President of Ecuador*

[TRANSLATION]

EXCELLENCY: It is known to various South American Governments, and I trust
that it has come to the knowledge of Your Excellency, what efforts His Majesty the
Emperor of Brazil, my august Sovereign, has made to assure the cooperation of the said
Governments toward one of the most magnificent enterprises that modern times have
seen; at the same time establishing on solid and enduring bases the peace and cordial
understanding which are indispensable in order that that undertaking may attain its
ends without hindrance, and promote, together with material prosperity, those sentiments of good will among neighboring peoples which should exist where there exist so
many common interests and so many bonds of natural sympathy.
    The high opinion which South America forms of the liberal policy of Your Excellency,
and the principles of progress which your Administration proclaims lead me confidently
to hope that the broad and generous policy of my august Sovereign will be understood
here, as it has been in other Republics; and that the special mission which His Majesty
the Emperor saw fit to entrust to me, and for the performance of which I have the honor
to deposit in Your Excellency's hands the Imperial Letter which accredits me in the
capacity of Resident Minister, will have a satisfactory result and one that is compatible
with the interests and with the honor of Brazil and of Ecuador.

[REPLY]

MR. MINISTER: In the pleasing and firm conviction that the broad and generous
policy of your august Sovereign rises to the high plane that the civilization of the
century through which we are passing indicates to us, and is demanded by the enlightened interests of America—this America of ours so lacking in population, so lacking
in circulating wealth, so lacking in that regenerating spirit of enterprise which, in more
fortunate countries, has caused great and powerful cities and even States to rise, as if
by enchantment, where days since there reigned only the silence and destitution of
uncultivated forests; it gives me satisfaction to assure you that you will find me disposed
to cooperate with the Government of His Imperial Majesty in the magnificent undertaking to which you have alluded, and which, based I doubt not, on amply liberal
principles, will surely open a new era of wealth, power and happiness—a new and
beautiful field of labor and hopes, of union and fraternity, to all our brother peoples.
    The choice of your person for the execution of such a pleasing project and for the deli-

tive to the question of the Amazon are clearly brought out in both documents, it is unnecessary for me to repeat them in this letter. You will judge
of these documents without the need of such explanations. Sr. Lisboa has
not yet initiated the special negotiation with which he is said to be charged.
When that happens we shall see the scope and significance of the policy of
my Administration.

What will be the opinion of the Government of the United States in this
matter, what will it do? I know well what the law permits; but I likewise
know what the interests of commerce and civilization counsel; and as I also
know the opinions of many other Governments on this matter,—to know
that of the United States is a desire more than natural and justifiable. The
conduct observed by the naval forces of the United States with respect to the
piratical forces of Flores has been truly unfortunate for the interests of both
Americas! Of course you are aware of the impressions which that conduct
has left upon the Colombian Republics, and very especially, which is natural,
upon the important Province of Guayaquil. I am far from attempting to
judge, much less express any opinion for or against such conduct, as befits the
post I occupy. I do take note of its consequences, and desire that they may
disappear, without leaving a trace, and may never return. * * *

2383

*Courtland Cushing, United States Chargé d'Affaires in Ecuador, to William L.
Marcy, Secretary of State of the United States* [1]

GUAYAQUIL, *October 31, 1853.*

SIR: I have the honor to inform you that I have taken leave of the Minis-
ter of Foreign Relations of Ecuador and expect to depart for the United
States to-day—A is a copy of my letter to the Minister on the occasion and
B of his reply.[2]

My successor Mr White not being here I have left the Archives and other
property of the Legation with M. P. Game Esqr., United States Consul, and
taken his receipt for the same, of which C. is a copy.—[3]

cate and interesting task of putting on a firm basis the peace and cordial understanding
which happily unite Ecuador and Brazil, is a further proof of the tact which governs all
the acts of His Imperial Majesty—an event upon which I congratulate myself because
it has furnished me the opportunity of knowing such a distinguished American as you—
and a sure presage of the successful outcome which your important mission must have.
In the performance thereof, depend upon the eminently American and progressive spirit
of the Ecuadoran Administration and people, and upon the well deserved sympathies
which you have gained for yourself already in this capital, as you did in the other States
of Colombia, where you have so worthily represented the interests and policy of your
beautiful country and your august Emperor.

[1] Despatches, Ecuador, vol. 2.   Received November 30.
[2] Neither is included in this publication.
[3] Neither C, nor D mentioned in the following paragraph, is included in this publication.

I will leave a letter for my successor of which D is a copy.

I have drawn on the Department under date of the 30th ins[t] in favor of M. P. Game Esqr. for one thousand one hundred and twenty five dollars on account of the expenses of my return.—

M[r] Lisboa, Envoy Extraordinary of Brazil, arrived here on the 26th ultimo on his way to the City of Quito.— While he was here I obtained some information relative to the object of his mission and the policy of Brazil in regard to the Navigation of the Amazon and immediately wrote to President Urbina on the subject. His replies indicate that the Government of Ecuador will not cooperate with M[r] Lisboa in the policy of Brazil.— This correspondence though not official, appears to me of sufficient importance to justify me in transmitting copies of so much thereof as relates to the subject, and more especially as in his letter of the 21st instant he expresses a desire to know the opinions and policy of the Government of the United States on the subject.— Inasmuch as he does not understand the English language I had to write to him in Spanish.

Of my first letter on the subject I did not keep a copy.[1]—E is a copy of my second [2] and F contains extracts from his replies.[3]

In my previous despatches I omitted to mention some facts worthy of note in respect to this Country.

Ecuador contains about one million of inhabitants—not more than one eighth part of whom are white.— At least one half are Indians and the balance Negros Mullattos and other mixed breeds.— Since the dissolution of the Colombian Confederacy Ecuador has had six different and distinct Constitutions, by all of which the Roman Catholic Religion was established to the exclusion of all others.— A large proportion of the Priests are fathers of children whom they openly recognize and support.

About the time I arrived in this Country and for some months thereafter there was a very bad state of feeling between the Governments of New Grenada [Granada] and Ecuador and iminent danger of war between the two Republics, chiefly in consequence of the fact that the then existing Administration of Ecuador encouraged by the Spanish, French, and Peruvian Chargés then in Quito, was doing all it could to check the progress of Democracy in New Grenada.— To this end the Government of Ecuador invited and received the Jesuits, whom the Government of New Grenada had just expelled; and sent money arms and amunition to the Province of Pasto to aid some Conservatives who were in rebellion against the Government of New Grenada.— The revolution which occurred in July 1851 and by virtue of which General Urbina became Supreme Chief of this Republic had the immediate effect of restoring good relations between the two Governments.—

[1] Probably the one of September 28, 1853, mentioned in Urbina's letter to Cushing, dated October 5, 1853, above, this part, doc. 2380.
[2] Above, this part, October 5, 1853, doc. 2379.
[3] *Ibid.*, October 5, 12, and 21, 1853, docs. 2379, 2381, and 2382.

The Jesuits were greatly dissatisfied with this result and were incessantly at work to destroy harmony between the Governments and impede their political progress.— In consequence of this intermeddling the National Assembly of Ecuador which met in Guayaquil in 1852, instructed President Urbina to expel them from the Republic which he did in the course of a few months thereafter.— While in Ecuador they exerted a powerful influence, especially upon the women of all classes and were well supplied with money when they left.— Some of them are in the adjoining provinces of Peru and are constantly plotting to get back into Ecuador, and it is said that with a view to this end they are cooperating with General Flores.

There is probably no state of like extent that has a more genial and salubrious climate or a greater proportion of luxuriant soil than Ecuador and it is amazing how little has been done to improve these natural advantages— There is but one saw mill in the Republic which belongs to the firm of Cox Game & Co, all foreigners.— But one foundry which was established and is owned by an enterprising Baltimore Mechanic.— There is not a carriage nor a wagon and not more than a dozen carts in the whole Republic.— Everything is transported on the shoulders of men or the backs of beasts or dragged upon the ground by oxen, mules and Jackasses.— Crooked sticks instead of ploughs are used in cultivating the Earth.— All vessels under the Ecuatorian flag united are not equal in tonnage to one of our first class Clipper ships.

I herewith send a copy of the Newspaper mentioned by President Urbina in his letter to me of the 21st instant[1] and have the honor [etc.].

2384

José Villamil, Ecuadoran Chargé d'Affaires at Washington, to William L. Marcy, Secretary of State of the United States[2]

[TRANSLATION]

WASHINGTON, *November 1, 1853.*

The Undersigned, Chargé d'Affaires of the Republic of Ecuador, has the honor of addressing himself, by order of his government, to H. E. the Secretary of State of the United States, in order to inform him that Ecuador is once more threatened with another piratical invasion, led by Juan Jose Flores, the proscribed of Ecuador; and that the expedition is being organized, in part, in San Francisco, upper California. This new and scandalous aggression had already been announced in various papers of this country, and if the undersigned has abstained from calling the attention of the Secretary

---

[1] See above, this part, doc. 2382, and note 3 thereto, p. 313, for the documents translated from the above-mentioned newspaper.   [2] Notes from Ecuador, vol. I.

of State, whom he is now addressing, to the subject, it has been because, after the tremendous and miserable failure of the former attempt, he did not believe that such could be the case; much less did he suppose that such an expedition would be composed, in part, of U. S. citizens who being so jealous of their freedom in their own country, ought to be, it would seem, the last men of whom any fear should be entertained, of their attempting in other countries, to put down that very liberty which has been required at the cost of rivers of blood.   But as this intelligence is now communicated by the Government of Ecuador itself, the Undersigned considers it his strict duty to ask, with due respect, of the government of the United States, through its organ H. E. the Secretary of State whom he is now addressing, that peremptory and definite orders may be given to the authorities of the State of California, directing them to break up all warlike preparations destined to disturb the peace at present enjoyed by Ecuador, a sister republic and the friend of the United States.

The Undersigned is aware that Ecuador does not dread this new aggression, any more than it did the last.   He knows that Ecuador will surrender her existence rather than see herself again humbled by a Satrap [Sp. "Satrapa."—Ed.] destitute of honor and decency; and he knows also, that nothing would be more painful to the country he represents in this, than to count among her enemies, citizens of the U. S.; and it is with a firm adherence to this conviction, that he begs the government of the U. S. to adopt such measures as may be necessary for preventing a country, which has taught the love of liberty to America, from being made the starting point of an armed expedition destined to crush liberty on that very continent; seeing that, "to attack liberty in Ecuador is to attack it in every section of South America."   This is a truth which cannot be hidden from the discriminating eye of the Government of the U. S.   The Undersigned avails himself of this occasion [etc.].

2385

Philo White, United States Chargé d'Affaires in Ecuador, to William L. Marcy, Secretary of State of the United States[1]

No. 3   GUAYAQUIL, *November 23, 1853.*

SIR: I have the honor to advise you, that I arrived here something more than a week since, where I have been detained by illness in my family: It is now my intention, however, within a day or two, to proceed up and over the Mountains to the City of *Quito*, the Seat of Government of this Republic; when I shall, without unnecessary delay, present my credentials as the Diplomatic Representative of the United States to the Supreme Authorities here.

[1] Despatches, Ecuador, vol. 3.   Received January 7.

I met my predecessor, Courtland Cushing, Esq.ʳ at Panama, on his return home.   He there handed to me some documents of public import, and communicated verbally much that will be serviceable in my intercourse with this Government.   And it is due that I should say, he has left a most favorable impression, with the authorities and the people here, of the friendly disposition of our Government towards this Republic.

The Envoy from Brazil, Don Miguel Marcia Lisboa, has already had his official presentation at Quito, and promptly entered upon negotiations there, with the well-understood design of restricting the benefits of the navigation and commerce of the River Amazon and its tributaries *exclusively* to the countries within whose territories its waters are confined.

With what success his mission here is likely to be attended, may be inferred from the fact, of which I am assured by the sight of a letter from a Deputy, that the Congress of this Republic has just passed a Decree, making the navigation of the waters of the Amazon within her borders free for the vessels of all nations.   One paragraph of the letter is in these words:

> Las Camaras cerrarán sus sesiones el 19 del presente, sin que se hayan acordado mas cosas de provecho que las leyes sobre libertad de estudios, remate de sales, (que objetado el Ejecutivo) las de conscripcion, y milicia nacional, y *la de abrir la, navigacion del Amazones á todo el mundo.*[1]

I shall take an early opportunity of procuring and forwarding to the Department a copy of this important Act, which assures us of the liberal and enlightened intentions of this Government.

I have received several numbers of a Pamphlet, published in Lima, and which came through the hands of M.ʳ Clay, our Minister to Peru wherein the restrictive and antiquated policy sought to be inculcated among these Southern Republics by Brazil, is most ably combatted.   I distributed them in the right quarter, and have the honor to inclose a copy for the information of the Department.[2]

My predecessor having resided in Guayaquil during nearly the entire period of his sojourn in this country I find a goodly portion of the Archives pertaining to the Legation with our Consul here, which are contained in five heavy boxes.   This property of the United States I shall forward to Quito, as that City is *fixed* in the Constitution as the political Capital of the Republic; and, in due time, will forward a bill of the Expense to the Dept.

I have already written to Mr. Clay, at Lima; and shall continue frequently

---

[1] A translation of this paragraph follows:

"The Chambers will close their sessions on the 19th instant, without any beneficial measures having been passed except the laws as to free instruction, public sale of salt (which was opposed by the Executive), those concerning conscription, and national militia, *and the one for opening the navigation of the Amazon to the whole world.*"

[2] Not found.

and freely, to communicate with him and others, on all matters interesting to our Government, or that may affect the rights of our citizens.

I have the honor [etc.].

2386

José Villamil, Ecuadoran Chargé d'Affaires at Washington, to William L. Marcy, Secretary of State of the United States [1]

[TRANSLATION]

WASHINGTON, *December 1, 1853.*

The undersigned, Chargé d'Affaires of Ecuador, deems it his duty to call the attention of H. E. the Secretary of State of the United States to an article headed, "Movements in South America" [2] which appears in the "San Francisco Commercial Advertiser" of the 29th of October, herewith enclosed to H. E.

It is not the anathema hurled against the worthy President of Ecuador, by a newspaper writer blind with passion, that the undersigned has to do with at present. This impotent anathema is of itself harmless: General Urbina [3] is beyond its reach. Still less does the undersigned mind the assertion of the newspaper writer, that the government of the United States, favors the traitorous designs of the life aspirant to the dominion of Ecuador. [4] It would be folly on the part of the Undersigned, to suppose for an instant, that the government of the United States can favor a man without any honorable antecedents, who has only studied the art of doing evil, and whose designs are known to be to subject once more the South American Republics to European dominion. The object of the Undersigned is to call the attention of H. E. the Secretary, to whom he addresses himself to the ostentatious declaration contained in the article alluded to, that the principal powers of Europe favor the designs of the reckless South American who meditates to subject once more South America to European dominion. Eternal God! America again subjected to Europe! No: let her first be blotted out from the face of the earth!

That a paper concocted in the dark dens of despotism should preach this monstrous doctrine, can be conceived; but that such a production should be issued from this classic land of liberty, and not be put down at once by public indignation, is beyond comprehension.

[1] Notes from Ecuador, vol. 1. Received December 2.
[2] Not included in this publication. Briefly, in this article, the writer states that the opening of the Amazon River can never be accomplished while Ecuador is under the despotic rule of President Urbina; that the people of that country, as well as those of Europe and of the United States, favor the restoration of Flores, and, because of this latter fact, Ecuador is unable to affect a loan to liquidate her heavy Brazilian debt.
[3] The translator of this note obviously mistook the "Ur" in Urbina's name for "Vo." In the Spanish original it was correctly written.   [4] He refers to General Flores.

Here the Undersigned ought to bring his note to a close, because he does not consider the liberty of South America to be in danger, so long as the northern eagle watches the slippery and tortuous course of the deceitful snake; but he may be allowed to make one single remark.   The *freshets* produced by the Mississippi, begin through a hole bored by a locust and end by inundating the whole country.   The first inroads of absolute despotism are even less perceptible and unhappy is that country that does not check them in time.   Let the tendencies of the repeated attacks made against Ecuador by the salaried agent of European power, be closely observed, and you will catch the tread of a vast scheme for European dominion in South America;—a dominion, which although it may never prove terrible to these "United Empires" could not avoid very soon affecting, to a considerable extent, their present commercial relations with South America; and would, at a later period, throw serious obstacles in the way of that immense increase of trade which they anticipate in the vast pacific Ocean.

With profound respect and due consideration [etc.].

2387

*Philo White, United States Chargé d'Affaires at Quito, to William L. Marcy,
Secretary of State of the United States* [1]

QUITO, *January 18, 1854.*

SIR: I have the honor to inclose, herewith, a printed copy of a Decree [2] passed by the Congress and approved by the Executive of this Republic, opening the *River Amazon* and its tributaries within the territorial limits of Ecuador to the commerce of all nations, and granting privileges and immunities to every class of traders and settlers within that region.

The project of the decree was under consideration by Congress on my arrival in the Republic.   And perceiving that this was a critical conjuncture with regard to this important measure,—the most interesting question, indeed, that was likely to arise during my mission to this country,—I deemed it incumbent upon me to act promptly, even before being recognized in my official capacity by the National authorities, in exerting what little influence I might possess, in expediting its passage through that body.   I accordingly distributed among the Members all the copies I could obtain of Lieut. *Maury's* pamph[l]et (translated into Spanish) on the advantages of the free navigation of the Amazon; as, also, another pamphlet, (in Spanish) urging the passage of the decree.

I likewise gave assurances to all connected with either the Legislative or

[1] Despatches, Ecuador, vol. 3.   Received March 6.
[2] Not included in this publication, since its content is adequately indicated within this despatch.

Executive Departments of the Government with whom I was enabled at the moment to communicate, that the measure was one of deep interest to the Government of the United States,—and that its adoption by Ecuador, would tend to draw more closely those ties of amity and political brotherhood, which already so cordially unite the two nations as neighbors and sister Republics.

The decree was passed, with much unanimity, despite the efforts to the contrary of Senhor Dñ *Miguel Maria Lisboa*, the Brazillian Envoy;—who departed for Peru soon after, satisfied, doubtless, that his mission would prove as fruitless in negotiation with the Executive, as his personal appliances had with the legislative bodies.

Mʳ Lisboa came with the reputation of an accomplished diplomatist; and, by his acquirements, and in his personal bearing is well qualified to represent his sovereign, with ability: But the *cause* in which he was employed is not tasteful to the present Government of Ecuador.

Every manifestation on their part which I have thus far witnessed, shows an enthusiastic admiration of our political institutions, and a cordial sympathy with our present Democratic Administration. The opening of the *Amazon* known to be an object anxiously desired by our Government, has become a paramount question with them.

I have deemed this matter of sufficient importance, to warrant me in translating and printing the Decree in Circular form, for the benefit of our merchants and others at home.

It was intended to make the decree as broad in its scope, and as liberal in its concessions, as could reasonably be desired by commercial nations: But should it not fully meet the views and expectations of the President and the Department, I shall feel honored with further instructions on the subject, not doubting a disposition on the part of this Government to concede any modification of the law that might be agreeable to us, and that would not compromit their honor, nor alarm the domestic interests of the country.

With sentiments of high regard [etc.].

2388

José Villamil, Ecuadoran Chargé d'Affaires at Washington, to William L. Marcy, Secretary of State of the United States [1]

[TRANSLATION]

WASHINGTON, *January 31, 1854.*

The Undersigned, Chargé d'Affaires of Ecuador, has received the note which H. E. the Secretary of State of the United States did him the honor of addressing him this day,[2] enclosing a copy of another dated the 23ᵈ of Decem-

[1] Notes from Ecuador, vol. I. The receipt date was not indicated.
[2] Above, this volume, pt. III, doc. 2325.

ber,[1] written by the competent authority of California to H. E., stating that there are no armed expeditions contemplated in that State hostile to Ecuador, and that in the event of any attempts being made to that effect, they would be suppressed and the offenders punished according to law.

The Undersigned duly appreciates the haste with which the Secretary whom he addresses has been pleased to allay his anxiety, in this respect, and feels likewise persuaded that the government he represents will also know how to appreciate this evidence of friendly interest which the government of the United States takes in the tranquillity and welfare of that republic.

The undersigned [etc.].

2389

Philo White, United States Chargé d'Affaires at Quito, to William L. Marcy, Secretary of State of the United States[2]

No. 15   QUITO, May 17, 1854.

SIR: At the request of President Urbina, communicated through Mr Espinel, Minister of Foreign Relations, who called at my house on the 25th ultimo, to confer personally with me in relation to a marauding expedition which, they had that moment been advised in a despatch received by express from their Consul at San Francisco, was actually fitting out in that Port against Ecuador, by the procurement and at the expense of their old enemy, *Gen'l. Flores*, whose son is now in California,—I took the liberty of writing to Major *General Wool* on the subject, as also to His Excellc'y *Gov. Bigler* of California, to *Commodore Dulaney* in command of our Pacific Squadron, and to M[r]. *Clay* our Minister at Lima,[3] advising them of the actual relations existing between Ex-President *Flores* and the present Government of Ecuador,—that there is a decree of *out-lawry* against him, for treason and other high crimes, in having waged war against and invaded the country at the head of a lawless buccaneer-band, murdering its citizens and pillaging their property,—and that, consequently, he and his followers will be summarily dealt with as *pirates*, should they fall into the hands of the authorities of this Republic.   And in my communications, I requested these Commanders to warn the misguided followers of such criminal enterprizes of the hazard to which they would be exposed, as well from the military and naval forces of the United States in the Pacific, as from the more sanguinary "tender mercies" of the race against whom they would be waging a lawless and unprovoked war of rapine.

I assured the Minister at the time, and have since reiterated that assurance

[1] Not included in this publication; its content is sufficiently reviewed within this note.
[2] Despatches, Ecuador, vol. 3.   Received June 26.
[3] For White's letters to Wool and Dulaney, see below, this part, p. 329, note 2.   Those to Bigler and Clay were not found.

to the President himself, that it was the fixed determination of my government to prevent, as far as practicable, all attempts of its citizens to get up or to join in marauding expeditions against the Republics of the South: And that the vigor and the vigilance with which the President and his Cabinet were now giving effect to the neutrality laws of the country, could not fail of resulting in the suppression of all piratical armaments within our borders.

And altho' I felt assured that my writing to *Gen. Wool* and *Commre Dulany* could avail nothing by way of imparting a renewed vigilance and efficiency to their operations against the "fillibusters", yet I found that my doing so would tend to allay to some extent the feverish anxiety on the part of the authorities here with regard to the rumors of invasion by which the country is so often agitated, and might, moreover, serve to strengthen their confidence in my reiterated assurances of the lively interest felt by my government for the continued progress and the permanent peace and prosperity of this Republic. I consequently did not hesitate in preparing and forwarding the communications above alluded to. And trust that my having done so, will meet the approval of the President and of yourself.

I have the honor [etc.].

2390

Marcos Espinel, Minister of Foreign Affairs of Ecuador, to Philo White, United States Chargé d'Affaires at Quito[1]

[TRANSLATION]

QUITO, *June 22, 1854.*

I have the honor to enclose to Your Honor a copy of a letter which was published in "El Heraldo de Lima" of the 16th of last month.[2] According to the text of the said letter, the citizens of the United States who are accompanying Mr. William Denison are going to take possession of the lands located on the shores of the Santiago River in the name of Peru and as colonists of that Republic.

Before this announced plan is put into effect, Your Honor must be informed—in order that you may kindly transmit the information to your nationals—that the two shores of the Amazon, from the river Chinchipe to Tabatinga, belong to the Ecuadoran people *de facto* and *de jure;* and that if Mr. Denison and his compatriots wish to establish themselves on Santiago territory, they can do so with the consent of the Ecuadoran Government, which has a most decided interest in welcoming industrious Americans in compliance with the law of November 26, 1853.

By this preliminary measure, contests and disagreeable occurrences which

[1] Despatches, Ecuador, vol. 3; enclosed with White to the Secretary of State, No. 19, July 5, 1854, below, this part, doc. 2392.   [2] Not found.

might be occasioned between Ecuadorans and Peruvians by this event will be avoided.

His Excellency Pedro Moncayo, Minister Plenipotentiary of this Republic near the Government of Peru, has spoken officially in this same sense to His Excellency Mr. Randolph Clay, Minister Plenipotentiary of the United States near the same Peruvian Government and it is to be hoped that both Your Honor and His Excellency Mr. Clay, as representatives of a just and eminently liberal Republic, will take an interest in the observance by your nationals of the rights and prerogatives which, strictly according to law, belong to Ecuador in the territories which are to be occupied by immigration from North America.

With sentiments of most distinguished consideration, I have the honor [etc.].

2391

Philo White, United States Chargé d'Affaires at Quito, to Teodoro Gómez de la Torre, Acting Minister of Foreign Affairs of Ecuador [1]

QUITO, *June 27, 1854.*

The undersigned has the honor to acknowledge the receipt of the communication addressed to him by His Excellc'y, Marcos Espinel, Minister of Foreign Relations, of date 22^d June instant,[2] in which he is advised that a party of American citizens, under the lead of Mr. Wm. P. Denison, have gone to take possession, in the name of Peru, of the land on the banks of the Santiago river at or near San Borja,—and desiring the undersigned to convey information to the said party of Americans, that both banks of the Amazon (or Marañon) from the river Chinchipe to Tabatinga belong of right and in fact to the people of Ecuador; but that if Mr Denison and his countrymen are desirous of establishing themselves in the territory bordering the Santiago River, they will be permitted to do so by the Government of Ecuador, which feels a deep interest in welcoming industrious Americans to the country as settlers, in accordance with the provisions of the Law of 26th September, 1853.

In view of the amicable relations now happily existing between Ecuador and the United States, and of the kindness and courtesy so uniformly manifested towards the undersigned by His Excellency the President, and the other Executive Functionaries of this Republic, motives of personal regard are superadded to a sense of official duty, in prompting the undersigned readily and cheerfully to comply with the request of His Excellency the Minister of Foreign Relations.

[1] Despatches, Ecuador, vol. 3; enclosed with White to the Secretary of State, No. 19, July 5, 1854, below, this part, doc. 2392.   [2] Above, this part, doc. 2390.

And the undersigned will feel doubly gratified, if his good offices exerted on this occasion shall contribute in any degree to "prevent the disagreeable contests between Ecuatorians and Peruvians" which the Minister fears may grow out of the event in question.

The undersigned will, therefore, avail himself of the first medium that offers of communicating with Mr Clay, the Minister of the United States in Lima, as also with Wm P. Denison and his party, for the purpose of advising them of the fact, that the territory where the latter contemplate locating,— but that, at the same time, should they desire to make permanent settlements at that point, they not have the consent but the invitation of the Authorities of this Republic to do so, the only prerequisite being a conformity with the Ecuatorian law above recited, which makes liberal colonists or settlers on the lands of Ecuador.[1]

With sentiments of high consideration [etc.].

2392

Philo White, United States Chargé d'Affaires at Quito, to William L. Marcy, Secretary of State of the United States[2]

No. 19   Quito, *July 5, 1854.*

SIR: A question of National Limits is pending between the Republics of Ecuador and Peru, and there have existed between them for some years conflicting claims to jurisdiction over a belt of territory on the Upper Amazon,— or Marañon.

A company of Americans having recently gone from Lima, with the view of locating within the disputed territory, under the inducement from the Peruvian government of obtaining grants of land, &c., the Ecuatorian Government has made that event the occasion of addressing an official communication to *me* on the subject: A copy of this communication, together with my answer, I have the honor to inclose herewith.[3]

I have the honor [etc.].

[1] The sentence is written thus in the manuscript volume, although parts of it have obviously been omitted.
[2] Despatches, Ecuador, vol. 3.   Received August 25.
[3] For these two notes, see above, this part, respectively, June 22 and 27, 1854, docs. 2390 and 2391.

2393

Philo White, United States Chargé d'Affaires at Quito, to William L. Marcy,
Secretary of State of the United States [1]

No. 20   QUITO, *July 6, 1854.*

SIR: You have doubtless been apprised, ere this, that Treaties of Limits, Amity, &c., were concluded in July last, between the Governments of New Granada and Brazil.

A pamphlet has recently been published at Bogota, which contains the texts of those treaties, (three in number, viz: a "Treaty of Amity and Limits,"—a "Convention of Fluvial Navigation,"—and a "Treaty of Extradition," &c.),—together with a Report from Sor. Lorenzo Maria Lleras, the New Granadian Minister of Foreign Relations, to the President of that Republic, embracing a synoptical view of the discussions had by the Plenipotentiaries of the two governments, in settling the mooted points presented in the protocols of each, with a passing commentary on the same by the Minister of New Granada.

The only copy of this pamphlet to be met with in Quito, is the property of President Urbina: And as he has loaned it to me for a few days, I have noted some of the most remarkable of the opinions broached, and the points discussed, by these Plenipotentiaries of two of the governments whose territories border the Amazon.

Such portions of these discussions, and their results, as are of most immediate interest to our country, and that seem most repugnant to a liberal and enlightened international policy, are found in what was said and done in negotiating the "Fluvial Convention", above mentioned. The first notable provision of this Instrument, is the abrogation of the *law* of New Granada, of 1852, opening the navigation of all her rivers to the people of every nation,— and which law, the New Granadian Plenipotentiary acknowledges he was among the most active (as a delegate in Congress) in procuring enacted. For this extraordinary change of (I will not say *opinion*, but) policy, he assigns this excuse, that "In considering the question, for the present, whether the opening of the Amazon to the flags of all nations, would enure to the advantage of the South American Republics conterminous with Brazil, I must say that, in spite of my own convictions and desires, I could not venture to decide affirmatively,—because the mournful, the painful experience of the past, admonishes me that the *losses* would be greater than the *gains*, by reason of the numerous claims that would be likely to arise against us, for damage done to foreign vessels navigating our rivers under such guaranties, by the Indians inhabiting their banks," and where the "civilized population is so sparse that the laws are inoperative in repressing the depredations of those savages." Moreover, he thinks the United States and England cannot

[1] Despatches, Ecuador, vol. 3. Received August 25.

with a very good grace, complain of the *exclusiveness* of the policy of the South American governments with regard to their "fluvial" intercourse, "until they make the navigation and commerce of the St. Lawrence River and *all its confluents*, as free to all the nations of the earth as to the people residing on their shores."

And the Brazillian Plenipotentiary, Sor. Miguel Maria Lisboa, with the restrictive policy of whose government the New Granadian Minister seems recently to have become indoctrinated, enunciates his views in the same strain, but of course in a more *ex cathedra* tone.   Holding, as he does, that "the international law, as acknowledged by most of the maritime countries of the world, concedes to those who possess both banks of a river, the right to open or close its navigation, according as it may suit their own interests and convenience," he asserts that "the United States of America alone have proclaimed the principle of free navigation to all who may inhabit one or both banks" of such river: And then proceeds to say, that "In spite of their illustrious career, and of their great influence as one of the principal powers of the world, they have never been able, with all the subtilty of their diplomacy, to apply that principle to the River St. Lawrence, in whose navigation they are so greatly interested:" That "notwithstanding they have, in their negotiations with England, argued with ability and astuteness, that the St. Lawrence was not a 'river', but rather a '*strait*' *between two seas*,"— contending, at other times, for the right to *continue* in the exercise of a privilege they had previously enjoyed while subject to Great Britain, and to share in all the natural advantages pertaining to a territory which was theirs by right of conquest and of continued occupancy;—yet, in spite of all these efforts, in spite of their being owners of and dwellers on the banks of that river and its confluents, "they have never succeeded in obtaining any other privilege than that of navigating said river in small vessels trading *bona fide* between Montreal and Quebec," &c.

And in another place Sor. Lisboa lays claim to especial liberality and generosity on the part of his government, in conceding, as a *boon*, to neighboring nations, inhabitants of the banks of the Amazon and its tributaries, the privilege of using the main trunk of that river to and from the sea; and he here takes occasion to institute a comparison between this magnanimous act of Brazil, and the course of policy still adhered to by England towards the United States, with respect to the navigation of the St. Lawrence.

Mr. Lisboa, I understand, was educated at the University of Edinburgh, (Scotland); has been much abroad and enjoys the reputation of being an astute diplomatist: It was therefore to have been expected, that he would inform himself *correctly* of the treaty stipulations between the United States and Great Britain, before making them the subject of so invidious a criticism as that contained in his communications with the New Granadian government.   He appears either to have been ignorant of the existence of the

"Ashburton Treaty," or to have *blinked* its stipulations before the eyes of the confiding Señor *Lleras*, the more readily to overcome the "convictions and desires" expressed by the latter in favor of free navigation, and thus easily draw him into the meshes of the selfish and *retrograde* policy of Brazil.

But as I have already intimated, the Pamphlet alluded to may have been forwarded to the Department directly from Bogota, and thus have put you in possession of its entire contents, which are worth noting in connexion with our South American diplomacy.

My principal motive, consequently, in bringing the subject to your attention at this time, is respectfully to ask information as to the *precise extent* of the rights and immunities enjoyed by the United States in the navigation of the St. Lawrence? Whether, by the provisions of the Ashburton treaty, that river has not, in its whole length, been rendered free to an unrestricted ingress and egress of our vessels, to the same extent that we demand of Brazil in regard to the Amazon, or as was conceded to Great Britain by the 8th Article of the Treaty of 1783, with respect to the Mississippi.

Mr. Lisboa seems to have relied wholly on the provisions of the 3d Article of the treaty of 1794, as a pretext for indulging in the "fling" with regard to the commercial relations between the United States and Great Britain. But having, myself, always supposed that the inequality of rights existing under the Treaty of 1794, was remedied by that concluded between Lord Ashburton and Mr. Webster in 1842, I have taken the liberty to inquire of the Honorable the Secretary of State, whether I am right in that supposition?

Not that I need new facts, &c., in my official intercourse with the Government of Ecuador, at this particular time, for they have conceded every thing that seems to be requisite on their part in relation to the navigation of the Amazon, and even express their readiness to accede to any reasonable modifications of their present law on the subject that we may suggest; but, as the matter is occasionally discussed in mixed company, it would be exceedingly satisfactory to me personally, and might, in a contingency not altogether improbable, become important in my official action, to be armed with an *authoritive* construction of the treaty stipulations that govern the commercial intercourse between the United States and Great Britain at this day, so far as *River* navigation is concerned.

I have the honor [etc.].

2394

Philo White, United States Chargé d'Affaires at Quito, to Marcos Espinel, Minister of Foreign Affairs of Ecuador[1]

F   QUITO, *July 29, 1854.*

The undersigned Chargé d'Affaires of the United States, having on the 25th of April last, at the solicitation of Your Excellency, written to Major Gen'l. John E. Wool, and to Commodore Bladen Dulany, commanding the Military and Naval Forces of the United States in the Department of the Pacific,[2] announcing to those Officers that the Executive Government of this Republic had received advices from their Consular Agent in San Francisco, to the effect that he had reason to believe a piratical expedition was in preparation at that Port, destined for the invasion of Ecuador, with the view of subverting its government and pillaging its citizens,—and Your Excellency

[1] Despatches, Ecuador, vol. 3; enclosed with White to the Secretary of State, No. 27, August 21, 1854, below, this part, doc. 2396.
[2] These two notes follow:

Philo White, United States Chargé d'Affaires at Quito, to Major General John E. Wool, in command of the United States Department of the Pacific

QUITO, *April 25, 1854.*

SIR: I take the liberty to address you at the special request of the President of this Republic, in relation to the marauding expedition said to be fitting out at San Francisco against Ecuador, ostensibly under the direction of Gen'l. Flores, formerly President of this Republic.

The Government here have letters from San Francisco, of the 15th ultimo, advising them that an expedition is positively in preparation there, destined against Ecuador. I have assured them that the Government of the United States will use all means at its command in the Pacific, to suppress these piratical enterprizes: And that, after your arrival at San Francisco, I feel assured your energy and vigilance will prevent the sailing of such unlawful expeditions.

Gen'l. Juan José Flores is out-lawed by the Government of Ecuador, for former acts of treason against the actual Government; and all who aid and abet his criminal attempts against this country, are declared "pirates", and will be summarily put to death, if caught.

Trusting that all buccaniering expeditions on foot in California, may be suppressed before leaving port,—and that you, General, are in the enjoyment of health,—

I have the honor [etc.].

Philo White, United States Chargé d'Affaires at Quito, to Commodore Bladen Dulaney, U. S. N., in command of the Department of the Pacific

QUITO, *April 25, 1854.*

DEAR SIR: The Government of this Republic have advices from California, of 15th ultimo, that a piratical expedition is fitting out there against Ecuador, under the countenance, if not indeed by the procurement, of the notorious *Flores*. He has been outlawed, and a price put upon his head; and his aiders and abettors are declared out-laws, and will be summarily put to death, if caught by the Authorities of this Republic.

I therefore take the liberty of writing you, respectfully to ask whether, if Guayaquil were to be attacked by these free-booters, you would feel at liberty to order a vessel of your Squadron to that point, for the protection of American citizens and property, and to aid the City against pillage by these pirates, the common enemies of mankind?

I shall feel obliged, if you will honor me with an answer.

With high regard and respect [etc.].

having requested, through the medium of the undersigned, that those commanding Officers would interpose the forces under their respective commands in thwarting the criminal designs of these common enemies of mankind.

The undersigned now has the pleasure of informing Your Excellency, that he has received despatches from General Wool, and from Commodore Dulany,[1] authorizing him to assure the Executive Government of Ecuador, that, to the best of their knowledge and belief there was not, at the time of their writing, any piratical expedition in preparation against Ecuador, nor did they believe any such marauding enterprize could for the present succeed against this Republic. But if, contrary to all probabilities at this time, Commodore Dulany should be apprized of the approach of any such expedition, he will promptly despatch a vessel of war to Guayaquil, as well for the purpose of protecting American interests, as for aiding in the cause of humanity, and contributing to the preservation of the lives and the property of the citizens of a friendly and neighboring Republic, from the rapine and murder to which they might be exposed from the irruption of a lawless band of desperadoes.

[1] They follow:

Major General John E. Wool, U. S. A. in command of the Department of the Pacific, to Philo White, United States Chargé d'Affaires at Quito

Head Quarters, Department of the Pacific,
SAN FRANCISCO, *June 13, 1854.*

SIR: I had the honor to receive your communication of the 25th of April, 1854 [Above, this part, p. 329, note 2.—Ed.], by the last Steamer from Panama.

In reply I would remark, that I am quite certain that no expedition is fitting out in California by Gen'l. Flores against Ecuador, or any other country. The rumor has probably arisen from the fact that the Mexican and French Consuls, aided by Count Rousset de Boulbon, have been engaged in fitting out expeditions against Sonora, in Mexico, but in which I have defeated them. The Mexican Consul was tried, and convicted: The French Consul was tried, but not found guilty,—the jury stood ten for conviction, and two for acquittal.

Watkins and Emory, have been tried, and convicted. Walker and his party have surrendered themselves, and have been turned over to the civil authorities for trial. Gen¹ Flores is not now in California.

I have the honor [etc.].

Commodore B. Dulaney, U. S. N. in command of the Department of the Pacific, to Philo White, United States Chargé d'Affaires at Quito

U. S. Flag Ship *St. Lawrence,*
CALLAO, *June 1, 1854.*

SIR: I have the honor to acknowledge the receipt of your letter of the 25th April ult. [Above, this part, p. 329, note 2, second document.—Ed.], asking that a vessel of the Squadron under my command should be sent to Guayaquil, in the event of a piratical expedition being directed against the Republic of Ecuador.

Notwithstanding the advices received by the Government of Ecuador, I have every reason to believe that there is not, at present, the least cause for apprehension. Should, however, a necessity arise for the intervention of an armed vessel of the United States, for the protection of American citizens and property, I shall, upon the earliest information, despatch one to Guayaquil, as you request.

I am, Sir, [etc.].

The high qualities of mind possessed by General Wool, and the illustrious professional reputation he has acquired in deeds of arms, gave assurance to the government of the undersigned, that in investing him with plenary powers as Commander in Chief of the Military Department of the Pacific, the most satisfactory results might be anticipated. And that distinguished Officer has already signally fulfilled the high expectations of his government, and of the nation, in having promptly suppressed the lawless enterprises that were on foot in California. Many of the criminal participators in those enterprizes, have already been prosecuted to conviction; and the last remnants of the piratical bands that ravaged a neighboring province, have been surrendered to the Commanding General, by whom they were turned over to the civil tribunals, at whose hands they will no doubt receive that condign punishment to which their crimes and their outrages upon humanity have consigned them.

The undersigned may be permitted to congratulate His Excellency the Minister of Foreign Relations, as well as the Executive Government of the Republic, upon a result so auspicious, as well to the peace and security of Ecuador, as to the safety and tranquility of all the governments whose Territories border the Pacific coast,

With sentiments of high consideration [etc.].

2395

Philo White, United States Chargé d'Affaires at Quito, to Marcos Espinel, Minister of Foreign Affairs of Ecuador [1]

K   QUITO, *August 15, 1854.*

SIR: In reference to Your Excellency's despatch of date of 22[d] June past,[2] in relation to the settlement of a party of North Americans at or near San Borja, within territory claimed by this Republic, the undersigned has the pleasure of informing your Excellency, that he has received a communication from Mr. Clay, Minister Plenipotentiary of the United States in Peru, in relation to the subject matter of said despatch.

M[r] Clay assures the undersigned, that he will avail himself of the first conveyance between Lima and the Santiago river, to forward the letter addressed by the undersigned to W[m] P. Denison, the leader of the party above named; but as there is no regular communication between those points, the opportunity of sending is very infrequent: Moreover, that it was rumored those Americans had become dissatisfied with their location, and a part of them, at least, had left for other regions.

[1] Despatches, Ecuador, vol. 3; enclosed with White to the Secretary of State, No. 27, August 21, 1854, below, this part, doc. 2396.   [2] Above, this part, doc. 2390.

And in this connexion, it affords the undersigned much satisfaction to say, that the further he pursues the investigation of the rights of Ecuador in regard to her Southern Boundary, the more fully is he satisfied of the legitimacy of her claim of jurisdiction to the banks of the River Marañon, (or Amazon) from Tabatinga to Chinchipe river.

With assurances of high regard [etc.].

2396

Philo White, United States Chargé d'Affaires at Quito, to William L. Marcy, Secretary of State of the United States [1]

[EXTRACT]

No. 27   QUITO, *August 21, 1854.*

SIR: I have the honor this day to forward to the Department, in separate envelops, copies of sundry Despatches.[2] . . .

I have the honor [etc.].

2397

Philo White, United States Chargé d'Affaires at Quito, to William L. Marcy, Secretary of State of the United States [3]

No. 28—Confidential.   QUITO, *August 22, 1854.*

SIR: Taking the liberty to invite your attention to my despatch N°. 19, dated 5ᵗʰ July, ultimo,[4] I may be pardoned for again adverting to the question of unadjusted Territorial Boundary between Ecuador and Peru, since events are daily transpiring which involve that question more and more intimately with another of greater magnitude to us,—that of the *free navigation* of the Amazon River.

From the investigations I have been enabled to make in regard to this question of territorial limits, and the information I have acquired touching the matter, I am clearly of the opinion that the Republic of Ecuador has a valid title to the entire left (or northern) bank of the Amazon, from the 78ᵗʰ degree of west longitude to the mouth of the Yavari river, the latter point being at the south-west angle of the boundary claimed by New Granada. Under the old Spanish Government, the Viceroyalty of Santa Fé de Bogotá extended still further south, including the mouths and portions of the trunks

[1] Despatches, Ecuador, vol. 3.   Received September 28.
[2] Those pertinent to this publication are above, this part, July 29 and August 15, 1854, docs. 2394 and 2395; and in notes on pages 329–30.
The omitted portion relates chiefly to the settlement of claims.
[3] Despatches, Ecuador, vol. 3.   Received September 28.   [4] Above, this part, doc. 2392.

of the Huallaga and Ucayali rivers, the right of the Vice Roys of Bogotá in their exercise of jurisdiction over all the "Mission of Maynas" south of the Amazon, never having been called in question.

It has been the great aim and constant endeavor of the Brazilian Government, to *control* the whole question of the navigation of the Amazon, in all its ramifications, and there to exclude *free trade* from that river.   To this end, all the arts of her diplomacy have been exerted to inveigle *Peru* into her toils; and in this it is to be feared she has been but too successful, evidence of which is found in the motives that prompted the issuing of the Executive decree of the Peruvian Government of the 4th of January last, wherein it was attempted virtually to repudiate those provisions of our Treaty with that Republic, and of their own Decree of the 15th April 1853, by which important privileges were conceded to our citizens in the navigation and commerce of the Amazon and its tributaries.

Brazil not being able, with any degree of plausibility, to lay claim in her own behalf to the Upper Amazon (or Marañon) between the points above indicated, she has found a convenient instrument for the effectuation of her schemes in the present Administration of Peru, as you will doubtless ere this have been advised by Mr. Clay, our Minister to that Republic: Accordingly we find that Peru, with the thinly-veil'd purpose of abetting the designs of Brazil, has unceremoniously taken possession of both banks of the Amazon, on the whole extent of the Ecuatorian frontier in that direction,—that she has appointed a Governor for *Loreto*, on the north side of the River,—and in fine, has usurped jurisdiction over a large extent of territory that most clearly belongs to Ecuador.

This Government has an able and discreet man, Doctor Pedro Moncáyo, as its Plenipotentiary at Lima; and they are now preparing to open negotiations with the authorities of that Government, and make a demand for an equitable settlement of the boundary difficulties existing between the two countries;—in which, I am inclined to think, Ecuador will be sustained by both New Granada and Venezuela, who are equally enterested with her in maintaining the integrity of their Southern boundary, as it existed not only under the Spanish authority, but likewise under that of the Colombian Republic, of which they were component parts,—their right to that ancient line of demarcation never having been alienated by any act of theirs, nor by any treaty stipulation has it ever been ceded to Peru.   More especially are New Granada and Venezuela likely to side with Ecuador in this question, since they both lay claim to the northern bank of the Amazon from the town of Loréto to the mouth of the Rio Negro.   And all three of these Northerly Republics, are borne out in their claim, it will thus be seen, by the favorite and conservative principle, among diplomatists, of *uti possidetis*.   Should Ecuador be thus backed, strong hopes are entertained that she will succeed in obtaining something like tardy justice,—at least so far as eventually to effect a compromise on the line of the Amazon, so as to render her a "riparian" State of the main channel of that river, from the mouth of the Yavari to the 78th degree of west longitude.

In the meanwhile, however, it behoves those Governments interested in the free commerce of the Amazon, to do something to strengthen the hands of Ecuador in her efforts to counteract the sinister policy of Brazil, thus attempted to be carried out through the agency of her supply ally, *Peru*.

And to this end, it has been suggested that the United States might exercise, in a legitimate way, a most salutary influence in determining the question auspiciously for free navigation by concluding *Additional Articles* to our existing *Treaty with Ecuador*.

In these Additional Articles, it might be stipulated that our citizens should enjoy the amplest privileges in the navigation of, and the carrying on commerce in, the Amazon and its tributaries,—to land and take in cargo duty free, &c., at sundry Ports to be designated, say those of "Loreto,"—"Pebas,"—"Oran,"—"Nauta,"—"San Borja," &c.: with an article granting privileges to Steam Vessls under our flag, such as the right of building work shops, establishing wood-yards, &c.&c.;—so as to place our rights in regard to the commerce of the Amazonian waters, on an equal footing with those of Ecuador.

Such a course on our part, would be lending an indirect countenance to the title of Ecuador to her territory on the Amazon now usurped by Peru. And it is more than probable that Peru herself, when she should see the United States thus tacitly acknowledging the claims of Ecuador, might retrace her retrograde movement of the 4th of January last,—or at least not attempt to carry out that invidious decree expressly aimed, as it was, at neutralizing the benefits that had previously been conferred upon our citizens, in common with others, in the commerce of the Amazon.

In such event, as we are not called on to take part in the dispute between them, we could avail ourselves after the conclusion of the Additional Articles with Ecuador, (whatever might be the fortune of the latter in the decision of the question of boundary) of the acts of Peru or of Ecuador as might best suit our interests.

Every decree or treaty stipulation of any of these Republics that invites us to carry on commerce with them through the waters of the Amazon, will add strength to our claim, that that River is a great National Highway. And it is not impossible that the step I have herein suggested, may exert a potent influence in persuading even Brazil eventually to relax in her selfish policy, and yield to the enlightened sentiment of the age in regard to *free trade*, and open the entrance of the Amazon to the commerce of all nations.

Should these views, thus imperfectly embodied, meet the concurrence of His Excellency the President, and of the Honorable the Secretary of State, I shall feel honored in being intrusted with authority to conclude such Additional Articles, or otherwise to give effect to the suggestions I have herein taken the liberty to make for the consideration of my Government.

And I must beg to add, should such a measure as I have recommended be deemed expedient, that there are weighty considerations in favor of prompt action in the matter.

With very great respect [etc.].

2398

Philo White, United States Minister Resident in Ecuador, to William L. Marcy, Secretary of State of the United States[1]

[EXTRACT]

No. 32   QUITO, *September 20, 1854.*

SIR: I have the honor to acknowledge the receipt of your despatch N°. 13, of date 12th August,[2] accompanied by a Commission from the President of the United States, empowering me to conclude a Convention with the Government of Ecuador, for "a grant to the United States and their citizens, to remove *Guano* from any or all of the Islands belonging to said Republic," &c.

And although the time allowed me, before the departure of the *monthly* mail for the United States, is too brief to admit of a lengthened answer to your communication, yet I ought not to delay briefly to state to you the unwelcome fact, that, after a thorough exploration, no guano can be discovered on the Galápagos Islands.

Captain *Game*, our Consul at Guayaquil, has just visited and explored those Islands. He is an experienced navigator, and was aided in his enterprize by this Government, they having put their small War Steamer "Guayas" under his direction for the purpose, and the President and Minister of Foreign Relations visited Guayaquil in person, to look after the arrangements for the expedition. Gen. Villamil accompanied our Consul in all his explorations.

Since Capt. Game's return, he has written to me that his expedition has proved an entire failure,—no *Guano*, worth the expense of removal, having been discovered by them; and Gen'l. Villamil himself has returned to Guayaquil, disappointed in his anticipations.

Yet, in pursuance of your instructions, I will endeavor to negotiate a Convention with the Authorities here for securing to our Government and citizens the *privilege* of removing Guano from any or all of their Islands and Territories whereon it may be discovered.

Under present discouragements, this Government may be disposed to

[1] Despatches, Ecuador, vol. 3. Received October 28.
[2] Above, this volume, pt. III, August 14, 1854, doc. 2326, is the one to which reference is erroneously made. No. 13 was dated June 1, 1854 and referred to a claim matter.

grant liberal concessions to those willing to incur the expense of making still further explorations.[1] . . .

I have the honor [etc.].

2399

Philo White, United States Minister Resident in Ecuador, to William L. Marcy, Secretary of State of the United States[2]

No. 37—Confidential.   QUITO, *November 22, 1854.*

SIR: You will have learned from my despatch of yesterday's date,[3] containing the Minutes of the conferences between myself and the Ecuatorian Plenipotentiary, that I have concluded a Convention with this Government, securing important privileges for our citizens in the trade in *huano* at the Galápagos Islands.

As the period is brief between the signing of the Treaty and the departure of *this month's mail,* I hasten to forward to the President of the United States as directed in your instructions, one of the two original transcripts of the Treaty, *in Spanish;*[4] and I shall avail myself of the intermediate time between this and the next monthly mail-day, to make an English translation of the document: Meanwhile, the Congress of Ecuador will undoubtedly have approved the Instrument, and thus enable me to forward by the *next* mail a ratified Treaty, that will lack only the approving action of the Executive and Legislative branches of our Government, to give it the full force of an international law.

I have found myself driven to the necessity of exercising a liberal discretion under your instructions, to effect any Treaty at all with this Government in relation to concessions to our citizens in the trade of huano at the Galápagos Islands.

In the first place, they would not listen to an offer for the *purchase* of the Islands, nor for an *exclusive* right to the huano thereon, except at a price that would have astounded our Government!—as may be inferred from the circumstance of their having at first demanded *five millions* as a "loan," in consideration of their agreeing to sell huano to our citizens at *one dollar* less per ton than to the rest of the world; their views, indeed, are astonishingly inflated in regard to the value of their deposits of huano. Nor would they give ear to my proposition to *fix the price,* either now or prospectively, by treaty stipulation: Such a measure, they think, will be compromitting their rights of "eminent domain." &c.,—altho' they promise to establish a rate lower than the article has ever hitherto been purchased at: And they perempt-

---

[1] The omitted portion relates to the imprisonment of a citizen of the United States at Tabatinga.   [2] Despatches, Ecuador, vol. 3.   Received December 27.

[3] Not included in this publication; its content is indicated within this paragraph.

[4] Not included in this publication.   In the manuscript volume there is a copy of the treaty in Spanish, signed and sealed, followed by a translation.

orily declined granting the privilege, under all circumstances, to Capitans of vessels to *excavate* and load the huano by the labor of their own hands, claiming the right to employ Ecuatorian laborers for placing the article on the beach, &c,

Yet, notwithstanding, I have obtained their assent to *concessions* which, I humbly conceive, are of so much value to a numerous class of our people, that justice to them would render it expedient for our Government to approve and ratify the Convention I this day inclose to the President:

1st: This Government having awarded one-fifth of all their huano to the discoverers,—in the proportion of one-third of that fifth to De Brissot, and of two-thirds of the fifth to Villamil,—which contract has been approved by Congress.—I have obtained its recognition by the stipulations of the Treaty:

2d: In consideration of an advance, or loan, (of a large sum, to be sure) to this Government, on which an interest of 5 per cent. per annum is to be paid, I have obtained the important concession to our citizens, of a reduction of *one dollar* per ton from the price to be paid by the citizens or subjects of all other nations:

3d: I have secured to our masters of vessels the privilege of *excavating* and loading the huano by means of their own crews and hands, in cases where there shall not be sufficient quantities of the article on the beach ready for shipment,—so as to prevent delays in despatching our vessels with cargoes:

4th: Full authority is granted to our Government to protect its citizens in their lawful pursuits on the Islands,—and, as a consequence, the right is conceded to protect the Islands themselves from incursions, depredations, &c.

Besides these special privileges and immunities, there are others contained in this Convention of a general nature, that will enure to the benefit of our people and our country.

Deferring further explanations until next mail, being pressed for time at this moment,—

I have the honor [etc.].

2400

Philo White, United States Minister Resident in Ecuador, to Franklin Pierce, President of the United States [1]

Confidential.   QUITO, *November 22, 1854.*

SIR: I have the honor to inform you, that I have just concluded a Convention with this Government, for regulating the commerce in *Huano* between her Islands and Ports and the United States, negotiated under authority of the special powers with which I was clothed by yourself for that purpose, and

---

[1] Despatches, Ecuador, vol. 3.   Received January 11.   Evidently this document was conveyed by a different route from the despatch of the same date to the Secretary of State, which was received December 27.

in conformity with instructions from the Honorable the Secretary of State:[1] And I hasten to inclose to you, by this month's mail, an original of that Convention,[2]—a translation of which I will make, and forward next month, by which time I shall be able to accompany another transcript of the Convention with the approval and ratification of the Congress of Ecuador.

Circumstances rendered it imperative, that I should avail, to a large extent, of the alternative discretion confided to me in the instructions of the Secretary. The Minutes of the several Conferences I held with the Ecuatorian Plenipotentiary in the negotiation of the Convention, a transcript of which I have inclosed to the State Department,[3] will enable you to estimate the difficulties encountered in agreeing upon terms more satisfactory to us than those I eventually obtained; and the incidents of these conferences will, I trust, serve as my justification in having exercised a rather full discretion in giving effect to the Secretary's instructions.

I am fully persuaded that this Government would have declined entering into *any* treaty stipulations, rather than have made further concessions than those contained in the Convention. And had I not now acceded to them, they would undoubtedly have made arrangements with European capitalists (who have already made tempting offers) for any reasonable amount of funds they may have stood in need of, and which could have been done at a decidedly lower rate of interest than that for which I have stipulated. So that, had I rejected their *ultimatum*, and thus have failed at this critical conjuncture to make the best terms practicable with them, I am convinced that any future attempt to treat with them for the valuable concessions we have now obtained would have proved as fruitless as all our efforts hitherto have [been?] to extricate our trade in huano with Peru from the vexations and *burdens* with which it is oppressed by the mo[no]polizing and odious policy pursued by that government.

The principle of an *obligatory* protection of the Galápagos Islands by the United States, was more pertinaciously contested by this government, than any other question mooted during the negotiation, except as to the policy of entering into any treaty stipulations at all on the subject of the huano trade: And on their finally surrending that point, the President especially insisted, as a consideration, upon raising the amount of the loan to $3,000,000, they having previously assented to its reduction to 2,000,000. And, judging of his motives *diplomatically*, I thought his mental purpose was so to increase the *interest* of the United States in the preservation of the Islands from lawless depradations, &c., as to add to the vigilance and increase the anxiety of our Government, in extending ample *protection* to them.

[1] For his instructions, see above, this volume, pt. III, August 14, 1854, doc. 2326.
[2] Not included in this publication, but for an explanation of the provisions of it, see below, this part, White's despatch No. 40, dated December 20, 1854, doc. 2402.
[3] He refers to White's despatch No. 36, dated November 21, 1854, which is not included in this publication.

The clause of the Convention relative to the right of the United States to protect its own citizens engaged in trade at the Galápagos, as well as the Islands themselves from forrays, and from interruptions to those employed in the huano business, leaves to our Government about as broad a discretion in carrying out that stipulation, as our treaty with Mexico does in regard to the protection of the Tehuantepec road.

Believing that the Convention I now have the honor to inclose to you, secures most important advantages to a numerous class of our countrymen, who are dependent largely upon that extraordinary fertilizer known as *huano*, for the successful tilth of their lands,—a portion of our citizens who have rarely shared in the beneficiary action of our Government; and feeling assured that an occasion will never again be presented to the Government for extending to them so acceptable a service, and to which they are so eminently entitled,—I trust that the Instrument I inclose will meet with the approval of Your Excellency, and be ratified by the action of the Senate and of the House of Representatives,—provided the deposits of huano on the Galápagos Islands shall prove, on the report of Messrs. Benjamin and Prats, to be as extensive as has been anticipated.

I have the honor [etc.].

2401

Philo White, United States Minister Resident in Ecuador, to William L. Marcy, Secretary of State of the United States [1]

No. 39—Confidential.   QUITO, *November 24, 1854.*

SIR: I had the honor to advise you by the regular mail on the 22[d] inst.,[2] of my having forwarded to the President of the United States, an original of a Convention or Treaty, just concluded with this Government, regulating the trade, &c. in *Huano* between the two countries: And I now avail myself of a brief space of time this morning before the departure of a *Government Express* hence to Guayaquil, to advise you of a singular diplomatic movement at this Capital, during two days past, for defeating the ratification of that Convention by this Congress.

Doctor Espinel, the Minister of Foreign Relations, called last night at my House, to advise me that Messrs. *De Paz* and *Villamus*, Chargés from Spain and France, Sor. *Sanz* the Peruvian Minister, and Mr. *Walter Cope*, the English *Consul*, called upon the Minister on Wednesday in a body, without the usual courtesy of asking in advance for a conference; and that they abruptly demanded the right to *Protest* against the ratification of our Treaty with Ecuador, in relation to the trade in huano, &c. &c.   The Minister consulted with me as to the proper course to pursue, and his reply was

[1] Despatches, Ecuador, vol. 3.   Received December 27.   [2] Above, this part, doc. 2400.

characterized by moderation and discretion: He asserted the full right of Ecuador to enter into treaty stipulation with all the nations of the earth, and to regulate her trade with them in regard to one or all articles of commerce; That the governments of the Protestants have an equal right with that of the United States, wherever they may choose to exercise it, to open negotiations with Ecuador for the regulation of the trade in *huano*, or other merchantable articles, with *their* respective countries, &c. &c.

Unfortunately the discussions in this Congress on *Treaties* as on all other subjects, *are public;* and in this way these diplomatic protestants became acquainted with the provisions of our Convention; and are, of course, exceedingly mortified that our country and our citizens should have secured advantages in the Galápagos huano trade *in advance* of the rest of the world! and they are particularly chafed, that the right should have been secured to the United States, (which I inserted in accordance with your instructions) of *protecting* their people in the enjoyment of those advantages,—and, as a corollary of that right, to *protect the Islands* where our people may be employed in the legitimate and necessary business of that trade, &c.

You will perceive that I have used the term "nacionales," in preference to that of "ciudadanos," in the 11th Art. of the Treaty, because nativity, or five years' residence, is requisite to constitute a "citizen" of the United States,—whereas, *every man employed under our flag*, is comprehended under the term "nacional," according to the most approved definition of the word among these people, in the connexion in which I have used it.

Dr Espinel informs me that our Convention is already approved by the Senate; and that it has passed to a second reading in the House, where it will again come up to-day, and before which the Minister himself will advocate its passage, as it is his prerogative to do. He feels assured of its passage, maugre all the attempts of the diplomatic protestants against it.

I trust, Sir, that this circumstance will serve as an additional incentive for *our* Government to approve and ratify the Treaty.

I have the honor [etc.].

2402

Philo White, United States Minister Resident in Ecuador, to William L. Marcy, Secretary of State of the United States[1]

No. 40—Confidential.   QUITO, *December 20, 1854.*

SIR: I have this day had the honor to forward to the President of the United States, a *duplicate* of the Convention concluded with Ecuador relative to the trade in *Huano* between the two countries, with a translation of the document subjoined,[2]—and, at the same time, to advise the President

[1] Despatches, Ecuador, vol. 3. Received January 26.
[2] Not included in this publication, since an explanation of the provisions of this treaty is given within this despatch. In the manuscript volume there is a copy of the treaty in

of the approval of the Treaty by Congress, and of the intention of this Government to send a Commissioner to Washington as bearer of the instrument, attested in due form as having been ratified by Congress and the Executive here: This Commissioner will be invested with power to effect an exchange of ratifications, should the Convention be acceptable to the President and Senate.

In giving a translation of the document, I have been careful to render the original as *literally* as the difference in the construction of the two idioms, and the verbally expressed *intentions* of the Ecuatorian Plenipotentiary, would seem to warrant. I may have amplified a little in rendering some few sentences of the Spanish text; but it has in all cases been done in strict accordance with the full and frank explanations that took place at our conferences, of the bearing and force of those sentences. In truth, as Doctor Espinel remarked, we have a guarantee that the provisions of this Treaty will be construed liberally in behalf of the United States, in the fact that the right of "protection" might involve, in certain contingencies, the power of interpretation.

Since my last despatch to you on this subject, (No. 39) [1] in which I alluded to an *extraneous* opposition to the approval of our Convention by the Ecuatorian Congress, circumstances go to strengthen a suspicion, previously entertained, that the same influences were exerted to embarrass the Executive during the *negotiation* of the Treaty.

An English Agent is here, urging upon this Government the acknowledgment of a large amount (some millions) of Old *Colombian* Bonds, which have served as "fancies" in the European stock markets for some thirty or forty years, and which the present holders obtained at a mere nominal price: This Agent, is backed by the British Consul for Ecuador, who has resided about thirty years in the country, and exercises no small influence through his extensive social intercourse. The paucity of the national resources was a serious obstacle to this Government's assuming large amounts of so old and rather questionable debts: A rumor therefore of the discovery of rich deposits of *huano* on the Galápagos, at this conjuncture, of course quickened the vigilance of the Agent, reanimated the zeal of the Consul, and brightened their hopes of an auspicious result to their financial mission. With the success of their countrymen in absorbing, to a large extent, the benefits resulting to the world from the discovery of the Peruvian huano before their eyes, it was worth an effort on their part to clutch the huano trade of Ecuador, and divert it to the advantage of English commerce and British capitalists, as had been done in the neighboring Republic. The English Consul, and the Agent of the British bondholders, therefore, conceived that

---

Spanish, signed and sealed, with a translation apparently made in the State Department, and also a bi-lingual text of it, signed and sealed.

[1] Above, this part, November 24, 1854, doc. 2401.

they were only discharging an incumbent duty in *protesting* to this Government against so hastily entering into a huano treaty with the United States; and they consequently endeavored to thwart its negotiation, and subsequently to defeat its approval by Congress.

The opposition of *Señor Sanz*, the Peruvian Minister here, was based upon his fears lest our treaty might throw open the trade in *huano* to the world upon liberal principles and thus serve to shame Peru out of her antiquated system of monopoly, and force an abandonment of her extortionate policy. He was foremost in the *protest*, and, with his Secretary, personally watched the discussions on the Treaty in Congress.

Señor De Paz, the Spanish Chargé, had negotiated a commercial convention with this Government during the past year; but it was rejected in the Senate, by the casting vote of the Post Master General, who holds a seat in that body: And although this recusant Senator was required to resign the Post Office,—yet Señor De Paz felt that the negotiation and ratification of an important Treaty with the United States, following so closely upon the heels of the rejection of an ordinary convention with Spain, would carry with it an odor of invidiousness, and leave the world in doubt as to the true relations existing between Ecuador and his Government: This state of things, doubtless, prompted him to join in the *protest*.

The new French Chargé, Mons. *J. A. Villamus*, was also an earnest participant in this diplomatic *episode:* And his opposition to the Treaty seems to be strongly spiced with jealousy of the growing power and political tendencies of the "Great Democracy" of the United States.

My proposition to treat with this Government on the subject of the Galápagos huano, and the arrival very soon thereafter of the Hon. J. P. Benjamin and Gen'l Villamil, created an extraordinary sensation in this Community: Visions of wealth and national aggrandizement filled the imaginations of the Officials, and inflated all their calculations from a basis of *milésimos* to one of *milionésimos!* In this extatic condition of the public mind, I found the Executive Officers of the Government slow in giving ear to anything like rational propositions for a huano treaty; and my first advances towards a negotiation, were met with dampening discouragements, —especially from the President of the Republic himself, as Senator Benjamin can inform you. They had already been approached with assurances of loans from Europe, on long time, at an interest of *three* per cent per annum,— and were given to understand, that almost any kind of protection they might desire for the Islands, would be accorded to them by the Great Powers of Europe.

Under these circumstances, I felt that the crisis demanded of me steps equally prompt and energetic: I saw that nothing short of considerations of the most marked character, could arrest the attention of the Authorities here, and induce them seriously to entertain my propositions. I accordingly, at our first conference, offered the Paper marked "Propositions" *first* and *second*,[1] a copy of which was forwarded by last month's mail. This presented the question in rather a novel point of view to them; and from that moment, their sympathies seemed to preponderate in favor of concluding some kind of arrangement with me.

Being on terms of intimacy with all the members of the Government, I was enabled to carry forward this somewhat novel, but, as the event has proved, opportune movement; and by gradually yielding the less important points, and obtaining in lieu some new concession, I eventually drew them into treaty stipulations, which I consider of vast importance to a paramount interest of our country, and which I verily believe are destined to save Ecuador and her huano trade from the clutches of European speculators, and to preserve this country from the thraldom of an *alien* influence, as paralyzing as that by which Peru is unfortunately held in commercial vassalage by the capitalists of the Old World.

Confronted as I thus had been by obstacles apparently insurmountable, the Diplomatic Representatives of other Powers here not only marvelled that I should have succeeded in negotiating a Convention with this Government at all, but that a Treaty making concessions so extraordinarily beneficial to the United States, as they deem them, and which, in their view, holds out such slender inducements to Ecuador in comparison with those offered on behalf of their constituents, should have been acceded to by the Executive, and hurriedly passed through Congress, was a startling announcement to them. Their active opposition, therefore, as well to the negotiation as to the subsequent ratification of the convention, is thus readily accounted for.

The benefits which the commerce and citizens of the United States may derive from the provisions of this Convention, will have been the legitimate results of the enterprize of *our* people in *discovering* the *huano*, and of the forecast and vigilance of our Government in being earliest in the field of negotiation with the proprietary nation, for placing our trade in that valuable fertilizer upon the most favorable footing: And the hostility of these diplomatic *protestants* to our treaty, is so manifestly the offspring of feelings of commercial and national rivalry, wounded at the prospect of our country's reaping the *first harvest* from the Huano fields of the Galápagos, that *their* opposition, I humbly conceive, should serve but to quicken the action of *our* Government in their approval of that instrument.

[1] These two propositions were briefly as follows: *First*, that Ecuador and the United States should have the exclusive privilege, for one year, of excavating and shipping guano from the Galápagos Islands; after which time the Government of Ecuador was to make the shipment free to all nations, under such regulations as she might from time to time adopt. *Second*, that Ecuador concede to citizens of the United States as well as to those of all other nations the right to use their own workmen in excavating and shipping guano; that all nations were to be charged the same rate; that the right be conceded to the United States to protect her citizens on the islands in conformity with international law and the recognized sovereignty of Ecuador.

As remarked in a former communication, I have been constrained to avail myself of the alternative discretion conveyed in your instructions. I have accepted less favorable conditions than the Government seems to have contemplated: But I have obtained concessions that excite the envy of all the other diplomatic Agents accredited at this Capital,—concessions never accorded to any other nation in regard to the huano trade of the world, and which in all probability, if not now accepted, never will be extended on any future occasion even to ourselves.

Not the least among the considerations that weighed with me in closing with the best terms I found it practicable to secure from this Government, and in concluding a convention with them at this particular juncture, was the fact, that had I protracted the discussion in our Conferences, with the contingent hope of still further modifying the conditions contained in the "ultimatums" they *more than once* presented, the negotiation would have been extended to a period beyond the adjournment of the Ecuatorian Congress, whose approval is requisite to consummate all international treaties: The measure would thus have been postponed for one year; and it is my settled conviction that the Ecuatorian Government would, in the meanwhile, have been irretrievably ensnared in the toils of the monied monopolists of Europe, and our people and our country thus have been as efectually cut off from an equal participation in her huano trade, as they now are from that of Peru.

*Article 1*ˢᵗ of the Treaty stipulated for an "advance" to Ecuador of $3,000,000. This is a large sum, and is the maximum of the amount I was authorized to offer for an *exclusive* right to the huano on one or more of the Islands, for a long term of years. The government would not listen, either to a *sale* of the Islands, or an *exclusive* right to the huano on them: and for a less "advance" than $3,000,000, I am persuaded I could not have concluded *any* treaty with them *at this time*,—and, for the reasons already stated, I believe this to be the *only* opportunity for obtaining anything like favorable terms. The first sum they named, was *five millions*,—which, or any reasonable amount, they intimated, could be obtained from other quarters, at a lower rate of interest than I would assent to. For the refunding of this 3,000,000, we shall have an ample guarantee in the pledge of all the huano on the Galápagos, should the article prove abundant there, if not, the Treaty will of course not be approved at Washington, but remain a dead letter.

*Article 2*ᵈ, reserves to Ecuador the exclusive right to fix the *price* of huano, and to alter and modify that price as her interest and circumstances may dictate: And they seem as little inclined to restrict themselves in that right by treaty stipulation, as to barter away the sovereignty of the Islands. This Article also recognizes the rights of the Discoverers (De Brissot and Villamil) in the only form I could persuade them to adopt,—they averring that the Executive *contract* securing those rights, having been approved by

Congress, is as binding upon the nation as a treaty stipulation: And although I combatted this view of the matter, they could not be prevailed on to use any more definite phraseology than that found in the Article. I inclose herewith a copy of the "contract" between Villamil and Benjamin, as discoverers, on the one part, and the Executive Government of Ecuador on the other,—which contract has since been ratified by Congress.

*Article 3*ᵈ concedes a most important discrimination in favor of our citizens and our commerce, as a consideration for the advance of $3,000,000. This point was prominent among the causes that led to the diplomatic *protest*, the provisions of this Article being considered especially obnoxious to the interests of the countries represented by the *protestants*. Assuming that the import of huano into the United States from the Galápagos Islands will amount to 300,000 tons per annum, and the deduction of $1 per ton from the ordinary price in favor of our citizens would be granting them a yearly *bounty* of 300,000 dollars.

*Article 4*ᵗʰ limits this discrimination in our favor, to the period during the existence of the Treaty.

*Article 5*ᵗʰ: If the discrimination of $1 per ton in favor of our citizens, shall prove a valuable consideration, the longer the provision is continued in force, the greater will be the aggregate benefit to be derived therefrom: Hence I concluded that a slow process of reduction would be preferable to a rapid one, and we fixed the rate at fifty cents a ton on account of principal, and f'ty. cents for interest,—which last, on the above basis, will yield $150,000, a sum adequate to discharge annually, or oftener, the five per cent. interest as it may accrue on the three millions advanced.

*Article 6*ᵗʰ guarantees the payment of interest on the "advance," at the rate of *five per cent.* It was with much difficulty I prevailed on them to allow more than *four* per cent., as loans were offered (to come from European capitalists) at *three* per cent., their payment to be guaranteed by the hypothecation of cargoes of huano. It is left to our Government to devise such measures as they may deem expedient, for the payment by Ecuador of the interest, and the gradual reduction of the principal of the debt, from funds that may arise from the reductions of $1 per ton, as stipulated in the preceding Article.

*Article 7*ᵗʰ permits Ecuador to reduce her debt, should she at any time desire to do so, at a more rapid rate than is provided for in Art. 5. This privilege they insisted on.

*Article 8*ᵗʰ secures to Ecuador the right of which the Government seems to be exceedingly tenacious, to employ her own people in excavating the huano and carrying it to the beach for embarkation, for which service they promise never to charge more than actual expenditures for labor, &c., the loading from the beach, the Captains will be permitted to perform by their own hands, in other words, they will buy the huano on the beach: But this important privilege is conceded to us, although it was grudgingly done, that, whenever there may be an insufficiency of huano ready on the beach to supply all vessels that may be waiting for cargoes, the Captains will be permitted to employ their own crews, &c., in those operations, thus obviating those vexatious and expensive delays experienced at the Peruvian Islands.

*Article 9*th places us, under all circumstances, hereafter, upon the best footing of the most favored nations.

*Article 10*th acknowledges the sovereignty of Ecuador over the Galápagos Islands.

*Article 11*th concedes to our Government the right of *protecting* its own people while engaged in the huano trade,—and, as a corollary of that right, to *protect the Island themselves*, as well as other points on the coast of Ecuador which might serve as convenient shelters for those marauding expeditions whose purpose might be rapine,—and who, for the consummation of their lawless designs, might attempt to seize upon the Islands, and thus interrupt our people in their lawful pursuits, and peradventure despoil them of their property. I have shaped this provision as nearly in accordance with your instructions as I found it practicable to do, in opposition to the strong desire of this Government to make the protection of the Islands *obligatory* upon the United States, without extending its benefits, *in terms*, to our citizens employed there, and of course only affording them an *incidental* protection: The following is the form of the Article they proposed, and strenuously contended for:

> *Articulo 11*: El Gobierno de los Estados Unidos se obliga á dar su proteccion á dichas islas de los Galápagos contra toda clase de invasiones, &c. &c.,—(the rest same as in the Article adopted.)

Translation:

> *Article 11*th: The Government of the United States *obligates* itself to give protection to the said Galápagos Islands, against all kinds of invasions, &c. &c.

In combatting this phraseology, I insisted that the *protection* to be exercised by the United States should be *permissive*, and not *obligatory*,—that the *primary objects* of that protection should be our own citizens, their property and their legitimate business, the protection of the sovereignty of Ecuador being only secondary and incidental; and this principle I made a *sine qua non* in assenting to the stipulations of this Article. Finally, in order to compromise this point, which I deemed of much importance, they agreed to surrender the *obligatory* clause provided I would consent to fix the "advance" at *three* instead of *two* millions, they having, at one stage of the negotiations consented to receive the last named sum: This I acquiesced in most reluctantly; but there was this additional motive that determined my acquiescence,—they had agreed to raise the rate of interest from *four* (their "ultimatum") to *five per cent*. We therefore eventually agreed to the Article in this form, to wit:

> *Article 11*: The Government of the United States will (or "can" which is synonymous) extend its protection to those of its own people, who may resort to the huano market in accordance with the provisions of this Convention,—as, also, to the Galápagos Islands themselves,—against all invasions, &c.

Article 12th, concedes to our Government the privilege of appointing a Vice Consul to reside on one of the principal of the Galápagos Islands, which we cannot do under the Old Treaty.

Article 13th relates to a scientific survey of the Islands.

Article 14th requires the payment of the $3,000,000, to be made in Washington; and

Article 15th provides, in the usual form, for the definitive ratification of the Convention at Washington, &c.

With this explanation of the provisions of the Convention, and an exposition of the motives of the negotiators in their final arrangement of its stipulations, I have the honor to commend the Instrument to the favorable consideration of the President.

NEW DISCOVERIES OF HUANO

I trust it will not be deemed inappropriate in this connection, to advise you of new discoveries of huano on Islands belonging to Ecuador. I have just received a communication from *M. P. Game*, Esqr, U. S. Consul at Guayaquil, informing me that he had returned to Port the day before, from an exploration of the Islands *near the coast* of Ecuador; and that he had discovered the genuine *Huano* on several of them: A sample of it was forwarded to Quito, and is now in possession of President Urvina [Urbina?]. Capt. Game estimates the quantity on "La Plata" Island (one of his discoveries) at 500,000 tons; and he thinks the deposits on another Island he visited, equally extensive. He fell in with, and examined several small rocky islets, which he found covered to a considerable depth with Huano.

Consul Game and his partner have "denounced" (as the phrase is in this idiom,) this discovery to the Government here; and in conversation with the President on the subject, I learned from him that the same proportion, (one-fifth) and the same terms, &c., that were accorded to Messrs. Villamil and DeBrissot, would be extended to Game & C°, the discoveries of the latter not being comprehended in the grant to the former, which is confined to certain specified Islands.

Judging from the sample of the last discovered huano, now in possession of the Executive here, I think it is of an inferior quality to that discovered by De Brissot.

It may be worthy of remark, that both *actual discoverers* of huano in Ecuador are citizens and natives of the United States,—Julius De Brissot, and Matthew P. Game. And I would respectfully submit, whether this circumstance ought not to weigh with our Government in behalf of the approval of the Convention, whose provisions will enable our countrymen to stamp the impress of *Americanism* on this branch of trade, now and for all time.

With very high regard [etc.].

2403

Philo White, United States Minister Resident in Ecuador, to Pacífico Chiriboga, Minister General of Ecuador [1]

C   QUITO, *December 26, 1854.*

The undersigned, Minister Resident of the United States, has the honor to inclose, herewith, to His Excellency the Minister General, the *form* of a "Declaration" in relation to Neutral Rights,[2] which he is instructed to submit to the Government of Ecuador,[3] for its approval and adoption.

It affirms the principle, that "free ships make free goods", contraband excepted; and that the property of neutrals, not contraband, found on board enemies' ships, is not confiscable.

These two principles have been adopted by Great Britain and France, as rules of conduct towards all neutrals in the present European war; and it is presumed that neither nation will refuse to recognize them as rules of international law, and to conform to them in all time to come.

The Emperor of Russia has lately concluded a Convention with the United States, embracing these principles as permanent and immutable, and to be scrupulously observed towards all powers which may accede to the same.

It is the intention of the United States to propose to the principal powers, to enter into treaty arrangements for the recognition of principles so enlightened and philanthropic.

And should the Government of this Republic be disposed to acquiesce in these views of the President of the United States, the undersigned is authorized to say, that the Government at Washington will promptly enter into Treaty stipulations with that of Ecuador upon the subject.

Awaiting the response of the Minister General to the Propositions contained in this communication,—that is to say, Whether the Government of Ecuador is prepared to join in a "Declaration" of Neutral Rights such as is

---

[1] Despatches, Ecuador, vol. 3; enclosed with White to the Secretary of State, No. 43, January 17, 1855, below, this part, doc. 2404.   [2] Not found.
[3] His instruction, dated October 18, 1854, was the same as the one sent to U. S. Minister Dana, in Bolivia, on the same date, for which, see above, vol. II, pt. I, doc. 391.

therein indicated, or to conclude treaty stipulations upon the basis of the accompanying *projet*,—the undersigned begs to reiterate [etc.].

2404

Philo White, United States Minister Resident in Ecuador, to William L. Marcy, Secretary of State of the United States[1]

[EXTRACT]

No. 43   QUITO, *January 17, 1855.*

SIR: . . . I also inclose a copy of the note (marked C,) I addressed, to the Minister on the 26th ult.,[2] in obedience to your instructions, on the subject of a *Declaration of Neutral Rights*, &c.[3] To that communication, I have received no response as yet, doubtless for the reason that the President of the Republic, (Gen'l. Urvina) and the Minister of Foreign Relations (Doct. Espinel) have not returned to the Capital from their visit to the "La Plata" and other Islands near the coast, on which, I had the honor to advise you last month, *Mr. Game*, our Consul at Guayaquil, had discovered large deposits of *Huano*.[4]

Anticipating a favorable response to this communication, on the return of those Functionaries, I would respectfully suggest to the Department whether I ought not to be *specially* authorized to sign the "Declaration" proposed, in conjunction with such Commissioner as may be appointed for the purpose by this Government? From the *attesting clause* in the Form with which I am furnished such *special powers* would seem to be contemplated by the Department.

And in regard to Treaty stipulations with this Government, for the recognition of the principles enunciated in such "Declaration", is it the desire of the Department that I should obtain the informal acquiescence of the Authorities here in those principles, in advance of my being specially empowered to negotiate such Treaty?

I have just received a communication from *Mr. Emile Prats*, whom I authorized, under your instructions, to proceed to the Galápagos Islands, and make such explorations and examinations as might be requisite, to determine the fact of the existence or non-existence of *Huano* thereon, as represented to the State Department by Mr. *Julius De Brissot*,—and, likewise, to make an approximative estimate of the *quantity* of that substance,

[1] Despatches, Ecuador, vol. 3. Received February 27.
The omitted portion relates to a claims case.
[2] Above, this part, doc. 2403.
[3] His instruction, dated October 18, 1854, was the same as the one sent to U. S. Minister Dana in Bolivia, on the same date, for which see above, vol. II, pt. I, doc. 391.
[4] See above, this part, December 20, 1854, doc. 2402.

should it be met with on those Islands: And I have to express my deep regret, that circumstances should have prevented Mr. Prats from making the examinations requisite to find the huano discovered by Mr. De Brissot. Mr. Prats, however, has full confidence in De Brissot's good faith, as has also the Hon. Mr. Benjamin, who accompanied Mr. P. to Albemarle Island. They visited no other Island; and the bearings of the only point they examined on that, not corresponding with those given by Mr. De Brissot, they are induced to believe that that point is not one of the localities he designated as containing deposits of huano, and that Mr. B. himself will be able readily to point out those deposits as represented by him to the Department and to them.

But in the mean while, the period within which our Treaty is required to be ratified by the Government at Washington, will have expired! And ulterior events, must determine its fate.

I have the honor [etc.].

2405

Philo White, United States Minister Resident in Ecuador, to William L. Marcy, Secretary of State of the United States[1]

No. 45   QUITO, *February 21, 1855.*

SIR: I have the honor this day to inclose to you, in a separate envelope, Nº 139 of "El Seis de Marzo," dated 16th February instant, (the Official paper of this Government) which contains a correspondence between the new "Liberator President" of Peru and his Minister of Foreign Relations, and the Executive Authorities here.[2]

You cannot fail to note the complacency, the enthusiasm indeed, with which President Urvina [Urbina?] greets the accession to power of the Revolutionary Chief in Peru. The entire Administration, in fact, and all their political friends, are jubilant over this (to them) auspicious issue of the civil war in their neighboring Republic.

And this sentiment is the more pervading, since it is notorious that *Echenique*, the ousted President of Peru, not only countenanced, but positively aided Gen'l *Juan José Flores* in his "piratical" invasion of Ecuador in 1852; and has ever since pursued a vexatious course of policy, and cherished illy concealed feelings of hostility, towards this Government;—while Castilla is a long-tried friend of Ecuador, especially of the present Executive incumbents, and an enemy of *Flores* and all his schemes of civil war and "restoration."

The suppression of the rebellion in New Granada, their adjoining neighbor North, and the restoration of the Constitutional Authorities there, is in

---

[1] Despatches, Ecuador, vol. 3.   The receipt date is not indicated.
[2] Not included in this publication; it occupies five full-length newspaper columns.

accordance with the interests and sympathies of both the Government and the people of Ecuador. But I find those best informed here, deplore the disorganizing tendencies that threaten to keep that unfortunate country painfully agitated.

With high respect [etc.].

2406

Philo White, United States Minister Resident in Ecuador, to William L. Marcy, Secretary of State of the United States [1]

[EXTRACTS]

No. 49   QUITO, *March 30, 1855.*

SIR: I have the honor to acknowledge the receipt of your despatches numbered 21 and 22, and your "Circular" of date 26th Febr'y.[2]

With the requirements of the latter, I shall endeavor to comply hereafter, as I now have a full supply of "despatch" paper, with ample margin.

In accordance with the suggestions contained in your despatch N°. 21, in relation to a "Declaration of Neutral Right", I shall seek the earliest convenient moment to communicate with the Minister of Foreign Relations on the subject, after he shall have conferred with the President in regard to the matter. It is a question in relation to which they will doubtless desire to counsel with each other, previously to determining what action to take in the premises. The President is now in Quito; but at his return he found the Minister confined to his rooms by indisposition: The numerous religious festivals about this season, materially interfere with the despatch of official business. . . .[3]

At the subsequent Congress, as you are aware, the subject of the *Huano Treaty* absorbed *all* my time and efforts, up to the last day of the sessions,— having had to fight the Treaty through, in opposition to domestic as well as extraneous influences, the foreign diplomatic body having *protested*, as well against its negotiation in the first instance, as its ratification by Congress subsequently. It would of course have been worse than useless, to urge the claim of the Messrs. Driggs, or any of the others in my hands, under such circumstances.

But this claim, having been already acknowledged by the Executive branch of the Government, should of course be the first to be liquidated. To accomplish which, my best efforts shall be exerted.

I have the honor [etc.].

[1] Despatches, Ecuador, vol. 3. Received May 25.
[2] None of these is included in this publication; No. 21 informs White briefly that, as soon as Ecuador has intimated her readiness to adopt the principles respecting the rights of neutrals, the necessary power will be forwarded to him to enter upon negotiations; No. 22 relates to a claim; and the content of the circular is indicated within this despatch.
[3] The omitted portion relates to a claim and the settlement thereof, delayed by the adjournment of the Ecuadoran Congress.

2407

Philo White, United States Minister Resident in Ecuador, to William L. Marcy,
Secretary of State of the United States [1]

No. 47   QUITO, *March 31, 1855.*

SIR: The Executive of this Republic is still absent, at his country Seat,
where his Principal Minister of State also spends a portion of his time:
Consequently I cannot, under these circumstances, obtain any definite
action by this Government on any ordinary measure of Foreign Policy.
Indeed, since the month of September last, when I first broached the subject
of our *Huano Treaty* to the Authorities here, they have been so thoroughly
absorbed with that matter,—and so frequent and lengthened have been the
absences of the President from the Capital since then,—that it has proved a
bootless task to endeavor to press any other question than that relating to
the *Huano* on their serious consideration. That seems to be the all-absorbing subject with them; and they are really oppressed with disappointment,
that I should not to this day have received anything authentic, either from
Mr. *Benjamin* or Mr. *De Brissot,* as to the verity of the alleged discoveries of
Huano on the Galapagos Islands by the latter. It is rumored, however, that
De Brissot is not at the Islands, whither Gen'l. *Villamil* repaired over a
month since; and a *hope* animates these people, that the existence of large
deposits of huano there will soon be demonstrated, beyond all cavil.

The "change of Administration" in Perú, has restored tranquility to the
southern border of Ecuador, and given this Government a reliable ally in
her next-door neighbor, where previously her diplomatic relations were
complicated and perplexing: Scarcely have they exchanged congratula-
tions, however, on this auspicious event, when they are again agitated by the
appearance of a cloud in the Southern horizon that portends new troubles
for their country: They scent mischief in the breeze from "Chile"!

A friend has sent me a Valparaiso newspaper, of date the 13th ult., containing articles that manifest an unfriendly spirit towards the United States,
and indicate a belligerent feeling for Ecuador, apparently aroused on
account of the readiness she has manifested to cultivate the most intimate
commercial and political relations with our country. And the Minister of
Foreign Relations of this Government has informed me, confidentially, that
they have advices from Valparaiso, to the effect, that *Gen'l. José Flores,* the
enemy of Ecuador and of the United States,—and, as I verily believe, a foe
to *all* "Democratic" forms of government,—against whom a decree of
outlawry now exists, for high crimes against his country,—has succeeded, by
his arts and his calumnies, in *disaffecting* the Government of "Chile"

---

[1] Despatches, Ecuador, vol. 3.   Received April 25.
White's despatches Nos. 46 and 47, both dated March 31, 1855, were of a later date than
his Nos. 48 and 49, which were dated respectively, March 24 and 30, 1855.   Nos. 46 and 48
are not pertinent to this publication.

towards both this country and the United States;—that the new Chilian Minister to be sent to Quito, altho' ostensibly charged with an amicable mission, is really invested with an ulterior discretion, either to enlist Ecuador in a Spanish-American "League" against the "encroachments" (!) of the United States,—or, in the last resort, to foment a *Revolution* here in favor of *Flores* and his confederates!—and thus to supplant *our friends* in Ecuador, and foist *our enemies* into its Government!   Hence the abuse and the slanders published in the Chile papers, in relation to our Huano Treaty now pending with this Government,—and which are said to be the production, or at least are prompted by Gen'l. Flores.   I shall of course be watchful of all these movements that may have a bearing upon the interests of our country.

The U. S. Steamer "Massachusetts," is now lying in Guayaquil Bay; and her commander has advised me that he was directed by Commodore Dulany to inquire of me whether her presence was required in the waters of Ecuador, &c.   Not conceiving that the exigencies of the moment demand the prolongation of his stay, at this particular juncture, either at Guayaquil or the Galápagos Islands, I have advised him to proceed to his destination, (California) in accordance with his original instructions from the Navy Department.

I have the honor [etc.].

2408

Philo White, United States Minister Resident in Ecuador, to William L. Marcy, Secretary of State of the United States [1]

No. 51   QUITO, *April 18, 1855.*

SIR: Since the date of my despatch Nº 50,[2] there have been some further developments in relation to the "conspiracy" to supplant the present incumbents of this Government, a new clue to the "plot" having been discovered in the contents of private letters found in possession of suspected persons.   More arrests have consequently been made; many of the "desterrados" have been sent off to the "Napo" region, which has been constituted, for the time being, a kind of "Botany Bay" for the *political delinquents* of Ecuador!—and several have obtained passports, on giving the required real estate security that they will forthwith depart the Republic, and not tarry on the Pacific side of the continent!   The purpose of the conspiracy, such as it was, seems therefore to have been defeated in its very inception.

Gen¹. *Juan José Flores*, the sworn enemy and evil genius of those in power here, has arrived in Peru, of which Mʳ Clay has doubtless ere this advised you.   His presence in such near proximity with Ecuador, which will increase his facilities of communicating with his proscribed partizans in this Republic, keeps the government authorities here and their friends in a

[1] Despatches, Ecuador, vol. 3.   Received May 25.
[2] Not included in this publication; it relates to the apprehended conspiracy of partisans of Flores to subvert the Ecuadoran Government.

feverish state of excitement and alarm, which indisposes and indeed disquali-
fies them, until more dispassionate councils shall prevail, for entering into
the consideration of the international questions I am endeavoring to adjust with them.

President Urvina [Urbina?] and his Ministers, however, feel well assured
that the present Ruler in Perú, Gen¹ Castilla, is a sincere friend of theirs,
and will not suffer *Flores* to remain there for the purpose of plotting revolutionary movements in Ecuador.

Gen'l. Gana, the new Plenipotentiary from Chile, has arrived in Ecuador,
and is daily expected in Quito. My confidential advices still assure me, that
one purpose of his mission is, (or was) to detach Ecuador from any "protectorate" or intimate alliance with the United States! What the state of our
relations with the Chilian Government at this time is, I am unadvised, not
having as yet received any response from Mr. Starkweather to the communications I have addressed to him on two occasions: But public sentiment in
Chile, to some extent, would seem to have been prejudiced towards our
Government: Indeed, I am advised from Guayaquil, that the new Minister's
mind, during his stay there, was disabused of absurd misconceptions of the
provisions as well as the object of the Huano Treaty I negotiated with
Ecuador.

It is known that the diplomatic "protestants" here against the Treaty,
(especially the French Chargé) were extraordinarily active in communicating
to the Chilian authorities every thing connected with the negotiation and the
ratification by the Congress here of the Treaty, and in prejudicing the
Chilians against it, as well as warning them against the alleged "sinister designs" of our Government, &c.! It is thought this Chilian Mission may be
the fruits of the extraneous Influence I have referred to.

I am, most respectfully [etc.].

2409

*Philo White, United States Minister Resident in Ecuador, to William L. Marcy,
Secretary of State of the United States* [1]

No. 53—Confidential. [QUITO], *April 25, 1855.*

SIR: On reading the expositions, by the Hon. Messrs Cass and Mason, in
the Senate of the United States, of the settled design of the Governments of
England and France, unwarrantably to interfere with the international rights
and interests of the United States,—I have thought it might be acceptable
to the President and yourself to receive translations of the following extracts
from a letter on that question, published in the Valparaiso "Mercurio,"
(loaned to me while I make the translation) and purporting to be written by a
respectable Frenchman, resident in Quito. The letter was undoubtedly
either written or dictated by *Mons. Villamus*, the French Chargé here. In
speaking of the incidents attending the interview between the diplomatic
protestants against our Huano Treaty, and the Minister of Foreign Relations,
the letter says:

> They (the protestants) represented to him (the Minister) the danger
> to which the security and independence of his country would be exposed,

¹Despatches, Ecuador, vol. 3. Received June 26.

if he relied upon a power, as a patron, whose ambitious views are so well known;—that the jealousy, and perhaps hostility, of their neighboring States, would thereby be provoked, because their political and commercial interests would be compromised;—and, in fine, they represented to him the opposition which a project that tended to *destroy the equilibrium of the forces (armaments) maintained in these seas,* would infallibly meet with from the European powers!

None of these considerations seemed to weigh much in his mind; and they (the protestants) retired with the conviction, that the thing had been predetermined upon; and that no impediment would deter Gen'l. Urvina (the President) from carrying out his project, the special benefits of which, in great part, are reserved for the men who compose his administration.

In view of the rate at which things are going on, it would not surprize me to see, within a few months, the Flag of the "Union" flying over the City of Guayaquil,—or at least at the Island of Puná, which commands the mouth of the River.

I hope that the Spanish American Governments, especially that of Chile,[1] will view this question as it has been viewed here,—that is, as leading to consequences destructive of the security and independence of South America.

In the conference of the diplomatic "protestants," with the Minister of Foreign Relations, *Mons. Villamus* was, as the Minister informed me, especially *brusque* and discourteous in his language and bearing: And on the Minister's reminding him of the diplomatic amenities due on such occasions, he gruffly replied, that he was "acting and speaking by command of His Imperial Majesty the Emperor of the French," &c. &c.

Now as the time was too brief since the initiation of the Huano Treaty, for him to have had any special instructions from his government in regard to *that* particular question, he must have been clothed with general and discretionary powers to intervene, to the detriment of the international interests of the United States, in all cases where *he* might deem it expedient,—or, he was guilty of an unwarrantable assumption, with the design of *bluffing* the Minister!

These incidents may serve to strengthen the convictions expressed by Messrs. Cass, Mason, and others, of the sinister designs of England and France, with regard to the international rights of our country.

With high regard [etc.].

[1] The following footnote was cited here in the text:
"And it is such insensate promptings as these, that have betrayed the Chilian Government into sending the present special Mission to Quito!"

2410

Philo White, United States Minister Resident in Eucador, to William L. Marcy Secretary of State of the United States [1]

No. 54—Confidential.   QUITO, *May 16, 1855.*

SIR: Since my despatch N⁰ 51, of date 18ᵗʰ ult.,[2] the deep sensation caused here by the recently detected "complot" to subvert the present Government of this Republic, which the sudden advent of Gen'l. Flores in Perú undoubtedly precipitated to a denouement unexpected to the "conspirators," the agitation of the public mind had much subsided after the principal persons implicated had been "desterrados": When a new cause of alarm arose, occasioned by a report that a formidable expedition was on foot in the United States, instigated by Gen'l. Flores, reputed to be under the leader-ship of Co¹ Clemons, and destined for revolutionizing Ecuador.

In addition to the newspaper publications with regard to such an expedition, this Government has received a communication from *Mr. Palmer;* their Consul Gen¹ at Washington, giving countenance to the rumors, which increased their fears of a buccaneering attempt from that quarter; and the publication, headed "Los Bandidos," which I inclose to you in a separate envelope, was issued from the Government Press in this City: It is indicative of the exasperated feeling that pervades the government officials here.

I have however assured them of my full belief, that if any such scheme has been concocted, it must utterly fail for lack of "material aid": That even if daring and lawless *men* should be found in sufficient numbers to render such an expedition formidable, the capitalists of our country could not be seduced into risking their *funds* in such criminal and hazardous adventures. By reason of these assurances on my part, the apprehensions of the government and its friends, of immediate danger from that quarter, are at this moment pretty much allayed. But the presence in Peru of their crafty and irreconcilable enemy, *Flores*, whose machinations against the peace and safety of the country are now carried on in immediate proximity with their territorial borders, tends not only to keep their minds in a feverish state of anxiety, but creates the necessity of augmenting their military armament, in field and in fortress, which is draining their already depleted exchequer to its dregs.

While on a visit at the national Palace, a few evenings since, *President Urvina* [Urbina?] sought a confidential interview with me, on matters principally relating to the huano Treaty and its concomitants: During this interview, the President was frank and unreserved, as he usually is, on such as well as all other occasions. He commenced by assuring me as he had repeatedly done before, of his partialities for the United States over all other foreign countries, and of his admiration for her political institutions. Animated by these sentiments, he said he had cheerfully embraced the oppor-

[1] Despatches, Ecuador, vol. 3.   Received June 27.   [2] Above, this part, doc. 2408.

tunity of conceding advantageous terms to our citizens, through Messrs. Benjamin and Villamil; as the reputed *discoverers* of huano on the Galápagos Islands; and that he had promptly and cordially acceded to the proffer by the Government of the United States to enter into the negotiation of a Convention for regulating the commerce of its citizens in that article, and making concessions highly favorable to our country and its interests.

The *initiative*, as he remarked, in all these transactions, was taken by the citizens and the government of the United States: And as I had been invested with full powers and a broad discretion to negotiate with Ecuador on behalf of the latter, and the private interests of the *discoverers* were represented by a gentleman whose character and position inspired universal respect and confidence,—the probabilities of a disappointment as to the *discovery* itself, or of a non-fulfilment of the stipulations of the contract with the discoverers or their agents, or even of the miscarriage of the Convention negotiated between the two governments,—had not seriously entered into the calculations of the Authorities here, in concluding and solemnly ratifying the Treaty and the Contract in question. Extravagant expectations were consequently raised, and the government came near being betrayed into financial operations based upon these high anticipations of an exuberant revenue.

After making this recital, in substance, he remarked, in rather a complaining mood, that the Government of Ecuador had now been kept six months in a state of perplexing suspense, with regard to the fate as well of the Treaty with our government as the Contract with Messrs. Benjamin and Villamil; that their relations with the principal powers of Europe, and with their neighboring Republic of Chile, had been complicated by the supposed partiality manifested in those transactions by the Government of Ecuador in behalf of the interests of the United States; that the continued doubt and apparent mystery in which the matter seemed to be involved, had led to gross and provoking misrepresentations of the provisions of the Treaty and of the Contract, as well as of the intentions and obligations of this government in relation thereto,—and out of which had grown a Special Mission from the Chilian government to that of Ecuador, whose eventual purpose it was to thwart any "aggressive" designs the United States may have cherished derogatory to the "nationality" of this Republic; that the authorities here are not only greatly annoyed, but conspiracy is actually fomented, by the sarcasms and the calumnies propagated by the partizans of Flores, *countenanced and incited by some of the foreign diplomatic agents here*, to the effect that this government has been *duped* by the crafty policy of the "Yankees," &c.; and that, as Messrs. Benjamin &c C° had obligated themselves to point out to the Officers of Ecuador the deposits of huano on the Galápagos, the supposed existence of which constituted the groundwork of their compact with the government, he thinks it most extraordinary that Mr. B. should so long have neglected to write, either to them or to myself, explaining the circumstances which have thrown so much doubt and suspicion upon the whole transaction, and afforded food for scandal among the enemies of both governments.

And he concluded by suggesting to me, whether there would be any impropriety in my writing to my government, to ask information on the subject, for the purpose of relieving the deep anxiety of the authorities and the people of Ecuador.

In reply, I assured the President that I sympathized with him and his Administration in their embarrassments, to which he had made reference; and regretted exceedingly that any action of mine, or of my government or my countrymen, should have tended to complicate the relations of Ecuador with other powers, or have added to their perplexities in the present critical conjunctures of their affairs; that I was equally surprised and mortified, that *Mr. Benjamin* had so long failed to write, either to myself or to this government, advising of the progress made, by himself and associates, in settling the question in regard to the huano deposits on the Galápagos, in fulfilment of their obligations under their contract with the government; and that the silence of Mr. Benjamin, and the erratic movements of Mr. De Brissot, were wholly inexplicable to me.

But, so far as my government was concerned, I would beg to remark, that the Treaty I had had the honor to assist in negotiating was based, as the President would bear in mind, upon a contingency which, until solved to the satisfaction of the authorities at Washington, precluded the Executive from taking action in regard to the ratification of the instrument; and that, while awaiting the requisite information to enable it to act understandingly in the matter, the circumstances of the case, as I conceived, were not such as necessarily to call for explanations from my government to that of Ecuador.

Yet, in consideration of our protracted disappointment in receiving information from the discoverers or their Agents,—and in view of the fact that the whole subject had assumed a prominence and excited a discussion here and at other points in the Pacific States, mortifying and embarrassing to the authorities of Ecuador,—I assented to the President's suggestion, to write to Washington in relation to the matter.

And in fulfilment of that assurance, I now have the honor respectfully to request information, whether Messrs. Benjamin, or Prats, or De Brissot, have communicated any facts to the Department, tending to throw light upon the alleged discoveries of the latter on the Galápagos Islands? Or whether the Treaty, concluded here on the 20th November last, is view [ed] by the President as having now become a *dead letter*, or is still open for future action on the part of either or both the contracting parties?

Some kind of response from Washington, however brief, would, I am induced to believe, in the present (*to them*) anomalous aspect of the huano question, serve as a cheering word to them, and tend to relieve their minds, in some degree, from the perplexities under which they are laboring, and restore a state of feeling better adapted to a dispassionate consideration of the *other matters*, to which I am endeavoring to draw their attention, in pursuance of instructions from the Department.

Mr. Game, our Consul at Guayaquil, still entertains a confident belief, that *Huano* actually exists on the Galápagos Islands; and he suggests that our Government order a suitable vessel of war to visit that groupe, and make a thorough survey of the *extent* and the *quality* of the deposits thereon. He has himself had a large experience as a navigator; and it is his opinion that the United States Steamer "Massachusetts," now in the Pacific, is admirably adapted to the service in question. In these suggestions, I most fully acquiesce: And should Mr. De Brissot fail of rendering *his* "discoveries" available, I would respectfully and ear[n]estly recommend to our Government, to detail a small vessel of war for the purpose of making the explorations indicated. Our citizens and our Government having taken the lead of all other nations in this enterprize, I may be pardoned for believing that considerations of national policy, as well as the interests of an important branch of our commerce, alike recommend to our Executive to adopt the readiest and most feasible measures for the prosecution of this enterprize to a *practical* and successful result,—and thus enable our own people to reap the harvest that may spring from the seed *they* have sown.

I would also respectfully inquire, whether, in the event of armed vessels, fitted out without the authority of any known "government," attacking the recognized territory of Ecuador, for purpose of pillage or of lodgment thereon, I should be warranted in advising the Commanding Officer of our Squadron to repress such marauding attacks, as lawless and piratical in their nature? I am advised by Mr. Clay, our Minister at Lima, that he has made a similar inquiry of the Department.

With high respect [etc.].

2411

Philo White, United States Minister Resident in Eucador, to William L. Marcy, Secretary of State of the United States [1]

No. 55   QUITO, *May 23, 1855.*

SIR: I take the liberty to inclose to you, herewith, "La Democracia", N° 109, of date 18th inst. This periodical is edited by high Officials in Quito; and the present N°, it will be perceived, is occupied almost exclusively, with matters relative to the designs of Gen'l *Juan José Flores*, and the asylum granted him in Perú, in immediate proximity with Ecuador, where, it is notorious, he is busy in endeavoring to fit out expeditions designed to revolutionize this Government.

That Chief has published an exculpatory communication in Perú, which

[1] Despatches, Ecuador, vol. 3.   Received June 26.

will be found in the "Democracia" I inclose.[1]   There is one paragraph in that publication, (indicated by red pencil) to which I would respectfully invite your attention, and of which I here give a translation, viz:

> . . . And if fortune shall some day place me in a situation to vindicate my rights; acknowledged by the representatives of England, France, Spain, the United States, and Chile, (who recognize the quarrel between myself and the violators of the public faith in Ecuador as a domestic affair) the people of Perú and their noble Chief shall receive my unfeigned acknowledgments and gratitude for their kind hospitality. J. J. Flores.

To enquiries whether the United States Government, or any of its representatives, have given the assurances attributed to them in this manifesto of Señor Flores, I have uniformly, for myself, disavowed any such doctrine, and declared my disbelief, that either the Government or any of the Diplomatic Agents of my country have ever expressed an opinion that would countenance any other "right" in Juan José Flores to fit out piratical expeditions against Ecuador, than pertains to all other lawless Chieftains or bands of "fillibusters."

But it would be more satisfactory to this Government, as well as gratifying to myself, if I were enabled *authoritatively* to make that disavowal.

I must beg, therefore, respectfully to ask the opinion of the Department in relation to this question.

With the highest respect [etc.].

2412

Philo White, United States Minister Resident in Ecuador, to Marcos Espinel, Minister of Foreign Affairs of Ecuador [2]

A   QUITO, *June 15, 1855.*

The undersigned, Minister Resident of the United States, has the honor to present to Dᣙ Marcus [Marcos] Espinel, Minister of Foreign Relations, and, through the medium of His Excellency, to the Executive Government of Ecuador, a printed copy of a Treaty between the United States and the Argentine Confederation, for the free navigaton of the Rivers *Paraná* and *Uruguay;* which Treaty was concluded July 10, 1853,—ratified July 5, 1854,—exchanged December 20, 1854,—and proclaimed by the President of the United States April 9, 1855.[3]

The undersigned begs to reiterate [etc.].

[1] Not included in this publication, since its content is adequately indicated within this despatch.

[2] Despatches, Ecuador, vol. 3; enclosed with White to the Secretary of State, No. 59, August 22, 1855, below, this part, doc. 2416.

[3] See Malloy, *Treaties, Conventions, etc., between the United States and Other Powers,* vol. I, p. 18.

2413

*Marcos Espinel, Minister of Foreign Affairs of Ecuador, to Philo White,
United States Minister Resident in Ecuador* [1]

[TRANSLATION]

QUITO, *July 20, 1855.*

The undersigned, the Minister of Foreign Affairs of Ecuador, had the
honor to receive and to inform his Government of the kind note which His
Excellency the Minister Resident of the United States was so good as to address to him,[2] enclosing the treaty concluded between Your Excellency's
country and the Argentine Republic regarding the free navigation of the
Paraná and Uruguay Rivers: And since the principles prevail in this treaty
which are professed by Ecuador and its Government, I have been instructed
by His Excellency the President of the Republic to congratulate Your Excellency and to thank you in his name for transmitting the printed copy
which has been received in this Ministry.

With sentiments of distinguished consideration [etc.].

2414

*Marcos Espinel, Minister of Foreign Affairs of Ecuador, to Philo White,
United States Minister Resident in Ecuador* [3]

[TRANSLATION]

[C]   QUITO, *August 9, 1855.*

The undersigned, the Minister of Foreign Affairs of Ecuador, has the honor
to write to His Excellency the Minister Resident of the United States, and to
enclose a certified copy of the Resolution issued by the Government of Ecuador,[4] declaring null and void the concession of the fifth part of the production
of "huano" declared by Mr. Benjamin, as the agent of Mr. de Brissot, both
citizens of the United States, and by General José Villamil, to exist on the
Galápagos Islands.   Although the Convention of November 26, 1854, concluded by the undersigned and His Excellency the Minister Resident lapsed
on April twentieth last, since the exchange of ratifications did not take place,
the Government of the undersigned has seen fit to inform the Government
of the United States, through the worthy medium of Your Excellency, of the

[1] Despatches, Ecuador, vol. 3; enclosed with White to the Secretary of State, No. 59,
August 22, 1855, below, this part, doc. 2416.
[2] See above, this part, June 15, 1855, doc. 2412.
[3] Despatches, Ecuador, vol. 3; enclosed with White to the Secretary of State, No. 59,
August 22, 1855, below, this part, doc. 2416.
[4] Not included in this publication, since its content is adequately indicated within this
note.

said resolution in view of the fact that, in Article 2 of the nullified arrangement referred to, reference was made to the concession granted to the supposed discoverers of huano.

The undersigned has the honor [etc.].

2415

Philo White, United States Minister Resident in Ecuador, to Marcos Espinel Minister of Foreign Affairs of Ecuador [1]

[C]   QUITO, *August 13, 1855.*

The undersigned, Minister Resident of the United States, has the honor to acknowledge the receipt of the despatch of His Excellency the Minister of Foreign Relations, of date 9th instant,[2] accompanied by a certified copy of a "Resolution" of the Executive Government of Ecuador, declaring a certain Contract, relative to the discovery of *Huano* on the Galápagos Islands, entered into between citizens respectively of Ecuador and of the United States on the one part, and the Government of Ecuador on the other, and bearing date the 30th of October, 1854,—as, also, a Convention negotiated between the undersigned and His Excellency the Minister of Foreign Relations, on behalf of their respective Governments, signed by the negotiators on the 20th of November, 1854, and ratified by the Congress and the Executive of Ecuador within a few days thereafter,—null, void, and of no effect.

Wa[i]ving other considerations involved in this "Resolution" of the Government of Ecuador, the undersigned is not disposed to question the *justice* of the measure as applicable to the case of the "Supuestos inventores del huano"; and he is prompt to acknowledge the courteous terms in which his Excellency the Minister of Foreign Relations has announced the fact, that the *Convention* in question has *lapsed*, (caducó) by reason of a failure in the final exchange of ratificatons, &c: Yet he deems this a fitting occasion to declare, that his Government is not legitimately responsible for the inauspicious result of the negotiation, nor for the somewhat anomalous circumstances which seem to have complicated the whole affair.

The Convention was negotiated in perfectly good faith by the Plenipotentiaries of both countries, for the *"sale and purchase of the 'huano' recently discovered on several of the"* [3] Galápagos Islands. But the alleged "discovery" having proved *illusory*, the instrument became *ipso facto* a nullity from the moment that that *illusion* was made manifest; and it would

[1] Despatches, Ecuador, vol. 3; enclosed with White to the Secretary of State, No. 59, August 22, 1855, below, this part, doc. 2416.

[2] Above, this part, doc. 2414. The accompanying resolution is not included in this publication, since its content is indicated within this despatch.

[3] Probably, through inadvertence, the closing quotation marks were placed here by the copyist, instead of after "Galápagos Islands."

have been none the less so, the undersigned conceives, even had the Government of the United States ratified it.   It is proper, however, that the undersigned should at the same time declare, that this state of the case has supervened from no voluntary agency of either of the contracting parties but has resulted from an adroit scheme, preconceived by the derelict individual who figured most prominently at the inception of the enterprize.

The undersigned will by the earliest conveyance, transmit to his Government copies of the documents furnished him by His Excellency the Minister of Foreign Relations.

And the undersigned avails himself of this occasion [etc.].

2416

*Philo White, United States Minister Resident in Ecuador, to William L. Marcy,
Secretary of State of the United States* [1]

[EXTRACT]

No. 59   QUITO, *August 22, 1855.*

SIR: I have the honor to report to the Department, that since my despatch N⁰ 58,[2] by last month's mail, *General Urbina*, the President of this Republic, has returned to the Capital from Guayaquil.   By reason of his illness, however, he was unable to give attention to Executive business during a week or two: And almost at the moment of his recovery, *Dr. Espinel*, the Minister of Foreign Relations, (and now Vice President elect of the Republic) suffered a dangerously inflammatory attack of Colic, from which he is yet scarcely recovered.

For these reasons, I have been unable to make much progress in our official business with this Government, since the date of my last previous communication.   The only matters, in fact, relative to which they have come to a determination, are,

1st: The President has decided, that he does not possess the requisite power to grant privileges to Sub-marine Companies, or to individuals, for fishing for pearls, &c., on the coasts of Ecuador,—the "Nautilus Sub-Marine Company" at Wilmington, Delaware, and a "Wrecking Company" at Boston, of which Mr. Joseph P. Couthony has been sent out here as Agent, having petitioned this Government for license to work their machinery in the waters of this Republic.   Document B, will show the correspondence between myself and the Minister on the subject;[3] from which, it will be seen that they refer the applicants to the National Congress: And,

---

[1] Despatches, Ecuador, vol. 3.   Received October 3.
[2] Not included in this publication.   It relates chiefly to internal politics.
[3] Not included in this publication.

2^d: The Galápagos Islands *Huano Contract* and *Treaty*,—both of which have been declared null and of no force or effect.   My correspondence, &c., in this matter, will be found marked C.[1]   Some passages in the letter of the Minister to myself,[2] as also the "Resolution" [3] of the President revoking the Contract and Treaty, may be worth noting: I annex a *printed* copy of the last-named document.

The paper marked A,[4] relates to our Treaty with the Argentine Confederation, for the Free Navigation of the River Paraná and Uruguy, a duplicate copy of which I presented to the Executive Government here.[5] . . .

With high regard [etc.].

2417

Philo White, United States Minister Resident in Ecuador, to Marcos Espinel,
Minister of Foreign Affairs of Ecuador [6]

A   QUITO, *September 3, 1855.*

The undersigned, Minister Resident of the United States, referring to verbal communications between himself and the Executive Government of Ecuador, some months since, in relation to a manifesto that had then been recently issued from Lima, by Gen'l *Juan José Flores*, in which that Chieftain alleged that what he characterized as his "rights," with reference to the questions growing out of the hostile demonstrations which he had for years been making with a view to the subversion of the settled and constitutional Government of Ecuador, had been "acknowledged by the representatives of England, France, Spain, the United States, and Chile,"—takes the liberty to remind His Excellency the Minister of Foreign Relations, that he took occasion at the instant to disavow, for himself, any such sentiment as is therein attributed to "representatives" of the nations indicated, so far as the United States is concerned,—and, at the same time, to declare his disbelief that any *other* diplomatic agent of his country had been so unmindful of his official obligations as this to scandalize the neutral relations of his Government with a friendly power.

And he now has the satisfaction to inform His Excellency the Minister of Foreign Relations, that he has just received a despatch from his Govern-

[1] See above, this part, August 13, 1855, doc. 2415.   [2] *Ibid.,* August 9, 1855, doc. 2414.
[3] Not included in this publication, since its content is sufficiently indicated within this despatch.
[4] Above, this part, June 15, 1855, doc. 2412, and, also, in the same part, see the reply, dated July 20, 1855, doc. 2413.
[5] The omitted portion relates chiefly to the remodeling of the diplomatic and consular systems, and, also, mentions enclosing a copy of a letter he addressed to the Ecuadoran Minister of Foreign Affairs, on the subject of neutral rights, not having had an answer from the latter to his note on this subject of December 26, 1854, above, this part, doc. 2403.
[6] Despatches, Ecuador, vol. 3; enclosed with White to the Secretary of State, No. 60, September 14, 1855, below, this part, doc. 2419.

ment,[1] in which he has been most fully borne out in the verbal assurances he has given the Executive Government of Ecuador in relation to this matter.

In this despatch the Honorable the Secretary of State of the United States remarks, that, "After the assurances so recently given to General Villamil, whilst that Gentleman was the Diplomatic Representative of Ecuador in the United States,—assurances which were confirmed by the active exertions of the Officers of the Government of the United States to maintain the integrity of the neutral laws, when there was reason to apprehend their violation by Gen'l Flores,"—he is of opinion "that the Government of Ecuador should not attach the slightest consequence to the vague intimations of Gen[1] Flores, when alluding, in his manifesto, to the acknowledgment of his rights by the representatives of the United States. Of itself, and with reference to its citizens, the Government of the United States will maintain the strictest neutrality towards the contending parties of other countries, recognizing the Government established by the popular will, and scrupulously repressing any known attempt on the part of its citizens to interfere with the tranquility of other nations."

The Executive Government at Washington "cannot of course know to what extent the private expression of opinion by the diplomatic agents of the United States in South America may have given color to the statement of Gen'l. Flores; but it has that confidence in their discretion, which warrants the belief that they would not, either officially or otherwise, afford the slightest encouragement to any individual or party, contemplating an invasion of a country at peace with the United States. On the contrary, it is well understood, that some of those Agents are using all proper influence to induce the Government to which they are accredited to discounten[an]ce and discourage the hostile movements which, it is feared, General Flores is endeavoring to organize against the present Administration of Ecuador."

With sentiments of high regard [etc.].

2418

Marcos Espinel, Minister of Foreign Affairs of Ecuador, to Philo White, United States Minister Resident in Ecuador [2]

TRANSLATION]

QUITO, *September 7, 1855.*

The undersigned, the Minister of Foreign Affairs of Ecuador, had the honor to inform his Government of the esteemed note which His Excellency

---

[1] Above, this volume, pt. III, July 11, 1855, doc. 2329.

[2] Despatches, Ecuador, vol. 3; enclosed with White to the Secretary of State, No. 60, September 14, 1855, below, this part, doc. 2419.

the Minister Resident of the United States was so kind as to address to him under date of the 3rd instant,[1] recalling the protest made by His Excellency the Minister Resident against the sentiments attributed to the Representatives of the United States by Juan José Flores, in a manifesto published in Lima, asserting that a number of nations, and among them, the American Union, had acknowledged his pretended rights over the Republic of Ecuador: In continuation, Your Execllency was so kind as to quote the principles of neutrality which the North American Government follows. and the laudable course of conduct which its diplomatic agents accredited near South American Governments have observed, trying to maintain the strictest neutrality on all occasions, recognizing the Governments established by popular vote, and scrupulously repressing any known attempt on the part of its citizens to interfere with the tranquillity of other nations.

The undersigned has the great satisfaction of declaring to His Excellency the Minister Resident that his Government is duly appreciative of the noble sentiments of the North American Government and is happy to acknowledge that it is the justice and rectitude of its intentions which have elevated your fortunate nation to its present position.

With sentiments [etc.].

2419

Philo White, United States Minister Resident in Ecuador, to William L. Marcy,
Secretary of State of the United States [2]

[EXTRACTS]

No. 60—Confidential.   QUITO, *September 14, 1855.*

SIR: I have had the honor to receive your despatch numbered 22, (doubtless 23) [3] containing the views of the Department in relation to the late manifesto and somewhat extraordinary assertion of Gen'l. Juan José Flores, that the "representatives" of the United States in South America sympathized in his illegal expeditions against Ecuador, and have communicated the substance of that despatch to the Minister of Foreign Relations here.

The President and his Cabinet feel gratified and honored by the prompt attention you have given to this matter, and express themselves duly grateful for the friendly interest you manifest in behalf of their Administration of this Government, and the magnanimous spirit displayed in your communication on the subject.   I inclose herewith copies of my correspondence with the Minister, marked A.[4] . . .

---

[1] Above, this part, doc. 2417.   [2] Despatches, Ecuador, vol. 3.   Received November 1.
[3] See No. 23, below, this volume, pt. III, July 11, 1855, doc. 2329.
[4] Above, this part, September 3 and 7, 1855, docs. 2417 and 2418.
The omitted portion relates chiefly to a claim, and to the receipt of books from the State Department.

Gen'l Gana, the Chilian Envoy, has concluded a Convention with the Executive here, which he transmitted to his Government some little time since: Nothing of its terms has come to my ears as yet; but as the action of Congress will be requisite to give validity to the instrument, I shall endeavor to ascertain its contents while under consideration by the two Chambers.

The personal as well as official relations between the Chilian Envoy and the French Chargé, (M. Villamus) appear to be of the most confidential nature: And the presence here of *Gen'l Gana*, is manifestly a cause of restiveness with the Executive Government. Much bad feeling is mutually harbored between the Administration and their friends and *Mons. Villamus*: And I hear that the latter frequently speaks disparagingly of our Government and our people, although he exhibits a plausible exterior in my presence, and our families are on social terms.[1] . . .

With high regard [etc.].

P.S. I inclose the "Seis de Marzo" of the 11th instant, in which this Government has published the correspondence between the Minister and myself, in relation to Gen'l Flores' manifesto:[2] This was done without my knowledge, and is not in accordance with my desire.

2420

Philo White, United States Minister Resident in Ecuador, to William L. Marcy, Secretary of State of the United States [3]

[EXTRACT]

No. 61   QUITO, *September 30, 1855.*

Postscript:[4]

Mons. Villamus, the French Chargé here, is again at serious variance with the Executive branch of this Govern⁺. While on a visit at my house, the other evening, with his family, he took occasion to complain in strong terms of the "bad faith" of this Government, in not paying promptly some deferred instalments of old claims recognized by a former Administration; and seemed to threaten, that they would have to negotiate with the French Admiral hereafter!

[1] In the omitted portion, he stated that the late guano treaty exerted an adverse influence over his prosecution of claims cases.

[2] The notes published were those above, this part, September 3 and 7, 1855, docs. 2417 and 2418. White's note of August 13, 1855, above, this part, doc. 2415, relating to the guano contract, was also published in this issue.

[3] Despatches, Ecuador, vol. 3. Received November 1.

[4] The body of this despatch relates to his expense account.

I now learn that he has demanded his passports, and that they have been sent to him.

I inclose, herewith, the President's Message to both Houses of the National Congress, now in session in Quito.

Respectfully

2421

Marcos Espinel, Minister of Foreign Affairs of Ecuador, to Philo White, United States Minister Resident in Ecuador [1]

[TRANSLATION

D   QUITO, *October 6, 1855.*

The undersigned, the Minister of Foreign Affairs of Ecuador, had the honor to inform his Government of the declaration made by the Government of the United States regarding the rights of neutrals, in conformity with the declarations made in similar cases by the Governments of England and France, and with a treaty concluded between the United States and the sovereign of Russia. These declarations, according to the explanation of His Excellency the Minister Resident of the United States, are "that free ships make free goods, contraband excepted; and that the property of neutrals, not contraband, found on board enemies' ships, is not confiscable." [2]

This solemn declaration has the effect of favoring commerce and the Government of Ecuador has found it commendable. Adopted by the principal powers, it may presently become a universal and invariable rule of international law, and will be most advantageous for the nations which, like Ecuador, on account of their own situation, maintain a strictly neutral policy in the questions of other peoples.

With sentiments of profound consideration, the undersigned has the honor [etc.].

2422

Philo White, United States Minister Resident in Ecuador, to Marcos Espinel, Minister of Foreign Affairs of Ecuador [3]

D   QUITO, *October 8, 1855.*

The undersigned, Minister Resident of the United States, has the honor to acknowledge the receipt of the despatch of His Excellc'y, the Minister of

[1] Despatches, Ecuador, vol. 3; enclosed with White to the Secretary of State, No. 62, October 17, 1855, below, this part, doc. 2423.
[2] See White's note above, this part, December 26, 1854, doc. 2403, from which this quotation has been made.
[3] Despatches, Ecuador, vol. 3; enclosed with White to the Secretary of State, No. 62, October 17, 1855, below, this part, doc. 2423.

Foreign Relations, of date 6[1] inst.,[1] in response to two communications from the undersigned in relation to an international declaraion of Neutral Rights, the first of which was addressed to the Minister General of Ecuador, under date of 26th December, 1854,[2] and the second to His Excell'cy. the Minister of Foreign Relations of 10th August last.[3]

And the undersigned will avail himself of this occasion to say, that it is to him a source of high gratification to learn from the despatch of His Excellc'y, the Minister, that the Government of Ecuador entertains views of international commerce so nearly in accordance with the liberal and philanthropic policy adopted at this day, not alone by the Government of the United States, but by the most powerful and enlightened nations of Christendom.

The dogma that claims for *belligerents* a law that takes precedence of *neutral* rights, is a relic of a barbaric age, and of despotic rule: Such a doctrine is equally repugnant to sentiments of humanity and to an advanced state of civilization.

Prompted by the ennobling and sagacious policy in question, Great Britain and the United States have recently concluded a mutually reciprocal Treaty, for giving a more complete and practical effect to this beneficent law of progress, which secures the rights of peaceful and of neutral commerce upon a basis of International Law paramount to all belligerent rules of action.

And as His Excellc'y the Minister of Foreign Relations concurs so fully in the sentiments cherished by the Government of the United States in regard to this important and interesting question, the undersigned feels warranted in construing the language of His Excellc'y D[r] Espinel, contained in his communication of the 6th inst., as an affirmative answer to the Proposition of the undersigned, made in his despatch to the Minister General on the 26th December, 1854, for a reciprocal Declaration by the two Governments with regard to the principles of Neutral Rights indicated therein: He will accordingly transmit to his Government the correspondence on the subject, and await instructions as to ulterior action in the matter.

With sentiments of high regard [etc.].

---

[1] Above, this part, doc. 2421.   [2] *Ibid.*, doc. 2403.
[3] Not included in this publication, since it was merely a reminder that his first note had not been answered.

2423

Philo White, United States Minister Resident in Ecuador, to William L. Marcy,
Secretary of State of the United States [1]

[EXTRACTS]

No. 62—Confidential.   QUITO, *October 17, 1855.*

SIR: I have the honor to inclose to the Department by this month's mail,
in a separate parcel, the different Reports that have been made to the National Congress of Ecuador, now in session at this Capital, by the Heads of
Departments of this Government: These Documents are comprised within
three pamphlets, and embrace an account of the operations of the Departments of "Foreign Relations," the "Interior," the "Hacienda," and that of
"War and Marine," during the past year.

Of these documents, the most interesting to us is the Report from the
Minister of Foreign Relations,[2] which contains more points than one worthy
of special note by our Government:

1st: We learn from it, that the Mission from *Chile* was precisely of the
character that I have heretofore indicated to the Department,—that is, it
was instituted (undoubtedly at the instigation of the French Chargé in
Quito, and the other Diplomatic Protestants against our Huano Treaty)
expressly for the purpose of counteracting what the jealousy of the Chilian
Government construed into an undue North American influence in Ecuador:

2d: That that Mission has eventuated, as I predicted it would, in a mortifying abortion!

3d: That in that Report, the Minister of Foreign Relations of Ecuador has
alluded to the incidents of this Chilian Mission, in such terms of half-con-
cealed sarcasm, as to provoke a piquant correspondence between the Envoy
and the Minister:

And 4th: That with the view of saving appearances, and blinking the fruit-
lessness of his Mission, the Chilian Minister has patched up a Consular Convention with this Government, which is little else than a re-affirmance of the
Consular stipulations already existing between the two countries.

From these results of this Mission "Extraordinary" from Chile, it may
very readily be inferred, that this self-constituted *Monitress* of the Spanish
American Republics, whose semi-sumptuary office involved nothing less
than a supervision of the political and diplomatic *associations* of the "family"
over which she assumed the functions of "Governess," *lectured* to intractable
pupils in Ecuador!

There is one thing in the Minister's Report, however, which I felt warranted in remonstrating against: It is the incorporating into it of my despatch
of the 3d of September,[3] containing the views of the Department discounte-

---

[1] Despatches, Ecuador, vol. 3.   Received December 1.
[2] Not found.   [3] Above, this part, doc. 2417.

nancing the assumption of Gen'l. Flores, that diplomatic agents of the United States recognized his "rights" in making a piratical war upon Ecuador. The Minister regrets having done anything to disturb the feelings of myself or my Government: But the document has gone forth to the world, and no remedial measures can help the matter. The truth is, there is such a deadly enmity between this Administration and Gen'l Flores, that they eagerly seize upon every incident that falls in their way, calculated to disparage and cast odium upon that chieftain.

French Claims: The difficulties between Mons. Villamus, the French Chargé, and the Government here, have been accommodated for the present: By the intercession of the British and Chilian diplomatic agents, this Government has been induced to guarantee the payment, on some little time, of the principal part of the claims that formed the pretext of Mons. Villamus's menaces against them.

Seth Driggs' Indemnity: The determination of this Government to pay these claims of French speculators, by reason of coercive appliances, of course opened the door for a remonstrance from myself,—which I promptly made in person, and persevered in, actually "badgering" the Minister and the Officers of the Treasury, until they issued to me a "libranza" on the Treasurer of the Custom House in Guayaquil, for one-half of the principal and interest of the claim of Seth Driggs, and will soon issue another document for the balance of the indemnity,—payable as soon as the previous hypothecations of the income of the Treasury will admit of. I should undoubtedly have constrained the payment of this claim something like a year ago, by *personal importunities*,—which seems to be almost the only effective method of bringing this people to positive results,—but for the intervention of our Huano Treaty, Messrs. Villamil and Benjamin's Galápagos Contract, &c., which operated as an estoppel upon all our other interests in this country, until the final catastrophy in the revocation by this Government of whatever remained of official vitality in those instruments, as seen in the Executive decree of the 9th of August last, a copy of which I forwarded to the Department by last month's mail.[1] . . .

Gen'l. Gana, Chilian Minister here, informed me while on a visit at my House the other day, that his Government had named him as Minister to France, to replace Admiral Blanco, his brother-in-law, now there, but who desires to return home.

Neutral Rights: The paper marked D, contains a further correspondence with this Government in relation to a reciprocal Declaration of Neutral Rights.[2] Their long-delayed response to my two written communica-

[1] Not included in this publication, since its content is sufficiently given in the Ecuadoran Foreign Minister's note to White of August 9, 1855, above, this part, doc. 2414.

The omitted portion relates to the payment of the Driggs claim, and, also, to the presentation of a book to the Ecuadoran Government.

[2] Above, this part, October 6 and 8, 1855, docs. 2421 and 2422.

tions,[1] and to my repeated personal intimations on the subject, is certainly not couched in those terms of frankness that I at one time had reason to hope for.—But at this particular juncture, their action is undoubtedly influenced by the *surveillance* of the Chilian Mission! I have, however, construed the communication of the Minister of Foreign Relations to me on the subject, as acceding to our proposition; and his omission to dissent from, is at least a tacit acquiescence in my conclusion. Should the Department, under these circumstances, deem it expedient to invest me with the requisite authority to enter into stipulations with this Government, similar to those with Russia, or Naples, it is my present opinion that they may come into the measure, after the departure of the Chilian Minister, which will probably take place soon after the adjournment of Congress, as the incumbent here has been offered the Mission to France.[2] . . .

I have the honor [etc.].

2424

Philo White, United States Minister Resident in Ecuador, to Franklin Pierce, President of the United States [3]

No. 3—Confidential.   QUITO, *April 16, 1856.*

SIR: I have the honor to transmit to you, herewith, the Articles of a Convention, with regard to the "Rights of Neutrals," [4] negotiated and concluded

[1] White's two communications were dated December 26, 1854 and August 10, 1855; the former is to be found above, this part, doc. 2403, and the latter is not included in this publication, since it was merely a reminder that his first note had not been answered.
[2] The omitted portion relates to the election of Dr. Espinel as Vice President of the Republic of Ecuador.
[3] Despatches, Ecuador, vol. 3.   Received June 2.
[4] The convention follows:

THE UNITED STATES OF AMERICA AND THE REPUBLIC OF ECUADOR, equally animated with a desire to establish and maintain, upon a permanent basis, the relations of friendship and good understanding which have at all times so happily subsisted between the two nations, as also between their respective peoples, and which shall confer reciprocal benefits upon both, have agreed to perpetuate, by means of a formal treaty, the principles of the rights of neutrals at sea, which they recognize as indispensable conditions of all freedom of navigation and maritime trade:

For this purpose the President of the United States has conferred full powers on Philo White, Minister Resident of that nation in Ecuador, and the President of the Republic of Ecuador has conferred like powers on the Hon. Francisco Pablo Ycaza, Minister of Finance of that Republic: WHO, after having exchanged their respective full powers, found in good and due form, HAVE CONCLUDED AND SIGNED THE FOLLOWING ARTICLES:

ARTICLE I

The United States of America, and the Republic of Ecuador, recognize as permanent and immutable the following principles, to wit:

1st: That "free ships make free goods,"—that is to say, that the effects or goods belonging to citizens or subjects of a Power or State at war, are exempt from capture or confiscation when found on board neutral vessels, with the exception of articles contraband of war:

2d: That the property of neutrals on board an enemy's vessel is not subject to confiscation, unless the same be contraband of war: They engage to apply these principles

between myself and a Plenipotentiary on behalf of the Ecuatorian Government, by authority of the Special Commission with which you honored me under date of the 3ᵈ of December, 1855, as also in pursuance of instructions from the Honbᵉ the Secretary of State, bearing the dates of 18ᵗʰ October 1854, and 3ᵈ Decʳ 1855.[1]

Various causes have prevented me from bringing this negotiation to an earlier issue, of which I have from time to time kept the Secretary of State fully advised: The primary of these causes, was the presence here of the Chilian Ambassador, whose Mission had an especial (if not an exclusive) reference to *our* relations with the Spanish American Republics; and which operated as a positive bar to this Government's entertaining my proposition at all during that functionary's sojourn in this Capital. Of the incidents

---

to the commerce and navigation of all such Powers and States as shall consent to adopt them on their part as permanent and immutable.

ARTICLE 2

The two high contracting parties reserve themselves to come to an ulterior understanding as circumstances may require, with regard to the extension to be given, if there be any cause for it, to the principles laid down in the 1ˢᵗ Article: But they declare from this time, that they will be governed by those principles, as a rule, whenever a question may arise for judging of the rights of neutrality,—the manner and form of carrying out the intentions of this Article, being made to harmonize with the stipulations of the Treaty of friendship and commerce already existing between the two countries, and which bears date the 13ᵗʰ day of June, A.D. 1839.

ARTICLE 3

It is agreed by the high contracting parties, that all nations which may acknowledge and accede to the rules laid down in the 1ˢᵗ Article of this Convention, by a formal declaration stipulating to observe them on their part, shall enjoy the rights resulting from such accession in as full and ample a manner as they shall be enjoyed and observed by the two Powers signing this Convention: They shall mutually communicate to each other the results of the steps which may be taken on the subject.

ARTICLE 4

In like manner the two high contracting parties declare, that they will not acknowledge as legitimate belligerents, armed ships or vessels that shall cruize, without being provided with the necessary commission or other papers, emanating from the Authorities of the country whose flag they may use, such commission or papers being deemed requisite in determining the legality of the cruize: Consequently, armed vessels that may be found cruizing without such credentials, will be considered piratical in their character and purposes.

ARTICLE 5

The present Convention shall be approved and ratified by the President of the United States, with the advice and consent of the Senate of the same, and by the President of the Republic of Ecuador, with the approbation of the Congress of that nation; and the exchange of these ratifications shall take place at Quito, within eight months, counting from this day, or sooner if possible.

In faith whereof, we, the Plenipotentiaries of the United States and of Ecuador, have signed this Convention, and affixed to it our respective seals, at Quito, the ninth day of April, in the year One Thousand Eight Hundred and Fifty-six.

PHILO WHITE (Seal)
F. P. YCAZA (Seal)

---

[1] For the former, a circular instruction, see above, vol. II, pt. I, under this date, doc. 391. The latter is not included in this publication, since its only pertinent part mentions briefly the transmission of a full power to negotiate a treaty on this subject.

connected with that Mission, and of its final catastrophe, I wrote fully and freely to the Secretary of State [1] at the time of their occurrence.

Another, and a scarcely less serious obstacle, was the pendency of our *Galápagos Huano Treaty*, which I found so much absorbed the minds of the public Authorities here, as to impede all further *progress* in my negotiations with them, until the Executive *abrogated* both that treaty, and the huano *contract* they had entered into with Messrs. Villamil and Benjamin.

And as this ill-starr'd *huano* affair served as the pretext for the officious intervention of the foreign diplomatic agents resident in Quito, and, eventually, was the ostensible motive for precipitating upon Ecuador an *extraordinary* Embassy from Chile, which, as well in its inception as its ulterior purpose, was exceedingly mortifying to the self-esteem of an independent power, —coupled with the miscarriage of the *three million* loan stipulated for in our treaty, and upon which they had based extravagant hopes of relief to their dilapidated exchequer,—the Executive Authorities here became nervously sensitive with regard to this whole matter; and the mere suggestion of a *new* treaty with our country, coming so closely upon the heels of the late *abortion*, I found to be decidedly distasteful to them.

I deemed it prudent, therefore, to await the subsidence of this effervescent feeling among the officials here, and not urge the subject of "neutral rights" further upon them at this particular juncture.

And accordingly I occupied myself in prosecuting the negotiation, with an Ecuatorian Commissioner appointed for the purpose, for the recognition, by this Government, of sundry claims of our citizens against Ecuador: Until, some two or three months past, believing there was a recurrence of feeling more propitious for a dispassionate consideration of our proposition in relation to this question of neutral commerce, I opened anew the negotiation on the subject: And, as the result, I now have the satisfaction of inclosing to you, herewith, the Articles of a Convention between the two Governments, agreed upon and signed by the negotiators on the 9th inst., the stipulations of which are substantially those of the Convention with Russia, of 22[d] July, 1854,—although, at the earnest desire of the Executive here, I consented to admit an additional article, proposed by them, with regard to the character of those who are entitled to claim the rights pertaining to "belligerents": This Article does not, however, as I conceive, injuriously affect the intent and meaning of the Convention as originally drawn by myself. The motive of this Government for desiring the insertion of this additional (the 4th) Article, will be found explained in my communication (and accompanying documents) addressed to the Secretary of State under this date.[2]

I trust that the Articles contained in this Convention may meet your

[1] Above, this part, *passim*.
[2] Below, this part, doc. 2425, and in note 1 thereto, p. 376, are the documents relating to this article.

approval; and that the Instrument may, consequently, obtain the advice and ratification of the Senate.

And in view of the exigencies of the case, I would respectfully suggest, provided the terms of the Convention be satisfactory, and you should be desirous to perfect the Instrument before the period for its full consummation lapses, that it be returned to Quito previously to the adjournment of the Ecuatorian Congress, whose approval is necessary to give it validity: And to attain this end, it would be requisite to forward the document by the mail Steamer for Panama on the 5ᵗʰ October, at the latest.

Begging to refer you, for further details with regard to the negotiation of this Convention, to my communication of this date addressed to the Honbⁱ. the Secretary of State,—

I have the honor [etc.].

2425

Philo White, United States Minister Resident in Ecuador, to William L. Marcy, Secretary of State of the United States [1]

[EXTRACT

No. 73—Confidential.   QUITO, *April 16, 1856.*

SIR: I have had the honor to transmit to the President of the United States, under this date, the Articles of a Convention, "in relation to Neutral Rights," [2] concluded and signed between myself and a Plenipotentiary acting on behalf of this Government, which has been negotiated by me in pursuance of your instructions, dated the 18ᵗʰ October, 1854, and 3ᵈ December, 1855, [3] —and by authority of a Special Commission from the President of the United States, bearing the date of your last instructions on the subject.

On [In?] reference to my first note addressed to the Minister of Foreign Relations of this Government in regard to the question of Neutral Rights, a copy of which (marked C,) [4] I inclosed to the Department along with my despatch of the 17ᵗʰ January 1855, (No. 43.) [5] it will be seen that more than fifteen months elapsed after I had initiated the negotiation, before I was enabled to bring the matter to an effective result. My several communications to the Department, numbered respectively 49,—51,—53,—54,—56, and 60, [6]—(and some others incidentally) will furnish you with explanations

[1] Despatches, Ecuador, vol. 3.   Received May 30.
[2] His despatch to the President is above, this part, doc. 2424, and the convention is in note 4 thereto, p. 372.
[3] See above, this part, p. 373, note 1, concerning these two instructions.
[4] Above, this part, December 26, 1854, doc. 2403.
[5] Above, this part, doc. 2404.
[6] Except No. 56, all are to be found above, this part, dated respectively, March 30, April 18, April 25, May 16, and September 14, 1855, docs. 2406, 2408, 2409, 2410, and 2419.

of the causes of the long-continued dalliance of the Executive Authorities here in regard to this question.

The interference with the negotiation of, and the "protest" against our Huano Treaty with Ecuador, by the English, French, Spanish, and Peruvian Diplomatic Agents resident in this Capital,—and the extraordinary and *admonitory* Mission sent hither by the Government of Chile, superinduced by the instigations of the foreign agents,—were among the most prominent of the obstacles that retarded the progress of this negotiation. A political *survelliance* was manifestly attempted to be exercised over the foreign relations of this Government, in which the officiousness of those diplomats was notoriously prominent, they availing themselves of the facilities afforded by the Chilian Embassy in this City.

In both cases, however,—(the Galápagos Huano Treaty, and the present Convention)—I have managed to carry out the main instructions of my Government, in despite of this combination of extraneous influences, which have been actively exerted to thwart our negotiations, with a design thus to prejudice our interests and cripple our commerce.

I inclose to you a copy of the *Memoranda* I noted down of the conversation at the Conferences between myself and the Ecuatorian negotiator.[1]   From

---

[1] It follows:

Memorandum of a conference on Neutral Rights, between Francisco Pablo de Ycaza, Minister of Foreign Affairs of Ecuador, and Philo White, United States Minister Resident in Ecuador

QUITO, *March 28, 1856.*

Memorandum: At a Conference between the Honorable Francisco Pablo de Ycaza, Plenipotentiary on behalf of Ecuador, and Philo White, Minister Resident, &c. on the part of the United States, held at the Office of the Department of the Treasury in Quito, on the 28th day of March, 1856, for the purpose of agreeing upon the terms of a Treaty between the two countries in relation to Neutral Rights, &c,—

Mr. White invited the attention of Señor Ycaza to two communications, of dates 26th December 1854, and 8th October 1855 [Both, above, this part, docs. 2403 and 2422.—Ed.], which he had the honor to address to the then Minister of Foreign Relations, expressing the readiness of his Government to enter into Treaty stipulations with that of Ecuador, for asserting the principles and defining the true interpretation of the rules of international law as applicable to the rights of neutral commerce.   From an examination of the contents of those two communications, in connexion with that of Mr. White bearing date 1st of February [Not included in this publication; it states chiefly that he has received a special commission to treat upon this subject.—Ed.], he believes Señor Ycaza will become fully apprised of the objects of the Government of the United States in instituting the present negotiation.

And here Mr. White would beg leave to remark, in which he trusts Señor Ycaza will coincide with him, that it fittingly pertains to the Government of the United States to take a leading part, in conjunction with philanthropic and enlightened Statesmen of other countries, in their efforts to ameliorate the cruel rigors of the restrictive jurisprudence of past ages with reference to the freedom of the Seas, because of the fact, well known to all Statesmen and intelligent commercial men, that no country has a deeper interest in the commerce of the world than the United States, the tonnage of her mercantile marine already exceeding that of any one other nation, while its ratio of increase promises to be equally rapid for the future: And because, 2dly, as may be seen by a historical reminiscense of the acts of the primitive Statesmen of that Republic, their earnest efforts were exerted in opposition to the prevalent dogmas of those days, the crude fancies of antiquated political economists, bearing no other recommendations to

these Minutes, as well as from the text of the Convention itself, you will perceive that I assented to the insertion of an Article, defining, to a limited extent, a class of cruizers deemed *not* to be entitled to the rights of "bellig-[er]ents".

At the invasion of Ecuador in 1852, it seems that *Gen'l. Flores*, the Chief of that lawless expedition, used the *Flag* of Ecuador on board the vessels that

favor than the usages of preceding centuries, or the edicts of despotic rulers of later eras, by whose arbitrary sanctions the private property of unoffending citizens or subjects on the ocean has been seized and pillaged by belligerent powers, as caprice might dictate, or their rapacious wants impel them: And those stern and consistent Statesmen, the early champions of free and beneficent institutions, never relaxed their endeavors in the philanthropic work of obliterating from the code of international law so iniquitous a species of licensed piracy on the high seas!

And consequent upon these ennobling principles, and the patriotic efforts of those Sages to render them universal, we see that the Foreign Policy inaugurated by them with regard to trade and commerce, is now coming to be acknowledged by the principal maritime countries of the world, as the simplest, the safest, and the wisest which any people ever adopted: "Peace, commerce, and honest friendship with all nations, entangling alliances with none",—is the axiom that served as the broad basis of their international Code. And this eminently practical and benign policy, thus sanctioned by the Fathers of the Republic, has been steadily pursued and faithfully carried out, by each successive Administration that has ruled the destinies of that Nation from the earliest period of its existence as an independent Sovereignty.

That "Free ships make free goods," is not a new maxim of International Law: It is coeval with Republican Government in the Western Hemisphere. That illustrious man and profound philosopher, *Doct. Benjamin Franklin*, to whom the civilized world accorded the reputation of purity of patriotism and far-seeing Statesmanship, was among the earliest of American Diplomatists who gave form and effect to this sentiment of expansive benevolence,—having incorporated the *very words* of this great axiom into a Treaty of amity and commerce, which he and his eminent colleagues, Messrs. *John Adams* and *Thomas Jefferson*, negotiated and perfected between the United States and Frederick the Great, of Prussia, in the year 1785.

That important Treaty served as the germ, whence has sprung a vigorous tree of Liberty, whose branches are o'erspreading the whole earth, giving shelter to trade and navigation, and now yielding fruits as abundant as they are life-invigorating, and of which the people of all nations are becoming eager to partake.

And it is believed that the present is a most favorable conjunction for establishing that maxim as an irrevocable law of commercial intercourse, whereby it may become as binding as any other well-settled principle of the international code. The three most potent nations of the Old World, now engaged in the bloody strife of arms, having adopted this benign principle for their own guidance with reference to neutral commerce, the horrors of war will be greatly mitigated during this sanguinary struggle, as well as all succeeding ones, so far as unoffending and peaceful neutrals are to be affected by the belligerent acts of the contending parties. Several other nations have recognized this great principle by treaty compacts, and still others are negotiating with a view to a participation in the benefits.

Mr. White would remark, further, that his Government, cherishing a deep interest in the well-being of Ecuador as a neighbor and an interesting Sister Sovereignty, instructed him more than a year since [See circular instruction, vol. II, Oct. 18, 1854, doc. 391.—Ed.], to propose to the Executive Government of this Republic to join with the United States in treaty stipulations in the sublime principle that "free ships make free goods." Having at that time performed the agreeable mission confided to him, he was subsequently assured by the then Minister of Foreign Relations, in a despatch bearing date the 6th of October last [Above, this part, doc. 2421.—Ed.], that the Government of Ecuador fully recognized the importance of the principle announced in Mr. White's communication of 26th December, 1854 [Above, this part, doc. 2403.—Ed.], and he expressed a belief that its benefits would especially enure to the advantage of nations whose policy it was, like that of Ecuador, to observe the strictest neutrality towards all belligerents.

In accordance with this declaration on the part of Ecuador, and in obedience to in-brought his motley band of adventurers hither, and claimed immunities for his ship as "belligerents" *under that flag!* It was with reference to any similar future abuse of their Flag, that they desired the insertion of the 4th Article in the present Convention.   I told Mr. Ycaza, that I viewed the Article as containing a mere reiteration of a *truism*, that could be of no practical benefit: But, believing that its incorporation into the Convention would

---

structions from his Government, Mr. White now has the honor to offer to the consideration of Señor Icaza [Ycaza?] a *Protocol* of a Treaty [Not found.—Ed.] between their respective Governments, designed to give effect to the principles of international commerce which have formed the subject matter of this Conference.

Mr. Ycaza then remarked, that he thanked Mr. White for having at the outset reduced his propositions to writing, including a protocol (draft) of a Convention embracing such stipulations as the Government of the United States are desirous of entering into with that of Ecuador.   And he would take this early occasion to say, that his government acquiesced entirely in the views of that of the United States, as now expressed by Mr. White, in relation to neutral Commerce, &c.   And he would refer to the provisions of the treaty of peace and amity already existing between the two countries, to show that they fully recognized those principles some 18 years ago: The stipulations of that Treaty, indeed, were so very explicit on this point, that it seemed to him, on first view, quite unnecessary to enter into any *new* convention for a re-assertion of the principles in question: But as he desired a little time to examine Mr. White's proposition in detail, he suggested an adjournment of the Conference until the 31st inst.,—to which Mr. White assented.

Monday, 31st March: In accordance with the desire of Mr. Ycaza, the conference was postponed until to-morrow.

April 1st: At the opening of this day's Conference, Mr. Ycaza observed, that after carefully examin'g the propositions offered by Mr. White, he came to the conclusion there ought to be a stipulation defining, to some extent, the kind of cruizers that were entitled to the rights and privileges of "belligerents."   In response, Mr. White remarked, that it was very apparent to *what* class of vessels such rights and privileges pertained;—every legally authorized cruizer, commissioned by a settled and recognized government, was legitimately entitled to the immunities of a *belligerent:* But if Mr. Ycaza would embody his views on this point, in a written form, perhaps Mr. White might not, on reflection, object to their adoption.   To which Mr. Ycaza assented; and, after some incidental conversation, the Conference was adjourned to the 3^d inst.

Thursday, 3^d April: At the Conference on this day, Mr. Ycaza presented the draft of an additional Article, substantially the same as the 4th of the Convention, Mr. White remarked, that he saw no objections to Mr. Ycaza's proposition, as an abstract declaration; but they were self-evident truths, that could not, as he conceived, gain additional strength from a reiteration in the present Convention, &c.   Mr. Ycaza replied, that the political history of Ecuador presented a case in point, which suggested to his government the possible utility of a stipulation such as he now had the honor to propose: "Juan José Flores, heading a band of lawless foreign adventurers, attacked Ecuador in 1852, the vessels of his marauding force making a piratical use of the *Flag* of Ecuador, thus exhibiting the monstrous outrage of 'pirates' claiming *belligerent rights* under *our* colors!"   And he said it was in view of possible repetition of similar outrages in buccaniering warfare, that he offered the additional Article in question.   Mr. White replied, that he knew how to sym[pa]thize in the excited feelings of the Authorities of Ecuador, with regard to the hostile demonstrations made by the Ex-Gen'l. Flores against this Republic in 1852: And as he could not perceive that his original draft would in the least be injuriously affected in its intent and meaning by Mr. Ycaza's proposed new article, he would defer to the wish of the latter, and consent to incorporate the amendment into the Convention.   After some further conversation, an adjournment of the Conference took place, until the 7th inst.

Monday, April 7:   The terms of all the Articles having been settled, arrangements were agreed upon for making clean duplicate copies of the Convention complete, in English and in Spanish; and Wednesday the 9th, was named for the last conference.

April 9th, 1856:   The clean copies of the Convention being ready on the afternoon of this day, the Negotiators affixed their signatures and seals to the duplicate copies, in the Office of the Ministry of the Hacienda, each taking a copy of the instrument.

not affect in the least the original intent of the Instrument, I would defer to his wish to give it a place therein.

You will also see, from my "Memoranda," that the Ecuatorian negotiator was of opinion (or so expressed himself) that no *new* Convention, or Declaration, in regard to the rights of neutrals, was called for, as between *our* respective governments,—because, as it seemed to him, those rights were distinctly asserted and amply secured by the provisions of the Treaty of amity and commerce already existing between the two countries, concluded in 1839. The stipulations of that Treaty are, in truth, more explicit with regard to the principles now sought to be made permanent and immutable, than perhaps any other of our general treaties: And to meet the views of the Executive in this respect, (for I found that the President and the Minister of Foreign Relations were consulted at short intervals throughout the entire negotiation) I consented to make special reference to that treaty in our present Convention, as you will see has been done in Article 2^d.

Hoping that the Articles of the Convention I now forward, may meet the approbation of the President and of yourself, I beg leave most respectfully to suggest, that, in such event, the Senate's approval be sought at an early day, and the ratified Convention be forwarded from New York by the Mail Steamer for Panama on the 5th of October at the latest, in order that it may reach Quito in time to receive the approval of the Ecuatorian Congress at its approaching session, and before the instrument lapses by its own limitations.[1] . . .

With the highest respect [etc.].

2426

Philo White, United States Minister Resident in Ecuador, to William L. Marcy, Secretary of State of the United States [2]

[EXTRACT]

No. 84   QUITO, *August 18, 1856.*

CLAIMS OF OUR CITIZENS

SIR: Circumstances, uncontrolable by myself, as they would have been by any other diplomatic agent that might have been sent here, have hitherto prevented a full adjustment of the *Claims* of American citizens for indemnity against this Government.

DIPLOMATIC QUESTIONS

It has been my fortune to encounter a group of *Diplomatic Questions*, which, for their number and the gravity of their import, have exceeded all

---

[1] The omitted portion cites five papers, enclosed with this despatch, none of which are included in this publication, except the one above, this part, p. 376, note 1, since they merely relate to the commissions of the two negotiators of the treaty and to the appointment of a day for a conference.   [2] Despatches, Ecuador, vol. 4. Received September 29.

other questions hitherto devolved upon any or all our Agents in charge of this Legation, since the establishment of diplomatic relations between the United States and Ecuador.

THE AMAZON QUESTION

My original instructions from the Department,[1] expressly made the Free Navigation of the Amazon, &c., "the most important question" that would demand my attention on this Mission. And from the first moment of my landing in the country to which I am accredited, I was confronted by obstacles of a formidable aspect in the management of that question. The Chavalier [Chevalier] *Lisboa*, a Brazillian Envoy, had preceded me at this Capital, having come from New Granada, where he had achieved a diplomatic triumph in the conclusion of a "Convention on Fluvial Navigation," by which that Republic was drawn into a close alliance with Brazil, in the maintenance of the restrictive policy of the latter with regard to river commerce &c. And he came specially charged with the negotiation of a similar compact with Ecuador, in which purpose he enjoyed the sympathies and availed himself of the covert aid of the foreign diplomatic agents resident in this Capital.

But notwithstanding the imposing *prestige* of his Mission, and the advantage of an advanced progress in his negotiations, I ultimately succeeded, after combatting the diplomatic arts, the influences and the prepossessions arrayed against our side of the question, in carrying my point, and in accomplishing all that I had been charged with by my Government in relation to that question, so far as any agency on my part was concerned. And in this, I believe I was more fortunate than any of my diplomatic colleagues in South America charged with a similar service.

HUANO TREATY

But scarcely had the Amazon question been put at rest, when I was commissioned to negotiate the somewhat notable *Galápagos Huano Treaty* with this Government.[2] That negotiation involved questions of the gravest importance, devolving on me duties of the most delicate nature, and imposing a degree of toil and anxiety hitherto unknown at this Legation. I found myself confronted in the prosecution of it, by the open hostility and the solemn *protests* of the entire body of Foreign Diplomatic Agents resident in this Capital; to which was subsequently superadded the efforts and the arts of an Extraordinary Embassy from the Republic of Chile, deputed hither by that Government with the express design of thwarting our negotiations here, and alienating the Authorities of Ecuador from any intimate alliance with us. And this war of diplomatic appliances was waged during some nine or ten months, with vast odds as to numbers against me. But, as the sequel will

[1] See above, this volume, pt. III, August 20, 1853, doc. 2322.
[2] *Ibid.*, August 14, 1854, doc. 2326.

show, this conspiracy against our interest, apparently so formidable in its means of annoyance, proved to be bootless in its results for mischief,—and I was ultimately successful in carrying the measure through all the perils it had to encounter, from the inception of the negotiation to the final consummation of the Treaty, which I had the satisfaction of forwarding to the President on the 22ᵈ November 1854.[1] And although the unfortunate upshot of this whole affair was sufficiently mortifying to *us*,—yet the officious and persistent interference in the matter on the part of the diplomatic *protestants* resident here, and the no less extraordinary intervention of a much vaunted *Special Mission* from Chile, eventuated in a still more humiliating *abortion* of the sinister purposes of our rivals.

CONVENTION ON NEUTRAL COMMERCE

While the Government and the people here were still agitated with the all-absorbing question of the Huano Treaty, and the Chilian Envoy continued his *ministrations* with the Executive Authorities, I received from Washington another Special Commission, authorizing me to negotiate a Convention with Ecuador in relation to Neutral Commerce, &c.[2] I accordingly presented the matter in due form to the Minister of Foreign Relations,[3] soon after receiving my instructions, and, in the name of my Government, requested that a Commissioner might be appointed in behalf of Ecuador to treat with me on the subject. But I found there was an insuperable disinclination on the part of this Government seriously to consider this matter, or any other of leading importance in relation to our country, while the Chilian Envoy tarried here, who manifestly exercised a degree of *surveillance* over their actions! And it was not until after the departure of that functionary from the country, that I was finally enabled to persuade this Government to appoint a Commissioner for the negotiation of a Convention with reference to this question. Ultimately, however, I was successful in carrying this last-named measure, as I had been in all the other diplomatic questions entrusted to my care. And on the 16ᵗʰ April past, I had the honor to transmit to the President of the United States the Convention in relation to Neutral Rights &c. agreed upon and signed by the Ecuatorian Commissioner and myself on the 9ᵗʰ of that month.[4]

Thus it will be seen, that these three leading diplomatic questions, with their *concomitants*, have occupied my time and mind, and imposed upon me almost constant labors, during nearly the entire period, thus far, of my

[1] See above, this part, doc. 2400. The treaty is not included in this publication. For an explanation of its provisions, however, see White's No. 40, dated December 20, 1854, above, this part, doc. 2402.
[2] See the circular instruction which went also to John W. Dana, U. S. Minister in Bolivia, on the same date, above, vol. II, October 18, 1854, doc. 391. It was not until December 3, 1855 that a full power to negotiate such a convention was sent to White.
[3] See above, this part, December 26, 1854, doc. 2403.
[4] See above, this part, doc. 2424, and note 4 thereto.

Mission in Ecuador. And in view of the formidable obstacles I had to contend with, the successful issue in each case, complete so far as *my* powers extended, attest at least the assiduity with which they have been managed.

CLAIMS FOR INDEMNITY

As by my instructions from the Department, a precedence was given to diplomatic questions over all other matters, except perhaps the "current business" of the Legation,—(which has been neither small nor infrequent, as my correspondence with the Department will show)—it was only at intervals of time that my attention could be devoted to the examination of the *Claims* of our citizens against Ecuador.[1] . . .

With sentiments of high regard [etc.].

2427

Philo White, United States Minister Resident in Ecuador, to Ramón Borja, Minister of Foreign Affairs of Ecuador [2]

A   QUITO, *September 25, 1856.*

The undersigned, Minister Resident of the United States, has been directed by his Government [3] to address His Excellency the Minister of Foreign Relations of Ecuador, on the subject of "*the declaration relative to Neutral Rights,*" adopted by the European powers who were parties to the late Paris Conference,—and to which "declaration," the undersigned learns from the recent Annual Exposition of the operations of the Executive Department under Your Excellency's charge, the diplomatic representatives of Great Britain and France "have solicited the adhesion of this Government." And it is presumed the same course has been adopted by those confederated powers towards other nations.

The undersigned having been specially commissioned by his Government for the purpose, had the honor, on the 9th of April last, in conjunction with the Honbl. *Francisco P. Ycaza*, Plenipotentiary on behalf of Ecuador, to conclude and sign a Convention between their respective governments, in relation to Neutral Commerce, &c.,[4]—which Convention contains provisions identical with the 2[d] and 3[d] propositions embraced in the Paris "declaration," and the fourth of those propositions is but the annunciation of a principle of international law now universally recognized. During the negotiations that preceded the signing of that Convention, the undersigned took

---

[1] The omitted portion relates to claims, and to the condition of the files of the legation.
[2] Despatches, Ecuador, vol. 4; enclosed with White to the Secretary of State, No. 88, October 8, 1856, below, this part, doc. 2429.
[3] This was a circular instruction and went on the same date to James A. Peden, U. S. Minister in Argentina, for which, see above, vol. I, July 14, 1856, doc. 32.
[4] See above, this part, p. 372, note 4.

occasion to allude to the fact, that his government had entered into similar treaty stipulations with several powers, and was in negotiation with other maritime countries [1] for the general adoption of the principles therein announced.　These principles have been long cherished by the United States, and inculcated, on all suitable occasions, in her intercourse with other nations: And the "declaration" of the confederated powers lately assembled at Paris, is but a tardy, and partial acquiescence in the truth and justice of these American axioms.　The peculiar form in which those powers have recognized these principles, however, divest them of the philanthropic tendencies designed by the American doctrine.

And the undersigned would here respectfully submit to His Excellency the Minister of Foreign Relations, whether the conditions which are to accompany the acceptance of the propositions of the Paris Conference, as presented to Ecuador for her "adhesion," will not necessarily, if accepted by her, render nugatory and of no effect the 2^d and 3^d Articles of the Convention just entered into between their respective Governments?　The undersigned is persuaded, in his own mind, that such an "adhesion" on the part of Ecuador, would be a virtual abrogation of the most essential stipulations of that Convention: Because, in the first place, all four of the Paris propositions must be taken, or none; and second, they must be taken not only indivisibly, but with the surrender of an important attribute of sovereignty,—that of negotiating with any nation on the subject of Neutral Rights,—unless such negotiation embrace *all* the propositions contained in the Paris "declaration."

Any American nation might well hesitate before surrendering so essential an element of her nationality, and subjecting herself to the overshadowing influences of a European Confederacy!

In the opinion of the undersigned, as well as of his Government, alarming consequences would be likely to result to most commercial nations from the new European doctrine now for the first time attempted to be introduced into the maritime code, and especially to those countries which are not burdened, or may not choose to burden themselves, with large naval establishments.

The right of a commercial State, when unhappily involved in war, to employ its mercantile marine for defence and aggression, has heretofore proved to be an essential aid in checking the domination of a belligerent possessed of a powerful navy: By the surrender of that sovereign right, one legitimate mode of defence is parted with, for a nominal surrender only by a strong naval power,—while in effect such a surrender places the weaker nation more completely at the mercy of the stronger.　By so unequal a surrender, the weaker loses, while the stronger gains; and the freedom of the seas is more effectually given up to a few great powers who may deem it expedient to maintain large navies.

[1] See his note above, this part, December 26, 1854, doc. 2403.

The undersigned is in expectation of soon receiving a more full development of the views of his Government, with regard to the operation of the first principle of the Paris "declaration,"—that in relation to the abandonment of the right to issue Letters of Marque,—in its reply to those powers which have invited its concurrence in that "declaration." Unless the Paris measure gives a full application to the principles upon which it is based, and is made to withdraw *private property* upon the ocean from seizure by public armed vessels as well as by privateers, it will be exceedingly injurious to the commerce of all those nations who may not keep up an expensive naval force.

In the mean while, by direction of the President of the United States, the undersigned has been instructed to present this general view of the subject to the Government of Ecuador: And he has respectfully to request, that His Excellency the Minister of Foreign Relations will cause this communication to be taken into consideration, as well by the Executive as by the National Chambers, (should the matter be submitted to legislative arbitrament) conjointly with the Paris propositions. And the undersigned cannot for a moment doubt, but that the decision of the Ecuatorian Government will be in accordance with an enlightened and sagacious State policy, and in exact fulfilment of all her obligations towards the United States, equally with other powers.

And the undersigned avails himself [etc.].

2428

Philo White, United States Minister Resident in Ecuador, to Ramón Borja, Minister of Foreign Affairs of Ecuador [1]

B   QUITO, *October 2, 1856.*

The undersigned, Minister Resident of the United States, presents his compliments to Dr. Borja, Minister of Foreign Relations of Ecuador, and has the pleasure to inclose to His Excellc'y, for the use of himself and the Executive Government of Ecuador, a printed copy of a despatch from the Secretary of State of the United States, addressed to the French Ambassador resident at Washington,[2] in response to a communication from him,[3] inviting the "adhesion" of the United States to the principles contained in the declaration concerning maritime law,"[4] adopted by the confederated powers recently assembled at Paris.

[1] Despatches, Ecuador, vol. 4; enclosed with White to the Secretary of State, No. 88, October 8, 1856, below, this part, doc. 2429.
[2] This note, dated July 28, 1856, is not included in this publication, since its content is sufficiently indicated in a circular instruction which went to the legations of the United States in Argentina and Ecuador, as well as to others, on the same date, and which is to be found above, vol. 1, August 29, 1856, doc. 34. It is printed, however, in *British and Foreign State Papers*, vol. 55, pp. 589–99.   [3] The reply is not included in this publication.
[4] In the file copy in the manuscript volume, there was no indication where this quotation began.

By the next Atlantic mail, the undersigned hopes to receive, and to present to Dr. Borja, a copy of this document in a more authentic and enduring form; but in the mean while, he hastens to communicate it to His Excellc'y in the shape of a Newspaper slip, as he is anxious that so important a State Paper should be placed in the possession of the Executive of Ecuador without delay, especially since the question which it so ably discusses has been brought to the consideration of this Government, as well by the diplomatic representatives of Great Britain and France, as by the undersigned in behalf of his Government.

And the undersigned [etc.].

2429

Philo White, United States Minister Resident in Ecuador, to William L. Marcy, Secretary of State of the United States [1]

No. 88   QUITO, *October 8, 1856.*

SIR: I have the honor to acknowledge the receipt, within a few days past, of your despatch N⁰ 32, of date 14th July.[2]   And in accordance with its instructions, I lost no time in addressing to this Government a communication on the subject,—a copy of which, marked A, is inclosed herewith.[3]

The subsequent mail from Guayaquil, brought me a newspaper copy of your despatch to *Count Sartiges*, of 28th July:[4] And in view of the great importance of the document, and of the urgency of the case,—the British and French Chargés resident in Quito having already communicated to this Government, for its action thereon, the "Declaration" of the Paris Conference,—I immediately inclosed your Answer to that "declaration" to the Minister of Foreign Relations here, in the form of a *newspaper slip:* A copy of my note on the occasion, I inclose herewith, marked B.[5]

By the next mail from the United States, I hope to receive your despatch to the French Minister, in a form more authentic than a newspaper copy; when I shall again take occasion to address this Government on the subject.

The present Administration will retire from Office, and a new one is to be inaugurated, on the 15th of this month; and I am not likely to obtain any definite expression of opinion in regard to this question from the old incumbents.

They however manifest no little curiosity, in this connection to learn what is the fate of the "Convention" I negotiated with them on "Neutral Rights," &c.   They will not suffer themselves to doubt of its ratification by the President and Senate,—because, as the original proposition came from

[1] Despatches, Ecuador, vol. 4.   Received December 1.
[2] Same as No. 20, of this date, to U. S. Minister Peden in Argentina, above, vol. 1, doc. 32.
[3] Above, this part, September 25, 1856, doc. 2427.
[4] Concerning it, see above, this part, p. 384, note 2.
[5] Above, this part, October 2, 1856, doc. 2428.

Washington, and the very terms of the Instrument were dictated from thence, they cannot think our Government will repudiate its own measure! More especially, since Ecuador is one among only *four* [1] (according to the newspaper copy of your despatch) of some forty nations with whom our Government offered to negotiate on the subject, who actually acceded to our propositions by entering into Treaty stipulations with us for giving effect to our favorite measure.

And I have respectfully to request, that, in due time, I may receive the requisite instructions from Washington, to enable me to satisfy the reasonable anxiety of this Government with regard to the fate of the "Convention."

With high regard [etc.].

2430

*Philo White, United States Minister Resident in Ecuador, to Antonio Mata,
Minister of Foreign Affairs of Ecuador* [2]

B   QUITO, *October 25, 1856.*

The undersigned, Minister Resident of the United States, has the pleasure to inclose herewith to His Excellency the Minister of Foreign Relations of Ecuador, a pamphlet copy of the despatch from the Secretary of State of the United States addressed to the Count de Sartiges, the French Minister at Washington, in response to an invitation from the confederated powers assembled, by representatives, in Paris at the beginning of this year, for the United States to *adhere* to the principles contained in a "declaration" there made "concerning maritime law." [3]

On the 25th ultimo, the undersigned had the honor to address His Excellency the Minister of Foreign Relations somewhat at length on this subject,[4] —and, on the 2[d] instant,[5] to inclose to him a *newspaper slip*, containing the important document above alluded to; and he has now respectfully to request, that the authentic copy of that document herewith inclosed, together with the three communications of the undersigned in relation to the matter, may take the same direction that was given to the joint communication on the subject from the Diplomatic Representatives of Great Britain and of France resident in this Capital,—which latter, as appears from the Annual Report of His Excellency the Minister of Foreign Relations, was referred to the National Congress, for such action thereon as might be deemed expedient by the legislative branch of the Government.   And the undersigned is the more desirous that his communications should be submitted to the same

---

[1] The names of the other three nations were not given in this communication.
[2] Despatches, Ecuador, vol. 4; enclosed with White to the Secretary of State, No. 91, November 1, 1856, below, this part, doc. 2431.
[3] Concerning it, see above, this part, p. 384, note 2.
[4] Above, this part, doc. 2427.   [5] *Ibid.*, doc. 2428.

arbitrament, because he deems it essential that the Representatives of the Nation should have before them a full exposition of the principles and the views of the Government of the United States in relation to this whole question, before coming to a final decision upon so important a matter.

In again recurring to this question, the undersigned begs to reiterate to His Excellency the Minister of Foreign Relations, and through him to the Government of Ecuador, that the President of the United States finds himself unable to agree to the first principle of the Paris "Declaration," contained in Protocol N° 23,—which proposes to abolish *privateering*,—or to the proposition in Protocol N° 24, which declares the indivisibility of the four principles of the "declaration," and surrenders the liberty to negotiate in regard to neutral rights except on inadmissible conditions.

It seems improbable that it could have been the object of the Governments represented in the Congress at Paris, to obstruct the adoption of principles which all approve, and are willing to observe, unless they are encumbered by an irrelative principle, to which some governments cannot accede without a more extended application of it than that which is proposed by the Paris Congress.

And the undersigned now has the honor to inform His Excellency the Minister of Foreign Relations, that he is instructed from the President of the United States, to propose to the Government of Ecuador to enter into an arrangement for its adherence with the United States to the four principles of the Paris "Declaration,"[1] provided the first of them is amended as specified in Mr. Marcy's despatch to the Count de Sartiges.[2] Without such amendment, the President of the United States is constrained, for many weighty reasons, some of which are stated in that despatch, to decline acceding to the first principle of the "declaration." The President, however, is ready to give his assent to the remaining three principles: And he entertains the hope, that the Powers represented in the Congress at Paris will take early measures to release each other from the restrictions imposed by Protocol N° 24. By the recollection that France, as well as Russia and Prussia, has heretofore favored liberal doctrines in regard to neutral rights and the freedom of the seas, the President is much encouraged in the hope that these powers will concur in the course suggested in the despatch addressed by Mr. Marcy to the Count de Sartiges.

The sincere desire of the President of the United States to maintain the most friendly relations with the Government of Ecuador, increases his solicitude to know what will be the treatment of American privateers upon the high seas and in the Ports of Ecuador, in case the United States should

[1] Same as the instruction, of the same date, to James A. Peden, U. S. Minister in Argentina, above, vol. 1, August 29, 1856, doc. 34.

[2] Mr. Marcy's proposed amendment was as follows: "And that the private property of the subjects or citizens of a belligerent on the high seas shall be exempted from seizure by public armed vessels of the other belligerent, except it be contraband."

unhappily be at war with any other power which has acceded to the "declaration." It is not reasonable to expect, that the United States will ever forego a resort to privateers in the event of becoming involved in war with a commercial State, unless the *amendment* she now proposes to the Paris declaration should be adopted as a settled principle of international law. If such war should happen with a nation which has acceded to the declaration proposed by the Congress at Paris, it is of much importance to know whether neutral nations which have also acceded to it, will treat our privateers in any respect differently from the manner in which they have been heretofore treated by them? Or whether the privateers of the powers which do not become parties to the declaration, will receive the same immunities in all neutral ports which have been heretofore accorded to such privateers? And in order to prevent future misunderstanding, it is quite essential that, on these points, the Government of the United States should be made acquainted with the views of the Governments which have agreed to that "declaration," or who may accede to it. With this view, the undersigned has been instructed, by order of the President of the United States, to make these inquiries of the Government of Ecuador, and to request a response thereto from His Excellency the Minister of Foreign Relations.

Although the President entertains no serious apprehensions, that the rights of the United States in regard to the employment of Privateers will be affected directly or indirectly by the new state of things which may arise out of the proceedings of the Congress of Paris, it would be gratifying to him to be assured by the Government of Ecuador, that no new complications in our relations with it are likely to result from those proceedings. And he trusts that, so long as Ecuador is, and he anxiously desires she should ever remain, a friendly power, her Ports will be, as they heretofore have been, a refuge from the dangers of the sea and from attack, as well for our privateers as for our merchant vessels and national ships of war, in the event of hostilities between any other power and our country.

Perhaps at no former period did the interests of commerce exercise a more potent influence in controlling the political destinies of the world than at this time. And the undersigned finds abundant cause for gratulation among all those nations whose interests and policy are averse to the maintenance of a large and burdensome war marine, in the fact that the eminently just and philanthropic principles enunciated and maintained by the Government of the United States, with regard to neutral commerce and the freedom of the seas, have been approved by not only all the most enlightened men of America, but have been favorably received and acquiesced in by liberal Statesmen throughout Europe. And it is an encouraging indication of an altered sentiment in Great Britain, favorable to the American doctrine, that many of the leading periodicals in that country, and among them the most influential journal in the world, (the London "Times,") acknowledge the beneficence and the equity of this American principle, and openly favor its incorporation into the maritime code. A confident hope may therefore be entertained, that the *amendment* proposed by the Government of the United States to the first Article of the Paris "declaration," will ere long be acceded to by the principal powers of Europe, and the code of international law be thus authoritively modified, in accordance with the principles of justice, and the sentiments of an enlightened philanthropy.

Respectfully requesting an early response to this communication, the undersigned reiterates [etc.].

2431

Philo White, United States Minister Resident in Ecuador, to William L. Marcy, Secretary of State of the United States [1]

[EXTRACT]

No. 91   QUITO, *November 1, 1856.*

SIR: I have the honor to acknowledge the receipt of your despatch N⁰ 33, dated 29th August,[2] respecting neutral rights, &c.; and I inclose herewith my communication to this Government, marked B,[3] made in pursuance of your instructions on the subject.

The Convention which I concluded with the Executive Authorities here, bearing date the 9th of April last,[4] was duly presented to Congress after the organization of the two Houses. But the failure of our Government to ratify that Convention, or even to acknowledge its receipt, (altho' other communications under the same envelope have reached their destination,) has induced the Chambers to suspend all further action in relation to the document.

The non-approval of this Convention at Washington, is incomprehensible to the Executive Officers of this Government, and is a subject of much conversation among the Members of Congress. In the absence of any advices from home on the subject, the matter is inexplicable with me, and I frequently feel embarrassed at my inability to satisfy the many queries propounded to me touching the fate of the Treaty. I would therefore respectfully inquire, whether it would be in accordance with the policy of the Department, to authorize me to give this Government any kind of explanation with regard to the non-action and total silence of the Washington Cabinet in relation to the matter.

Being on cordial terms of official and social intercourse with the President and his Ministers, as well as with the prominent Members of both Houses of

[1] Despatches, Ecuador, vol. 4. Received December 5.
[2] Same as No. 24, of this date, to James A. Peden, U. S. Minister in Argentina, above, vol. I, pt. I, doc. 34.
[3] Above, this part, October 25, 1856, doc. 2430.   [4] Above, this part, p. 372, note 4.

Congress, they converse with me freely and frankly on subjects of public interest. But in regard to my last communications to them, inviting their attention to the question of the abolition of Privateering, &c., there is a hesitancy on their part to act,—not, however, from any positive indisposition to favor our doctrine, for, so far as, my observation goes, they acknowledge the justice and the philanthropy of our principle, but they seem rather in doubt as to the *mode* in which it would be expedient to give expression to their acquiescence in your last propositions. Intimations have been thrown out, although vaguely, that the *ignoring* of its own Treaty by my Government, raises a question of self-respect and of national dignity with them, in their future consideration of the matter. It was remarked to me the other day, that had the United States ratified the Convention they instructed me to negotiate with them on this very subject, the question would have been divested of its present complications,—as "Additional Articles" might, in such case, have been appended to that Convention, embracing the "Arrangement" proposed in your despatch of the 29ᵗʰ August, for an "adherence" on the part of Ecuador "with the United States" in her views relative to the "declaration" of the Paris Congress. As a ready solution, however, of the perplexities attending the question, the Executive Government has adopted the expedient of referring the whole matter to Congress, to be disposed of as the Representatives of the Nation may deem most expedient.

I would therefore, in the present aspect of the case, beg leave respectfully to ask instructions as to the *form* of "an arrangement for the adherence" of Ecuador "with the United States to the four principles of the Declaration of the Congress" of Paris, &c. &c., which I am directed by the President to propose to this Government.[1] . . .

I have the honor [etc.].

2432

Philo White, United States Minister Resident in Ecuador, to William L. Marcy,
Secretary of State of the United States [2]

No. 95   QUITO, *November 19, 1856.*

SIR: After my despatches by last month's mail were sent off, I learned the purport of Article 10, of the Treaty of Friendship, Commerce, &c. lately negotiated at Santiago de Chile, between that Republic and those of Peru and Ecuador. By the stipulations of that Article, *Privateering* is abolished, and declared "piratical," as between those three contracting parties; and their citizens are inhibited from engaging in the fitting out or the manning of any Letter of Marque under the flag of another nation. These are the sole provisions of the Article.

[1] The omitted portion relates to the building of a railroad from Guayaquil to Quito.
[2] Despatches, Ecuador, vol. 4. Received December 15.

The present Session of the Ecuatorian Congress will terminate before the close of this month; and the question of "Neutral Rights," &c.,—embracing the "four points" of the Paris "declaration," and your proposition for an *amendment* to that Declaration,[1]—is now under discussion in both Houses. Translated copies of my three communications to the Foreign Minister on the subject[2] are before them, together with a full and correct translation of your despatch to Count Sartiges,[3] with which I have furnished the Senate in *printed form.*

To me personally, they express their entire concurrence in our doctrine of exempting all private property, at sea as well as on shore, from becoming the lawful spoil of war; and unless some sinister influence should bear sway with the majority, I am inclined to hope the Chambers will sanction a declaration to that effect.

It has been known here during two weeks past, that New Granada and Costa Rica have recognized our principle, of exempting all private property from capture at sea in time of war, in a Treaty just concluded between those Republics. Had I been instructed to that effect, I am quite confident that this Government would have acquiesced in the insertion of an Article in our Convention of the 9th of April last, recognizing this our doctrine in all of its breadth.

With very high respect [etc.].

2433

Philo White, United States Minister Resident in Ecuador, to William L. Marcy, Secretary of State of the United States [4]

No. 98—Confidential.   QUITO, *December 31, 1856.*

SIR: The Congress of Ecuador adjourned on the 28th ultimo; and the question of Neutral Rights, Privateering, &c., has been *accommodated*, after a fashion, (as they hope) by the *ratification* of all in relation to the matter that was presented to the Chambers in a shape legitimately to call for legislative action.

At the time your new instructions in relation to this question reached me, the Chargés of England and France had just received directions from their Governments to present the "four points" of the Paris Declaration to the Government of Ecuador, for its "adhesion" to the same. Our Convention

[1] See above, this part, p. 387, note 2.
[2] Above, this part, September 25, October 2, and October 25, 1856, docs. 2427, 2428, and 2430.
[3] Not included in this publication, since its character is sufficiently indicated in the circular instruction which went to the legations of the United States in Argentina and Ecuador, as well as to others, on the same date, and which is above, vol. 1, pt. 1, August 29, 1856, doc. 34. It is printed, however, in *British and Foreign State Papers,* vol. 55, pp. 589–99.
[4] Despatches, Ecuador, vol. 4. Received January 30.

(of the 9th of April last)[1] had been presented to Congress at the commencement of its session by the Executive; and in accordance with the instructions contained in your despatches numbered 32 and 33, of the dates 14th July and 29th August,[2] I presented the question to the Minister of Foreign Relations in my communications of 25th September and 25th October,[3] (copies of which I have hertofore forwarded to the Department) and urged upon this Government, somewhat at length, the views of the President of the United States touching the question, as contained in your communications to me, above recited, and in your despatch to Count Sartiges of the 28th July.[4]   And, as I have already advised you, the whole matter was referred to Congress by the Executive.

In frequent and frank conversations I have held with the Executive Authorities, as well as with many of the most intelligent Members of Congress, they uniformly expressed an acquiescence in, and, as I think, really *felt* a sympathy for our views of this question, in preference to those of the confederated monarchies of Europe, as enunciated in the Paris Declaration. They were consequently slow in embracing the European dogma; and it cost the Representatives of those Powers here a good deal of effort, accompanied by personal importunity with the Members, before they could persuade the Chambers to declare their adhesion to the "four points."

But preliminary to this "adhesion", and in deference to the strong representations I had made of the views of my Government, they had unconditionally ratified our Neutral Rights Convention of the 9th of April, knowing at the time that it could not be confirmed at Washington until the *next* session of our Congress, although by the terms of the Instrument its ratification by the United States should have preceded that by Ecuador.   And I am well persuaded, that had the *amendment* proposed by yourself to the "four points,"[5] been embraced in the provisions of the Convention, it would as promptly have received the approval of this Government, as it now has under the present rather anomalous aspect of the case.

From the isolated position of Ecuador with reference to the commerce of the world, and from the fact that this Government possesses little or no war or mercantile marine, her Statesmen do not very readily comprehend the importance of the question of Neutral Rights, as practically applicable to their case; and there is a manifest desire on their part to avoid any further action in the matter, lest troublesome discussions should be excited with Chile, or their relations with England and France be marred.   On the return of President Robles from Guayaquil, however, I shall urge the Minister to a decision with regard to your proposition for *amending* the "four points," &c.

With high regard [etc.].

[1] Above, this part, p. 372, note 4.
[2] Same as instructions Nos. 20 and 24 of these dates, to James A. Peden, U. S. Minister in Argentina, above, vol. 1, docs. 32 and 34.   [3] Above, this part, docs. 2427 and 2430.
[4] Not included in this publication.   Concerning it, see above, this part, p. 391, note 3.
[5] See above, this part, p. 387, note 2.

2434

Philo White, United States Minister Resident in Ecuador, to William L. Marcy, Secretary of State of the United States [1]

No. 99—Confidential.   QUITO, *December 31, 1856.*

SIR: I have the honor to inclose, herewith, a despatch for the President of the United States, containing a certified copy, marked F, of the Decree of the Ecuatorian Congress,[2] ratifying our *Neutral Rights* Convention with this Government, concluded by myself on the part of the United States, the 9th April last, in pursuance of authority from the President, and instructions from yourself on the subject, and which was forwarded to the President on the 16th April.[3]

I have the honor [etc.].

2435

Philo White, United States Minister Resident in Ecuador, to William L. Marcy, Secretary of State of the United States [4]

Confidential.   QUITO, *February 20, 1857.*

SIR: A diplomatic episode has recently been enacted in this Capital, of which it may not be amiss for me to advise the Department, since it is likely to interrupt, for a time, the cordial relations between this Government and a principal Power of Europe.

I have from time to time kept the Department fully advised of what has transpired here with regard to the question of the "Four Points" enunciated by the Congress of Paris, and the proposition of our Government to *amend* the European dogma[5] by incorporating therein the principle that *private property* should enjoy the same immunity from capture by a belligerent *at sea* as *on shore.*

This whole matter having been referred to the National Congress by the Executive,—including the communication of the English and French Chargés asking the "adhesion" of Ecuador to the "four points," and my several representations to the Minister on the subject,[6] in exposition of the principles and views of our Government,—the *Chambers* became the forum where the question was to be discussed and determined. And as I have stated on former occasions, *personal appliances* were resorted to by the Chargés in question, for the purpose of obtaining a declaration of the Chambers adverse

[1] Despatches, Ecuador, vol. 4.   Received January 29.
[2] Neither one is included in this publication.   His despatch to the President is substantially in the same wording as this one to the Secretary of State, and the content of the decree is adequately indicated within this despatch.
[3] See above, this part, doc. 2424, and in note 4 thereto is the convention of April 9, 1856.   [4] Despatches, Ecuador, vol. 4.   Received March 30.
[5] Above, this part, p. 387, note 2, is the proposed amendment.
[6] Above, this part, *passim.*

to our principle.   As might have been expected, bad feeling on the part of the irascible French Chargé grew out of this undignified mode of conducting a diplomatic discussion!

As this Government possesses neither a war nor mercantile marine to speak of, the question of Neutral Rights, &c., in all its phases, is an utter *abstraction* to them.   And in the issues that are presented to them by other nations touching this matter, their first desire is to *accommodate all* friendly powers by an *acquiescence* in their propositions, where by so doing they can preserve the semblance of consistency; but if this cannot be done, their next aim is, to "shirk" these issues!

This was, in effect, the "decision" come to in the last Congress,—for they ratified, unqualifiedly, our Convention of the 9th of April last[1] in relation to Neutral Commerce, &c., and would most unquestionably have been equally prompt in its approval had what is called "Mr. Marcy's amendment" been incorporated into that instrument, and they likewise, without reservation, declared their "adhesion" to the "Four Points"!

Not long after the adjournment of Congress, at an interview I had with the Minister of Foreign Relations, the matter of our Convention on Neutral Commerce became the subject of conversation; in the course of which, he remarked that, in his private judgment, our proposition for exempting private property from capture, &c., was as correct in principle as it was philanthropic in its scope and tendencies; and he expressed his belief that it would soon become a settled principle of international law.   He at the same time promised to furnish me with a copy of the Decree of Congress approving our Convention; which he did, shortly after, and which I inclosed to the President of the United States on the 24th December.[2]

This last circumstance,—that is, conceding to me a priority as to time in furnishing us with copies of the Congressional approvals of our respective propositions, afforded a pretext for an *explosion* between the French Chargé and the Minister of Foreign Relations, which resulted in a suspension of diplomatic intercourse with Mons. Andres Villamus by this Government!

The two Chargés having learned that I had been favored with a copy of the Decree of the Chambers by which our Convention was ratified, in anticipation of their being furnished with the Act of *adhesion* to their "four points," sought and obtained an interview with the Minister; and in the course of explanations with regard to the object of the interview, Mons. Villamus became excited, and, despite Mr. Cope's efforts to restrain him, he indulged in undiplomatic language, charging the Ecuatorian Government with duplicity, with disingenuousness, &c.: To which, the Minister retorted sharply; and but for the peace-restoring offices of Mr. Cope, (the English Chargé) there might have been a personal rencounter!

[1] Above, this part, p. 372, note 4.
[2] The decree was sent to the President on December 31; it is not included in this publication since its content is sufficiently indicated within this despatch.

By the first mail-steamer from Guayaquil for Europe after this occurrence, the Ecuatorian Government sent instructions to their Chargé in Paris, to request of the French Emperor the *recal* of Mons. Villamus! And it was not until after the departure of that Steamer, that they advised the Chargé of what they had done! Thus getting one month's start of him in *their own* representation of the circumstances attending the *imbroglio!*

This Mons. Andres Villamus, is the same personage who gained a somewhat equivocal notoriety for the busy and officious part he enacted in the diplomatic opposition with which I found myself confronted in the negotiation of our *Galápagos Huano Treaty;* and who was afterwards one of the most persistent and clamorous of the agents who instigated the Chilian Government to send an Embassy Extraordinary to Quito, with the sole design of thwarting the objects of that Treaty, and of neutralizing an alleged undue North American influence in Ecuador. Troubled waters seem to constitute that gentleman's favorite element.

With high respect [etc.].

2436

Philo White, United States Minister Resident in Ecuador, to Antonio Mata, Minister of Foreign Affairs of Ecuador [1]

A   QUITO, *February 25, 1857.*

The undersigned, Minister Resident of the United States, takes the liberty to call the attention of His Excellc'y the Minister of Foreign Relations of Ecuador, to a communication which he had the honor to address to His Excellency under date of the 13th of December last.[2]

Through the medium of that communication, the undersigned took occasion to make certain propositions to the Government of Ecuador, by express direction of the President of the United States, touching the privileges and immunities that should of right be extended to neutral vessels during the conflicts of belligerent powers on the high seas, and to which he invited the assent of this Government. And on subsequent occasions, he took the liberty verbally to iterate and reiterate that request, at interviews with His Excellc'y the Minister, who, as the undersigned understood him at the time, expressed his (Dr. Mata's) personal acquiescence in those propositions, which he admitted were fair and equitable, and based upon just and humane principles,—assuring the undersigned, at the same time, that an answer to his

[1] Despatches, Ecuador, vol. 4; enclosed with White to the Secretary of State, No. 106, March 13, 1857, below, this part, doc. 2438.
[2] Not found under this date, nor under the date, December 3, as it is referred to in the Minister of Foreign Affairs' reply to this note, below, this part, March 11, 1857, doc. 2437. From the resumé of its contents within this note, however, it seems to be substantially the same as his note of October 25, 1856, above, this part, doc. 2430.

communication should speedily be given, a pressure of other duties upon the Executive Departments having prevented an earlier attention to the matter.

Since the date of that communication, information has been received, that the Emperors of Russia and of France, and the Prime Minister and Press of Great Britain, have expressed their full approval of this measure of philanthropy and of justice; and by no one of the nations of Christendom with whom communications have been held on the subject, have those propositions been dissented from,—while, on the contrary, the Government of the United States has been commended by enlightened Statesmen and the good men of all nations, for having been the first to propose, and ever since zealously to advocate, this great measure of wisdom and of humanity, which is destined ere long to become a universally recognized principle in the maritime law of the world.

Confiding in the liberal and enlightened counsels which so happily bear sway in the Administration of the Ecuatorian Government, the undersigned will not allow himself to doubt, that the decision of its Executive in relation to this interesting question, will be in entire accordance with the beneficent principles of the age, and in full harmony with those sentiments of an expansive philanthropy which pervade the Christian world at this day.

But should Ecuador, in her sovereign capacity, see fit to assume a position with regard to this measure peculiar to herself, the undersigned could only express his regret at her determination, without undertaking to question her prerogative in the adoption of whatever course of policy she might deem it expedient to pursue under the circumstances: Yet, let the decision of this Government in regard to the question under discussion be what it may, the undersigned believes, in view of the amicable relations now existing between the two countries, that the requirements of diplomatic usage entitle him, after the lapse of more than two months from the date of his communication, to again urge a response from His Excellc'y the Minister of Foreign Relations to so reasonable and courteous a request, without any further delay than circumstances of the most imperative kind shall absolutely demand.

And the undersigned begs to reiterate [etc.].

2437

Antonio Mata, Minister of Foreign Affairs of Ecuador, to Philo White, United States Minister Resident in Ecuador [1]

[TRANSLATION]

B   QUITO, *March 11, 1857.*

Having submitted to the examination and consideration of His Excellency, Charged with the Executive Power the dispatch of December 3,[2] in which His Excellency the Minister Resident was so good as to propose formally to the adhesion of Ecuador the principle by which the Government of the United States has amplified the first of the four points of the Declaration of the Congress of Paris, together with the communications which His Excellency the Minister had addressed to this office under dates of September 25 and October 25 of the preceding year,[3] and the reply of the Government of the United States to Count de Sartiges, Minister of France[4] upon the proposed acceptance of the said declaration; the undersigned has been directed by His Excellency to reply to His Excellency Mr. Philo White in the following terms:

The Ecuadorean Government believes to be just, philanthropic, and very adequate for diminishing in great part the evils which private property and the commerce of belligerent nations suffer on the high seas in time of war, the principle that "the private property of the subjects or citizens of a belligerent is exempt on the high sea from capture by publicly armed ships of the other belligerent, excepting contraband of war"; and he has implicitly expressed this same opinion heretofore, when, acceding to a request of His Excellency the Minister Resident, he submitted this matter to the deliberation of the Legislative Chambers which were in session during the latter months of the year just past.

The conduct observed by the Government of the undersigned upon that occasion was founded upon the circumstance that the Executive Power lacked the necessary authority to express its adhesion to the principle mentioned by a solemn act which would have the force of a law of the Republic; and as the reason for such procedure still obtains, it is not within the power of the Government of Ecuador to satisfy the just desires manifested by His Excellency Mr. White more fully than by offering to again call the attention of the next Legislature to this matter, which it was unable to consider at the preceding sessions.

The undersigned [etc.].

[1] Despatches, Ecuador, vol. 4; enclosed with White to the Secretary of State, No. 106, March 13, 1857, below, this part, doc. 2438.
[2] Not found.   See above, this part, p. 395, note 2.
[3] Both are above, this part, docs. 2427 and 2430.
[4] Not included in this publication, since its character is indicated in the circular instruction sent to the legations of the United States, in Eucador, Argentina, and several other countries, above, vol. I, August 29, 1856, doc. 34.   It is printed, however, in *British and Foreign State Papers*, vol. 55, pp. 589–99.

2438

Philo White, United States Minister Resident in Ecuador, to Lewis Cass, Secretary of State of the United States [1]

No. 106   QUITO, *March 13, 1857.*

SIR: I have the honor to inclose, herewith, copies of two communications (marked A and B)[2] that have recently passed between myself and the Minister of Foreign Relations here, in regard to the question of exempting private property from the hazards of War on the high seas.

It will be seen from the Minister's last note to me on the subject, dated the 11th inst., and marked B, that I have finally succeeded, after persistently following him up with written communications and personal conferences during nearly four months past, in drawing out the Executive Government of Ecuador from the non-committal stand it had hitherto maintained with regard to Mr. Marcy's *amendment*[3] to the "four points" of the Paris Declaration. This Government has now unreservedly declared itself satisfied of the justice and philanthropy of our favorite principle, and expressed its full belief that the measure we propose will prove efficacious in relieving private property and the commerce of the world from most of the disasters they have heretofore suffered on the high seas in time of war.

The President, however, assumes that the Executive is not clothed with adequate power to enter into any arrangement more formal than this declaration in regard to the measure, without express authority from the National Congress,—which authorization had to be obtained previously to his declaring the adhesion of Ecuador to the "four points." And he has proffered to recommend our proposition to the attention of the Ecuatorian Congress at its next session.

With the highest regard [etc.].

2439

Philo White, United States Minister Resident in Ecuador, to Antonio Mata, Minister of Foreign Affairs of Ecuador [4]

A   QUITO, *March 20, 1857.*

The undersigned, Minister Resident of the United States, presents his compliments to His Excellency the Minister of Foreign Relations of Ecuador,

[1] Despatches, Ecuador, vol. 4.   Received April 30.
[2] Both are to be found above, this part, February 25 and March 11, 1857, docs. 2436 and 2437.
[3] See above, this part, p. 387, note 2.
[4] Despatches, Ecuador, vol. 4; enclosed with White to the Secretary of State, No. 108, April 4, 1857, below, this part, doc. 2441.

and takes the liberty to transmit to His Excellency a *printed slip* (affixed hereto) purporting to be a translation of the *tenth Article* of a Tripartite Treaty, (or Alliance) between the Republics of Ecuador, Peru, and Chile, bearing date the 15th day of September last, and which was approved and ratified by the Executive and Legislative branches of this Government in the month of November following.[1]

When this Treaty was under consideration by the National Chambers, rumor gave to some of its provisions an interpretation in conflict with the principles uniformly held and maintained by the Government of the United States, subversive of the rights of that nation, and prejudicial to the interests of its citizens,— rights and principles long acknowledged, and sanctioned as well by international law as by the practical usages of the principal Powers of Christendom.

> *Article 10:* The high contracting parties shall adopt, for their mutual relations, the following principles: A neutral flag covers the merchandize belonging to the enemy, except contraband of war; neutral merchandize is free on board a hostile ship, and shall not be subject to confiscation except in the case of contraband of war: Likewise they agree to give up the employment of Privateers as a means of hostility against any of the contracting parties, and to consider and treat as pirates those who do not conform to this Article; likewise they will consider and treat as pirates their native or naturalized citizens who may accept Letters of Marque, or commissions for aiding and co-operating in a hostile way, with the enemy of any of them.

And at an interview with which *Dr. Mata* then honored the undersigned, the *tenth Article* was, as a matter of courtesy, shown to him in the form in which it appeared in the official draft of the Treaty in possession of the Ecuatorian Government, without however permitting the undersigned,—as it was quite proper he should not have been, nor did he ask to be permitted,—to examine any other portion of it: And His Excellc'y took that occasion, in view of the prevalent rumors in relation to the matter, to assure the undersigned, that the declaration of *outlawry* against "Privateers," as contained in said Article, and the denunciation against that class of cruizers and their armaments the like summary and sanguinary penalties of destruction and death that are affixed to the crime of *piracy*, were not intended to be made applicable to vessels commissioned by the Government of the United States, but referred solely to "Corsairs" pertaining to, or manned by the citizens, or sailing under the respective flags, of those nations alone who were parties to the Treaty.   And this explanation and disavowal on the part of His Excellc'y the Minister, seemed to the undersigned entirely reconcilable with the phraseology of the Article as he then read and understood it.

The affixed article appeared thus in the manuscript volume.

But it seems that some of the public journals in the United States are disposed to put a less favorable construction upon that Article; and as the undersigned cannot, from the casual reading he was enabled to give it at the moment it was exhibited to him, recal its precise phraseology,—he would esteem it a favor, were His Excellc'y the Minister to inform him, whether the translation of the Article in question (hereto affixed) is a faithful rendition of the original as contained in the ratified Treaty? And whether the conversation between D^r. Mata and the undersigned, on the occasion above referred to, with regard to the true interpretation of the 10th Article, is in substance correctly narrated herein?

And the undersigned [etc.].

2440

Antonio Mata, Minister of Foreign Affairs of Ecuador, to Philo White, United States Minister Resident in Ecuador [1]

[TRANSLATION]

B

Quito, *April 1, 1857.*

The undersigned, Minister of Foreign Relations of Ecuador, has had the honor to receive the despatch dated the 20th ultimo,[2] which His Excellency the Minister Resident of the United States has addressed to him with the purpose of requesting the undersigned to state whether, in reference to the project of the Treaty of Union celebrated between this Republic and the Republics of Peru and Chile, the English translation of Article 10 thereof, which His Excellency the Minister has enclosed in said despatch,[3] does or does not conform to the original filed in this Ministry, and moreover to state whether the account of the meeting which took place between His Excellency the Minister and the undersigned in regard to this matter is correctly related by His Excellency the Minister in the note to which this is a reply.

The undersigned is pleased to assure His Excellency the Minister Resident of the United States that the translation of Article 10 of the above-cited Treaty of Union does not conform prefectly with the original before him; since in place of the phrase, "*y en considerar y tratar como piratas à los que lo hicieren en el caso à que se refiere este articulo,*" ("and to consider and treat as pirates *those who shall have practised it in the case referred to in this article,*" have been substituted the words of the English which correspond to these words: "*y én considerar y tratar como piratas à aquellos que no se conformaren con este articulo.*" ("and to consider and treat as pirates *those who do not conform to this Article.*") This alteration in the words produces, naturally, a

---

[1] Despatches, Ecuador, vol. 4; enclosed with White to the Secretary of State, No. 108, April 4, 1857, below, this part, doc. 2441. [2] Above, this part, doc. 2439.
[3] The article is printed in the body of the text of White's note, above, this part, March 20, 1857, doc. 2439.

complete variation in the sense.   The article as worded in the original clearly confines to the contracting parties themselves the abolition of privateering and the penalty decreed to make this abolition effective.

But the translation submitted by His Excellency the Minister furnishes sufficient reason for believing that the signatory Nations of the Treaty have desired to impose their stipulations upon other sovereign States, thus attributing to themselves the faculty, which they do not possess, nor can any Nation in the world possess, of dictating laws to others.

Even should the terms of the Article in question give occasion for doubt (which they do not) the rules of good interpretation would prevent a meaning being attributed to them which is absurd in every light; and such has been the character which some newspapers of the United States have been inclined to give to them, as pointed out by His Excellency the Minister.

With respect to the interview recorded by His Excellency the Minister, the undersigned is pleased to affirm that the conversation and confidential exhibition of Article 10 of the Treaty, which took place in that conference, happened exactly in the manner related by His Excellency the Minister Resident in his esteemed despatch.

May His Excellency [etc.].

2441

Philo White, United States Minister Resident in Ecuador, to Lewis Cass, Secretary of State of the United States [1]

No. 108   QUITO, *April 4, 1857.*

SIR: In my despatch N⁰ 95, dated the 19th November,[2] I had the honor to advise the Department of the result of my inquiries, up to that period, with regard to the rumored provisions of a "Treaty of Union" then recently negotiated between Chile, Peru, and Ecuador.

While the consideration of that Treaty was pending before Congress, (both Houses possessing an advisory prerogative in the ratification of treaties) common fame attributed to it stipulations subversive of our national rights, and in conflict with the principles of maritime warfare uniformly held and acted upon by our Government.   I consequently thought it my duty to seek a conference with the Minister of Foreign Relations, and call his attention to the subject.   At this conference I inquired of him, confidentially, whether the Treaty contained any stipulation that could rightfully be construed as giving countenance to these rumors, as affecting the belligerent rights of the United States?   To assure me that it did not, the Minister brought out the authenticated copy of the Instrument which was on file in his Department, and exhibited to me, in confidence, the *tenth Article*, which

---

[1] Despatches, Ecuador, vol. 4.   Received May 30.   [2] Above, this part, doc. 2432.

he averred was the only provision it contained material to the point in question. According to my own rendition of that Article, its prohibitions, denunciations &c., did not seem to affect the rights or privileges of any other nations than those who were parties to it: And I so informed the Department at the time.

But it seems that a Lima correspondent of a New York newspaper, by clandestine means, obtained access to the entire document, and published a translation of it in advance of its final conclusion by an exchange of ratifications between the three contracting parties. The *tenth article* of this translation seeming to me to be somewhat discrepant with my recollection of the true import and apparent intent of the original, as exhibited to me by the Minister of Foreign Relations in November last, I took the liberty to invite his attention to this surreptitiously promulgated version of the Treaty, in a communication dated the 20th ultimo,—a copy of which I herewith inclose, marked A[1]: To this the Minister promptly responded, and I now have the honor to inclose you a copy of his answer, marked B,[2] for the information of the Department.

It will be seen that the Minister treats the *tenth article* of the translation, as a perve[r]sion of the true interpretation of the original; and frankly acknowledges that the defective rendering of that article, as it stands in the translation, fully warranted me in instituting an inquiry into its authenticity. And he characterized as absurd the bare supposition that the three States, parties to the Treaty in question, would for a moment assume to dictate to other and sovereign powers new dogmas of international law, &c., without their full acquiescence therein.

Whatever may have been the occult motives of that leading State whose promptings unquestionably gave birth to this "triple Alliance," in counseling a measure so equivocal in its bearings upon the interests of the United States, yet I cannot discern any thing so materially objectionable in the phrase of the document, when taken in connexion with the Ecuatorian Minister's explanations and disavowals, as to warrant me in entering a special *protest* against the *implied* jealousy manifested therein towards our country.

I shall therefore await other developments in regard to this Hispano-American "Alliance," or be governed by instructions from home, before taking further action in the matter.

With sentiments of high regard [etc.].

[1] Above, this part, March 20, 1857, doc. 2439.   [2] *Ibid.*, April 1, 1857, doc. 2440.

2442

Philo White, United States Minister Resident in Ecuador, to Lewis Cass, Secretary of State of the United States [1]

No. 119   QUITO, *June 30, 1857.*

SIR: Begging to refer to my despatch Nº 106, of date 13th March last,[2] as well as to the communications accompanying it, (marked A and B,) from the Minister of Foreign Relations of this Government,[3]—I would most respectfully inquire, whether it is the desire of the President and yourself, that I should follow up the course of proceedings I had already instituted under instructions from your predecessor, with regard to obtaining the adhesion of this Government to the *amendment* proposed by ours to the Paris "Four Points" in relation to maritime law, Viz: That *all private property* shall henceforth be exempt from the hazards of capture and confiscation by belligerents on the high seas?

I have heretofore had the honor to advise the Department, that the Executive Branch of this Government referred the matter of the *"four points"* of the Paris Declaration, proposed for their adhesion by the Representatives of England and France, to the National Congress for a decision of the question, —and that the action of the Chambers thereon was affirmative.   The present Administration, although it will have been seen that they acquiesce in the justice and philanthropy of "Mr. Marcy's *amendment*," (so called) have now proposed to give the question of adhesion to *our new principle*, the same direction they did that of the "four points," for its solution.

The Congress of Ecuador will assemble for the despatch of business in September; and I should be gratified if you could honor me, at as early a day as practicable, with instructions which shall serve as my warrant, either to urge the question to a final result at the approaching session of the National Chambers, or to leave it in *abeyance* until further advised on the subject.

With sentiments of high regard [etc.].

2443

Philo White, United States Minister Resident in Ecuador, to Lewis Cass, Secretary of State of the United States [4]

No. 136   QUITO, *January 1, 1858.*

SIR: In acknowledging the receipt of your despatch Nº 40, dated 18th. September,[5] in which you inform me "that it is not the intention of the Presi-

[1] Despatches, Ecuador, vol. 4.   Received July 28.   [2] Above, this part, doc. 2438.
[3] Above, this part, February 25 and March 11, 1857, docs. 2436 and 2437, are the documents so marked; "A" however, is a note from White to the Minister of Foreign Affairs.
[4] Despatches, Ecuador, vol. 5.   Received March 1.
[5] Not included in this publication, since its content is indicated within this despatch.

dent, at this time, to pursue the consideration of the subject" of the *amendment*[1] proposed by the late Secretary of State to the "Four Points" of the Paris Congress in regard to the property of neutrals, I have the honor to state that immediately on receipt of your despatch, I communicated the determination of my Government to the Minister of Foreign Relations, requesting that he would advise the Senate, who then had the subject under consideration, (it having previously received an affirmative vote in the House of Representatives) of my own and my Government's desire that no further proceedings in relation to the matter should take place in that body.

But learning that the Senate would probably take a final vote on the question at their night session of that same day, and fearing lest the Minister might not procure a translation of my Note for a day or two, I repaired in person to the Senate Chamber, to indicate to that body the altered state of the case, with an expression of my wish that their action thereon might be deferred until the Minister could communicate with them in regard to the matter.   To which they politely assented; but during their next day's sitting, a final vote was taken on the pending question without hearing from the Minister,—the Senate, through that vote, expressing it as their opinion, that the object sought by the United States, could be more effectually accomplished by *negotiation* than by legislative enactment!

When it was suggested by some of the Members, that the Senate would stultify themselves by such a vote, inasmuch as they had already acted in a case identical with this, having last year adopted the "Four Points" of the Paris Congress as a *law* of this Republic,—it was answered on the part of the majority, that since the Executive Administration had deemed it expedient to conclude a *Treaty* with the Minister of the United States resident in Ecuador, he having been invested with ample powers from his Government for that purpose, in which were enunciated most of the principles of international law embraced in the Paris Declaration, and which Treaty was approved and ratified by both Houses of the Ecuatorian Congress, but which the Cabinet at Washington, although it was a measure of their own prompting, had suffered to lie dormant ever since,—it were an easy task for the Diplomatists having the matter in charge, to give effect to the proposed *amendment* by appending it to the Convention of the 9th April 1856,[2] as a Supplemental or *Additional Article*.   The treaty-making power having been resorted to from choice by the North American Government, for proclaiming to the world these axioms of maritime law, any desired alteration or amendment of the original declaration could, in the opinion of the Senators, be more appropriately attained by treaty stipulation than by legislative action,"— &c. &c.

The President of the Senate, fearing lest the rather clumsy proceedings of that body in their final disposition of the question of the "Fifth Point,"

[1] See above, this part, p. 387, note 2, for the amendment.   [2] *Ibid.*, p. 372, note 4.

(thus styled by the Minister of Foreign Relations,) might prove distasteful to me, addressed me a familiar and apologetic Note on the subject; to which I responded with equal frankness, that the question, at that stage of the Senate's action upon it, did not as I conceived involve that body in any parliamentary dilemma, but admitted of a very ready solution, in perfect accordance with Senatorial dignity and diplomatic etiquette. But as there was now no practical point at issue, I begged to assure him, that no considerations of mere etiquette could, in the least degree, lessen the sincere regard and high respect I cherished for the Honorable Body over which he presided.

The Senate is politically disaffected towards the present Administration; and their perverse action with regard to the question of the "Fifth Point," is attributed to the fact, that it was urged upon their attention as a "Ministerial measure." Another circumstance, however, may have had no small influence in determining their final vote: A rumor seems to have come to their ears, through a channel inexplicable to me, that the Executive Authorities of the United States had ratified the Treaty concluded with *Perú*, affirming that "free ships make free goods," &c., while the Convention previously entered into with Ecuador, containing similar stipulations in all respects, had been treated with silence and neglect by the Cabinet at Washington. I promptly expressed my disbelief in the rumor at the time, altho' I could not authoritively contradict it. Very recently, however, I have met with the annexed Article[1] in the newspapers, the purport of which seems to have come to the knowledge of the politicians here long ere I was apprised of any such report.

It would of course be a source of very great relief to this Government, as well as to myself, could we have any assurance as to the intentions of the President and yourself, with regard to an eventual ratification of the Convention I concluded with this Republic on the 9th April 1856, and referred to above.

With very high respect [etc.].

[1] Not included in this publication. This brief article, dated Washington, November 6, 1857, stated that a treaty had been proclaimed between the United States and Peru providing that "free ships make free goods, and that the property of neutrals on board enemy's vessels is not subject to detention or confiscation, unless the same be contraband of war," and that these principles are to apply to the commerce of all Powers that consent to adopt them as permanent and immutable.

2444

Philo White, United States Minister Resident in Ecuador, to Lewis Cass, Secretary of State of the United States [1]

[EXTRACT]

No. 144   QUITO, *April 17, 1858.*

SIR: . . . Much bad blood continues to manifest itself between Ecuador and Peru. The question of territorial limits, is for the moment held in abeyance, while the new Minister Resident from Perú, (Señor Juan C. Cavero) is engaged in an acrimonious discussion,—or rather *controversy,*—with this Government, on frivolous points of international etiquette; in which, it seems to me, both parties manifest a forgetfulness of, or a culpable unacquaintance with those diplomatic courtesies which should never be lost sight of in both official and personal intercourse between the representatives of friendly powers. As a sample of the asperity of style of these people in their official disputations, I inclose herewith N⁰ 277 of "El Seis de Marzo," containing the initial communications of a lengthened correspondence between the Peruvian Minister Resident and the head of the Foreign Office here,[2] in which they upbraid each other, in the *most expressive terms*, with a violation of those rules of international comity, which the diplomatic code recognized by all civilized nations has made imperative in the intercourse between the accredited Agents of independent sovereignties.

Notwithstanding this bellicose tone of the two Ministers, it is nevertheless not at all probable that their respective Governments will thereby be precipitated into relations any more belligerent than have existed between them for several years past. . . .

With sentiments of high respect [etc.].

2445

Francisco Pablo Ycaza, Minister of Foreign Affairs of Ecuador, to Philo White, United States Minister Resident in Ecuador [3]

A   QUITO, *March [May] 6, 1858.*

My Government has received reliable information to the effect that an attempt has been made abroad to give a sinister interpretation to the Con-

[1] Despatches, Ecuador, vol. 5. Received May 31.
The omitted portions at the beginning and end of this despatch relate, chiefly, to the temporary appointment of Sr. Ycaza as Minister of Foreign Affairs, and to the recall of all the diplomatic agents of Ecuador abroad, because no appropriation for their salaries had been made in the last Congress.   [2] Not included in this publication.
[3] Despatches, Ecuador, vol. 5; enclosed with White to the Secretary of State, No. 147, May 19, 1858, below, this part, doc. 2446.
No doubt, inadvertently, in the Spanish copy in the manuscript volume, from which this translation was made, the date of this note was written "6 de Marzo" instead of "6 de Mayo." See reference to it in the accompanying despatch.

vention which it celebrated with its British creditors on the appropriation (adjudicación) to them of various portions of wild land of the Republic, in payment of that part of the Colombian debt which fell to its share, and in fulfillment of previous laws and conventions.

Being unable, therefore, to accept such interpretations, discreditable to Ecuador and to the Governments with whom it is supposed to have contracted I have been directed by His Excellency the Vice-President, Charged with the Executive Power, to apprize Your Excellency of the true terms of the Convention[1] to which I refer, which will be found in official periodical No. 281 which Your Excellency will find attached to the present communication; my

The articles of this convention, printed in *El Seis De Marzo*, dated May 7, 1858, follow:

[TRANSLATION]

QUITO, *September 21, 1857.*

Article 1. In payment of the value of the provisional Ecuadorian bonds which have been issued in London by the Commission established for the purpose, award is made to the holders of said bonds, and in conformity with Article 24 of the Convention of November 6, 1854, of the public lands described below.

One hundred thousand square "cuadras" between the Mataje and Tola rivers and one hundred thousand square "cuadras" on the Salima, Atacames, and Sua rivers, starting from the common confluence of the three rivers: all these lands being in the province of Esmeraldas, at the price of three pesos a "cuadra."

One million square "cuadras" on the banks of the Zamora River, starting from the nearest possible point of the town of Gualaquiza, at the price of four reales per "cuadra."

One million square "cuadras" in the canton of Canelos, province of Oriente, on the banks of the river Bobonaza, and running from the confluence of the latter with the Pastaza toward the west, at four reales per "cuadra."

Four hundred and ten thousand and two hundred square "cuadras" between the river Cañar which descends to Jesus María, toward the north and the road to the town of Pucará, to Balao, at the rate of three pesos a "cuadra."

Article 2. In case there should be no public lands, or not in sufficient quantity, in the last region indicated in the preceding paragraph, the bondholders promise to take an equal quantity, and for the same price, in the province of Esmeraldas.

Article 3. The immigrants who are to inhabit the lands which have been adjudicated by virtue of the preceding articles shall be subject to the following conditions and shall enjoy the following privileges:

1. They shall recognize now and forever the sovereignty of Ecuador over the said lands and over the towns which may be established there;

2. They shall be subject to the Constitution and laws of the Republic and to the established authorities or those which may hereafter be established;

3. Immigrants shall enjoy the rights of natives and citizens of Ecuador, in conformity with the Constitution of the Republic, provided that they comply with the requirements which it establishes;

4. They shall be exempt for fifteen years from every kind of taxes or personal contribution which may exist, or which may be established hereafter, as well as from the payment of tithes and first fruits;

5. They shall likewise be exempt, for the same period, from all military service, except in case of a piratical invasion of the Republic, or the invasion of the said colonies by any barbarous tribe.

Article 4. The governors of the provinces in which the lands to which this convention refers are situated, shall give to the bondholders possession of said lands, upon order of the Executive Power. Expenses for surveying shall be borne equally by the contracting parties.

Sole section. For the better understanding of this article, it is declared: that the Government of Ecuador shall, in delivering the adjudicated lands, deal only with the Commission of Bondholders, established in London, or with its duly authorized representative, and never separately with the holders of said bonds, nor with the colonists who may present themselves to occupy the said lands, the distribution of which is the

Government hoping that this publication alone will suffice to assure the Government which Your Excellency represents of the legitimacy of those proceedings.

To this end I have the honor [etc.].

2446

Philo White, United States Minister Resident in Ecuador, to Lewis Cass, Secretary of State of the United States [1]

No. 147—Confidential.   QUITO, *May 19, 1858.*

SIR: I took the liberty to inform the Department, in my Nº 144, of date 17th April ultº,[2] that an *imbroglio* between Ecuador and Perú had grown out of the dispute as to the territorial boundaries of the two Republics. Their discussions, instead of leading to a solution of their difficulties, appear to have aggravated them, until the question has become entangled in rather an ugly complication, involving other powers and extraneous matters.

Some of the English holders of the Old Colombian Bonds, despairing of being able to effect any ready liquidation of Ecuador's proportion of that Debt, agreed to take wild lands for colonization, in part satisfaction of their Bonds; and they sent an Agent and Engineer out here, to select the lands that might be awarded by this Government for that purpose. It was in the *location* of these "tierras baldías," that the Peruvian Minister, who appears to be an erratic genius, found occasion to initiate a rather bellicose discussion with this Government,—which has eventuated in solemn "Protests," and, it would seem, in an appeal to *France* for her *intervention* in behalf of Peru, to protect the integrity of her soil against the *encroachments* of the United States and Great Britain!!

The Government of Ecuador considers the misrepresentations by the Peruvian Minister of the true merits of the question between them, of so sinister and grave a nature, as to warrant it in addressing to me an official despatch on the subject,—(see the Minister's letter, 6th inst., marked A,

---

duty of the Commission which has negotiated them, and which represents all parties interested in them.

Article 5. In taking possession of the public lands, the holders of provisional bonds shall deliver said bonds to the Government of Ecuador to an amount equal to the value of the lands which they receive, the debt recognized as due them being thus cancelled at the rate of 21½ per cent of the interest due and not paid by January 1, 1855, accruing on the loans made to Colombia in 1822 and 1824.

And in order that the preceding articles may have full public faith and may be fulfilled and observed on the part of the Government of Ecuador and of the holders of the bonds, we sign this agreement in duplicate and affix our rubrics thereto.

F. P. ICAZA.
GEORGE S. PRITCHETT.

[1] Despatches, Ecuador, vol. 5.   Received June 28.   [2] Above, this part, doc. 2444.

accompanied by a printed copy of the Agreement with the English Bond Holders, which is attached,)[1]—with a request that the same may be communicated to my Government, as affording a truthful exposition of the matter of the "tierras baldías."

The Peruvian Minister,—who, the diplomatic wags about Quito say, has been chafed into a "medio-loco" state of mind by a quixotic controversy with the Editors of "La Democracia" newspaper, who are more than a match for him,—by implicating myself and my Government in the imbroglio between Peru and Ecuador, has been guilty of so gratuitous and discourteous an act, that I felt called upon to address M*r*. *Cavero* an official Note on the subject, in order to disabuse his mind of the utterly groundless impressions with which it seems to have been possessed in regard to our course of policy. —A copy of my communication to M*r* C., is hereto annexed, marked B.[2]

All of which, I trust, so far as my agency is concerned, will meet the approval of the Honorable the Secretary of State.

With very high respect [etc.].

[1] Above, this part, March [May] 6, 1858, doc. 2445, and note 1, p. 407.
[2] In this communication to Cavero, which follows, White states, in a footnote to the extract contained therein, that "I have made the foregoing translation from a Spanish extract obtained from an indisputable source, as the true language contained in Mr. Cavero's despatches on the Boundary Question":

Philo White, United States Minister Resident in Ecuador, to Juan Celestino Cavero, Peruvian Minister Resident in Ecuador

B   QUITO, *May 11, 1858.*

The undersigned, Minister Resident of the United States, presents his compliments to His Excellency the Minister Resident of the Republic of Perú accredited near the Government of Ecuador, and begs to inquire of Mr. Cavero whether the following extract, which has been communicated to M*r* White as having been taken, word for word, from an official despatch addressed by Mr. C. to his Government,—and which is said to have been made the basis of a formal proposition to a Principal European Power, for an intervention in behalf of Peru, against alleged designs of the Governments of Great Britain and the United States, subversive of the territorial rights of Perú on the Upper Amazon,—has been correctly reported as contained in such despatch?

[EXTRACT—TRANSLATION]

" * * * That it was proposed to appropriate (*adjudicar*) to the Government of H. B. M. large tracts of land situated on the Northern banks of the Amazon, which is exclusively the property of Peru; and to concede, besides, to the United States the free navigation of the interior rivers, over which Peru holds dominion equally as certain: And that, by reason of Mr. Cavero's vigilant forecast and well directed investigations, it subsequently came to his knowledge that the Government of Quito had not confined itself to a mere project, but that these designs had been carried into effect by actual and minute surveys made by competent Engineers; and by mutual Agreement between the Diplomatic Agents of the United States and Great Britain, contracts were concluded with them which guaranteed these cessions,—contracts which have finally been submitted for approbation to their respective Governments."

Mr. White would fain hope, that some mistake has occurred in transcribing the foregoing extract: Should it, however, prove to be the veritable language used in the despatch in question, Mr. White feels it incumbent on him to disabuse the mind of Mr. Cavero of the very material misapprehensions and misinformation, which seem to have betrayed him into strange errors with regard to the policy of the United States, and the action of her representative here, touching the pending questions between Peru and Ecuador.

2447

Philo White, United States Minister Resident in Ecuador, to Lewis Cass, Secretary of State of the United States [1]

No. 148   QUITO, *June 1, 1858.*

SIR: I took the liberty to inclose to the Department, on the 19ᵗʰ ultᵒ, (accompanied by my despatch Nᵒ 147,) a copy of a communication which I felt it my duty to address to the Peruvian Minister Resident at this Capital,[2] by

It would seem to have escaped the memory of Mr. Cavero, that Mʳ White distinctly informed him, at an informal interview between them at the house of the latter, that his Government had expressly instructed him, some two or three years since, to suspend further negotiation with Ecuador in regard to the free navigation of the Upper Amazon, until the question of territorial boundaries between Perú and this Republic should be definitively *settled by themselves;* with which instruction, Mr. White has scrupulously complied.

And from the tenor of the foregoing extract, it is clearly inferable that, notwithstanding all Mʳ Cavero's *acertadas averiguaciones*, he was, at the time of inditing the despatch under consideration, wholly unapprised of the existence of the Decree of the National Congress of Ecuador, enacted the 26ᵗʰ November, 1853, and promulgated to the world immediately thereafter, by which the commerce of her navigable rivers was made *free to all nations*, and the people of every country invited to colonize her public domain. Under the allurements held out by this munificent Law of the Nation, whose liberal offers were extended equally to Peruvians, to Englishmen, to Frenchmen, as well as to North Americans and all others, a number of Mr. White's countrymen came to locate in the Upper Napo country, as peaceful colonists on Ecuatorian territory, and in the midst of an Ecuatorian population, presided over by an Ecuatorian Governor and other Provincial Officers. All of these colonists, however, are at this time either dead or have gone to other parts, with a solitary exception, an individual who has "squatted" so high up on the waters of the Napo, as, it is believed, takes him quite beyond the extreme limit to which Mr. Cavero would seriously extend the territorial claim of Peru; so that this man has clearly never trespassed on disputed territory.

No especial privileges or immunities were extended to these isolated American colonists over the citizens or subjects of other countries, by any act of Mʳ White or of this Government; but they located themselves on Ecuatorian soil, solely under the guarantees held out by the above-recited National Decree, whose promises are as freely offered to Peruvians and all others who choose to avail themselves of its provisions as to North Americans. And no design has at any time been entertained by Mʳ White or his Government,—no act done by them, nor any *project* concocted, or understanding entered into, with the Representative of any other Power, intended in the least degree to affect, or which could have the remotest bearing upon, the vexed question of territorial jurisdiction between Perú and Ecuador.

So far, therefore, as Mʳ White and his Government are concerned, the *acts* and *designs* imputed in the extract above quoted, are wholly unfounded, and inapplicable to them. And as these imputations are utterly unsustained by any conceivable arrangement of *facts* connected with the official agency of Mʳ White, he is seriously apprehensive lest his estimable Colleague from Peru may have fallen a victim to the sinister arts of a class of incorrigible *quidnuncs*, who are wont to congregate about all National Capitals, and whose favorite vocation it is to propagate, *ex cathedra*, the *vagaries* of their own theories as realities and legal entities,—to the great annoyance of new-comers, and, peradventure, to the scandal of the current diplomacy of the day.

But, as Mʳ White has already intimated, he sincerely trusts, and would be highly gratified to hear, that there is something wrong in the *transcription* of the language of the "*extract*" which forms the subject of this communication.

In the mean while, Mr. White avails himself of the occasion to assure Mʳ Cavero, of the sincere regard and high estimation in which he has the honor to subscribe himself Mr. C's. very Obedient Servant.

[1] Despatches, Ecuador, vol. 5.   Received July 28.
[2] The despatch is to be found, above, this part, doc. 2446, and the enclosure with it in note 2, p. 409 thereto.

way of disabusing his mind of erroneous impressions with regard to the acts and intentions of our Government, touching the territorial rights of Perú on the Amazon river. I now have the honor to inclose, herewith, M.ʳ Cavero's answer (marked A)[1] to my communication. But he seems so grudgingly to acknowledge himself wrong in imputing to us any part or lot in the imbroglio

[1] This communication follows:

Juan Celestino Cavero, Peruvian Minister Resident in Ecuador, to Philo White, United States Minister Resident in Ecuador

[TRANSLATION]

QUITO, *May 19, 1858.*

The undersigned Minister of Peru has received the very estimable communication of His Excellency Mr. Philo White of the 11th instant [Above, this part, p. 409, note 2.— Ed.], in which he is pleased to state that it has come to his knowledge that the under- signed had advised his government (Peru) that Ecuador "proposed to appropriate (*ad- judicar*) to the government of Her Britannic Majesty large tracts of land situated on the Northern banks of the Amazon, which is exclusively the property of Peru,—and to concede, besides, to the United States the free navigation of the interior rivers," &c.

In view of this, His Excellency Mr. White offers some reflections upon the just, lawful and consistent policy of the Government of the Union which he represents, declaring "that some two or three years since his government (that of the United States) had expressly instructed him to suspend further negotiations in regard to the Upper Amazon until the question of territorial boundaries between Peru and this government (that of Ecuador) should be definitely settled."

No other policy could be expected from a government so respectable, so austere in its international relations, and so scrupulously observant of the perfect rights of other nations. Thus, if the undersigned Minister has advised his government of the prospec- tive navigation of the Napo and other eastern rivers confluents of the Amazon, he has been compelled to do so by reason of the universal public rumor that steamers for the purpose were assuredly being constructed in England and the United States to navigate said rivers on the strength of the law of November 26, 1853, which granted to the world the free navigation of said rivers; as well as by reason of the very significant declaration which His Excellency Mr. White made to the undersigned at the house of the Chargé d'Affaires of Her Britannic Majesty, Mr. Cope, on December 10 last, when, the latter having remarked that British Steamers would soon navigate the eastern rivers, His Excellency Mr. White added that within a few months the American flag would like- wise wave in those waters. The undersigned having replied to His Excellency Mr White that those rivers were not under the dominion of Ecuador alone, but of all the other riparian States, namely, Peru, New Granada, Venezuela, and the Empire of Brazil, His Excellency (Mr. White) replied that we would come to an understanding with those States, and that the Government of the Union had nothing to do with them, —a circumstance that must not have escaped the memory of His Excellency.

And as on the other hand His Excellency Mr. White is not ignorant of the fact that the representative of Peru, Mr. D. Mariano Saenz, protested against the said law of Novem- ber 26, 1853, subversive of the rights of the said republics to the waters of the eastern rivers, and to the territory situated on their banks; since Ecuador was directing river navigation of those places without notice to or consent of the nations holding joint ownership. The Chargé d'Affaires of New Granada likewise protested against the law of September 24, 1852, in that it authorized the executive power of Ecuador to formulate agreements with Señor Elias Mocatta, commissioned by the Anglo-Ecuadorean bond- holders, for the payment of the external debt with wild lands: And notwithstanding these protests, His Excellency the American Minister will have observed that this same contract [Above, this part, p. 407, note 1.—Ed.] has been realized, as may be seen in the official periodical "*El Seis de Marzo*," No. 281, which the undersigned has the honor to submit herewith to His Excellency in order that he may be so good as to bring it to the attention of his Government.

Therein is registered the alienation of the *Canton of Canelos*, province of Oriente, on the banks of the river Bobonaza, up to its confluence with the Pastaza. This territory, by the Spanish laws of July 15, 1802, and subsequent confirmatory law of October 7,

between Peru and Ecuador, that I deemed it proper, in order to correct all misapprehension as to our course of policy, to put in a rejoinder to his despatch,—a copy of which, marked B,[1] also accompanies this. These people are such incorrigible controversalists, that it becomes necessary, in carrying

---

1805, has been expressly and incontestably separated from the former Intendency of Quito and added to Peru; And when those countries became independent of Spain Peru was in possession of said territory of Canélos, conformably to the *uti possidetis* of 1810.

Consequently, Mr. White will already have observed, with his wisdom and profound knowledge of the political and statistical history of these places, that the Government of Ecuador has committed the most shameful usurpation in appropriating to its British creditors an indisputable territory of Peru. And even should there have been any doubt concerning the ownership of this territory, the fact that it had been claimed by Peru, and that there existed the Treaty of Guayaquil of 1829, which designates the manner of peacefully resolving boundary controversies, should have been sufficient to prevent Ecuador from taking it upon herself to dispose of the territory in question, overlooking the consideration and respect due to two Nations such as Peru and New Granada, and thereby disregarding all the fundamental principles of international law, thus giving the injured republics a perfect and undisputed right to employ the strong measures and recourses permitted by the law of nations in such cases.

Therefore, the very fact of the appropriation by the government of Ecuador to its creditors of territory belonging exclusively to Peru, with shameful disregard to pending treaties, is decisive proof of the truth contained in the extract given in the said note of the 11th instant, without regard to whether the undersigned may or may not have informed his government thereof in such terms.

With respect to the free navigation of the eastern rivers which flow into the Amazon the undersigned is especially gratified, and will take pleasure in informing the Government of Peru of the solemn declaration made by His Excellency the Minister of the United States "that his government has not and will not enter into any agreement with Ecuador regarding the free navigation of the Upper Amazon until the question of boundaries between Peru and Ecuador may be definitively settled."

It would be desirable, and is the sincere hope of the undersigned, that such may be the intentions of Great Britain in this respect, and that the reports and rumors which have been disseminated regarding this matter may prove to be erroneous.

Assuring His Excellency Mr. Philo White of his deepest respect and most distinguished esteem [etc.].

[1] In White's communication which follows, a footnote to the words "a principal European Power," in the second paragraph, indicated that the Power referred to was France:

Philo White, United States Minister Resident in Ecuador, to Juan Celestino Cavero,
Peruvian Minister Resident in Ecuador

QUITO, *May 25, 1858.*

The undersigned, Minister Resident of the United States, has had the honor to receive the polite Note of His Excell'cy the Minister Resident of the Republic of Perú, of date the 19th inst. [Above, this part, p. 411, note 1.—Ed.], and begs to make his acknowledgments for the prompt and courteous response contained therein to the Note of the undersigned of the 11th instant [Above, this part, p. 409, note 2.—Ed.].

But while cordially thankful for the frank and friendly sentiments manifested in Mr. Cavero's note, Mr White deeply regrets to learn from it, that the statements which at first came to his knowledge in an apocryphal shape, and which he had hoped would not bear the test of a rigid scrutiny, have now assumed the form and substance of responsible *facts*,—to wit, that Mr. Cavero and his Government have made a formal appeal to a principal European Power, for its intervention in behalf of Perú, by reason of alleged *projected* violations of her territorial rights by Great Britain and the United States!

Mr. White had hoped that he succeeded, in his note of the 11th instant, in showing the entire innocence of himself and his Government of any act or design which could be construed into a trespass on Peruvian rights of territory bordering on the Upper Amazon, or from which any aggressive intent could be apprehended or even deductively inferred. He must therefore hold himself and his Government wholly guiltless of the grave responsibility of having, in the least degree, contributed towards precipitating

on a correspondence with them, to use a piquant style in order to satisfy them of the earnestness of your purpose.

It is now understood, in diplomatic circles, that Señor Cavero will soon demand his passports, and take his departure from this Capital, *"under pro-*

Peru into the extraordinary alternative of seeking relief from her governmental troubles at the footstool of a European monarchy!

Such a suicidal procedure on the part of an *American Republic*, M͞r White cannot but view as fraught with portentous mischiefs, present and prospective, to the cause of free institutions all over the world. Naught but the extremest political exigency,—no impending calamity short of a menaced destruction of all the guarantees of public security and private rights, could justify American Rulers in immolating the liberties and independence of their country at the shrine of a monarchical power in the Old World! The very proposition implies remorse for past political heresies!—and affords a sad commentary on man's capacity for self-government! Can it be, that Perú is reduced to so deplorable a strait in her struggles to maintain an independent political existence among the nations of the earth, as thus in effect to pronounce the elective franchise an illusion! —and Republican Government a failure! Or is this erratic movement on the part of that Government and her Representative in Ecuador, the effect of a momentary hallucination, by which chimeras dire have disturbed their imaginations while laboring to work out the problem of democratic institutions?

In view of this hypothesis, and of the implied admissions contained in Mr. Cavero's communication of the 19ᵗʰ, a reluctant conviction is forced upon the mind of the undersigned, that it is but too true, as intimated in his note of the 11ᵗʰ inst., that gratuitous and evil counsels had been obtruded upon the confiding attention of His Excellc'y, the Representative of Peru, with regard to the scrupulously neutral policy which has ever served to guide the United States and her Representatives in their diplomatic intercourse with other powers.

And although not doubting that the Peruvian's Minister's confidence had been thus insidiously betrayed by the sinister arts of professed friends, and his mind thereby become deeply imbued with prepossessions, yet Mr. White cannot but marvel at M͞r Cavero's mistaking the whisperings of coteries for a *"universal rumor"*!—And thus to have been led, as by an *ignis fatuus*, to implicate the undersigned and his Government in *designs* which are as utterly unreal as the "baseless fabric of a vision"!

The "declarations" imputed to the undersigned, with regard to the navigation of the Amazon, were random words, casually spoken; but which, nevertheless, so far as they went, and when rightly understood, express the sentiments and represent the views of himself and his Government, touching the great principles under review, and which have already been practically recognized as maritime law by the principal commercial powers of Europe as well as by the United States.

In the progress of human events, it has already become apparent to the most enlightened and most progressive of the nations of the earth, that the expansive tendencies of the principles of Free Trade are calculated to exert a more benign influence in the development of a high grade of civilization, and to advance the material interests and fulfil the destined mission of man on earth, than all other human agencies.

And as a sequence of these ameliorating axioms, destined soon to be invested with all the authority of international law, it is now held by the United States, and widely acquiesced in throughout the Old World, that great *navigable Rivers*, which serve as outlets and path-ways to market of extensive and productive regions of country, ought, in reason and of right, to be considered as much the *common high-ways* of all the nations whose territories extend to the navigable channels of such rivers, as of those who possess both banks of their *mouths*,—and that the latter are not necessarily invested with any right to inhibit the ingress or egress of vessels freighted with the commerce of the "ribereños" nations above.

Now all that Mr. White said on the occasion referred to by Mr. Cavero, was briefly to reiterate these principles of a more liberal commercial code. But it seems that M͞r Cavero misapprehended his language in regard to the floating of the American flag on the waters of the Amazon: M͞r White, speaking in the *subjunctive* mood, remarked, that *if* the right of Ecuador to the Northern bank of the Amazon were established, he would not be surprised to see the flags of North American trading vessels flying on those navigable streams before the lapse of many months,—as they could come there under the guarantees held out by the Ecuatorian law of the 26ᵗʰ November, 1853: And this

test!"   This Government, however, affect not to apprehend an open rupture
with Peru, consequent on the bellicose tone of their Representative here:
Yet it is manifest that *recruiting* for the army, just now, is going on more
briskly than at any other period for more than a year past: Press-gangs patrol
the streets for the purpose of *nabbing* the material for soldiers,—that being
the ordinary method in this country of filling up their rank and file!   It is
quite doubtful, however, whether the present incumbents of the Peruvian
Government, although not lacking the *animus* as regards Ecuador, can find
leisure to undertake a foreign war at this particular juncture, as a mutinous

---

was spoken mainly with reference to the antiquated dogma adhered to by Brazil, that
the possessor of "ribereños" territory has the right to shut out foreign commerce from
even an *arm of the sea*, provided such possessor owns on both sides of the estuary.

Nothing was said in the course of these remarks, that implied a menace against Peru;
because the hypothesis on which the words were based, presupposed the claim of Ecuador to the northern bank of the river would be settled,—and that, in such event, Perú
could have no color of right, not even according to the exploded doctrine of Brazil, to
interfere with the commerce on the opposite side of the river to her own possessions.

Now if the simple advocacy of these beneficent principles of free trade, in a random
conversation conducted in the best possible humor, constitutes the burden of Mr.
White's offense against Perú, and forms the sole groundwork of an arraignment of himself and his Government by His Excellc'y the Peruvian Representative, for intentional
acts of *aggression* against the territorial rights of that Republic,—then it may not be
altogether a fanciful idea, that the *nervous system* of that State is illy calculated to withstand the turbulent ordeal incident to democratic institutions!—and the notion of
spreading her political bed in the lion's lair *as an asylum*, is not so irrational as, under
less anomalous circumstances, might be imagined!

But, sympathizing as Mʳ White does in the common-weal of a brother Republic, he
would, in all kindness towards Mʳ Cavero and his Government, most respectfully suggest to them, whether they may not have mistaken the Arbiter before whom to lay their
plaint!   However fully they may confide in the friendly offices of the Potentate to whom
they are said to have appealed for a solution of their troubles,—and not doubting his
paternal inclinations towards his suppliants from the "Inca"—land,—a question arises
whether he is not estopped from extending to them the potent aid they crave in checking
the prevalence of the modern principles of an expansive commerce, by himself having
recently become an illustrious propagandist of those very principles?   For it ought to
be known to the Peruvian Government and its Representatives abroad, that, at this
very moment, in alliance with another great power, that monarch is using zealous efforts, backed by the *argumentum ad hominem* of naval and military armaments, to
inculcate upon the perverse understandings of a numerous and marvellous people in the
Eastern Hemisphere,—who, by the way, like the dwellers South of the Amazon, are
peculiar for their *restrictive* policy in regard to foreign commerce,—the vast benefits to
the world which will accrue from the universal adoption of the new maritime code.

And in conclusion, Mʳ White may be allowed to express an anxious hope, that Mr.
Cavero and his Government will re-consider their reputed purpose of submitting the
destinies of their country to the arbitrament of a European throne!—That they will not
lightly abandon the American brotherhood of free and independent Sovereignties; but
that they will patriotically resolve still to bear the ills inseparable from all forms of
government, rather than resort to the perilous experiment of "flying to others they
know not of."

With an identity of interests, and a congeniality of political sentiments, the undersigned and his Government cherish a deep solicitude for the well-being of all the Republics on this Continent: They are desirous of seeing them remain peaceful, prosperous and
happy: And they ardently hope that the vexed questions which have disturbed the relations of good neighborhood between Peru and Ecuador, may soon be happily adjusted;
and that those fraternal feelings of cordial amity which should always subsist between
brother Republics, may be speedily and abidingly re-established among their people.

And the undersigned begs to assure His Excellc'y the Minister Resident of Perú,
[etc.].

spirit is still rife at home, which demands their vigilant attention within their own borders.

President *Francisco Robles* still remains at Guayaquil, with his family; and Vice President *Marcos Espinel*, continues "Encargado del Poder Ejecutivo." General *José Maria Urvina* [Urbina?], Ex-president, having absolutely abandoned the Mission to Rome and Brazil, has refunded most of the $20,-000 he received as *out-fit*, &c.   So that there is not, at this time, any apparent cause for *internal* agitation in this Republic.

With high respect [etc.].

2448

Philo White, United States Minister Resident in Ecuador, to Lewis Cass, Secretary of State of the United States [1]

No. 149   QUITO, *June 18, 1858*.

SIR: Since writing my despatch Nº 148, of the 1st instant,[2] the movement of troops, and the revelations of high Officials of this Government, indicate a greater apprehension on their part of an open rupture with Peru, than I had supposed.   Señor *Francisco Pablo Ycaza*, the Minister of Finance, called on me the other evening to take leave, on his departure for Peru as Special Envoy to that Government, and offered to become the bearer of any despatch I might desire to forward to the United States Minister at Lima. Although somewhat reserved as to all the purposes of the Mission, I learned from him, in general terms, that he goes as a messenger of peace between the two Cabinets,—for this Government is well persuaded that *Señor Cavero*, the Peruvian Minister Resident here, has represented their *imbroglio* in a most tortuous, untruthful point of view; and the main design of Señor Ycaza's mission is to lay the true state of the case before the Executive Authorities of Peru.   And I can the more readily appreciate the new Envoy's opinion of the unscrupulousness of the Peruvian Minister's course as a Diplomatist, from my own correspondence with him,[3] as well as from the representations of Walter Cope, Esqr., the English Chargé d'Affaires here, who charges him with the grossest misrepresentations to the British and French Governments, to whom he has rendered discrepant versions of the same facts!

I accordingly wrote to Mr. Clay, our Minister in Lima, commending Soř. Ycaza to his polite attentions; and expressing a hope that, should circumstances seem to render it proper for him to do so, he would use his good offices in favoring the peaceful mission of the Ecuatorian Envoy.

I take the liberty to inclose, herewith, Nº 282, of the Official Gazette of this Government, ("El Seis de Marzo,") containing their recognition of the

---

[1] Despatches, Ecuador, vol. 5.   Received July 28.   [2] Above, this part, doc. 2447.
[3] *Ibid.*, p. 411, note 1, and p. 412, note 1.

appointment of M*r* *Thomas V. Clarke*, as Vice Consul of the United States at Guayaquil.   And in doing so, I may be allowed to remark, that, so far as I can learn, Mr. Clarke has given full satisfaction in discharge of the duties of that Consulate.

In this connexion, it may not be inappropriate for me to state, that since I last wrote to the Department, M*r* *Augustus Cooke*, who was (and possibly may be still), an applicant for that Consulate, has left Guayaquil,—a feud having been engendered between him and his patron, *Dr. J. H. D. Sigur*, which resulted in leaving Mr. Cooke quite destitute of resources.   M*r* Clarke, the Vice Consul, however, succeeded in obtaining for him a clerkship somewhere on the Pacific coast.

I have the honor [etc.].

2449

Philo White, United States Minister Resident in Ecuador, to Lewis Cass, Secretary of State of the United States [1]

No. 152   QUITO, *July 2, 1858*.

SIR: I have the honor to inclose, herewith, a copy of a second Note from *Señor Juan C. Cavero*, the Peruvian Minister Resident at this Capital, marked A,[2]—in which, it will be seen, he tacitly admits what I had surmised,

[1] Despatches, Ecuador, vol. 5.   Received August 28.
[2] Cavero's second note (the first one, dated May 19, 1856, is to be found above, this part, p. 411, note 1) follows:

Juan Celestino Cavero, Peruvian Minister Resident in Ecuador, to Philo White, United States Minister Resident in Ecuador

[TRANSLATION]

QUITO, *June 16, 1858*.

I have received the very estimable communication of His Excellency Mr. White dated May 25 last [Above, this part, p. 412, note 1.—Ed.], in which he is good enough to declare anew the intentions and policy of the Government of the Union in refraining from entering into any agreement with Ecuador concerning the acquisition of territory or navigation of confluent rivers of the Amazon so long as the pending questions on boundaries between Peru and Ecuador are not definitively settled; to assert the respect which His Excellency Mr. White and his government have always professed for the principles of neutrality and non-intervention in diplomatic commerce with all independent powers; to offer some remarks, moreover, regarding the disadvantages resulting from a treaty between Peru and any European power; and, finally, to manifest the desires animating His Excellency for the consolidation of peace in Peru, for its prosperity, and for a fraternal and peaceful solution of the differences which have arisen between the Ecuadorean Republic and Peru.

Duly appreciating the expression of the generous sentiments of His Excellency respecting Peru, I can do no less than applaud the political system of neutrality and respect for the rights of these republics engaged in territorial questions which His Excellency for the second time declares his government will observe as a rule of conduct.

I did not, in my reply of May 19 last [Above, this part, p. 411, note 1.—Ed.], nor must I in the present communication, take up the matters, explained at such length by His Excellency the Representative of the United States, to prove the disadvantage of any treaty on the part of Peru with Powers, granting such a fact, since I know nothing in this respect, nor have I received any information from my government.

that he was duped by the sinister arts of political and diplomatic busybodies about the Capital, in imputing to myself and my government collusive and aggressive purposes with regard to the territorial rights of Perú on the Upper Amazon.

And from the generalizing style of his response to my allusion to the *appeal*, which it is believed Perú has made to the French Emperor for his protective aid against the alleged *aggressive designs* of Great Britain and the United States upon Peruvian rights, and the careless manner in which he slurs over the matter, I think there can be very little doubt but that negotiations are actually on foot between Peru and France, the ulterior design of which is an intervention by the latter in behalf of the former; and that *Mons Villamus*, the French Chargé here, and who gained an unodorous notoriety by his officious interference with, and *protest* against, the negotiation of our Galápagos Huano Treaty in 1854, is the putative foster-father of this embryo Franco-Peruvian *Protectorate*.

I also inclose herein, a copy of my third Note to Senor Cavero, marked B[1]
I have the honor [etc.].

Moreover, if my government should consider it to its advantage to enter into any treaty with one or more powers of the European continent, it would do so in the exercise of the sovereign and imprescriptible rights which are inherent in every state.
With assurances of deepest respect [etc.].

[1] White's note follows:

Philo White, United States Minister Resident in Ecuador, to Juan Celestino Cavero, Peruvian Minister Resident in Ecuador

QUITO, *June 28, 1858.*

The undersigned has been honored with the polite Note of His Excell'c⁷ the Minister Resident of Peru, bearing date the 16th instant [Above, this part, p. 416, note 2.—Ed.], and begs to tender his acknowledgments to Mr. Cavero for the courteous terms employed and the kindly sentiments manifested in that communication.

Although the undersigned fears Mr. Cavero is not yet fully impressed with a right comprehension of the non-interfering policy of the United States with respect to international questions arising between and solely affecting other powers, nor of the scrupulous avoidance by Mr. White and his government of any act that might embroil them in the unfortunate *imbroglio* between Peru and Ecuador with regard to their conflicting claims of territorial jurisdiction on the Upper Amazon,—yet, the ruling purpose which led to the initiation of this correspondence, will have been mainly accomplished by the virtual admissions of His Excell'c⁷ the Peruvian Minister Resident, to the effect that the United States and her Representative here were wrongfully implicated in alleged acts and designs, whose tendency it was charged would be *aggressive* upon the territorial rights and eminent domain of Peru, which had been imputed to them in Mr. Cavero's despatches to his government, an *extract* from which was quoted in Mr. White's Note of the 11th ultimo [Above, this part, p. 409, note 2.—Ed.].

Recognizing, as the United States does, the "imprescriptible" rights of sovereignty as inherent in every independent State,—whether she may be the feeblest among Republics, or the most puissant of Empires,—it would be doing injustice to the intentions of the undersigned to attribute to him (which Mr Cavero seems to do inferentially,) a disposition to interfere with or in any way to disparage the treaty-making prerogative of Peru: And he feels assured that dispassionate parties will accord to him justificatory motives for the course he has pursued in the conduct of this correspondence.

The Minister Resident of Perú had erroneously implicated the undersigned and his government in sinister designs against that Republic; and it was known that negotiations had been set on foot by the latter, whose purpose is believed to have been the

Footnote 1, p. 417—*Continued*

petitioning for a *protectorate* from a European monarch, as a shield of the suppliant State against fancied territorial aggressions by the United States and another principal power.

In so extraordinary a conjuncture, where the aspect of the external relations of Peru was equally ominous and enigmatical,—and where the figment of an *aggressive intention* unadvisedly attributed to the government of the undersigned, was made the pretext of an anomalous procedure on the part of the complainant State,—Mr White would have been derelict in duty to his country and to himself, had he not promptly and emphatically disavowed any such design, and declared himself and his government wholly guiltless of all participation in, or of responsibility for, any of those untoward events which seem to have so complicated the governmental affairs and impaired the self-reliance of an American Republic, as to drive her into a virtual abandonment of her nationality, as a dernier measure of external safety and of internal quiet and security.

Although the injustice of thus coupling the name of the United States in the *plaint* which the Peruvian Representative and his government are reputed to have made to a European potentate, would have fully warranted the strictures which the undersigned felt called on to bestow upon the subject in his two former Notes,—yet, independently of this consideration, the proposition itself involves matters of such grave import to the whole family of independent American States, as to bring it within the rule of a paramount international question on this Continent. It becomes, consequently, a legitimate topic of diplomatic discussion, and challenges the critical investigation, as well as the serious consideration, of all the parties whose interests are involved in its solution.

It is a trite axiom of international law, as well as of natural right, that an independent State is properly the arbiter of her own political destinies. And though the dogma of absolute governments makes the allegiance of the subject untransferable, and denies to him the right of voluntary expatriation, no such disability attaches to a State, whose *volition* is her paramount law, and whose prerogative is held to extend even to self-denationalization, either by a waiver of her sovereignty under a *protectorate*, or by an absolute surrender of her franchises into the keeping of a tutelary superior. And so, in this view of the matter, a State has an undoubted *right* to commit an act of *felo-de-sé*, without incurring a *legal* attainder; while, by the laws of both God and man, the individual citizen or subject, who perpetrates self-destruction, is accursed of all in Heaven and all on earth,—and, by common acclaim, is denied the consolations of a Christian Sepulture!

But while such are some of the abstract prerogatives of a State, her rights and her immunities, as well as her duties and her obligations, are *correlative*, and can only be made legitimately effective by the interpretations of international law: That law gives no license to a State, while in the exercise of her own natural rights, to infringe the privileges of good neighborhood, or in anywise to disturb the peace or endanger the political safety of a co-equal sovereignty. And applying these general propositions to the case under consideration, Mr. White believes himself justified in claiming for his government, as a member of the fraternity of American States, a voice in the pregnant question, whether it would be politic or safe to accept, much less to *invite*, the intervention of any European monarchical power as an arbiter in the political troubles of this Hemisphere. For he verily believes that, under however paternal a *guize* the good offices of a despotic Ruler in the Old World might be proffered, the *finale* of any such ostensibly *protective* mission, would be the subversion of the Republican institutions, and the ultimate extinction of free government in the *beneficiary* State.

To avert a catastrophe so disastrous to the hopes of the friends of political and civil liberty throughout the world, the undersigned conceives it to be not only his right, but an incumbent duty, as the representative of one of the independent States most deeply interested in perpetuating our present system of Republican Government, to warn a sister Republic against any such hazardous measure as that which it is feared Perú and her Representative in Ecuador are intent upon consummating.

Entertaining these views, and cherishing sentiments of cordial friendship towards Perú, it is a source of much relief to the undersigned to learn from Mr. Cavero's last Note, that he has no certain knowledge whether his government has or has not effected any diplomatic arrangement for a European *protectorate* on the shores of the Pacific. And as an earnest of the warmth of his political sympathies, and in view of a community of interests, as well as of the common national destiny of their respective States, Mr White may be permitted to express an ardent hope that Perú will take counsel from the patriotism and the valor of her Revolutionary Worthies, and continue to struggle on with heroic endurance in her seemingly adverse fortunes, until, by availing of her own

2450

Antonio Mata, Minister of Foreign Affairs of Ecuador, to Philo White, United States Minister Resident in Ecuador [1]

[TRANSLATION]

QUITO, *July 8, 1858.*

In number 2,271 of the *Gazeta Oficial* of New Granada, among the documents that have been published with the purpose of submitting to the judgment of public opinion the conduct which the Granadian Government and Senate are observing with respect to Ecuador, in consequence of some pending questions now being discussed between the two Cabinets, there is recorded a note addressed by His Excellency the Minister Resident of Peru in this Republic to Sr. Ramon Maria Orejuela, Consul General of New Granada, containing the statement that Your Excellency had positively assured His Excellency Señor Cavero that the Ecuadorean Government had conceded to the United States the *favor (gracia)* of allowing its vessels freely to navigate the Amazon and its affluents: and as the Ecuadorean law of November 26, 1853, which declared the navigation of those rivers free with respect to the part belonging to Ecuador, inasmuch as it makes a concession to the vessels, not of this or that Nation, but to those of all the land, can in no manner be qualified by a favor granted to the United States, it is to be supposed with much reason, that as many as read the said dispatch may judge that Señor Cavero has alluded, not to the law mentioned, which, being general, can not properly be denominated a *favor (gracia)*, but to a special Convention, by which my Government should have conceded to that of Your Excellency the privilege concerning the existence of which it is sought to arouse suspicion.

This consideration and the desire to avoid the misrepresentation of facts, with consequent disgrace to the honor and probity of the Governments of Ecuador and the United States, have determined His Excellency charged with the Executive Power to direct me to address Your Excellency in order to request you to be so good as to state whether, during the long period of time in which Your Excellency with notable judgment and prudence has discharged the duties of the Legation of North America, you have concluded any Convention with my Government, by which the ships of the United States were granted the favor of which Señor Cavero speaks, or have had

ample resources and indomitable energies, she shall have surmounted all her perplexities without a resort to the perilous alternative of calling in the aid of a European potentate, whose views of government among men are antagonistic to free institutions, and whose *interests* would prompt him to blot out the last vestige of rational liberty on earth.

And the undersigned avails himself of the occasion [etc.].

[1] Despatches, Ecuador, vol. 5; enclosed with White to the Secretary of State, No. 155, July 23, 1858, below, this part, doc. 2453.

any knowledge that such a Convention had been effected before the arrival of Your Excellency in this Republic.

My Government does not doubt that Your Excellency, realizing the importance of nullifying the authorized statement which is being printed in the official periodical of New Granada, will be good enough to comply with the just request contained in this dispatch, for which purpose, I enclose herewith an authentic copy of the above-mentioned note of His Excellency Sr. Cavéro [Cavero].[1]

I take this opportunity [etc.].

2451

Philo White, United States Minister Resident in Ecuador, to Antonio Mata, Minister of Foreign Affairs of Ecuador [2]

[QUITO], *July 15, 1858.*

DEAR SIR: I take much pleasure in acknowledging Your Excellcy's communication of the 8th inst.,[3] and am cordially thankful for the copy you inclose me of an official despatch from His Excellc'y Juan C. Cavero, Minister Resident of Perú in this Republic, addressed to Dr. Ramon Maria Orejuela,[4] the New Granadian Consul General at Quito, and which the latter caused to be published in the Bogota Official Gazette N⁰ 2,271.

I am the more gratified with the receipt of this communication and its accompaniment, because it affords me a fitting occasion to declare to Your Excellc'y and your Government, what I have already declared to the Peruvian Minister himself, that, so far as my Government and myself are concerned, the publication made at Bogota is as flagrantly unjust as it is unfounded in fact, not only with respect to alleged acts imputed, but to the sinister intentions insinuated against us.

It came to my knowledge more than two months since, that Mr. Cavero had, in despatches to his own as well as to foreign governments, imputed aggressive purposes to me and my government, as well as to the worthy Representative of Her Britanic Majesty here, with regard to the question of territorial boundaries between Ecuador and Perú. I accordingly lost no time in opening a correspondence with the Peruvian Minister,[5] in which, after quoting an *extract*, which has been furnished me as correctly copied from one of his despatches, and which is similar in purport to that published at Bogota, I reminded Mr. Cavero of my having distinctly stated to him, soon after he took charge of the Peruvian Mission here, that my

---

[1] Not included in this publication, since its character is sufficiently indicated within this note.

[2] Despatches, Ecuador, vol. 5; enclosed with White to the Secretary of State, No. 155, July 23, 1858, below, this part, doc. 2453.   [3] Above, this part, doc. 2450.

[4] Not included in this publication, since its character is sufficiently indicated in the Ecuadorian Minister of Foreign Affairs' note, dated July 8, 1858, above, this part, doc. 2450.

[5] Above, this part, *passim.*

Government had instructed me to refrain from entering upon negotiations with Ecuador in relation to the navigation of the Upper Amazon, until the mooted question between the two claimants to jurisdiction on those waters should be settled *between themselves;* and that, in accordance with those instructions, I had scrupulously abstained from all action in relation to the matter. After he had been thus premonished, it was with much surprise I saw the extraordinary assertions promulgated by him through official despatches!

I also expressed to M͞r Cavero my surprise, that, after claiming for himself the credit of having made *acertadas averiguaciones* into the intricacies of the case, he should have come out of that investigation wholly unadvised of the existence of the important and commendable Decree of the Ecuatorian Congress, of the 26th November 1853, by which the commerce of the navigable rivers of this Republic was made free to all nations, and liberal inducements held out to the people of every country to colonize her public domain, —since his ignorance of that Decree was clearly inferable, from the fact that he erroneously characterized as a *special favor* conceded to the United States, what I expressly claimed for my countrymen as a *legal right,* under the general provisions of that Decree, to navigate the waters of the Amazon, always subject to the contingency, that the rightful jurisdiction of Ecuador to one bank at least of those waters, was first to be established.

And, in view of these hallucinations of my colleague from Perú, I did not conceal from him an expression of my fears, that he may unfortunately have fallen a victim to the sinister arts of a class of incorrigible *quidnuncs,* who are wont to congregate about all National Capitals, and whose favorite vocation it is to propagate, *ex cathedra,* the vagaries of their own theories as realities and legal entities,—to the great annoyance of new-comers, and peradventure to the scandal of the diplomacy of the vicinage.

Equally uncalled for and irreconcilable with fact, is M͞r Cavero's *flout* against the North Americans who settled on the River "Napo," and who, he depreciatingly alleges, were *"inundating"* the wild lands in controversy between Ecuador and Perú. The story of these luckless colonists, is a brief one: Under the allurements held out by the Decree of the Ecuatorian Congress of 1853, whose liberal offers extended as well to *Peruvians* as to all others, some isolated Americans went to locate on the head-waters of the "Napo," where they were surrounded by a settlement of Ecuatorian citizens, and domiciled in the midst of the Provincial Officers of that Government. No special favors were conceded to these immigrants by Ecuador, more than to those of all other nations; but they went there solely under the guarantees of the National Decree of 1853, as the people of every other country were encouraged to do. But of those American immigrants who went there, one solitary individual alone remains in that region, the others having either died or abandoned the enterprize.

And in all kindness towards my colleague and the nation he represents, I may here be allowed to remark, that it would be a source of gratulation to every true philanthropist, and gladden the hearts of all friends of progressive civilization, were Mr. Cavero's naturally heroic countrymen to *emulate*, rather than *disparage*, the *productive* enterprize of the *Anglo-American* race; —in whose migratory career Heaven's injunction to man is in rapid process of fulfilment, as by their peaceful and irrepressible labors *wildernesses* are being *subdued*, and the earth is made to yield its bountiful fruits as a rich reward for their industry thus dutifully bestowed in God's earthly vineyard; —and following close upon whose footsteps, the world has rarely failed to witness a high grade of civilization, with all its blessed concomitants of fruitful fields, smiling plenty, and a diffusive prosperity cheering to the heart of man in his earthly heritage.

And God grant that the Peruvian Nation may henceforth listen to the counsels of true friendship and matured wisdom, and *lay* that fiend of *civil war* which has been so ruthlessly devouring them, and devote their *peaceful* energies to *productive* enterprises: Far better would it be, for the cause of humanity and a happy solution of all their troubles, to fertilize their generous soil with the sweat from industry's brow, than to drench it in fraternal blood, amidst those deplorable scenes of sanguinary strife and carnage hitherto so often witnessed there,—and over which the genius of rational Liberty mourns the degeneracy of her professed worshippers, while the friends of Free Government have been deeply scandalized in the eyes of a philanthropic and Christian world!

In this connexion, however, I ought perhaps to state, with regard to the Peruvian Minister's course, that he now expresses a regret that his despatch should have found its way into the Bogota Official Gazette, as it was not destined by him to the notoriety it seems now to have attained. And he further assures me, that he did not intend to cite the U. S. Vice Consul at Guayaquil as authority for the mendacious rumor, attributing to the United States Government an intention to buy up the wild lands in controversy between Ecuador and Peru, &c.: He acquits the Vice Consul of having made any such statement to him, or to his correspondent.

And I will here take occasion further to state, that Mr. Cavero has inclosed to me a copy of a document, which he informs me he has caused to be delivered to the members of the Foreign Diplomatic Corps in Quito, as a *Circular Letter*,—in which he qualifiedly recants the imputations contained in his published despatch to the prejudice of my government and myself. A copy of that "Circular" is herewith inclosed.[1]

But as affording a refreshing contrast to the Machiavelian diplomacy too prevalent at this day, I cannot close this communication without bearing cheerful testimony to the marked courtesy, the honorable bearing, and the

[1] Not found.

fair dealing I have uniformly experienced, during the somewhat lengthened official and intimate relations I have sustained with all branches of the Ecuatorian Government.

And I avail myself of this renewed occasion [etc.].

2452

Philo White, United States Minister Resident in Ecuador, to Lewis Cass, Secretary of State of the United States [1]

[EXTRACT]

No. 154 [QUITO], *July 16, 1858.*

SIR: . . . *Internal* quiet and general contentment, prevail throughout Ecuador,— although portending *external wars* seem to be looming up in their Northern as well as Southern horizons,—that restless architect of diplomatic mischief, Señor *Juan Celestino Cavero*, the Peruvian Minister Resident here, having busied himself in fomenting *imbroglios* between both New Granada and Peru with Ecuador! So far, however, as he had coupled me and my Government in any of those *imbroglios*, I have been so frank and out-spoken in my disprovals of his unwarrantable implications, that he seems latterly to have been dis[ci]plined into quite a gentle mood in all his references to us. In proof of this, I herewith inclose, (marked A,) a *"Circular"* [2] he has sent to all the Foreign Diplomatic Agents accredited here, in which he makes a qualified *recantation* of what he had gratuitously insinuated to our prejudice. I also inclose (marked B,) a copy of a third letter from Señor Cavero,[2] in response to my last communication,—which, it will be seen, is couched in quite a subdued tone.

A preposterous rumor, to the effect that the U. States Government was about to buy up certain Ecuatorian Land Scrip in the hands of English bond holders, having found its way into the Bogota (New Granada) Gazette in connexion with a despatch from Sor̃. Cavéro at Quito, wherein the U. S. Vice Consul at Guayaquil was given as authority, Sor̃. S. [C?] has addressed me quite an affectionate letter, (private) wholly acquitting the V. Consul of having intimated any such thing to him or his correspondent,—the V. Consul having previously utterly denied the "impeachment," in a note to me. Turbid and troubled waters, seem to be the congenial element of this Peruvian Diplomat.

I have the honor [etc.].

[1] Despatches, Ecuador, vol. 5. Received August 28.
The omitted portion relates to the election of a vice president of Ecuador.
[2] Not found.

2453

Philo White, United States Minister Resident in Ecuador, to Lewis Cass, Secretary of State of the United States [1]

No. 155   [QUITO], *July 23, 1858.*

SIR: There are continually new developments of the mischiefs resulting from the unscrupulous course pursued by the Peruvian Minister accredited at this Capital, *Señor Juan C. Cavero.* It now appears, from a communication addressed to me by the Minister of Foreign Relations of this Government, a copy of which is inclosed herein,[2] that one of the prominent incitements operating with the New Granadian Congress in their impending *Declaration of War* against Ecuador, is a despatch from Señor Cavero, sent from Quito, which is made up of fallacies and fictions! A copy of my response to the Ecuatorian Minister, is also inclosed herewith.[3]

The idea, however, of New Granada's going to war with her near neighbor, on the merest shadow of a pretence, in the present collapsed state of her *Finances,* as shown by the annexed exhibit from her Minister of the Hacienda, is quite farcical!—especially while an ugly question with the United States remains on her hands unadjusted!

With high respect [etc.].

2454

Francisco Pablo Ycaza, Minister of Foreign Affairs of Ecuador, to Charles R. Buckalew, United States Minister Resident in Ecuador [4]

[TRANSLATION]

A   GUAYAQUIL, *April 27, 1859.*

From the moment the naval forces of Peru arrived off the Ecuadorean coasts with the object of notifying and making effective the blockade which their Government believed it its right to decree, those forces have committed every kind of abuse, violating international law, the law of war, and the practice constantly followed by Nations whose conduct serves as a rule in such cases.

The notoriety given to the acts and to the notes exchanged between the Commander of the Peruvian Squadron and the authorities of Guayaquil which have been published, makes the task of specifying and detailing the abuses committed during the six months of the existence of the blockade

[1] Despatches, Ecuador, vol. 5. Received August 28.
[2] Above, this part, July 8, 1858, doc. 2450.
[3] *Ibid.,* July 15, 1858, doc. 2451.
[4] Despatches, Ecuador, vol. 2; enclosed with Buckalew to the Secretary of State, No. 8, May 18, 1859, below, this part, doc. 2456.
Charles R. Buckalew, of Pennsylvania, to whom this was addressed, was commissioned minister resident to Ecuador on June 14, 1858. He left his post for the United States on July 10, 1861.

both unnecessary and tiresome. It suffices to say that in its execution no other rule has been followed than the caprice of the blockading force.

Entrance to ships of one Nation has consequently been seen to be permitted, at the same time that others were repulsed, and unwarranted exceptions made between vessels covered by the same flag. Even the meaning of words has been observed to be altered, operations being designated as blockade which would perhaps not be ventured and are even prohibited in the case of a declared war.

How shall we characterize, in effect, the night attack which the Peruvian forces with four hundred disembarked men, supported by the whole Squadron, made upon the village of Puná, where there were only eighteen men to do police service in that port?

How shall we characterize the daily excursions which are made by armed launches and boats into the interior rivers with the purpose of destroying all ships they may meet in transit and their cargoes, and this in places where, by reason of their distance from the city, they can not be suspected of intending to force the blockade, without exempting from a like fate the vessels which are in dock or barred from egress?

How shall we characterize the attempt on the part of the blockading vessels to force from their position in front of the city, as has already happened, provoking iminent conflicts, the vessels which by reason of the poor position of the Peruvian forces or their lack of skill or carelessness have been able to enter the port and now find their egress barred?

How shall we characterize the interference with the interior river traffic and even of the water traffic within the city?

How shall we characterize the abandonment of persons having the misfortune to encounter a Peruvian vessel on some part of the destroyed vessels from which they have been miraculously saved?

How shall we characterize man hunting, of which there has been more than one example?

How, in fine, shall we reconcile all this with the response of the Government of Peru to the Minister Plenipotentiary of Chile, in which he says— "that the Commander of the blockading forces is conducting the operations in a manner strictly in accordance with International Law"?

Nevertheless, the Government of Ecuador, animated by sentiments of conciliation, and the desire to prevent a greater disgrace to the American name, and to avoid a conflict which would expose the city of Guayaquil, defenseless against naval forces, to destruction together with its immense neutral interests: out of consideration for the Nations which have presented their good offices for the settlement of the pending question,—has up to the present tolerated such excesses, confining itself to protesting against them to the Commander of the Squadron and the Government of Peru through one of the mediators.

But seeing that the spirit which has guided its tolerance has so far been misunderstood; that those abuses increase each day; that the fact that the mediation of two friendly Governments has been accepted and that all the negotiators have now met in Lima, has in no way modified the hostilities of the Peruvian forces, but that on the contrary these hostilities, suspended for some days, have been renewed following the arrival of the last packet-boat from Peru, and have been made intolerable in every degree, "what should have been a vehicle of peace being converted into a strategem of war," as the Commander of the Squadron said on March 19 last, and it being logically deducted from this conduct that there is a deliberate intent to seek disputes which will make peace impossible, the Government of Ecuador finds itself confronted by the grievous alternative of consenting to the complete humiliation of the Republic or accepting the conflict into which it has for some time been desired to embroil it.

In such a case there is no question as to the resolution which should be adopted by a Government which recognizes its duty to itself and to the country which has entrusted its destiny to it; and the Government of Ecuador is therefore resolved to repress hereafter every abuse on the part of the blockading forces and to repel force with force.

Inasmuch as serious conflicts or perhaps war may result from this resolution which the Government has been forced to adopt by reason of the conduct of Peru, His Excellency the President has directed me to address this declaration to all the honorable members of the diplomatic Corps residing in the Republic, in order to disavow its responsibility for later events which it has been powerless to avoid, and in order that foreigners residing in the country, apprized of the circumstances, may adopt the course they deem best to safeguard their persons and interests, the Government on its part offering them all the aid and protection that it may be possible for it to lend them.

But at the same time I should here state that although the unqualifiable hostilities of the Peruvian Squadron at the precise moment of entrance into peace negotiations, have placed the Government of Ecuador under the sad necessity of adopting the resolution just referred to, this fact has not thereby altered in the least its plan of conciliation and its vehement desire that peace may be established as soon as possible, with which object it will not omit any step or any sacrifice which can accomplish that purpose without disgrace to the national honor.

The undersigned [etc.].

2455

Charles R. Buckalew, United States Minister Resident in Ecuador, to Francisco Pablo Ycaza, Minister of Foreign Affairs of Ecuador [1]

B   QUITO, *May 12, 1859.*

SIR: I have the honor to acknowledge the receipt of your communication dated the 27th day of April [2] on the subject of the difficulties with Peru and announcing the determination of the Government of Ecuador to repel force by force.—

I embrace the occasion [etc.].

2456

Charles R. Buckalew, United States Minister Resident in Ecuador, to Lewis Cass, Secretary of State of the United States [3]

No. 8   QUITO, *May 18, 1859.*

SIR: Since my last communication,[4] political events of some importance have occurred in this country.

I have received a communication from the Minister of Exterior Relations reciting certain grievances against Peru in connection with the blockade of Guayaquil (which yet continues) and announcing the determination of this Government to repel force by force—I enclose a copy of this communication, and of my reply, marked A. and B.[5]

On the first of this month a revolution directed against the existing Government of Gen. Robles, broke out in this city and it has been to a considerable extent successful.—A Provisional Government, consisting of a Triumvirate, has been established and steps taken to extend the movement throughout the country.   The province of Imbabura on the north, and Leon and Chimborazo on the south, have joined with Pichincha (of which Quito is the capital) but an attempt at revolution in Cuenca, further south, was put down by the troops stationed there.—We have no news from the remaining mountain Province of Loxa [Loja?], adjoining Peru, but it probably has been, or will shortly be, occupied by the Peruvian forces, without resistance from the people.—The province of Cuenca & the Pacific provinces of Guayaquil, Manabi, and Esmeraldas, are those which adhere to the regular Government, but changes may occur in either at any moment.

[1] Despatches, Ecuador, vol. 5; enclosed with Buckalew to the Secretary of State, No. 8, May 18, 1859, below, this part, doc. 2456.   [2] Above, this part, doc. 2454.

[3] Despatches, Ecuador, vol. 5.   Received June 28.

[4] Not included in this publication, since it relates chiefly to the removal of the executive authorities of the government to Guayaquil, to the injurious effect of the Peruvian blockade of Guayaquil on the finances of Ecuador, and to the reported acceptance of the mediation of Chile by Peru.

[5] These two notes are above, this part, respectively, April 27 and May 12, 1859, docs. 2454 and 2455.

I suppose my duty will be to recognize the Revolutionary Government only in the event of its being generally established, & especially at Guayaquil, where our relations with the country are most important.—

I send, directed to the Department, several Newspapers and printed Bulletins relating to the revolutionary movement—to its commencement and progress.—

I am, with great respect [etc.].

2457

Charles R. Buckalew, United States Minister Resident in Ecuador, to Lewis Cass, Secretary of State of the United States [1]

[EXTRACT]

No. 11   QUITO, *August 24, 1859.*

DEAR SIR: Since my last despatch [2] the revolutionary party here has been entirely put down, the Government has returned to Quito, and a session of the Congress called for the 15th, of September—the regular time.

But the Peruvian difficulty continues.   The mediation by Chili and New Granada has fallen through, and the Ministers of those Powers publish a Statement reflecting in somewhat strong terms upon the Peruvian Government.—

In the early part of this month the Peruvian forces blockading Guayaquil determined to cut off the supply of water from the city.—Their boats, sent for that purpose, came into collision with the Ecuatorian troops, and several lives were lost.—Whereupon, on the 8th., the Peruvian Commander gave notice to the inhabitants to evacuate the city in three days, as he intended to attack and take it.—At the latest accounts the attack had not been made, but was still threatened.—Meantime, shore-batteries have been erected for defence, and a fight is probable.—

On the 12th. our war Steamer, the "Saranac", arrived in port and was to remain until the 20th. when it would proceed to Panama.—Perhaps its presence may have delayed hostilities.—I am informed that most of the inhabitants have left the city, and doubtless they have undergone much loss & suffering.—

The blockade has now lasted ten months, much to the discredit of Peru and with great loss to this country.—Originally instituted upon insufficient pretexts, it has been continued to aid the revolutionists in this country, and probably with the ultimate object of seizing and appropriating the valuable province of Guayaquil.—I believe the leading reason alleged by Peru for hostilities is the dismissal of her Minister to this country (Cavero) which

---

[1] Despatches, Ecuador, vol. 5.   Received September 16.
The omitted portion at the end of this despatch relates to the sending of newspapers and, also, to consular affairs.   [2] His No. 10 relates to his salary.

was a similar act to the dismissal of Crampton & quite as justifiable.—I may add, that the blockade has been irregularly conducted, and a recognition of its validity expressly refused by the English Government. . . .

With high regard [etc.].

2458

Aaron H. Palmer, Consul General of Ecuador in Washington, to Lewis Cass, Secretary of State of the United States [1]

WASHINGTON, *August 30, 1859.*

SIR: I have the honor of enclosing to you herewith an Official communication of mine published in the New York Herald of the 27th Inst. "On the contested Boundary Between Peru and Ecuador; and the combination of Peru and Brazil to exclude Ecuador from the free navigation of the Amazon" &c.[2]

Deeming the subject of immediate political as well as commercial importance to the United States, in view of the early contemplated opening of that river, and its principal affluents, to American Steam Navigation and commercial enterprise, I am induced to submit the communication to you for your information; and have the honor to be,

With the highest respect [etc.].

2459

Charles R. Buckalew, United States Minister Resident in Ecuador, to Lewis Cass, Secretary of State of the United States [3]

No. 12   QUITO, *September 20, 1859.*

SIR: Shortly after the date of my last despatch an arrangement was entered into between the Commander of the Peruvian forces blockading Guayaquil and General Franco Commander of the Ecuatorian troops in the city, under which the blockade was suspended.—The main feature of the agreement provided for the organization of a local, independent government for the city, by the citizens—This agreement has been approved by Gen. Castillo, the President of Peru, and the blockade declared raised.—The Peruvian vessels, however, remain off the city.—

About the end of August President Robles left this city and proceeded toward the coast.— Upon arriving at Bodegas (Babahoyo) he resigned the office of President and then went on to the Island of Puna below Guayaquil, where at the last accounts he was awaiting the Steamer of the 19th. (yesterday) in order to withdraw himself to Chili.—

[1] Notes from Ecuador, vol. 1. Received August 30.   [2] Not included in this publication.
[3] Despatches, Ecuador, vol. 2. Received October 29.

About the time he left Quito, the revolutionary party rose in the province of Imbabura (north) and, assisted by some New Granadians who came over the line, subdued the Government forces.—On Sunday, September 4th—the citizens rose at Quito, and after an hour's fighting took the cuartel, or Soldier's quarters, and re-established the authority of the Provisional Government of May— Nine or ten persons were killed in the fight.— Subsequently, most of the interior towns, and the province of Manibi upon the coast, have declared for the Provisional Government and it is likely it will soon be recognized by the whole country except Guayaquil.—What will happen there cannot be foreseen.—For my own part I have a strong impression that Peru intends eventually to seize and hold that city and the province connected with it, but it may turn out otherwise.—

Jose N. Casanova Esq. appointed Consul at Guayaquil has arrived at that port and entered upon the discharge of his official duties on the 23^{d} of last month.—

I have to acknowledge the receipt of Despatch No. 3. from the Department, dated 20 July last.[1]—

I remain [etc.].

2460

Charles R. Buckalew, United States Minister Resident in Ecuador, to Lewis Cass, Secretary of State of the United States [2]

No. 14   QUITO, *November 22, 1859.*

SIR: Since my despatch of Septr 20th.[3] was written, the following events have occurred in this country.—

The Provisional government at Quito has established its authority in all the Provinces except Guayaquil, where a local government exists under Gen Franco.—

In October Gen Castilla, the President of Peru, came in one of his vessels off Guayaquil, had an interview on board with Gen Franco, and sent a request to Quito for another interview with Gabriel Garcia Moreno, the leading man of the Provisional party.—He then issued a notice to the effect that the Ecuatorians must unite and establish a single government, or he would proceed to seize upon Guayaquil, after which he retired to Payta.— To that place he was followed by Garcia Moreno, & in the interview between them he made the unreasonable demand of twelve millions as the condition of peace.—Garcia Moreno returned in disgust to Quito.—

On the 8th. instant, Castilla returned & took position off Guayaquil with a dozen vessels of all sorts, and a force of four or five thousand men, but up to the 15th (the date of our latest news from the Coast) no landing had been effected or attack made.

[1] It was not pertinent to this publication.
[2] Despatches, Ecuador, vol. 5.   Received January 7.   [3] Above, this part, doc. 2459.

Ecuador is badly prepared for resistance, and it is reasonable to conclude that the city and province of Guayaquil will pass into the hands of Peru—
I am, very obediently [etc.].

2460a

Charles R. Buckalew, United States Minister Resident in Ecuador, to Lewis Cass, Secretary of State of the United States [1]

[EXTRACT]

No. 17   QUITO, *March 22, 1860.*

SIR: The regular mails between Quito and the coast have been interrupted by the civil war since sometime in January. I now write by an Express employed by the Foreign Ministers resident here.

The Provisional Government of Quito has succeeded in extending its authority over all the mountain country, including Cuenca and Loxa.— The Government of Gen Franco at Guayaquil is therefore confined to the lowlands west of the mountains. The negotiation of a Treaty by the latter with Peru, for the cession of the extensive unsettled region claimed by Ecuador east of the Andes, under pretence of adjusting boundary, has rendered that Government weak; has been followed by many popular protests from Municipalities, and has tended to strengthen the Provisional Government. . . .
I am, very truly [etc.].

2461

Roberto de Ascásubi, Secretary General of the Provisional Government of Ecuador, to Charles R. Buckalew, United States Minister Resident in Ecuador [2]

[TRANSLATION]

A   QUITO, *October 2, 1860.*

The undersigned, Secretary General of the Provisional Government, has the honor of communicating to the Honorable Minister Resident of the United States, that in consequence of the complete and decisive victory which the national army in Guayaquil achieved on the 24th of the past month, over the forces of the traitor William Franco, the Provisional Government is the only one acknowledged in all the extent of the Republic.—
The undersigned has also the pleasure of informing the Hon. Minister

[1] Despatches, Ecuador, vol. 5. Received April 19.
The omitted portion discusses consular affairs, and also relates to an enclosed newspaper containing the treaty discussed above in this despatch.
[2] Despatches, Ecuador, vol. 5; enclosed with Buckalew to the Secretary of State, No. 24, November 20, 1860, below, this part, doc. 2463.

Resident of the United States, that His Excellency the Supreme Chief & Director of the War, in pursuance of the ample powers with which he is invested, has thought proper to reestablish the ancient Ecuatorian flag, as appears by the Decree, of which, by the order of the Government I have the honor to transmit herewith an authorized copy.[1]—

With sentiments of particular regard [etc.].

2462

Charles R. Buckalew, United States Minister Resident in Ecuador, to Roberto de Ascásubi, Secretary General of the Provisional Government of Ecuador [2]

B   QUITO, *October 20, 1860.*

The undersigned, Minister Resident of the United States, has the honor to acknowledge the receipt of the note of the Honorable Secretary General, Señor Ascasubi, stating the extension of the authority of the Provisional Government to all parts of the Republic, and communicating the decree of His Excellency the Supreme Chief, dated at Guayaquil the 26th. ultimo, in relation to the National Flag.[3]—

The undersigned has to express his gratification at the termination of the civil war, and the restoration of peace.—The public events which began with the blockade of Guayaquil by Peru two years since and ended recently with the expulsion of Gen Franco from the country, afford an instructive lesson which ought not to be lost upon the people of Ecuador.—They prove the necessity of union and subordination to lawful authority, and that internal divisions provoke insult and injury from foreign Powers: They prove, also, that integrity and energy, united with patriotic intentions, will, in the end, always prevail over corruption and faction.—

That your country, Mr. Secretary General, may prosper in future; that it may retain its independence and attain to high character among the nations, is the sincere and earnest desire of the undersigned, who renews to the Honorable Señor [etc.].

[1] Not included in this publication.
[2] Despatches, Ecuador, vol. 5; enclosed with Buckalew to the Secretary of State, No. 24, November 20, 1860, below, this part, doc. 2463.   [3] Not included in this publication.

2463[1]

Charles R. Buckalew, United States Minister Resident in Ecuador, to Lewis Cass, Secretary of State of the United States [2]

No. 24   QUITO, *November 20, 1860.*

SIR: I have to inform you that an Election is appointed to take place in this country on the 29th. instant and the three following days, of Delegates from the several Provinces to a Convention which will meet at Quito on the 8th. of January next.—That body will reestablish a regular constitutional Administration.—

By a recent decree, the old flag of the Republic of Colombia is restored as the national flag of Ecuador.—I send, herewith, a copy of this decree and copies of notes that have passed between the Secretary General of the Provisional Government & myself upon the subject,[3] and upon the restoration of peace in the Republic.—The papers are marked A. and B. and are accompanied with the necessary translations.—

The additional volumes of the "Wilkes Exploring Expedition", received some time since, have been duly delivered to the Provisional Government, and their receipt politely acknowledged.—

I have the honor [etc.].

[1] Number 2466 follows this document. In numbering the documents, the numbers 2464 and 2465 were inadvertently omitted and the omission was discovered too late to warrant the numerous changes necessary for correction.

[2] Despatches, Ecuador, vol. 5. Received December 27.

[3] Above, this part, October 2 and 20, 1860, docs. 2461 and 2462.

PART V
COMMUNICATIONS TO FRANCE

COMMUNICATIONS TO FRANCE

2466

*Edward Livingston, Secretary of State of the United States, to William C. Rives,
United States Minister to France* [1]

[EXTRACT]

No. 42   WASHINGTON, *February 4, 1832.*

SIR: . . .[2] We are involved in some difficulty by a pretension of the
Buenos Ayrean Government to the exclusive possession of the Falkland
Islands, which they claim as part of the former Vice Royalty of La Plata,
and their title to which it is necessary to investigate.   The first permanent
settlement on these Islands appears to have been made by France some time
in 1766, or thereabouts.   Spain, a year or two afterwards was in possession
of this settlement, and under it disputed the title with the English.   I have
been unable to ascertain in what manner the possession passed from France
to Spain.   You probably can get this information, and if you can I could
wish to have a copy of the treaty or act of cession. . . .[3]

I am, with great respect, your obedient servant.

2467

*John Forsyth, Secretary of State of the United States, to Edouard Pontois,
French Minister to the United States* [4]

WASHINGTON, *May 4, 1838.*

SIR: I hasten to acknowledge the receipt of your note of yesterday's date,
together with the enclosed extract [5] of a despatch addressed to you on the
16th ultimo, by the Baron Deffaudis, notifying this Government, agreeably
to the orders of His Majesty the King of the French, that, in consequence of

---

[1] Instructions, France, vol. 14.
William C. Rives, of Virginia, to whom this instruction was addressed, was commissioned
as envoy extraordinary and minister plenipotentiary to France, on April 18, 1829.   He took
leave on September 27, 1832.   On July 20, 1849, he was again commissioned as envoy extraordinary and minister plenipotentiary to France, taking leave on May 12, 1853.
[2] In the omitted portion, Rives is informed of the ratification of the convention he had
negotiated.   [3] The omitted portion deals with routine matters.
[4] Notes to France, vol. 6.
Edouard Pontois, to whom this note was addressed, presented his credentials, as envoy
extraordinary and minister plenipotentiary of France, on April 14, 1837.   He took leave on
April 22, 1839.
[5] See below, this volume, pt. VI, doc. 2516, for the note from Pontois.   The extract enclosed therewith is not included in this publication.

the refusal of the Mexican Government to accept the ultimatum offered to it in March last by the French Government, with the view of effecting a reconciliation of the differences between them, all the ports of Mexico are declared to be in a state of blockade—and that this blockade was to be enforced, with regard to Vera Cruz, from and after the 15th of April; and has doubtless been since extended to the other ports of the Republic.

I have lost no time in submitting these papers to the President for his consideration, and in adopting such measures as were best calculated to give the earliest notice of this event to the American Public.

I have the honor [etc.].

2468

Aaron Vail, Acting Secretary of State of the United States, to Lewis Cass, United States Minister to France [1]

No. 26   WASHINGTON, *September 27, 1838.*

SIR: You are requested to obtain, if practicable, and forward to this Department, a copy of the "Convention entre la France et l'Espagne touchant les Possessions sur les Iles de Falkland—1767," noticed in Martens' "Guide Diplomatique," vol. 1, p. 52. It appears not to have been printed; but it is probable that no objection will be made, on an informal application at the office of Foreign Affairs, to furnish you with a transcript of it.

Your despatch of 14th August last, (without a number) [2] has just been received.

I am, Sir, respectfully, your obdt servant.

2469

Aaron Vail, Acting Secretary of State of the United States, to Lewis Cass, United States Minister to France [3]

No. 30   WASHINGTON, *October 29, 1838.*

SIR: The President sees with deep regret the continuance of the unfortunate controversy between France and Mexico, and it would afford him sincere pleasure if his agency could be employed in bringing it to a termination which would prove satisfactory to both parties. At the time the dispute began to assume its present hostile character, the relations between the United States and Mexico were of a nature which made it very difficult, if

[1] Instructions, France, vol. 14.
The name of the addressee, Lewis Cass, was written in pencil in the file copy of this instruction. For a biographical sketch of him, see above, vol. 1, doc. 36, note 2, p. 53.
[2] It probably should have been No. 59. See below, this volume, pt. VI, doc. 2524.
[3] Instructions, France, vol. 14.

not impossible, for this Government to take any steps in furtherance of so desirable an object.   Since then, however, the character of those relations has undergone a material change; negotiations entered into with a conciliatory disposition on the part of both Governments have resulted in the conclusion of a treaty by which, when it shall have been ratified, most of the matters in controversy between them, are to be submitted to the arbitrement of a friendly Power; and there is reason to believe that the residue will likewise be adjusted in a friendly spirit, although this expectation has not yet approached so near its realization as to authorize the resumption, on our part, of direct diplomatic relations with Mexico.   The President, therefore, would no longer feel any delicacy in tendering his good offices to contribute in bringing about an adjustment of the difference between Mexico and France, were he not precluded from the adoption of any specific steps in the matter by the information which has reached him that a movement to the same effect had been made in the shape of an offer of mediation by the Government of Great Britain, which he feels satisfied will do all in its power towards the attainment of the object in view.   He has, however, instructed me to make you acquainted with his sentiments in relation to this subject, and to authorize you to express to the French Government, or in any other quarter you may have reason to believe that the communication would be useful and acceptable, his readiness to afford his assistance in any form in which it may appear likely to prove beneficial to the parties concerned.   A communication of the same import with this, is this day addressed to the Minister of the United States at the British Court.

I am, Sir, [etc.].

2470

John Forsyth, Secretary of State of the United States, to Lewis Cass, United States Minister to France[1]

No. 39   WASHINGTON, *October 31, 1839.*

SIR: You will receive, enclosed, a petition recently addressed to this Department by M#r# Robert Upton, of Salem, in the State of Massachusetts, together with copies of correspondence and other documents [2] fully setting forth the particulars in regard to the seizure of the American brig Eliza Davidson, under the pretext that she had violated the blockade last year declared by His Majesty the King of the French against the Government of Buenos Ayres.   This vessel was arrested in March last, by the corvette "Perle," belonging to the French fleet, at the port of Loberia Chica on the coast of Patagonia, one hundred miles south of the river La Plata—she was carried back to Montevideo, anchored as a prize under the guns of the

---

[1] Instructions, France, vol. 14.   [2] Not included in this publication.

French Admiral's ship, and, after being detained a few days, was restored, but prohibited from returning to the same port to complete her cargo, by which means her voyage was entirely broken up, to the great loss and damage of the complainant.

You will find, upon an examination of the facts of this case, that the capture of this American vessel was made under circumstances which the French Government cannot, it is presumed, attempt to justify. It will only be necessary, therefore, to protest against this lawless exercise of authority on the part of France—to invite a disavowal of any intention on their part wantonly to harass our commerce,—and to claim from His Majesty's Government, in behalf of the memorialist, as it is the President's wish you should do, without needless delay, the redress of the petitioner's wrongs, and indemnification for his losses.

I have the honor [etc.].

2471

Daniel Webster, Secretary of State of the United States, to Lewis Cass, United States Minister to France [1]

No. 60   WASHINGTON, *January 27, 1842.*

SIR: I have received your despatch N⁰ 138, of the 17ᵗʰ ultimo,[2] transmitting the copy of a letter addressed to you by the diplomatic representative at the French Court of the Oriental Republic of Uruguay,[3] in which, under instructions from his Government, that Minister proposes to adopt initiatory measures for the negotiation of a Treaty of Friendship, Commerce, and Navigation, between the United States and that Republic. Having submitted these papers to the consideration of the President, I am directed to inform you, in reply, that, however desirous he may feel to extend and improve our commercial and friendly relations with the Governments of this hemisphere, and to place them under the high sanction of conventional stipulations; under existing circumstances, and especially whilst the difficulties between Buenos Ayres and Uruguay remain unadjusted, and the whole country continues in an unsettled and excited state as little favorable to the development of its natural resources and to the interests of its inhabitants as to the existence of useful diplomatic relations with other States, he cannot recognise in the present a fitting occasion of exemplifying his amicable dispositions towards that Republic, and must therefore defer, till a more auspicious season, any negotiation having that end in view.

I am, Sir, [etc.].

---

[1] Instructions, France, vol. 14.   [2] Below, this volume, pt. VI, doc. 2542.
[3] *Ibid.*, December 14, 1841, doc. 2541.

2472

John C. Calhoun, Secretary of State of the United States, to William R. King,
United States Minister to France [1]

No. 4   WASHINGTON, *August 12, 1844.*

SIR: I have laid your despatch N? 1 [2] before the President, who instructs
me to make known to you, that he has read it with much pleasure, especially
the portion, which relates to your cordial reception by the King, and his assurance of friendly feelings towards the United States.   The President, in
particular, highly appreciates the declaration of the King, that, in no event,
would any steps be taken by his Government in the slightest degree hostile,
or which would give to the United States just cause of complaint.   It was
the more gratifying, from the fact, that our previous information was calculated to make the impression, that the Government of France was prepared
to unite with Great Britain, in a joint protest against the annexation of
Texas, and a joint effort to induce her Government to withdraw the proposition to annex, on condition, that Mexico should be made to acknowledge her
independence.   He is happy to infer from your despatch, that the information, as far as it relates to France, is, in all probability, without foundation.
You did not go further than you ought in assuring the King, that the object
of annexation would be pursued with unabated vigor, and in giving your
opinion, that a decided majority of the American People were in its favor, and
that it would certainly be annexed at no distant day.   I feel confident, that
your anticipation will be fully realized at no distant period.   Every day will
tend to weaken that combination of political causes, which led to the opposition to the measure, and to strengthen the conviction, that it was not only
expedient, but just and necessary.

You were right in making the distinction between the interest of France
and England in reference to Texas; or rather, I would say, the apparent interests of the two countries.   France cannot possibly have any other than
commercial interest in desiring to see her preserve her separate independence;
while it is certain, that England looks beyond, to political interests, to
which she apparently attaches much importance.   But in our opinion the
interest of both against the measure, is more apparent than real; and that
neither France, England, nor even Mexico herself, has any in opposition to
it, when the subject is fairly viewed and considered in its whole extent and in
all its bearings.   Thus viewed and considered, and assuming that peace, the
extension of commerce, and security, are objects of primary policy with them,
it may, as it seems to me, be readily shown, that the policy on the part of

[1] Instructions, France, vol. 15.
  William R. King, of Alabama, to whom this instruction was addressed, was commissioned
envoy extraordinary and minister plenipotentiary to France, on April 9, 1844.   He took
leave on September 15, 1846.   Prior to this, he had been commissioned secretary of legation
to Russia, on April 23, 1816.   His successor was commissioned on November 30, 1818.
[2] Below, this volume, pt. VI, July 13, 1844, doc. 2551.

those Powers, which would acquiesce in a measure so strongly desired by
both the United States and Texas for their mutual welfare and safety, as the
annexation of the latter to the former, would be far more promotive of these
great objects, than that which would attempt to resist it.

It is impossible to cast a look at the map of the United States and Texas,
and to note the long, artificial and inconvenient line, which divides them,
and then to take into consideration the extraordinary increase of population
and growth of the former and the source from which the latter must derive
its inhabitants, institutions, and laws, without coming to the conclusion,
that it is their destiny to be united; and of course that annexation is merely
a question of *time* and *mode*. Thus regarded, the question to be decided
would seem to be, whether it would not be better to permit it to be done
now, with the mutual consent of both parties, and the acquiescence of these
Powers, than to attempt to resist and defeat it. If the former course be
adopted, the certain fruits would be the preservation of peace, great extension of commerce by the rapid settlement and improvement of Texas, and
increased security, especially to Mexico. The last, in reference to Mexico,
may be doubted; but I hold it not less clear than the other two.

It would be a great mistake to suppose, that this Government has any
hostile feelings towards Mexico, or any disposition to aggrandize itself at her
expense. The fact is the very reverse. It wishes her well, and desires to see
her settled down in peace and security; and is prepared, in the event of
annexation of Texas, if not forced into conflict with her, to propose to settle
with her the question of boundary and all others growing out of the annexation, on the most liberal terms. Nature herself has clearly marked the
boundary between her and Texas by natural limits too strong to be mistaken.
There are few countries whose limits are so distinctly marked; and it would
be our desire, if Texas should be united to us, to see them firmly established,
as the most certain means of establishing permanent peace between the two
countries, and strengthening and cementing their friendship.

Such would be the certain consequence of permitting the annexation to
take place now with the acquiescence of Mexico; but very different would be
the case, if it should be attempted to resist and defeat it; whether the attempt should be successful for the present or not. Any attempt of the kind
would, not improbably, lead to a conflict between us and Mexico, and involve
consequences in reference to her and the general peace, long to be deplored
on all sides, and difficult to be repaired. But should that not be the case,
and the interference of another Power defeat the annexation for the present,
without the interruption of peace, it would but postpone the conflict, and
render it more fierce and bloody, whenever it might occur. Its defeat would
be attributed to enmity and ambition on the part of that Power by whose
interference it was occasioned, and excite deep jealousy and resentment on
the part of our People, who would be ready to seize the first favorable

opportunity to effect by force, what was prevented from being done peaceably by mutual consent. It is not difficult to see how greatly such a conflict, come when it might, would endanger the general peace, and how much Mexico might be the loser by it.

In the mean time, the condition of Texas would be rendered uncertain, her settlement and prosperity in consequence retarded, and her commerce crippled, while the general peace would be rendered much more insecure. It could not but greatly affect us. If the annexation of Texas should be permitted to take place peaceably now, as it would without the interference of other Powers, the energies of our People would, for a long time to come, be directed to the peaceable pursuits of redeeming and bringing within the pale of cultivation, improvement, and civilization, that large portion of the continent, lying between Mexico, on one side, and the British possessions on the other; which is now, with little exception, a wilderness, with a sparse population, consisting, for the most part, of wandering Indian tribes. It is our destiny to occupy that vast region; to intersect it with roads and canals; to fill it with cities, towns, villages, and farms; to extend over it our religion, customs, constitution, and laws; and to present it as a peaceful and splendid addition to the domains of commerce and civilization. It is our policy to increase by growing and spreading out into unoccupied regions, assimilating all we incorporate. In a word, to increase by accretion, and not through conquest by the addition of masses held together by the cohesion of force. No system can be more unsuited to the latter process, or better adapted to the former, than our admirable Federal System. If it should not be resisted in its course, it will probably fulfil its destiny, without disturbing our neighbors, or putting in jeopardy the general peace; but, if it be opposed by foreign interference, a new direction would be given to our energy much less favorable to harmony with our neighbors, and to the general peace of the world. The change would be undesirable to us, and much less in accord with what I have assumed to be primary objects of policy on the part of France, England, and Mexico.

But, to descend to particulars; it is certain, that while England, like France, desires the independence of Texas, with the view to commercial connections, it is not less so, that one of the leading motives of England for desiring it, is the hope, that, through her diplomacy and influence, negro slavery may be abolished there, and ultimately, by consequence, in the United States, and throughout the whole of this continent. That its ultimate abolition throughout the entire continent is an object ardently desired by her, we have decisive proof, in the declaration of the Earl of Aberdeen delivered to this Department,[1] and of which you will find a copy among the documents transmitted to Congress with the Texan Treaty. That she de-

[1] For this declaration, dated December 26, 1843, see below, vol. VII, pt. II, footnote to Pakenham's letter of February 26, 1844, doc. 2826.

sires its abolition in Texas, and has used her influence and diplomacy to effect it there, the same document, with the correspondence of this Department with Mr. Pakenham,[1] also to be found among the documents, furnishes proof not less conclusive.   That one of the objects of abolishing it there, is to facilitate its abolition in the United States, and throughout the continent, is manifest from the declaration of the abolition party and societies, both in this country and England.   In fact, there is good reason to believe, that the scheme of abolishing it in Texas, with the view to its abolition in the United States and over the continent, originated with the prominent members of the party in the United States; and was first broached by them in the so called World's Convention, held in London, in the year 1840, and, through its agency, brought to the notice of the British Government.

Now, I hold, not only that France can have no interest in the consummation of this grand scheme, which England hopes to accomplish, through Texas, if she can defeat the annexation; but that her interests, and those of all the continental Powers of Europe, are directly and deeply opposed to it.

It is too late in the day to contend that humanity, or philanthropy, is the great object of the policy of England in attempting to abolish African slavery on this continent.   I do not question but humanity may have been one of her leading motives for the abolition of the African slave trade; and that it may have had a considerable influence, in abolishing slavery in her West Indian possessions; aided, indeed, by the fallacious calculation that the labor of the negroes would be at least as profitable, if not more so, in consequence of the measure.   She acted on the principle, that tropical products can be produced cheaper by free African labor and East India labor, than by slave labor.   She knew full well the value of such products to her commerce, navigation, navy, manufactures, revenue, and power.   She was not ignorant, that the support and the maintenance of her political preponderance depended on her tropical possessions; and had no intention of diminishing their productiveness, nor any anticipation that such would be the effect, when the scheme of abolishing slavery in her colonial possessions was adopted. On the contrary, she calculated to combine philanthropy with profit and power, as is not unusual with fanaticism.   Experience has convinced her of the fallacy of her calculations.   She has failed in all her objects.   The labor of her negroes has proved far less productive, without affording the consolation of having improved their condition.

The experiment has turned out to be a costly one.   She expended nearly one hundred millions of dollars in indemnifying the owners of the emancipated slaves.   It is estimated that the increased price paid since by the People of Great Britain for sugar and other tropical productions, in consequence of the measure, is equal to half that sum; and that twice that amount

[1] See Pakenham's notes, dated April 19 and 30, 1844, below, vol. VII, pt. II, docs. 2828 and 2829; and Calhoun's notes to Pakenham, dated April 18 and 27, 1844, below, vol. VII, pt. I, docs. 2678 and 2679.

has been expended in the suppression of the slave trade; making together two hundred and fifty millions of dollars as the cost of the experiment. Instead of realizing her hope, the result has been a sad disappointment. Her tropical products have fallen off to a vast amount. Instead of supplying her own wants and those of nearly all Europe, with them, as formerly, she has now, in some of the most important articles, scarcely enough to supply her own. What is worse, her own colonies are actually consuming sugar, produced by slave labor, brought direct to England, or refined in bond, and exported and sold in her colonies as cheap, or cheaper, than they can be produced there; while the slave trade, instead of diminishing, has been, in fact, carried on to a greater extent than ever. So disastrous has been the result, that her fixed capital vested in tropical possessions, estimated at the value of nearly five hundred millions of dollars, is said to stand on the brink of ruin.

But this is not the worst. While this costly scheme has had such ruinous effects on the tropical productions of Great Britain, it has given a powerful stimulus, followed by a corresponding increase of products, to those countries which have had the good sense to shun her example. There has been vested, it is estimated, by them, in the production of tropical products, since 1808, in fixed capital, nearly four thousand millions of dollars, wholly dependent on slave labor. In the same period, the value of their products has been estimated to have risen from about seventy-two millions of dollars annually to nearly two hundred and twenty millions, while the whole of the fixed capital of Great Britain, vested in cultivating tropical products, both in the East and West Indies, is estimated at only about eight hundred and thirty millions of dollars, and the value of the products annually at about fifty millions of dollars. To present a still more striking view. Of three articles of tropical products, sugar, coffee, and cotton, the British possessions, including the West and East Indies, and Mauritius, produced, in 1842, of sugar only, 3,993,771 pounds, while Cuba, Brazil, and the United States, excluding other countries having tropical possessions, produced 9,600,000 pounds; of coffee, the British possessions produced only 27,393,003, while Cuba and Brazil produced 201,590,125 pounds; and of cotton the British possessions, including shipments to China, only 137,443,446 lbs. while the United States alone produced 790,479,275 lbs.

The above facts and estimates have all been drawn from a British periodical of high standing and authority,[1] and are believed to be entitled to credit. This vast increase of the capital and production on the part of those Nations, who have continued their former policy towards the negro race, compared with that of Great Britain, indicates a corresponding relative increase of the means of commerce, navigation, manufactures, wealth, and

[1] There is an asterisk at this point in the document referring to a footnote which reads, "Blackwood's Magazine for June, 1844."

power. It is no longer a question of doubt, that the great source of the wealth, prosperity, and power of the more civilized Nations of the temperate zone, especially Europe, where the arts have made the greatest advance depends, in a great degree, on the exchange of their products with those of the tropical regions. So great has been the advance made in the arts, both chymical and mechanical, within the few last generations, that all the old civilized Nations can, with but a small part of their labor and capital, supply their respective wants, which tends to limit, within narrow bounds, the amount of the commerce between them, and forces them all to seek for markets in the tropical regions, and the more newly settled portions of the globe. Those who can best succeed in commanding those markets, have the best prospect of outstripping the others in the career of commerce, navigation, manufactures, wealth, and power.

This is seen and felt by British statesmen, and has opened their eyes to the errors which they have committed. The question now with them is, how shall it be counteracted? What has been done cannot be undone. The question is, by what means can Great Britain regain and keep a superiority in tropical cultivation, commerce, and influence? Or, shall that be abandoned, and other Nations be suffered to acquire the supremacy, even to the extent of supplying British markets to the destruction of the capital already vested in their production? These are the questions which now profoundly occupy the attention of her statesmen, and have the greatest influence over her councils.

In order to regain her superiority, she not only seeks to revive and increase her own capacity to produce tropical productions, but to diminish and destroy the capacity of those who have so far outstripped her in consequence of her error. In pursuit of the former, she has cast her eyes to her East India possessions; to Central and Eastern Africa, with the view of establishing colonies there, and even to restore, substantially, the slave trade itself, under the specious name of transporting free laborers from Africa to her West India possessions, in order, if possible, to compete successfully with those who have refused to follow her suicidal policy. But these all afford but uncertain and distant hopes of recovering her lost superiority. Her main reliance is, on the other alternative, to cripple or destroy the productions of her successful rivals. There is but one way by which it can be done, and that is, by abolishing African slavery throughout this continent; and that she openly avows to be the constant object of her policy and exertions. It matters not how, or for what motive, it may be done; whether it be by diplomacy, influence, or force; by secret or open means; and whether the motive be humane or selfish, without regard to manner, means, or motive,—the thing itself, should it be accomplished, would put down all rivalry, and give her the undisputed supremacy in supplying her own wants and those of the rest of the world; and thereby more than fully retrieve what she has lost by her errors.

It would give her the monopoly of tropical productions, which I shall next proceed to show.

What would be the consequence, if this object of her unceasing solicitude and exertions should be effected by the abolition of negro slavery throughout this continent, some idea may be formed, from the immense diminution of productions, as has been shown, which has followed abolition in her West India possessions.   But as great as that has been, it is nothing, compared to what would be the effect, if she should succeed in abolishing slavery in the United States, Cuba, Brazil, and throughout this continent.   The experiment in her own colonies was made under the most favorable circumstances. It was brought about gradually and peaceably, by the steady and firm operation of the parent country, armed with complete power to prevent or crush at once all insurrectionary movements on the part of the negroes, and able and disposed to maintain, to the full, the political and social ascendency of the former masters over their former slaves.   It is not at all wonderful, that the change of the relations of master and slave took place, under such circumstances, without violence and bloodshed, and that order and peace should have been since preserved.   Very different would be the result of abolition, should it be effected by her influence and exertions, in the possessions of other countries on this continent, and especially in the United States, Cuba, and Brazil, the great cultivators of the principal tropical products of America.   To form a correct conception of what would be the result with them, we must look, not to Jamaica, but, to St. Domingo, for an example. The change would be followed by unforgiving hate between the two races, and end in a bloody and deadly struggle between them for the superiority. One or the other would have to be subjugated, extirpated, or expelled, and desolation would overspread their territories, as in St. Domingo, from which it would take centuries to recover.   The end would be, that the superiority in cultivating the great tropical staples would be transferred from them to the British tropical possessions.

They are of vast extent, and those beyond the Cape of Good Hope possessed of an unlimited amount of labor, standing ready, by the aid of British capital, to supply the deficit which would be occasioned by destroying the tropical productions of the United States, Cuba, Brazil, and other countries cultivated by slave labor on this continent, so soon as the increased price, in consequence, would yield a profit.   It is the successful competition of that labor, which keeps the prices of the great tropical staples so low, as to prevent their cultivation with profit in the possessions of Great Britain, by what she is pleased to call free labor.   If she can destroy its competition, she would have a monopoly in those productions.   She has all the means of furnishing an unlimited supply; vast and fertile possessions in both Indies; boundless command of capital and labor; and ample power to suppress disturbances, and preserve order throughout her wide domains.

It is unquestionable, that she regards the abolition of slavery in Texas, as a most important step towards this great object of policy, so much the aim of her solicitude and exertions, and the defeat of the annexation of Texas to our Union, as indispensable to the abolition of slavery there. She is too sagacious not to see, what a fatal blow it would give to slavery in the United States, and how certainly its abolition with us would abolish it over the whole continent, and thereby give her a monopoly in the productions of the great tropical staples, and the command of the commerce, navigation, and manufactures of the world, with an established naval ascendency and political preponderance. To this continent the blow would be calamitous beyond description. It would destroy, in a great measure, the cultivation and production of the great tropical staples, amounting annually in value to nearly three hundred millions of dollars; the fund which stimulates and upholds almost every other branch of its industry; commerce, navigation, and manufactures. The whole, by their joint influence, are rapidly spreading population, wealth, improvement, and civilization over the whole continent, and vivifying, by their overflow, the industry of Europe, thereby increasing its population, wealth, and advancement in the arts, in power, and civilization.

Such must be the result, should Great Britain succeed in accomplishing the constant object of her desire and exertions, the abolition of negro slavery over this continent; and towards the effecting of which she regards the defeat of the annexation of Texas to our Union so important. Can it be possible that Governments so enlightened and sagacious as those of France and the other great continental Powers can be so blinded by the plea of philanthropy, as not to see what must inevitably follow, be her motive what it may, should she succeed in her object? It is little short of mockery to talk of philanthropy, with the examples before us of the effects of abolishing negro slavery in her own colonies, in St. Domingo, and the northern States of our Union; where statistical facts, not to be shaken, prove, that the freed negro, after the experience of sixty years, is in a far worse condition, than in the other States, where he has been left in his former condition. No; the effect of what is called abolition, where the number is few, is not to raise the inferior race to the condition of freemen, but to deprive the negro of the guardian care of his owner, subject to all the depression and oppression belonging to his inferior condition. But, on the other hand, where the number is great, and bears a large proportion to the whole population, it would be still worse. It would be to substitute, for the existing relation, a deadly strife between the two races, to end in the subjection, expulsion, or extirpation of one or the other, and such would be the case over the greater part of this continent, where negro slavery exists. It would not end there; but would, in all probability extend, by its example, the war of races over all South America, including Mexico, and extending to the Indian as well as to the African race; and make the whole one scene of blood and devastation.

Dismissing, then, the stale and unfounded plea of philanthropy, can it be, that France and the other great continental Powers, seeing what must be the result of the policy for the accomplishment of which England is constantly exerting herself, and that the defeat of the annexation of Texas is so important towards its consummation, are prepared to back, or countenance, her in her efforts, to effect either? What possible motives can they have to favor her cherished policy? Is it not better for them, that they should be supplied with tropical products, in exchange for their labor, from the United States, Brazil, Cuba, and this continent generally, than to be dependant on one great monopolizing Power for their supply? Is it not better, that they should receive them at the low prices, which competition, cheaper means of production, and nearness of market would furnish them by the former, than to give the high prices, which monopoly, dear labor, and great distance from market would impose? Is it not better, that their labor should be exchanged with a new continent, rapidly increasing in population, and the capacity for consuming, and which would furnish, in the course of a few generations, a market nearer to them, and of almost unlimited extent, for the products of their industry and arts, than with old and distant regions, whose population has long since reached its growth?

The above contains those enlarged views of policy which, it seems to me, an enlightened European statesman ought to take, in making up his opinion on the subject of the annexation of Texas, and the grounds, as it may be inferred, on which England mainly opposes it. They certainly involve considerations of the deepest importance, and demanding the greatest attention. Viewed in connection with them, the question of annexation becomes one of the first magnitude, not only to Texas and the United States, but to this continent and Europe. They are presented, that you may use them on all suitable occasions, where you think they may be with effect, in your correspondence, where it can be done with propriety, or otherwise. The President relies with confidence on your sagacity, prudence, and zeal. Your mission is one of the first magnitude, at all times, but especially now; and he feels assured, nothing will be left undone on your part to do justice to the country and the Government in reference to this great measure. I have said nothing as to our right of treating with Texas, without consulting Mexico. You so fully understand the grounds on which we rest our right, and are so familiar with all the facts necessary to maintain them, that it was not thought necessary to add any thing in reference to it.

I am, Sir, very respectfully [etc.].

2473

John C. Calhoun, Secretary of State of the United States, to William R. King, United States Minister to France [1]

No. 6   WASHINGTON, *August 26, 1844.*

SIR: I have the honor to acknowledge the receipt of your despatch Nº 2, dated July 31ˢᵗ,[2] and to express my gratification at the result of your conversation with Mr. Guizot; especially that part of it which refers to the rumored protest of the French Government, conjointly with that of Great Britain, against the proposed annexation of Texas to the United States. Such a step, had it been taken by France, must have excited unkind feelings, and given to the United States just cause of complaint. The Government of the United States will confidently rely on the assurances of Mr. Guizot; and it is hoped that, neither separately, nor jointly with any other Power, will France adopt a course which would seem so little in accordance with her true interests, or the friendly relations which have so long subsisted between the two countries.

My reply [3] to your first despatch [4] which was forwarded by the last steamer, renders it unnecessary for me to enlarge on the topics presented in your last. In regard to Mr. Guizot's inquiry respecting a proposed guaranty of the independence of Texas, your reply was well-timed and judicious. The settled policy of the United States has been to avoid entering into such guaranties, except in cases of strong necessity. The present case offers no reasons to warrant a deviation from that policy. On the contrary it presents a strong additional reason why it should be adhered to, as such a guaranty would permanently defeat the proposed measure of annexation which both countries seem anxious to advance. A suggestion of the same purport was made to me, by the British Minister here, Mr. Pakenham, during a casual conversation, soon after I came into office; and he was promptly informed that the Government of the United States could not accede to such a proposition.

I am, Sir, respectfully [etc.].

¹ Instructions, France, vol. 15.   ² Below, this volume, pt. VI, doc. 2552.
³ Above, this part, August 12, 1844, doc. 2472.
⁴ Below, this volume, pt. VI, July 13, 1844, doc. 2551.

2474

John C. Calhoun, Secretary of State of the United States, to William R. King,
United States Minister to France [1]

No. 9   WASHINGTON, *September 12, 1844.*

SIR: I herewith transmit to you a copy of a despatch to the Honorable
Wilson Shannon our Minister at Mexico,[2] in order that you may be possessed
of the views of your Government in regard to Texas, and the proposed invasion by Mexico. The despatch is also designed as a reply, incidentally, to
the appeal made by Mexico to the Ministers of Foreign Powers.

I am, Sir, respectfully [etc.].

2475

James Buchanan, Secretary of State of the United States, to William R. King,
United States Minister to France [3]

No. 18   WASHINGTON, *March 25, 1845.*

SIR: Your despatch, N⁰ 11, under date of the 27th ultimo,[4] has been received and submitted to the President. In commencing his administration,
he had confidently hoped, that the Government of France was animated by
the same kind spirit towards the United States which inspires the Government and People of this country in all their conduct towards their ancient
Revolutionary ally. This agreeable impression was made upon his mind by
the emphatic declaration of His Majesty to yourself, on the 4th July last,
when speaking on the subject of the annexation of Texas to our Union, "that
in any event no steps would be taken by his Government, in the slightest
degree hostile, or which would give to the United States just cause of complaint." [5] The President was also gratified with the subsequent assurance
of Mr. Guizot given to yourself, that France had not acted, and would not
act, in concert with Great Britain for the purpose of preventing annexation,
but that, in any course she might pursue, she would proceed independently of
that Power. You may then judge of the surprise and regret of the President,
when he discovered from your last despatch [6] that the Governments of
France and Great Britain were now acting in concert and endeavoring, by a
joint effort, to dissuade the Government and People of Texas from giving
their consent to annexation. Nay, more, that so intimate has been their

[1] This instruction was copied from Instructions, Netherlands, vol. 14, since an index entry in Instructions, France, vol. 15, stated that No. 9, to Minister King, was the same as
No. 22, of this date, to Minister Hughes, at The Hague.
[2] See below, instruction No. 6 to Shannon, dated September 10, 1844, vol. VIII, pt. I,
doc. 3243.
[3] Instructions, France, vol. 15.   [4] Below, this volume, pt. VI, doc. 2557.
[5] See King's No. 1, below, this volume, pt. VI, July 13, 1844, doc. 2551.
[6] No. 11, below, this volume, pt. VI, February 27, 1845, doc. 2557.

alliance to accomplish this purpose, that even "the instructions of the French Government to its representatives in Texas had been communicated to Lord Aberdeen."

The People of Texas are sovereign and independent. Under Providence, they hold their destiny in their own hands. Justice to them requires that they should have been left free to decide the question of annexation for themselves, without foreign interference, and without being biased by foreign influence. Not a doubt exists but that the People of the two Republics are anxious to form a reünion. Indeed the enthusiastic unanimity which has been displayed by the citizens of Texas in favor of annexation is unexampled in the history of Nations. Little reason, then, have we to anticipate that whilst the two Republics were proceeding to adjust the terms for accomplishing this reünion, that France, in concert with Great Britain, and under the lead of that Power, should interpose her efforts and her influence to paralyze and arrest the free action of the People of Texas, and thus place herself in an unfriendly attitude towards the United States.

The President leaves it to your sound discretion to decide whether you ought not to embrace a favorable opportunity to communicate, formally or informally to the Government of France, the painful disappointment which he has experienced from a review of these circumstances.

I am, Sir, respectfully [etc.].

2476

James Buchanan, Secretary of State of the United States, to William R. King, United States Minister to France

No. 32   WASHINGTON, *May 14, 1846.*

SIR: [Same as instruction No. 24, of this date, to W. A. Harris, Esquire, chargé d'affaires of the United States at Buenos Aires.[1] It announced the declaration of war between the United States and Mexico.]

[1] Above, vol. I, doc. 17.

2477

*James Buchanan, Secretary of State of the United States, to Alphonse Pageot,
French Minister to the United States* [1]

WASHINGTON, *July 16, 1847.*

SIR: I have the honor of transmitting to you a copy of the explanation
made by Commodore Sloat to the Secretary of the Navy, on the 2^{d} ultimo,[2]

[1] Notes to France, vol. 6.
Alphonse Joseph Yver Pageot served as minister plenipotentiary *ad interim*, of France,
from November 14, 1842, until January, 1848. He presented his credentials, as envoy
extraordinary and minister plenipotentiary of France, in January 1848. His services terminated on March 29, 1848.
[2] This communication from Sloat to the Acting Secretary of the Navy follows:

Commodore John D. Sloat to John Appleton, Acting Secretary of the Navy

NEW YORK, *June 2, 1847.*

SIR: I have the honor to acknowledge the receipt of your letter of the 29th ult^{o} with
its enclosure. [Not included in this publication.—Ed.] In reply, I have to state that
no "unpleasant correspondence" occurred between the Acting French Consul at
Monterey and myself in consequence of his protesting against my taking possession of
California. A correspondence of that character however did take place respecting the
apprehension and detention of a Frenchman, named Cambuston, who, some days after I
took possession, joined a Mexican officer and his party, and left Monterey to join
General Castro.
A few miles from Monterey they seized Augustine Escobar, a native farmer, at his
house, tied him, and abused him in a shameful manner. Cambuston held a loaded
pistol in his hand, threatening him, while the party robbed him of his rifle, pistols, ammunition, money and several horses. All this was proved by the affidavit of Escobar,
who is a respectable man, known to all the American and English residents of Monterery.
Cambuston went with the party and joined Generals Pico and Castro at Santa Bar-
bara. They, knowing his character, availed themselves of his services, and ostensibly
sent him back to deliver a letter to me from Gen! Pico, which letter was not of the least
consequence, and was merely a cover to enable him to bring communications to their
friends. He came into town stealthily at night on foot, and succeeded in avoiding our
sentinels, and delivered his despatches, said to have come under cover to the French
Consul, soon after which he was made prisoner.
He did not deliver the letter for me until two or three days subsequent, when he had
become alarmed, fearing he would be treated as a spy. I did not, however, think it
advisable to proceed against him as such, being desirous to avoid any difficulty with the
French Consul, knowing he was disposed to be troublesome. I therefore concluded to
turn him over to the civil authority to be tried for robbery and maltreatment of a citizen. The Alcalde immediately admitted him to bail. Out of the above occurrence,
and the seizure by Capt. Mervin (who commanded the town), of about two gallons of
liquor of another French subject by the name of Oliver, who had opened a grog-shop
(not a grocery store), within a few yards of the quarters of our men, contrary to an
ordinance posted up about the town.
It so happened that shortly after the latter occurrence, I was on shore and met the
acting French Consul for the first time at Capt. Mervin's quarters, where the circumstances was [*sic*] enquired into in his presence. Oliver denied having sold any liquor,
but admitted it was exhibited in his shop. Capt. Mervin had discovered it immediately
after his doors were opened, and before he had had an opportunity to dispose of any.
He was extremely insolent to Capt. Mervin, who was confident he would furnish it to his
men if he had an opportunity: he therefore directed it to be emptied on the sand. No
indemnity was promised him by me! All that was said was that if his future conduct
was unexceptionable I would take his case into consideration: nor was he ever required
or asked to come on board the Savannah to be paid. The truth is, the Acting French
Consul was extremely inimical to us, and was also exceedingly discourteous (indeed I might
use much stronger terms), in his communications to me, which, however, I took no notice of, except by discontinuing the correspondence. At this time, I transferred the

in answer to the charges of misconduct preferred against him by Mr. Gasquet, the Acting Consul of France at Monterey, and by Messrs. Cambuston and Olivier, French subjects, and which you communicated to the Department by your informal note of the 30th April last.[1]

From the known prudence and discretion of the Commodore, I was persuaded at the time that these charges could not have been well-founded: and I think you will agree with me that so far as he is concerned, they have been entirely refuted. Commodore Stockton who succeeded him in the command of our naval forces may soon be expected in Washington. Upon his arrival, he will also be asked for explanations: and his answer shall be immediately communicated to you.

It is to be regretted that the Acting Consul of France so far forgot his duty and the relations of cordial amity existing between the two Governments as to have officially protested against Commodore Sloat for having taken possession of California in the exercise of the rights of war. This act, with the subsequent unfriendly conduct of Mr. Gasquet, was well calculated to induce French subjects in that remote region to believe that they would be acting in conformity with the wishes of their own Government in taking part with the enemy. Such an impression may have given rise to the very exceptionable proceedings of Mr. Cambuston; and I am gratified that the manner in which he was treated by Commodore Sloat was so mild and forbearing.

I avail myself of this occasion [etc.].

2478

John M. Clayton, Secretary of State of the United States, to William C. Rives, United States Minister to France [2]

No. 9   WASHINGTON, *January 26, 1850.*

SIR: It being very desirable that France should coöperate with the United States in a guaranty to protect any works which may be undertaken

---

command to Commodore Stockton, with copies of all the correspondence. From the course the Consul had pursued since my arrival at Monterey, the Commodore considered it necessary for our safety, and to prevent further difficulties, to direct him to retire some distance in the country, giving him forty-eight hours to remove, with which he refused to comply. At the end of the time, the Com. confined him to his own house. I have the correspondence so far as it was entered into by me, and the affidavit of the farmer Augustine Escobar, and can furnish the Department with it if desired: indeed, I am anxious that the Government should fully understand the course I pursued towards that troublesome functionary.

I return, herewith, the memorandum as requested; and have the honor [etc.].

[1] Below, this volume, pt. VI, doc. 2583.
[2] Instructions, France, vol. 15.
Instruction No. 2 to Rives, dated August 16, 1849, written to him apparently before he left the United States, directed him to stop in London on his way to Paris and to carry out

to facilitate the intercourse between the Atlantic and Pacific Oceans, I have to request that you will bring the subject to the notice of the French Government, with the view of ascertaining what it will be willing to do towards carrying this object into effect. You will, for this purpose, first ascertain whether the French Government is disposed to enter into treaty stipulations with New Granada and Nicaragua similar to the stipulations contained in our late treaties with those Republics. If France should be disinclined to such a measure, you then might propose to that Government that it should enter into a treaty with the Government of the United States upon the same subject. Should your first proposition, however, be favorably received, it might not be necessary at present to mention the second. You will accordingly lose no time in informing the Department of the result, when we will instruct our Diplomatic Agents in Central America and New Granada to make it known to the Governments of those countries, in order that they may adopt the necessary measures to conclude suitable treaty stipulations upon the subject with the Government of France. If, however, that Government should be averse to treating directly with the Governments of the Spanish American States, but should still be willing to treat with this Government, you will also promptly inform the Department of the fact, when the necessary powers, with instructions relative to the details of the negotiation, will be transmitted to you.

You are aware that there are three routes for the proposed interoceanic communication. It is not unlikely that they may all ultimately be used for this purpose. A wise forecast therefore would seem to dictate that any stipulations which may be entered into with the view to protect any one of them should be applicable for the same purpose to the others, and should be equally acceptable to the parties to any treaty upon the subject. We have not yet concluded any convention with Mexico in regard to Tehuantepec; but our Minister to that Republic is instructed to propose one to the Mexican Government.

The obstruction which the route by the way of the river San Juan and the lakes of Nicaragua may possibly meet with from the pretensions of Great Britain; the grounds of those pretensions; and the views of this Government with regard to them, you are already well acquainted with. In order, however, to enable you to furnish the French Government with specific information upon these points, should it be desired, a copy of the instructions to the United States' Legation at London,[1] in regard to them, is herewith transmitted. Copies of the treaty between the United States and New Granada,

---

instructions which had been previously given to Bancroft as minister to Great Britain (see below, vol. VII, pt. I, No. 55 to Bancroft, under date of May 2, 1849, doc. 2690), i. e., if Bancroft himself had not already done so. Because of the nature of this instruction to Rives, it has been included below, vol. VII, pt. I, doc. 2694.

[1] This probably refers to instruction No. 4 to Lawrence, under date of October 20, 1849, below, vol. VII, pt. I, doc. 2697.

of the 12th December, 1846, and a transcript of the 35th article of our recent treaty with Nicaragua—which treaty will soon be submitted to the Senate—are also herewith enclosed.[1]

I have lately had reason to hope that Great Britain may settle the Nicaragua controversy with us by a friendly treaty—of which I will give you the earliest advice.

I am, Sir, respectfully [etc.].

2479

John M. Clayton, Secretary of State of the United States, to William C. Rives, United States Minister to France [2]

No. 12   WASHINGTON, *April 27, 1850.*

SIR: I informed you in my despatch N° 9, of the 26th January last,[3] that I had reason to hope that Great Britain would settle the Nicaragua controversy with us by a friendly treaty, of which I would give you the earliest advice.   In fulfilment of this promise, I now have the satisfaction of acquainting you that Sir H. L. Bulwer concluded a Convention with me on the 19th instant for facilitating and protecting the construction of a ship canal between the Atlantic and Pacific Oceans, which is alike honorable to both countries.   This Convention provides that neither party to it shall make use of any protection or alliance for the purpose of occupying, fortifying, colonizing, or assuming or exercising any dominion whatsoever over any part of Central America or the Mosquito Coast.   Virtually it makes provision also for the protection of the Company which already has the charter from Nicaragua, and which is protected by Squier's treaty, as well as for the future protection of the Tehuantepec and Panamá routes, and all other practicable routes across the Isthmus.   It prohibits the blockade of vessels traversing the canal; it liberates all Central America from foreign aggression; and it will, in short, when known, be hailed as a declaration of Central American Independence.   The Convention is now before the Senate, which will no doubt consent to its ratification, when a copy of it will be transmitted to you, in order that, at the proper time, you may invite the French Government to enter into the treaty of accession for which the Convention provides.   A full power for this purpose will hereafter be forwarded to you.

I am, Sir, respectfully [etc.].

---

[1] For the text of the former, see Malloy, *Treaties, Conventions, etc., between the United States and Other Powers*, vol. I, pp. 302–314, and for the latter, which is, presumably, a reference to the article of that number, in the treaty of September 3, 1849, see above, vol. III, doc. 922, note 2, p. 360.   [2] Instructions, France, vol. 15.   [3] Above, this part, doc. 2478.

2480

*John M. Clayton, Secretary of State of the United States, to William C. Rives,
United States Minister to France* [1]

WASHINGTON, *May 26, 1850.*

SIR: Enclosed herewith, I send you a printed copy of the "Convention
between the United States of America and Her Britannic Majesty, concluded at Washington the nineteenth day of April, A. D. eighteen hundred
and fifty," [2] which was ratified by the Senate on Wednesday last, by a vote
of forty-two against ten.   I also enclose a copy of the President's message
communicating the Convention to the Senate.   I have every reason to believe that the treaty will soon be, (if it has not already been,) ratified by the
British Government.

As it is desired by the United States and Great Britain that the great
interoceanic communication across the Isthmus contemplated in the treaty
shall also be open on equal terms to the citizens and subjects of every other
State which is willing to grant thereto such protection as the United States
and Great Britain engage by the treaty to afford, I hope you will lose no time
in bringing this subject to the notice of the Minister of Foreign Affairs of
France, and negotiating with the French Government a convention in the
very words, as far as the same are applicable, of the one concluded between
the United States and Great Britain.

I am, Sir, [etc.].

2481

*Daniel Webster, Secretary of State of the United States, to Sain de Boislecomte,
French Minister to the United States* [3]

WASHINGTON, *August 24, 1850.*

SIR: I have received your note of the 20th instant, [4] relative to the coöperation of this Government with the Governments of Great Britain and France,
for the purpose of protecting the Dominican Republic against the incursions
of the Haïtian Government.

In reply, I have the honor to state, that all the information possessed by
this Department with regard to the subject, beyond what you have just
communicated to it, is contained in two notes which passed between Mr.
Clayton and Her Britannic Majesty's Minister in this city, in May last.

[1] Instructions, France, vol. 15.
[2] For the text of this convention, see Malloy, *Treaties, Conventions, etc., between the United States and Other Powers,* vol. 1, p. 659.
[3] Notes to France, vol. 6.
Ernest André Olivier Sain de Boislecomte, to whom this note was addressed, presented his credentials as envoy extraordinary and minister plenipotentiary of France on March 18, 1850.   He took leave on May 6, 1851.   [4] Below, this volume, pt. VI, doc. 2617.

Sir Henry Bulwer, in his note to M.ʳ Clayton of the 11.ᵗʰ of that month,[1] represented that the French Government had expressed its willingness to unite with that of Her Britannic Majesty and of the United States for the purpose of arresting the conflict between the different races in S.ᵗ Domingo, and that Lord Palmerston considered that the best course to be pursued for this purpose, would be to instruct the representatives of the three Governments in Haïti to make a joint and concurrent representation to the Haïtian Government to induce them to consent to a treaty of peace and friendship with the Dominican Republic; and Mr. Clayton, in his reply, under date of the 20.ᵗʰ of May,[2] stated to Sir Henry Bulwer, that this Government had sent Special Agents to that Republic, from time to time, for the purpose of enquiring into its condition, with a view to enable the Government of the United States to decide upon the expediency of acknowledging its independence; that a person, (Mr. Green), who had for some time been acting in the character of Agent on behalf of this Government, was daily expected to return; and that it was the intention of the President to lose no time in communicating to the Senate the instructions to, and the correspondence of,[3] that Agent, "with a nomination of a Chargé d'Affaires to the Dominican Republic": when, "if that enlightened body should think proper to confirm the nomination, the President will be prepared to coöperate with Great Britain and France, by employing the good offices of this Government to bring about a lasting peace between that Republic [the Dominican] and its adversary in the Island of S.ᵗ Domingo."

From this, it would appear that, at the date of the letter of Mr. Green to the Minister of Foreign Affairs of Haïti,[4] a copy of which accompanies your note of the 20.ᵗʰ instant,[5] he could not have been aware of the correspondence between Sir Henry Bulwer and Mr. Clayton which has just been referred to. Mr. Green returned home in June last, and has been since engaged in preparing his final report, which has only recently been received at this Department.[6] So soon, however, as the President shall be authorized to open regular diplomatic intercourse with the Dominican Republic, you shall be advised of the fact, in order that this Government may then join with England and France in bringing about a peace between the Dominican Republic and Haïti.

If reasons should be found to exist rendering inexpedient the appointment of a regular Chargé d'Affaires to Dominica, the propriety of deputing a Special Agent to coöperate with the Agents of England and France in that Island,

---

[1] Below, vol. VII, pt. II, doc. 2911.
[2] *Ibid.*, pt. I, doc. 2706.
[3] See instructions to Green, above, this volume, pt. I, June 13, 1849 and February 16, 1850, docs. 2193 and 2194.   For despatches from Green, and accompanying enclosures, see above, this volume, pt. II, between the dates August 27, 1849, and June 15, 1850, inclusive.
[4] See above, this volume, pt. II, doc. 2230, note 1, p. 83, dated May 8, 1850.
[5] Below, this volume, pt. VI, doc. 2617.
[6] See above, this volume, pt. II, June 15, 1850, doc. 2230.

with reference to this whole subject, will then be taken into early consideration by the President.

I avail myself of this opportunity [etc.].

2482

Daniel Webster, Secretary of State of the United States, to Sain de Boislecomte French Minister to the United States [1]

WASHINGTON, *March 21, 1851.*

SIR: I have the honor to acknowledge the receipt of your note of the 20th instant,[2] covering a copy of the declaration which was made by the Agents of the United States, France, and Great Britain, under date of the 11th ultimo, to the Government of Haiti,[3] with the view of bringing about a pacification of that Island; and to thank you for your kindness and attention on the occasion.

I avail myself of this opportunity [etc.].

2483

John J. Crittenden, Acting Secretary of State of the United States, to William C. Rives, United States Minister to France [4]

No. 34   WASHINGTON, *September 29, 1851.*

SIR: Your despatches to N⁰ 102,[5] inclusive, have duly come to hand. In that of the 10th instant, speaking of the late events in Cuba as then occupying public attention in Paris, you say: "It is no doubt known to you that this Government some time since entered into an arrangement with that of England to employ their joint naval forces on the West India Station to aid in maintaining the authority of Spain, in certain contingencies, over the Island of Cuba," &ᶜ. Rumors of a like nature have heretofore reached the Department through the public journals and other similar channels, but no intimation of the existence of such an arrangement has been received from any official source; and upon enquiry the Department is assured by Mr. Crampton, the British Chargé d'Affaires, that no knowledge whatever of any conventional stipulations on the subject is possessed by either the

[1] Notes to France, vol. 6.   [2] Not included in this publication.
[3] See above, this volume, pt. II, p. 96, in footnote 2; enclosed with Walsh's No. 2 to the Secretary of State, dated February 14, 1851, doc. 2238.
[4] Instructions, France, vol. 15.
John J. Crittenden, Attorney General of the United States, who signed this instruction, was designated Acting Secretary of State, by President Fillmore, on September 25, 1851, to act during the absence of the Secretary of State (Daniel Webster) from the seat of government.   [5] For No. 102, see below, this volume, pt. VI, September 10, 1851, doc. 2619.

British or French Legation here. It is, however, obviously important to
ascertain the facts of the case with certainty, so that the precise nature and
terms of the arrangement or understanding between France and England,—
if it really exist,—may be known here; and with this view the President is
desirous that you should use your best endeavors to obtain them, and report
them without unnecessary delay to this Department.

I am, Sir, respectfully [etc.].

2484

John J. Crittenden, Acting Secretary of State of the United States, to Count
de Sartiges, French Minister to the United States [1]

WASHINGTON, *October 22, 1851.*

The Undersigned, Acting Secretary of State of the United States, has the
honor to remind M. de Sartiges, Envoy Extraordinary and Minister Plenipotentiary of the French Republic, that in the interview which he had with
him on the 8th instant, he stated that he might have occasion to address him
in writing upon the subject of the information which M. de Sartiges then
communicated, that the French Government had issued orders to its ships
of war in the West Indies to give assistance to Spain, and to prevent, by
force, any adventurers of any nation from landing with hostile intent on the
Island of Cuba.

Having imparted that information to the President, the Undersigned has
now the honor, by his direction, to address M. de Sartiges in regard to it.

M. de Sartiges is apprized that a few days prior to the interview adverted
to, the Chargé d'Affaires of Her Britannic Majesty had given to this Department official notice that his Government had issued similar orders to its
naval forces. The President had regarded this as a matter of grave importance but its gravity is greatly increased by the concurrence and coöperation
of France in the same measure.

It cannot be doubted that these orders have been occasioned by the recent
unlawful expedition of less than five hundred men, which, having evaded
the vigilance of this Government and escaped from New Orleans, were landed
by the steamer Pampero upon the Island of Cuba and were soon captured
and many of them executed. That such an accident should have incited the
combined action of two great European Powers, for an object to which
neither of them is a direct party, and in a manner that may seriously affect
the People of the United States, cannot fail to awaken the earnest consideration of the President.

[1] Notes to France, vol. 6.
Count Etienne Gilbert Eugène de Sartiges, to whom this note was addressed, presented
his credentials as envoy extraordinary and minister plenipotentiary, on May 29, 1851. He
left about May 20, 1859.

He cannot perceive the necessity or propriety of such orders—while he entertains the strongest apprehensions that their execution by French and British cruisers will be attended with injurious and dangerous consequences to the commerce and peace of the United States. They cannot be carried into effect without a visitation, examination, and consequent detention of our vessels, on our own shores, and in the great channels of our coasting trade; and this must invest British and French cruisers with the jurisdiction of determining, in the first instance, at least, what are the expeditions denounced in their orders, and who are the guilty persons engaged in them.

It is plain, however different may have been the intention of the respective Governments, that the exercise of such a power and jurisdiction could hardly fail to lead to abuses and collisions perilous to the peace that now so happily prevails. By such an interference, those Governments seem to assume an attitude unfriendly to the United States. The President will not, however, allow himself to believe that this intervention has been intended as an admonition or reproach to this Government. He has signally manifested his condemnation of all such lawless enterprizes, and has adopted active measures for their prevention and suppression. It must also be known to the Governments of France and England, in common with all the world, that this Government, since it took its place among nations, has carefully preserved its good faith, and anxiously endeavored to fulfil all its obligations, conventional and national. And this it has done from motives far above any apprehension of danger to itself. From its beginning under the present Constitution, it has sedulously cultivated the policy of peace, of not intermeddling in the affairs of others, and of preventing, by highly penal enactments, any unlawful interference by its citizens to disturb the tranquillity of countries with which the United States were in amity. To this end, many such enactments have been made—the first as early as the year 1794, and the last as late as 1838. The last having expired by its own limitation, and all the preceding legislation on the subject having been comprehended in the act of Congress of the 20th April, 1818, it is unnecessary to do more than to refer M. de Sartiges to its provisions as marking the signal anxiety and good faith of this Government to restrain persons within its jurisdiction from committing any acts inconsistent with the rights of others, or its own obligations. These laws were intended to comprehend, and to protect from violation, all our relations with, and duties to, countries at peace with us, and to punish any violations of them by our citizens, as *crimes* against the United States. In this manifestation of its desire to preserve just and peaceful relations with all nations, it is believed that the United States have gone before, and further than, any of the older Governments of Europe. Without recapitulating all the provisions of those laws by which the United States have so carefully endeavored to prohibit every act that could be justly offensive to their neighbors, it is deemed enough for this occasion to say, that they denounce all such enterprizes or expeditions as those against which the orders in question are directed.

The Undersigned thinks it is of importance enough to call the attention of M. de Sartiges more directly to this law. A literal copy of it is accordingly herewith communicated.

Besides the ordinary legal process, it authorizes the President to employ the military and naval forces of the country for the purpose of preventing such expeditions and arresting for punishment those concerned in them. In the spirit of this law, the President condemns such expeditions against the Island of Cuba as are denounced by the orders in question, and has omitted nothing for their detection and prevention. To that end, he has given orders to civil, naval, and military officers from New York to New Orleans, and has enjoined upon them the greatest vigilance and energy. His course on the subject has been in all things clear and direct. It has been no secret, and the Undersigned must presume that it has been fully understood and known by M. de Sartiges. An appeal might confidently be made to the vigilant and enlightened Minister of Spain that his suggestions for the prevention of such aggressions, or the prosecution of offenders engaged in them, have been promptly considered, and if found reasonable, adopted by the President. His course, it is believed, has been above all question or just cause of complaint. This Government is determined to execute its laws, and in the performance of this duty can neither ask nor receive foreign aid. If, notwithstanding all its efforts, expeditions of small force, hostile to Cuba, have, in a single vessel or steamer, excited by Cubans themselves, escaped from our extensive shores, such an accident can furnish no ground of imputation, either upon the law or its administration. Every country furnishes instances enough of infractions and evasions of its laws, which no power or vigilance can effectually guard against.

It need not be feared that any expeditions of a lawless and hostile character can escape from the United States, of sufficient force to create any alarm for the safety of Cuba, or against which Spain might not defend it with the slightest exertion of her power. The President is persuaded that none such can escape detection and prevention, except by their minuteness and insignificance.—None certainly can escape which could require the combined aid of France and England to resist or suppress.

Cuba will find a sure, if not its surest, protection and defence in the justice and good faith of the United States.

There is another point of view in which this intervention on the part of France and England cannot be viewed with indifference by the President. The geographical position of the Island of Cuba, in the Gulf of Mexico, lying at no great distance from the mouth of the river Mississippi, and in the line of the greatest current of the commerce of the United States, would become, in the hands of any powerful European nation an object of just jealousy and apprehension to the people of this country. A due regard to their own safety and interest must therefore make it a matter of importance to them who shall possess and hold dominion over that Island. The Government of France and those of other European nations were long since officially apprized by this Government that the United States could not see without concern that Island transferred by Spain to any other European State. President Fillmore fully concurs in that sentiment, and is apprehensive that the sort of protectorate introduced by the orders in question, might, in contingencies not difficult to be imagined, lead to results equally objectionable.

If it should appear to M. de Sartiges that the President is too apprehensive on this subject, this must be attributed to his great solicitude to guard the friendly relations between the two countries against all contingencies and causes of disturbance. The People of the United States have long cherished towards France the most amicable sentiments, and recent events which made her a Republic have opened new sources of fraternal sympathy. Harmony and confidence would seem to be the natural relations of the two great Republics of the world—relations demanded no less by their permanent interests than by circumstances and combinations in Continental Europe, which now seem to threaten so imminently the cause of free institutions. The United States have nothing to fear from those convulsions, nor are they propagandists; but they have at heart the cause of freedom in all countries, and believe that the example of the two great Republics of France and America, with their moral and social influences coöperating harmoniously, would go far to promote and to strengthen that cause.

It is with these views that the President so much desires the cultivation of friendly feelings between the two countries, and regards with so much concern any cause that may tend to produce collision or alienation. He believes that this Cuban intervention is such a cause.

The system of Government which prevails most generally in Europe is adverse to the principles upon which this Republic has been founded; and the Undersigned is well aware that the difference between them is calculated to produce distrust of, if not aversion to, the Government of the United States. Sensible of this, the People of this country are naturally jealous of European interference in American affairs. And although they would not impute to France, now herself a Republic, any participation in this distrustful and unfriendly feeling towards their Government, yet the Undersigned must repeat that her intervention in this instance, if attempted to be executed in the only practicable mode for its effectual execution, could not fail to produce some irritation, if not worse consequences. The French cruisers sailing up and down the shores of the United States, to perform their needless task of protecting Cuba, and their ungracious office of watching the people of this country, as if they were fruitful of piracies, would be regarded with some feelings of resentment, and the flag which they bore—a flag that should always be welcome to the sight of Americans—would be looked at as casting a shadow of unmerited and dishonoring suspicion upon them and their Government.

The Undersigned will add that all experience seems to prove that the rights, interests, and peace of the Continents of Europe and America will be best preserved by the forbearance of each to interfere in the affairs of the other. The Government of the United States has constantly acted on that principle, and has never intermeddled in European questions.

The President has deemed it proper to the occasion that his views should be thus fully and frankly presented for the friendly consideration of M. de Sartiges and his Government, in order that all possible precaution may be used to avert any misunderstanding, and every cause or consequence that might disturb the peace, or alienate, in the least, the sentiments of confidence and friendship which now bind together the Republics of the United States and France.

The Undersigned avails himself of this occasion [etc.].

2485

Daniel Webster, Secretary of State of the United States, to Count de Sartiges, French Minister to the United States [1]

WASHINGTON, *November 18, 1851.*

The Undersigned, Secretary of State of the United States, has the honor to acknowledge the receipt of the note of M. de Sartiges, Envoy Extraordinary and Minister Plenipotentiary of the French Republic, of the 27th ultimo,[2] upon the subject of the orders given by the Government of that Republic to its naval commander on the West India station, directing him to prevent, by force, the landing of adventurers from any nation with hostile intent upon the Island of Cuba.

The Undersigned has the honor to acquaint M. de Sartiges, that he has submitted the same to the President, who has directed him to state, in reply, that the apprehensions of this Government, and the reasons therefor, in regard to the orders referred to, are considered to have been frankly and fully stated in the note of Mr. Crittenden, of the 22[d] of October last.[3] And, inasmuch as M. de Sartiges now avers that the French Government had only in view the execution of the provision of its maritime code against pirates, further discussion of the subject would seem to be for the present unnecessary.

The Undersigned avails himself of this occasion [etc.].

[1] Notes to France, vol. 6.   [2] Below, this volume, pt. VI, doc. 2623.
[3] Above, this part, doc. 2484.

2486

Daniel Webster, Secretary of State of the United States, to Count de Sartiges, French Minister to the United States [1]

WASHINGTON, *April 29, 1852.*

The Undersigned has the honor to acknowledge the receipt of M. de Sartiges' note of the 23^d instant,[2] together with the copy of the instruction from M. Turgot, the French Minister of Foreign Affairs, to M. de Sartiges, bearing date the 31st ultimo.[3]

There is no doubt that M. Turgot has justly described the course of policy which has influenced the Government of the United States heretofore in regard to the Island of Cuba.   It has been stated and often repeated to the Government of Spain, by this Government, under various administrations, not only that the United States have no design upon Cuba themselves, but that if Spain should refrain from a voluntary cession of the Island to any other European Power, she might rely on the countenance and friendship of the United States to assist her in the defence and preservation of that Island; at the same time, it has always been declared to Spain that the Government of the United States could not be expected to acquiesce in the cession of Cuba to an European Power.   The Undersigned is happy in being able to say, that the present Executive of the United States entirely approves of this past policy of the Government, and fully concurs in the general sentiments expressed by M. Turgot, and understood to be identical with those entertained by the Government of Great Britain.   The President will take M. de Sartiges' communication into consideration, and give it his best reflections.   But the Undersigned deems it his duty at the same time to remind M. de Sartiges, and, through him, his Government, that the policy of that of the United States has uniformly been to avoid, as far as possible, alliances or agreements with other States, and to keep itself free from national obligations, except such as affect directly the interests of the United States themselves.   This sentiment has been strongly felt and uniformly entertained in the councils of this Government from its earliest history.   How far, therefore, it may be necessary to make this case of Cuba an exception and especially how far any motive may be found for entering into treaty stipulations or exchange of official declarations with the Governments of France and Great Britain, in the existing state of things, upon the subject of Cuba, are questions which, as the Undersigned has already intimated, will be maturely considered.

The Undersigned avails himself of this opportunity [etc.].

[1] Notes to France, vol. 6.   [2] Below, this volume, pt. VI, doc. 2628.
[3] See below, this volume, pt. VI, p. 636, note 3.

2487

Charles M. Conrad, Acting Secretary of State of the United States, to William C. Rives, United States Minister to France [1]

No. 52   WASHINGTON, *October 14, 1852.*

SIR: Intelligence has recently been received of a serious rupture having occurred between the Government of the "Equatur" and the Chargé d'Affaires of France to that Republic, which has ended in his abrupt departure from the country. The conduct of that functionary as well as that of the Commander of the French Naval forces in those seas was certainly extraordinary and this together with other circumstances, have caused suspicions to be entertained by that Government, and which appear to be shared by our Chargé d'affaires, that this occurrence was the result of a foregone conclusion, and that the circumstance which apparently gave rise to it was merely seized hold of as a pretext to justify a course already determined on.[2]

It is also said that the expedition of Flores against that Republic, which has recently terminated in a disastrous failure, was encouraged if not secretly instigated by France; and that another attempt will be made to restore him to power. The motive for all this is said to be hostility to Republican institutions.

You will please endeavor, (of course indirectly and without any formal inquiry) to ascertain as far as practicable, whether there be any foundation for these suspicions and what measures, if any, the French Government has adopted or intends to adopt in reference to the difficulty between her Representative to the "Equator," and the Government of that Republic.

I am, Sir, very respectfully [etc.].

2488

Edward Everett, Secretary of State of the United States, to the Count de Sartiges, French Minister to the United States [3]

WASHINGTON, *December 1, 1852.*

SIR: You are well acquainted with the melancholy circumstances, which have hitherto prevented a reply to the note which you addressed to my predecessor on the 8th of July.[4] That note and the instruction of M. de Turgot of the 8th of April[5] with a similar communication from the English Minister[6] and the *projet* of a Convention between the three powers relative

---

[1] Instructions, France, vol. 15.
[2] See Chargé d'Affaires Cushing's despatch No. 23, September 1, 1852, above, this volume, pt. IV, doc. 2365.   [3] Notes to France, vol. 6.   [4] Below, this volume, pt. VI, doc. 2630.
[5] See below, this volume, pt. VI, p. 636, note 3, but dated March 31, 1852.
[6] For communication of April 8, 1852, see below, vol. VII, pt. II, doc. 2974, note thereto.

to Cuba[1] have been among the first subjects, to which my attention has been called by the President.

The substantial portion of the proposed Convention is expressed in a single article in the following terms:

> The high contracting parties hereby severally and collectively disclaim now and for hereafter all intention to obtain possession of the Island of Cuba, and they respectively bind themselves to discountenance all attempt to that effect on the part of any power or individuals whatever.
>
> The high contracting parties declare severally and collectively that they will not obtain or maintain for themselves or for any one of themselves any exclusive control over the said Island nor assume nor exercise any dominion over the same.

The President has given the most serious attention to this proposal, to the notes of the French and British Ministers accompanying it, and to the instructions of M. de Turgot and the Earl of Malmesbury transmitted with the project of the Convention and he directs me to make known to you the view which he takes of this important and delicate subject.

The President fully concurs with his predecessors, who have on more than one occasion authorized the declaration referred to by M. de Turgot and Lord Malmesbury, that the United States could not see with indifference the Island of Cuba fall into the possession of any other European Government than Spain; not however because we should be dissatisfied with any natural increase of territory and power on the part of France or England. France has within twenty years acquired a vast domain on the Northern coast of Africa with a fair prospect of indefinite extension. England within half a century has added very extensively to her Empire. These acquisitions have created no uneasiness on the part of the United States.

In like manner the United States have within the same period greatly increased their territory. The largest addition was that of Louisiana, which was purchased from France. These accessions of territory have probably caused no uneasiness to the great European powers, as they have been brought about by the operation of natural causes, and without any disturbance of the international relations of the principal States. They have been followed also by a great increase of mutually beneficial commercial intercourse between the United States and Europe.

But the case would be different in reference to the transfer of Cuba from Spain to any other European power. That event could not take place without a serious derangement of the international system now existing, and it would indicate designs in reference to this hemisphere which could not but awaken alarm in the United States. We should view it in somewhat the same light in which France and England would view the acquisition of some

[1] See below, this volume, pt. VI, p. 636, note 3, second document.

important island in the Mediterranean by the United States; with this difference, it is true, that the attempt of the United States to establish themselves in Europe would be a novelty, while the appearance of a European power in this part of the world is a familiar fact but this difference in the two cases is merely historical; and would not diminish the anxiety, which on political grounds would be caused by any great demonstration of European power in a new direction in America.

M. de Turgot states that France could never see with indifference the possession of Cuba by *any* power but Spain, and explicitly declares that she has no wish or intention of appropriating the Island to herself, and the English Minister makes the same avowal on behalf of his government.   M. de Turgot and Lord Malmesbury do the Government of the United States no more than justice in remarking that they have often pronounced themselves substantially in the same sense.   The President does not covet the acquisition of Cuba for the United States.   At the same time he considers the condition of Cuba as mainly an American question, and to a limited extent only a European question.   The proposed Convention proceeds on a different principle.   It assumes that the United States have no other or greater interest in the question than France or England; whereas it is necessary only to cast one's eye upon the map, to see how remote are the relations of Europe, and how intimate those of the United States with this Island.

The President, doing full justice to the friendly spirit, in which his concurrence is invited by France and England, and not insensible to the advantages of a good understanding between the three powers in reference to Cuba, feels himself nevertheless unable to become a party to the proposed compact for the following reasons:

It is in the first place in his judgment clear, (as far as the respect due from the Executive to a co-ordinate branch of the Government will permit him to anticipate its decision), that no such Convention would be viewed with favor by the Senate.   Its certain rejection by that body would leave the question of Cuba in a more unsettled position than it is now.

This objection would not require the President to withhold his concurrence from the convention if no other objection existed, and if a strong sense of the utility of the measure rendered it his duty, as far as the Executive action is concerned, to give his consent to the arrangement.—Such however is not the case.

The Convention would be of no value unless it were lasting.   Accordingly its terms express a perpetuity of purpose and obligation.   Now it may well be doubted whether the Constitution of the United States would allow the treaty-making power to impose a permanent disability on the American Government, for all coming time, and prevent it under any future change of circumstances, from doing what has been so often done in times past.   In 1803 the United States purchased Louisiana of France; and in 1819, they

purchased Florida of Spain.   It is not within the competence of the treaty
making power in 1852 effectually to bind the government in all its branches,
and for all coming time, not to make a similar purchase of Cuba.   A like
remark I imagine may be made even in reference both to France and England,
where the treaty making power is less subject than it is with us to the control
of other branches of the Government.

There is another strong objection to the proposed agreement.   Among the
oldest traditions of the Federal Government is an aversion to political alliances with European powers.   In his memorable farewell address, President Washington says:

> The great rule of conduct for us in regard to foreign nations is in
> extending our commercial relations, to have with them as little political
> connection as possible.   So far as we have already formed engagements
> let them be fulfilled with perfect good faith.   There let us stop.

President Jefferson in his inaugural address in 1801 warned the country
against "entangling alliances."   This expression, now become proverbial,
was unquestionably used by Mr. Jefferson in reference to the alliance with
France of 1778; an alliance at the time of incalculable benefit to the United
States; but which in less than twenty years came near involving us in the
wars of the French revolution, and laid the foundation of heavy claims upon
Congress not extinguished to the present day.   It is a significant coincidence
that the particular provision of the alliance which occasioned these evils
was that under which France called upon us to aid her in defending her West
Indian possessions against England.   Nothing less than the unbounded
influence of Washington rescued the Union from the perils of that crisis, and
preserved our neutrality.

But the President has a graver objection to entering into the proposed
convention.   He has no wish to disguise the feeling, that the compact, although equal in its terms, would be very unequal in substance.—France
and England by entering into it would disable themselves from obtaining
possession of an Island remote from their seats of government, belonging to
another European power, whose natural right to possess it must always be
as good as their own; a distant island in another hemisphere and one which
by no ordinary or peaceful course of things could ever belong to either of
them.   If the present balance of power in Europe should be broken up, if
Spain should become unable to maintain the Island in her possession, and
France and England should be engaged in a death struggle with each other,
Cuba might then be the prize of the Victor.   Till these events all take place
the President does not see how Cuba can belong to any European power but
Spain.

The United States on the other hand, would by the proposed Convention
disable themselves from making an acquisition which might take place with-

out any disturbance of existing foreign relations and in the natural order of things. The island of Cuba lies at our doors. It commands the approach to the Gulf of Mexico, which washes the shores of five of our States. It bars the entrance of that great river which drains half the North American Continent, and with its tributaries forms the largest system of internal water communication in the world. It keeps watch at the door way of our intercourse with California by the Isthmus route. If an Island like Cuba belonging to the Spanish crown guarded the entrance of the Thames and the Seine, and the United States should propose a Convention like this to France and England, those powers would assuredly feel that the disability assumed by ourselves was far less serious than that which we asked them to assume. The opinions of American statesmen, at different times and under varying circumstances, have differed as to the desirableness of the acquisition of Cuba by the United States.—Territorially and commercially it would in our hands be an extremely valuable possession. Under certain contingencies it might be almost essential to our safety. Still for domestic reasons, on which in a communication of this kind, it might not be proper to dwell, the President thinks that the incorporation of the island into the Union, at the present time, although effected with the consent of Spain, would be a hazardous measure; and he would consider its acquisition by force, except in a just war with Spain, should an event so greatly to be deprecated take place, as a disgrace to the civilization of the age.

The President has given ample proof of the sincerity with which he holds these views. He has thrown the whole force of his constitutional power against all illegal attacks upon the island. It would have been perfectly easy for him, without any seeming neglect of duty, to allow projects of a formidable character to gather strength by connivance. No amount of obloquy at home, no embarrassments caused by the indiscretions of the Colonial government of Cuba have moved him from the path of duty in this respect. The Captain General of that island, an officer apparently of upright and conciliatory character, but probably more used to military command than the management of civil affairs, has on a punctilio in reference to the purser of a private steamship, (who seems to have been entirely innocent of the matters laid to his charge), refused to allow passengers and the mails of the United States to be landed from a vessel having him on board. This certainly is a very extraordinary mode of animadverting upon a supposed abuse of the liberty of the press, by the subject of a foreign government in his native country. The Captain General is not permitted by his government, three thousand miles off, to hold any diplomatic intercourse with the United States. He is subject in no degree to the direction of the Spanish Minister at Washington; and the President has to choose between a resort to force to compel the abandonment of this gratuitous interruption of commercial intercourse, (which would result in war) and a delay of weeks and months necessary for a negotiation with Madrid, with all the chances of the most deplorable occurrences in the interval; and all for a trifle that ought to have admitted a settlement by an exchange of notes between Washington and the Havana. The President however has patiently submitted to these evils, and has continued faithfully to give to Cuba the advantage of those principles of the public law, under the shelter of which she has departed in this case from the comity of Nations. But the incidents to which I allude and which are still in train are among many others which point decisively to the expediency of some change in the relations of Cuba; and the President thinks that the influence of France and England with Spain would be well employed in inducing her so to modify the administration of the government of Cuba, as to afford the means of some prompt remedy for evils of the kind alluded to, which have done much to increase the spirit of unlawful enterprize against the Island.

That a convention such as is proposed would be a transitory arrangement, sure to be swept away by the irresistible tide of affairs in a new country, is, to the apprehension of the President, too obvious to require a labored argument. The project rests on principles applicable if at all to Europe, where international relations are in their basis of great antiquity, slowly modified for the most part in the progress of time and events; and not applicable to America which but lately a waste, is filling up with intense rapidity, and adjusting on natural principles those territorial relations, which, on the first discovery of the Continent, were in a good degree fortuitous.

The comparative history of Europe and America even for a single century shews this. In 1752, France, England, and Spain were not materially different in their political position in Europe from what they now are. They were ancient, mature, consolidated States, established in their relations with each other and the rest of the world, the leading powers of Western and Southern Europe. Totally different was the state of things in America. The United States had no existence as a people. A line of English colonies not numbering much over a million of inhabitants, stretched along the coast.— France extended from the bay of St. Lawrence to the Gulf of Mexico and from the Alleghanies to the Mississippi; beyond which Westward the continent was a Wilderness occupied by wandering savages, and subject to a conflicting and nominal claim on the part of France and Spain. Every thing in Europe was comparatively fixed; every thing in America provisional, incipient, and temporary, except the law of progress, which is as organic and vital in the youth of States as of individual men. A struggle between the provincial authorities of France and England for the possession of a petty stockade at the confluence of the Monongahela and the Alleghany kindled the seven years war; at the close of which the great European powers, not materially affected in their relations at home, had undergone astonishing changes on this continent. France had disappeared from the map of America, whose inmost recesses had been penetrated by her zealous Missionaries and her resolute and gallant adventurers; England had added the Canadas to her transatlantic dominions; Spain had become the Mistress of Louisiana, so that in the language of the Archbishop of Mexico in 1770 she claimed Siberia as the Northern boundary of New Spain.

Twelve years only from the treaty of Paris elapsed, and another great change took place,—fruitful of still greater changes to come. The American revolution broke out. It involved France, England, and Spain in a tremendous struggle, and at its close the United States of America had taken their place in the family of Nations. In Europe the ancient States were restored substantially to their former equilibrium; but a new element of incalculable importance in reference to territorial arrangements is henceforth to be recognized in America.

Just twenty years from the close of the war of the American revolution, France by a treaty with Spain, of which the provisions have never been disclosed, possessed herself of Louisiana; but did so only to cede it to the United States; and in the same year Lewis and Clark started on their expedition to plant the flag of the United States on the shores of the Pacific. In 1819 Florida was sold by Spain to the United States, whose territorial possessions in this way had been increased threefold in half a century. This last acquisition was so much a matter of course, that it had been distinctly foreseen by the Count Aranda, then prime Minister of Spain, as long ago as 1783.

But even these momentous events are but the forerunners of new territorial revolutions still more stupendous. A dynastic struggle between the Emperor Napoleon and Spain commencing in 1808 convulsed the Peninsula. The vast possessions of the Spanish Crown on this continent,—Viceroyalties and Captain Generalships filling the space between California and Cape Horn,—one after another asserted their independence. No friendly power in Europe at that time was able, or if able was willing to succour Spain, or aid her to prop the crumbling buttresses of her colonial empire. So far from it, when France in 1823, threw an army of 100,000 men into Spain to control her domestic politics England thought it necessary to counteract the movement by recognizing the independence of the Spanish Provinces in America. In the remarkable language of the distinguished Minister of the day, in order to redress the balance of power in Europe, he called into existence a new world in the West; somewhat overrating perhaps the extent of the derangement in the old world, and not doing full justice to the position of the United States of America, or their influence on the fortunes of their sister republics, on this continent.

Thus in sixty years from the close of the seven years war, Spain like France, had lost the last remains of her once imperial possessions in this hemisphere. The United States meantime were by the arts of peace and the healthful progress of things, rapidly enlarging their dimensions and consolidating their power.

The great march of events still went on. Some of the new Republics, from the effect of a mixture of races, or the want of training in liberal institutions, shewed themselves incapable of self government. The province of Texas revolted from Mexico, by the same right by which Mexico revolted from Spain. At the memorable battle of San Jacinto in 1836 she passed the great ordeal of nascent states, and her independence was recognized by this government, by France, by England, and other European powers. Mainly peopled from the United States, she sought naturally to be incorporated into the Union. The offer was repeatedly rejected by Presidents Jackson and Van Buren, to avoid a collision with Mexico. At last the annexation took place. As a domestic question it is no fit subject for comment in a communication to a foreign Minister. As a question of public law, there never was an extension of territory more naturally or justifiably made.

It produced a disturbed relation with the government of Mexico; War ensued and in its results other extensive territories, were, for a large pecuniary compensation on the part of the United States, added to the Union. Without adverting to the divisions of opinion which arose in reference to this war,—as must always happen in free countries, in reference to great measures,—no person surveying these with the eye of a comprehensive statesmanship, can fail to trace in the main result the undoubted operation of the law of our political existence. The consequences are before the world. Vast provinces which had languished for three centuries under the leaden ways of a stationary system are coming under the influences of an active civilization. Freedom of speech and the press, the trial by jury, religious equality, and representative government have been carried by the constitution of the United States into extensive regions in which they were unknown before. By the settlement of California the great circuit of intelligence round the globe is completed. The discovery of the gold of that region leading as it did to the same discovery in Australia, has touched the nerves of industry throughout the world. Every addition to the territory of the American Union has given homes to European destitution and gardens to European want. From every part of the United Kingdom, from France, from Switzerland and Germany, and from the extremest north of Europe a march of immigration has been taken up, such as the world has never seen before. Into the United States grown to their present extent in the manner described, but little less than half a million of the population of the old world is annually pouring, to be immediately incorporated into an industrious and prosperous community, in the bosom of which they find political and religious liberty, social position, employment, and bread. It is a fact which would defy belief were it not the result of official inquiry, that the immigrants to the United States from Ireland alone, besides having subsisted themselves, have sent back to their kindred for the three last years nearly five millions of dollars annually; thus doubling in three years the purchase money of Louisiana.

Such is the territorial developement of the United States in the past century. Is it possible that Europe can contemplate it with an unfriendly or jealous eye? What would have been her condition in these trying years, but for the outlet we have furnished to her starving millions?

Spain meantime has retained of her extensive dominions in this hemisphere but the two islands of Cuba and Porto Rico. A respectful sympathy with the fortunes of an ancient ally and a gallant people, with whom the United States have ever maintained the most friendly relations, would, if no other reason existed, make it our duty to leave her in the undisturbed possession of this little remnant of her mighty transatlantic empire. The President desires to do so; no word or deed of his will ever question her title or shake her possession. But can it be expected to last very long? Can it resist this mighty current in the fortunes of the world? Is it desirable that it should do so? Can it be for the interest of Spain to cling to a possession that can only be maintained by a garrison of twenty five or thirty thousand troops, a powerful naval force, and an annual expenditure for both arms of the service of at least twelve millions of dollars? Cuba at this moment costs more to Spain, than the entire naval and military establishments of the United States cost the Federal Government. So far from being really injured by the loss of this island, there is no doubt that were it peacefully transferred to the United States, a prosperous commerce between Cuba and Spain resulting from ancient association and common language and tastes, would be far more productive than the best contrived system of Colonial taxation. Such notoriously has been the result to Great Britain of the establishment of the independence of the United States. The decline of Spain from the position which she held in the time of Charles the fifth is coeval with the foundation of her colonial system; while within twenty five years and since the loss of most of her colonies, she has entered upon a course of rapid improvement unknown since the abdication of that Emperor.

I will but allude to an evil of the first magnitude, I mean the African slave trade, in the suppression of which France and England take a lively interest, an evil which still forms a great reproach upon the civilization of Christendom and perpetuates the barbarism of Africa; but for which it is to be feared there is no hope of a complete remedy, while Cuba remains a Spanish colony.

But whatever may be thought of these last suggestions it would seem impossible for any one, who reflects upon the events glanced at in this note, to mistake the law of American growth and progress, or think it can be ultimately arrested by a Convention like that proposed. In the judgment of the President it would be as easy to throw a dam from Cape Florida to Cuba, in the hope of stopping the flow of the Gulf Stream, as to attempt by a compact like this to fix the fortunes of Cuba "now and for hereafter;" or as expressed in the French text of the Convention "for the present as for the future," (*pour le present comme pour l'avenir*), that is for all coming time. The history of the past,—of the recent past,—affords no assurance that twenty years hence France or England will even wish that Spain should retain Cuba; and a century hence judging of what will be from what has been, the pages which record this proposition, will like the record of the family compact between France and Spain, have no interest but for the antiquary. Even now the President cannot doubt that both France and England would prefer any change in the condition of Cuba to that which is most to be apprehended viz⁺ an internal convulsion which should renew the horrors and the fate of San Domingo.

I will intimate a final objection to the proposed Convention. M. de Turgot and Lord Malmesbury put forward as the reason for entering into such a compact "the attacks which have lately been made on the Island of Cuba by lawless bands of adventurers from the United States with the avowed design of taking possession of that Island." The President is convinced that the conclusion of such a treaty, instead of putting a stop to these lawless proceedings, would give a new and powerful impulse to them. It would strike a death-blow to the conservative policy hitherto pursued in this country toward Cuba. No administration of this government however strong in the public confidence in other respects, could stand a day under the odium of having stipulated with the great powers of Europe that in no future time, under no change of circumstances, by no amicable arrangement with Spain, by no act of lawful war, should that calamity unfortunately occur, by no consent of the inhabitants of the Islands should they like the possessions of Spain on the American continent succeed in rendering themselves independent, in fine by no overruling necessity of self preservation, should the United States ever make the acquisition of Cuba.

For these reasons, which the President has thought it advisable, considering the importance of the subject, to direct me to unfold at some length, he feels constrained to decline respectfully the invitation of France and England to become parties to the proposed Convention. He is persuaded that these friendly powers will not attribute this refusal to any insensibility on his part to the advantages of the utmost harmony between the great maritime States upon a subject of such importance. As little will Spain draw any unfavorable inference from this refusal the rather as the emphatic disclaimer of any designs against Cuba on the part of this Government, contained in the present note, affords all the assurance, which the President can constitutionally or to any useful purpose give, of a practical concurrence with England and France in the wish not to disturb the possession of that island by Spain.[1]

I avail myself, Sir, of this opportunity [etc.].

[1] This poorly constructed sentence follows faithfully the file copy.

2489

Edward Everett, Secretary of State of the United States, to William C. Rives,
United States Minister to France [1]

No. 56   WASHINGTON, *December 17, 1852.*

SIR: Your despatches up to the 25th November,[2] have been duly received
at the Department.   Circumstances which will readily occur to you have
prevented them from being promptly acknowledged.

Your despatch N° 174 of the 25th November was received yesterday.   It
announces the result of the appeal to the People of France, on the subject of
the restoration of the Empire, as far as the return of the votes had come in.
That event has already no doubt been consummated and the Empire
formally proclaimed.   This change will of course in no degree affect the
friendly relations between the United States and France.   A deep interest
was felt by the Government and people of this Country in those events of
February 1848, which for a while promised to assimilate the institutions of
France with our own.   But it is the fundamental law of the American Republic, that the will of the People constitutionally expressed is the ultimate
principle of Government and it seems quite evident that the People of France
have with a near approach to unanimity desired the restoration of the Empire.

The President has regarded with great satisfaction the wise and pacific
sentiments to which the Prince President gave utterance on more than one
recent occasion; and you will take a proper opportunity to tender to his
Majesty the sincere wish of the President that his elevation to the imperial
throne by the popular will and voice may conduce to his own true glory, the
happiness of France, & the prosperity of the great family of Nations.   The
vast increase of commercial intercourse and of the facilities of communication
have rendered the relations of States far more intimate than at any former
period; and it is not too much to say that every country in Christendom has
an interest in the welfare of such a great and central power as France.

It is not supposed by the President that the restoration of the Empire will
have presented any subject of delicacy to you, as a member of the diplomatic
corps.   On the contrary supposition, the good judgment evinced by you, on
occasion of the Coup d'état last year, supersedes the necessity of any instructions from this Department even had it been possible that instructions
should be framed to meet events so contingent.

Some concern has lately been felt in the United States at two occurrences
to which it may be proper to call your attention.   One is the reported movement in the Mexican State of Sonora, where a battle is said to have been
fought between the Mexican Government or Commander General Blanco and

[1] Instructions, France, vol. 15.
[2] Rives's No. 174 of November 25, 1852 is not included in this publication.   Its content is
partially revealed in this acknowledgment.

a French adventurer, Count Raousset Boulbon, in which the former has been defeated. The conflict grew out of the disputed occupation of a mine. The Newspapers report that Boulbon had declared the annexation of Sonora to France. There is no authentic account of this occurrence even as a matter of fact. If it has taken place, it is to be considered as the unauthorized act of an adventurer, seeking to gain strength by associating his operations in this way with the name of a strong foreign Government. On speaking to M. de Sartiges about it he told me he considered it a "Mauvaise plaisanterie", and I have in conversing with him, treated it in that light. It may not be amiss for you to allude to it in that way in conversing with the French Minister.

The other matter is more serious. It is a report which first appeared in a respectable French Journal at New York, on the authority of a private letter from St. Domingo to the effect that the Independent Government of Dominica has ceded the Bay and Peninsula of Samana to France, as a permanent Naval station, and with a view to the exercise of a protectorate over that part of the Island, in virtue of a Convention negotiated with France in 1844 but not executed by Louis Philippe. The French Minister has no information on this subject beyond what is contained in the journal referred to, which however is declared by its Editor to be from a reliable source. M. de Sartiges appears to be however of opinion that the report may be founded in fact, though he does not think more has been done, than to propose an arrangement for a permanent Naval station in the Bay of Samana for the French Squadrons having occasion to visit the Antilles.—

I transmit you a document printed by order of the House of Representatives which will acquaint you with the steps taken by France, England, and the United States, to preserve the tranquillity and integrity of the Eastern portion of the Island of San Domingo. The policy pursued by the United States in this respect has been wholly disinterested. It has been no doubt in our power to obtain a permanent foothold in Dominica; and we have as much need of a Naval station at Samana as any European power could possibly have. It has however been the steady rule of our policy, to avoid as far as possible, all disturbance of the existing political relations of the West Indies. —We have felt that any attempts on the part of any one of the great Maritime powers to obtain exclusive advantages in any of the Islands where such an attempt was likely to be made, would be apt to be followed by others and end in converting the Archipelago into a great Theatre of national competition for exclusive advantages and territorial acquisitions which might become fatal to the peace of the world.

The subject is somewhat delicate, and in any conversation you have with the French Minister you will naturally approach it with caution. It will be best to endeavor to ascertain the precise facts before making any remark on our policy. It is possible that the report is wholly unfounded. I shall be anxious to hear from you on this subject.

It was my wish to send to you and Mr. Ingersoll a copy of my note to the Ministers of England and France,[1] declining to enter into a tripartite Convention, with those powers to guaranty the actual state of Cuba. The length of the note under the existing pressure upon the Department has made it inconvenient to multiply copies. The purport is briefly indicated in the message, and it is not unlikely that it will be called for by Congress and printed.

I have the satisfaction to inform you that I have been directed by the President, with the unanimous approval of the Cabinet, to commence a negotiation with the British Minister on the subject of the Fisheries and Commercial reciprocity with the Provinces on a basis which promises success and will I think result in a liberal and comprehensive settlement of both questions. This will be an event of great importance politically and otherwise. You will perhaps find an opportunity incidentally to let the French Minister perceive that our relations with England are on an excellent footing.

I am, Sir, respectfully [etc.].

2490

Edward Everett, Secretary of State of the United States, to William C. Rives, United States Minister to France [2]

No. 61   WASHINGTON, *February 23, 1853.*

SIR: Your despatches to Nº 190,[3] inclusive, have been duly received at this department.

With reference to that part of your last despatch which relates to the rupture between the Republic of Ecuador and the late Chargé d'Affaires of France to that Republic, I transmit to you, herewith, the copy of a despatch upon the same subject just received from the Chargé d'Affaires of the United States at Guayaquil;[4] and am, Sir, respectfully, Your obedient servant,

[1] See above, this part, December 1, 1852, doc. 2488.
[2] Instructions, France, vol. 15.
[3] No. 190 is below, this volume, pt. VI, February 2, 1853, doc. 2634.
[4] There is no enclosure with this instruction, but, undoubtedly, it refers to Chargé d'Affaires Cushing's despatch dated January 6, 1853, for which, see below, this volume, pt. IV, doc. 2370.

2491

William L. Marcy, Secretary of State of the United States, to John Y. Mason, United States Minister to France [1]

No. 4   WASHINGTON, *December 17, 1853.*

SIR: The enclosed extract from the instructions given by this Department to Mr. Buchanan, under date of the 2ⁿᵈ of July last,[2] indicates the views of the President in relation to the intervention of Great Britain and France in the affairs of Cuba, and is communicated to you for your information.

I am, Sir, respectfully [etc.].

2492

William L. Marcy, Secretary of State of the United States, to John Y. Mason, United States Minister to France [3]

No. 5   WASHINGTON, *December 22, 1853.*

SIR: I transmit to you, herewith, an extract from a despatch dated the 27ᵗʰ Ultimo this day received from Jonathan Elliott, Esqʳᵉ, the Commercial Agent of the United States in St. Domingo.[4]   It will be seen that this extract relates to the supposed intention of France to overthrow the present President of the Dominican Republic and place Ex-President Baez again in power. You will accordingly, on your arrival at Paris, take an early opportunity to set on foot an enquiry into the matter, and use your best endeavors to ascertain for the information of this Government, how far the suspicion referred to is well or ill-founded.

I am, Sir, respectfully [etc.].

2493

William L. Marcy, Secretary of State of the United States, to John Y. Mason, United States Minister to France [5]

No. 8   WASHINGTON, *March 17, 1854.*

SIR: The seizure of the Steamship "Black Warrior" by the authorities of Spain at Havana has created an unusual degree of excitement throughout the Union.   In order that you may be kept fully advised of all that is transpiring here in relation to the subject I transmit, herewith the message of the President to the House of Representatives and the documents by which it was acompanied.[6]

I am, Sir, respectfully [etc.].

[1] Instructions, France, vol. 15.
John Y. Mason, of Virginia, was commissioned as envoy extraordinary and minister plenipotentiary to France, on October 10, 1853.   He died, at his post, on October 3, 1859.
[2] For the instructions to Buchanan, see below, vol. VII, pt. I, doc. 2734.
[3] Instructions, France, vol. 15.   [4] Above, this volume, pt. II, doc. 2251.
[5] Instructions, France, vol. 15.   [6] Not included in this publication.

2494

William L. Marcy, Secretary of State of the United States, to John Y. Mason, United States Minister to France [1]

No. 20—Confidential.   WASHINGTON, *June 27, 1854.*

SIR: On the 15th of March last the President pursuant to a call, submitted to Congress all the Documents then in this Department relative to the seizure and detention of the American Steam packet, the Black Warrior, at the Port of Havana, on the 28th of the previous month.   These documents, together with the President's message, were printed and a copy thereof transmitted to you.[2]   Mr. Soulé our Envoy Extraordinary and Minister Plenipotentiary to Spain was directed to demand satisfaction of the Spanish Government for this outrage.   I herewith send you a copy of the Despatch sent to him marked (A.)[3]   Some intermediate correspondence took place between him and the Spanish Minister of Foreign Relations before he received a final reply to the demand of this Gov^t[4]   On the 8th day of May that reply was received,[5] and on the 10th transmitted to this Government.[6]   It justified the Cuban authorities in all they had done.   I need not herein describe to you the character of that reply nor state the grounds why it was deemed by the President entirely unsatisfactory.   Some of these grounds are disclosed in a despatch to Mr. Soulé of the 22nd inst, a copy of which is hereto subjoined marked (B).[7]   For the purpose of advising you of the further steps which the President intends to take in this matter I also send you a copy of a confidential despatch to Mr. Soulé marked (C.)[8]   These documents will put you in full possession of the views of the President in regard to the affair of the "Black Warrior".

The purpose of purchasing Cuba has been revived and Mr. Soulé has been instructed to open that matter if circumstances should, in his judgment, present a favorable opportunity.   He is authorized to increase twenty, or

---

[1] This instruction was taken from Instructions, Great Britain, vol. 16, since there was no document of this date in the body of the manuscript volume, Instructions, France, vol. 15; but in the index of that volume, under this date, appeared the following entry: "No. 20 *Confidential.*   Transmitting copies of instructions to Mr. Soulé respecting Cuba and the 'Black Warrior' case.   Remarks on the subject.   (Vide Instructions to Ministers to London, page 300)."   Also, at the end of this document a note stated that it was sent to Mr. Mason *mutatis mutandis* as No. 20.

[2] Above, this part, March 17, 1854, doc. 2493.

[3] See below, volume and part containing Communications to Spain, No. 10 to Soulé, dated March 17, 1854.

[4] See notes from Soulé, under the dates, April 8, 11, 12, 13, and 20, 1854, and notes from the Spanish Minister of Foreign Relations under the dates, April 11, 12, and 18, 1854, below, in the volume and part containing Communications from Spain.

[5] Below, volume and part containing Communications from Spain, but dated May 7, 1854.

[6] See below, volume and part containing Communications from Spain, Soulé's No. 14 of May 10, 1854.

[7] Below, volume and part containing Communications to Spain, instruction No. 16 to Soulé.

[8] Probably that of June 24, 1854, below, volume and part containing Communications to Spain.

even thirty per cent, the maximum sum mentioned in Mr. Saunder's instructions.   The Gov᭣ is not yet advised that Mr. Soulé has taken any steps under his instructions for that purpose.

I have just received a despatch from our Consul at Havana[1] in which he states that a special messenger had arrived there in the last British Steamer from the Spanish Minister at Paris (who is a brother of the Captain General) with a Treaty between France and Spain and with an assurance from the Brother that France would take sides with Spain in case of any attempt by the U. S. to take possession of Cuba.

If there be any Treaty embodying such a provision or any explicit understanding to that effect between France and Spain it is quite important that this Government should get at that fact.   I hope you will do what you can to get reliable information on that subject.   France, which has undoubtedly strong sympathies with Spain, and strong prejudices against the United States, will adopt the Spanish version of the affair of the Black Warrior, and no doubt has been furnished with Mr. Calderon's reply[2] to our demand.[3]

It has occurred to me that there would be no harm done should you (if a fair occasion offered) read to M. Drouyn de Lhuys the copy of my response[4] to that reply.   I have not an opportunity to consult the President on this point as he is now absent from this City—I leave this matter entirely to your discretion—If you should conclude to do so (to read it but not furnish a copy)—I do not wish that you should convey the impression that you act in the matter by instructions from your Government, but let the French Minister believe that you are induced to do so by the strong desire you have that the French Gov᭣ should not remain under erroneous impressions as to the true character of the transactions at Cuba.   Considering the prejudices which the French Government seem to have against this Country in regard to the Black Warrior case as well as to all others with which Cuba is connected, I am disposed to let it see our side of the question in that particular case.   If you see fit to act upon this suggestion I of course shall take the responsibility of the measure.   I do not wish France to know—it is important she should not know or have any intimation of the ulterior course indicated in the Despatch to Mr. Soulé of the 24ᵗʰ instant.[5]

I am, Sir, respectfully [etc.].

[1] Not included in this publication.
[2] Below, the volume and part containing Communications from Spain, under date May 7, 1854.
[3] Ibid., Soulé's notes of April 8 and April 11, 1854.
[4] Below, the volume and part containing Communications to Spain, instruction No. 16, to Soulé, under date of June 22, 1854.
[5] Marked confidential, below, the volume and part containing Communications to Spain.

2495

*William L. Marcy, Secretary of State of the United States, to John Y. Mason,
United States Minister to France* [1]

No. 26   WASHINGTON, *August 16, 1854.*

SIR: With this note you will receive a copy of two despatches to Mr. Soulé,
Nos 18 and 19.[2]   In the latter as you will perceive it is proposed that yourself
and Mr. Buchanan should have an interview with Mr. Soulé for the purpose
of conferring on our affairs with Spain.   This whole subject in its widest
range is opened to your joint consideration.   From the better knowledge
you will possess derived from your different positions the President expects
to receive useful information and suggestions in regard to this very difficult
and highly important matter.

It is left to Mr. Soulé to designate the place and time of meeting.   It is
hoped that nothing will prevent your meeting at the earliest practicable
period.

I am, Sir, respectfully [etc.].

2496

*William L. Marcy, Secretary of State of the United States, to John Y. Mason,
United States Minister to France* [3]

No. 33   WASHINGTON, *November 14, 1854.*

SIR: I transmit for your information a copy of an instruction of yesterday
which by the President's direction has been addressed to Mr. Soulé[4] relative to
your recent conference with Mr. Buchanan and him upon the subject of the
relations between the United States and Spain, with particular reference to
the Island of Cuba.

I am, very respectfully [etc.].

2497

*William L. Marcy, Secretary of State of the United States, to John Y. Mason,
United States Minister to France* [5]

No. 75   WASHINGTON, *February 1, 1856.*

SIR: When Mr. Alberdi, the Minister from the Argentine Confederation
was here on his way to Europe, it was the determination of this Government
to transfer our Minister Resident, appointed to Buenos Ayres to the Argen-

[1] Instructions, France, vol. 15.
[2] See below, the volume and part containing Communications to Spain, both under date of
August 16, 1854.   [3] Instructions, France, vol. 15.
[4] See below, the volume and part containing Communications to Spain, No. 27, to Soulé.
[5] Instructions, France, vol. 15.

tine Confederation to which he had been accredited as well as to Buenos Ayres, and to suspend diplomatic relations with the latter. Great Britain had not recognized Buenos Ayres as an independent Government, but the French Government had done so.

Though formerly Buenos Ayres was one of the States of the Argentine Confederation, she had withdrawn therefrom on account of the treaties which that Confederation had made with the United States, Great Britain, and France. By those treaties the La Plata and some of its tributaries were opened to foreign Commerce, and it was supposed that this provision in those treaties was the real cause of the secession of Buenos Ayres from the Confederation. Though she avowed her willingness to make free the navigation of the La Plata.

Had that been the real ground of the secession of Buenos Ayres, neither the United States, Great Britain, nor France, ought to have countenanced her conduct, and they would have been fully justified for that cause were there no other, in refusing to recognise her as an independent Power, Before any further step was taken in carrying out the policy indicated in the instructions to Mr. Buchanan[1] the aspect of the case was changed by information received from our Minister to Buenos Ayres. He stated in one of his despatches to this Government that a treaty had been concluded between the Argentine Confederation and the State of Buenos Ayres,[2] but did not specify any of its provisions.

The fact that the Argentine Confederation had made a treaty with Buenos Ayres seemed to justify the pretensions of the latter to be regarded as an independent State by other Powers: I therefore thought it necessary, before going any further in the direction indicated when Mr. Alberdi was here, to get further information respecting the Treaty concluded between the two States.

I have written to our Minister at Buenos Ayres for particular information as to the object and provisions of that treaty. That treaty may change the policy of Great Britain and the United States towards Buenos Ayres and render it proper for both to recognize her independence.

It was in furtherance of the views of the Argentine Confederation which had regard to the extension and freedom of foreign commerce, that this Government and that of Great Britain were inclined to withhold their recognition of the independence of Buenos Ayres. But if the Argentine Confederation have admitted that independence by entering into treaty relations with her, it cannot be expected that other nations should not do the same thing. I have hitherto deferred addressing you on the subject until I should receive further information from our Minister to Buenos Ayres in relation to the

[1] See below, No. 93 to Buchanan, under date of June 16, 1855, vol. VII, pt. I, doc. 2755.

[2] This statement does not appear to have been made by Peden, the United States minister at Buenos Aires, in any portion of his despatches which are included in this publication, and which were received at the Department between the date of the instructions to Buchanan, June 16, 1855, and the date of this instruction to Mason.

treaty between that State and the Argentine Confederation. If the latter has recognized the independence of the former, this Government could not with propriety ask that of France to change its relations with Buenos Ayres and conform to the course proposed to be pursued by Great Britain and the United States towards her. As soon as I hear from our Minister I shall communicate again with you on the subject.

I am, Sir, respectfully [etc.].

2498

William L. Marcy, Secretary of State of the United States, to Count de Sartiges, French Minister to the United States [1]

[EXTRACTS]

WASHINGTON, *February 26, 1857.*

The Undersigned, Secretary of State of the United States, has laid before the President, the petition or reclamation of persons styling themselves French subjects, residents at Greytown, presented through the medium of the Count de Sartiges, the Envoy Extraordinary and Minister Plenipotentiary of the Emperor of the French, by the approval of his Government.[2]

Upon full consideration of the subject embraced in the note of the Count de Sartiges,[3] the President has not been able to find any grounds of right, or even equity, upon which such a reclamation can be sustained. The losses for which indemnity is sought resulted from the bombardment of Greytown on the 13th of May, 1854 by the U. S. Sloop of War "Cyane." The appeal is not made in the name of the French Government, yet by its approval the French Minister has presented the case to the notice of this Government. On this account it has received the most respectful consideration; but such consideration could not be given to it without bringing into view questions of international law which can only be appropriately discussed on a direct issue between independent powers. The claim to indemnity in this case is not placed distinctly on the ground of right, nor is the justice or propriety of the conduct of the United States towards the community at Greytown called in question. Should this point be raised by any party having a right to bring it into discussion, there would be no difficulty in justifying the bombardment on well settled principles of international law, and by memorable examples in the conduct of the most enlightened nations. The President, in his annual message to Congress of the 4th of December, 1854, presented his views on that subject, and a reference to that document will render it unnecessary to reproduce them in a reply to the note of Count de Sartiges.

[1] Notes to France, vol. 6.
[2] The petition here referred to is not included in this publication.
[3] Not included in this publication.

In disposing of the present application, the United States are not called on to vindicate their course towards those who were members of the community at Greytown, for the provocation and the propriety of the chastisement, so far as that community is concerned, are not to be brought into discussion, but the manner of inflicting the punishment, and the consequences in regard to foreign residents, are supposed to furnish grounds for an equitable claim upon this Government for their losses on that occasion.

It is presumed that there will be no attempt to maintain that individual members of an organized political body, in a case like this, can be allowed to separate themselves from the collective community, and claim rights and immunities which do not belong to the whole association. It would be preposterous to hold that the associated body deserved the punishment inflicted upon it and the individuals composing it are entitled to indemnity for their sufferings.

If there were persons in Greytown when it was bombarded, who did not belong to the political organization there established, and who suffered in consequence of that bombardment, they can only resort for indemnity, if entitled to it, to that community. It was to that community they committed their persons and property, and by receiving them within its jurisdiction, it assumed the obligation of protecting them. Nothing can be more clearly established than the principle that a foreigner, domiciled in a country, can only look to that country for the protection he is entitled to receive while within its territory; and that if he sustain injury for the want of that protection, the country of his domicil must indemnify him. It is scarcely necessary to refer to cases to establish this position; a few, however, will be alluded to for that purpose. . . .[1]

The Undersigned has thus far considered the case as it would stand, if the claimants were what they represent themselves to be, merely foreign residents of Greytown, and if Greytown was then in fact, what the note of the Count de Sartiges assumes it to have been a Sovereign State. He speaks of the difficulty between that place and the United States as "a difference originating between two Sovereign States".

Taking this view of the establishment at Greytown, though it is not one in which the Government of the United States is inclined to concur, it will be proper to consider the relation and connection which the applicants had with it in the character of a sovereign State. If it should be made to appear that they were constituents of the Greytown community, and not foreign resident traders, it will be impossible to find any foundation for their claims against the United States. It is admitted that the people at Greytown assumed to be an independent State; they had a constitution and a government with Executive Legislative and Judicial Departments, and this political organization was in practical operation when Greytown was bombarded. Actual

[1] The omitted portion cites several similar cases arising in the past.

residence conferred the right of suffrage. Those who took any part in organizing that Government, or who subsequently held office under it, or exercised the right of suffrage, cannot be allowed to deny its existence as a responsible Government or object to being dealt with as members of that political society. Their former citizenship was merged in that which they acquired by this new political association, and while this association lasted and they remained in it, they could not be citizens or subjects of any other State. They owed allegiance to the Government of Greytown, and not to any other country, and the duty of protecting them, devolved upon that Government alone; they could rightfully look to no other power for security or indemnity, nor could they reasonably expect that any other would voluntarily interpose in their behalf, if their proper guardians failed in duty to them.

Their relation to the Country of their birth while at Greytown under these circumstances cannot be distinguished from that which a resident of foreign birth bears to this Country, who has become a regularly naturalized citizen of the United States. Having become such a citizen, the duty of protection if he needs and deserves it, belongs to this country and not to that of his nativity.

The names of the persons who make reclamation for losses at Greytown, in the assumed character of French subjects resident there, are not given in the note of the Count de Sartiges but they have been obtained from other sources, and their political relation to what they regarded and still regard, as the Government of Greytown is well ascertained. Almost every one of them was a member of the political organization established at that place; they enjoyed the franchises of citizens; had the right of voting at elections and exercised it; and several of them held high and responsible offices under that Government.

No persons could be found there who had taken a more active part in public affairs, or were more directly responsible for the conduct of that political community towards the United States, than most of those who now seek reclamation in the character of French subjects. They certainly cannot expect to be indemnified by this Government for losses resulting from the just chastisement, brought upon themselves by the conduct of the community of which they were members; nor is it believed that they can enlist in their behalf the sympathy of the country of their birth, by attempting to renounce their actual citizenship and recover that which they had cast off on becoming constituents of the Greytown Government.

It is confidently believed that when the actual relation of these claimants to the political community of Greytown is fully disclosed to the French Government, it will not consider them entitled even to its friendly interposition.

If it should be found on further examination that there were a few persons, and if any, the number must be very small, who could be fairly regarded as domiciled French subjects in Greytown at the time of the bombardment, and who sustained losses by that act, it is very clearly established by the views herein presented that they can have no claim against the United States. They deliberately placed themselves and their property under the protection of the community of Greytown.   By receiving and subjecting them to its jurisdiction that community assumed the duty of protection and if the conduct of their chosen protectors towards a foreign power has involved them in losses to these protectors, and to them only can they look for redress.   The practice of nations has settled this doctrine, and a different rule would require in prosecuting hostilities in an enemy's country a discrimination between citizens and domiciled foreigners, which could never be made, and in the practice of nations has never been attempted.

The Undersigned is not aware that the principle that foreigners domiciled in a belligerent country must share with the citizens of that country in the fortunes of the war, has ever been seriously controverted, or departed from in practice.

No power assailing an enemy's country is required to discriminate between the subjects of that country and foreigners domiciled therein, nor can the latter with any better right than the former, claim indemnity in any case except from the Country under whose jurisdiction they have placed themselves.

It is possible that applicants to this Government for indemnity on account of losses occasioned by the bombardment may attempt to avoid the conclusiveness of the objections herein presented by considering Greytown as a mere municipality under the sovereignty of a tribe of Indians called the Mosquitoes.   Nothing favorable to the pretensions of the claimants would be gained by such a hypothesis.   If it be assumed that this tribe had sovereign authority over a territory including Greytown, the argument which has been presented to show that the United States are not responsible for the property destroyed by the Bombardment will lose none of its force or applicability by the transfer of the sovereignty of that place to the Mosquitoes. Those who were a part of or participated in, the municipal Government of Greytown, can hardly be allowed to assume the character of foreign residents; and if they or others; could invest themselves with that character, their condition as claimants against the United States would not be improved. They were under the protection of the sovereign power of the Country and if that power appertained to the tribe of Mosquito Indians and not to the association at Greytown, as before assumed, they could only look to the Mosquitoes for the redress of wrongs from which the Government of the Country wherein they voluntarily placed themselves was bound to shield them.   International law opens to them no other source of reclamation. The obligation to protect and in the event of a failure, to indemnify would devolve upon Greytown in one case and upon the Mosquito Indians in the other.

Regarding the Mosquitoes as possessing the sovereignty over Greytown, it was for them to complain of the proceedings of the United States towards the people at that place, and to make reclamation if any was due, for injuries to foreigners whom they had received within their jurisdiction and whom they were consequently under obligation to protect. The Mosquitoes seem to be well satisfied with the treatment received by Greytown from the United States, for they have not complained of it, nor asked for any indemnity for either their citizens or foreign residents who sustained losses by the bombardment. If the sovereign power of a country acquiesces in, and apparently approves of the chastisement by a foreign power of those under its protection it certainly will not be concluded that the sufferers by that chastisement are entitled to indemnity from that foreign power, for losses thereby sustained.

The stren[g]th of the positions herein taken are not impaired by the fact that in some cases the claimants might be turned over for redress to a feeble power. It should be recollected that in this instance it was to such a power without anything in its character or composition to justify confidence that the applicants committed their property, and they cannot reasonably ask to have a well settled principle of international law changed in order to meet the exigency of their case.

The Undersigned has discussed the case upon the basis on which the applicants have placed it. They have assumed that Greytown was a sovereign State at the time it was bombarded, and that they were there as foreign merchants engaged in trade.

It is not presumed that they will shift their position and adopt that which the United States have heretofore taken and still maintain in regard to the character of Greytown. Though the people at that place had adopted the form and arrangements of a political organization, their character and conduct did not in the opinion of this Government entitle them "to stand before the world in the attitude of an organized political society." During the period of their association they had earned for themselves no better character than that "of a marauding establishment, too dangerous to be disregarded and too guilty to pass unpunished." If the subjects or citizens of foreign States, chose to become dwellers among such an assemblage, and entrust their property to such a custody, they can have no just cause to complain nor good grounds for the redress of injuries resulting from the punishment inflicted upon that offending community. In this aspect of the case the situation of these foreigners would not be unlike that of a person who should indiscreetly place his property on board of a piratical ship. If that ship were captured, and the property destroyed or lost, the owner could have no pretence of claim against the captors. It was his fault that he inconsiderately exposed it to such a contingency.

Though an issue is not made in respect to the right of the United States to inflict the punishment they did upon the people of Greytown, it is assumed that there was a harshness in the proceeding which commends the present application to the equitable consideration of this Government. This view is not only not sustained but is directly opposed, by the facts of the case.   Before the arrival of the Cyane in the harbor of San Juan notice had been given to the whole population at Greytown by the Commercial Agent that this Government claimed satisfaction of that community for injuries and insults, and that if it was withheld, a United States vessel of War would be sent to inflict proper chastizement but no steps were taken to avert it.   After the Cyane arrived the demand for satisfaction was repeated and formal proclamation issued by the Commander of that ship stating that if nothing was done by way of rendering satisfaction within a specified period, the place would be bombarded.   It is true that only twenty four hours were allowed by the proclamation, to comply with that demand.   It however should be recollected that the United States Commercial Agent had made a similar previous demand which had been treated with open contempt, and further violence to American citizens and their property publicly threatened."[1]   At the same time the proclamation was published "foreigners generally and those favorable to the United States were notified that a steamer would be in readiness on the morning of the day of the bombardment, to carry such as were disposed to a place of safety."   Not only was this proffer of means for security declined by those who now claim to have been foreign traders there, but they made no appeal to the Commander of the Cyane for his favorable consideration of their case nor for that discrimination between themselves and the other dwellers at Greytown which they now wish to have made.   Had there been just grounds for such discrimination, it is fair to presume they would have asked for it, and that, if practicable it would have been granted.   As they did not claim it when it might have been available they cannot with a good grace do so now to sustain extravagant demands for their losses.   They then chose to share the common fate which awaited the guilty community in which they lived and the Undersigned has not been able to discover any principle of international law, or rule of equity, which places them in any better condition in regard to redress from the United States than that of all other residents of Greytown.

The French Government having consented that its much respected diplomatic representative here should be the medium of preferring the claims referred to, the Undersigned has pursuant to the wishes of the President, given the application a more deliberate consideration on that account, than would otherwise seem to be due to it, and has shown in a satisfactory manner as he believes that neither upon the ground of right nor

[1] It is thus in the file copy in the manuscript volume, although there was no indication of the beginning of this quotation.

justice nor by any considerations addressed to its sense of equity is this
Government obliged or required to make compensation for the losses occasioned by the bombardment of Greytown.

The Undersigned avails himself of this opportunity [etc.].

2499

*Lewis Cass, Secretary of State of the United States, to John Y. Mason, United
States Minister to France* [1]

No. 109   WASHINGTON, *May 16, 1857.*

SIR: Herewith I send you the copy of a note of the 22nd Ultimo addressed
by this Department to Lord Napier, the British Minister in this City.[2]
It has reference to our relations with New Granada, and is forwarded to you
for your information, and for that of Count Walewski, to whom you will
take an early opportunity of reading it.

I am, Sir, respectfully [etc.].

2500

*Lewis Cass, Secretary of State of the United States, to Count de Sartiges,
French Minister to the United States* [3]

WASHINGTON, *September 21, 1857.*

The Secretary of State presents his compliments to the Count de Sartiges,
and in compliance with his oral request, has the honor to transmit to him,
herewith, the copy of a note of the 10th instant from this Department to Lord
Napier,[4] relative to a joint convention between the United States, England,
and France, for the purpose of securing the freedom and neutrality of the
transit route over the Isthmus of Panama.

2501

*Lewis Cass, Secretary of State of the United States, to John Y. Mason, United
States Minister to France* [5]

No. 131   WASHINGTON, *November 23, 1857.*

SIR: I have to inform you that a treaty was signed here on the 16th instant
by Mr. Yrisarri [Irisarri], the Minister of the Republic of Nicaragua and by

---

[1] Instructions, France, vol. 15.   [2] See below, vol. VII, pt. I, doc. 2776, April 22, 1857.
[3] Notes to France, vol. 6.   [4] See below, vol. VII, pt. I, doc. 2782, Sept. 10, 1857.
[5] This document was copied from Instructions, Great Britain, vol. 17, since no copy was
found in the appropriate volume containing instructions to France. In the index of Instructions, France, vol. 15, however, a note stated that No. 131, to Mason, went on this date,
mutatis mutandis, as No. 86, to Minister Dallas in London.

me pursuant to which this Government guaranties to that Republic the transit route through her territories between the two oceans in consideration of certain advantages to the United States and their citizens in respect to said transit. The design of this Government in entering into this stipulation was not selfish or exclusive. Any other nation may form the same engagement with Nicaragua and may expect the same equivalent. It is also believed that the terms of the Treaty will not conflict with those of that commonly called the Clayton Bulwer Treaty, signed by the Plenipotentiaries of the United States and Great Britain on the 19th of April 1850.

I am Sir, Your obedient servant.

2502

Lewis Cass, Secretary of State of the United States, to John Y. Mason, United States Minister to France [1]

No. 146　　　　　　　　　　　　　　　WASHINGTON, *June 9, 1858.*

SIR: Accompanying this letter you will receive a condensed statement of the affairs of the United States with Nicaragua,[2] and of the reports, which have reached here touching the conduct of Mr. Filix [Felix] Belly, a French man, who has recently made himself quite conspicuous in that country, and in Costa Rica, by his opposition to the interests of the U. States.

There is reason to believe that he has produced the impression there, that he is an Agent of the French Government, and has exerted the influence which that impression and other circumstances have given him, to our serious detriment. And it is probably owing to his interference, his promises and statements, that the President of Nicaragua has been induced to withhold his ratification from a recent treaty with the United States, after the Treaty had met with the concurrence of the Constituent Assembly. This refusal has tended still more to complicate our relations with that Republic.

I had a conversation with Mr. de Sartiges yesterday, who expressed his conviction that this Mr. Belly is not an Agent of the French Government, but that he has gone to Central America upon some speculation, furnished with the necessary means by persons embarked with him in the enterprize. It is quite possible that Mr. de Sartiges is right, and that this man is a mere adventurer, acting for private purposes and supported by private means. But the subject should be brought to the notice of the French Government, and I will thank you, in conversation with Count Walewski, to make known to him these circumstances, and ascertain whether Mr. Belly has had the authority of the Government for his proceedings. I need hardly say, that this inquiry is one which should be made with a good deal of discretion, and

[1] Instructions, France, vol. 15.　　　　[2] Not found.

not in the nature of a peremptory demand. If Mr Belly has assumed a character to which he is not entitled, Count Walewski will doubtless be glad of an opportunity to disavow his pretensions.

I am, Sir, respectfully [etc.].

2503

Lewis Cass, Secretary of State of the United States, to John Y. Mason, United States Minister to France [1]

No. 166   WASHINGTON, *November 5, 1858.*

SIR: Your despatches to N$^{\circ}$ 353 [2] have been received. The information which you have transmitted respecting M. Belly has been highly acceptable. No uneasiness however, is felt here in regard to the proceedings of that person.

I am Your obedient servant.

2504

Lewis Cass, Secretary of State of the United States, to John Y. Mason, United States Minister to France [3]

No. 167   WASHINGTON, *November 10, 1858.*

SIR: I herewith transmit to you, for your information the copy of a despatch of the 25th of July last, addressed by this Department to General Lamar, [4] relative to our complaints against the Governments of Nicaragua and Costa Rica. This Despatch was communicated by the General to the Governments of those countries, with the exception of the paragraph marked in pencil, which he thought proper to omit, and in this shape has found its way into the newspapers.

I am, Sir, respectfully [etc.].

[1] Instructions, France, vol. 15.
In the date of the file copy of this instruction, the year was written as 1859, apparently an error of the copyist. The figures "58" appeared in pencil over the figures "1859."
[2] Although "N$^{\circ}$ 353", appearing in the file copy of this instruction, had been later changed with pencil to read, "N$^{\circ}$ 323," it refers evidently to Mason's despatch No. 353, below, this volume, pt. VI, October 12, 1858, doc. 2656.
[3] This document was copied from Instructions, Great Britain, vol. 17, since no copy was found in the appropriate volume containing instructions to France. In the index of Instructions, France, vol. 15, however, a note stated that No. 167, to Mason, went on this date, *mutatis mutandis*, as No. 139, to Minister Dallas in London.
[4] Above, vol. IV, pt. I, doc. 1100.

2505

Lewis Cass, Secretary of State of the United States, to John Y. Mason, United States Minister to France [1]

No. 169   WASHINGTON, *November 26, 1858.*

SIR: You will receive herewith the memorandum of a Conversation I held a few days since with M. de Sartiges.[2]   The subject has assumed a very grave aspect and it is necessary I should communicate to you the views of the Government that you may be able to explain them fully in conversation to Count Walewski, and for that purpose it will be proper to embrace the first favorable opportunity which an interview with the Minister may give you.

The general policy of the United States concerning Central America is familiar to you.   We desire to see the Isthmian routes opened and free for the commerce and intercourse of the world and we desire to see the States of that region well governed and flourishing and free from the control of all Foreign Powers.   The position we have taken we shall adhere to, that this country will not consent to the resubjugation of those States, or to the assumption and maintenance of any European authority over them.

The United States have acted with entire good faith in this whole matter. They have done all they could do to prevent the departure of illegal Military expeditions with a view to establish themselves in that region, and at this time measures are in progress to prevent the organization and departure of another, which is said to be in preparation.   Should the avowed intention of the French and British Governments be carried out and their forces be landed in Nicaragua, the measure would be sure to excite a strong feeling in this Country and would greatly embarrass the efforts of the government to bring to a satisfactory close these Central American difficulties which have been so long pending.

You will be good enough to suggest to Count Walewski, that considering the circumstances I have stated, and also the friendly relations which have so long existed between the United States and France, the President indulges the confident hope that the French Government will abstain from all forcible interference in the affairs of Central America and will use its influence to bring the existing embarrassments there to a speedy and satisfactory conclusion.

I am, Sir, [etc.].

[1] Instructions, France, vol. 15.
[2] He refers evidently to the document dated November 21, 1858, above, vol. IV, doc. 1111, note 4, p. 134.

2506

Lewis Cass, Secretary of State of the United States, to Count de Sartiges, French Minister to the United States [1]

WASHINGTON, *March 15, 1859.*

SIR: I have the honor to acknowledge the receipt of your note of the 12th instant,[2] inquiring in behalf of your Government what position the American Companies which claim to have special rights of transit through the territory of Nicaragua and Costa Rica are now understood to occupy in reference to the Governments of those Countries.

In reply to the inquiry I cannot do better than enclose to you herewith a copy of the letter which was addressed by this Department to the American Minister in Central America, on the 25th of July 1858,[3] and which states very fully the views of this Government upon the subject of the transit contracts to which your note refers.

I ought to add that I am not aware that the American contracts have been surrendered or declared forfeit in the manner described in my letter to General Lamar.

Be pleased Sir, to accept [etc.].

2507

Lewis Cass, Secretary of State of the United States, to John Y. Mason, United States Minister to France [4]

Private and Confidential.   WASHINGTON, *April 12, 1859.*

DEAR SIR: I desire to write you more freely than I could do in a public despatch, and therefore address you this private communication. It will put you in possession of the state of our relations with Nicaragua and enable you to make known to Count Walewski the serious complaints we have against that state, and the course we shall pursue so far as we have determined on it. I think in a day or two I shall write you a public despatch which you can show to Count Walewski; but in the meantime the statements of this letter will be sufficient for the purpose of all necessary explanations. We are desirous that the French Government should understand our condition and purposes, for I am sure it will recognise not only the injuries we have sustained, but also the moderation we have exhibted under circumstances which have now reached a crisis calling for prompt and efficient action on our part.

You know the difficulties we have had with England respecting the affairs of Central America. It was hoped that these would be adjusted by the

---

[1] Notes to France, vol. 7.   [2] Below, this volume, pt. VI, doc. 2666.
[3] See above, vol. IV, pt. I, instruction No. 9 to Lamar, doc. 1100.
[4] Instructions, France, vol. 15.

Clayton Bulwer Treaty, but the parties differed so widely in its construction that the most serious results were apprehended. At length a proposition was made by the British Government to accept substantially our construction of that instrument and to dispose of the Mosquito question by the abandonment of the protectorate, and by providing a suitable reservation and annuity for the Indians and by recognising the dominion of Nicaragua over the whole country. The Bay Islands dispute was to be adjusted by the surrender of the whole group to Honduras, and by making some reasonable provision for the security of bona fide settlers, and also for the benefit and protection of trade. We have every reason to believe that the English Government is resolved to carry this arrangement honestly into effect. With that view Sir W. Gore Ouseley came here last season on his way to Central America, with the purpose we understood of communicating freely with this Government and making known his instructions. He did not, however, do so, and we do not know what his instructions were or whether he received them before he left here. We have no reason to doubt, however, that they were in conformity with the previous understanding.

When Sir W. Gore Ouseley left here we supposed that on his arrival in Nicaragua our treaty with that country would be taken up and acted on without delay, as we knew he would have much influence as the Representative of England, and Lord Napier had informed us, that his Government approved the treaty, and had recommended its ratification to the Nicaraguan Government. We have, however, been much disappointed. The Cass-Irissarri [Irisarri] treaty has been wholly neglected, and propositions made for its modification, as you will perceive, to which this Government will not accede. In the meantime Sir W. Gore Ouseley has negotiated a treaty with the Nicaraguan Government for a transit route and commercial Treaty, thus securing all needful advantage for England without any concession, the Mosquito protectorate and the Bay Islands being yet retained. I do not know the cause of this postponement of the Mosquito question, nor do I believe it will be approved by the British Government. I think the error will be corrected by prompt action. But in the meantime its effect upon the public mind here has been very injurious, increasing the excitement and inducing the belief that the execution of the Clayton Bulwer Treaty is to be ultimately evaded. We have communicated with the British Government upon this subject freely but in the best spirit.

Both Lord Napier and the Count de Sartiges are well acquainted with our negotiations, with the present condition of our relations with that State, and I feel justified in saying that both of them are satisfied that the United States have just and serious causes of complaint against Nicaragua.

We are desirous that this subject should be fully made known to the French Government, that it may be able to appreciate not only the injuries and indignities we have suffered but also the redress to which we are entitled.

I shall send you herewith copies of various documents,[1] which taken in connection with those you have already received will put you in possession of the state of our affairs with Nicaragua, and you will please to embrace the first favorable opportunity to communicate freely with Count Walewski and explain to him our views and position.

In addition you will also receive a copy of Count de Sartiges letter to me of March 12th 1859[2] and of my answer[3] explanatory of our views respecting the rights of American citizens who have formed contracts with the Govt of Nicaragua for opening and using the transit routes. These views we shall inflexibly adhere to.

You will impress upon Count Walewski that we want nothing of Nicaragua which is not honorable to her and what[4] we have not a fair right to demand. We shall under no circumstances abandon the determination, that the transit routes across the Isthmus shall be kept open and safe for all commercial nations. The Nicaraguan Government is making an experiment upon this subject in which it must fail.

You will perceive that the Steamers of an American Company have been seized, and the route actually closed. It has been stated that M. Belly has obtained an influence in Central America which he is exerting to our injury. The purposes of that gentleman, so far as regards the opening of routes across the Isthmus, are nothing to us so far as they do not interfere with the vested contract rights of our citizens. We recognize the right of Nicaragua to authorize any individuals or any companies to make roads or canals through its territories but we do not recognize its right arbitrarily to annul contracts made with American citizens, and I am sure the French Government will assent to the justice of this principle.

We have a considerable Naval force on each side of the Isthmus, and this will probably be increased without delay. Orders have been reiterated to the respective commanding officers to afford all necessary and proper protection to the persons and property of American citizens. Desirous as we are to avoid actual collision with Nicaragua, yet the intercourse we have had with the Government of that Country strongly inclines us to believe that we shall obtain the justice to which we are entitled only by the employment of force.

[1] Most of the documents, which accompanied this communication, are elsewhere in this publication. Those printed are as follows: Secretary Cass to Lamar, No. 12, of November 2, 1858, No. 20, of March 4, 1859, No. 22, of April 1, 1859, and No. 24, of April 4, 1859, above, vol. IV, docs. 1105, 1112, 1113, and 1114; Lord Malmesbury to Lord Napier, December 8, 1858, in footnote to Napier's note, of December 30, 1858, below, vol. VII, pt. II, doc. 3114; Count de Sartiges to Cass, March 12, 1859, below, this volume, pt. VI, doc. 2666; Cass to Count de Sartiges, March 15, 1859, above, this part, doc. 2506; Cass to Dallas, No. 168, of April 12, 1859, and Cass to Lord Napier, November 8, 1858, both below, vol. VII, pt. I, docs. 2801 and 2794.   [2] See below, this volume, pt. VI, doc. 2666.
[3] Above, this part, March 15, 1859, doc. 2506.
[4] It is thus in the file copy in the manuscript volume. The word "which" was written above, in pencil, in a different handwriting.

Contrary to my expectation I have been enabled to send the public despatch referred to, at this time.[1]

I am, Dear Sir, [etc.].

2508

Lewis Cass, Secretary of State of the United States, to John Y. Mason, United States Minister to France [2]

No. 179   WASHINGTON, *April 12, 1859.*

SIR: The state of our relations with Nicaragua has occasioned much solicitude to the Government, and they have recently assumed a very grave aspect, from which serious consequences may be apprehended. The President is desirous that the French Government should be made acquainted with the conduct of Nicaragua towards the United States, and the necessity we are under to assert the honor of our Country and redress the injuries which have been inflicted upon our Countrymen. You are aware of the differences which have for some years existed between the United States and Great Britain arising out of the condition of Central America and of the failure of the Clayton-Bulwer Treaty satisfactorily to terminate them. More recently however Great Britain has proposed to accept substantially our construction of that treaty, and though unexpected embarrassments have prevented the anticipated measures from being carried into effect, yet the President is convinced, that these impediments have not been owing to Her Britannic Majesty's Government and that they will be removed and the proposed arrangement be carried into effect by that Government in good faith and without delay.

You will receive herewith copies of various despatches,[3] which in addition to those heretofore transmitted to you will convey to you all the necessary information upon this subject. It is the desire of the President that you seek an interview with Count Walewski, and communicate to him the condition of our affairs with Nicaragua. As my letter to Mr. Dallas of this date contains our general views upon this subject, a copy is hereto annexed for your information[4] and to enable you to conduct your conversation with a full knowledge of the facts. It may be that in your conversation with the Minister of Foreign Affairs you may find it expedient to refer to other facts connected with this subject, with a view to its full comprehension, and that justice may be done to the forbearance of the United States. Should such be the case, the accompanying papers will furnish you with all necessary information. You may leave with Count Walewski a copy of my letter of April 1.[5]

[1] The public despatch, also of April 12, 1859, immediately follows this document.
[2] Instructions, France, vol. 15.   [3] See above, this part, p. 496, note 1.   [4] *Ibid.*
[5] This refers apparently to instruction No. 22 to Lamar, dated April 1, 1859, which is listed as being among the papers enclosed   See above, vol. IV, doc. 1113.

The letter to Count de Sartiges of the 15th ultimo, a copy of which and a copy also of his letter to me, referred to in the former are both enclosed,[1]— contains the views of this Government respecting vested rights of American citizens acquired by contract with the Nicaraguan Government and the determination of the President to maintain and protect them. There are no circumstances which can induce the Government of the United States to abandon this position.

We want no war with Nicaragua, but the measure of our forbearance is filled, and the President has determined upon the adoption of such a course as is demanded by the honor and interests of the United States.

I am, Sir, [etc.].

2509

Lewis Cass, Secretary of State of the United States, to John Y. Mason, United States Minister to France [2]

No. 194   WASHINGTON, *September 19, 1859.*

SIR: You will receive herewith the copy of a letter addressed to this Department by Mr. Mata, the diplomatic Representative here of the Government of Mexico as recognised by the Government of the United States and copies also of the notes which accompanied the letter of Mr. Mata.[3]

It appears from these documents that contrary to the arrangements made with the merchants forwarding the specie, which left the City of Mexico by the conducta [*sic*] which arrived at Vera Cruz in June, last, and much to their dissatisfaction, orders were given to change its direction from Vera Cruz route and direct it to the Port of Antigua or Macombo and there to have the specie embarked on board the foreign vessels of war. Orders were also given under certain circumstances to detain the conducta at Jalapa, and there to await the directions which might be received from the City of Mexico. This proceeding was a breach of good faith for which there was no justification, but the unfortunate consequences which might otherwise have resulted from it were averted by the firm and judicious measures taken by Mr. McLane, the Minister of the United States to the Republic of Mexico, I have been officially informed that with this conducta, there was a large amount of specie belonging to citizens of the United States, and to citizens of Bremen, whose interests Mr. McLane had been requested to attend to,

[1] For the former, see above, this part, doc. 2506, and for the latter, see below, pt. VI, March 12, 1859, doc. 2666.
[2] This document was copied from Instructions, Great Britain, vol. 17, since no copy was found in the appropriate volume of instructions to France. However, a note in the index of Instructions, France, vol. 15, stated that No. 194, to Mason, went on this date, *mutatis mutandis*, as No. 194, to Minister Dallas in London.
[3] See below, in the volume and part containing Communications from Mexico, the note from Mata to the Secretary of State, of July 30, 1859, which is, presumably, the note to which reference is made, and the footnote thereto concerning enclosures.

and this interference therefore gives to this Government just cause of complaint. Having no diplomatic communications with the Miramon authorities at the City of Mexico, the President is not prepared at present to seek redress at that place. And the outrage being disavowed and censured by the Constitutional Government we are unwilling to add to its embarrassments by holding it responsible for this occurrence. But it appears from the statement made in the name of General Miramon that the course he adopted upon this occasion was determined upon in concurrence with the Foreign Ministers at the City of Mexico, including necessarily the Ministers of France and Great Britain, the matter being arranged with them as General Miramon states.

If this be so the proceedings of those two Ministers representing Governments having the most friendly relations with the United States are certainly liable to censure. I do not wish you to make a formal written representation upon the subject, but upon some proper occasion you will in conversation bring the matter to the attention of Count Walewski, and I do not doubt but that the Count if he finds the facts correctly stated will manifest his displeasure at this interference of the French Minister.

I desire to say to you confidentially, that I find it difficult to conjecture the motives which could have dictated the conduct of the British and French Ministers unless indeed the object was to prevent the Jaurez [Juárez] government from collecting the usual tax upon the specie exported and thus injure it by diminishing its resources. If this were the design it was an unjustifiable interference in the political contests in Mexico incompatible with their respective diplomatic positions, and I am confident unacceptable to their governments.

A similar communication has been addressed to the Minister of the U. S. at London.

I am, Sir, respectfully [etc.].

2510

Lewis Cass, Secretary of State of the United States, to Charles J. Faulkner, United States Minister to France [1]

No. 27   WASHINGTON, *August 31, 1860.*

SIR: Since I resumed my duties at this Department a few days since, my attention has been directed to your despatch N° 39[2] and I desire to say in reference to it, that the position of this Government in relation to the condi-

[1] Instructions, France, vol. 15.
   Charles J. Faulkner, of Virginia, to whom this instruction was addressed, was commissioned as envoy extraordinary and minister plenipotentiary to France, on January 16, 1860. He took leave on May 12, 1861.
[2] See below, this volume, pt. VI, July 30, 1860, doc. 2671.

tion of Mexico has been fully made known to the French and Spanish Representatives here in conversation with them respectively.

The statement made to you by Mr. Thovenel [*sic*] of the Report of the Chargé of France upon this subject is substantially correct, with the exception however, that I have no recollection that the Government of Spain was referred to as taking part in the effort at conciliation.

The facts in connection with this measure, are as follows.   The Governments of France and England were anxious for the restoration of tranquility and of order in Mexico, and with that view it was proposed that the United States, France and England should express to both the Rival Governments in that country, the interest they feel in the accomplishment of this desirable object, and should recommend to them to come together and to agree to put an end to their hostilities, and should unite upon the basis of a free and liberal Government and submit the result of their labors for the acceptance of the Mexican people.   All design to interfere by force in the matter or to influence the action of the Mexican authorities or people in any other manner than by friendly representations, was peremptorily disavowed, and it was intimated, that the cooperation of the United States in this endeavor was desired by the two Powers proposing it.   Our established policy, however, being opposed to intervention in the internal affairs of other countries, the President did not think proper to take any part in this proceeding.   It is understood that the effort was made and proved abortive.

The French Chargé in his report to his Government has stated correctly the assurance he gave that France had not the slightest idea of resorting to force upon this occasion.   He stated also that if the rights and interests of French citizens should be violated in Mexico, the Government of France would feel itself at liberty to adopt such measures for their redress or protection, as might be deemed expedient.   Upon this I informed him, that the United States did not call in question the right of France to compel the Government of Mexico by force, if necessary to do it justice, but that the permanent occupation of any part of the territory of Mexico by Foreign Power, or an attempt in any manner forcibly to interfere in its internal concerns or to control its political destiny, would give great dissatisfaction to the United States.   Our policy upon this subject as you are aware is well known by all the Powers interested in the question; and it will be adhered to under all circumstances.

Upon some favorable opportunity, you will be good enough to communicate the substance of these views to Mr. Thouvenel.

I am, Sir, respectfully [etc.].

PART VI

COMMUNICATIONS FROM FRANCE

COMMUNICATIONS FROM FRANCE

2511

William C. Rives, United States Minister to France, to Edward Livingston, Secretary of State of the United States[1]

[EXTRACT]

No. 95   PARIS, *January 8, 1832.*

SIR: I have the honor to enclose a communication recently addressed to me by the minister of Brazil at this court, which, besides the information it contains repecting an interesting point in the political combinations of Europe at the present moment, refers to a project which may re-act on the interests of our own continent. In my acknowledgement of its receipt, a copy of which is also enclosed,[2] while I thought it due to the character of our

[1] Despatches, France, vol. 26. Received February 26.
The brief omitted portion at the end of this despatch relates to the writer's illness, and comments upon European affairs.
[2] These two documents follow:

The Chevalier de la Rocha, Brazilian Minister to France, to William C. Rives, United States Minister to France

PARIS, *December 29, 1831.*

The Undersigned Envoy Extraordinary, and Minister Plenipotentiary of His Majesty the Emperor of Brazil, near the Court of France, is under the necessity of addressing Mʳ Rives, the Envoy Extraordinary and Minister Plenipotentiary of the United States of North America, for the purpose of directing his attention to the subject of a plan, which according to information received, is now in agitation among certain European Powers.—It is well known that Don Pedro the First Emperor of Brazil, was called to the throne by the voice of the Nation, after it had atchieved its independance —that he afterwards abdicated the crown, which according to the Constitution devolved upon his son who was proclaimed and recognised as the Second Emperor of Brazil—and that Don Pedro then returned to Europe, and has since resided in this City.—

It now appears, that he has changed the intention which he publickly avowed, of living here as a private individual, and has set on foot an expedition against Portugal, for the ostensible purpose of placing on the throne of that kingdom, his daughter Donna Maria who has been acknowledged as Queen by several Powers, but as many think with the determination in reality, of annulling the abdication of the Portuguese crown made in her favour and placing it on his own head. Whether this design was suggested to him by others, or by his own imagination, it is needless to inquire.

The opposition made by Spain to the return of Don Pedro to Portugal, and her wish to keep Don Miguel on the throne, have been openly evinced; such opposition could hardly have been of much avail, while the other European Powers favoured the restoration of the Young Queen, and the nomination of her Father as Regent, until he could find an opportunity of seizing the reins himself; but the overthrow of Poland has caused a change in the views of those Powers, and produced a desire to conciliate Spain. A proposition has consequently been made (as the Undersigned has been informed from good authority) to Ferdinand the 7ᵗʰ, that he should consent to the deposition of Don Miguel, and to placing Donna Maria on the throne, under these three Conditions namely,

(1) that there should be no Constitution in Portugal unless Ferdinand 7ᵗʰ pleases.
(2) that Don Pedro shall never set foot in Portugal.

503

government to give the fullest assurances of the deep interest it takes in the destinies, and especially the inviolable independence of our sister States of the South, I yet sought to avoid a form of expression which might give sanction to an opinion that the policy of the United-States, with regard to any ulterior measures of protection, had ever been fixed by a competent constitutional authority.

The apprehensions of the Brazilian minister, I am inclined to think, have been suggested rather by a jealous and patriotic watchfulness on his part, than by any precise schemes of interference formally embraced by any of the Powers of Europe. The attention of our government, however, cannot be too early drawn to the possibility of such an occurrence. . . .

I have the honor to be [etc.].

---

(3) that the King of Spain shall have the right of selecting a husband for Donna Maria.

In addition to these, the Undersigned knows that a promise has been made to Don Pedro of replacing him on the throne of Brazil.—The Undersigned does not pretend to make any observations on these arrangements with respect to Portugal, but he cannot be indifferent to those however absurd, which refer to Brazil. Don Pedro has of his own accord abdicated the throne of Brazil, his abdication was unanimously accepted by the Nation, and in accordance with the Constitution, his Son succeeds him. Now any attempt on the part of the European Governments to interfere with the internal regulations of our Country, would assuredly occasion a war, which must be very prejudicial to its prosperity, even should we prove victorious.—But will such intervention in the affairs of any American State by Europeans be tolerated?

The Undersigned has before him, the able message of the Illustrious President of the United States to Congress, sent December 7th 1824; in it he finds recorded, the sacred principle of "allowing no interference in the Concerns of American States, by European Powers;" and he flatters himself that it extends to the Empire of Brazil. Persuaded of this, the Undersigned has taken the liberty of addressing M[r] Rives, and requesting that he would communicate to his Government, the intelligence here conveyed, which it cannot receive so soon by way of Brazil, as the Undersigned is now awaiting the departure of the packet, which will carry it to the latter country.—The Undersigned embraces this opportunity of assuring M[r] Rives of his high consideration.—

William C. Rives, United States Minister to France, to the Chevalier de la Rocha, Brazilian Minister to France

PARIS, *January 3, 1832.*

SIR: I have been prevented by an indisposition which has confined me hitherto to my bed, from acknowledging the receipt of your interesting communication of December 29th, respecting the plans of certain European Governments, for disturbing the tranquillity of the Brazilian Empire. I am highly obliged by such a proof of confidence on your part, and will hasten to transmit to my Government, the information and observations of Your Excellency, with a firm persuasion that they will be received with interest, as the inviolability of American independance is always with us an object of the greatest solicitude, and every attempt to attack that of any Nation on our Continent, must excite our most vigilant attention.—

I take with pleasure [etc.].

2512

William C. Rives, United States Minister to France, to Edward Livingston, Secretary of State of the United States [1]

[EXTRACTS]

No. 113   PARIS, *May 18, 1832.*

SIR: In conformity to the wish expressed by you in your despatch of 4th Feb last,[2] I have endeavoured to procure through the Department of foreign affairs, all the information which the archives of this government afford, respecting the manner in which the possession of the Falkland Islands passed from France to Spain. The delicate health of Count Sebastiani still preventing him from occupying himself with business, except in a very limited degree, my communications on the subject have been chiefly with Monsieur de Sage, now the sole *Directeur* of the political *Division* in that Department.

The subject of the enquiry falling mainly within the province of the Marine and Colonial Department, Mr. De Sage applied to that Department for a communication of such documents as might be found there in relation to it. Several of the original *letters* of Captain Bougainville, to the Minister of Marine and the Colonies, were sent in answer to the application, and were read to me by Mr. De Sage, in an interview I had with him a few days ago. From these letters, it results that the Falkland Islands, (les Isles Malouines) were taken possession of by Captain Bougainville on the 5th of April 1764 and were subsequently delivered over by him to the authorities of Spain on the 1st of April 1767. It farther appears from the letters of Captain Bougainville that this delivery of possession to Spain was in pursuance of express *instructions* received from his government, and that a formal *act* of *cession* was executed by him, at the time of delivering possession. No copy, however, of this act of cession, could be found in the Marine and Colonial Department. Mr. De Sage promised that he would cause an examination to be made, in the general repository of the public archives for a copy of this instrument, as well as for any convention which may have been concluded between the governments of Spain and France on the subject, and if a discovery of either should be made, he would inform me of the fact.

If you should desire to possess copies of Captain Bougainville's letters, I think it probable they might be obtained by a formal and written application for them: but Mr. De Sage making no offer to put me in possession of them, and hinting, indeed, that copies could be had only through the medium of such an application, I await your farther instructions to enlighten me on the propriety and expediency of making it.—

Of the fact itself of a formal and conventional transfer of these islands, from France to Spain, I think there can be no doubt. Besides the evidence

[1] Despatches, France, vol. 26. Received July 13.
[1] Above, this volume, pt. v, doc. 2466.

of it furnished by the letters of Captain Bougainville, the historical accounts
of these islands treat it as a fact, belonging to the domain of general notoriety.
Among these accounts, one which, I have been induced to believe, may be
found particularly useful in the investigation of the point in question, is a
history of Bougainville's expedition &c. by Pernetti Member of the Academy
of Sciences at Berlin, who accompanied the expedition as historiographer.
The work is, I believe very rare and difficult to be found.   A copy of it, however, was recently met with at Paris by Lieut. A. B. Pinkham of the U. S.
Navy, who has taken it with him home, and would, I am sure, be most happy
to put it at your disposition.

Although the derivation of title to Spain from France, appears to have
been regular and unexceptionable, it is to be hoped, considering the importance of the free entry of these islands to our South Sea trade, that other
grounds will not be wanting to oppose successfully the claim of exclusive
sovereignty over them now set up by the Government of Buenos Ayres.[1] . . .

We have had no news recently of Don Pedro's operations or prospects.
For some time past, it has been supposed that the strong representations of
the English and French governments had turned Spain from her original purpose of aiding Don Miguel, and that the two brothers would be left to decide
their quarrel with their own resources.   I need not add that the turn which
the pending ministerial crisis may take in England, is likely to have fully as
important a bearing on this question, as on any other of European politics.

I have the honour to be [etc.].

2513

Edward Livingston, United States Minister to France, to Louis McLane,
Secretary of State of the United States [2]

[EXTRACT]

No. 12   PARIS, *November 14, 1833.*

SIR: . . . Affairs in Spain are still involved in great uncertainty.
Nothing yet is known of the movements of Don Carlos, although the accounts, or rather the rumours of the day speak of formidable insurrections in
various parts of the kingdom, and of very doubtful conduct on the part of
General Saarsfield, who you know commanded the army of observation on
the frontiers of Portugal.   He gave in his adherance [*sic*] to the Queen, and
marched against the Carlists at Bilbao, but his movements have been so

[1] The omitted portion discusses the question of precedence between ministers from foreign
countries and the heads of departments, and also comments upon European political affairs.
[2] Despatches, France, vol. 27.   Received January 11.
The omitted portions at the beginning and end of this despatch relate to claims against
France, and to Livingston's reply to the Minister from Central America to France, in which
the former declines to enter into the question raised by the latter, in regard to the refusal
of the French Government to grant the latter's request for his passports.

slow, that apprehensions are entertained of his loyalty. Should he declare for Don Carlos the Queen will be hard pressed; and if the French government fulfils its engagements, it must cross the Bidassoa, and light up the flame of a general war. In that event the succour of England must be bought, and it has been hinted to me from a respectable quarter, that the price demanded will be the island of Cuba. Although I do not place entire confidence in this, yet I shall endeavor (and I think I shall succeed) to procure the earliest intelligence of any such design, and transmit it to you with the speed that its importance to us demands. . . .

I have the honour [etc.].

2514

Charles E. Anderson, United States Chargé d'Affaires ad interim at Paris, to John Forsyth, Secretary of State of the United States [1]

[EXTRACTS]

Private. PARIS, *June 6, 1837.*

SIR: In a private letter of the 1 May,[2] I had the honor to relate to you a conversation I had had with a distinguished member of the Diplomatic Corps relating to the Spanish Minister, and at the same time mentioned the subject of the Cuba loan, about which both the French & English papers are now so full of speculations. Yesterday I received a confidential note from the Minister of Foreign Affairs, requesting me to come, if possible, to see him this morning at an early hour. At this interview which was long and confidential, he told me: that it was his wish, that we should have a mutual understanding on the subject of the proposed Spanish loan: that, although he had reason hitherto to think the application to England for a guarantee would have no more success than that to France, he still considered it our duty to be watchful: that if the island of Cuba was not to remain in the possession of Spain, the policy of France would be to see it independant; and in this, he beleived, he would be fully seconded by the policy of the United States. I answered; that the question of a change in the political position of Cuba was not a new one in the United States; and that I could not be wrong in saying, that there would be but one voice against any measure which should place it in the dependance of any other power than that

[1] Despatches, France, vol. 28. Received July 15.
Charles E. Anderson, of New York, the writer of this despatch, was commissioned secretary of legation to France, on October 4, 1836. He acted as chargé d'affaires *ad interim*, from April 3 to November 29, 1837. He resigned on April 1, 1839.
[2] No letter under the above date was found, but apparently he refers to his private letter of May 2, which reported, among other things, a rumor that Spain had attempted a loan pledging as security the revenues of Cuba, and that those to whom the application was made asked as additional security that France and England should guarantee the payment. It is not included in this publication.

of Spain.   He asked me, if I had any official communication on the subject; to which I replied: that I had not: that, after having had the assurance from him, that no attempt of the kind manifested in the negotiation of this loan would be in any way countenenced by France, I had looked upon the news-paper paragraphs on the subject as unfounded rumours.   I then asked him, if he had positive reasons for viewing them differently.   He then again re-peated: that *hitherto* he had not: for that he had been assured through a re-sponsible source of information, that Lord Palmerston would not listen to such a proposal: and besides, that if he did, it would not receive the sanction of one third of the votes of Parliament.   Now however, he saw grounds for apprehension, and therefore urged me to write to you at once, again, on this matter: but in other respects to regard the conversation between us as strictly confidential.

There was a meeting of the Diplomatic body last evening to offer their re-spects to the Duchess of Orleans.   I think it perhaps is not unworthy of re-mark,—and I avail myself of this occasion to mention it,—that the Duchess went so far beyond the usual ceremonial phrases as to express her satisfaction that the relations between "America" and France were now so friendly, and her hopes that they might always continue so: to which I replied in like man-ner and with the same sincerity.   Lord Granville was not present at this reception, being confined to the house by a severe attack of the gout.   I asked Mr Aston, who represented him, "if it was true, that he was going to guarantee so heavy a loan to our neighbour, the Spanish Minister."   His manner in denying the whole report assured me that it was without founda-tion; or at least that he was not in the secret.[1] . . .

I will avail myself of every opportunity to get all the correct information I can obtain on the principal subject of this letter, which I will have the honor to transmit to you, and will take the earliest favorable opportunity of inform-ing Mr Stevenson of it.

I am, Sir, very respectfully [etc.].

2515

Charles E. Anderson, United States Chargé d'Affaires ad interim at Paris, to John Forsyth, Secretary of State of the United States[2]

[EXTRACT]

PARIS, *August 3, 1837.*

SIR: . . . Count Molé entered into the question of the long agitated treaty between England and Spain very fully, and was kind enough to give

[1] The omitted portion contains a financial discussion which took place between the French Minister of Foreign Affairs and Mr. Anderson.

[2] Despatches, France, vol. 28.   Received September 17.

The omitted portions of this despatch relate to a claims question, and to commercial relations between the United States and France.

me a full and detailed account of all the measures proposed and combatted at different times, with reference to the aid which England was to give to the cause of the Queen in raising a loan. He thinks, now, that it is the intention of the English Government *to guarantee to the* QUEEN *the possession of Cuba.* He feels himself hurt, and, I think, much disappointed at the want of frankness shewn in the whole of this transaction both at Madrid and at London; and among other things, he said, that a positive declaration had been given to him that a treaty had not been made, and that Lord Palmerston had not denied this declaration whereas now he had every reason to think that the Treaty was actually in existence and had been carried by Mr Marliani to London, there seen and returned to Madrid.

Before being signed by the Queen it is necessary that it should be laid before the Cortes, and he told me, that the presentation of this Treaty to the Cortes would not be an unexpected event to him. . . .

Your ob. Se^r.

2516

Edouard Pontois, French Minister to the United States, to John Forsyth, Secretary of State of the United States [1]

[TRANSLATION]

WASHINGTON, *May 3, 1838.*

SIR: The Mexican Government having refused to accept the Ultimatum which, with a conciliatory intent, the French Government had addressed to it under date of March 21 last, the Minister of the King in Mexico, who is at present on board the frigate *L'Herminie*, has just informed me, by the brig-of-war *l'Eclipse*, sent for this purpose to Pensacola, both of this refusal and of the measures which it gave rise to on the part of the Captain Bazoche, commanding officer of the French naval forces; and, in compliance with the orders of His Majesty, I hasten to inform the Government of the United States of the following official notification:

All the ports of Mexico are declared in a state of blockade. This blockade became effective for Vera Cruz on the 16th of last month, and was not to delay becoming so for the other ports of the Republic.

The orders which the commandant, Mr. Bazoche, received for the execution of the mission entrusted to him are entirely in conformity with the liberal principles which France professes on the subject of blockades, as you will see, Sir, by the attached extract from the despatch which I received from Baron Deffaudis,[2] and are drawn in such a way as to spare neutrals, principally the navigation of the United States, impediments which are not

---

[1] Notes from France, vol. 11. Received May 3.   [2] Not included in this publication.

absolutely indispensable for attaining the legitimate end which the Government of the King intends.

In addressing this communication to you, Sir, I have the honor to request you to be so good as to acknowledge its receipt as promptly as possible, in order that the departure of the brig *l'Eclipse* which is awaiting my reply at Pensacola, may not be too long delayed.

I avail myself of this opportunity [etc.].

2517

Lewis Cass, United States Minister to France, to John Forsyth, Secretary of State of the United States [1]

[EXTRACT]

Private.   PARIS, *May 5, 1838.*

DEAR SIR: . . . I had a long conversation with the Chilean Chargé the other day. He is a discreet intelligent man, and he is in great trouble, at the state of their affairs with France, arising out of one of these claims to be exempted from local jurisdiction The French government demand for their Consuls authority over French subjects in Chili, and if I did not misunderstand the Chargé some violences have been committed by the Admiral upon that Station, in order to enforce the demand. Chili has represented the nature of its constitution, and the exclusive jurisdiction, confided to it's Courts, and has referred to the relations upon this subject, between the United States and France, and offered to confer upon the French Consuls the same power they have in our Country. But in vain. I met the Chargé this week, at dinner, and he told me, the matter was in statu quo. I comforted him by referring to our history, and telling him, after we were obliged to submit to the law of force for thirty years, we had acquired strength enough to resort [to?] the great arbiter war, and this, I supposed, must be in time their case, in the course of time.

I am, Dear Sir, [etc.].

<hr>

[1] Despatches, France, vol. 28. Received June 6.
The omitted portion discusses a note from the French Foreign Minister, in which he places in the same category, exemption from United States jurisdiction on the high seas, and exemption from United States jurisdiction in United States ports.

2518

Lewis Cass, United States Minister to France, to John Forsyth, Secretary of State of the United States [1]

[EXTRACT]

Private. PARIS, *May 30, 1838.*

DEAR SIR: . . . Mr. Henderson, the Texian representative is here. He has not yet succeeded in seeing Count Molé or in getting from him an answer to his note, announcing his arrival and objects. I have had much conversation with Mr Henderson, and have felt disposed to afford him all the aid in my power, *unofficially*. There is obviously no intention, on the part of the French government to recognize the independence of Texas at present. And it seems doubtful whether they will even make a commercial arrangement, like that which has been made with England, for the admission of vessels reciprocally. Perhaps Mr Henderson may be able to move a little better, after the session, but now, the ordinary administrative business seems alone to be done.

I am satisfied, that the resolution in the Texian legislature, withdrawing their proposition for admission to our Union, originated with Mr Henderson, in consequence of suggestions, made to him in England. He was given to understand, that while such a matter was pending his chance of recognition would be small, and there is no doubt, but the desire to see Texas independent, rather than connected with us, led to the intimation. He told me his views before the arrival of the information of the introduction into the Texian legislature of the resolution.

It is a strange fact, but so it is, nevertheless, that the Slave question is felt even in the application of Texas. Mr. Henderson tells [me?] this was distinctly avowed by Lord Palmerston in England not as making a difficulty in the views of the government, but as operating upon the community, and thus complicating the matter. Mr Henderson met the suggestion promptly, as one to which they never would listen, and one, which England had no right to make.

Here the same feeling is evident. And I am not sure, but it will operate more decidedly. I have not yet met a man in Europe, who understands our peculiar situation upon this subject. I consider myself pretty philosophical in the government of my temper, but this is the only question, about which I have suffered myself to be moved in conversation. In fact, I have determined not to run the risk of being provoked, by talking any more about it. They are ignorant of the historical incidents of slavery among us, of its first introduction by the British. They are ignorant of our division of political

[1] Despatches, France, vol. 28. Received July 13.
The omitted portion discusses consular matters, and the writer's contemplated trip to England.

power, and that this is a matter left to the State governments, with whom the general government has no concern. They know nothing of the condition of the Slaves, nothing of their treatment, nothing of the danger of immediate emancipation to such an immense number of uneducated persons. But every other consideration is absorbed in the word freedom, and right or wrong, it must be had.

I had a conversation with the Mexican Minister yesterday. I find the course, taken by France irritates him exceedingly. He says he came on last October to arrange this matter, and that it was a month before they found time to receive him. He was desirous of referring the matter to some other government, but this was declined. He thinks his Country will hold out to the last. But as I have not much faith, either in their principles or firmness, I look to the success of the French, as nearly certain.

If there should be nothing important to be done here in September, I propose to make a quick trip *incognito* to Milan to see the ceremony there. I have quite a passion for these old fashioned sights, and as I do not think I can stand it more than two or three years I mean to embrace the opportunities, that present themselves. The publick business shall not suffer, nor shall you ever again be troubled by a claim for compensation, for a Chargé officiating in my———[1] I will never present one, without recording in writing, that he expects no additional allowance for his services.

I am, Dear Sir [etc.].

2519

Count Louis M. Molé, Minister of Foreign Affairs of France, to Lewis Cass, United States Minister to France [2]

[TRANSLATION]

PARIS, *May 31, 1838.*

MR. GENERAL: The Mexican Government having refused to rectify the numerous grievances for which the Minister Plenipotentiary of the King in Mexico had been instructed to request reparation from it, the Commander of the French naval forces before Vera Cruz found it necessary to adopt, as he was authorized to do by his instructions, the measures which, in such a case, the dignity of France and the justice of her claims required. Accordingly, all the ports of Mexico have been declared to be in a state of blockade and this blockade, which became effective for Vera Cruz on April 16 last, was to become effective without delay for the other ports of Mexico likewise.

---

[1] The original of this despatch was bound so closely and written so badly in the manuscript volume that it was impossible to ascertain fully the omitted word here. The beginning of the word appears to be "abs" as if it were "absence," which apparently would fit the case.

[2] Despatches, France, vol. 28; enclosed with Anderson to the Secretary of State, July 3, 1838, below, this part, doc. 2521.

In informing you of the provisions thereof, Mr. General, I hasten to add that the orders given by the Government of the King to insure the execution [of the blockade] are conceived in such a way as to reconcile the practical exercise of a legitimate right with the respect which is due the freedom of flags and with the sincere desire to impede neutral navigation as little as possible.

I beg you to be so good as to inform the Federal Government of this notification.

Please accept [etc.].

2520

Count Louis M. Molé, Minister of Foreign Affairs of France, to Lewis Cass, United States Minister to France [1]

PARIS, *June 16, 1838.*

MR. GENERAL: The Consul of the King at Buenos Ayres having unsuccessfully exhausted the methods of negotiation to secure reparation of the serious violations of international law of which the Government of that State has been guilty towards French nationals residing in its territory, the commander of the French naval forces in southern waters, in conformity with instructions which he had received for this eventuality, on March 28 last declared the port of Buenos Ayres and all the littoral belonging to the Argentine Republic to be in a state of blockade. This blockade, of which the agents of foreign powers in Buenos Ayres were immediately notified by him, became effective on the same day—March 28. Further, the measures adopted to insure the efficacy thereof are entirely in accord with the liberal principles professed by France in the matter of maritime law and in this respect, Sir, I can only refer to the statement contained in the letter which I had the honor to address to you on May 31 relative to the blockade of the ports of Mexico.[2]

I beg you to be so good as to inform the Government of the United States of this communication.

I have the honor [etc.].

2521

Charles E. Anderson, Secretary of the United States Legation at Paris, to John Forsyth, Secretary of State of the United States [3]

PARIS, *July 3, 1838.*

SIR: Enclosed are copies of two letters received from the French Minister of Foreign Affairs relative to the blockade of the Mexican and Argentine

---

[1] Despatches, France, vol. 28; enclosure with Anderson to the Secretary of State, July 3, 1838, below, this part, doc. 2521.
[2] Above, this part, doc. 2519.   [3] Despatches, France, vol. 28.   Received August 15.

ports.[1] The letter of the 31st May, alluded to in the subsequent letter appears not to have been sent to this office. A copy of it was not obtained until yesterday.

I am, Sir, very resp[ly] [etc.].

2522

Lewis Cass, United States Minister to France, to John Forsyth, Secretary of State of the United States [2]

No. 57   PARIS, *July 14, 1838.*

SIR: Finding that the letter of the Minister of Foreign Affairs, announcing the blockade of Mexico,[3] embraced, in its terms, as well the coast of that republick upon the Pacifick, as upon the Gulf of Mexico, I have asked from him an explanation,[4] stating, that not having understood, there was any French naval force to give effect to a blockade of the Western Coast of Mexico, I presumed the measure announced extended only to its ports upon the Gulf. I shall communicate the answer as soon as it is received.

I have the honor [etc.].

2523

Count Louis M. Molé, Minister of Foreign Affairs of France, to Lewis Cass, United States Minister to France [5]

[TRANSLATION]

PARIS, *August 8, 1838.*

SIR: You have expressed to me a desire to know whether the blockade of the Mexican ports of which I have had the honour to notify you extends to those on the Pacific.[6]

To the present time, this blockade applies only to the Mexican ports situated on the Atlantic; but if the King's Government, should judge proper to extend it hereafter to the ports on the opposite coast, care will be taken to do all which may be necessary for the purpose of assuring its efficiency on that side, and to notify the Federal Government of it previously.

Accept Sir [etc.].

[1] See above, this part, May 31 and June 16, 1838, docs. 2519 and 2520.
[2] Despatches, France, vol. 28.   Received August 8.
[3] See above, this part, May 31, 1838, doc. 2519.
[4] Not included in this publication.   Its content is sufficiently revealed within this despatch.
[5] Despatches, France, vol. 28; enclosed with Cass to the Secretary of State, [No. 59], August 14, 1838, below, this part, doc. 2524.
[6] The note from Cass, dated July 11, is not included in this publication.   Its content is sufficiently revealed within this despatch.

2524

Lewis Cass, United States Minister to France, to John Forsyth, Secretary of State of the United States [1]

No. [59 ?]   PARIS, *August 14, 1838.*

SIR: The enclosed paper is a copy of a communication from Count Molé [2] in answer to my letter of the 11th July 1838,[3] asking an explanation with regard to the extent of the blockade of Mexico.

I am, Sir, [etc.].

2525

Lewis Cass, United States Minister to France, to Count Louis M. Molé, Minister of Foreign Affairs of France [4]

PARIS, *December 7, 1838.*

SIR: I have it in charge from my government to represent to your Excellency, that the commanding officer of the United States Ship *Erie* has received from the officer commanding his Majesty's blockading squadron off the coast of Mexico, under date of August 28th 1838, a letter, by which it is announced, that thereafter all neutral vessels appearing off the ports of the Gulf would be presumed to come with the intention of violating the blockade and would be seized & detained till the government of his majesty should pronounce their sentence, without any previous notice being given to them; thus changing in a material degree, the mode of conducting the blockade as originally announced to other nations.

I persuade myself, Mr le Comte, that the commanding officer of the French blockading squadron, has mistaken the intentions of his Majesty's Government & that the proper remedy will be applied to restore the conduct of this blockade to the principles originally announced, & for this purpose I beg leave to ask the interposition of your excellency.

I avail myself [etc.].

[1] Despatches, France, vol. 28.   Received September 27.
In the manuscript volume, the serial number of this despatch was omitted, but apparently it should have been "No. 59," since it follows No. 58, of July 29, 1838, and immediately precedes No. 60, of September 22, 1838.
[2] Above, this part, August 8, 1838, doc. 2523.
[3] Not included in this publication. Its content is sufficiently indicated within this despatch.
[4] Despatches, France, vol. 28; enclosed with Cass to the Secretary of State, No. 67, December 15, 1838, below, this part, doc. 2528.

2526

Lewis Cass, United States Minister to France, to John Forsyth, Secretary of State of the United States [1]

No. 64   PARIS, *December 10, 1838.*

SIR: I enclose the copy of a communication from Count Molé respecting the arrangement made in 1767 between France and Spain on the subject of the Falkland Islands.[2]

Mr Vail in his dispatch of September, 29th 1838 [3] asking for a copy of this arrangement suggested an informal application for it.   I found however that an official communication was necessary, and the request therefore assumed that form.   I state this fact, not because it is of any importance, but to account for the apparent variation between the instructions and their execution.

I am, Sir, very respectfully [etc.].

2527

Count Louis M. Molé, Minister of Foreign Affairs of France, to Lewis Cass, United States Minister to France [4]

[TRANSLATION]

PARIS, *December 12, 1838.*

SIR: I have received the letter which you did me the honour to write to me on the 8th of this month [5] relative to a communication addressed on the 28th of August to the Captain of the American corvette Erie, by the Commander of the French Naval forces employed in blockading the Mexican-

[1] Despatches, France, vol. 28.   Received January 24.
[2] This communication follows:

[MEMORANDUM—TRANSLATION]

There was no diplomatic convention between France and Spain in 1767 relative to the possession of the Falkland Islands.

In the comment which he made on page 52 of his *Guide Diplomatique*, Martens doubtless meant to speak of a known historical fact, the result of which we will briefly set forth.

After the peace of 1763, Bougainville was sent by Louis XV to attempt discoveries in the southern seas and laid the foundations of a colony in one of the Iles Malouines. As a result of the negotiations then taking place between France and Spain, the former power sent Bougainville to Madrid to request authorization of the Spanish Cabinet to continue the proposed settlement, or to propose to it the cession of the islands. Charles III accepted the latter part of the proposal.   Orders were given on both sides to the Navies of the two States: Admiral Bougainville joined two Spanish frigates, left Montevideo and arrived at the Iles Malouines or Falkland Islands March 23, 1767. On the following April 1, the officers of His Catholic Majesty took possession of these islands.

[3] He evidently refers to the Acting Secretary of State's instruction of September 27, 1838, above, this volume, pt. v, doc. 2468.
[4] Despatches, France, vol. 28; enclosed with doc. 2528, December 15, 1838, below, this part.
[5] He presumably refers to the note of the 7th from Cass, above, this part, doc. 2526. This was probably the mistake of the amanuensis in the legation.   This translation was evidently made in the Department, and was filed with a French copy in the manuscript volume.

ports, for the purpose of informing him that from that day every neutral vessel appearing before one of those ports should be considered as seeking to violate the blockade and should be in consequence captured and detained until the French Government should pronounce sentence with regard to her.

The King's Government had foreseen the wish expressed by you, and made adequate provision, by addressing instructions to Admiral Baudin, to make no change in the rules previously adopted, with respect to the blockade of the Mexican ports, as communicated to the Federal Government by the King's Minister at Washington.[1]

The Minister of Marine has nevertheless been made acquainted with the contents of the letter to which I have now the honour of replying, and has been requested to prescribe any new measures, which he may judge necessary, in conformity with those already determined on.

I have the honour [etc.].

2528

Lewis Cass, United States Minister to France, to John Forsyth, Secretary of State of the United States [2]

No. 67   PARIS, *December 15, 1838.*

SIR: I have the honor to inform you, that immediately after the receipt of despatch N⁰ 32, of 6ᵗʰ November 1838, from the Department,[3] I sought an interview with the Minister of Foreign Affairs to bring to his knowledge the change made in the principles established by the French government for the blockade of the Mexican ports, as announced in the letter, of the 28ᵗʰ August, from the commanding officer of the French naval forces in the Gulf of Mexico to the Captain of the sloop of war "Erie". I found that this change had been made without any authority and was disavowed by the Government. On my return I addressed to the Minister a letter of which a copy is enclosed, and have just received the satisfactory answer, a copy of which is herewith transmitted to you.[4]

It is proper to add, that upon this as upon former occasions, when I have

[1] He evidently refers to a note of Pontois to the Secretary of State of October 12, 1838, which is not included in this publication. It is a denial by the French Government that it had ever prescribed the measures reported by the Captain of the *Erie*, and asserts, on the contrary, that it had recommended again to its naval forces forbearance towards all neutrals. This note was in response to a vigorous protest from the Secretary of State, of July 19, in which an explanation of the alterations, made by the French squadron in regard to neutral vessels, was demanded.

[2] Despatches, France, vol. 28. Received January 21.

[3] Not included in this publication. This instruction pointed out that the principles which the French commander proposed to enforce, in relation to the blockade of Mexican ports, were still at variance with the official notification given to the United States government, and would likely lead to inconveniences to our commerce, and, it was supposed, had not the sanction of the French Government; Cass was instructed to take the matter up again with the French Foreign Minister.

[4] For these two notes, see above, this part, December 7 and 12, 1838, docs. 2526 and 2527.

conversed with Count Molé upon the subject of this blockade, he has expressed the determination of the King's government to relax the rigour of the recognized principles respecting blockades, as far as could be done, consistently with the end they had in view, and to inflict the least practicable injury upon the commerce of other nations.

I am, Sir, very respectfully [etc.].

2529

Lewis Cass, United States Minister to France, to John Forsyth, Secretary of State of the United States [1]

No. 69   PARIS, *December 21, 1838.*

SIR: I thought it better, in carrying into effect Despatch N⁰ 30[2] from the Department respecting the friendly mediation of the United States in the difficulties between France and Mexico, to communicate directly and frankly with Count Molé rather than indirectly and through the intervention of any third person; not only because the proceeding directed was honorable to the United States and could not be misapprehended, but because whatever channel were adopted it would not escape the penetration of an ordinary man, and still less of Count Molé, that the proposition must have been previously authorized by the government of the U States. I therefore embraced the first favorable opportunity of conversing with the Minister on the subject.

After a full explanation of the feelings of the government of the United States, Count Molé expressed his conviction that the most friendly views had dictated the proceeding, but that under existing circumstances the King's government could not adopt any measures of a pacific character, till the receipt of despatches from the French squadron in the Gulf of Mexico. He stated that advices had just been received from the Admiral announcing his arrival upon the Mexican coast and that a messager [*sic*] had been dispatched to the Capital with the ultimatum. He mentioned two points in which this ultimatum was less exceptionable than the ultimatum, so called, presented by the Baron Deffaudis, the French Minister. First, that the removal of the Mexican judge was not demanded, and second that the terms of payment of the indemnity required were prolonged. He expressed his belief that the propositions, now made, would be accepted; but if they were not that the hostile operations of the French force, which would be immediately commenced, would reduce the Mexican government to the necessity of an arrangement. He expressed great confidence in Admiral Baudin, and

---

[1] Despatches, France, vol. 28. Received February 26.
[2] Above, this volume, pt. v, October 29, 1838, doc. 2469.

considered his force quite sufficient for the accomplishment of the objects proposed.   He did not conceal his dissatisfaction at the course of proceeding, which had been adopted, stating his conviction, that if his instructions had been followed, the affair would have been terminated, within three months from the commencement.   He considered the course adopted by the French Minister at Mexico towards that government as too peremptory, and calculated to wound the selfrespect of any nation; and he was dissatisfied with some part of the conduct of the French commanding officer, who, I presume, will be brought to trial.

The state of affairs connected with Mexico occasions much inquietude here, and the result is looked for with no little solicitude.   It is expected that the first arrival will bring some decisive intelligence; and this it is, as you will perceive, which renders the government unwilling to take any new measure at the present moment.   Count Molé did not state whether a proposition of mediation, if made, would be accepted or declined, but contented himself with expressing his conviction of the good faith of the U. States, and saying that the government had every reason as I have mentioned, to expect immediate intelligence that the difficulty was terminated.   Under these circumstances the conversation closed, and I took my leave.

You will know, ere this reaches you, how far events will have realized this expectation.   It is possible, should they have proved adverse, that the intermediation of the United States may be desirable.

I shall not lose sight of the matter, and shall advise you of any proceeding I may adopt.

I am, Sir, very respectfully [etc.].

2530

Edouard Pontois, French Minister to the United States, to John Forsyth, Secretary of State of the United States [1]

[TRANSLATION]

WASHINGTON, *January 9, 1839.*

SIR: I regret that I am unable to furnish you the information which you did me the honor to request of me in your letter of the 7th this month,[2] on the present state of the blockade of the ports of Mexico by the French naval forces.   I have no other information in this respect than that which was given me by the Chief of Staff of Admiral *Baudin* and which is exactly the same as that contained in the American newspapers on the capture of Fort St. Jean d'Ulloa, and the surrender which followed.

I have the honor [etc.].

[1] Notes from France, vol. 11.   Received January 9.
[2] Not included in this publication.   Its purport is adequately revealed herein.

2531

Lewis Cass, United States Minister to France, to John Forsyth, Secretary of State of the United States [1]

Private.   PARIS, *July 12, 1839.*

MY DEAR SIR: I wrote you, at the time, a private letter,[2] informing you of the intermediation, I had undertaken between Count Molé and Gen. Henderson, at the request of the former. Gen. Henderson, the Texian Minister here, who is a most worthy modest man, after waiting some time, was desirous of returning, seeing no prospect of accomplishing the objects of his Mission. However Count Molé desired him to stay, saying that M. de Saligny had been directed to proceed to Texas, and to make a report upon the condition of the Country. After that the state of affairs here rendered it impossible for the Ministry to take any steps in this matter, their situation being so uncertain. But now a more permanent administration being formed, Gen. Henderson thought it best to raise the subject, in order, that it might be brought before Marshal Soult. It was known too, that Saligny's report had been rec'd and that it was favourable. Under these circumstances, Gen Henderson wished I should see the Marshal and explain to him, what had taken place, and why he had remained here. I accordingly went there, and M. Pontois accompanied me to explain what I had to say, more clearly than I could [do?] it. I told the Marshal, I did not come to ask the recognition of Texas, that that was a subject, it was not proper for me to present to the French government, particularly, as our relations with Mexico were amicable. And that I came unofficially, as a private man, merely to express the wishes of Gen. Henderson, that the state of uncertainty, respecting himself personally & his Country might be terminated, and that if nothing could be affected, that he might return home. I then explained the relation I had occupied between Gen. Henderson and Count Molé, which led to my present application. Marshal Soult was wholly unacquainted, as I supposed, with the affair, and seemed very desirous of procuring all possible information. I ought however to have mentioned, that the Journal des debats, in an article, a few days before, on the occasion of Admiral Baudin's visit to Mexico had exhibited an evident leaning towards the Texian question. M. Pontois explained the whole matter very well to the Marshal and presented some considerations, derived from the interest of France and the condition of Texas, which seemed to have great weight. The result of the whole was the distinct avowal by the Marshal of his disposition to recognize Texas, and a pretty strong hint, that it would be speedily done. He said he should wait the arrival of Admiral Baudin who is expected every day, in order to get his views. These views

---

[1] Despatches, France, vol. 29. Received September 9.
[2] Presumably, the letter of May 30, 1838, above, this part, doc. 2518.

are known to be friendly, and I think, ere long, you will see the act of recognition.   The Marshal asked me to request Henderson to call upon him, which he has since done, and to day he told me he was invited to dine there. The first official attention, he has rec'd in France.

I am, Dear Sir, [etc.].

2532

Lewis Cass, United States Minister to France, to John Forsyth, Secretary of State of the United States [1]

No. 82   PARIS, *September 28, 1839.*

SIR: I have the honor to inform you that a Treaty has been signed between the French government and the Minister of Texas, by which France recognizes the independence of that country.   The treaty besides contains commercial stipulations.   The Texian Minister has been received by the King.

I am, Sir, [etc.].

2533

Lewis Cass, United States Minister to France, to John Forsyth, Secretary of State of the United States [2]

No. 87   PARIS, *December 6, 1839.*

SIR: I learned incidentally, a day or two since, that a Buenos Ayrean Privateer had been captured by the French blockading squadron in the river La Plata, and had been sent by the commanding officer to France to be tried as a pirate.   She was commanded by an Englishman, who had been many years in the service of the Argentine republic, and had a crew of twelve persons, six of whom claimed to be American citizens.   They were confined on board the vessel in the harbor of Brest, awaiting the decision of the authorities upon their case.   We have no Consul at that port, and I did not receive any application from the prisoners, perhaps because they had not the means of making their cases known to me, but I had the general facts from such a quarter as to admit no doubt of their truth.   Tho' I learned nothing concerning the national character of these men, but from declarations proceeding from themselves.   I could not interfere in a formal manner, but I thought it proper to see the Minister of Foreign Affairs, and to remonstrate, if necessary against a pretension, wholly unfounded in the law of nations. You recollect, no doubt, that Admiral Baudin while blockading the Mexican coast, issued a proclamation, or species of manifesto, threatening to inflict summary punishment as pirates upon all persons, taken in Privateers, com-

[1] Despatches, France, vol. 29.   Received January 19.   [2] *Ibid.*   Received January 9.

missioned by the Mexican government.   I refer to this paper, from memory, not having time to advert to it, and I am under the impression, it required, that at least two thirds of the crew of each Mexican Privateer should be Mexican citizens, to give to it the character of a lawful cruizer.   At any rate, such is said to have been the declaration of the French Commanding Officer in the River La Plata, and the failure to comply with it the motive for sending this prize to France, for trial, as a pirate.

Her Captain had appealed for himself and for the English part of his crew to the British government, and the British Ambassador had received instructions to remonstrate against the trial of these men as pirates, and to demand that they should be considered as Prisoners of war.

I explained to Marshal Soult my position with respect to the American part of the crew, that I had received no application from them, nor any direction from the government to interfere in their favor, but I thought it proper to speak to him informally upon the subject, and to express the persuasion, that they would be considered as Prisoners of war, and not as pirates.   He told me he had examined the matter, and it was his conviction that they could not be viewed as pirates; and that he had communicated that opinion to the Minister of Marine, to whose Department the subject belonged.   He had recommended, that they should be considered as prisoners of war.   So, the matter will terminate by a practical abandonment of this innovation upon the law of nations.

Certainly this mode of carrying on war, by preying upon unarmed commerce is not entitled to much favor at this day, nor have our citizens who expatriate themselves to engage in such expeditions a right to expect the aid of their government in their difficulties.   Still, they ought not to be put out of the protection of the law of nations, by the mere will of one of the parties engaged in the contest.

I have the honor [etc.].

2534

Lewis Cass, United States Minister to France, to Marshal Soult, Duke of Dalmatia, Minister of Foreign Affairs of France [1]

Paris, *December 9, 1839.*

M. le Maréchal: I have the honor to enclose the substance of a statement made by Robert Upton,[2] a citizen and merchant of the United States, to the American government representing the capture of the Brig "*Elisa Davidson*" by the French vessel of war "*La Perle*" on the coast of Patagonia in March last, and I have been instructed to present this case to Your Ex-

[1] Despatches, France, vol. 29; enclosed with Cass to the Secretary of State, No. 90, January 12, 1840, below, this part, doc. 2536.

[2] Neither this nor the correspondence mentioned in the succeeding paragraphs was found.

cellency and to express the conviction of the government of the United States, that the government of His Majesty will not hesitate to grant a full indemnification to Mᵣ Upton for the loss consequent upon the illegal capture of his vessel.

The circumstances of the capture are fully stated in the correspondence, which took place between Commodore Nicolson, commanding the American Squadron upon that Station, and Admiral LeBlanc, commanding that of France. The letters from Admiral LeBlanc to Commodore Nicolson bear date the 20th, 21st, 23rd, 23rd Meridian, and 24th March 1839, and those from Commodore Nicolson to Admiral LeBlanc are dated, 21st, 22nd, and 23rd March 1839. In his letter of March 23rd the Admiral states, that he shall transmit to his government an exact account of all that had occurred in relation to this matter, together with the copy of the correspondence of Commodore Nicolson upon the subject. Presuming M. le Maréchal, that these papers have reached you, and that the letters of Commodore Nicolson have been translated into French, I shall not trouble you by annexing the English copies to this letter. But I beg leave to refer you to them, as well for all the circumstances of the capture, as for the clearest evidence of the justice of the demand for indemnification. Should however, any circumstances have prevented these papers from reaching you, I will cause copies of them to be immediately transmitted on receiving an intimation that they are deemed necessary.

It results from this correspondence that the place of capture was not within the limits of the blockade, as established by the French Admiral, and that if it had been, the force employed in that quarter was altogether insufficient to give it effect. And the French Admiral, satisfied, I presume, that the capture was illegal, at the termination of the correspondence with Commodore Nicolson, directed the restoration of the vessel.

I enclose copies of the statements, rendered by the owner of this vessel and by his agents at Montevideo and Buenos Ayres, estimating the injury, which resulted from her seizure.

I am also instructed, M. le Maréchal, to protest against this lawless exercise of power by the French naval officers, and to ask from the government of his Majesty a disavowal of any intention to harass the commerce of the United States. A disavowal, which the peculiar circumstances of this case render necessary, and which I feel persuaded the French government will not hesitate to make, as the part, which France has so long and so efficiently taken in the support of the most liberal principles of maritime law is a pledge, that whatever unlawful injuries may be inflicted by her armed force, upon the commerce of neutral nations, in operations arising out of a state of war, this result is due to the officers charged with their conduct and not to the instructions of the government.

I avail myself of this occasion [etc.].

2535

Marshal Soult, Minister of Foreign Affairs of France, to Lewis Cass, United States Minister to France [1]

[TRANSLATION]

PARIS, *December 30, 1839.*

SIR: I have received with its accompanying papers the letter [2] with which you honoured me respecting the seizure for a moment, of the American brig *Eliza Davidson* by [the?] French sloop of war *Pearl* one of the vessels employed in the Blockade of Buenos Ayres—for which seizure the owner of the *Eliza Davidson* considers himself justified in demanding indemnification to the amount of twenty five thousand dollars.

I transmitted your communication to the Minister of Marine, with a request that he would afford me some explanations as to the facts to which it relates, and I shall answer you without delay so soon as I have received those explanations.

As to the demand made by you, Sir, that the King's Government should disavow all intention to impede the commerce of the United States, I am at the same time surprised and grieved, that the good faith (*loyauté*) of which it has given so many incontestible proofs should not have caused a conviction that such a demand was at the least superfluous.   France in establishing and maintaining as she has, the right, the blockade to which she has been forced by her interests and dignity to resort with regard to the Argentine Republic, has demonstrated sufficiently her desire to reconcile as far as possible the exercise of such right with due regard for the navigation of neutral Powers; while at the same time it is no less manifest that if this blockade should be prolonged farther than might have been expected the responsibility ought not to rest upon her.   France would certainly not wish at the present day to disavow principles of maritime right which she has maintained at the cost of so much blood and at so many sacrifices; and the officers of the Royal Navy are too well assured of this not to make it the constant rule of their conduct.   So that if in certain cases, appearances give grounds for accusation against those officers, you will admit Sir that before condemning them, the King's Government, would be imperatively obliged as a duty to examine with care the circumstances of the facts with which they are charged and the real bearing of the accusation.   It was under these views that I have thought proper to communicate to the Minister of Marine the complaint which Your Government has charged you to advance, and I have the honour [etc.].

[1] Despatches, France, vol. 29; enclosed with Cass to the Secretary of State, No. 90, January 12, 1840, below, this part, doc. 2536.
[2] Above, this part, December 9, 1839, doc. 2534.   No copies of the accompanying papers were found.

2536

Lewis Cass, United States Minister to France, to John Forsyth, Secretary of State of the United States [1]

No. 90   PARIS, *January 12, 1840.*

SIR: I have the honor to transmit the copy of a letter, which I addressed to the Minister of Foreign Affairs,[2] in conformity with your instructions of the 31st October last,[3] and also of the answer I have received.[4]

The latter as you observe does not contain any answer to my demand of indemnification for the capture of the *Elisa Davidson* but announces, that the proper measures have been taken to procure the necessary information, previously to the decision of the government. From the delay, which similar subjects experience here, I anticipate it will be some time, before any definite action is obtained. In the mean time, however, it is proper to remark, that the case will not turn alone upon the point, which seems exclusively to have occupied the attention of the claimants, as well as of Comodore Nicolson, and to which the papers are directed, that of the original extent of the blockade of the *River Coasts* of the Argentine republic, as established by the French Admiral in his notification of 28th March 1838, because by a subsequent act of the French government of 16th June 1838,[5] and which was transmitted to the Department of State from this Legation the 3rd July 1838 [6] the blockade was extended to all the coasts of the Argentine republic, and embraced therefore in its terms the place, where this ship was captured. Still there can be no doubt, but that the capture was entirely illegal, as there was actually no force, South of the mouth of the River La Plata, and it appears that the French Admiral was so conscious of this defect, that the cruizer was instructed upon this occasion, merely to warn off the vessels found upon the coast, and eventually the captured vessel was released. As you will perceive, I have assumed, that the capture was illegal, without stating the grounds, not choosing to provoke an unnecessary discussion, until I ascertain, whether reparation will be delayed, and if so, for what reason.

To the demand of disavowal, which I made conformably to your instructions, the answer, as you no doubt foresaw, expresses surprise that such an application should be made. But at the same time, while protesting against such a demand, there is in fact a distinct disavowal of any intention on the part of the French government to inflict unnecessary injury upon our Commerce. I have merely acknowledged the receipt of the letter, and stated, that I should transmit it for your consideration. My own impression

[1] Despatches, France, vol. 29.   Received March 20.
[2] Above, this part, December 9, 1839, doc. 2534.
[3] Above, this volume, pt. v, doc. 2470.
[4] Above, this part, December 30, 1839, doc. 2535.
[5] Above, this part, doc. 2520.   [6] *Ibid.*, doc. 2521.

however is, that the answer, so far as respects a disclaimer, is as satisfactory, as we could expect.

I am, Sir, very Respectfully [etc.]

2537

Marshal Soult, Minister of Foreign Affairs of France, to Lewis Cass, United States Minister to France [1]

[TRANSLATION]

PARIS, *January 22, 1840.*

GENERAL: I had the honour to announce to you on the 30th of December last [2] in reply to your communication [3] relative to the American brig *Eliza Davidson* that I had asked information from the Department of Marine as to the reasons and the circumstances of the temporary seizure of that vessel by the Corvette *La Perle* employed in the blockade of the Argentine Republic.

The Minister of Marine not having received from the Commander of the French Squadron in the Plata any report upon that affair, regrets that he cannot at this moment furnish you with the proper information, in order to enable you to see the matter in its true light. But when Counter Admiral [*Fr. Contre-Amiral; Rear Admiral*] Le Blanc returns to France, as he soon will, he will hasten to ask information of that officer. You will see Sir by this explanation that the delay in examining the complaint which forms the subject of your letter of December 9th is not to be attributed to the French Government.

I have the honour [etc.].

2538

Lewis Cass, United States Minister to France, to Marshal Soult, Minister of Foreign Affairs of France [4]

PARIS, *January 25, 1840.*

MONSIEUR LE MARÉCHAL: I have had the honor to receive your letter of the 22nd inst, [5] and while I thank you for the application you had made to the Minister of Marine for the necessary information in relation to the capture and detention of the American Brig "*Elisa Davidson*" by the Corvette "*La Perle*," and for the assurance that the delay in the investigation of this

[1] Despatches, France, vol. 29; enclosed with Cass to the Secretary of State, No. 91, February 6, 1840, below, this part, doc. 2540.
[2] Above, this part, doc. 2535.   [3] *Ibid.*, December 9, 1839, doc. 2534.
[4] Despatches, France, vol. 29; enclosed with Cass to the Secretary of State, No. 91, February 6, 1840, below, this part, doc. 2540.   [5] Above, this part, doc. 2537.

matter does not proceed from the government of the King, permit me to remark, M. le Maréchal, that if Admiral Leblanc is expected in France before orders to report upon this subject would probably reach him in the La Plata, then the proposition to await his arrival is one, to which I could make no objections.   But if the period of his absence is doubtful, I beg leave to suggest the expediency of asking the Minister of Marine to call upon him for a report of all the circumstances of this case which may be necessary to enable the government of his Majesty to do justice to the demand I have been instructed to make.   Such a report would cause little trouble to the Admiral, and indeed it is probable some accident has prevented its arrival before this time, because he stated in a letter dated Montevideo March 23ʳᵈ 1839, to the American Commodore Nicolson, that he should render to his government a strictly exact account of what had passed and also transmit the correspondence to allow a full explanation with the Government of the United States.

Under the most favorable circumstances, M. le Maréchal, the application of my countryman, the owner of the brig captured, for indemnity in consequence of his losses will necessarily by exposed to much delay.   And in this consideration, I trust, you will find my excuse for desiring that the decision of this affair may not await the return of the Admiral, if the report would probably precede his return.

I avail myself [etc.].

2539

Marshal Soult, Minister of Foreign Affairs of France, to Lewis Cass, United States Minister to France [1]

[TRANSLATION]

PARIS, *January 29, 1840.*

GENERAL: I received the letter which you did me the honour to write to me on the 25ᵗʰ of this month in answer to mine of the 22ⁿᵈ[2] and in which, supposing the period of the return of Counter Admiral Le Blanc to be doubtful, you express the idea that it would be proper to write to him, and ask of him a report of the circumstances of the affair of the seizure of the American Ship *Eliza Davidson*.   This would be really the most natural course, if the absence of M. Leblanc were to be prolonged much further, without a certainty of its termination.   But that General Officer having been replaced in the command of the French Naval forces in the Plata by Countre Admiral Dupotet who quitted France in the latter part of October past; there is every reason to believe that he is now on his way, returning to Brest, and

---

[1] Despatches, France, vol. 29; enclosed with Cass to the Secretary of State, No. 91, February 6, 1840, below, this part, doc. 2540.

[2] For these two notes, see above, this part, docs. 2537 and 2538.

that he will arrive there immediately.   The letter which might be addressed
to him to ask information, would certainly not find him before Buenos Ayres
or Montevideo; and the information which he can give will be soon obtained
on his return.   Therefore I think that it is better to wait for the arrival
(which will doubtless be soon) of Counter Admiral Le Blanc

I embrace the opportunity [etc.].

2540

*Lewis Cass, United States Minister to France, to John Forsyth, Secretary of
State of the United States* [1]

No. 91   PARIS, *February 6, 1840.*

I have the honor to enclose a copy of the letter from the Minister of Foreign Affairs of the 22nd January last in answer to my letter to him of the 9th
December 1839 [2] respecting the "*Eliza Davidson*" a copy of which was transmitted to the Department by my despatch of 12th Jan[y] 1840, No. 90.[3]

As the letter from the Foreign Office left the question of adjustment entirely indeterminate, I thought it necessary to ask for a reconsideration of the
matter, and accordingly wrote the letter of the 25th January last,[4] a copy of
which is enclosed.   I send also a copy of the answer,[5] which is entirely satisfactory.

I am, Sir, very respectfully [etc.].

2541

*José Ellauri, Uruguayan Minister to France, to Lewis Cass, United States
Minister to France* [6]

PARIS, *December 14, 1841.*

Mr. MINISTER: I have just received the Powers and instructions from the
Government of the Republic of Uruguay to conclude a Treaty of Friendship,
Commerce and Navigation with the Government of the United States of
North America, and as it is impossible at this time for me to leave this
Capital, where most important negotiations detain me, I hasten to inform
you of this fact, Mr. Minister, that you may notify your Government thereof;
and, if my proposals are accepted, the Government of the United States
could grant the Powers to the person who might deserve its confidence in

[1] Despatches, France, vol. 29.   Received March 22.
[2] For these two notes, see above, this part, docs. 2534 and 2537.
[3] Above, this part, doc. 2536.   [4] *Ibid.*, doc. 2538.   [5] *Ibid.*, January 29, 1840, doc. 2539.
[6] Despatches, France, vol. 29; enclosed with Cass to the Secretary of State, No. 138,
December 17, 1841, below, this part, doc. 2542.

order that he might make arrangements with me on this subject and immediately enter on the necessary conferences.

Please accept [etc.].

2542

Lewis Cass, United States Minister to France, to Daniel Webster, Secretary of State of the United States [1]

No. 138   PARIS, *December 17, 1841.*

SIR: I have the honor to transmit the copy of a letter just received from the Minister of the Republic of Uruguay at this Court,[2] and to add that should the President be pleased to entrust to me the negociation of a Treaty of Commerce with the Minister of that power, I should execute the duty punctually under such instructions as you might give. I am the more free to express this sentiment, as I should neither expect nor receive any compensation for the service.

I am, Sir, very respectfully [etc.].

2543

Lewis Cass, United States Minister to France, to François Guizot, Minister of Foreign Affairs of France [3]

PARIS, *May 17, 1842.*

SIR: I have been instructed by my Government[4] to bring to the attention of the Government of His Majesty, the case of the American schooner the *Josephine*, captured on the 20th May 1840 by the French vessel of war *l'Eclair* off the Coast of Buenos Ayres, for an alleged violation of the blockade of a part of the Coast of that Republic established by authority of the French Government, and to ask, that full compensation may be made to the owner, for the injury he has sustained.

It is certain that this blockade did not extend to that part of the Coast, off which the *Josephine* was captured, nor was she at the time attempting to violate the blockade as the same was made known to neutral Nations. Of these two facts their exists no doubt. And under these circumstances, no belligerent rights were contravened, nor could there be any legitimate seizure of a neutral vessel.

[1] Despatches, France, vol. 29. Received January 26.
[2] Above, this part, December 14, 1841, doc. 2541.
[3] Despatches, France, vol. 30; enclosed with Ledyard to the Secretary of State, No. 14, August 5, 1843, below, this part, doc. 2548.
[4] This instruction, dated April 6, 1842, is not included in this publication. Its purport is adequately given in this note.

It was expressly declared by the French Consul at Montevideo, 14ᵗʰ November 1839, by the authority of the French Admiral, to the Foreign Agents at Montevideo, that the blockade of the Argentine Coast did not extend to the ports outside of and to the South of Cape St Antonio. That the place of capture was beyond this cape is shown by the very chart annexed to the proceedings of the Prize Court at Montevideo, on which the point is indicated where the *Josephine* was taken.

That this Schooner was not attempting to violate the blockade as established is proved by the procès-verbal of the capturing vessel. It is there expressly said, that she followed the *Josephine* from the very harbour of Montevideo, because she *Seemed suspicious to her*. The French vessel was stationed before a neutral port to watch neutral vessels at anchor there, and to follow them because they might possibly attempt to violate the blockade. The only ground of suspicion stated in the procès-verbal is that the *Josephine* steered towards the passage, into which "*she hoped to* enter, should the wind, the fog, and the state of the sea permit." Such vague suppositions do not justify the exercise of this extreme right of capturing the vessels of a neutral and friendly power.

I must beg your attention, Sir, to the remarks of Mʳ Binard, Avocat aux Conseils du Roi, herewith enclosed,[1] which place in a clear light the illegality of the proceedings with respect to the capture and condemnation of the American vessel.

In the protest of the American Captain it is stated, that the provisions and stores of the *Josephine* were consumed by the capturing crew. I bring this circumstance before you, not from its importance, but because I am certain that such irregularities if committed are unknown to the French Officers, and totally contrary to the instructions of the Government. It is well to point out the assertion that the truth of it may be ascertained. If found to be true, I am well aware the Government of His Majesty will take care to express their disapprobation at such conduct.

All the documents in relation to this case are understood to be within Your Excellency's reach, and to them I beg to refer you for a full understanding of the whole matter.

I avail [etc.].

[1] Not found.

2544

François Guizot, Minister of Foreign Affairs of France, to Lewis Cass, United States Minister to France [1]

[TRANSLATION]

PARIS, *June 8, 1842.*

MY DEAR GENERAL: I have received, along with its enclosures, the letter which you did me the honor of writing me [2] to protest against the capture of the American vessel Josephine, seized by a vessel of the Royal Navy of France during the blockade of the ports of the Argentine Republic and declared to be a lawful prize by the Prize Commission of Montevideo.

I transmitted the protest and the documents accompanying it to the Minister of Marine, with the request that he furnish me the information with which to reply to your communication. The Council of State is, moreover, charged with the investigation of the affair of the Josephine, and we can only await its decision, which I intend to expedite so far as it lies in my power.

Please accept [etc.].

2545

Henry Ledyard, United States Chargé d'Affaires ad interim at Paris, to François Guizot, Minister of Foreign Affairs of France [3]

PARIS, *February 15, 1843.*

SIR: On the 17th May last General Cass had the honor, in compliance with the instructions of his Government,[4] to address a letter to Your Excellency calling the attention of the Government of His Majesty to the case of the American Schooner *Josephine* captured on the 20th May 1840 by the French vessel of war *L'Eclair* off the coast of Buenos Ayres for an alleged violation of the blockade of a part of the coast of that Republic, and asking that full compensation may be made to the owner for the injury he has sustained.

On the 8th June last a reply was received from Your Excellency [5] stating that you had transmitted this claim to the Minister of Marine requesting certain information from his Department, and that this case being before the Council of State you proposed to hasten its decision as much as possible.

Not having had the honor to hear from Your Excellency since that time I

---

[1] Despatches, France, vol. 30; enclosed with Ledyard to the Secretary of State, No. 14, August 5, 1843, below, this part, doc. 2548.
[2] Above, this part, May 17, 1842, doc. 2543.
[3] Despatches, France, vol. 30; enclosed with Ledyard to the Secretary of State, No. 14, August 5, 1843, below, this part, doc. 2548.
[4] Above, this part, doc. 2543, is the note from Cass. The instruction to him of April 6, 1842 is not included in this publication, but its purport is given within this note.
[5] *Ibid.*, doc. 2544.

beg leave to recall the matter to your attention in the confident expectation
that a decision may be speedily given in favor of this claim of my countryman.

I avail [etc.].

2546

*Henry Ledyard, United States Chargé d'Affaires ad interim at Paris, to
François Guizot, Minister of Foreign Affairs of France* [1]

PARIS, *April 17, 1843.*

SIR: I had the honour on the 15th February last [2] to call Your Excellency's
attention to the case of the American Schooner *Josephine* captured in May
1840 by the French vessel of war *L'Eclair* off the coast of Buenos Ayres for an
alleged violation of a part of the Coast of that Republic, and at the same
time I expressed a hope that a speedy decision would be given in favor of the
claim of the owner.

Not having had the honour to hear from Your Excellency I beg leave to
renew my request for its consideration and earnestly to ask that it may receive an early settlement.

I avail [etc.].

On the 23rd May another letter was addressed to Mr Guizot,[3] pressing a
settlement of the claim of the owner of the *Josephine.*

2547

*François Guizot, Minister of Foreign Affairs of France, to Henry Ledyard,
United States Chargé d'Affaires ad interim at Paris* [4]

[TRANSLATION]

PARIS, *July 28, 1843.*

SIR: You have several times called my attention to the case pending before the Council of State with regard to the capture of the American schooner
Josephine by one of the King's vessels employed in the blockade of the Rio
de la Plata in 1839.[5]

I take pleasure in advising you that the Council of State, by an order of the
17th instant has invalidated the capture of the Josephine and has ordered
that the proceeds of the sale of that vessel and of her cargo be delivered, with

---

[1] Despatches, France, vol. 30; enclosed with Ledyard to the Secretary of State, No. 14,
August 5, 1843, below, this part, doc. 2548.   [2] Above, this part, doc. 2545.   [3] Not found.
[4] Despatches, France, vol. 30; enclosed with Ledyard to the Secretary of State, No. 14,
August 5, 1843, below, this part, doc. 2548.
[5] See above, this part, February 15 and April 17, 1843, and see, also, a note from Cass to
Guizot, dated May 17, 1842, docs. 2545, 2546, and 2543.

the ship's papers, to the owners or their representatives.   You will find a copy of the order enclosed.[1]

I avail myself [etc.].

2548

Henry Ledyard, United States Chargé d'Affaires ad interim at Paris, to Abel
P. Upshur, Secretary of State of the United States [2]

No. 14   PARIS, *August 5, 1843.*

SIR: On the 6th April 1842 (N⁰ 63), General Cass was instructed by the Secretary of State[3] to bring before the French Government the case of the American Schooner "Josephine" captured, in May 1840, off the coast of Buenos Ayres, by the French vessel of war "L'Eclair," for an alleged violation of the blockade of part of the coast of that Republic established by the French Government.

I have now the honour to transmit copies of the correspondence between this Legation and the Minister of Foreign Affairs upon this subject.[4]   By M[r] Guizot's letter to me dated 28th July last you will see that the capture of the "Josephine" has been invalidated by the Council of State and that the proceeds of vessel and cargo have been ordered to be paid to the owners or to their representatives.

I am, Sir, very respectfully [etc.].

2549

Henry Ledyard, United States Chargé d'Affaires ad interim at Paris, to John
Nelson, Acting Secretary of State of the United States [5]

No 28   PARIS, *April 6, 1844.*

SIR: I have the honor to enclose a copy of the answer of the Minister of Foreign Affairs to the several applications from this Legation for an indemnity to the owners of the American brigs *Elisa Davidson,* and *America* for the loss and injury sustained by the detention of these vessels by the French blockading force off the coast of Buenos-Ayres in March 1839.[6]

[1] Not included in this publication.
[2] Despatches, France, vol. 30.   Received September 25.
   Henry Ledyard, of Michigan, the writer of this despatch, was commissioned secretary of legation, August 7, 1839.   He acted as chargé d'affaires *ad interim*, from November 12, 1842, to June 10, 1844.   He left September 17, 1844.
[3] Not included in this publication.   Its purport is adequately given within this despatch.
[4] See above, this part, under the dates May 17 and June 8, 1842; February 15, April 17, and July 28, 1843, docs. 2543, 2544, 2545, 2546, and 2547.
[5] Despatches, France, vol. 30.   Received June 11.
[6] Not included in this publication.   Its contents are adequately reviewed within this despatch.

You will perceive that M⁫ Guizot denies that the French Government is in any manner responsible for their detention, which, he asserts, was owing to the refusal of their captains to show their ships-papers to the French officer charged to ascertain their nationality. Commodore Nicolson [Nicholson?] admits in his letter to Admiral Leblanc dated 23ʳᵈ March 1839. that the captains did refuse to furnish this evidence and that they were wrong in so doing. M⁫ Guizot justifies the detention on this ground and expresses a hope that the Government of the United States will be convinced that the French authorities did all that could be properly required of them in the first instance by the restoration of these vessels to their owners as soon as their character was ascertained. He does not enter upon a consideration of the points raised by Commodore Nicolson in his correspondence with Admiral Leblanc touching the validity of the blockade and which were afterwards assumed by General Cass in his letter to Marshal Soult, then Minister of Foreign Affairs, a copy of which was sent to the Department with his despatch (Nᵒ 90.) dated 12, January 1840.[1]

I am, Sir, very respectfully [etc.].

2550

Henry Ledyard, United States Chargé d'Affaires ad interim at Paris, to John C. Calhoun, Secretary of State of the United States[2]

No. 29   PARIS, *April 30, 1844.*

SIR: I had the honour, on the 5ᵗʰ August last,[3] to transmit to the Department the decision of the Council of State in the case of the American Schooner "Josephine" which vessel had been captured by part of the French blockading force on the coast of Buenos Ayres in May 1840, for an alleged violation of the blockade of the coast of that Republic established by orders of the French Government.

As this decision, while declaring the capture illegal, awarded the proceeds only of the sale of vessel and cargo, which were sold at a great sacrifice, to the claimants, I thought it my duty to endeavor to obtain a more ample indemity for the loss they had sustained by the seizure of their property by the Officers of the French Government. As soon, therefore, as the summer vacation was over and the Minister of Foreign Affairs had returned to town, I addressed him a letter dated 23ʳᵈ September,[4] asking that the principle of

---

[1] See above, this part, doc. 2536; and, also, in the same part, the enclosure dated December 9, 1839, doc. 2534.   [2] Despatches, France, vol. 30.   Received June 11.

[3] See above, this part, doc. 2548, and for its enclosure referred to below, see above, this part, July 28, 1843, doc. 2547.

[4] Neither this nor any of the subsequent correspondence with the French Foreign Minister mentioned in this despatch, is included in this publication, since their substance is adequately reviewed herein.

the decision of the Council of State should be carried out and that the claimants should be placed in the position they were in at the time of the capture of their vessel. To this after renewed applications I received a reply dated 20. Dec. in which M.ͬ Guizot stated it was evident from the terms of the decision that it was the conviction of the Council of State that the captain of the American Schooner intended to violate the blockade and it was owing simply to a neglect of a superogatory form by the captors that the proceeds of the sale of vessel and cargo had been adjudged to the claimants. He adds that in his opinion substantial justice had been awarded. I replied by my letter of the 5ᵗʰ January, in which I denied that any such inference was warranted by the terms of the decision, and renewed my demand for a full indemnity. On the 4ᵗʰ March M.ͬ Guizot answered that the Council of State having given their decision, it had become a matter adjudged, (*chose jugée*), and that my application could not be complied with.

I determined, however, to make one more application and accordingly wrote to M.ͬ Guizot on the 24ᵗʰ March declaring that it was upon the decision of the Council of State that the capture was illegal that I founded my demand for compensation; I added that the United States could not admit that a neutral should be made to suffer by the neglect of proper forms on the part of a belligerent nor that these forms were superogatory as they were termed in his former letter. I concluded by requesting that the case should be taken up and reconsidered. This appeal has proved as unsuccessful as the former ones as you will perceive by his letter of 2ⁿᵈ April, in which he refers me to his communication of 4ᵗʰ March as containing his final answer.

The award of the Council of State appears to me exceedingly unjust and as it has now been twice formally sanctioned by the Government, I have the honor to submit a copy of the correspondence which has passed between the Minister of Foreign Affairs and myself for your consideration and instructions as to what steps are now to be taken in the matter.

I am, Sir, very respectfully [etc.].

2551

William R. King, United States Minister to France, to John C. Calhoun, Secretary of State of the United States [1]

[EXTRACT]

No. 1   PARIS, *July 13, 1844.*

SIR: I have the honor to inform you that I arrived in Havre on the 7ᵗʰ, and at this place, on the 10ᵗʰ of last month. As soon as the necessary arrangements could be completed I sought an audience of the King in order to pre-

[1] Despatches, France, vol. 30. Received August 3.

sent my letter of Credence.   The 1ˢᵗ of July was appointed for this purpose, and accordingly, on that day, I repaired to Neuilly where the Court resides at this moment.   In presenting the letter of the President to His Majesty, the King of the French, I made the brief Address, a copy of which (A.)[1] is subjoined.   Nothing could be more cordial than the reply and reception of the King.   He reciprocated very warmly my assurances of national and personal good-will, and acknowledged with marked sensibility the just tribute which I paid to the virtues of his family.   Referring to my allusion to the assistance rendered to the United States at the period of their revolutionary struggle, he observed that the recollection of it, afforded him great satisfaction, and added, in emphatic words and manner, that he ever considered America the natural ally of France.   Much more to this purport and in this strain, the King delivered in very good English, expressed in warm and well chosen terms.   I was afterwards presented to the Queen and to the Duke de Némours, by whom I was received with equal kindness and consideration.   The next day, I received an invitation for myself and Secretary of Legation to dine with his Majesty on the fourth of July, a compliment which derived its chief value from the selection of the day.   On that occasion, after dinner, the King, in a familiar conversation, broached the subject of Texas, and asked why the Treaty had been rejected by the Senate, the news of which had just been received.   I seized this opportunity to assure him that the rejection was caused by political considerations of a domestic nature; that the object would, in my opinion, be prosecuted with unabated vigor; that it was my firm belief that a decided majority of the American people were in favor of the measure, which would certainly be consummated at no distant period.   Thereupon the King frankly observed that it was his desire to see Texas remain an independent state, and spoke of commercial advantages secured to France by treaty with that Republic.   I replied that the interests of France, which were purely commercial, were totally distinct from those of England, and that they would be promoted by the annexation of Texas to the United States.   His Majesty admitted that the colonial possessions of Great Britain in North America involved that power in political considerations which did not affect France, with reference to this question, and he finally assured me, or gave me, at least, distinctly to understand, that in any event, no steps would be taken by his government, in the slightest degree hostile, or which would give to the United States, just cause of complaint.   This declaration I consider of no small importance, for although a constitutional monarch, the King of the French is no cypher, but substantially his own prime minister, and a minister moreover, who does not hold his place by the uncertain tenure of a fluctuating majority in the Chamber of Deputies.

In the course of the conversation, his Majesty informed me that his

[1] Not included in this publication.

emphatic advice to the Mexican government, had been, as the best policy for that state and for others, to acknowledge at once the independence of Texas. Among other topics, the King took occasion to observe that some anxiety had been felt by the French government with regard to supposed designs of the United States upon the Sandwich islands. I promptly reassured him upon this subject, with the declaration that the interests of the United States in the Pacific being purely commercial, nothing more was desired by them than to prevent any European power from acquiring a preponderance in that quarter, which might prove detrimental to American navigation, so extensive and so valuable in the South Seas.

A few days after, I requested of M. Guizot, Minister of Foreign Affairs, an interview for the purpose of holding a free conversation upon topics interesting to the two countries   He expressed a corresponding desire, but upon the plea of numerous engagements, requested a postponement of the conference, until next week, to which as I had no specific proposition to communicate, I was constrained to defer.   Indeed, the conversation which I have had in a higher or rather the highest quarter, makes me less solicitous about the delay, though I shall omit no proper steps to obtain an early interview, and an explicit understanding, the result of which I shall not fail to transmit by the first opportunity.

The general impression in the best informed circles here, is that England, at this moment, exerts a marked influence upon the councils of the French government, and particularly upon the mind of M. Guizot, who is the ruling spirit, of the Cabinet, as well as the ablest expounder and defender of its principles and policy in the tribune.

Still the policy of the King is essentially pacific and conservative, and, I am persuaded, that however much he or his ministers may desire to maintain a cordial understanding with the cabinet of St James, that disposition, as the King assured me, will not proceed to the extent of acts hostile or unfriendly to the United States, in reference to the Texas question,   Indeed, domestic embarrassments, and European questions, among which those of Algiers and Morocco preponderate at present, necessarily indispose the governments both of England and France, from involving themselves in active difficulties in remote quarters, whatever may be the feeling with which they, and particularly the former, contemplate any measure calculated to augment the territory and power of the United States.   About the time of my arrival, much was said about a joint protest of France and England against the annexation of Texas to the United States, and indeed Mr Smith the Chargé d'Affaires of the former Republic, informed me that he had reason to believe that such a step had been taken.   I have not been able to satisfy myself that such a document exists, and, indeed, what I have gathered, leads me to the opposite conclusion.   If it does, and I shall not hesitate to ask M. Guizot the question, however much it may be regretted, as proof of the malign influence exerted by Great Britain upon the councils of the French government, in a matter which concerns the latter so remotely, it should be regarded as of little weight after the assurances of the King to which I have referred, and the other considerations upon which I have touched.[1] . . .

I have the honor [etc.].

2552

William R. King, United States Minister to France, to John C. Calhoun, Secretary of State of the United States [2]

[EXTRACT]

No. 2　　　　　　　　　　　　　　　　　　　　　　PARIS, *July 31, 1844.*

SIR: In my first despatch,[3] I had the honor to state, that I had requested and obtained the promise of an interview with Mʳ Guizot, the Minister of Foreign Affairs, for the purpose of conferring with him upon topics interesting to my government. A week or ten days having elapsed without hearing further from him, and being somewhat anxious to have an explicit understanding with him upon topics of no small importance, I reiterated my request in writing, whereupon the twentieth of July, was appointed for the desired interview.

I commenced the conversation with Mʳ Guizot, by observing that I wished to confer with him upon a subject in which the government and people of the United States felt a deep interest—the annexation of Texas. I remarked that on my arrival here, I was met by rumors that the government of France had united with that of England in a formal protest against the proposed annexation; that, convinced that such a step did not comport either with the interests or policy of France, I had attached little or no importance to rumors so improbable, which I had even dismissed from my mind after the assurances, received in my conversation with the King, which I had the honor to communicate in my last and first despatch; that nevertheless subsequent information of a character and from a source, which I did not feel myself authorized, altogether to disregard, had reached me, which had induced me, reposing entire confidence in the well-known frankness of His Majesty's government, to put an end to conjecture, by seeking information from a source upon which I could altogether rely.—With considerable animation if not some impatience, Mʳ Guizot, at once assured me that no such step as that referred to, had been taken; that on this subject France had acted for herself and in connection with no other power; that the French government

[1] The omitted portion relates to a swindler who had taken refuge in Switzerland, and also relates to the favorable impression Mr. Ledyard, the writer's immediate predecessor, had made on the French authorities.
[2] Despatches, France, vol. 30. Received August 22.
[3] Above, this part, July 13, 1844, doc. 2551.

did, indeed, desire to see the independence of Texas maintained, but that I might be assured, its action, whatever that might be, would be entirely independent of that of England whose interests in relation to this question were different from those of France, which were purely commercial. I expressed my gratification at these assurances, remarking that a movement such as that which had been, I was happy to learn, erroneously imputed to the French government, would have seriously impaired the friendly, nay, I might also say affectionate feelings entertained for the French nation by the American people, a result which no one would have regretted more than myself. Mr Guizot then observed, with evident allusion to the rejection of the Treaty by the Senate—"but the subject of annexation is at an end." I told him, at once, that I owed it to frankness to say, that I by no means considered it so; that public opinion was all-powerful in the United States, and that whoever might be called to administer the government, must be controlled by it; that, according to my belief, a large majority of the American people were in favor of the proposed annexation, not from a desire to obtain more territory, but from a pervading conviction, that it was necessary to the security of the country. To his enquiry if this feeling was not confined to one of the great political parties, I replied—certainly not—though more general with that called the democratic. He then asked me if my government would be satisfied with a guarantee of the independence of Texas without conditions. To this query, I replied that I could give no assurances on this point, upon which I was not instructed, but that it was of such vital importance to us that no foreign power should obtain a preponderance in Texas, that we should view with great distrust any movement calculated to place that republic under foreign and particularly British influence; that, England, having once refused to unite with France and the United States to urge upon Mexico the acknowledgement of the independence of Texas, was a circumstance calculated to excite suspicion of her views and intentions. I added that Mexico was known to be very much under her control, and it was not to be disguised, that, whether impelled by that influence or not, the Mexican Republic was hostile to the United States, and, indeed, to France also; that so great had been the emigration to Texas from the British dominions, of late years, as to threaten, should it continue, to give, sooner or later, a predominating influence to England in that wide region, and I observed that he must see the necessity on our part of guarding against such control, for the security of the peculiar property of the South, to say nothing of the exposed situation of New Orleans, the great emporium and outlet of the West should a hostile power spring up in its immediate vicinity. Leaving the subject of Texas, Mr Guizot enquired whether the slave population of the United States increased rapidly. I replied, more rapidly in proportion than the white, a proof that the slaves were well-treated, well-fed, and not overworked. He then asked if they seemed contented with their situation. I replied that a more contented and cheerful population of laborers did not exist either in Europe or America, and to this conclusion, every intelligent, enquiring and unprejudiced traveller had come.   He made no comment upon this, whereupon I rose and took my leave with the remark that I would communicate to my government the substance of the conversation which I had had the honor to hold with him, and which could not fail to prove highly satisfactory.

I will take this occasion to express my confidence that the course of the American government upon the important question which was the principal subject of my conference with Mr Guizot, will not be influenced by rumors of dangers from abroad which do not exist, and which, if they were real, it would be our true policy to face with a calm but firm aspect.   However desirous France may be to see the independence of Texas preserved, her opposition, if assurances from the highest sources may be relied upon, will not assume an unfriendly attitude, nor will that of England proceed to the extremities which have been so fearfully paraded in certain quarters.   However earnest her resistance to the annexation of Texas to the United States, and I am by no means disposed to underrate it, I have no idea, that Great Britain will for this object, hazard the employment of any arms, besides those of diplomacy, a cheap instrument if it prove successful.   I have been much gratified to find a healthy state of feeling upon this subject among our countrymen abroad of all parties, whose patriotism seems to expand as they recede from the sphere of domestic conflicts of opinion.   They look upon this question as one involving considerations of national dignity and power, and they feel that it would be folly as well as weakness to be deterred from the right course by the frowns, the menaces, or even the hostile acts of any foreign power.   This much I thought it my duty to say.[1] . . .

I have the honor [etc.].

2553

William R. King, United States Minister to France, to John C. Calhoun, Secretary of State of the United States [2]

[EXTRACT]

No. 4   PARIS, *October 6, 1844.*

SIR: I have the honor to acknowledge the receipt of your despatches Nos. 4, 5 and 6.[3]   It affords me great satisfaction to learn that the President approves of my course in the interviews which I had with the King and M^r

---

[1] The omitted portion relates to a fugitive from justice, and to the propriety of negotiating an extradition convention with Switzerland.

[2] Despatches, France, vol. 30.   Received October 29.

[3] For Nos. 4 and 6, dated August 12 and 26, 1844, respectively, see above, this volume, pt. v, docs. 2472 and 2473.   No. 5 relates to a consular appointment and is not included in this publication.

Guizot; and that the assurances which I received upon those occasions are deemed acceptable.— I am also happy to find the opinions which I expressed, corroborated by the views so amply and ably developed in your despatch of the 12ᵗʰ August, which I shall not fail to present and enforce upon all suitable occasions.

Since I last wrote,[1] I have nothing of particular interest to communicate. The Texas question has ceased to be a topic of interest or even of allusion here, though it is not improbable, now that the harmonious relations of France and England have been at least temporarily restored, the designs of Mexico against the young republic may once more direct the attention of the French cabinet to that remote quarter. Prudent, however, as is the King of the French, and ever solicitous to maintain peace and good will, both for his own sake, and that of France, whose strength and resources are rapidly developing with this temperate policy, I entertain very little apprehension, that he will connect himself actively, if at all, with the hostile manoeuvres of England in relation to the annexation of Texas to the United States, from a mistaken view of the true interests of this country in the question, and at the hazard of forfeiting the friendship and regard of the American government and people. I delayed writing with the hope that the steamers from New York and Boston would bring me something from Washington, but I was disappointed although despatches were received by Messʳˢ Wheaton and Irving, who are in Paris, at this time. The former gentleman was kind enough to show me the copy of your despatch of the 10ᵗʰ September to Mʳ Shannon,[2] on the subject of the threatened invasion of Texas by Mexico, a transcript of which, I make no doubt was also directed to me, as its early receipt at this legation, was of no slight urgency and importance. The failure or delay of this important communication makes a word opportune with regard to the transmission of my correspondence from the Department of State.[3] . . .

I am, Sir, [etc.].

[1] Not included in this publication, since it was a discussion of European political affairs and also related to an extradition convention between the United States and Switzerland.

[2] See below, vol. VIII, pt. I, doc. 3243.

[3] In the omitted portion he suggests that instructions to him be sent by steamer instead of by the ordinary packet, because of the delay in transmission by the latter method.

2554

William R. King, United States Minister to France, to John C. Calhoun, Secretary of State of the United States [1]

[EXTRACT]

No. 6   PARIS, *November 15, 1844.*

SIR: I have the honor to acknowledge the receipt, since my last communication, of your Despatches Nos. 9, 10, and 11.[2] The first which came last, having been received but a few days ago, has been already referred to in my despatch of the 6th of last month.[3] I shall not fail to expose and to press, the able considerations which it presents, on all suitable occasions and in all proper quarters. The Texas question seems to awaken little or no interest here at present, nor can I perceive that it has assumed any new aspects. Its fate is considered to be very much involved in the Presidential contest, the result of which may revive that solicitude which is now permitted to slumber. In my conversations here, I have ever sought to treat it as a national rather than a political or party question, dependent for its solution upon personal or temporary considerations. In taking this elevated and, as I flatter myself, patriotic view of the subject, events will soon prove whether I am right, or whether I have over estimated the sensibility of the great mass of the American people to considerations of national dignity and power.

Perhaps the recent difficulties between the French Minister and Mexico, have rendered this government more insensible to the supposed rights or wrongs of the Mexican Republic. Be this as it may, as long as the *action* of France is not hostile, or does not lend itself to the unfriendly designs of England towards the United States, we have no right to complain of her sentiments with regard to Texian independence, however much we may wish that they were more politic for herself, and more favorable to us. The avowed policy of the King of the French, is peace, and non-intervention as the best means of securing peace; therefore, even had I not his declarations and those of his minister, I would not easily apprehend that so wise and wary a monarch would permit himself to be entangled in the meshes of a knotty question, and one altogether profitless, with the certainty of alienating the American people, the "natural allies" of France, by such wanton interference. Upon his favorite topics of peace and non-intervention, His Majesty dwelt emphatically in a late interview, when he expressed sentiments and opinions which though not uttered with reference to the United States, Mexico and Texas, were strikingly applicable to the existing relations of the three republics.

[1] Despatches, France, vol. 30.   Received December 23.
[2] No. 9 is above, this volume, pt. v, September 12, 1844, doc. 2474.   The others are not included in this publication.   No. 10 requested the purchase of a book, and No. 11 transmitted letters of felicitation upon the occasion of two royal births.
[3] Above, this part, doc. 2553.

The Map of Texas from the Topographical Bureau, which accompanied the copy of Your Despatch to Mr Shannon is of opportune interest.[1] . . .
    I am [etc.].

2555

William R. King, United States Minister to France, to John C. Calhoun, Secretary of State of the United States [2]

[EXTRACT]

No. 9   PARIS, *December 31, 1844.*

SIR: I have the honor to acknowledge the receipt of your Despatch No. 12,[3] and shall, without delay, deliver to the authorized representative of the Spanish government, coupons corresponding to the amount of sixty thousand dollars.

The decisive result of the Presidential election, which was not anticipated in Europe, has given a new interest to American questions, and especially to that of Texas.

The election of the unsuccessful candidate was counted upon with certainty to extinguish annexation forever. Although I still believe that the French government will take no actively offensive steps in this matter, I cannot shut my eyes to the fact that its wishes at least, coincide with those of England, and that its influence may be lent, to a certain extent, to the support of British policy with reference to this question. The King is, for various reasons, anxious to conciliate England. That country was the first to acknowledge the government of July, which has never been viewed with a favorable eye by the great continental monarchies. The King of the French feels that the British government is his main stay, and that with the English alliance he is able to maintain the paramount object of his policy which he deems essential to the security of his dynasty, as well as to the prosperity of France—I mean the peace of Europe. I make every allowance for the difficulties of his position, amidst hostile or unsympathizing dynasties, and threatened at every moment by the revolutionary tendencies of Europe and of France in particular. Still these apprehensions may precipitate him into dangers of another character, and in wishing to secure a powerful friend in this hemisphere, he may alienate the "natural ally" of France in America. But though too anxious, perhaps, to conciliate England, I do not suspect the King of unfriendly dispositions towards the United States. I confess I have not quite the same confidence in his minister Mr Guizot. Though an able, and, I believe, a virtuous man, his systematic devotion to England, blinds

[1] The omitted portion is not pertinent to this publication.
[2] Despatches, France, vol. 30. Received January 27.
[3] Not included in this publication.

him to other interests of hardly less importance. He is a man of the cabinet rather than of the world, and carries into public affairs the rigid theories of the speculative politician. He pursues his objects with inflexible resolution, but without a sufficient regard for the opinions, the sentiments, the prejudices if you will, of the French people. So far from seeking to win popularity, even by honorable compliances, he is suspected of taking pride in the defiance of public opinion. He has rendered the English alliance almost odious in France, by an ostentatious, if not a defying, parade, of deference to English policy. In the discussions upon the Right of Search Treaties, he was forced indeed to succumb, but without the grace of good will. He unhesitatingly declared that the English alliance was more important, politically and morally, than any modification of the Treaties. Fortunately public opinion, even among the supporters of the Administration, is unchangeably hostile to these obnoxious Treaties.

It is thought that one of the objects of the late Royal visit to England, when the King was accompanied by his Minister, was to obtain the modifications of these Treaties and the abrogation of the last Convention, which must remain a dead letter for every purpose, but that of keeping alive national antipathies. The British government might have conceded the point, had it not been deterred by apprehension of offending the fanatics, who from their numbers and influence however diminished, must yet be treated with a certain consideration.

Upon the whole, I apprehend nothing from European influence upon American questions, if we have the firmness to despise and resist the brutum fulmen of mere diplomatic remonstrance. Public sentiment in France restrains the British tendencies of the Minister, and even renders his tenure of power, precarious by reason of these obvious dispositions. The cold reception of the Royal Speech at the opening of the Session of the Chamber of Deputies, was mainly caused by this feeling, and was a significant indication for the King and his Ministry. The éclat of the African victories was tarnished in French estimation by the eagerness to tranquillize British susceptibilities, as evinced by the conclusion of a treaty with the Emperor of Morocco without the exaction of substantial guarantees, and the evacuation of Mogadore even before the ratification of the Convention. As to France, then, the fears of her government, if not the wisdom of her Rulers, will deter her from multiplying the difficulties of her foreign relations which have proved to her already a source of so much embarrassment.

From England, there is not, in reality, more to apprehend. Her debt, her financial difficulties with a property tax in time of peace, her East India embarrassments, her Canadian troubles, the scarcely slumbering volcano of Ireland, are all salutary checks upon her hostile disposition. She will be but too happy, if she can thwart the policy of the United States by the cheap weapons of diplomatic remonstrance or newspaper menace. I trust, then, as

I have remarked in a former communication, that the course of our government will be determined by duty and patriotism alone, and that it will not
permit itself to be influenced, in the slightest degree, by the empty demonstrations which timid politicians dread, or artful ones affect to apprehend.

I confess I fear more from Texas herself, than from European hostility.
It is to be apprehended that two rejections of proffered annexation have
given some effect to foreign intrigue, if they have not somewhat cooled the
disposition of her people for union with the United States.   The hostility to
annexation of the new Administration in Texas, is hardly concealed, and it
may not be amiss to state that the late Chargé d'Affaires of that republic
here, who will probably be the new Secretary of State, frankly avowed to
myself as well as to others, his opposition to the measure.   Nothing will be
left undone by England, and perhaps by France, to foster this adverse feeling, and this, doubtless, is the direction which their hostility will take, it is to
be feared not without effect.   But it is superfluous to press considerations
which have, without doubt, suggested themselves to your mind, with sufficient clearness and force.[1] . . .

I am [etc.].

2556

William R. King, United States Minister to France, to John C. Calhoun,
Secretary of State of the United States [2]

[EXTRACTS]

No. 10   PARIS, *January 29, 1845.*

SIR: The publication of your instructions and despatches to me,[3] produced
quite a sensation here, as well as in England.   On the other side of the channel the effect was disappointment and anger.   The British papers not only
accused this government of neglecting the interests of France in the Texas
question; they did not hesitate to charge it with duplicity and treachery
towards England.

The public impression here was that of satisfaction, mingled with some
regret on the part of the opposition that the ministry had not been guilty
of the unwise and impolitic course of which it had been suspected and accused.   I have deemed it the part both of policy and dignity to presume that
the declarations of the government are entirely to be relied upon, unless
retracted or modified in an authentic quarter.   Of course I have not permitted myself to interrogate the ministry so long as it remained silent; but
I have narrowly watched the course of its acknowledged organs.   These have

[1] The omitted portion relates to a passport question.
[2] Despatches, France, vol. 30.   Received February 22.
[3] Presumably those of August 12, August 26, and September 12, 1844, above, this volume,
pt. v, docs. 2472, 2473, and 2474.

published your despatches without a word of contradiction or even of comment. The King and his minister have both had opportunities of conversing with me upon the subject; but as they did not take advantage of them, I maintained a proper and prudent reserve. Public opinion would have strongly condemned any action of this government, unfriendly to the United States in their difficulties or disagreements with Mexico and England, and, as I have just observed, the Opposition was very sorry to be deprived of so popular a ground of attack. Indeed, I have supposed, that in the present critical conjunction of affairs, the Ministry was happy to be relieved of an imputation, which, if just, would have rivetted the leading reproach against it, of excessive, if not humiliating deference to England. Whatever then, may be the personal dispositions of the Cabinet, or rather of its leader, irresistible popular opinion would forbid offensive or active interference against the annexation of Texas, even were the Ministry not restrained by embarrassments which almost threaten its existence.[1] . . .

Should the present ministry fall, Count Molé will probably be at the head of the new cabinet, and it is understood that M⁏ Thiers has promised him the support of his friends. M⁏ Thiers has, in conversation, expressed his unqualified disapproval of the surmised cooperation of France with England upon the Texas question, and his sentiments upon this subject have been strongly reflected by his acknowledged organ of the press. Count Molé has been generally considered the representative of the Russian *alliance* as contradistinguished from the English alliance; but this is a circumstance of little significance at this moment, as he has declared himself favorable to the maintenance of friendly relations with England, while he has condemned the exaggeration of this policy which he characterized as "la politique à outrance," a principle strained to a dangerous extreme.[2] . . .

I have the honor [etc.].

2557

William R. King, United States Minister to France, to John C. Calhoun, Secretary of State of the United States [3]

[EXTRACT]

No. 11   PARIS, *February 27, 1845.*

SIR: The news of the passage, in the House of Representatives, of a bill for the annexation of Texas, created no little sensation here. The general impression was favorable, & the idea that the measure might lead to a war

---

[1] The omitted portion relates to the ministerial crisis and to the suppression of the slave trade.

[2] The omitted portion relates to the rescue of part of the crew of the United States Ship *Elizabeth* by a French vessel, and to other matters not pertinent to this publication.

[3] Despatches, France, vol. 30. Received March 21.

with England, is now universally abandoned.   As I have always said, nothing is to be apprehended from the open hostility of any European power, but much is to be feared from adverse influences exerted upon the councils of Texas herself, & I regret that my opinion is confirmed that the efforts of France are united with those of England to induce the young Republic to maintain her separate existence.   Gurantee of independence, commercial advantages, proffers of pecuniary assistance &c, have been or will be, probably, held out to tempt her to reject the advances of the United States. It is to be regretted that this government is so blinded by its devotion to the English alliance, as not to see that its true policy in this question is neutrality if not active sympathy with the United States.   France is not & probably can never be a predominant naval power.   Her arm at sea, must ever rest upon that of America, and it is only by cooperation with us that she can hope to withstand the formidable maritime power of England.   There are no points of political or territorial rivalry between us, and what makes us strong, so far from rendering her weak, must bring her strength in the hour of trial which is destined, sooner or later, to come.   Unfortunately the present administration of the government, with no inimical disposition towards the United States, have lost sight of these obvious considerations, in their anxiety to maintain a thoroughly cordial understanding, upon all points, with Great Britain.   I have every reason to believe that before my arrival, this government had in a measure pledged itself to cooperate with England, on the Texas question, & that if it subsequently modified its resolution, it was only to the extent of abstaining from overt & offensive acts of opposition to the measure of annexation.   I have even been informed from a creditable source, that a protest was actually sent to the French minister at Washington but withheld by the advice of Mr Pakenham, lest it should have an effect the opposite to that intended.   There can be no doubt that French influence both at Washington & in Texas, is cooperating with that of England, actively, perseveringly, and it is to be feared, efficiently.   Secret opposition is more to be feared than open hostility, which latter would certainly promote, while the former may defeat, the measure in question.

Mr Terrell the new Texian Chargé d'Affaires, has arrived in Paris, after spending some time in London.   He is an avowed opponent of annexation, and thinks that his opinion is rapidly gaining ground in Texas.   He had frequent interviews with Lord Aberdeen, with whom it is to be presumed he has a cordial understanding.   My conversations with him confirm the opinions above expressed, and which I had previously entertained. I learned from him incidentally, that the instructions of the French government to its representative in Texas had been communicated to Lord Aberdeen, a significant indication of the harmonious views & action of the two cabinets.   All these circumstances prove the necessity of prompt, able, &

vigilant counteraction of the combined policy of England and France in Texas. The unfortunate rejection of the treaty, has naturally cooled the ardor of the people for annexation, and every moment of delay, weakens our hands, while it strengthens those of our persevering adversaries. The question is now to be decided, not in London or Paris, or even Washington, but in Texas.[1] . . .

I have the honor [etc.].

2558

William R. King, United States Minister to France, to James Buchanan, Secretary of State of the United States [2]

[EXTRACT]

No. 13   PARIS, *April 29, 1845.*

SIR: I have the honor to acknowledge the receipt of Despatches, Nos. 15, 16, 17 & 18,[3] to the last of which I proceed to make a brief reply.

I am not astonished that the President feels "regret and surprise" at the course of the French government with regard to the annexation of Texas. Its policy in this question is neither wise nor consistent with the sympathy which unites the people as it should the governments of France and the United States. It does not, I am persuaded, spring from a wish to injure us, but from an overweening desire to conciliate England, the fixed idea of the King as well as of his able, but obsequious minister. They allege, indeed, that French cooperation with England is only apparent, being nothing more than a fortuitous coincidence of policy. But were there not more positive indications of a cordial understanding between the two governments in this matter it is obvious that such complete coincidence could not arise & continue without deliberate concert of action.

Nevertheless in the exercise of that discretion which the President is good enough to leave to me, I do not deem it advisable, for the present, at least, to express to the government of France, the "painful disappointment" which he has experienced from a review of these circumstances.[4] I think it my duty to abstain from doing so, because I do not believe that the influence of France can make much impression upon the councils of Texas; because it is too late for remonstrance to have a salutary effect, even supposing, which is not at all probable, that it would change the policy so justly complained of; and last, though not least, because in the present critical state of our rela-

---

[1] The omitted portion refers to the ministerial crisis, and also to the forwarding of a book.
[2] Despatches, France, vol. 30. Received May 21.
[3] For No. 18, see above, this volume, pt. v, March 25, 1845, doc. 2475; the first three are not pertinent to this publication.
[4] This quotation is taken from the last sentence of the Secretary of State's instruction of March 25, 1845, above, pt. v, doc. 2475; and, obviously, there should have been no quotation marks after "disappointment," but it was thus in the original of this document.

tions with England, it would not be wise or expedient to commence an irritating controversy, without urgent necessity, with a government whose people at least would not see us, with an unfriendly or indifferent eye, stand up against their formidable rival, long their deadly adversary. Nevertheless, I shall not omit, as I have not hitherto lost, any opportunity of asserting and vindicating in the highest quarters, the rights, the sentiments, & the expectations of the American government & people, upon this important question.[1] . . .

I have the honor [etc.].

2559

William R. King, United States Minister to France, to James Buchanan, Secretary of State of the United States [2]

[EXTRACT]

No. 14   PARIS, *June 16, 1845.*

SIR: . . . I enclose, a copy of the supplement to the Moniteur of the 11th inst. which contains the report of a debate which took place in the Chamber of Deputies the day before, of considerable interest to the United States.[3] It was commenced by a distinguished member of the Opposition, M[r] Billault, who has signalized himself by his able & persevering hostility to the Right of Search Treaties. He attacked the whole foreign policy of Ministers, and criticized more particularly their course with reference to the Texan question, which he denounced as unwise and gratuitous; servile to England & offensive to the United States.

In his reply, M[r] Guizot strongly denied that the French government had sought to control the will of the people of Texas with regard to annexation, while he admitted that the "weight of its influence, and the expression of its opinion" had been exerted in favor of the independance of Texas, which he justified upon the ground that it was the interest of France to sustain the separate existence of a power with which she had contracted Treaties, as well as to prevent the excessive preponderance of any one of the great powers established upon the American Continent. Such he declared were the motives of her conduct, and within these limits had her action been confined. M[r] Guizot did not deny, however, the fact which I have already communicated to you, and which was asserted in the debate, that the instructions of the French government to its representative in Texas, had been communicated to Lord Aberdeen, a significant indication of the cordial

[1] The omitted portion relates to the Oregon question and to other matters not pertinent to this publication.
[2] Despatches, France, vol. 30.   Received July 21.
The omitted portion refers to an extradition treaty between the United States and France.
[3] Not included in this publication.   It occupies ten and one half full-length newspaper columns.

understanding upon this question of the French and British cabinets. I have very little doubt, indeed, that at an early period, certainly before my arrival in France, this government had committed itself to a policy, in this matter conformable to the wishes of England. Still nothing has transpired, either in this debate or before, sufficiently positive or palpable, in my opinion to justify or render expedient a recourse to diplomatic remonstrance. The recent reply of Mʳ Guizot to Mʳ Billault is substantially that which he had made to me and which was communicated to the Department. But if there be not matter for official complaint, there is legitimate cause for dissatisfaction with the course of France upon this question, inasmuch as she has avowedly lent her influence against us, gratuitously or upon very slight pretences. Fortunately that influence upon the councils or the determination of the people of Texas cannot have much weight and is chiefly to be regretted as calculated to impair the friendly sentiments which have hitherto, so happily subsisted between her and the United States.

It may be well enough to add, that although I have not deemed it advisable to remonstrate officially against French interference in the Texas question, this government is fully aware of the feeling with which its unwise and unfriendly course has been viewed by me, and what is more important, by the American government and people. I am glad to be able to state that the French people by no means participate in the exclusive sympathy with England which pervades the foreign policy of their government, and is more particularly evinced by its opposition to the annexation of Texas to the United States.[1] . . .

I have the honor [etc.].

2560

Jacob L. Martin, United States Chargé d'Affaires ad interim at Paris, to James Buchanan, Secretary of State of the United States [2]

[EXTRACT]

No. 15 *bis*   PARIS, *July 15, 1845.*

SIR: On the 4ᵗʰ of July Mʳ King and his family left Paris, for the North of Italy, Switzerland and the Rhine, in search of health and needful recreation. They will be gone about two months probably, during which time the duties devolve upon me as Chargé d'Affaires *ad interim.*

[1] The omitted portion refers to the slave trade convention.
[2] Despatches, France, vol. 30. Received August 3.
The original despatch, No. 15, was not pertinent to this publication.
Jacob L. Martin, of North Carolina, the writer of this despatch, was commissioned secretary of legation to France on April 15, 1844, and acted as chargé d'affaires *ad interim* from July 4 to October 14, 1845, and from September 15, 1846 to July 24, 1847. Prior to this, on July 15, 1840, he had been appointed chief clerk in the Department of State. He was superseded by the appointment of Daniel Fletcher Webster on March 6, 1841. On April 7, 1848, he was commissioned chargé d'affaires to the States of the Church. He died at this post, August 26, 1848.

I have nothing of importance to communicate by the Steamer of the 19th. The French Chamber of Deputies has adjourned and the Peers will soon follow the example.   The Ministry, upon the whole, find themselves stronger than at the commencement of the Session, and it is now doubted that they will resort to a dissolution of the Chambers.   The success of the recent negotiation for a new slave-trade convention with England, and the acquiescence of the Roman authorities in the removal of the Jesuits from France are considered auspicious events for the Cabinet.   The Morocco and Tahiti questions, at one time very embarrassing to the government, have ceased for the present to agitate the public mind.

If the opposition had deemed the Texas question of sufficient importance or urgency they might have rallied upon it with some effect, for no part of the policy of the Ministers is more generally condemned, than the disposition evinced by them to thwart the United States in the matter of annexation. If it is painful to witness the impotent inclinations of the government in this affair, it is gratifying to observe how pervading and instinctive is the opposite feeling among the people.   But the question was too remote to become a subject of direct and earnest agitation between the contending parties, and some of the leaders of the opposition discountenanced the proposition to give it prominency in the assaults upon the ministry.   French influence was deemed by us of so little weight upon the result, that we regretted its adverse exertion chiefly as evincing an unfriendly spirit towards the United States, or rather an invidious preference for England in a question of vital importance to us, in which France had, at best, a very slight interest.

The early assurances of Mr King that European opposition to the annexation of Texas to the United States would be confined to diplomatic intrigue and newspaper declamation, are confirmed by the event.   In England nothing is said now about hostile interference, and in France such an idea was never hinted.   The notion that it was a casus belli, is now treated with contempt, and the British papers begin to express a sullen acquiescence in what seems to be an inevitable result.   Their last hope vanished with the departure of Mr Ashbel Smith.   The mission or rather roving commission to Europe, of that gentleman was an obvious counterpart to the mysterious expedition of Mr Commissioner Elliot to Mexico.   A few days after Mr Smith's arrival in London, it was authoritatively announced in a leading English paper, that President Jones, despising the clamor of the least intelligent or respectable portion of the Texan people, would not anticipate the regular meeting of the Congress in December.   But these lofty pretensions and the high hopes which they manifested were quickly dashed by the news that popular opinion in Texas was overwhelming in favor of annexation, and that President Jones had been compelled to summon Congress to meet in June.   Mr Smith has gone back a friend to annexation!   I must not omit to mention that he made a brief visit to Paris, where he had an interview with Mʳ Guizot, which must have been a meeting of mutual condolence rather than of congratulation. How any one at home could doubt, the inveterate hostility to annexation, of President Jones and all his emissaries and measures, is to us here, matter of no little surprise.[1] . . .

I have the honor [etc.].

2561

Jacob L. Martin, United States Chargé d'Affaires ad interim at Paris, to James Buchanan, Secretary of State of the United States [2]

[EXTRACTS]

No. 17   PARIS, *August 15, 1845.*

SIR: The unanimous adoption of the Annexation resolutions by the Texan Congress, and the equally united rejection by the Senate of the preliminaries of a Treaty with Mexico, under the auspices of France and England, have created quite a sensation in Europe. We hardly doubted this result, but we did not count upon so prompt and united a decision. The astonishment of the governments of England and France, at the utter failure of their intervention, is equalled only by their mortification. They can hardly persuade themselves that their influence in the American hemisphere is so null. The English papers of all parties vent their spleen in unmitigated abuse of the United States. But it is mere wordy wrath; insulting, not menacing. They treat annexation as an "accomplished fact," and do not hint the idea of further resistance. Their scolding is the empty echo of their impotent diplomacy.

All the French papers which are not ministerial, express their unqualified gratification, which is the public feeling here. They take particular pains to prove that the French people do not sympathize with the hardly credible policy of the government in the Texas question. With one strain, they decry its interference as gratuitous and impolitic, while they, ridicule without stint, the lame and impotent conclusion of its perverse policy. They dwell with peculiar gust, upon the circumstance that the treaty was not even honored with a consideration until precluded by the adoption of the annexation resolutions. It is impossible to exhibit a more sorry figure than the French government in this business. The ministerial organs are dumb; they cannot find a word in mitigation of Mʳ Guizot's foolish and frustrated diplomacy.[3] . . .

---

[1] The omitted portion relates to a claims case and other matters not pertinent to this publication.   [2] Despatches, France, vol. 30.   Received September 5.

[3] In the omitted portion he states that the French people were humiliated by the obsequiousness of their government to England on the Texan question, and comments upon Mr. Guizot as a political figure. He also states that the United States cannot count upon the friendship of the French Government.

American character has risen in Europe by reason of the brilliant termination of the Texan question. All admit that it has been managed by our government with singular skill, prudence and firmness. A flattering surprise is manifested that so little importance was attached, and so little heed given to European intervention in this great American question.   The event too, has confirmed the very slight estimate placed by Mr King upon French influence in Texas. He thought it was hardly worth a quarrel, and wisely deemed that the best rebuke of this ridiculous intermeddling was the proof of its impotency.

Considerable sensation has been excited here and in England by the publication of a quasi declaration of war against the United States, on the part of Mexico. Its ambiguous character, and premature date, 4th June, before the meeting of the Texan Congress, make me attach to it very little importance. It has been the signal for renewed abuse of us in the English papers, which however disclaim all cooperation with Mexico. The will, would not be wanting, were there not more to be lost than gained. The feeling excited by this publication in France, is decidedly favorable to us. One ministerial paper timidly hints at dangers to our commerce from intrusive privateers. This would easily be prevented by, if the determination of our government were known, to treat all hostile ships as piratical, a large proportion of the officers and crews of which were not national.[1] I think England announced such a determination at the commencement of the hostilities with China.

There is a sort of political interregnum here at this time. The Court is at Eu, on the coast of Normandy, and Mr Guizot at his countryseat in the same province where a portion of his constituents lately gave him a public dinner, at which he made a speech magnifying his prowess and policy, but studiously eschewing all allusion to the sore subject of Texas. In the mean time the Department of Foreign Affairs is in the charge of the Minister of the Interior. Mr King who is slowly returning through Germany, is expected here in a few weeks. I heard from him some days since, when, I am happy to state, he was in good health.[2] . . .

I have the honor [etc.].

[1] This sentence follows faithfully the original.   Probably "by" should have been omitted.
[2] The omitted portion refers to a claim and to a consular matter.

2562

William R. King, United States Minister to France, to James Buchanan, Secretary of State of the United States [1]

[EXTRACT]

No. 19   PARIS, *October 31, 1845.*

SIR: The intelligence by recent arrivals of the almost certain abandonment by Mexico of hostile designs against the United States, has extinguished whatever hope may have lingered in Europe of successful resistance to the annexation of Texas. It is now acquiesced in universally, as an "accomplished fact." Even the irritation which it excited on the other side of the Channel is gradually subsiding as reason resumes her sway, and a fairer view of the question is embraced by the public mind. The evident impossibility on the part of Mexico to recover possession of her victorious province the independence of which had been acknowledged by several of the great powers of Europe, the tardiness and hesitation with which the United States acceded to the almost unanimous wishes of the kindred people of Texas, these are but a few of the considerations which to the sober and unprejudiced mind, make annexation upon our southwestern border seem a less harsh and violent process, than that which is habitually and systematically practised in other regions which it is not necessary to designate.

The prompt and easy success of the measure convinces me of the correctness of my course, in not entering a formal protest against the part which France thought proper to take in this exciting question. Having convinced myself, and, indeed, received positive assurances that her opposition to the measure would not assume a hostile character I did not attach sufficient importance to her interference, however gratuitous and unfriendly, to make it the subject of national quarrel, especially at a moment when it was not desirable to add a new difficulty to those in which the question was already involved. I contented myself, therefore, with pointing out the impolicy and impotence of the meditated intervention, and with urging upon my own government the importance and dignity of acting with, promptitude and firmness, from its own sense of duty and interest, without regard to the gratuitous opposition of foreign powers. The best triumph, I argued, was success, and the most effectual rebuke of hostile machinations, to defeat them. I was gratified to find that the course which I thought the proper, prudent, and dignified one, was approved of, and I am now happy to be able to congratulate my government upon the successful result of its firm, independent and judicious bearing during the progress of this great question which has excited such strong and general feeling both at home and abroad.[2] . . .

I have the honor [etc.].

---

[1] Despatches, France, vol. 30.   Received December 8.
[2] The omitted portion refers to a claim and to a treaty of extradition.

2563

William R. King, United States Minister to France, to James Buchanan,
Secretary of State of the United States [1]

[EXTRACT]

No. 20   PARIS, *November 14, 1845.*

SIR: . . . The interference of France and England in the affairs of Buenos
Ayres and Montevideo caused no little surprise, as the ministers of both
countries had, not very long since, echoing each other, publicly deprecated
such intervention as unwarranted and impolitic.   The French government
was stimulated thereto by the opposition press which habitually represents
Rosas as a sanguinary tyrant, although his enduring popularity and liberal
treatment of foreign merchants of whom so many are established in his
country, might well have furnished some counterpoise to the extravagant
denunciations of his enemies.   Persons entitled to express an opinion with
whom I have conversed here, think that if he is firm and the people united in
his support, he may defy for a long time if not ultimately defeat the intrusive
intervention. . . .

I have the honor [etc.].

2564

William R. King, United States Minister to France, to François Guizot, Min-
ister of Foreign Affairs of France [2]

A   PARIS, *January 4, 1846.*

SIR: I have the honor to call the attention of Your Excellency to the
following paragraph from the London "Times" of the 1ˢᵗ inst.

> Mʳ Calhoun and Mʳ King stated in their official correspondence, with
> an assurance that has seldom been equalled, that they received from the
> King of the French a pledge that France would offer no opposition to the
> work they had in hand.   That statement was utterly false; for although
> France, like England, did not conceive that her interest in the province
> or state of Texas was sufficiently strong to justify a declaration of war
> against the aggressor, she did protest as energetically as England,
> against the violation of those principles which are the basis and the
> safeguard of international relations.

Upon the decency of such language, so applied, or of the taste which toler-
ates it, it is not my purpose to animadvert.   This is not the first time that

[1] Despatches, France, vol. 30.   Received December 8.
The omitted portions at the beginning and end of this despatch, relate to the changes in
the French ministry, to the difficulties between France and Turkey, and to other matters
not pertinent to this publication.
[2] Despatches, France, vol. 30; enclosed with King to the Secretary of State, No. 24,
January 29, 1846, below, this part, doc. 2569.

the veracity of my despatches and of those of the late distinguished Secretary of State of the United States, has been assailed in the same quarter, in terms of gross outrage.   I would continue to treat such calumnies with the contempt they deserve, did they not receive some sanction from their republication in the "Journal des Débats" of this morning, a paper which, if not official, is, from its character and relations, stamped with a certain degree of authority.   The respect which I owe to myself, and still more that which is due to my government, will not justify me in permitting such charges, thus persisted in, and thus reproduced, to pass any longer uncontradicted.   The courtesies of private life, not to speak of those due to public station, must not be violated with continued impunity.

Your Excellency will perceive that Mᴿ Calhoun's published Despatch of the 12ᵗʰ August 1844,[1] which is obviously referred to in the paragraph copied by the "Journal des Débats", is egregiously perverted, so that the charge of audacious falsehood, with which that eminent statesman and myself are so coarsely stigmatized, rests, to say the least, upon a rash misstatement. Noticing in a summary way the information of my having received satisfactory assurances that, though preferring the independence of Texas, in no event would the French Government take steps in the slightest degree hostile, or which would give to the United States, just cause of complaint, the Despatch referred to, contains the following language.

> I have laid your Despatch No. 1 [2] before the President, who instructs me to make known to you, that he has read it with much pleasure, especially the portion which relates to your cordial reception by the King, and his assurance of friendly feelings towards the United States.   The President, in particular highly appreciates the declaration of the King. That in no event any steps would be taken by his Government in the slightest degree hostile, or which would give to the United States just cause of complaint.   It was the more gratifying from the fact that our previous information was calculated to make the impression that the Government of France was prepared to unite with Great Britain in a joint protest against the annexation of Texas, and a joint effort to induce her Government to withdraw the proposition to annex, on condition that Mexico should be made to acknowledge her independence.   He is happy to infer from your Despatch, that the information, as far as it relates to France, is, in all probability without foundation.

To the joint effort to induce Texas to withdraw her proposition to annex, my Despatch had not alluded, and I am not aware that any protest, joint or single, against the annexation of Texas, has ever been presented to the American Government.

A little farther on, the preference entertained by the French Government for the continued independence of Texas, is alluded to in these terms.

[1] Above, this volume, pt. v, doc. 2472.   [2] Above, this part, July 13, 1844, doc. 2551.

You were right in making the distinction between the interests of France and England in reference to Texas, or rather, I would say, the apparent interests of the two countries. France cannot possibly have any other than commercial interest in desiring to see her preserve her separate independence, while it is certain that England looks beyond to political interests to which she apparently attaches much importance.

This Despatch has now been before the public more than a year, and although the subject of it has been referred to in conversations with Your Excellency, and has been discussed in the Chambers, when, if my memory serves me well, both the *concerted* action, and conjectured *protest* were disclaimed, I have never received the slightest intimation from the French government that its statements were questioned. The positive allegations of the paragraph I have quoted, conveyed in language of characteristic coarseness, which should not lightly be applied to men who have in eminent and responsible stations, long enjoyed to [*sic*] the confidence of their government and country, having been conspicuously reproduced by a leading ministerial paper, under the eye of the French government, to remain silent any longer, were to manifest an unworthy indifference to private reputation, as well as public consideration. The former has never before been assailed; when the latter can be with impunity, I can no longer serve my country with honor and advantage.

I feel it my duty then, before giving a public contradiction to these charges, at once to request Your Excellency to enable me to state that they have not in the slightest degree the authority or sanction of the French government. Whatever feeling may have been excited by recent political transactions, I cannot but persuade myself that it will give Your Excellency great pleasure promptly to exonerate from such unworthy imputations, a distinguished citizen who has occupied the most eminent stations, including that of Vice President of the United States, as well as him who has the honor to be their representative near His Majesty the King of the French.

I avail myself of this occasion [etc.].

2565

François Guizot, Minister of Foreign Affairs of France, to William R. King, United States Minister to France [1]

[TRANSLATION]

B. Private. PARIS, *January 9, 1846.*

SIR: I have received the letter which you did me the honor to write to me, on the 4th of this month,[2] and I hasten to reply to it. The *Journal des*

[1] Despatches, France, vol. 30; enclosed with King to the Secretary of State, No. 24, January 29, 1846, below, this part, doc. 2569. [2] Above, this part, doc. 2564.

Débats is not, in any manner, the organ of the Government of the King, which cannot and should not be considered responsible for what is published therein, whether for articles emanating from that Journal itself, or those borrowed from foreign journals. I add, that in regard to the question of Texas, at the same time that the Government of the King has pursued the course which seemed to it in conformity with the views of a wise policy, and the interests of France, it has never had, as you have already received the assurance, the intention to do anything hostile to the United States, or which might give them a just cause of complaint.

I take pleasure in repeating it to you.

Receive, I pray you, Sir, the renewed assurance of my high consideration.

2566

William R. King, United States Minister to France, to François Guizot, Minister of Foreign Affairs of France [1]

C   PARIS, *January 9, 1846.*

SIR: I have the honor to acknowledge Your Excellency's note of this morning.—My letter was not written upon the assumption that the *Journal des Débats* was the organ of the Government of His Majesty, although in the very article copied, that Journal is qualified as the "principal organ of the French government." Its object, as stated, was to vindicate my reputation, public and private, so grossly assailed under the very eye of the Government, in a place and form which gave to the calumny a certain degree of authority before the world. I presume, therefore, that in marking your note, "private" (particulière) it is not intended by Your Excellency that it is not to be used by me in any manner which I might think proper to attain that end.

I avail myself of this occasion [etc.].

2567

François Guizot, Minister of Foreign Affairs of France, to William R. King, United States Minister to France [2]

[TRANSLATION]

PARIS, *January 21, 1846.*

SIR: The Governments of France and Great Britain, had charged their Plenipotentiaries to interfere between the two States at war, on the banks of

[1] Despatches, France, vol. 30; enclosed with King to the Secretary of State, No. 24, January 29, 1846, below, this part, doc. 2569.
[2] Despatches, France, vol. 30, enclosed with King to the Secretary of State, No. 22, January 27, 1846, below, this part, doc. 2568.

the Rio de la Plata, in order to put an end to the hostilities, which have so long desolated these countries; the Government of Buenos Ayres, having refused to accede to the propositions of conciliation, which have been addressed to it, the Plenipotentiaries of the two Kingdoms found themselves under the necessity of placing the ports and coasts of the Province of Buenos Ayres, under blockade from and after the 24th of September last. They have however endeavoured to lessen the injury, which such a measure may cause to the navigation of neutrals, by granting delays as long as possible for the departure of merchant vessels.

I pray you, Sir, to communicate the present notification to your Government.

Receive, Sir, the assurances [etc.].

2568

*William R. King, United States Minister to France, to James Buchanan,
Secretary of State of the United States* [1]

No. 22   PARIS, *January 27, 1846.*

SIR: I have the honor to transmit herewith the official notification on the part of France of the blockade of Buenos Ayres, by the combined forces of France and England.[2] Whatever may be my views upon this "conciliatory" transaction, you will perceive by the accompanying note,[3] that I have thought proper to confine myself to the acknowledgement and transmission of the notification, unless the marked repetition of its somewhat singular phraseology, be considered the expression of an opinion upon this high-handed act of "intervention." Unfortunately it is generally approved of by the opposition in this country, whose friendly attitude, so opportunely taken, with regard to the Texas and Oregon questions, was an additional reason to dissuade me, in my representative capacity, from taking the initiative in remonstrating against a measure injurious to American interests and, to say the least, unpalateable to American pride and principles. Besides, to protest, when resistance is not probable and may not be politic, is hardly compatible with a proper sense of national dignity. The serious disapprobation of the government and people of the United States, of the course of France and England, in this question, is no secret.

I have the honor [etc.].

[1] Despatches, France, vol. 30. Received February 22.
[2] Above, this part, January 21, 1846, doc. 2567.
[3] Not included in this publication. The purport of this brief note is adequately given within this despatch.

2569

*William R. King, United States Minister to France, to James Buchanan,
Secretary of State of the United States* [1]

No. 24   PARIS, *January 29, 1846.*

SIR: I have the honor to transmit the accompanying copy of a correspondence with the Minister of Foreign Affairs of this government on the subject of
my despatches upon the Texas question.[2]   I had occasionally noticed in the
English journals confident assertions that M⋅ Calhoun and myself, had mis-
represented and even deliberately falsified the declarations made to me by
the French Government with regard to its course in reference to the annexation of Texas.   However annoying "these positive allegations,[3] I could
not with propriety take notice of the unauthenticated assertions of British
newspapers.   On the 1ˢᵗ of this month, however, there appeared an article in
the London "Times" reasserting these charges of falsehood in terms of
the grossest outrage.   This was copied into the "Journal des Débats" of the
4ᵗʰ inst, which paper, always hostile to us, had, in the irritation caused by the
President's Message, thrown off the habitual reserve of a ministerial organ.
Under these circumstances, I could no longer remain silent, and on the very
day of the republication of the obnoxious article, I addressed the communication (A) to M⋅ Guizot requiring him promptly to state, that the opprobrious
imputation had not in the slightest degree the authority or sanction of the
French government.   Before answering my letter he requested an interview
in which he used every effort to induce me to be satisfied with the assurance
that the "Journal des Débats" was not the organ of the government, which
had never complained of my despatch, and should not be held responsible for
unauthorized newspaper publications.

To all this I replied that the "Journal des Débats" a leading ministerial
paper, was considered in some degree as a government organ, and was so represented, indeed, in the very article copied from the London "Times;" adding that unless he was prepared to confirm the accuracy of the statements in
my despatch, so authoritatively called in question, I should feel myself
compelled from a sense of duty to myself and to my country to suspend all
further relations with the French government.   To this he replied that he
hoped I would not take such a step which was not called for by the occasion,
and that if I insisted upon it he would write me a note repeating the assurances
which had been given to me that on the Texas question France would take no
steps hostile to the United States, or which would give to them just cause of
complaint.   He objected, however, to the inferences drawn by M⋅ Calhoun
from these assurances.   I replied that in the conference which I had had

---

[1] Despatches, France, vol. 30.   Received February 21.
[2] Above, this part, dated, respectively, January 4, 9, and 9, 1846, docs. 2564, 2565, and
2566, and referred to below in this document as enclosures A, B, and C.
[3] Apparently there should have been a closing quotation mark after "allegations."

with him, subsequently to writing my despatch, he expressly stated that France had not and would not unite with England in protesting against the annexation of Texas, and that upon this question she would act for herself, and in concert with no other power. The first part of this statement he admitted, but added that he did not recollect having said that there would be no concert of action with reference to the Texas question. I assured him that he had used the precise words, that my recollection of them was perfect, and that I had noted down the conversation the very day on which it had taken place. He insisted that I had misunderstood him, probably because he did not express himself clearly in English, which language by the by, he speaks very well, and I so assured him. I mentioned to him my regret that I had not submitted to him at the time, my note of the conversation referred to, in order that he might verify its correctness. This, to my great surprise, although a common and proper diplomatic usage, he declared he would not have done!

The next day, Mr Guizot forwarded to me the promised note (B) disclaiming the "Journal des Débats" as a government organ, and confirming *totidem verbis* the statements of my despatch! He took the precaution however, to mark it "private, or unofficial" (particulière), but I declined to consider it such, in a note (C) which I immediately addressed to him, and which has remained without a reply written or verbal, although I have met with him since. I do not consider any part of the correspondence confidential, and it was indeed, my intention to make it public, at once, but the Texas discussion coming on in the Chambers and assuming a favorable turn, I abstained from doing so, lest I should be thought to be blending myself, at a critical moment, with the party contests of the country. In this view I was confirmed by persons, whose judgment and experience give authority to their opinions. I deem it my duty however to add, that the correspondence has been freely shown to American and other friends, and that its import is no mystery. I now transmit it to the Department, which will judge of the propriety of laying it before the public. Should it determine to do so, I will take the liberty to suggest that it be accurately printed. Justice to Mr Guizot requires that his letter, I allude particularly to the French original should not appear without careful correction, especially as it regards the accents, which when omitted or misplaced have a very awkward effect.

I have the honor [etc.].

2570

William R. King, United States Minister to France, to James Buchanan,
Secretary of State of the United States [1]

[EXTRACT]

No. 25 PARIS, *January 30, 1846.*

SIR: The relations of France with the United States, have formed a prominent topic of discussion in the Chambers. It was generally expected that Mr Guizot would seize the first opportunity to reply with severity to the strictures in the President's Message upon the conduct of the French government in the Texas question. But reflection brought with it cooler counsels, and when the subject was opened in the Chamber of Peers by an attack upon the policy of the government, Mr Guizot replied with a calmness and moderation, as it regards the form at least, which took every one by surprise. He referred to the Message with respectful courtesy, disclaimed all hostility to the United States, and even passed a qualified eulogy upon their political institutions and social polity. He, however, sought to justify his opposition to the annexation of Texas upon the ground that the United States had become strong, and were growing rapidly stronger, and that they, therefore required to be watched with a vigilant if not jealous eye. He, at the same time developed and defended with elaborate sophistry his famous theory, of American equilibrium, and the policy of preventing the great and growing American republic, from absorbing her feebler neighbours, in the western hemisphere. The speech was effective as a rhetorical effort, but it captivated without convincing. It did not reconcile public opinion to an intervention which was not only gratuitous but had cooled the affection of an old and natural ally without even having had the merit of success.—

The discussion was not pursued in the Chamber of Peers, but was soon resumed, with greater animation in the other House, where Mr Thiers delivered, upon this question, the most brilliant and effective speech to which the Session has yet given birth. It was characterized by great moderation and prudence, as from one who had been, and might be again, Minister, which gave to it greater effect. He attacked the interference of the French government in the Texas question, as gratuitous and impolitic. He blamed it severely, as offensive to the United States the traditionary ally of France. He exposed the emptiness of the commercial pretext, and asserted that the intervention was the price stipulated for the consent of England, to the abrogation of the obnoxious Right of Search Treaties. He expressed with cutting sarcasm and happy effect, Mr Guizot's specious and novel theory of American equilibrium, the true name of which he said was English equilibrium, for it redounded to the benefit of Great Britain alone. He painted with bright and rapid touches the wonderful progress of the United States, and declared

[1] Despatches, France, vol. 30. Received February 21.

that besides that of France, he desired the greatness of no other nation save the United States, from which no possible danger but much benefit would accrue to France.   Mͬ Thiers was listened to with almost religious attention, and it was obvious that he had the silent approbation of even the Conservative majority, so strongly pledged to the support of the ministry.   His speech was an important demonstration, and has not been without an echo in the country, which is beginning to be aroused from the torpor into which it had lapsed.

The debate was adjourned till the next day, when Mͬ Guizot replied to his distinguished rival, but as, is generally admitted, with but faint success.   He somewhat changed or enlarged the ground upon which he had defended his Texan intervention by attributing it to a desire to indicate at an early moment, his intention to assume a neutral attitude in the Oregon difficulty.   It would seem to plain minds that the best way to indicate neutrality is to practise it, and at all events his "indication" was not very clear, for it was generally interpreted as an evidence of sympathy with England in her differences with the United States.   One thing has been gained by this discussion; the French government has been constrained to make a public declaration of neutrality with regard to the future which had not been so distinctly intimated in Mͬ Guizot's first speech.   It is confidently asserted that his colleagues, apprehensive of the effect of his speech in the Chamber of Peers, had required him to give more explicit and satisfactory assurances in his second discourse.

Mͬ Guizot was followed by Mͬ Billaut, an eminent advocate, who has distinguished himself by his opposition to the Right of Search Treaties. He proved to the conviction of the Chamber that the French government had not acted in this question, as had been alleged, at the instance of the government of Texas, but by the instigation of that of England and, had by no means confined itself to giving friendly counsels to Texas or Mexico, but had assumed towards the United States, an offensive attitude.   Both the speakers on this side deprecated the course of France as precluding her from interposing her good offices between the United States and Great Britain should the peril of war become serious.

Upon the whole the Ministry has been damaged not a little by this debate which has had a salutary influence in drawing out public opinion against the policy of the French government in opposition to the United States.   Even the Conservatives, devoted as they are to the present administration, disapprove of its course in this matter.   The will may not be wanting in the government to cooperate, at least indirectly, with England, against us, but it is restrained by irresistible public opinion.   From all quarters I receive assurances to this effect, and I have every reason to believe that the voice of Mͬ Thiers echoes the real sentiments of a large majority of the French people.   The ministry, I have no doubt regret the part they have played in this business, first, because it failed, and then, because it is deeply unpopular. Their object was unquestionably to conciliate England, and all Mʳ Guizot's ingenious reasons for interference are of subsequent invention.   He has too many good reasons for doing a bad thing.   The truth is, that he was assured the Whig candidate would be elected to the Presidency, and annexation consequently be renounced by the American people, and he therefore imagined he might meddle with the question, without involving himself in serious consequences.   He was also made to believe by interested parties, that there was a large portion of the people of Texas, opposed to annexation.   He was deluded by his agents abroad, who instead of telling him plain truths, however, unpalateable, wrote only to gratify his inclinations, and as the French express it, abounded in his sense.   He affords another example that to be crafty is not to be wise, and that crooked paths are generally slippery ones.

What is most important to us, is that there is nothing to apprehend from this government, and country.   The latter is with us, and will restrain the former from being against us.[1] . . .

I have the honor [etc.].

2571

William R. King, United States Minister to France, to James Buchanan, Secretary of State of the United States [2]

[EXTRACTS]

No. 26   PARIS, *February 28, 1846.*

SIR: . . . The Correspondence which I had the honor to transmit in relation to my despatch communicating the declarations of the King of the French with reference to the Texas question,[3] was soon after published by a London journal.   I had sent it to Mʳ McLane and requested him to exercise his discretion with regard to the propriety of its publication, at once, in the quarter where the obnoxious imputations had first been promulgated. After due reflection and consultation, it was thought advisable to give it to the press.   This brought, as was to be expected, additional vituperation from the newspaper convicted of falsehood, but the effect has been salutary in putting an end to a calumny which, silently whispered, or publicly rumored for more than a year, was calculated to impair the consideration of the government and its representatives.

[1] The omitted portion refers to the Oregon question.
[2] Despatches, France, vol. 30.   Received March 21.
The omitted portion relates to tobacco contracts.
[3] Presumably he refers to his correspondence with the Foreign Minister, above, this part, January 4, 9, and 9, 1846, docs. 2564, 2565, and 2566, enclosed with his despatch No. 24, above, this part, January 29, 1846, doc. 2569.

Since the termination of the discussion upon the Address in the French Chambers, the Texan question has ceased to excite interest in this country. A large and complaisant majority was satisfied with the declarations of the Minister that nothing hostile or unfriendly had been designed or was yet entertained, against the United States.—The effect of the impression made there by Mᵣ Guizot's speeches, remains to be seen. But the ministerial majority is so large, and the discouragement of the opposition so complete, that hardly anything would now suffice to stimulate effective resistance to the course of the Cabinet.[1] . . .

Much has been said lately with respect to a project of establishing a monarchy in Mexico, with a European prince upon the throne, by the help of England, and France, and perhaps Spain. Remote hopes or vague ideas of such a character may be entertained, but I have no reason to think, that they have assumed a more definite shape. They are grounded upon the opinion that the evils of anarchy are disgusting the people of Mexico with their abortive experiment of republican liberty. If they have any chance of realization, this will depend upon public sentiment in Mexico. Some years ago, a distinguished and wealthy citizen of that republic, publicly recommended such a change, but so little ripe was the public mind for it then, that he was obliged to conceal himself, till he could take refuge in exile. The idea is naturally agreeable to European monarchists. A marriage of the Duke de Montpensier, the youngest son of Louis Philippe, with the infanta, sister of the Queen of Spain, has been spoken of in connection with this project. The idea of such an alliance has probably been entertained, but as the health of the young Queen, is not strong, and her sister is heir apparent to the Spanish throne, the arrangement would hardly be palateable to England. I transmit the Journal des Débats of this day, and would call your attention to an article which it copies from the "Heraldo," of Madrid,[2] which shows that Castilian pride is flattered, in no small degree, by the idea of placing a Spanish prince upon the ancient throne of Montezuma.

The appeal to Europe against the preponderating influence of the United States beyond the Atlantic, savors somewhat of the famous doctrine of the "American equilibrium."

I have the honor [etc.].

[1] The omitted portion relates to the Oregon question.
[2] Not included in this publication.

2572

William R. King, United States Minister to France, to James Buchanan,
Secretary of State of the United States [1]

No. 28   PARIS, *June 1, 1846.*

SIR: I have the honor to acknowledge your despatches up to No. 32 inclusive, which last was accompanied by a copy of the proclamation of the
President announcing that war exists between the United States and Mexico.[2]
I regret that the "Union" of the 11th and 12th May containing the President's
Message and all the proceedings upon it in Congress which you state was
forwarded to me, has not been received. Its detention would have been
very unfortunate if I had not found these proceedings, though abridged and
mutilated, in the New York papers.

It is impossible yet to know the effect of this announcement abroad; but
it may be confidently asserted that the promptitude and energy displayed by
the American government in all its departments, in this emergency, will have
a salutary influence upon public opinion in Europe which had been somewhat
unfavorably impressed by the delay and neglect of preparation which characterized the action of Congress, on the Oregon question. An agreeable
feature of the late proceedings is the unanimity which distinguished them,
and which as you truly remark, will serve to convince the world that in our
country when it becomes necessary to assert the national rights and vindicate the national honor, all party distinctions vanish. A late number of the
Journal des Débats the leading ministerial paper, adopting the tone as it em-
ulates the hostility of the British press, dealt with malevolent satisfaction
upon the total want of military preparation and resources to maintain the
pretensions of the United States. It will be obliged now to drop that note.

In my communications with this government I shall not fail to impress
upon it the fact that we have entered upon this contest with great reluctance
after much forbearance, and that while resolved to prosecute it with vigor
both by land and sea, we have undertaken the war solely for the purpose of
conquering an honorable and permanent peace. I shall also seize the first
opportunity to comply with your instructions, by announcing to the Minister
of Foreign Affairs, that it is the intention of the Government of the United
States to establish with adequate force, a strict blockade of the ports of
Mexico both on the Atlantic and Pacific, with a view of bringing her speedily
to reasonable terms by interrupting her commerce and cutting off the principal source of her revenue.

I perceive that some apprehensions are manifested that Mexico will arm
numerous privateers against our Commerce. As she has no navy, these

---

[1] Despatches, France, vol. 30. Received June 20.
[2] For the text of No. 32, a circular instruction, see above, vol. 1, May 14, 1846, doc. 17,
note 2, p. 33.

must come from other countries.   With most of them we have treaties sanctioning the principle of international law which regards such acts of hostility by the subjects or citizens of governments at peace, as piracy.   I trust we shall not hesitate to treat all hostile crews not principally Mexican, and these it is easy to distinguish, as of this character.   A few summary examples would soon put an end to such annoyance.

I must not disguise my opinion that the feelings of this government will be adverse to us in the contest which has just commenced, partly from antipathy to the republican cause assailed in Mexico by European intrigue in combination with domestic treachery; partly from devotion to the English alliance which continues to be the fixed idea of the King and consequently of his cabinet.   Still there is no ground to apprehend hostile interference, in the absence of friendly offices, because they would not be tolerated by an overwhelming majority of the French people, already irritated by the course of the government upon the Texas question.   A great, immediate danger will not be incurred to ward off the remoter and less palpable one of republican power and example.   In confirmation of this opinion I may state that in a recent debate, M̱ Guizot found himself constrained when assailed again for his abortive Texas demonstration, to proclaim the high respect and consideration which he entertained for that "great nation" (the United States), and to reiterate in the strongest terms the determinaton of the French government to maintain a neutral attitude for the future.   Whatever importance may be attached to the former declaration, I find a sufficient guaranty for the latter in the irresistible force of public opinion.   Still I would counsel, as I shall observe, the most courteous relations with the French Government and authorities everywhere, that no ground or pretext of offence may be given to the French people, which might embolden and empower the government to display towards us an unfriendly attitude.   His Majesty the King of the French rarely suffers an occasion to pass without assuring me of the great friendship and regard which he entertains for the United States.   It is well that policy counsels the expression of such sentiments.

Since writing the above I had an interview with His Majesty at 1 P.M. for the purpose of presenting the letter of the President, congratulating him upon the birth of the Princess Marguérite Adelaide Marie of Orleans.   I have only time left to say in the briefest manner, that the King conversed with me very freely upon our relations with Mexico, expressing his great regret that hostilities had taken place, but declaring his firm determination to abstain from all participation, direct or indirect in the contest.   He referred also to the monarchical projects in Mexico, with indifference if not contempt; not only to the desire of Paredes for the adoption of a Spanish prince, but to the old project of placing a prince of his own family upon the throne, of which he had entirely disapproved.   As these declarations are not without interest and importance I give them in this crude and hasty manner, with the remark that as they proceed from the sovereign and not from his constitutional advisers, this is an additional reason why they should not reach the public eye.

I have the honor [etc.].

2573

William R. King, United States Minister to France, to James Buchanan, Secretary of State of the United States [1]

[EXTRACT]

No. 29   PARIS, *June 30, 1846.*

SIR: . . . The news of the signal victories of our troops on the Rio Grande was very grateful, as I had felt no little anxiety for the situation of General Taylor. These achievements have made a very salutary impression abroad, as is strikingly manifested by the tone of the public press and of conversation. Our institutions and character are no longer deemed so ill adapted to military emergencies. Had we been defeated in the late brilliant encounters, as the large odds against us made it not improbable, those who are not well disposed to us on this side of the water, might have been emboldened to unfriendly or offensive demonstrations.

I persist in believing that this government views with no cordial feelings our successes on the Mexican frontier. The King, indeed, declares that he will take no part in the conflict, but my recollections of the Texas question, cause me to receive these general declarations with some distrust.

I have no apprehension that any steps of open hostility will be taken against us, because they are forbidden by common prudence, and would hardly be tolerated by the French people. If England, however, should attempt to resist our legitimate pretensions, the diplomatic efforts of this government will doubtless, be directed in the same channel. At present the French government has not made up its mind what course to take, but is obviously waiting to see what England will do. Its hesitation is increased by the change in the British ministry. The new Cabinet does not inspire it with quite the same confidence as the old one, although I am persuaded that no alteration will be effected thereby in the foreign policy of Great Britain. The persevering and unfair hostility of the "Journal des Débats," is a manifestation of the feeling towards the United States of the French government, which is confirmed by other indications. One of the principal editors of this paper, a member of the Chamber of Deputies, who writes most of the articles, unfriendly to our government and people, remarked the other day, that he doubted whether the European powers would look patiently on the threat-

[1] Despatches, France, vol. 30. Received July 24.
The omitted portion relates to the Spanish debt to the United States. It also relates to the assistance rendered by a French ship to a United States steamer.

ened conquest or mutilation of Mexico. The general tone, however, of the French press, is unfavorable to a policy adverse to the United States.

You have doubtless been apprized of the strengthening of the French squadron in the Gulf of Mexico. Mʳ Guizot informed me in the conversation in which I notified him of the intention of the American government to blockade the Mexican ports, on both sides of the Continent, that this was done only with reference to the protection of French commerce. It is a circumstance, however, not without political significance. Mʳ Guizot must be unfaithful to his absurd doctrine of American equilibrium, if he does not try, by diplomatic means, at least, to resist any further accession to the territory of the United States. Fortunately the "entente cordiale" though strong between the governments of France and England, is less so between the nations, whose ancient animosity does but slumber, and is easily awakened. For this reason it is our obvious policy to cultivate the kind feelings of the French people, and to give their government no pretext for quarrelling with us. For my part, I shall watch narrowly the course of this government, and do everything in my power to prevent, or to detect and counteract any hostile influence that may be exerted.

I am glad to learn that there is a prospect of terminating the La Plata difficulties. The governments of England and France are heartily sick of their unjustifiable intervention, and will take advantage of the first favorable pretext to bring it to an end. Such an opportunity is furnished by the close of Oribe's presidential term, and I have good reason to believe that it will be turned to account. I have long been aware that the King is not friendly to the policy of intervention, and he, indeed, assured me some time ago, that not a soldier should France send to carry it out, adding, with more than usual candor, that he had been drawn into it, by the desire to please England. Now that the latter is disposed to retire, France will hardly be willing to persist alone in this unprofitable and abortive intervention to which she was impelled not only by anxiety to please England, but by the absurd clamors of the opposition, in this matter, less wise than the government.[1] . . .

I have the honor [etc.].

[1] The omitted portion relates to the commercial treaty of 1822 between France and the United States.

2574

William R. King, United States Minister to France, to James Buchanan,
Secretary of State of the United States [1]

[EXTRACT]

No. 31   PARIS, *July 20, 1846.*

SIR: . . . All eyes are now turned towards Mexico. I am glad to see that peace is to be conquered by vigorous war, the only means of securing it with such a people. The blows already inflicted have been felt abroad as well as in Mexico. They have shown what we can and will do, if molested, however pacific and commercial our natural and general policy. They have *commanded* respect and secured a perhaps doubtful neutrality. Whatever may be the disposition of this government with regard to the maintenance of the "balance of power" in the American hemisphere, it will not venture to take any active part against the United States in its difficulties with the Mexican republic. Its experience of the Texas questions is not encouraging to further interference.

In a late conversation with the King, when assuring him of the sincere desire of the United States for a prompt and permanent peace, I took occasion to say that the obstinacy of Mexico proceeded doubtless from the hope of aid from European governments. Which? he quickly asked, and I as promptly replied, France and England; whereupon he declared in the most emphatic and explicit manner, that no such assistance would be rendered by France, and he thought he could assure me, by England neither. I have had no recent conversation with Mr Guizot, who left Paris, some days since for his seat in Normandy.

I have the honor [etc.].

2575

Jacob L. Martin, United States Chargé d'Affaires ad interim at Paris, to James
Buchanan, Secretary of State of the United States [2]

[EXTRACTS]

No. 34   PARIS, *August 31, 1846.*

Sir: . . . Further indications are given that this government will maintain a neutral position if not spirit, in our difficulties with Mexico. The diplomatic journal, the "Partfeuille," [Portefeuille] conducted somewhat under ministerial auspices, and deriving not unfrequently information from the

---

[1] Despatches, France, vol. 30. Received August 11.
The omitted portion relates to the Spanish debt to the United States, to the writer's contemplated trip, and to the settlement of the Oregon question.
[2] Despatches, France, vol. 30. Received October 1.
The omitted portions of this despatch discuss the French King's speech, French affairs in Tahiti, and other matters not pertinent to this publication.

Department of Foreign Affairs, strongly inculcates this policy. Whatever may be the sentiments of the King or of M.ʳ Guizot, the Conservative party, does not approve and would not suffer, that exclusive devotion to British interests, particularly upon American questions, which was the recent tendency of the Administration. My own opinion upon this subject was lately strengthened by that of a distinguished and moderate member of the Chamber of Deputies. Besides, although the irritation caused by the recent discussion of the Spanish marriage has somewhat subsided, the new Whig ministry in England does not inspire the same confidence and sympathy as the Tory Administration. The recent debate, too, in the British parliament upon Mexican affairs, and the feeling with which it was received by the public, show that prudent sentiments also prevail in the English Cabinet. Both the English and French governments are dissatisfied with their unwise and unjustifiable interference on the shores of the La Plata, & it is hoped that the mission of M.ʳ Hood, will lead to a speedy and satisfactory adjustment of the difficulty: The Whigs when out of power strongly condemned the intervention and the King of the French who never had it at heart, from the first refused to send the necessary contingent of land forces. . . .

I have just received a letter from M.ʳ King, dated at Liverpool 28.ᵗʰ August, informing me that he will be in Paris, in a few days.

I have the honor [etc.].

2576

Jacob L. Martin, United States Chargé d'Affaires ad interim at Paris, to James Buchanan, Secretary of State of the United States [1]

[EXTRACTS]

No. 1   PARIS, *October 1, 1846.*

SIR: M.ʳ King having presented his letter of recall on the 15.ᵗʰ, inst.[2] I on that day assumed the duties of this Legation as Chargé d'Affaires.[3] . . .

I learn nothing positive of the result of M.ʳ Hood's Mission to La Plata. A recent number of the London "Times" contains a statement of the terms upon which he is authorized to treat with President Rosas, which are these —1: the evacuation of the territory of Monte Video, by the Argentine troops; 2: a free election of deputies in the capital and departments; [3:?] the reunion of these deputies in some point completely removed from all influence of the belligerents, whether on Brazilian soil, or on board neutral vessels of war; and there to elect a president; 4: that should Oribe be chosen,

[1] Despatches, France, vol. 30. Received October 23.
[2] It is thus in the manuscript volume, although obviously the writer should have written "15.ᵗʰ ultimo."
[3] The omitted portion relates to European political affairs and also to tobacco contracts.

he should be as admissible as any other; 5: reciprocal guarantees in favor of all the belligerents.   I called to this statement, the attention of M͇ Rosalés the Chargé d'Affaires of Chili, who, although regretting very much the introduction of his name in the publication, informed me that the terms were in the main correctly reported.   His opinion is entitled to confidence because, he is the friend, personal and political, of the Argentine Minister at this court, and is privy to all his proceedings.   M͇ Rosales feels confidence that the question will be settled by the Hood Mission, President Rosas, as he alleges, having been always willing to accept such terms, and the opposition to Oribe in the Oriental Confederacy being confined to a small faction in Monte Video, a free and fair election must restore him to the Presidency.—

His Majesty, Louis Philippe, who has been always averse to the intervention undertaken to please England, has no longer that inducement to persevere.

I have the honor [etc.].

2577

Jacob L. Martin, United States Chargé d'Affaires ad interim at Paris, to James Buchanan, Secretary of State of the United States [1]

[EXTRACT]

No. 4   PARIS, *October 31, 1846.*

SIR: . . . As to any leaning towards the United States, I have not the smallest reliance upon such an inclination.   It would be a desperate and dernier resort.   We are the subject of unmitigated political dislike.   Frederick the Great declined to assist the infant cause of America, because "his trade was to be a King."   His Majesty Louis Philippe thinks that our republican experiment, so conspicuous and successful, interferes seriously with this royal trade, and his monarchical "esprit de corps" is heightened by the circumstance, that he was but recently admitted into the company of Kings, and is eager to give proofs that he is worthy of the "order."   Of this morbid anxiety, I could give some curious illustrations, if this were the place or time. A smile from the pettiest prince of the old stock, is more grateful to him, than the good-will of the greatest of republics.   No new rich man, or lucky "tradesman in the city" is more ambitious of "good society".

As to M͇ Guizot he is an inveterate dogmatist of the ultra-conservative school, more royalist than the King, and entertains for republicanism, the feeling which a fanatic cherishes for a hostile sect, or a metaphysician for a rival theory.   I would not express such opinions, if I had not very good reasons, to know that they are correct.   We must never count upon the good

---

[1] Despatches, France, vol. 30.   Received November 19.
The omitted portions of this despatch discuss European political affairs, the failure of the potato crop, and other matters not pertinent to this publication.

will of this French government, and I am not solicitous about it, for our true interest and dignity rest upon ourselves. We owe it chiefly to our strength aided by distance, and to the reacting danger of meddling with us, that all idea is abandoned here of intervention in our relations with Mexico. They are looked upon with no friendly eye, but the probable acquisition of territory in that quarter, is now, forsooth, treated, as a matter of little import to France, although it must be confessed that California weighs something in the American "balance of power." . . .

I have the honor [etc.].

2578

Jacob L. Martin, United States Chargé d'Affaires ad interim at Paris, to James Buchanan, Secretary of State of the United States [1]

[EXTRACTS]

No. 5   PARIS, *November 16, 1846.*

SIR: The remarks in my last despatch [2] concerning the feelings and policy of this government towards the United States may have appeared somewhat harsh, but they were amply justified a day or two after, by the publication of an article in the ministerial paper, the "Journal des Débats," denouncing the course of the American Government towards Mexico, as one of theft, (larcin) holding up our institutions and people to the odium of Europe, and charging the President with treachery and bad faith, for ordering General Taylor to terminate an armistice which was referred to his approbation by the very terms of the capitulation! Nothing so uncandid or malignant has appeared in the English newspapers. It excited great indignation among our countrymen in Paris of all parties. It was answered with point and effect by the republican paper, the "National;" and has since been condemned as untrue and malevolent by the "Presse," a more independent Conservative journal, which generally treats American affairs with candour and impartiality.

As the "Débats" is not an official paper, the government does not hold itself responsible for what appears in its columns, though it would be absurd to suppose that anything is admitted, which might be thought disagreeable to the King or the ministry. The influence of the government upon its tone is proved by the following incident. Some time ago the paper indulged in harsh reflections upon the King of Prussia, which caused his late minister, Count d'Arnim to remonstrate verbally to Mʳ Guizot, who replied that he was very sorry, but could not help it. "If you cannot, I will," rejoined the Minister, "for I will cause an order to be issued that it shall not pass the Prussian frontier." Thereupon the obnoxious articles ceased to appear.

[1] Despatches, France, vol. 30. Received December 20.
[2] Above, this part, October 31, 1846, doc. 2577.

The diatribes in the "Débats" are generally written by the notorious political prostitute, Michel Chevalier, the ex-St Simonien, who feeling that he had some talent and no principle, walked through the streets of Paris, in a turban and petticoats, until he had made himself sufficiently conspicuous, when he turned short round and sold himself outright to the government, to render republican institutions odious in France, by maligning our government and people, of which, having enjoyed their hospitality, he knows just enough to give plausibility to his calumnies in the eyes of the ignorant or imperfectly informed reader.   There is some consolation in knowing, that of all public men in France, he is the most despised by all parties.   Even those who employ him are ashamed of him.

Much importance is not to be attached to the good or ill will of this government which is impotent to serve or to harm us.   The best rebuke of such calumnies is to despise them, and to carry out our policy vigorously, without reference to the opinions of those who are jealous of our power and progress.   Our brilliant military achievements, and the peaceful and prosperous developement of our institutions, excite no little solicitude in the breasts of European monarchs.   They fear the silent yet effective propagandism of American example.   So that they keep their hands off, I am unmoved by evil wishes or words which betray an uneasiness that is more flattering than would be their indifference or even their friendship.   In the mean time I deem it prudent to maintain with the authorities here, the necessary intercourse of official courtesy.   The case is not worth a quarrel.[1] . . .

There is much doubt thrown upon the result of Mr Hood's mission to La Plata.   M. de Sarratea, the Argentine minister himself begins to entertain them, though he counts firmly upon the ultimate success of the negotiation.   They will not be removed until the arrival of Mr Hood who is expected soon.   As all parties had agreed to the terms proposed, the difficulty must grow out of the manner of executing them, and is variously attributed to President Rosas, and to the authorities of Montevideo.   It is believed that the regular plenipotentiaries, especially Baron Deffaudis, are inclined to throw obstacles in the way.[2] . . .

I have the honor [etc.].

[1] The omitted portion relates to European political affairs.
[2] The omitted portion relates to gun cotton experiments and also acknowledges the receipt of a despatch.

2579

*Jacob L. Martin, United States Chargé d'Affaires ad interim at Paris, to
James Buchanan, Secretary of State of the United States* [1]

[EXTRACT]

No. 6   PARIS, *November 30, 1846.*

SIR: . . . Much disappointment has been caused by the failure of M[r]
Hood's mission to La Plata; but I am again assured from reliable quarters,
that this check is only the postponement of an inevitable arrangement.
The refusal of Baron Deffaudis, the French Minister to acquiesce in the
modification of the terms previously agreed upon, to the effect that the evacuation of Monte Video and the raising of the blockade of Buenos Ayres,
should take place simultaneously, has been disapproved of and instructions
have been or are about to be sent, to remove this obstacle to pacification.
All parties are tired of this protracted and ruinous quarrel.

The free trade party is making slow but sure progress in the public opinion
of this country, where protection means prohibition. Distinguished and
influential names are enlisting themselves in the cause, and the discussions
of the "society of free exchanges" begin to attract much interest. The
government, feeling its servitude to the ultra-protectionists who are pre-
dominent in the limited class of electors, is disposed to go as far, as inveterate
prejudice or influential interest will permit it. But the first step which was
the most difficult, has been taken.

I have the honor [etc.].

2580

*Jacob L. Martin, United States Chargé d'Affaires ad interim at Paris, to
François Guizot, Minister of Foreign Affairs of France* [2]

A   PARIS, *February 11, 1847.*

SIR: In compliance with the request of Mr Desages with whom at the suggestion of Your Excellency I had the honor to converse yesterday upon the
subject of the communication of the American Consul at Marseilles that a
Mexican Agent had arrived in that port authorized to issue letters of marque
against the commerce of the United States, I hasten to transmit a brief
abstract of the legislation of the United States [3] with reference to hostile
attempts within their jurisdiction or territory against the citizens, subjects
or property of a foreign power with which they are at peace.

[1] Despatches, France, vol. 30. Received December 20.
The omitted portion relates to European political affairs.
[2] Despatches, France, vol. 30; enclosed with Martin to the Secretary of State, No. 11,
February 28, 1847, below, this part, doc. 2582.   [3] Not included in this publication.

Your Excellency will observe that among these various effective enactments, is included the very case in question, it being declared a high misdemeanour punishable with severe fine and imprisonment, for any person to deliver a commission within the territory or jurisdiction of the United States, to be employed for the unlawful purpose indicated.

Relying upon the fair and friendly sentiments of the Government of His Majesty, as proved by the instructions already given to maintain the neutrality of France in the contest between the United States and Mexico, I feel persuaded that I have but to signalize the unlawful designs of the Mexican agent referred to, that prompt and effective steps may be taken to prevent them from being carried into effect; measures obviously dictated by justice, reciprocity and an enlightened regard for the mutual interests of France and the United States.   Sincerely entertaining this confidence I feel that it would not become me at this moment to discuss the propriety or necessity of the desired interdiction, but in view of the urgency of the case, and of the uneasiness which prevails to a certain extent, in commercial circles, I deem it my duty, respectfully but strenuously to invoke the prompt and effectual attention of the competent authorities to this subject.

I avail myself of this occasion [etc.].

2581

François Guizot, Minister of Foreign Affairs of France, to Jacob L. Martin,
United States Chargé d'Affaires ad interim at Paris [1]

[TRANSLATION]

B   PARIS, *February 26, 1847.*

SIR: I have received with the document annexed to it, the letter which you did me the honor to write, to me, on the 11th instant,[2] relative to the arrival in the Port of Marseilles, of a Mexican agent, authorized, as it appears, to deliver letters of Marque against the United States.

You have relied Sir, on this occassion, with perfect justice, upon the sentiments of France towards the friendly power, which you represent.   I have submitted to the Minister of Marine, the communication which you addressed to me, but I did not, on that account, delay to act agreeably to your request.   Having been informed in the month of December last, of the issue of letters of Marque and certificates of naturalization, by the Mexican Government, I had immediately made known the fact to Admiral de

---

[1] Despatches, France, vol. 30; enclosure with Martin to the Secretary of State, No. 11, February 28, 1847, below, this part, doc. 2582.

[2] Above, this part, doc. 2580.   The document annexed to it is not included in this publication, since its purport is adequately reviewed in Martin's note to Guizot.

Mackau, in order that he might[1] proper measures, as far as possible, to prevent our sea men, from contracting any engagement of this kind.

Receive Sir, the assurance [etc.].

2582

Jacob L. Martin, United States Chargé d'Affaires ad interim at Paris, to James Buchanan, Secretary of State of the United States [2]

[EXTRACTS]

No. 11   PARIS, *February 28, 1847.*

SIR: . . . Some time ago I received a letter from our Consul at Marseilles, in reply to my circular, informing me that a Mexican agent had arrived in that port, authorized to deliver letters of marque against the United States, but stating that he did not think he was likely to succeed in disposing of any. I immediately waited upon Mr Guizot who expressed his regret and surprise at the circumstance, and desired me as he was compelled to go immediately to the Chamber, to confer freely upon the subject with Mr Desages, a person high in the Department, who enjoys his entire confidence. This gentleman informed me that effective instructions had already been given to enforce the neutrality of France, and expressed his conviction that everything would be cheerfully done, to accomplish that object. I explained to him our legislation upon this subject, and stated to him that as the issuing of letters of marque in the United States, against the commerce of a friendly power was a highly penal offence, we should expect a similar protection of American interests in France. He assured me that everything practicable would be done, and desired me to furnish him with an abstract of our legislation in relation to this question which I did, and it will be found appended to a letter which I addressed to the Minister of Foreign Affairs, a copy of which (A) I have the honor to transmit.[3] Since then I have obtained satisfactory assurances, that what I requested has been done, and after commencing this despatch I received from Mr Guizot an acknowledgement of my communication a copy of which (B.) I also transmit.[4] Joined to the verbal assurances of the government, I have but little apprehension, that Mexican agents will be able to effect anything in this country against the commerce of the United States, in which impression I am confirmed by the circumstance that I have heard nothing more from Mr Crosall, while our

[1] Obviously, the word "take" has been omitted in this translation. In the French copy of this note, it appears as follows: "afin qu'il pût prendre les mésures convenables."

[2] Despatches, France, vol. 30.   Received March 23.

The omitted portion discusses European political affairs.

[3] Above, this part, February 11, 1847, doc. 2580.   The appended document is not included in this publication. Its purport is adequately reviewed in Martin's note to the French Foreign Minister.   [4] Above, this part, February 26, 1847, doc. 2581.

consuls in the other ports of France have remained entirely silent.   The Department may rest assured that I shall not fail to keep a vigilant eye upon such proceedings.[1] . . .

I have had some conversation with Lord Howden, the newly appointed British Minister to Brazil and La Plata.   He goes out, I feel pretty sure, with instructions to terminate the intervention in La Plata, upon conditions substantially those proposed by Mr Hood, which were frustrated by the opposition or obstinacy of the French and English Ministers.

I have the honor [etc.].

2583

*Alphonse Pageot, French Minister to the United States, to James Buchanan,
Secretary of State of the United States* [2]

Informal.   WASHINGTON, *April 30, 1847.*

At the time that Commodore Sloat, Commander of the Naval forces of the United States in the Pacific, took possession of California, in consequence of the hostilities that had broken out between Mexico & the United States, the Acting Consul of France at Monterey, Mr *Gasquet*, thought proper to protest against this act of Commodore Sloat.   A correspondence, of an unpleasant character between the Commodore & the acting Consul, sprung out of this protestation.

A short time after, Commodore Stockton superseded Commodore Sloat, in the command of the American Naval forces in the Pacific; the correspondence between his Predecessor & the Acting Consul was submitted to him, & he immediately wrote to the latter that, in consequence of the insolent language he had used towards Commodore Sloat, he ceased to recognize him as the Representative of the French Government & ordered him to leave the city, in 24 hours, under penalty of being arrested & imprisoned.   On the refusal of the acting Consul to comply with this injunction, the Commodore assigned to him his own house as a prison, wherein he remained the space of 50 days, at the end of which he was released.

Simultaneously to this occurrence, a french Citizen, by the name of *Cambuston* was arrested by order of the American Commander, on the charge of being engaged with the ennemy, against the authority of the United States.   He was taken on board the frigate *Savannah*, and after a preliminary examination, was delivered over to the Alcade of Monterey, who sentenced him to a fine of 20 dollars.

Another french subject, by the name of *Olivier* who kept a Grocery store, where spirituous liquors were found, was subjected to the seizure & destruction of these liquors, on the ground that a recent police regulation had pro-

---

[1] The omitted portion relates to a commercial convention.
[2] Notes from France, vol. 13.   Received June 25.

hibited their sale. On his proving that he had not offered any for sale, since the publication of the regulation, the Commodore promised him an indemnity, for his loss, but refused to pay it over to him, unless he came, in person, on board of the Savannah, to receive it.

2584

Jacob L. Martin, United States Chargé d'Affaires ad interim at Paris, to James Buchanan, Secretary of State of the United States [1]

[EXTRACT]

No. 13   PARIS, *May 15, 1847.*

SIR: The news from Mexico cheered every American heart, and confounded the predictions of the European revilers of our country. The vigor of our policy and the extraordinary success of our arms have exalted the national character and astounded those who asserted that our institutions and habits were not adapted to military emergencies. With whatever feeling European governments contemplate our triumphs, and there is good reason to believe that it is not a very favorable one, they do not seem disposed to interfere with them, and were they so inclined, their distresses and perplexities would not permit it.

I regret to be obliged to inform you that information has been received that a Mexican vessel of war, the Unico, forty days from Vera Cruz, Capt. D. Laurenzo Sisa, armed with one gun and thirty three men, captured in the waters of Ivica, and carried into Barcelona on the 2^{d} May the American brig or schooner "Carmelita," Capt. Edwin, forty days from Ponce, laden with coffee for Trieste. I have no doubt, if the information be correct, that our Minister at Madrid, will take such steps with the Spanish government, as the case demands. I immediately wrote to the Navy Agent at Marseilles and the American Consul at Gibraltar requesting them to give the earliest possible intelligence of the fact to the most accessible of our ships of war either in the Mediterranean or on the African station. I have no means of knowing the present position of our naval forces on those stations and indeed I have been informed by a merchant from Marseilles that we have none left, within the straits of Gibraltar, a circumstance which I can hardly credit.

The Mexican Consul at Havre has protested against the measure we have adopted of establishing an American tariff in the ports of Mexico, and warns merchants that if they take advantage of it, they will ultimately be obliged to indemnify his government. The French papers maintain that the American government is bound to protect foreign merchants from these consequences, and call upon their government to obtain guarantees to that effect.—As we

[1] Despatches, France, vol. 30. Received June 5.

have an undoubted right to exclude commerce altogether, to permit intercourse at all is purely ex gratia, and at the risk of those who avail themselves
of the privilege. I do not hesitate, however, to express the opinion that the
equity of our government will in a treaty of peace provide for the protection
of the interests which its policy has invited. Perhaps the announcement
of such an intention would be judicious, as it would encourage foreign commerce to avail itself of the new regulations.

Some time ago I was informed by a person whom I suppose to be a Carlist
officer, that since the failure of the contemplated expedition of the Count de
Montemolin, the Mexican minister or consul in London, had engaged about
a hundred Carlist officers to enter the Mexican service. The same information has also reached me through another channel. The terms on which
they are engaged, are a free passage, ten pounds bounty, naturalization and
certain boons upon arriving in Mexico, and a further inducement was held
out that the course of events in that country might finally enure to the benefit of a prince of their party. My informant who represented himself as their
friend, assured me that his only motive in giving me the information was the
hope that I might be able to take steps to prevent them from engaging in a
service that must end in disappointment if not destruction to these deluded
men. As they were to embark from the 10th. to the 15th. inst. at different ports
with Mexican passports, it was impossible to prevent them from going if they
have not been deterred by the recent news from Mexico. I subjoin a list of
their names as furnished to me.[1] . . .

I have the honor [etc.].

2585

*Jacob L. Martin, United States Chargé d'Affaires ad interim at Paris, to
James Buchanan, Secretary of State of the United States* [2]

[EXTRACT]

No. 14   PARIS, *May 31, 1847.*

SIR: The topic of greatest interest when I last had the honor to address
you,[3] was the reported capture of an American vessel in the Mediterranean
by a Mexican Ship of war. The rumor proved, in the main, correct but the
captor turned out to be a privateer with a crew of Spanish desperadoes.
She has been detained by the Spanish authorities in Barcelona, and the crew
are to be tried for a violation of the Treaty between Spain and the United
States. I do not enter into more details because all the circumstances, are
minutely recapitulated in a despatch from the Chargé d'Affaires *ad interim*

---

[1] The omitted portion relates to French political affairs.
[2] Despatches, France, vol. 30.   Received July 6.
[3] His No. 13, above, this part, May 15, 1847, doc. 2584.

in Madrid, which will reach the Department by the same conveyance that carries this letter. The alarm excited in commercial circles by this incident has almost entirely subsided, especially as nothing has been heard of the other vessels which it was rumored, had been fitted out for the same purpose. These, if there was any foundation for the rumor, have probably been discouraged by the ill-success of the "Unico."

From a note just received from the American Consul at Algiers, written in Cadiz, there is good reason to believe that the abortive cruiser was fitted out at Oran, in Algeria, which is within French jurisdiction. I have no cause to doubt the repeated assurances of the French government, that no hostile proceedings against the commerce of the United States, would be tolerated in its ports, and I am persuaded that the authorities were ignorant of this criminal attempt. Nevertheless, I feel it my duty promptly to call the attention of the French government to this audacious violation of its neutrality, and to insist upon the exertion of an effective vigilance throughout all its borders. Good intentions are nothing without corresponding efficient action.[1] . . .

I have the honor [etc.].

2586

Jacob L. Martin, United States Chargé d'Affaires ad interim at Paris, to James Buchanan, Secretary of State of the United States [2]

[EXTRACT]

No. 15 PARIS, *June 16, 1847*.

SIR: As soon as I received information that the Mexican privateer the "Unico" had been fitted out at Oran in Algeria I called the attention of Mr Guizot to the circumstance, who expressed his surprise and regret, and assured me that the proper steps should at once be taken to prevent the recurrence of such criminal attempts. At his suggestion I addressed him the letter (A) [3] his reply to which, this instant received, informs me that as the measures required by the case, must proceed from the Department of the Marine, he had hastened to refer my communication to the Duke de Montebello. I do not doubt the entire good faith of the French government in this matter, and rely with confidence upon the assurance I have received that the proper steps will be cheerfully taken. All alarm upon the subject has disappeared, and I have no reason to believe that such criminal enterprizes will be renewed.[4] . . .

I have the honor [etc.].

[1] The omitted portion relates to the United States naval force in the Mediterranean, to the imprisonment of a citizen of the United States, and to European political affairs.

[2] Despatches, France, vol. 30. Received July 30.

[3] Neither this letter, nor the reply was found in the manuscript volume.

[4] The omitted portion reports the death of a consul.

2587

Richard Rush, United States Minister to France, to James Buchanan, Secretary of State of the United States [1]

[EXTRACT]

No. 9   PARIS, *December 10, 1847.*

SIR: . . . Mr. Martin has heard through a respectable channel, that Gustierez d'Estrado, the Mexican who published a pamphlet in favor of Monarchy in Mexico, is striving to recussitate [resuscitate?] that cause in Europe; that to this end he has been in intercourse with M. de Lutzou, the Austrian ambassador at Rome, where he failed; but that he has since had interviews with Lord Palmerston, who, it is said, will be passive under the project of making the duke of Montpensier king of Mexico, for *that*, it seems, is the great project held up to the king of the French; Gustierez d'Estrado alleging, in interviews he has had with the King, that he has received communications from distinguished persons in Mexico to the effect that the only refuge now left for their country, is in the monarchical principle supported by European power and means.

These rumors being afloat, I give them. The idea has been of twenty years standing and more, to raise up a throne in one and another of the Spanish American States, and stock it with blood royal from Europe. Time has been more and more showing its futility; and now that the seal seems to have been finally put to its utter hopelessness, in Mexico at least, by the triumphant progress and success of the arms of the United States, it comes forward again. If Louis Philippe can seriously entertain it though coming under the lure of parental partiality or ambition, the world might have to abate something of the wisdom it gives him credit for: nevertheless, there is probably no incumbant of any throne in Europe, who likes republicanism less than he does.[2] . . .

I have the honor [etc.].

[1] Despatches, France, vol. 31.
The omitted portion relates to an application made to the French Government for an ancient map of New Orleans.
Richard Rush, the writer of this despatch, of Pennsylvania, was commissioned envoy extraordinary and minister plenipotentiary to France, on March 3, 1847. He took leave on October 8, 1849. Prior to this, he had been commissioned, in October 1817, as envoy extraordinary and minister plenipotentiary to Great Britain. His commission was confirmed on December 16, 1817. Albert Gallatin, of Pennsylvania, envoy extraordinary and minister plenipotentiary to France, was associated with him, May 22, 1818, "to conclude treaties for the renewal of the convention of July 3, 1815, and for commerce." Mr. Rush took leave on April 27, 1825.
[2] The omitted portion relates to the termination of the war in Switzerland.

2588

Richard Rush, United States Minister to France, to James Buchanan, Secretary of State of the United States [1]

[EXTRACT]

No. 12   PARIS, *January 14, 1848.*

SIR: . . . The President's message was received here on the second of this Month. Our war with Mexico caused this document to be looked for with extraordinary interest this year, and its arrival did not disappoint expectation. If waited for with anxiety, its authentic statements of the successful progress and brilliant events of the war, coupled with its enlarged views of the belligerent policy of the United States, commanded deep attention and respect. The press spoke out emphatically in its favor as soon as it arrived. I account it still higher homage to have afterwards heard, as I did, deliberate testimonials to its wisdom energy and moderation from persons who stand among the very highest in this great capital in intellect, fame and rank; and whose impartial positions give intrinsic weight to their judgments. May I dare to add the solid satisfaction which, individually and officially, I experienced on finding that the doctrines of the message in regard to Mexico sustained, though far more cogently and broadly, some of those which I had ventured upon intimating beforehand in my conversations with the King, as likely to mark the policy of my government. . . .

I have the honor [etc.].

2589

Richard Rush, United States Minister to France, to Jules Bastide, Minister of Foreign Affairs of France [2]

PARIS, *July 20, 1848.*

The Undersigned, envoy extraordinary and Minister plenipotentiary of the United States, has the honor to bring to the notice of his Excellency the Minister of Foreign affairs of the French Republic, a case in which American interests have been affected by the French Naval forces in the River La Plata.

The case has been thus represented to the Undersigned:

That in the month of November last, Samuel B. Hale and John Langdon, citizens of the United States, then residing and doing business as merchants at Buenos Ayres, shipped on board the brig "Independentia Americana"

[1] Despatches, France, vol. 31. Received February 18.
The omitted portions of this despatch relate to French political affairs, and to other matters not pertinent to this publication.
[2] Despatches, France, vol. 31; enclosed with Rush to the Secretary of State, No. 45, July 29, 1848, below, this part, doc. 2590.

merchandise consisting of wool, sheepskins, and other articles, to the value of several thousand dollars. That the vessel was bound to Monte Video [Montevideo], and regularly cleared from the custom house at Buenos Ayres on or about the 26th of November. That on the 3rd of December, she was arrested and detained by the French brig of war Pandour, stationed in the outer Roads, off the port of Buenos Ayres, because of a doubt entertained by the commander of the French brig whether the vessel was bound to Monte Video or not. That the French Commander told the captain that if he would procure a certificate from the shippers that his vessel was bound to Monte Video, he would allow her to pass; and granted him permission to go ashore at Buenos Ayres for that purpose. That the Captain returned with such a certificate, in the form of a letter to the French commander from the shippers. That notwithstanding this evidence of the truth of her destination, the vessel was detained; on which the consignees of the cargo at Monte Video addressed a note of remonstrance to the French admiral in command on that station, requesting her release. That instead of acceding to this request, the admiral replied that the *Independentia* [*Independencia*] *Americana*, would be proceeded against with all strictness; and that, accordingly, she was condemned by a prize court created at Monte Video, and vessel and cargo sold, without the parties interested having had any opportunity to make their defence.

The before named American citizens who were in part shippers of the cargo, declare that their shipment was regular; that they had no intention of committing any infringement of the belligerent or blockading rights of the French government or any of its officers; that their papers were such as numerous other vessels had been furnished with, who were allowed to pass the French vessels of war off Buenos Ayres without molestation; and that they are at a loss to know why their property was condemned, unless, as they have heard, on account of conduct in the Captain disrespectful to the officers of the French squadron. If this were so, they state that they were ignorant of it, and would disapprove of it; but to whatever extent it may have gone, and however otherwise reprehensible, they cannot think that the justice of this government will allow its penalties to fall upon innocent shippers of the cargo.

In support of the foregoing statements, the Undersigned begs leave to enclose herewith the document Marked A, being the protests of the two American shippers taken at the American consulate, Buenos Ayres, on the 27th and 29th of December 1847; and the document marked B, being an official certificate of the consul,[1] of the number of vessels sailing under the

---

[1] The protests of the American shippers and the official certificate of the consul, dated January 5, 1848, follow:

    TO ALL TO WHOM THESE SHALL COME OR MAY CONCERN:

I, Joseph Graham, Consul of the United States of America for the Port of Buenos Ayres in South America, Send Greeting: Know Ye, that on the 27 day of December in

Footnote 1, p. 584—*Continued*

the year of our Lord one thousand eight hundred and forty seven appeared at this consulate, Samuel B. Hale a citizen of the United States of America residing in Buenos Ayres, and required me to note and extend his protest for the uses and purposes hereinafter mentioned and after having been by me, duly sworn according to law, avers and declares as follows, that is to say that in the month of November last he shipped on the Brig "Independencia Americana" whereof was Master Juan B. Repetto, thirty five bales containing Nine hundred and thirty six dozens Sheep Skins and eight bales containing eight thousand and eighty six pounds of wool, that the residue of the cargo of said brig consisting also of the produce of Buenos Ayres was shipped by English and other Foreign Merchants in Montevideo either to be sold there or reshipped, that the above mentioned 43 bales owned and shipped by him the said Hale were consigned to Messrs Zimmermann, Frazier & Co to be transhipp^d to the United States, that on or about the 26th day of November last the said Brig Independencia Americana with her cargo aboard was regularly cleared from the Custom house in Buenos Ayres and sailed for Monte Video with the first favorable wind thereafter, that on the 3^d day of December inst as the said brig was passing the French Vessels of War stationed in the outer roads of the Port of Buenos Ayres, she was boarded and captured by the officers and crew of the French brig Pandour—that on the 6th inst the said J. B. Repetto, Master of the said brig was permitted to come ashore at Buenos-Ayres, when he statted to the shippers, that the Commander of the said French Brig of War *Pandour*, said that he had detained the said Brig "Independencia Americana" because he doubted if she were really bound to Montevideo, and further said that if he the said Captain, would procure a certificate from the shippers, that the real destination of the said brig & Cargo was Montevideo, that then he would permit him the said Captain to pursue his voyage, with the said brig & Cargo, whereupon he the said Hale, together with the other shippers wrote and delivered to the said Master of the "Independencia Americana" a note of which the following is a true copy. viz

BUENOS AYRES, *December 6, 1847.*

To the Commander of the French Squadron in the Outer roads of Buenos Ayres.

DEAR SIR: The undersigned the freighters of the Brig "Independencia Americana" now laying in the outer roads, beg leave to say that the aforesaid Brig "Independencia Americana" has been loaded by us with a cargo of Pipes of Tallow, Bales of Wool & Sheep skins, Hides & Horns, with the intention of discharging or transhipping the same in the Port of Montevideo, and we have to ask that the aforesaid vessel, may be allowed to proceed to the Port of Montevideo without delay, in order to prevent any extra risks of the river navigation, and prevent demurrage on Freight engaged in Montevideo of the aforesaid cargo, and are respectfully

Your obt servts

(Signed)   ROBERT BARBOUR
"   SAMUEL B. HALE.
         GEORGE BELL
         JOHN LANGDON

The said Hale further states that the said Master of the Brig "Independencia Americana" returned aboard immediatly carrying with him the said letter, he further states that he received a letter from his consignees in Montevideo (Mess. Zimmermann Frazier & Co) with date of the 17th inst informing him that the said brig with her cargo had been detained, by the Officers of the French Squadron, and taken into the harbour of Montevideo, but that they the said consignees, felt confident she would be released. He further states that this day he received another letter from his said Consignees, with date of 22^d Inst. informing him that they, together with the other consignees of the Cargo of the said Brig, seeing there was delay in releasing said Cargo addressed a joint and respectful note to the French Admiral Commanding that station [Not found.—Ed.], requesting that the said Cargo might be released, to which they received a reply of which the following [is?] a copy.

Footnote 1, p. 584—*Continued*

> *Rear Admiral F. Le Predour, French Commander in Chief of the Brazil and La Plata stations, to Messrs. Henry A. Green, Zimmermann, Frazier & Co., Henrique [Enrique] Dowse, Merchants at Montevideo*

[TRANSLATION]

ROADSTEAD OF MONTEVIDEO, FRIGATE *La Charte, December 20, 1847.*

SIRS: I have received the letter which you did me the honor to write me [Not found.— Ed.] to request me to put again at your disposal the brig "Independencia Americana" seized by the French vessel blockading Buenos Ayres. I regret, gentlemen, that I cannot accede to the desire expressed in your letter, but the circumstances which gave rise to the seizure of the vessel which you claim are so serious, there was something so offensive in the conduct of your Buenos Ayres correspondent toward the officer commanding the blockade, that by all the means in my power, I shall exact exemplary justice in the case of the "Independencia Americana".

Please accept, Gentlemen, the assurance of my consideration.

That said consignees further inform him that on the 21st inst, they had been told a prize court had been convened and had condemned said brig Independencia Americana and her cargo, and they were advertised to be sold the 28th inst. He further states that no other letter or communication of any kind, was addressed by him, or as he is informed and believes, by any of the other shippers by said brig, to any Commander or officer of the French Navy or to any person connected therewith than the one herein copied dated the 6th of December 1847 [Above, in this footnote—Ed.] and addressed "to the Commander of the French Squadron in the outer roads of Buenos Ayres" and that said letter was not written or signed by him or any of the shippers, with the expectation or intention of exciting the *indignation* or *ire* of Admiral Predour [Le Predour] or of any other person connected with the French Navy or Government, and that said letter furnishes no just or tenable reason for the seizure and confiscation of his property, or for influencing the said Admiral to exact his powerful influence in Montevideo to have said Brig & Cargo condemned. He further states that he shipped his 43 bales in said Brig in the prosecution of his regular and legal business, without any intention of committing any infringement upon the Belligerent or Blockading rights of the French Government, or any of its officers, that the shipment was made in a vessel with [the?] same kind of papers and under the same circumstances with numerous others, which pass daily and nightly in full view of the French vessels of War stationed off Buenos Ayres, without being hindered or molested, that during and ever since the month of June last, the French vessels *said* to be blockading the Port of Buenos Ayres, have not prevented or *pretended* to attempt to prevent their free entry, and departure at Buenos Ayres of vessels to and from Montevideo, especially when it was known the cargo of said vessels had or would pay duties or charges in Montevideo, that hundreds, he believes thousands of vessels have passed monthly during the aforesaid months, and are still continuing to pass, with Cargoes to and from Montevideo, without any kind of attempt being made or pretended to be made to prevent them by the French or any other vessels of War off Buenos Ayres or at any other place. He further states that the said unjust and illegal seizure and confiscation of his aforesaid sheep skins & Wool, has damaged him to the amount of three thousand six hundred spanish dollars.—

(Signed) SAMUEL B. HALE.

WHEREFORE the said Samuel B. Hale on his own behalf and on the part and behalf of all others interested in said Sheepskins & Wool or anything connected therewith hath protested, and I the said Consul at the request of the said Hale, do hereby solemnly, PROTEST against the Officers Commanding the French Vessels of War off Buenos Ayres at the time of the seizure, against Admiral Predour, against the so called prize Court at Montevideo, against the French Government, and the King of the French, and against all persons, officers, or Governments, whomsoever or whatso[e]ver in any way or manner connected with or taking part in the aforesaid seizure, condemnation and confiscation of the aforesaid property for all losses, damages or detriments of whatsoever nature, which the said Samuel B. Hale, or any other person interested therein, may have sustained or may hereafter sustain in consequence. Thus done and Protested this 27th day of December in the year of our Lord One thousand eight hundred and forty seven.

(Signed) JOS. GRAHAM
U. S. Consul

Footnote 1, p. 584—*Continued*

I, Joseph Graham, Consul of the United States of America for the Port of Buenos Ayres, DO FURTHER CERTIFY, that on the 29th of December 1847 also appeared at this Consulate John Langdon a citizen of the United States of America, residing in Buenos Ayres and required me to note and extend his protest and after being by me duly sworn according to law, solemnly avers and declares that in the month of November last he shipped on board the brig "Independencia Americana" mentioned in the foregoing protest of Samuel B. Hale, eleven thousand five hundred and eighty four prime bullock horns, which were consigned to Henry Dowse, Merchant of Montevideo to be sold there or transhipped, and after having carefully read the foregoing protest of said Hale, he avers and declares that his said horns, were shipped at the same time and under the same circumstances with the bales mentioned in the foregoing protest, were seized condemned and confiscated, at the same time, in the same way and under the same circumstances, with the said bales of the said Hale, and further that he is cognizant of all the circumstances, in said foregoing protest and knows them to be true and that he was damaged by the said seizure and confiscation of his said horns to the amount of seven hundred and fifty dollars.—

(Signed)   LANGDON.

WHEREFORE the said John Langdon on his own behalf and on the part and behalf of all others interested in the said Horns, hath Protested, and I the said Consul at the request of the said John Langdon do hereby protest against all persons, officers, Courts and Governments, named in the said foregoing protest, in the same manner and form as is done therein, for all losses, damages or detriments of whatsoever nature, which the said John Langdon or any other person interested therein, may have sustained or may hereafter sustain in consequence of the seizure, condemnation and confiscation of the aforesaid Horns, thus done and protested this 29th day of December, 1847.

(Signed)   JOS. GRAHAM.
U. S. Consul

CONSULATE OF THE UNITED STATES OF AMERICA, BUENOS AYRES.

I, Joseph Graham, Consul of the United States of America, for the Port of Buenos Ayres, DO HEREBY CERTIFY that the foregoing is a true copy of the protests of Samuel B. Hale and John Langdon Citizens of the United States of America residing in Buenos Ayres, as extended signed and recorded in this Consulate.

In witness whereof I have here unto set my hand and official seal this 30th day of December 1847.

(Signed)   JOS. GRAHAM.
U. S. Consul

CONSULATE OF THE UNITED STATES OF AMERICA,

BUENOS AYRES, *January 5, 1848.*

I, Joseph Graham, Consul of the United States of America for the port of Buenos Ayres —DO HEREBY CERTIFY, that according to the official report of the Captain of this port, the which in my opinion is worthy of full credence, there have entered, since the first of June last, at this port and others adjacent in this Province, chiefly at this Port, Two thousand one hundred and forty five "*National*" vessels, and one hundred and forty one Foreign vessels—there have cleared and sailed during same time, chiefly from here, Two thousand five hundred and sixteen (2516) "*National*" and seventy one foreign vessels, up to the first of Jany 1848. Of these vessels, some have been stopped, when passing the French vessels of war claiming to blockade this Province, but all, with one single exception, have been permitted to proceed on their voyage with their cargoes. The Brig "Independencia Americana" was captured about the third of December last on her voyage from this Port to Monte Video, and afterwards taken to Monte Video by officers of the French navy, and with her cargo was there condemned and sold, as a prize. The "Independencia Americana" belonged to that class of vessels called "National" and sailed with same kind of papers as the others—her cargo consisted of the produce of this country—part of which belonged to Citizens of the United States.

I FURTHER CERTIFY that since the 1st of June last, up to the first of this year, there has been shipped from this Port and Enderado, chiefly from this Port, to the United States direct or to be reshipped at Monte Video for the U. S., produce of this country, to the value of about three hundred and seven thousand, nine hundred and fifty ($307.950) Spanish dollars, estimated at prime cost here, and that none of this property

same circumstances as the *Independentia* [*Independencia*] *Americana*, that
had been allowed to pass the French blockading squadron.   The latter
document will also show the amount of exports to the United States from
Buenos Ayres during a period of six months.   Those exports were shipped
first to Monte Video, and thence transshipped to the United States, not for
any advantage to the American shippers, but the contrary; the object being
that the goods might be made to pay duties at Monte Video to the anomalous
government in that place.

In corroboration of this, the Undersigned also encloses an extract of a
communication from the Chargé d'affaires of the United States at Buenos
Ayres, dated the 9th of March,[1] in which he describes the nature and irregu-

---

Footnote 1, p. 584—*Continued*

has been captured by the French except that aboard the said "Independencia
Americana."

In witness whereof I have hereunto set my hand and official seal at Buenos Ayres, this
5th January 1848.

(Signed)   JOS. GRAHAM.
U. S. Consul

[1] It follows:

*William A. Harris, United States Chargé d'Affaires at Buenos Aires, to Richard Rush,
United States Minister to France*

[EXTRACT]

BUENOS AYRES, *March 9, 1848.*

Mr Samuel B. Hale, whose papers for a reclamation on the government of France,
will come into your hands with this note, is a gentleman of the highest integrity and
respectability.   He is a citizen of the United States, residing in this city, and carrying
on business extensively as a merchant.   He, with others of our countrymen, as well
as all foreigners, has unfortunately suffered much, by the long deranged and extraordinary state of things in the River Plate.   And he, with M[r] Langdon, another of our
fellow citizens, is now seeking a restitution of the amount of property recently taken
by the French in the prosecution of their *quasi* blockade of this port, and taken to
Monte Video and sold under the judicial order of a nominal prize court.

By the long established usages in relation to blockade, and by the well known principles of the law of nations, which have by the common consent of mankind, become
the rule by which the conduct of each has been regulated and controlled, the greater
part of these proceedings, by the English and French—and lately especially by the
French—must be held, upon strict scrutiny, to be illegal and unwarrantable.   It has
not been the lawful exercise of a belligerent right, to coerce a stubborn party to speedy
terms, and in which neutrals would be bound to acquiesce, but it is a measure, which,
as Lord Howden himself—with a perfect knowledge of all the facts—officially declared,
had "entirely lost its original character of a coercive measure against General Rosas,
and had become *exclusively* a mode of supplying with money, partly the government of
Montevideo, and partly certain foreign individuals there"; and, with this view of the
subject, he ordered the English forces to be withdrawn from all further participation in
it.   This act of itself, as well as the reasons upon which it was founded, changed the
character and nature of the blockade.   In fact, in every just legal sense, it annulled it
entirely.   The measure originally, was a *joint* proceeding, by the parties to it; mutually
and jointly declared, and conjointly and equally proceeded in; and, when one party,
in effect, declared it *unlawful,* and withdrew from it, it was in all legal acceptation, an
abrogation of the entire measure.   The mere unauthorized declaration of a French
Chargé d'Affaires and Consul General, that it would be continued as originally established, was not the usual or legal mode of establishing a proper blockade, but was only
a renewal of the original outrage, in a more exceptionable form.   So conscious, indeed,
seemed the parties themselves, of the unjustifiable character of this last measure, that
for a long time, there was only one small French vessel of war, stationed off this port,

larity of the blockade in the River Plate [Plata]; and it is known to the Undersigned how injurious has been its operation upon the neutral commerce of the United States.   He makes this communication one of the enclosures of this note, as further explanatory of the condemnation complained of; the chargé d'affaires testifying also to the entire respectability of the characters of the two American citizens thus divested of their property.

If therefore the circumstances of this condemnation as herein set forth, shall be found correct, the Undersigned has the honor to request that the government of the Republic will be pleased to cause such retribution to be made to these two American citizens as justice demands.

And he prays the Minister of foreign affairs to accept the assurances of his high consideration.

---

and was the only solitary vessel, under the new declaration of the French, blockading a sea and river coast, of some five or six hundred leagues.

Soon after this, the Authorities in Monte Video, openly declared, by an official publication, that it was necessary to their support, and even to their existence as a government, that neutral commerce should be made to stop at Monte Video, and find its way to and from the ports of Buenos Ayres, in the small craft of the River.   These small vessels of the River, which brought goods to Montevideo, and carried thither the produce of this Province, were not only permitted, but were even encouraged by the French to pass freely, so long as it was known that they were contributing by the duties which they paid in Monte Video, to replenish its coffers and to fulfill the object of this extraordinary proceeding.   I should not omit to inform you, that vessels from beyond sea, bound to any of the ports of the River, were forced to stop at Monte Video; there was paid the usual enormous import duty upon their merchandize; upon this same merchandize, an export duty was paid, when it was shipped in small craft to Buenos Ayres, or to any other ports in the River; and an import and export duty, was in the same way, levied upon all the produce of the country, carried to Montevideo, and shipped from thence to ports beyond sea.   You will at once perceive the advantage to them, of this operation.   It was to make Montevideo the only port for the commerce of the world, for all this region of country; obliging that commerce, both foreign and domestic, to pay an enormous import and export duty, for the support of the anomalous government in Montevideo.   And, this same merchandize, which had been compelled to stop at Montevideo and pay an import and export duty there, had to pay the usual import duty here.   And the produce which was sent from this place, as a return cargo, had to pay the export duty here, and an import and export duty in Montevideo; so that a Merchant of this city, or of any other port of the confederation, had to pay *six* duties, upon an inward and outward cargo, instead of *two*.   Such has been the working of this system, upon the rights and interests of neutrals.

But, the whole blockade, as a measure, wrong and unjustifiable as it is, in its principles, its objects, and its management, yet derives an additional shade of enormity, from the caprice and uncertainty with which it is now carried on.   Some days it appears to be strict; at other times so lax, that scarcely any notice is taken of vessels entering or leaving the port.   Sometimes vessels are stopped for a short time, and then set at liberty; at other times, under exactly similar circumstances, they are detained and declared lawful prize.   And, even the absence of a refined manner, or the use of language by the captains or owners of vessels thus detained, construed as uncourteous by the French Commander, it is said, has, in one instance at least, been assigned as cause for condemning them to be sold as lawful prize.

I have made these observations, not for the purpose of giving you a full history of this unprecedented blockade, nor as an argument against its unjust and injurious effects upon ourselves and others, but simply to give you in a few words, some idea of its true character, and of the manner in which it is now conducted.

2590

Richard Rush, United States Minister to France, to James Buchanan, Secretary of State of the United States [1]

No. 45   PARIS, *July 29, 1848.*

SIR: Shortly before the late insurrection, I received a communication from two American citizens at Buenos Ayres, Samuel B. Hale and John Langdon, who are residing there as merchants, informing me that a vessel called the "Independencia Americana", in which they had shipped goods to Montevideo, was captured off Buenos Ayres by the French blockading squadron, and their property illegally condemned by a prize court at Montevideo in December last; and seeking redress, through me, from the French government.

I enclose a copy of their letter marked A. dated the 4ᵗʰ of March,[2] which in part makes known the circumstances of their case.   They also sent me their

[1] Despatches, France, vol. 31.   Received August 21.
[2] This note follows:

Samuel B. Hale and John Langdon, United States citizens, merchants in Buenos Aires, to Richard Rush, United States Minister to France

BUENOS AIRES, *March 4, 1848.*

SIR: We the undersigned citizens of the U. S. residing in this city beg leave respectfully to call your attention to a just claim, we consider we have, on the Government of France, for the illegal seizure of our property in front of this port, by the French naval forces off here.

Enclosed we hand the Protest & other documents relating to this affair [See above, this part, p. 584, footnote 1.—Ed.], for your attentive perusal; and then, we are convinced, you will concur with us, as well as the U. S. authorities here, that the French Government ought, & must in justice refund to us our property.   We say this with due respect to the King of France, and his Government; & the facts too notorious to be questioned, will bear us out in our demands for justice.   We can safely state that there are not in this city two individuals, who have respected more the orders of the French Admirals in this river during the time they have been at variance with the Government of Buenos Ayres than us.   After witnessing day and night fleets of 40 & 50 sail, sailing in & out in view of the French forces off here, who have tacitly allowed it because it was too notorious to pretend to be ignorant of it; we finally shipped our goods on board the Brig "*Independencia Americana*" bound to Montevideo where the goods were to be reshipped for the United States.   The "*Independencia Americana*" had the same papers & same flag of the numerous Vessels running in & out dayly, and therefore our property, the property of two American citizens, ought to have been allowed to pass unmolested, as well as the property of Brazilians, French, Italians, Spaniards, English &c which passes daily.   Why make an exception & seize our property & make us sufferers, who are the friends of France; and allow property belonging to the citizens of Buenos Ayres, with whom France is at variance, to pass for so long a time unmolested.

On the application of Commandant Tilton of the U. S. Brig "Perry" who was then at Montevideo, when the vessel was taken; & later of Commodore Storer of U. S. Ship "Brandywine" the French Admiral LePredour stated, that it was too late for him to act, because the prize court which he had created at Montevideo, had condemned and sold the property; and the case had been remitted to the French Government; and besides that the Captain of the "Independencia Americana" was disrespectful and even insolent to the French Officers commanding the forces off this Port at the time of seizure.   Now we beg leave to do away with the reasons above alledged as causes why our property was not immediately restored to us.

First, We ask what right has a Prize Court in Montevideo to judge our case, & condemn our property, without allowing us to defend our cause & plead our case?—

protest made on the 29th of December before the consul of the United States at Buenos Ayres, in which the circumstances are all set forth in more detail. I transmit a copy of it marked B; together with the copy of an official certificate, marked C, from the consul, containing some further explanatory particulars.[1]

In addition to these documents, I received at the same time a note from Mr. Harris, our chargé d'affaires at Buenos Ayres, dated the 9th of March,[2] which not only assured me of the respectable characters of these citizens of the United States, but also embraced valuable remarks, presented with clearness and force, on the irregular nature of the blockade.

On considering all the circumstances of this capture as they were thus laid before me, I determined, regarding as I did the condemnation to be unwarrantable, to address an official note to this government, though necessarily without your instructions, asking the redress which justice seemed to demand. Before I could act, the insurrection broke out, which stopped business and overset the late Executive government; and for nearly a month afterwards, as seen by my number 42,[3] there was no reinstatement in the foreign office, of a permanent or known minister. On the day after Mr. Bastide's re-appointment was officially announced, viz, the 20th of this month, I drew up and sent to him a note, of which a copy is enclosed marked D;[4] and to which I beg leave to refer as embracing a synopsis of the case. Be-

---

Secondly, are we to be marked out as victims, because an illbred insolent Captain offended the French Commander?—We in this letter publicly disapprove in the most positive manner, the highly improper conduct of the Captain, of whose character we are completely ignorant; all our business having been transacted with the owner of said vessel.

Will the U. S. Government & people, allow the property of their poorest citizen to be illegally & unjustly seized, tried and condemned, and sold by French Naval Officers far from France, where the party agreaved had no hearing, nor hope of justice being done him?

Will the United States allow property of their citizens to be wrested from them when the property of other countries, weak and insignificant compared with them, is allowed to be conveyed freely from port to port.

We are morally convinced that before the enlightened and upright Tribunal in France, where this our case will be brought by you, that justice will be done us without delay. To save expenses and trouble, it would be preferable, if you could in your official capacity recover our property from the French Government.—We subscribe ourselves resp[y] [etc.].

N. B. In case you should be obliged to carry our Claim before the competent French Court please inform us that we may send our power of Attorney to you, or such agent as you may recommend to us. This letter with the documents accompanying it will be handed to you by S[or] D[n] Juan Martin Puyrredon who is authorized by us to pay any expenses necessary to the recovery of our property.

(Signed) SAMUEL B. HALE.
JOHN LANGDON.

[1] For Hale's protest, dated December 27, Langdon's protest, dated December 29, 1847, and the official certificate from the consul, dated January 5, 1848, see above, this part, p. 584, note 1.
[2] Only an extract of this note was found in the manuscript volume. It is above, this part, p. 588, note 1.
[3] Not included in this publication.   [4] Above, this part, July 20, 1848, doc. 2589.

sides the other documents, I accompanied it with an extract from Mr. Harris's note, a copy of which I transmit, marked E.[1] I will take care to inform you of Mr. Bastide's answer as soon as I may receive it, and in the meantime, unless you instruct me otherwise, will not overlook the case.

I have the honor [etc.].

2591

Jules Bastide, Minister of Foreign Affairs of France, to Richard Rush, United States Minister to France [2]

[TRANSLATION]

PARIS, *August 28, 1848.*

SIR: You did me the honor to address a note to me, under date of July 20 last,[3] relative to the seizure, in the Plata, by the French brig-of-war *le Pandour* and for violation of the blockade of Buenos Ayres, of the merchant vessel the *Independentia [Independencia] Americana*, having on board some merchandise belonging to Messrs. Hale and J. Langdon, American merchants established in that city. It appears from this note and from the documents accompanying it that the *Independentia [Independencia] Americana* was subsequently condemned by the prize court at Montevideo, and sold.

I am requesting the Minister of Marine to transmit to me any information he may possess on this matter, and I am urging him, in case no report has yet reached his department, to be so good as immediately to request explanations of the Rear Admiral commanding the station of the Plata. In addition, I must point out to you at this time, that the way of recourse to the Council of State against the decision of the Montevideo prize court is open to the interested parties.

Please accept, Sir, [etc.].

2592

Richard Rush, United States Minister to France, to James Buchanan, Secretary of State of the United States [4]

[EXTRACT]

No. 49   PARIS, *August 30, 1848.*

SIR: Referring to my number 45,[5] respecting the capture of the "Independentia Americana," by the French blockading squadron off Buenos

---

[1] Above, this part, March 9, 1848, p. 588, note 1.
[2] Despatches, France, vol. 31; enclosed with Rush to the Secretary of State, No. 49, August 30, 1848, below, this part, doc. 2592.   [3] Above, this part, doc. 2589.
[4] Despatches, France, vol. 31.   Received October 2.
The brief omitted portion of this despatch relates to the exchange of articles of military equipment between the French and the United States departments of war.
[5] Above, this part, July 29, 1848, doc. 2590.

Ayres, I have now the honor to enclose the copy of a first reply dated the 28th instant,[1] which I have received from the Minister of Foreign Affairs upon that subject. . . .

I have the honor [etc.].

2593

Jules Bastide, Minister of Foreign Affairs of France, to Richard Rush, United States Minister to France [2]

[TRANSLATION]

PARIS, *September 8, 1848.*

SIR: Your Government was duly informed of the blockade of Buenos Ayres established September 24, 1845,[3] by the combined naval forces of France and England. I have the honor to announce to you that this blockade, in which the English forces had last year ceased to participate, was lifted by the French naval forces during the month of June last, but that the latter have maintained the blockade of the parts of the coast of the Eastern territory occupied by the troops under the command of General Oribe.

I beg you, Sir, to be so good as to bring this information to the knowledge of your Government.

Accept, Sir, [etc.].

2594

Richard Rush, United States Minister to France, to Jules Bastide, Minister of Foreign Affairs of France [4]

PARIS, *September 12, 1848.*

SIR: I have the honor to acknowledge the receipt of your Excellency's note of the 8th instant,[5] informing me that the blockade of Buenos Ayres established the 24th of September 1845 by the combined naval forces of France and England, but in which the English forces ceased to cooperate last year, was raised in the month of June by the French forces; but that the latter maintained the blockade of the parts of the coast of the Oriental territory, occupied by the troops under the orders of General Oribe.

I will not fail to communicate this information to my government. It will be received with satisfaction I am sure; a satisfaction which I beg leave to say would but have been increased had the blockade been given up entirely.

I pray you, Sir, to receive [etc.].

[1] Above, this part, doc. 2591. It is in answer to Rush's note to him, of July 20, 1848, above, this part, doc. 2589.
[2] Despatches, France, vol. 31; enclosed with Rush to the Secretary of State, No. 51, September 14, 1848, below, this part, doc. 2595.
[3] See above, this part, Guizot to King, January 21, 1846, doc. 2567.
[4] Despatches, France, vol. 31; enclosed with Rush to the Secretary of State, No. 51, September 14, 1848, below, this part, doc. 2595.   [5] Above, this part, doc. 2593.

2595

Richard Rush, United States Minister to France, to James Buchanan, Secretary of State of the United States [1]

No. 51   PARIS, *September 14, 1848.*

SIR: The day after my number 50,[2] I received from Mr. Bastide a note of which I enclose a copy,[3] giving me official information of the fact, already generally known, viz., that the blockade of Buenos Ayres, established in September 1845 by France and England, but from which England withdrew last year, has at last been given up by France also. I have lost no opportunity since being here, of raising my voice against this blockade, as injurious to neutral commerce; and in my answer to Mr Bastide, of which a copy is also enclosed,[4] whilst assuring him that his communication would be received with satisfaction by my government, I let him understand that it would have been more complete if it had informed me that the whole blockade in those waters had ceased; for it will be seen by his note that it is still maintained on the parts of the coast of the Oriental territory occupied by the troops of General Oribe.

I have the honor [etc.].

2596

Drouyn de Lhuys, Minister of Foreign Affairs of France, to Richard Rush, United States Minister to France [5]

[TRANSLATION]

PARIS, *March 1, 1849.*

SIR: My predecessor had the honour to inform you on the 28 of august last,[6] that he had asked from the Department of the Marine, for information respecting the capture, off Buenos Ayres, of a ship called the *Independencia Americana*, of which he had spoken to you, in his [of which you had apprized him by a] note of the 20th of July previous.[7]

The Minister of Marine has just communicated to me a report of the Prize Commission, in which are expressed the reasons for the seizure of the vessel in question. I have the honour to send you herewith, a copy of this docu-

---

[1] Despatches, France, vol. 31. Received October 6.
[2] He probably intended to say, "the day after I wrote my despatch No. 50." It is not pertinent to this publication.
[3] Above, this part, September 8, 1848, doc. 2593.
[4] *Ibid.*, September 12, 1848, doc. 2594.
[5] Despatches, France, vol. 31; enclosed with Rush to the Secretary of State, No. 79, March 9, 1849, below, this part, doc. 2597.
[6] Above, this part, doc. 2591.
[7] Above, this part, doc. 2589, is Rush's note of this date. The copy in French in the manuscript volume of the above sentence reads, "dont vous l'aviez entretenu par une note," etc., and this is obviously a faulty translation of it.

ment,[1] presenting the circumstances in a manner entirely different from that in which they are viewed, in the papers accompanying your note.[2]

The Minister of the Marine moreover informs me, that the proceedings in this case, have been submitted on the 14th of November last, to the Council of State, which will decide upon the validity of the claims connected with it.

Accept, Sir, [etc.].

[1] A translation of this document follows:

Report of the French Prize Commission of the La Plata River regarding the Seizure of the Brig Independencia Americana

[TRANSLATION]

MONTEVIDEO, *December 20, 1847.*

The Prize Commission instituted, agreeably to the Decree of 6 Germinal of the year VIII, and by Consular Ordinance of November 6th last.

Having considered the *procès verbal* of the seizure of the brig *Independencia Americana,* under the Argentine flag, drawn up on board of the French brig *Pandour,* under date of the 11th of this month of December, and the annexed documents [Not found.], as well as the preparatory instructions in virtue of the said decree.

Considering that it is shown by these documents, that on the 3rd instant, the brig *Independencia Americana,* leaving Buenos Ayres under the Argentine flag, while that port was blockaded, for Rio Grande, has been seized by the French cruisers, and brought under the guns of the brig *Pandour;* that the commander of the latter vessel enjoined upon the Captain of the *Independencia Americana,* under pain of seizure, to carry her back to Buenos Ayres, from his desire to accord to her the toleration, granted to other vessels under similar circumstances, and that the Captain had refused to obey this injunction, alleging that he had received orders from his owners, not to go back, in case he should be required to do so by the cruisers;

Considering that, although from this fact alone, he had placed his vessel under liability of seizure, he had asked and obtained leave from the Commandant of the *Pandour* to go on shore in order to receive new instructions from his owners, and to justify himself with regard to them, and that on his return, he persisted, after their formal and repeated orders, in his refusal to carry the brig *Independencia Americana,* back to Buenos Ayres, offering to the cruisers no other alternatives than those of allowing him to continue his voyage freely, or of carrying him under escort, to Montevideo, the place for which he declared himself bound, a refusal which afforded grounds for the definitive seizure of the said vessel, on the 11th instant.

Seeing moreover from all these acts and documents, that the Captain of the *Independencia Americana,* has knowingly placed himself in the attitude of a violator of the blockade, with intention and resistance, aggravating his culpability.

Seeing that, on the other hand, according to the terms of the declaration of blockade of the Argentine coasts, the delay allowed for the departure of the vessels which were then lying in the blockaded ports, has long since expired.

From these motives and reasons, the Commission is of opinion, that the brig *Independencia Americana,* seized under the Argentine flag, and her cargo, are and ought to be considered as good prize.

Thus decided by the members of the Commission, on the days, month, and year above stated.

A true copy.

A. DEVOIZE.

(Signed)   A. SOULÉ.   J. CHARRY-JUNᵗ

[2] See above, this part, p. 584, note 1 and p. 588, note 1.

2597

Richard Rush, United States Minister to France, to James Buchanan, Secretary of State of the United States [1]

No. 79   PARIS, *March 9, 1849.*

SIR: On the 20th of last July I addressed a note to the Minister of Foreign Affairs a copy of which was transmitted with my number 45,[2] on the capture of the vessel called the "Independentia [Independencia] Americana" by the French blockading squadron off Buenos Ayres, and the condemnation by a prize court at Monte Video of certain property on board belonging to American citizens. My note alledged the illegality of the capture, and made application for the proper redress.

The first answer from the Minister was chiefly in the nature of a general acknowledgment of my note. It was dated the 28th of August, and a copy sent to the department with my number 49.[3]

With my number 51, of the 14th of September, was enclosed the copy of a note from the same Minister of Foreign Affairs, then Mr. Bastide, dated the 8th of September,[4] officially communicating to me for the information of my government, the fact that the blockade of Buenos Ayres was raised in the month of June preceding by France (England having previously withdrawn from it entirely), except as to the parts of the Oriental territory occupied by the troops under the orders of General Oribe. A copy of my answer to this note was also enclosed.[5]

A few days ago I received a note from the present Minister of Foreign Affairs, Mr Drouyn de L'huys, dated the first instant, referring to my original note to Mr. Bastide of the 20th of July and Mr. Bastide's first answer to it on the 28th of August, and informing me that the Minister of Marine had just communicated to him the decision of the prize commission setting forth the motives which gave rise to the arrest of this vessel. I enclose a copy of the Minister's Note,[6] and also of the decision of this prize commission at Monte Video.[7] It will be seen by the latter document, that the whole proceeding and condemnation of the vessel and cargo, are assumed to be regular and justified.

Under my present lights, I do not view the grounds of the decision as satisfactory, but the contrary. But as I presented the case to the notice of this government without instructions, as intimated in my number 45,[8] and have heard nothing from the department on the subject since, I have deemed

---

[1] Despatches, France, vol. 31. Received April 9.
Although this despatch of March 9, 1849, was addressed to Buchanan as Secretary of State, he had retired on March 4 and had been succeeded on March 7 by Clayton.
[2] His despatch No. 45, dated July 29, 1848, and the enclosure referred to here, are above, this part, docs. 2589 and 2590.
[3] His despatch No. 49, dated August 30, 1848, and the accompanying enclosure, are above, this part, docs. 2591 and 2592.
[4] His despatch and the accompanying enclosure are above, this part, docs. 2593 and 2595.
[5] Above, this part, September 12, 1848, doc. 2594.   [6] *Ibid.*, March 1, 1849, doc. 2596.
[7] *Ibid.*, p. 595, note 1.   [8] *Ibid.*, July 29, 1848, doc. 2590.

it most judicious to pause at the present point in order that, if the Legation is to go on with the demand for redress, it may do so under a special instruction from the department, if thought proper to be given; which would carry more weight than when the Minister acts on his general power only.   This course will lead to but slight additional delay after the time already unavoidably gone by before this government, after receiving my first note, could get its own report from a place so distant as the seat of the capture and condemnation.   Perhaps also the department may now have information or views on the subject, of which the Legation is not in possession, yet fit to be imparted; and even should any thing exist of a nature to impair the case in any way, of which I may hitherto not have been aware, the Legation would thus have an opportunity of knowing it if within the knowledge of the department.   As to the intimation in Mr Bastide's note of the 28th of August, and in that of the present Minister of the first of this month, that redress is open to the parties by an application or appeal to the council of State in Paris, I regard it as little relevant, since, if the condemnation be unwarrantable, the government itself, whose armed forces committed the wrong, is responsible; and moreover the records of this Legation in the case of the Josephine, as reported to the department by Mr. Ledyard on the 20th of April 1844,[1] would show how inadequate is the redress which can alone be obtained from the council of state after one of these captures by the French squadron in La Plata, followed up by a condemnation there.

Furthermore.   I am under the belief, that the government of the United States protested, from the very beginning, against this extraordinary blockade in those waters by France and England; so near akin to the incipient movements of the former power at least, when, at a later period, she would have checked by her interference our national course under the plea of adjusting balances in a more northern part of the American Continent.   But there is no official evidence in this Legation of any such protest, and the Minister when going on with the case might find it advantageous to be able to assert and recall, authoritatively, this fact, if it be so, to the French government.

In conclusion I beg to state, that after receiving the note of the Minister of Foreign Affairs of the first instant, I thought it proper, before making you this communication, to ascertain with precision what was the actual state of this blockade at the present juncture; for the frequent change in its phases, has been but the natural result of its intrinsic irregularity and injustice. Accordingly, I applied in person to the Minister for information, who told me that it continues to rest upon the footing announced in Mr. Bastide's Note of the 8th of September last, communicated to the department in my dispatch N° 51, of the 14th of that Month.

I have the honor [etc.].

[1] He erroneously refers to Ledyard's despatch of April 30, 1844, above, this part, doc. 2550.

2598

*Richard Rush, United States Minister to France, to Drouyn de Lhuys, Minister
of Foreign Affairs of France* [1]

PARIS, *April 21, 1849.*

SIR: The note which your Excellency did me the honor to write to me on
the first of March relative to the case of the vessel Independencia Americana,
captured by the French blockading squadron off Buenos-Ayres in December
1847, I transmitted to my government by an early opportunity after its
receipt. [2]

But before receiving any answer, I hasten to lay before Your Excellency
the enclosed copy of a letter from the members of the prize commission at
Montevideo which I have received only recently, addressed to the Chargé
d'Affaires of France [3] simultaneously with the proceedings of the prize court
on the occasion in question. [4]   By this document it will be perceived that the
prize commissioners who adjudged the vessel and cargo, as lawful prize to
the French squadron, absolved, in effect, those most interested in both from
all blame; declaring also that they condemned the conduct of the Captain,
which alone had led to the capture.   Furthermore: that the Commissioners
did actually claim indulgence for the owners, from the vice admiral in command of the squadron, as well as from the tribunal called upon to revise the
decision of the court.

[1] Despatches, France, vol. 31; enclosed with Rush to the Secretary of State, No. 89, April
24, 1849, below, this part, doc. 2599.
[2] It was enclosed with his despatch No. 79 to the Secretary of State, dated March 9, 1849.
Both of these documents are above, this part, docs. 2596 and 2597.
[3] A translation of this letter follows:

*The members of the Prize Commission, appointed to adjudicate on the seizure of the Brig
Independencia Americana, to A. Devoize, French Chargé d'Affaires at Montevideo*

MONTEVIDEO, *December 22, 1847.*

SIR: In pronouncing an unfavourable opinion, in the case of the—*Independencia Americana,* We have had principally in view, to establish that fraud could not be authorised,
by the toleration of the blockaders, so far as to force them to an absolute abdication of
their rights; but we have acquired the conviction, that the persons most interested in the
vessel, and her cargo, *have remained unconnected with the obstinacy,* which the Captain
has displayed, in breaking the blockade, and that they have strongly condemned his
inexplicable conduct.
It is from this consideration that we now claim your *indulgence,* M̲ᵣ Chargé d'Affaires,
and that of the Rear Admiral or that of the Court, *which has been convened to revise the sentence passed by us,* and to pray you to add a copy of this present letter, to the documents
of the proceedings.
We have the honour to be

A. SOULÉ.   J. CHARRY JUN̲ᵣ

The present letter shall be added to the file of papers, in the case of the *Independencia
Americana,* to be used as there may be need.
A true Copy from the original, deposited in the office of the Council of State.

BOURGUIGNAT—Keeper of the Archives of the Council of State.

[4] Above, this part, p. 595, note 1.

Referring Your Excellency to the note which I had the honor of addressing to your predecessor, on the 20th of July last[1] on this whole subject, I now naturally give way to the hope, seeing that the prize commissioners themselves thought the American owners of the cargo innocent, that this government will desire to do them justice by awarding them indemnity to the amount of the loss sustained by the above capture and condemnation of their property.

I gladly seize this new opportunity of tendering to Your Excellency [etc.].

2599

Richard Rush, United States Minister to France, to John M. Clayton, Secretary of State of the United States [2]

No. 89   PARIS, *April 24, 1849.*

SIR: With my number 79, I transmitted a note from the Minister of Foreign Affairs[3] containing an unfavorable answer to mine of the 20th of July last[4] on the case of the "Independentia [Independencia] Americana," the vessel captured in December 1847 by the French squadron off Buenos Ayres, which has so long maintained its irregular and objectionable blockade in those waters.

It had been my intention to wait whatever instructions you might deem it proper and convenient to honor me with in this case before taking any further step in it; but I lately got possession of a document hitherto unknown to me, which bears strongly upon its merits. It is a Letter from the very commissioners of the French vice Admiral's prize court that condemned the property at Monte Video, to the chargé d'affaires of France at that station, absolving, in effect, the owners of the cargo (in part the two American citizens for whom I claim justice) from all blame on the occasion, and even recommending their case to every indulgent consideration. I enclose a copy of the Letter,[5] by which this will be seen; the more especially when read in connexion with the summary of facts given in my representation of the case to the Minister of Foreign affairs in my Note to him of the 20th of last July.

I got possession of this Letter through a French lawyer here, who acts for other shippers of the cargo. How it happens that the Minister of Foreign affairs was unacquainted with it when writing to me on the first of March, I know not, as it appears to have been in the Registry of the Council of State in Paris. If known to him, I should have supposed it would have been no-

[1] Above, this part, doc. 2589.   [2] Despatches, France, vol. 31.   Received May 14.
[3] For the note and the despatch which it accompanied, see above, this part, March 1 and March 9, 1849, docs. 2596 and 2597.   [4] See above, this part, doc. 2589.
[5] Above, this part, December 22, 1847, p. 598, note 3.

ticed; or rather let me say, have changed the nature of this government's decision on this international claim—looking to its equitable grounds. Under this view of the Letter I could not hesitate to write a fresh note to the Minister upon the subject, even without the benefit of your instructions.

Accordingly, on the 21st instant, I addressed one to him covering a copy of this document from the prize commissioners, making the use of it for the American claimants which it seemed to me to justify. I enclose a copy of my note[1] and have the honor [etc.].

2600

Drouyn de Lhuys, Minister of Foreign Affairs of France, to Richard Rush, United States Minister to France[2]

[TRANSLATION]

May 14, 1849.

Sir: You did me the honor to transmit to me a letter written to the Consul General and Chargé d'Affaires of France at Montevideo by the assistant judges[3] who, acting with him as a prize commission, judged the case of the *Independencia Americana*, the purpose of which letter is to request in favor of the interested parties the indulgence of the French agents or the court appealed to to revise the verdict which they rendered. A copy of this document forms part of the official file in the case, which is subject to the Council of State and regarding which I am going to address thereto my observations. The spirit of equity which animates French courts should assure you that claims brought before the Council of State will be investigated with the most absolute impartiality.

As regards the document which you transmitted to me, I must point out to you, Sir, that it would be difficult to understand how the grounds for indulgence indicated by the members of the prize commission could be applied to the shippers from Buenos Ayres, since the Captain of the *Independencia Americana*, after he had twice gone ashore to confer with these shippers, preferred to let the vessel be seized rather than run it back to port, as ordered by the French Cruiser. However, I only bring this point up in order to show that the letter of the members of the prize commission does not, perhaps, have all the value in this respect which you may have attributed to it.

Accept, Sir, [etc.].

---

[1] Above, this part, doc. 2598.
[2] Despatches, France, vol. 31; enclosed with Rush to the Secretary of State, No. 92, May 15, 1849, below, this part, doc. 2601.
[3] See above, this part, December 22, 1847, p. 598, note 3. It was transmitted to him in Rush's note of April 21, 1849, above, this part, doc. 2598.

2601

Richard Rush, United States Minister to France, to John M. Clayton, Secretary of State of the United States [1]

[EXTRACT]

No. 92   PARIS, *May 15, 1849.*

SIR: I have just received and have the honor to enclose a copy of it, an answer, dated yesterday, from the Minister of Foreign affairs to my note of the 21st of April on the case of the 'Independentia [Independencia] Americana', transmitted with my number 89.[2]

It appears that the document from the prize commissioners at Monte-Video [Montevideo] which I sent to the Minister,[3] has had no effect, its bearing upon the equity of the case not being admitted. The Minister's Note contains other statements at variance with the facts that were represented to me, and as I set them forth in my first Note to this government on the 20th of last July.[4]

The root of the evil is in the irregular, not to say illegal, blockade itself. Such a blockade was objectionable enough in its infringements of the fair rights of American commerce throughout that continent, when sustained by France *and* England, conjointly. But doubly more so did it become when enforced by France alone, after England had fully and formally before the world withdrawn herself from it—the power heretofore charged with a proneness to stretch the claim of blockade as far as possible where it could be done. It was *after* that withdrawal that France, by her single squadron, made this capture and condemnation of American property, to which she now so decidedly adheres.

As to what is said in the Minister's Note of the spirit of equity animating the French tribunals, I regret that the records of this Legation in the case of the Josephine as referred to in my number 79[5] oblige me to say, that where American property has formerly been seized and illegally condemned by France under this blockade, and so admitted to have been, the spirit of equity here invoked has proved an inadequate reliance to the wronged American citizens.[6] . . .

I have the honor [etc.].

[1] Despatches, France, vol. 31. Received June 4.
[2] For the Foreign Minister's reply, see above, this part, May 14, 1849, doc. 2600, and also, in the same part, Rush's despatch No. 89, dated April 24, 1849, doc. 2599, and its enclosure of April 21, 1849, doc. 2598.   [3] Above, this part, p. 598, note 3.
[4] *Ibid.*, doc. 2589.   [5] *Ibid.*, March 9, 1849, doc. 2597.
[6] The omitted portion refers to French political affairs.

2602

*William C. Rives, United States Minister to France, to John M. Clayton,
Secretary of State of the United States* [1]

[EXTRACTS]

PARIS, *October 3, 1849.*

MY DEAR SIR: I arrived here on the 27th ult. I am, of course, prepared at any moment to enter upon the discharge of my official duties. But Mr. Rush has not yet taken leave of the government, & 'till he does so, I cannot regularly present myself as his successor.[2] . . .

I addressed to you from London several communications on the subject of the Nicaragua & Mosquito question,[3] on which you instructed me to hold a conference with Lord Palmerston on my passage thro' England. In my last despatch, I gave you a full detail of that conference, which indicated a far better spirit in the British Government than had been previously manifested, & I cannot but think from the conciliatory temper then shewn by Lord Palmerston & the objects avowed & disavowed by him, that Mr. Lawrence will be able to come to a friendly arrangement with him of the whole subject. Certainly, all that passed in the conference led me to believe that such a result was practicable, as it would, undoubtedly, be auspicious to the interests of both countries. I trust that, on my part, there was no misapprehension of the spirit of your Instructions or the policy of our government; and that what was said & done by me will meet the approbation of the President & yourself.[4] . . .

I remain, my dear sir, [etc.].

2603

*William C. Rives, United States Minister to France, to John M. Clayton,
Secretary of State of the United States* [5]

[EXTRACTS]

No. 16   PARIS, *January 9, 1850.*

SIR: For the last ten days, the National Assembly has been occupied mainly with a very interesting discussion on the affairs of the La Plata States. The Government had submitted a proposition for the payment of the subsidy stipulated in favor of Montevideo. On this proposition a general discussion arose on the relations of France with both Montevideo and Buenos Ayres.

[1] Despatches, France, vol. 32. Received October 23.
[2] The omitted portion reports that his predecessor was sailing from Liverpool for the United States on the 20th instant, and adds that he received a telegraphic instruction directing him to be presented to the French Government as soon as possible.
[3] See below, vol. VII, pt. II, docs. 2869, 2870, 2871, and 2872, under dates of September 6, 14, 21, and 25, 1849.   [4] The omitted portion relates to European political affairs.
[5] Despatches, France, vol. 32. Received January 28.

The Government avowing it's dissatisfaction with the terms of the Treaty negotiated with Rosas by Admiral Le Predour and its determination not to submit it to the National Assembly for ratification, declared its purpose to be to renew negotiations in the *ordinary form* to obtain modifications of such of the articles as it objected to.   A very large portion of the Assembly seemed to prefer a more energetic mode of proceeding, and a proposition was submitted to open a credit to the Ministers of War and the Marine with a view to sending out an expedition of eight or ten thousand men to support and enforce the negotiation.   This proposition was referred to a Committee, of which Mʳ Daru was Chairman, who made an elaborate report, and concluded with a resolution in favor of an *armed* negociation.   The Report was opposed by the Government, which still adhered to the policy of a negotiation in the usual pacific forms, but with the declared determination to maintain the rights and honor of the Country, and the interests of the French Citizens established on the La Plata, with vigor and firmness.   The Report was sustained with great ability, and extraordinary fullness of information on South American affairs, by Monsieur Thiers.   His speech seemed to produce a great effect upon the National Assembly, and it was thought at one time, would lead to a decision against the policy of the Government, the defence of which rested mainly upon Mʳ Rouher, the Minister of Justice, supported by occasional explanations from Genˡ La Hitte, the Minister of Foreign Affairs. Finally, however, the views of the Government prevailed, and a resolution, sanctioned by them, was carried by a majority of 338 to 300.

The whole debate, as touching the affairs of our Hemisphere, and marked by frequent and always respectful allusions to the policy of the United States, cannot fail to be interesting to us.   I send a report of it herewith [1] in three successive noˢ of the Moniteur, the only Journal in which it is adequately reported.   You will perceive that, among the various propositions submitted, was one to invite the United States and England to unite with France in a final and comprehensive settlement of the La Plata troubles; but this, with various other amendments, was put aside by the resolution which was finally adopted.[2] . . .

I enclose herewith a copy which appeared in one of the Journals of Paris yesterday, of the Treaty negotiated by Admiral Le Predour with Rosas,[3] without being able to vouch for its authenticity, as it has not been officially made known to the public.

I have the honor [etc.].

[1] Not found.
[2] The omitted portion refers to other questions under discussion in the National Assembly not pertinent to this publication.   [3] Not included in this publication.

2604

Memorandum on inter-oceanic communication, rail and canal, presented by William C. Rives, United States Minister to France, to General de La Hitte, Minister of Foreign Affairs of France [1]

PARIS, *February 27, 1850.*

The enterprises which have been set on foot to unite the Atlantic and Pacific Oceans by a Rail-way across the Isthmus of Panama and by a grand Canal through the Territory of Nicaragua present themselves as objects of the highest interest to all the commercial Powers of the world. The Government of the United States, far from wishing to obtain any exclusive privilege or advantage in these great high-ways of commerce, which promise such important benefits to humanity at large, is desirous of seeing their free use and enjoyment secured to all nations, on terms of just reciprocity. To attain this end the more effectually and to guard against the interruption which a state of war and contingencies of a like kind might occasion in the use of these grand communications, it has seemed to the Government of the United-States to be highly desirable to place them under the protection of a solemn and permanent international guarantee, to which the principal Powers, seperately or jointly, should be parties.

The United States have already entered into a stipulation of this character with the Government of New Granada in reference to the Panama Rail-Road, which will be found in the XXXVth article of their Treaty of June 10th 1848 with that State, and have recently negotiated a Treaty of a similar nature with the State of Nicaragua, respecting the Nicaragua Canal, which is probably before the Senate of the United States for ratification. In the vast career which will be opened to the trade, navigation and industry of France by means of these new channels of commercial intercourse, as well as in her known sympathy with whatever is grand and noble in schemes proposed for the general benefit of mankind, the enlightened Government of the French Republic will, it is believed, find every inducement to give its cordial concurrence to a large and liberal policy for the promotion of these high interests.

The points on which it is desired to ascertain the views of the French Government, at present, are—

1st whether it would be disposed to guarantee the neutrality of these great highways of commerce by the Isthmus of Panama and Central America in consideration of reciprocal advantages to be granted by the States through whose territories they respectively pass, such as those stipulated in the Treaty between the United States and New-Granada?—And if so,

2[d!y] whether the French Government would prefer forming separate

---

[1] Despatches, France, vol. 32; enclosed with Rives to the Secretary of State, No. 23, March 6, 1850, below, this part, doc. 2605.

Treaties with the States of Nicaragua and New-Granada for the objects in question, or joining the United States and such other Powers as may entertain corresponding views in a common Treaty, founded on reciprocal stipulations with the States above mentioned, and designed to secure by the mutual and solemn engagement of all the parties the perpetual neutrality of the contemplated inter-oceanic passage.

2605

William C. Rives, United States Minister to France, to John M. Clayton, Secretary of State of the United States [1]

No. 23   PARIS, *March 6, 1850.*

SIR: Your Despatch N° 9,[2] with the accompanying papers, was received here on the 21st ult.

I lost no time in bringing the subject of it to the notice of General La Hitte, the Minister of Foreign Affairs. I explained to him fully the policy of the United States in regard to the freedom of the contemplated inter-oceanic communications by the Isthmus of Panama and Central America, and the expediency of placing them under the efficient protection of an inter-national guarantee. He expressed, in a very emphatic manner, his approbation of the large and liberal views by which the Government of the United States was actuated, and gave his adhesion, in very distinct terms, to the general principle of a mutual guarantee. In regard to the details of any specific arrangement for carrying it into effect, he reserved his opinion till it should be formed upon fuller reflection and investigation, and said he would, without delay, submit the whole question to the deliberations of the Council of Ministers.— I left with him one of the copies of our Treaty with New-Granada which you sent me, and called his attention particularly to the XXXVth Article as showing the nature of the stipulation we have entered into with that Government for the guarantee of the Panama Rail-Road. I did not deem it necessary or expedient to communicate to him the extract of the Treaty recently negotiated with the State of Nicaragua, respecting the Nicaragua Canal, as that Treaty had not yet been acted upon by the Senate; but I mentioned to him the fact that such a Treaty had been negotiated, and that it awaited only the advice and consent of the Senate for it's ratification.—

In this first interview with the Minister of Foreign Affairs, I thought he indicated a preference for a common Treaty of guarantee to which France, the United States and other commercial powers should be parties, rather than entering into seperate and distinct Treaties with the two States

---

[1] Despatches, France, vol. 32. Received March 25.
[2] Above, this volume, pt. v, January 26, 1850, doc. 2478.

exercising or claiming the Territorial sovereignty over the contemplated lines of communication. This impression has been confirmed by several conversations I have had with him since our first interview, and also since the subject has been under the consideration of the Council of Ministers. In all these conferences, he has given a very cordial sanction to the *principle* of guaranteeing the neutrality of these great high-ways of commerce, but seems to think it would be a manner of proceeding more suitable to the grandeur of the object & in other respects preferable, to carry it into execution by the common accord of all the principal commercial powers embodied in one and the same Treaty, if such a course should be found practicable. He has promised, however, to give me an answer in writing; and to enable him to do it more satisfactorily, he requested me to furnish him with a memorandum of the precise points on which we desire to know the views of the French Government. I accordingly drew up and handed him, some days ago, the memorandum, of which a copy is herewith enclosed;[1] and I yet have some hope of receiving his answer in time to go with this despatch by the Liverpool Steamer of the 9th instant. Nothing, I am satisfied, will prevent it but the pressure at this moment, upon his Department of some troublesome questions connected with the controversy between Prussia and Switzerland respecting the principality of Neufchatel, and the embroiled condition, generally, of the German Powers.—

The French Government, I think, regards the pretensions of Great Britain, on behalf of the socalled King of Mosquito, to dominion over the mouth of the River San Juan as futile and untenable. I have drawn this inference from general allusions made occasionally in conversation, rather than from any explicit avowal of opinion to that effect. A consideration, indeed, of no small weight against those pretensions is drawn from one of the Maps annexed to a very clever work on the Nicaragua communication which was written and published in England by the President of the Republic in 1846, when he was a private citizen. In that Map No. II, which is presumed to have been framed according to the best authorities, political and geographical, then accessible in England, the delimitation of the Mosquito Coast, as well as the State of Nicaragua, is distinctly laid down, and the extension given to the Mosquito Coast, it will be seen, stops far short of the River San Juan.

Though the French Government, from very natural and obvious motives of policy at the present moment, might not be inclined to enter into positive stipulations, either with Nicaragua or the United States, which would be calculated to involve the Republic in hostile collision with England, yet I cannot but think that in a diplomatic congress of the Commercial Powers to concert a common guarantee of the inter-oceanic passage through Central America, (which seems to be the mode of proceeding preferred by the Minister of

[1] Above, this part, February 27, 1850, doc. 2604.

Foreign Affairs here), the weight of France would be thrown decidedly against the exclusive pretensions set up by England in the name of the Mosquitos.

I have the honor [etc.].

2606

Memorandum presented by General de La Hitte, Minister of Foreign Affairs of France, to William C. Rives, United States Minister to France [1]

[TRANSLATION]

PARIS, *March 6, 1850.*

The Government of the United States of North America has expressed the desire to know if the French Government would be disposed to guarantee the neutrality of the great commercial high-ways which it is proposed to establish across the Isthmus of Panama and Central America, in consideration of reciprocal advantages to be granted by the States whose territories they will traverse, and whether, in case of an affirmative answer to that question, it would prefer forming seperate Treaties with the States of Nicaragua and New-Granada, or joining the United States and other powers entertaining similar views in a common Treaty.

Before explaining itself formally on these two points, the French Government has need to inform itself, with more of precision than it can do at this moment, of the nature of the advantages which would flow to it from the fact of it's guarantee; it is also necessary to know the duties attached to this guarantee; lastly, the answer which other Governments, to which the same proposals may be addressed, should think proper to return to them, would, to a certain degree, influence it's determination. But it does not hesitate to declare at once that the truly liberal views, which accompany the queries contained in the Memorandum of M⊺ Rives,[2] obtain all it's approbation, and that it will esteem itself happy to be able, after a mature examination, to accede to the project which is thus presented to it.

[1] Despatches, France, vol. 32; enclosed with Rives to the Secretary of State, No. 24, March 7, 1850, doc. 2608.
[2] Above, this part, doc. 2604.

2607

General de La Hitte, Minister of Foreign Affairs of France, to William C. Rives,
United States Minister to France [1]

[TRANSLATION]

PARIS, *March 6, 1850.*

General de La Hitte has the honor to address to Mr. Rives a Memorandum [2] in answer to that which he was pleased to deliver to him [3] on the
subject of the guarantee of the neutrality of the great commercial high-ways
between the two Oceans.

He hopes that the Minister of the United States will find in it the expression of the desire of the Government of the Republic to accede to the
project which he has presented in the name of his Government.

Gen[l] de La Hitte has the honor [etc.].

2608

William C. Rives, United States Minister to France, to John M. Clayton,
Secretary of State of the United States [4]

No. 24   PARIS, *March 7, 1850.*

SIR: I enclose herewith a copy of the answer of the Minister of Foreign
Affairs to the Memorandum I presented to him on the 27th ult.[5] respecting
the proposed guarantee of the neutrality of the passage between the two
Oceans by the Isthmus of Panama and Central America.   It was received
last evening, but too late to accompany my despatch of yesterday,[6] though it
is hoped to be yet in good time to go out by the Liverpool Steamer of the
9th instant.

The answer, though avoiding commitment on specific points, which was
hardly to be expected in the present stage of the business, expresses in strong
terms, as I supposed it would, the approbation felt by the French Government of the liberal views of the Government of the United States, and the
hope to be able, upon farther examination, to give its co-operation in carrying them into effect.   I had informed Gen[l] de La Hitte that I had as yet
received no powers to negotiate with him in relation to this subject, but that
if the French Government should be willing to treat with us upon it, you
proposed to send me the necessary powers, with the detailed instructions for

[1] Despatches, France, vol. 32; enclosed with Rives to the Secretary of State, No. 24, March
7, 1850, doc. 2608.   [2] Above, this part, March 6, 1850, doc. 2606.
[3] *Ibid.*, February 27, 1850, doc. 2604.
[4] Despatches, France, vol. 32.   Received March 25.
[5] See the Minister of Foreign Affairs' note and accompanying memorandum, above, this
part, both dated March 6, 1850, docs. 2605 and 2606, and, also, in the same part, under its
date, Rives's memorandum, doc. 2604.   [6] Above, this part, doc. 2605.

their execution. His answer, therefore, may be considered as laying the foundation for future negotiation.

A rumor has reached us here that you have already concluded a convention with the British Government in regard to the Nicaragua communication. I presume there can be but little doubt that France will be willing to enter into any arrangement which may have been concluded with England.

I have the honor [etc.].

2609

William C. Rives, United States Minister to France, to John M. Clayton, Secretary of State of the United States [1]

[EXTRACT]

No. 40   PARIS, *June 13, 1850.*

SIR: . . . For the last eight or ten days a very lively solicitude has been manifested here in the diplomatic circles, as well as by the Government and the Press, in regard to the Cuban expedition and the measures taken by our Government for it's repression. The enterprise has been universally considered a very lawless one, as attempted to be organised and set on foot in the Territory of a neutral and friendly power, and great satisfaction has, therefore, been expressed at the news received yesterday of it's failure. Much speculation and commentary have been indulged in [by?] the Press as to the manner in which it was viewed by our Government, and illiberal and unfriendly insinuations have sometimes been made that it was *winked at* by the public authorities of the United States. In my intercourse with the Government here and with the members of the Diplomatic corps, I have not failed to profit of every opportunity to give them correct views of the good faith and energy with which the United States have fulfilled, and were determined to fulfill, their neutral obligations in regard to this and every other similar enterprise attempted upon the peace or dominions of friendly powers from our shores. The Spanish Ambassador here, the Duke of Sotomayor, is a man of very high and honorable character; and I have the satisfaction to believe that with the materials I have been enabled, in our social intercourse, to lay before him, evincing the scrupulous anxiety and the firm determination of our Government to perform it's duties according to the most just and elevated conception of them, he fully appreciated the good faith and honor which have marked all our proceedings. It is now much to be hoped that a firm execution of our laws against those who have violated them, and thereby compromised the peace and honor of the country,

[1] Despatches, France, vol. 32. Received June 28.
The omitted portion relates to a proposition to increase the allowance, made to the President of the French Republic, for incidental expenses of his official position.

will be superadded to fortify the confidence of the just and liberal-minded portion of mankind in our national integrity, and at the same time to refute the illiberal insinuations of our detractors.

I received yesterday your Despatch dated 26ᵗʰ May 1850,[1] (but not numbered), transmitting a copy of the Convention concluded on the 19ᵗʰ of April last, between the United States and Great Britain, and shall lose no time in bringing the subject to the notice of the Minister of Foreign Affairs here.

I have the honor [etc.].

2610

William C. Rives, United States Minister to France, to General de La Hitte, Minister of Foreign Affairs of France [2]

PARIS, *June 14, 1850.*

MONSIEUR LE GÉNÉRAL: In the Memorandum I had the honor to submit to you on the 27ᵗʰ February last,[3] I mentioned to you the desire which was felt by the Government of the United States to promote, in concurrence with other powers, the opening of a Ship Canal through Central America to unite the Atlantic and the Pacific Oceans, and to place that great work and such other commercial highways as might be established between the two Oceans, under the protection of an inter-national compact which would guarantee their neutrality, and secure their use and enjoyment to all on terms of entire reciprocity. A Convention, having these objects in view, has recently been concluded at Washington between Great-Britain and the United-States, a copy of which I have the honor herewith to send you.[4] Both of the contracting parties, as you will perceive from the provisions of the Convention are desirous that the great inter-oceanic communications therein contemplated shall also be open, on equal terms, to the citizens and subjects of every other State which is willing to grant thereto such protection as the United States and Great Britain engage by the said Treaty to afford. I have been instructed, therefore, to bring the subject without loss of time to the notice of your Excellency, with a view to the conclusion of a Convention with France in the very words, so far as the same are applicable, of the one I have the honor to communicate herewith, if it should meet the approbation of the Government of the Republic.

I pray your Excellency to accept [etc.].

[1] Above, this volume, pt. v, doc. 2480.
[2] Despatches, France, vol. 32; enclosed with Rives to the Secretary of State, No. 41, June 20, 1850, below, this part, doc. 2611.   [3] Above, this part, doc. 2604.
[4] For the text of the Clayton-Bulwer Convention, dated April 19, 1850, see Malloy, *Treaties, Conventions, etc., between the United States and Other Powers,* vol. I, p. 659.

2611

William C. Rives, United States Minister to France, to John M. Clayton, Secretary of State of the United States [1]

[EXTRACT]

No. 41   PARIS, *June 20, 1850.*

SIR: In my last despatch N$^{\circ}$ 40, written on the 13th instant,[2] I acknowledged the receipt, the day before, of your despatch dated the 25th of May,[3] transmitting a copy of the Convention concluded at Washington on the 19th of April between the United States and Great Britain respecting the contemplated Ship Canal through Central America to unite the Atlantic and Pacific Oceans.   As you expressed the desire that I should lose no time in bringing the subject to the notice of the Minister of Foreign Affairs here, I immediately turned my attention to the proper mode of doing it under the instructions contained in your despatch.   Those instructions being of a precise and specific character, restricting any negotiation which might take place here, to the very words of the Convention concluded at Washington between the United States and Great Britain, so far as the same are applicable, I thought it proper to present that proposition distinctly to the mind of the Minister of Foreign Affairs, and, in order to avoid the possibility of error or misconception, to do it in writing.— I enclose herewith a copy of the note I addressed to him on the 14th instant,[4] in which you will see I adhered strictly, as seemed to me, under the circumstances, both necessary and proper, to the language used by you in your despatch.

I have since called upon the Minister of Foreign Affairs for the purpose of conversing with him upon the subject.   He told me he had been so much occupied with the more pressing affairs of his Department that he had not yet had time to examine the Treaty, but he hoped to be able to do so soon, when he would be very happy to communicate with me farther in regard to it.[5] . . .

I have the honor [etc.].

[1] Despatches, France, vol. 32.   There was no receipt date on the file copy in the manuscript volume.   [2] Above, this part, doc. 2609.
[3] He refers erroneously to the Secretary of State's instruction to him, of May 26, above, this volume, pt. v, doc. 2480.   [4] Above, this part, doc. 2610.
[5] The omitted portion discusses European political affairs.

2612

*William C. Rives, United States Minister to France, to John M. Clayton,
Secretary of State of the United States* [1]

[EXTRACT]

No. 42   PARIS, *June 27, 1850.*

SIR: . . . The uncertain position of the Ministry, while this state of
things continued, is, doubtless among the circumstances which have prevented the Minister of Foreign Affairs from heretofore turning his attention
to the subject of the Convention for the protection of the Nicaragua Ship
Canal. I saw him yesterday and he again apologised to me for not having
yet been able to turn his attention to the subject as seriously as it's importance required. He said that although the principal question between them
and England in relation to the Greek affair had been adjusted by the agreement to revert to the London Convention, there were yet some *delicate*
matters to arrange previous to a formal resumption of diplomatic intercourse,
and these had necessarily occupied, and still continued to occupy, much of
his attention. He said, however, he proposed to submit my communication,[2] with the copy of the Convention concluded between the United States
and England, to the Council of Ministers at a very early day, and he should
then be prepared to enter into farther communication with me on the subject.
It is very certain that the recent misunderstanding with England, on the
occasion of the proceedings against Greece, has deeply enlisted the feelings
as well as engaged the attention of this Government, and although the external forms of friendly intercourse will probably, be soon resumed, my
conviction is that a real and mutual *coolness* exists, and is likely to exist for
an indefinite time, between the two Governments.

I have the honor [etc.].

2613

*General de La Hitte, Minister of Foreign Affairs of France, to William C. Rives,
United States Minister to France* [3]

[TRANSLATION]

PARIS, *July 5, 1850.*

MONSIEUR: I have received the letter which you did me the honor to
write to me the 14th. of June[4] on the subject of the Convention concluded the

---

[1] Despatches, France, vol. 32. Received August 6.
The omitted portion relates to allowance, made to the President of the Republic, for incidental expenses.
[2] Above, this part, June 14, 1850, doc. 2610.
[3] Despatches, France, vol. 32; enclosure with Rives to the Secretary of State, No. 46,
July 10, 1850, below, this part, doc. 2615.   [4] Above, this part, doc. 2610.

19th of April last at Washington between the United States and England. The stipulations of that Treaty appear to me in general to conform to the liberal views announced in the *Memorandum* you put into my hands on the 27th of February.[1] In this respect, we can not but be altogether disposed to give our adhesion to it. Nevertheless, before calling for a decision of the Government of the Republic upon the subject, there are some points on which I would desire to obtain farther information, *(des éclaircissemens)*.

In the *Memorandum* to which I have referred above, the neutrality of the inter-communications between the two oceans was considered as proper to be established, either by separate Treaties which each maritime power should contract with the states of Nicaragua and New Granada, or by a common Treaty which the different powers, entertaining the same views, should conclude with those two states. The convention which you have communicated to me makes mention only in an indirect manner of the states thro' whose territory the proposed communications are to pass. The 6th article declares that the contracting parties agree each to conclude treaties with the states of Central America, as they may judge it advisable to do so, for the purpose of more effectually promoting the great object of the convention. I am aware that this course *(marche)* may have been adopted in order to arrive more speedily at a settlement of the difficulties which existed between the United States and England; but it seems to me that the mode of proceeding at first contemplated by the Government of the United States would have been preferable in itself. However this may be, Monsieur, I should deem it of importance, (se methais [mettrait?] du prix), to know whether your Government has any fixed views respecting the arrangements to be formed with the State of Nicaragua, and to learn also, if it be possible, the substance of those arrangements.

On an other hand, the convention of the 19th April recognises in such persons as should already have concluded a contract with any State thro' whose territory the proposed canal may pass, a right of priority to the protection of the two parties upon certain conditions—and particularly upon the condition that the stipulations of the said contract are not of a nature to give rise to just causes of objection. In this connection, I remark that the contract concluded last year between the Government of Nicaragua and an American company represented by Mr White, contained some clauses susceptible of grave objections. Among other stipulations, it provided that all vessels belonging to the company and all merchandise which it should transport by the Canal from one sea to the other, should be exempt from every species of duty or impost on the part of the Government. I do not think that such a privilege could be admitted, particularly if the voyages of these vessels were to extend beyond the limits of the canal and for distant destinations, *(pour le long cours)*, for it would be to be feared in that case

---

[1] Above, this part, doc. 2604.

that the transportations of the company, already too much favored by the gratuitous use of the canal, would take an unlimited extension, and that the principle of equality for all flags laid down in theory would be thus destroyed in practice. It would be highly important to prevent all difficulty on this subject by a precise understanding beforehand on the nature and limits of the privileges which should be recognised in the canal company.

Other provisions of the before-mentioned contract would likewise require to be modified — particularly the 9.th article which stipulates that the greater part of the stock of the canal should always be owned by citizens of the United States. This clause, which appeared natural so long as the Government of the United States presented itself as the sole protector of the canal, would ill accord with the actual principle of a protection in common.

I shall receive with great interest, Monsieur, the communications which you shall have it in your power to make me on the several points I have just indicated.

Receive, Monsieur, the assurance [etc.].

2614

William C. Rives, United States Minister to France, to General de La Hitte, Minister of Foreign Affairs of France [1]

PARIS, *July 7, 1850.*

MONSIEUR LE GÉNÉRAL: I have had the honor to receive the letter which you were pleased to address to me on the 5.th instant in answer to that which I wrote to your Excellency on the 14.th ultimo [2] on the subject of the Convention concluded at Washington on the 19.th April last between England and the United States. I shall hasten to transmit it to my Government, by whom I shall, doubtless, be enabled to furnish you fuller and more precise information than it is, at present, in my power to give you on the points on which you desire to obtain farther explanations.

The Treaty between Nicaragua and the United States which I mentioned, in the *Memorandum* of the 27.th February last,[3] as having been submitted to the Senate of the United States for their advice and consent had not been definitively acted on at the date of my last intelligence from Washington; and as it is quite possible that it may have undergone, or will undergo, some modifications in it's passage thro' that Body, I am not now able to inform you with exactness what arrangements may have been made, or are expected to be made, between the two Governments respecting the great

[1] Despatches, France, vol. 32; enclosed with Rives to the Secretary of State, No. 46, July 10, 1850, below, this part, doc. 2615.
[2] For these two notes, see above, this part, under their dates, docs. 2610 and 2613.
[3] Above, this part, doc. 2604.

inter-oceanic communication in question. I will simply remark, however, that under the convention of the 19th april between England and the United States, if France should become a party to it, whatever rights or advantages may be acquired from Nicaragua by the United States for their citizens, in regard to commerce and navigation thro' the proposed canal, would immediately & ipso facto enure, in the same extent and upon the same terms, to the benefit of France and her citizens.

In regard to the contract which has been entered into with the State of Nicaragua by the American Company represented by Mr White, I am entirely unacquainted with it's details, never having seen a copy of the contract, or an abstract of it's provisions; nor am I yet informed whether it has received the approbation of the Sovereign parties to the convention of the 19th April. The 5th article of the convention, in reserving to the parties, either separately or jointly, the faculty of withdrawing their protection from the canal, in case of mal-administration or improper practises by the company, seems to have been intended to furnish a security against, as well as a remedy for, the possible abuses which your Excellency supposes might grow out of the nature and extent of the privileges accorded to it.

But upon this, as well as the other points indicated in your letter, I shall embrace, with great pleasure, the earliest opportunity of laying before you such farther information as I may be enabled by my Government to communicate to you.

I pray you, Monsieur le Général, to accept [etc.].

2615

William C. Rives, United States Minister to France, to John M. Clayton, Secretary of State of the United States [1]

No. 46 PARIS, *July 10, 1850.*

SIR: I enclose herewith a letter received a few days since from the Minister of Foreign Affairs in answer to the note I had addressed to him [2] on the subject of the convention concluded on the 19th April last between the United States and England in relation to the contemplated inter-oceanic communication thro' Central America.

You will perceive that the Minister, while expressing the disposition of the French Government to give it's adhesion to the general principles of the Convention, desires to obtain farther information on particular points

[1] Despatches, France, vol. 32. Received July 26.
[2] Both of these notes are above, this part, dated respectively, June 14 and July 5, docs. 2610 and 2613.

before coming to a final conclusion on the subject. These points refer to the treaty arrangements proposed to be made by the United States with the State of Nicaragua, and also to the contract concluded with that State by the American company undertaking to construct the Canal. Having observed from the correspondence between yourself and Sir Henry Bulwer, which was communicated to the Senate with the convention of the 19th of April, that modifications (the nature of which was not explained) were contemplated to be made in the Treaty between the United States and Nicaragua then pending before that Body, I was, of course, unable to answer the Minister with certainty and precision on the first point; and having never seen any copy of the contract between the Canal company and the State of Nicaragua, and being unapprised of the views of the Government in regard to it, I could give him no specific explanations on the second. My answer, therefore, (a copy of which is also enclosed),[1] was necessarily confined to a few general views founded on the text of the convention itself, and a promise to forward his letter to you for such farther explanations as you might deem necessary and proper.

The object of the first enquiry propounded by the Minister of Foreign Affairs is, doubtless, to know what advantages are to be granted by the State of Nicaragua in return for the obligations assumed by the other powers to protect the Canal and guarantee it's neutrality. As the prospect of these advantages will form a part, at least, of the motive with the French Government for entering into the proposed guarantee, it desires to know beforehand the value and extent of the proffered advantages; and the same consideration would, not improbably, lead it to prefer that the State of Nicaragua should be *directly* a party to any arrangement to be concluded on the subject between France and other powers—a mode of proceeding which, you will perceive, the Minister of Foreign Affairs says he should have considered preferable in *itself* to that actually adopted. In regard to the contract concluded with the State of Nicaragua by the Canal company, I have reason to believe that misconceptions have prevailed here, not only respecting the contract itself, but the relations of the protecting powers to it. General de Lahitte mentioned to me, in a casual conversation last evening that the President had been informed by some one that the Protecting Powers were to guarantee to the Canal Company a certain profit upon their investment. The idea, I told him, was disproved by the Convention itself, which contained no such stipulation. He at once recognised the sufficiency of the answer, and said he was persuaded there was no foundation for the notion.

I have the honor [etc.].

---

[1] Above, this part, July 7, 1850, doc. 2614.

2616

William C. Rives, United States Minister to France, to Daniel Webster, Secretary of State of the United States [1]

[EXTRACTS]

EDINBURG, *August 9, 1850.*

MY DEAR SIR: The last Steamer has brought us the news of the formation of a new Cabinet at Washington & of your acceptance of the post of Secretary of State in it. A name so well known to the whole world cannot fail to conciliate the respect of Foreign powers, & will, I am sure, inspire all the governments of Europe with entire confidence in the justice, good faith & wisdom with which our exterior relations will be conducted. You will permit me, I hope, to express the satisfaction I feel at being thus brought into communication with one so eminently fitted to preside over the diplomatic intercourse of the country.

My health being somewhat enfeebled by my long confinement in Paris, & the most of the Diplomatic corps having left there in consequence of the hot season, I have been making an excursion for the last two or three weeks & chiefly in this Island. You will perceive from the communications addressed to your Department that there was a necessary pause in the only negociation entrusted to me, in consequence of the French Government desiring information on certain points which could be elucidated only by explanations from Washington.[2] . . .

About the time I left Paris, a rumour was circulating there that the Spanish Government had proposed to France, & afterwards to England, a joint convention for the protection of their West-India possessions against the *acts of piracy*, (so called), which might be committed against them under shelter of the *anormale* legislation of the United States. The terms in which this story was couched, (the tenor of which is given in the enclosed news-paper scrap),[3] seeming to me to be injurious to the good faith & integrity of the Government of the United States, I thought it well enough, in an incidental way, to afford General de La Hitte an opportunity of explanation respecting it. He assured me with great frankness, that it was entirely unfounded—that the only communication ever made to him by the Spanish Government on the subject was to possess him of a copy of the letter written by Mr. Pidal, Spanish Minister of Foreign Affairs, to Mr. Calderon at Washington respecting the Cuban expedition sailing from the ports of the United States—and that the only thing which had been done by the French Government on the occasion was to send instructions to their naval commander in the West-Indies having in view *exclusively* the protec-

[1] Despatches, France, vol. 32. Received August 24.
[2] The omitted portion refers to the death of President Taylor, and, also, mentions enclosing a newspaper relating to the unfortunate seizures of French vessels at San Francisco.
[3] Not found.

tion of *their own citizens*, if any contingency should arise affecting their safety or interests.   I had previously profited of my kindly personal relations with the Duke of Sotomayor, the Spanish ambassador at Paris, to place in his hands your remarks in the Senate as containing the fullest & most weighty exposition of the policy of the Government of the United States towards Spain & particularly in regard to Cuba.

I will only add that it will be a source of pride & pleasure to me, at all times, to assist in carrying out your enlightened views of our foreign policy; & I pray you, my dear Sir, to accept [etc.].

2617

Sain de Boislecomte, French Minister to the United States, to Daniel Webster, Secretary of State of the United States [1]

[TRANSLATION]

WASHINGTON, *August 20, 1850.*

MR. SECRETARY OF STATE: Your predecessor having expressed a desire to my colleague, the British Minister, and to myself, that England and France might combine with the United States in protecting the Dominican Republic against the incursions of the Haitian Government,[2] we have been instructed by our respective Governments to act accordingly in furtherance of that object; and I had the honor to inform the Honble Mr Clayton of our intentions to that effect, who assured me verbally, that the American Agent at Port au Prince should be instructed to act in the same spirit as those of France and of England.

It appears, however, from a document of which I have received a copy, and which I herewith enclose,[3] that Mr Green, the agent of the Government of the Union, under the plea of urging the claims of certain American citizens, has taken steps with the Government of Haiti, towards producing a complete cessation of hostilities against the Dominican Republic.

Mr. Green has taken these steps alone; and without the knowledge of the English and French agents, and in doing so, he has declared himself formally authorized by the instructions of his government.   This assertion appears to me so utterly at variance with the assurances which I received from your predecessor on the subject, that I cannot believe otherwise but that Mr. Green must have exceeded his powers; and I have no doubt that the Government of the Union, which has manifested so much good faith in its inter-

[1] Notes from France, vol. 14.   Received August 19.   Apparently this document was dated one day ahead or the receipt date was inadvertently written "19" instead of "20."
[2] See Clayton's note to Bulwer, dated May 20, 1850, on this subject, below, vol. VII, pt. I, doc. 2706.   Clayton's note to the French representative was not found.
[3] Above, this volume, pt. II, May 8, 1850, p. 83, note I.

course with other nations, will hasten to put an end to this misunderstanding on the part of its agents at St Domingo, by instructing them to act in unison with those of England and of France in procuring the pacification of the Island.

Please to accept [etc.].

2618

Sain de Boislecomte, French Minister to the United States, to Daniel Webster, Secretary of State of the United States [1]

[TRANSLATION]

WASHINGTON, *December 21, 1850.*

MR. SECRETARY OF STATE: Sir Henry Bulwer, Her Britannic Majesty's minister, has communicated to me, before sending you a copy of the same, the instructions which he has forwarded to Her Majesty's Consul at Haiti,[2] with a view of securing [pour obtenir] the pacification of the two sides of the Island, and, I hasten to assure you that the aforesaid instructions harmonize entirely with those which the Consul of the French Republic has received upon the same subject. I hope that the Government of the United States will coöperate with our respective governments in an act which is to contribute so much to the good of humanity.

Please to accept [etc.].

2619

William C. Rives, United States Minister to France, to Daniel Webster, Secretary of State of the United States [3]

No. 102   PARIS, *September 10, 1851.*

SIR: . . . The principal topic, however, which has occupied the public attention here for the last four or five days is the late events in Cuba. The comments of the Press here, as well as in England, on those painful occurrences are highly colored by the mingled prejudice and jealousy with which the Governments of Europe look upon the United States, their Republican Institutions, and their extraordinary progress in all the elements of national power and strength. No one can be insensible to the exceedingly grave character of the possible consequences which may grow out of those events, and I hope you will find it convenient, and not deem it inexpedient, to possess me, as soon as possible, of the light in which they are viewed by the

[1] Notes from France, vol. 14. Received January 8, 1851.
[2] For a copy of these instructions, see footnote to Bulwer's note to the Secretary of State, dated December 21, 1850, below, vol. VII, pt. II, doc. 2938.
[3] Despatches, France, vol. 33. Received September 25.
The omitted portion refers to the minister's vacation and, also, to French political affairs.

Government of the United States. Whether American citizens, who may have honestly believed, however the result may have shewn their delusion, that they were going to the aid of an oppressed people engaged in a serious effort to effect their liberation by a recurrence to arms, (forbidden tho' their enterprise was by the laws of their own country), can be properly considered as *pirates* and *robbers*, and shot down in cold blood upon the public place as such, with every circumstance of revolting brutality, is a question upon which I await the firm and conscientious decision of my own Government, enlightened as it will be by a knowledge of all the facts and a profound consideration of the great questions of public law and national dignity involved, without permitting my equanimity to be disturbed by the wild chorus of denunciation commenced by the English Press and re-echoed by that of this country. It cannot be denied, however, that the language of the Press, in Europe, however passionate and unreasoning, has a powerful influence in moulding public opinion, and thro' that, directing and controuling the policy of Governments.

It is, no doubt, known to you that this Government some time since entered into an arrangement with that of England to employ their joint naval forces on the West India Station to aid in maintaining the authority of Spain, in certain contingencies, over the Island of Cuba. This arrangement I believe to have been dictated by the habitual jealousy of the British Government with regard to the growing power of the United States, and the policy of the French Government, at the present moment, to maintain a close understanding with that of England. But I shall be slow to believe, in the event of serious national difficulties between the United States and Spain growing out of the late occurrences in Cuba, that France will be prepared to sacrifice her ancient friendly relations with the United States and the vast interests to her involved with those relations, to a new and far less natural connection, however assiduously that connection has been mutually courted and cultivated for the last three or four years.

I have the honor [etc.].

2620

William C. Rives, United States Minister to France, to Daniel Webster, Secretary of State of the United States [1]

No. 103   PARIS, *September 18, 1851.*

SIR: I had yesterday a long and free conversation with the Minister of Foreign Affairs on the subject of our relations generally with France, but more particularly as they might be affected by questions growing out of the recent events in Cuba. There had been for several days past rumours

---

[1] Despatches, France, vol. 33. Received October 4.

thro' the Press of conferences at the Elysée between the Spanish Minister, the English Ambassador, and the French Minister of Foreign Affairs with regard to those events and the questions they might give rise to between Spain and the United States. Those rumours I had reason to believe were without foundation. But the *Constitutionnel* of yesterday morning, which is supposed here to represent more particularly the personal opinions of the President, contained a paragraph, of which I enclose a copy,[1] stating in substance that it was said the French Government would address a communication to the Government of the United States on the affairs of Cuba and that the English Government had announced to this government it's intention to do the same thing. So formal an intervention as this paragraph announced of two of the powers of Europe in a question to which neither of them could be considered as properly a party, and in a spirit, to say the least, somewhat equivocal, seemed to me both to justify and to require a direct appeal on my part to the Minister of Foreign Affairs for some *éclaircissement* on the subject. He assured me in most positive and emphatic terms, and repeated the assurance again and again, that there was not the least foundation for the paragraph in question—that it was not for the Government of France to give any lesson to the Government of the United States respecting it's rights or it's duties—that it, moreover, recognised and rendered the fullest justice to the good faith and sincerity with which the Government of the United States had endeavoured to repress the late enterprises against the neighbouring possession of Spain, and that there was no reproach to be addressed to it as the organ and central authority of the Union in respect of the late deplorable occurrences.

After this earnest and repeated disclaim by Mr Baroche of the intention imputed to the French Government by the paragraph of the Constitutionnel, the conversation took a wider range, and I thought the occasion not an unsuitable one for rectifying the false notions which had been so industriously propagated by the European Press in regard to the piratical motives and objects of those who, however unlawful the enterprise in which they were engaged, were, many of them undoubtedly actuated by aims and considerations very different from plunder, and also to explain to him how naturally the needless and revolting barbarity of the Spanish Authorities, (waiving the question of *right* under the law of nations to put in practise the sanguinary severity invoked by them upon these misguided men), had excited a feeling of horror, not unmixed with indignation, among many of the most peaceful and conscientious citizens of the United States. Mr Baroche did not controvert the justice of these observations, but on the contrary, seemed to me to feel the weight of the considerations they suggested. He, however, expressed the hope that the feelings of excitement which had arisen or might

[1] Not included in this publication. The substance of this brief clipping, occupying about eight and one half lines of newspaper type, is given adequately below, in this despatch.

arise between the two nations from the late unfortunate occurrences would be calmed down by reflection and the mutual love of peace, and said that whatever moral influence the French Government could properly employ with either party would be exerted to that end.

In the course of this conversation, the Minister of Foreign Affairs declared frankly the desire which the French Government felt that Spain should preserve her territorial possessions in different quarters of the world. But, at the same time, he expressed the deep interest they felt in maintaining their ancient friendly relations with the United States and the desire of guarding those relations from the danger of interruption by the constant practice of mutual cordiality and candour. Believing that it is of reciprocal importance to the United States to maintain a cordial good understanding with France, and, in the contingency to which we are always more or less exposed of a collision with another great power of Europe by a commercial and maritime rivalry existing in the nature of things, that her friendship would be almost a *vital* interest to us, my attention has been earnestly directed, as well during my former mission in Europe as the present, to the study of the causes which seemed most to endanger the stability of our ancient connection with France. I feel it my duty to state to you, as the result of these observations long and carefully pursued, my conviction that the chief, if not the sole, danger to the continuance of our harmony with France lies in the habitual jealousies of the power just referred to, and her traditional policy, handed down from one generation to another, to embroil the United States and France with each other, remaining herself, if possible, at peace with both.

I have already had occasion to mention to you the evidences I had seen of the great anxiety of the English Legation here that the United States should put themselves forward invidiously in the controversy between France and the Sandwich Islands, while England herself had the clearest and strongest ground for remonstrance in the formal Treaty Stipulations by which France was bound directly to *her* to respect the independence of those Islands. And yet so desirous has she been to avoid the risk of giving offence to France and of transferring that ungracious office to us that she has never to this day, so far as I have been able to learn, uttered a single word of protest or remonstrance against the proceedings of the French Government in that affair tho' professing to us the strongest disapprobation of them.

I have every reason to believe that, pursuing steadily the same policy, she has done all she could to instill into the French Government distrust respecting the supposed designs of the United States upon the Island of Cuba, and to induce this Government to take an attitude in that question which might compromise it's friendly relations with the United States. The measures announced by the President of the French Republic in his message to the National Assembly in the month of November last as having been taken by him to aid in defending the Island of Cuba against the incursions of adventurers from the United States were, I have been informed from a reliable source, the result of an arrangement with the British Government for the joint employment of the naval forces of the two countries to that end; and yet neither in the Queen's speech to Parliament nor in any other official Document of the British Government have we seen any allusion made to this arrangement, lest, it is to be presumed, the susceptibility of the people or Government of the United States might be touched by it. At the present moment, in like manner, it is easy to see that the influence of the British Government is exerted, directly and indirectly, to stimulate this Government to commit itself on the side of Spain in any further questions which may spring out of the events in Cuba between her and the United States, while England, I am persuaded, will hesitate long before she openly assumes herself any attitude that may endanger her peaceful relations with the United States.

Delicate as I feel these matters to be, I have yet thought it my duty to bring them to your consideration. Unceasing and systematic as are the efforts to embroil the United States and France with each other, I believe they may be frustrated by a policy of mutual frankness, cordiality and manliness on the part of both Governments. I ought to mention to you, in this connection, that the French Government has been a good deal disappointed by the delays which have taken place in the adjustment of the reclamation for the Seizures at San Francisco, the principle of which they considered as having been long since recognised by the Government at Washington. Mʳ Baroche has several times alluded to the subject with great delicacy, but not without anxiety lest the delays which had taken place should give rise to unpleasant *interpellations* in the National Assembly. In the conversation I had with him yesterday, he begged me to invite your attention to the subject at as early a period as your numerous official engagements would admit.

I have the honor [etc.].

2621

William C. Rives, United States Minister to France, to Daniel Webster,
Secretary of State of the United States [1]

No. 105   PARIS, *October 2, 1851.*

SIR: The questions to which the late events in Cuba have given rise still continue to occupy much of the public attention here. Of this, there are daily proofs in the Press; and dining with the President of the Republic a few days ago at Sᵗ Cloud, he introduced the subject himself in conversation with me. Referring to the anxieties which had been excited lest the general peace of the world might be disturbed by a renewal of similar attempts, he

[1] Despatches, France, vol. 33. Received October 20.

suggested the idea of some joint agreement between the United States, England and France in regard to Cuba. Being frequently interrupted by the arrival of other guests, he did not explain to me the precise nature or terms of such a joint agreement as he supposed might be desirable, but referred me to the Minister of Foreign Affairs, who, he said, would enter into the subject more fully with me. I told the President that I had no powers or instructions from my Government on the Question, but that I should be happy to converse with the Minister of Foreign Affairs and learn what were the views of the Government of France.

The hurried and imperfect conversation which passed with the President, in the midst of a large company, did not enable me to judge how far he might have adopted the idea which has been broached in England of a joint guarantee by that Power, France and the United States of the Spanish Dominion over the Island of Cuba. I availed myself of the first moment of leisure to see Monsieur Baroche, as the President had requested me to do, and had a full conversation with him yesterday morning at the office of Foreign Affairs. He commenced by asking me if I had not recently seen the President and had some conversation with him on the subject of Cuba. I told him I had, and repeated to him, what I had said to the President, that I was entirely without powers or instructions from my Government in relation to the question, but was always happy to converse with him frankly on any subject which he deemed to be of common interest to both countries. I then added that if the President's suggestion contemplated any thing like a guarantee of the permanent sovereignty of Spain over the Island of Cuba, I thought there would be insuperable objections to it on the part of the United States, for, while I well knew that the Government of the United States had no illegitimate aims on the Island of Cuba, it could never join in, or be indifferent, even, to any interference of third powers to prevent the people of the Island from asserting their own Independence, if, in the course of future events, they should desire and endeavour to effect it.

Monsieur Baroche declared in the most explicit terms that, on that point, there was a perfect accord between the views of the French Government and that of the United States—that France would never consent to guarantee the Island of Cuba to Spain against interior insurrection or any genuine and spontaneous movement of the people of the Island, to effect their Independence—that the suggestion which had been made did not contemplate, indeed, a formal *guarantee* to Spain of any kind, but simply a common declaration by the Governments of the United States, France and England, in the interest of the general tranquility of the world and to allay the jealousies and apprehensions which had been excited by recent events, that neither of the three powers would seek to get possession of the Island. He said that the French Government had the most perfect confidence in the loyalty and honorable intentions of the Government of the United States with regard to Cuba; but the public mind both in Europe and America having been painfully agitated by recent events and serious apprehensions perceived for the general peace of the world, it was thought that a common declaration of the kind he had suggested, united in by three such powers as the United States, France and England, would have a salutary effect in restoring general confidence and quiet.

I said to Monsieur Baroche in terminating our interview, that being entirely without instructions from my Government, I could say nothing to him officially on the subject he had mentioned, but that I would communicate to you the views and sentiments he had expressed. I understood him to say it was his intention also to write to Monsieur de Sartiges to present the subject to your consideration.

I have the honor [etc.].

2622

William C. Rives, United States Minister to France, to John J. Crittenden, Acting Secretary of State of the United States [1]

No. 108   PARIS, *October 23, 1851.*

SIR: I received the day before yesterday your despatch N⁰ 34,[2] in which, referring to an allusion made in my despatch No. 102[3] to an arrangement entered into by the Government of France with that of England for the employment of their joint naval forces on the West India station to protect, in certain contingences the Spanish possession of the Island of Cuba, you inform me of the President's desire that I should communicate to the Department of State, with as little delay as possible, any evidence I may possess or be able to obtain of the existence & nature of any such understanding or arrangement between France & England. You inform me at the same time that on enquiry addressed to Mʳ Crampton, the British Chargé d'Affaires at Washington, the Department of State has been assured by that gentleman that no knowledge whatever of any *conventional stipulations* on the subject is possessed by either the British or French Legations in the United States.

I am quite aware that no *conventional stipulations* have existed on the subject, nor is it usual, I apprehend, that arrangements of the kind alluded to, take the shape of formal diplomatic *conventions*. It is not the less true, however, I am persuaded, that an arrangement, of the nature above mentioned, the result of mutual understanding & communications between the two Governments, has for some time past existed & still exists between England & France in regard to the Island of Cuba. In the message of the

---

[1] Despatches, France, vol. 33. Received November 10.
[2] Above, this volume, pt. v, September 29, 1851, doc. 2483.
[3] Above, this part, September 10, 1851, doc. 2619.

President of the French Republic to the National Assembly on the 12ᵗʰ day of November last, the nature of the measures adopted by the French Government on this subject was openly declared. The following is the translation of the passage in the Message relating to Spain & Cuba, the original of which is subjoined to this despatch.

> In Spain, we have seen with pleasure the ties which unite the two countries strengthened by the mutual sympathy of the two Governments. As soon as the French Government heard of the criminal attack directed by adventurers against the Island of Cuba, we sent new forces to the Commander of the station of the Antilles, with order to unite his efforts to those of the Spanish Authorities to prevent the renewal of similar attempts.

The measures thus announced by the President as having been taken by the French Government to aid in protecting the Spanish dominion over the Island of Cuba against certain dangers which were supposed to threaten it, were universally considered at the time, & so treated in all the diplomatic circles of Europe as well as by the Press, as the result of a joint arrangement between England, France, & Spain. It was well known that active communications had been going on between the three Governments on the subject; & the general sentiment of the Diplomatic Corps here, which is rarely misled on such a question, assigned to the English Government a part in these negotiations, second only to that of the party primarily & immediately interested. I will add also that a gentleman of the highest respectability, not connected with the Diplomatic Corps, informed me at the time that a distinguished Admiral of the French Navy, a member of the National Assembly & now forming a part of the *Commission de permanence*, told him that the orders issued by the French Marine Department to the Commander of their Naval forces in the Antilles were founded on a distinct understanding with the British Government that corresponding orders were to be given to the English Squadron on the same station.

In farther justification of the opinion which has been invariably & universally held here, that England, next to Spain, has been the leading party in these arrangements, I may refer to a declaration made in the Spanish Cortes on the 16ᵗʰ day of July last, by the Minister of Foreign Affairs, the Marquis of Miraflores, who, in answer to a question put to him by a member of that body, while declining to enter into details which might "*compromise*" the Government in it's relations with other powers, is reported to have used this significant language.—"All I can say to Senor Badia is that, at the present time the *Naval* force of *England* & France, & the state of our relations with those countries offer us the certain means of preserving the integrity of our valuable Island."

Conclusive as all these circumstances were to my mind of the existence & reality of the arrangement between England & France alluded to in my despatch N? 102, I yet felt it my duty, after the receipt of your despatch of the 29th ult? to endeavor, if possible, to obtain more direct evidence of the fact from the highest official source. I knew there were considerations which made both this Government & that of England desirous that they should appear to have acted *independently* of each other in the measures which they may have adopted respecting the Island of Cuba, & the part taken by the latter, indeed, had never yet been avowed in any public act or document. I was sensible, therefore, that the subject was a delicate one to enter upon with the Minister of Foreign Affairs. I, nevertheless, determined to see him & to give such a direction to our conversation, without being unduly inquisitive or importunate, as might incidentally put me in possession of the facts which it was most important to know.

I accordingly called upon Monsieur Baroche at the Office of Foreign Affairs yesterday morning, & found him disposed to converse with me freely respecting the questions to which the late events in Cuba had given rise. He made no secret of the orders which had been given to the French Naval Forces in the West Indies to aid the Spanish Authorities in Cuba to defend the Island against invasion, & he said that he had instructed Monsieur de Sartiges to state frankly to the Government of the United States that such orders had been given & what the nature of them was. When I referred to the understanding which I supposed had been entered into with England on the subject, he seemed anxious to preclude the idea, as I anticipated he would, that the two Governments were co-operating with each other, *in virtue of any formal stipulations*. He distinctly admitted, however, that there was an express understanding between them as to the measures they had respectively adopted—that there had been repeated conferences between the British Ambassador & the Government here on the subject—and that the orders given to the French Naval Commander on the West India Station were, when framed, formally communicated to the British Government, & that Lord Palmerston had, in like manner, communicated to the French Government that similar orders had been or would be given to the English naval forces on the same Station.

It appears then unquestionable, from these statements made to me by Monsieur Baroche with his usual frankness & clearness, that the *same* measures have been concurrently adopted by the French & English Governments in regard to the Island of Cuba, *after* repeated conferences between their respective organs on the subject, & that the orders separately given by the two Governments for carrying those measures into effect were, when perfected, formally communicated by the one to the other as the fulfilment of a common understanding.— An arrangement of this kind loses nothing of it's real character from it's not having been reduced to the shape of formal *conventional stipulations*. The omission of those formalities, indeed, without changing, in any manner, the intrinsic nature of the arrangement, would better serve the policy of that one of the parties who, although the original mover of it, (as I have always believed), preferred, instead of appearing in an equal line as a contracting party on the face of a formal Convention, that another should *seem* to have taken the initiative of an act, which was not without some risk of arousing the susceptibility of an important third power.

The precise import of the orders which have been given to the naval forces of France & England, under this arrangement, is not very clear; & I thought it the less necessary to insist upon that point as Monsieur Baroche informed me that Monsieur de Sartiges had been instructed to give you the fullest explanations in regard to it.   While directed professedly against invasions of an irregular & unlawful character like that of Lopez, it is not impossible that the orders which have been issued by the two Governments partake of the vagueness of the apprehensions & suspicions which prompted them. As yet nothing amounting to an absolute *guarantee* of the Island of Cuba to the Spanish Crown against eventualities of every sort, has been concluded with any power, I am sure, tho' negotiations for that purpose, *it has been said*, are now pending at Madrid, connected with conditions for the gradual abolition of slavery & certain administrative changes in the Island.   The views of this Government on the subject of *guarantee*, as expressed to me by Monsieur Baroche, I have already communicated to the Department in my despatch N⁰ 104.[1]

The President has not yet been able to form a new Ministry & the former Heads of the respective Departments still continue provisionally to direct their administration.

I have the honor [etc.].

2623

Count de Sartiges, French Minister to the United States, to John J. Crittenden, Acting Secretary of State of the United States [2]

[TRANSLATION]

WASHINGTON, *October 27, 1851.*

The Undersigned, Minister of France has received the note dated the 22ᵈ of October, which, the Acting Secretary of State addressed him,[3] subsequently to the conversation he had the honor of holding with him, on the 8ᵗʰ of the same month, in the course of which, Mʳ de Sartiges had, in a kind and friendly manner, informed Mr. Crittenden, who appeared to be ignorant of the fact, of the character of the instructions issued by the government of

---

[1] He refers erroneously to his despatch No. 105, dated October 2, 1851, above, this part, doc. 2621.   No. 104 is not pertinent to this publication.
[2] Notes from France, vol. 15.   Received October 29.
[3] Above, this volume, pt. v, doc. 2484.

the Republic, to the commanding officer of the French Station at Havana, as soon as it was known in Paris, that the first detachment of adventurers, commanded by Lopez, which announced itself, as the advance guard, of a larger expedition, had succeeded in getting off to sea.

Notwithstanding the spirit of kindness in which that communication was made, Mr Crittenden reserved himself to point out, in writing, if, upon reflection, he should deem it expedient, the considerations, which it might give rise to; both in the mind of the President and his own.   Mr de Sartiges thanks him for having done so; for while he sees, in the note addressed to him, renewed assurances of the strongest sympathy, on the part of the American Government, and of the American people, for France and her government, he also finds occasion, to recall certain points of his conversation, which, it would appear, were not, at first, presented by him, with sufficient clearness. Mr de Sartiges had endeavored to establish, in a distinct manner, the two following points; *first*—that the instructions issued by the government of the Republic, were spontaneous and isolated; *secondly*, that those instructions were exclusive, for an exclusive case, and applicable only to the class, and not to the nationality, of any pirate or adventurer, that should attempt to land, in arms, on the shores of a friendly power.   He had added, that the existing laws, in regard to the right of search, laws, about which, the susceptibilities of the French Government, are as forcibly roused, as those of the government of the United States—were neither directly, nor indirectly affected, by the order to repel violence by force, since the instructions which have been issued to the commanding officer of the French Station, were only intended to apply to a case of piracy, the article of the maritime code, in force, concerning pirates.   In again asserting these two points categorically, as he now does, the Undersigned thinks that he has removed all cause of prejudice, on the part of the President, both as regards the importance of an act, agreed upon, in advance, on the part of France and England, and the likelihood, that the laws which govern the right of search, will be, in the least, affected.   He will add, that the attitude assumed by President Fillmore, and by his Cabinet, under these lamentable circumstances, has been so upright, that the French Government, so far from intending to imply doubts, which did not exist, by the measures it spontaneously adopted, it had, on the contrary, reason to believe, that it would find, in those same latitudes, the American Squadron, acting in the same spirit, and pursuing a similar object. This consideration must prevent any false construction, tending to give to this act of the Republican Government, the appearance of an admonition, or of a reproach, tacitly addressed to the Government of the United States, and never contemplated by the French Government.

Mr de Sartiges begs to thank Mr Crittenden, for having sent him, the text of the law of 1818, actually in force, for preventing the crime of armed invasion of a territory, belonging to any friendly power.   He is happy to find, that the opinion of the Representatives of the American Nation, is in honest opposition to this species of aggressions; and that Congress has furnished the President with sufficient means to arrest them. These means, placed in strong and able hands, and, of which, the President openly declares, that he will make an energetic use, if, unfortunately, the occasion for resorting to them, should again occur, become the much more precious for the peace of the world, as America is closely connected with Europe,—being only separated from the latter, by a distance scarcely exceeding eight days' journey,— by one of the most important of general interests,—the interest of commerce. The nations of America and of Europe, are, at this day, so dependent upon one another, that the effects of any event, prosperous or otherwise, happening on one side of the Atlantic, are immediately felt on the other side. The Undersigned finds among other proofs, an evidence of the interest which binds the Government of the United States, to the other Governments of the world, in several passages of the note of October, 22^{d}, wherein, Mr. Crittenden, in appealing to the liberal ideas of France, intimates, that the continuance of those sentiments of confidence, and fraternal sympathy, which so happily unite the two countries, is calculated to make the cause of free institutions, in Europe, prevail. The result of this community of interests, commercial, political, and moral, between Europe and America,—of this frequency and rapidity of intercourse between them, is, that it becomes as difficult to point out the geographical degree, where American policy should terminate, and European policy begin, as it is, to trace out the line, where American Commerce begins, and European Commerce terminates;—where may be said to begin or to terminate, the ideas, which are in the ascendant, in Europe and in America.

The Undersigned has likewise the honor of reminding the Acting Secretary of State, that the territories belonging to the various European powers, either on the seas, or on the American Continent, are considered by the States to which they appertain, as constituting part of the system of their general policy. France has never admitted that her possessions, in the Antilles, might enjoy any other political rights, than those which are universally recognized in Europe; it is the same with England;—the same with Spain; in regard to their American possessions. It is in virtue of this principle of common law, which no power has as yet repudiated, either on its own account, or in behalf of its neighbors, that the Government of the Republic has been able to show the interest it feels, as it has done, for the security of an Island, recognized as Spanish territory, by treaties actually in force, which security has been threatened in the midst of Universal peace.

These general considerations, do not prevent the Undersigned from acknowledging, that the interest which a country feels for another, is naturally increased by reason of proximity, and, his government, which understands the complicated nature, as well as the importance of the relations existing between the United States and Cuba, has seriously considered the declaration formerly made by the government of the United States, and which has been renewed on this occasion, "That that Government, could not see with indifference the Island of Cuba, pass from the hands of Spain into those of another European State." The French Government, is likewise of opinion, that, in case it should comport with the interests of Spain, at some future day, to part with Cuba, the possession of that Island, or the protectorship of the same, ought not to fall upon any of the great Maritime powers of the world.

The Undersigned hopes, that this frank declaration, which, he feels himself justified in making, in regard to the disinterested views of his Government, as to the future destiny of Cuba, and which breathes the same spirit, as that of the declaration which the United States Government made on the subject, and the categorical explanations he has given, relative to the character of the instructions exclusively sent to the French Station at Havana, will put an end to all the uncertainty, which the late events, that befell on the occasion of Lopez's expedition, might have given rise to, in the mind of the President, and that His Excellency will rest satisfied, as to the great value, which, the Government of the Republic attaches, to the maintenance and development of those frank, and sympathetic relations, at present existing between the two countries.

The Undersigned avails himself of this occasion [etc.].

2624

William C. Rives, United States Minister to France, to Daniel Webster, Secretary of State of the United States [1]

[EXTRACT]

No. 111   PARIS, *November 5, 1851.*

SIR: . . . The National Assembly, in pursuance of their adjournment, met yesterday, & the Message, of the President, which had been looked to with great interest & anxiety not only here, but through Europe, was laid before them. It's important feature is the recommendation, in unequivocal terms, of the repeal of the law of the 31st May 1850, & the reestablishment of Universal Suffrage on the broad basis on which it stood under the Constituent Assembly.—I enclose a copy of the Message,[2] & annex to this despatch a translation of the two paragraphs of it which have a special interest for the United States.

[1] Despatches, France, vol. 33.   Received November 24.
  The omitted portion refers to the acceptance by Napoleon III of the office of arbiter tendered to him by the United States and Portugal, relating to the claims for the destruction of the ship *General Armstrong.*   [2] Not included in this publication.

In the first of these paragraphs you will recognise a full confirmation of what I have said in several of my despatches & particularly that of the 23ᵈ ultº (Nº 108),[1] respecting an *arrangement* between England & France for the joint employment of their naval forces for the protection of the Island of Cuba. The President of the Republic says in so many words "*we associated ourselves to England*, (en nous associant à l'Angleterre), to offer the *co-operation* of our naval forces to the Cabinet of Madrid, in order to repel the audacious enterprise against the Island of Cuba", thus not only proclaiming the existence of a mutual & common arrangement, but implying by a significant phraseology that England, as I have always supposed, had really taken the lead in it, & that France joined in it as her associate. It is due to the French Government, in this connection, to mention what Monsieur Baroche said to me in my last conversation with him on this subject—that in the orders given to the French Naval Forces, they were expressly instructed, in any operations they might engage in, to respect the flag of the United States wherever it might appear, & to commit no act of hostility upon any vessel or armament under it's protection.

I have the honor [etc.].

EXTRACTS FROM THE MESSAGE OF THE PRESIDENT OF THE FRENCH REPUBLIC OF THE 4ᵀᴴ INSTANT.

Our good relations with Spain cause us to hope an early & definitive adjustment of the differences on the subject of the boundary of the Pyrenees. We have seized with eagerness the occasion to give to Spain a proof of the sincerity of our relations, in associating ourselves to England (*en nous associant à l'Angleterre*), to offer to the Cabinet of Madrid the co-operation of our naval Forces in order to repel the audacious enterprise against the Island of Cuba. Moreover, our Minister at Washington has been instructed to give his support in a friendly manner (*appuyer amicablement*), to the reclamations of the Court of Madrid—reclamations whose justice has been loyally recognised by the Federal Government.

 . . . . .

The reclamations which a great number of French Merchants & Shipowners have to pursue against the Government of the United States, on account of arbitrary seizures made by the Custom-Houses of California, are not yet liquidated & paid; but the American Congress & the Cabinet of Washington have formally acknowledged their justice, and we shall not be long in obtaining a legitimate satisfaction of them.

[1] Above, this part, doc. 2622.

2625

William C. Rives, United States Minister to France, to Daniel Webster, Secretary of State of the United States [1]

[EXTRACT]

No. 112   PARIS, *November 13, 1851.*

SIR: . . . Not having yet received an answer to the enquiries I addressed to the proper official Department here for information on the points mentioned in your communication of 10th ultimo,[2] it is not in my power to add any thing of importance to what I had the honor to lay before you in my Despatch Nọ 110,[3] respecting the Legislation of France on those points. In addition to the instances, however, mentioned in that despatch of manifest connivance on the part of European Governments at military expeditions fitted out within their respective jurisdictions against foreign countries, I am now enabled to give you some particulars of one which, from the consideration of the parties concerned, it may be of special interest to recall. Ex-President Flores of the Republic of Ecuador, on his expulsion from that country, took refuge in Spain, & there openly commenced & prosecuted, with the encouragement & assistance of the Spanish Government, the enlistment of men & officers, & other military preparations for the invasion of that Republic & the accomplishment of a counter-revolution in that part of South America.

A branch of the same expedition was organised in England, of which you will find a notice in the British Annual Register for the year 1847, under the date of the 4th of January of that year, in the part of the work which is devoted to the *chronicle* of current events, p. 4. Complaints being made to the British Government of the hostile preparations going on in England, that Government was compelled to interfere, & seized & confiscated the three vessels, one a large India-man & the other two heavily armed Steamers, which had been engaged to convey the expedition. In the notice of the expedition contained in the Annual Register, you will observe it is stated that the funds for carrying it on were reported to be furnished by the Spanish Queen Mother Christina, one of whose sons by Munos (the Duke of Rianzares), was said to be destined to the sovereignty of the country, which was the object of this unlawful enterprise.

[1] Despatches, France, vol. 33. Received November 28.
The omitted portion relates chiefly to a discussion in the French National Assembly relative to the military force of the country.
[2] Neither the instruction nor the note of Rives to the French Government is included in this publication. The points mentioned in the brief instruction to him were as follows: "Is there any law in France which prohibits the enlistment of troops within the Republic, to be employed in wars abroad?" and "Is there any law of the French Republic which prohibits its own citizens from fitting out or setting on foot military expeditions in France, intended to act against other Governments or to take part in wars in other countries?"
[3] Not included in this publication, since it cited past instances of the fitting out, in France, of hostile expeditions against European, and not American governments.

Spain was the principal theatre of the preparations made for it. It was there that the chief of the expedition established himself, & there men & officers were openly enlisted, organised & trained, to the number of many hundreds.   Recruiting stations were publicly opened in Madrid & several of the principal towns of Spain, & no concealment whatever made of the object of these preparations. A gentleman of the highest respectability who then resided in Spain, & had the best means of information, assures me that he has seen a letter from the Inspector General of the Spanish Army to General Flores informing him that discharges were daily granted to soldiers in the Spanish Army to enable them to join the expedition, & another from the Minister of War, holding out to Spanish officers the assurance that they should retain their rank in the Spanish service notwithstanding their temporary absence, in order to induce them to engage in the expedition.

All these things were going on for months under the eyes & with the encouragement of the Spanish Government, during the ministry of the same Senor [Señor] Isturiz, who a few months since as Ambassador of Spain in England, put forth a statement denouncing as piratical & atrocious an expedition which, in no single respect, was more unwarrantable than that which was aided & abetted by the public authorities of his own country, while he was it's prime minister, & which they never, at any time, did the slightest thing to repress, the expedition having fallen thro' solely from the seizure of the vessels in England which were engaged to convey it to it's destination.

I have the honor [etc.].

2626

William C. Rives, United States Minister to France, to Daniel Webster, Secretary of State of the United States [1]

No. 140   PARIS, *April 3, 1852.*

SIR: I received on the 1ˢᵗ Instant a note from the Minister of Foreign Affairs requesting me if convenient, to call at the Foreign Office the following day.   I did so accordingly, when the Marquis Turgot opened the conversation by saying he desired to see me to inform me that it was the intention of the French Government to send a Minister very soon to South America for the purpose of entering into commercial arrangements with the States bordering on the La Plata & it's—tributaries—that the recent events in that quarter, afforded an appropriate occasion for securing, in the general interest of all nations, the free navigation of those great confluents—& that the French Government wished to profit of the opportunity, at the same time, for extending the market for the productions of French industry.   He said it was not the wish or the intention of the French Government to ask for any exclusive privileges or advantages for their trade.   On the contrary, it de-

[1] Despatches, France, vol. 33.   Received April 28.

sired only such arrangements as would be open to the rest of the world & alike beneficial to all nations.   This being the case, he thought it proper, in the spirit of frankness & friendship which he hoped to see always prevail in the relations between our two countries, to make me acquainted at once with the intentions of the French Government, that I might communicate them to my own.   I said to him that I was persuaded the Government of the United States would justly appreciate this mark of consideration on the part of the Government of France, & added that the commercial policy of the United States had always been founded on the liberal & catholic principles which he announced as forming the object of the contemplated negotiations in South America.   At the same time, I certainly think the Government of the United States should lose no time in placing, by it's own vigilance & care, the commerce of our citizens on a footing of equal advantage with that of other nations in a part of the world where, in a race of fair & equal competition, we cannot fail to secure the most brilliant prizes.

After this subject was disposed of, the Marquis Turgot adverted to the reports which have prevailed here for a week or two past, & to which one of the leading Parisian-Journals has given an undue importance, of another expedition against Cuba being in preparation at New-Orleans.   He said it was with great regret that the French Government had seen these reports, & that it had been constrained by it's engagements to renew the orders that had been heretofore given to their naval force in the West-Indies, restricting itself, however, to a simple renewal of those orders in the terms in which they had been given with reference to the last expedition.   I called the attention of the Marquis Turgot to the correspondence which had already taken place between the Department of State & Monsieur Sartiges on this subject, & sought to impress upon him the unpleasant & dangerous consequences which might arise from the orders which had been issued by the English & French Governments to their respective squadrons in the West-Indies & which were, last autumn, notified to the Government of the United States.[1]   He said, that as these orders were directed exclusively against piratical attempts & that as the flag of the United States would, in every case be respected, he did not see that any danger of collision with the United States could grow out of them.   I told him the subject had been fully discussed in the correspondence to which I referred, & I hoped the French Government would weigh well the considerations that had then been presented. I subjoin to this despatch the newspaper article above alluded to,[2] which appeared in the *Journal des Debats* & is vouched, as you will perceive, by the signature of it's principal Editor & proprietor.

I have the honor [etc.].

[1] See the notes of Acting Secretary of State Crittenden and Secretary of State Webster to Sartiges, above, this volume, pt. v, October 22 and November 18, 1851, docs. 2484 and 2485; and see, also, the note of Sartiges to Crittenden, above, this part, October 27, 1851, doc. 2623.
[2] Not included in this publication.

2627

Count de Sartiges, French Minister to the United States, to Daniel Webster,
Secretary of State of the United States [1]

[TRANSLATION]

WASHINGTON, *April 22, 1852.*

The Minister of France, charged by his Government to present a communication to the Secretary of State in company with the Minister of England, requests him to be good enough to indicate the day and hour when he can receive him.   He begs him to accept the assurance of his high consideration.

2628

Count de Sartiges, French Minister to the United States, to Daniel Webster,
Secretary of State of the United States [2]

Confidential.   WASHINGTON, *April 23, 1852.*

SIR: I have the honor to send you herewith the copies of the dispatch and convention [3] which formed the subject of the conversation which Mr. Crampton and I had the honor to have with you this morning.

[1] Notes from France, vol. 15.   The receipt date was not indicated.   [2] *Ibid.*
[3] They follow:

Marquis de Turgot, Minister of Foreign Affairs of France, to Count de Sartiges, French
Minister to the United States

[Translation]

PARIS, *March 31, 1852.*

SIR: The flagrant attacks recently directed against the island of Cuba by bands of adventurers organized on the territory of the United States with the boldly avowed design of taking that ancient possession from Spain, have upon several occasions, as you know, invoked the serious attention of the Government of the Republic; and it has regretted them all the more in that they might eventually compromise the friendly relations so happily existing between France and the United States.   We have therefore sent to the Commanders of the French naval forces in the Gulf of Mexico instructions to take all necessary measures, should the occasion arise, to cooperate with the Spanish authorities in the defense of the island and in the maintenance of the sovereignty of Spain over this important colony.   The Government of Her Britannic Majesty, animated by the same sentiments of respect for the rights of the Spanish Crown, and governed by the same principles, has adopted similar resolutions for the preservation of the present state of possession of the island of Cuba, which is of no less importance to the relations of the great maritime Powers than to the interests of Spain herself.   The two cabinets of Paris and London have also exchanged communications on this subject with that of Washington, which evidence their solicitude for the maintenance of rights consecrated by treaties and by time and the federal Government for its part, in disavowing in the most formal manner expeditions which were prepared on its territory, and which sheltered themselves under its flag, declared that it would not see with indifference the island of Cuba fall into the power of any other European power than Spain.   As we ourselves could not see with indifference this important colony fall into the power of any other maritime Power than Spain, we have wondered, in the presence of these facts, whether it would not be possible, in order to avoid in the future all chance of friction and

The opinion and sentiments which you have expressed to us upon this subject with such frankness and precision, are so perfectly in accord with those expressed by the government of the Republic, and are such a complete application of the principles announced by President Fillmore upon several occasions, and especially in his last annual message to Congress, that it would be a great satisfaction to me to be able to transmit them to Marquis

---

to remove more surely all disagreeable complications between the great States, which alone might be supposed to hold ambitious designs upon Cuba, to proclaim in common accord, by an act or exchange of declarations, the sentiments which animate them, and the official declaration of which would be of a nature effectively to prevent any future attempt towards an opposite end.   It is in this spirit that we have communicated with the Government of Her Britannic Majesty on this question, and we have become assured that it was ready, as we ourselves are, to engage not to profit in any case from events which could result in causing this colony to pass into its power.   If, therefore, the Government of the United States shared our view that the best method of guaranteeing the good harmony of our mutual relations, against the dangers which would threaten from the renewal of culpable aggressions which are ever to be dreaded, would be to proclaim anew our disinterested intentions regarding the island of Cuba, we would be prepared to sign with it and the Government of Her Britannic Majesty a mutual engagement which would establish, by the same act and in the same form, our respective renunciations of the eventual possession of a colony, whose importance would not permit its abandonment, without defence, to the possibilities of aggression condemned by the law of nations and incompatible with the interests of all maritime Powers.

I attach hereto, in the event that the federal Government should prefer a convention to the exchange of notes, a draft project which, in the opinion of the Government of the Republic, would answer the purpose proposed, and I request you to submit this project to the approval of the Washington Government.   Please accompany this communication with all the arguments and explanations you consider susceptible of influencing the acceptance by the federal Government of the proposition which I have just presented to you.

You will please read the present dispatch to the Secretary of State for Foreign Affairs, and leave a copy with him.

Accept [etc.].

DRAFT CONVENTION

[Translation]

Preamble

Her Majesty the Queen of the United Kingdom of Great Britain and Ireland,
The Prince President of the French Republic,

and the United States of America, having judged it useful, with a view to strengthening the friendly relations which happily exist between them, to declare and determine by a convention their views and intentions relative to the island of Cuba, have to this end appointed their respective plenipotentiaries, to wit:

Her Majesty the Queen of the United Kingdom of Great Britain and Ireland, etc., etc.
The Prince President of the French Republic, etc., etc.
The President of the United States of America, etc., etc.

Who, after having communicated their respective full powers and found them in good and due form, have agreed upon and adopted the following articles:

Article 1

The high contracting parties, by the present convention, disavow individually and collectively, for the present as well as for the future, all intention of obtaining possession of the island of Cuba, and they engage respectively to prevent and to repress, so far as may lie in their power, every attempt undertaken toward this end by any power or individual whatsoever.

The high contracting parties declare individually and collectively that they will not assume or maintain, either for all or for one of them, any right of exclusive control over the said island, and that they will not assume nor exercise any authority there.

Turgot in the exact terms employed by you.   If, therefore, you should think it à propos in acknowledging receipt of the present communication, to reproduce them succinctly in the form which would appear to you to be most desirable, I would thus be put in a position to transmit them *confidentially* to my government in a form which, I am certain, would be extremely pleasing to it.

Accept, Sir, the assurance of my highest esteem.

2629

Count de Sartiges, French Minister to the United States, to Daniel Webster, Secretary of State of the United States [1]

[TRANSLATION]

WASHINGTON, *April 29, 1852.*

SIR: I have received the note which you were good enough to write to me in response to the letter I had addressed to you on the 23d,[2] confidentially in accordance with your suggestion, and following the interview which I had with you on the 22 instant in company with the Minister of England.[3]

It is with sincere satisfaction that I find the assurance in your note that the proposition contained in the dispatch of March 31 from Marquis Turgot [4] will be taken into consideration by President Fillmore, who will give it his most serious attention.   While recognizing that this important question merits the mature reflection of the Government of the United States, I dare to hope, Sir, that the parity of views of my Government and the Government of the United States upon the subject of the future of Cuba, which you set forth in your note, will facilitate the prompt and satisfactory solution of this question.

Accept, Sir, the assurance of my high esteem.

Article 2

The present convention shall be ratified and the ratifications exchanged at Washington as soon as possible within the period of .... months from the date of the convention.

In faith whereof the respective plenipotentiaries have signed this act and affixed thereto their seals.

Done at Washington the .... of the year of our Lord 1852.

[1] Notes from France, vol. 15.   The receipt date was not indicated.
[2] For the former note, see above, this volume, pt. v, April 29, 1852, doc. 2486, and for the latter, see above, this part, doc. 2628.
[3] Sartiges applied for an interview on the 22d, for which see above, this part, doc. 2627, but the first paragraph, in his note to the Secretary of State, dated April 23, for which see above, this part, doc. 2628, refers to this interview as having occurred "this morning."
[4] See above, this part, p. 636, note 3.

2630

Count de Sartiges, French Minister to the United States, to Daniel Webster,
Secretary of State of the United States [1]

[TRANSLATION]

WASHINGTON, *July 8, 1852.*

MR. SECRETARY OF STATE: In reply to the communication which I had
the honor to present to you April 23, which comprised a draft convention
relative to the island of Cuba, and the copy of the instructions which had
been sent to me upon that occasion by the Minister of Foreign Affairs of the
Prince President, you addressed a note to me on the 29th of the same month
in which you assure me that the communication which I had had the honor
to make to you would be taken up for consideration by President Fillmore
and given his most serious attention.[2]   Two months have elapsed since then,
and I desire to ask you to be good enough to inform me of the intentions of
the American Government on the subject of the invitation which I had the
honor to address to you in the name of my Government, and by which the
Government of the United States is invited to join its declaration to that
which the French Government, in agreement with the English Government,
has resolved to make, and which consists in a common renunciation, under
every condition and by every means whatsoever, of the possession of the
island of Cuba.   At the same time I shall call your attention in writing to
several of the observations in support of this proposition, which, in common
with the Minister of England, I presented to you in the conversation which
Mr. Crampton and I have already had with you on this subject, and which,
I at least hope, are of a nature to put the question in its true light, and remove every false interpretation which might be attached to the acts and
words emanating from one of the three Governments.

First, as to the right of possession and sovereignty, Cuba is a Spanish
province by the most sacred of titles, discovery and uninterrupted possession.   Spain intends to preserve her province; the Spanish subjects who inhabit it wish to remain united to the Mother country.   This right of possession is indisputable and undisputed, and the Government of the United
States upon every occasion, I am pleased to recognize, has hastened to proclaim its respect for this right.   Therefore, is it not the simple recognition of
this right that the Government of the Prince President proposes by the
declaration which it announces its willingness to make simultaneously with
the Government of the Queen of England and, we hope, with the Government of the United States?   What is proposed is, in guarding against future

[1] Notes from France, vol. 15.   Received July 8.
[2] For the note of Sartiges to the Secretary of State and its enclosures, see above, this part,
doc. 2628, and footnote 3 thereto, p. 636; and for the reply, see above, this volume, pt. V,
doc. 2486.

eventualities, to end a situation which is too strained, from the point of view of the relations between Spain and the other Powers in general with respect to Cuba, and delicate from the point of view of the relations between the great maritime Powers themselves.

In effect, today when the maritime commerce of the world tends to take the shorter routes of the isthmuses of Central America to pass from one ocean to the other, the island of Cuba, a veritable continent placed on this route, finds itself in a geographical situation such that the nation which possesses it, provided its naval armaments are considerable, can at will protect or intercept interoceanic communication. Now if the maritime Powers must, out of respect for the acquired rights of Spain and for international law, abstain from every ulterior design upon the eventual possession of Cuba, they owe it to the protection of the interests of their subjects, to the protection of the commerce of all nations, all of which have the right to use the same maritime routes, to proclaim and secure, so far as lies in their power, the present and future neutrality of the island of Cuba. France has allowed no occasion to pass of manifesting with regard to Cuba its respect for the sovereign rights of the Spanish Crown, its disinterested sentiments concerning the present and future of that possession. England in like acts has witnessed a similarity of sentiments and views in this regard, and the Government of the United States has itself declared upon several occasions that it could not be expected to acquiesce in the cession of Cuba to any European Power.

This declaration of the Government of the United States partakes of the nature of that made by the Governments of France and England, which they propose to the American Government to consign in common in an official act. Only, my Government, and likewise the English Government, at the same time that it declares that it cannot be expected to acquiesce in the cession of Cuba to any maritime Power, adds that it frankly renounces it upon its own behalf both for the present and for the future. I do not doubt that the Government of the United States, in making its declaration, has been animated by the same motive as that which inspired the declarations of the French and English Governments. However, the word *"European"* coupled with the word Power may cause our Governments to hesitate as to the meaning of this declaration of the Government of the United States, and may give rise to the thought that the latter Government, while excluding other nations from the possibilities of the future, takes care to reserve the advantages thereof for itself. Between Powers such as the United States, France, and England, one does not search to give other than their exact import to political words and acts. By the acceptance of the draft of the common declaration which I have had the honor to remit to you April 23, the import of the declarations made by the Governments of the United States, France and England, on the subject of the future of the island of Cuba, will be exactly determined. It is important, for the reasons stated above, that the question as to the future of Cuba be fully settled today. It is important to all of us that it be determined, in so far as the permanent neutrality of the island is concerned, and for the following reason:

You are aware that the French Government and that English and French subjects are in various ways creditors of Spain for considerable sums. The expense involved in the maintenance of a strong army of 25,000 men in the island of Cuba, constitutes a serious drain upon its treasury, which impedes the efforts it is making to fulfill its financial engagements towards us. By removing the cause of the fear which leads to these expensive armaments, the Spanish treasury would be left more latitude to meet its engagements. This applies more particularly to Spain, France and England; but what applies to the commerce of all the nations, and particularly to American commerce, the most important to Cuba, is that in the present state of things, Spain can not reasonably be expected to adopt any measure tending to modify in a more liberal sense, its tariff at Habana, which is complained of in the United States, and which has often been advanced as justification for aggressions against the island. But if on the strength of the guaranty of peaceful possession, which the great maritime Powers would give to it by the declaration which they propose to make in common, Spain could without danger decrease the number of its troops in Cuba, this lessening of its burdens would doubtless permit it to lower the duties which bear heavily upon foreign commerce, in which you have the largest part.

The project which I have been charged to present to you, Mr. Secretary, contains but one article, having in view two objects: one, "renunciation of the eventual heritage of Cuba"; the other, "engagement to cause this renunciation to be respected". These two objects appear to have already occupied the attention of the American Government, and in order to preserve the sovereignty of Spain over the island of Cuba, this Government has upon several occasions thought of having recourse to vigorous measures, among others, at a time when the rumor was spread, wrongly no doubt, that it was the intention of a Spanish General to withdraw to Cuba and there declare his independence under the protection of one of the large maritime Powers, the Government of the United States thought it its duty to offer to the Spanish Government in preparation for such a contingency the assistance of its army and navy.

Today France in concert with England does not ask the United States to do as much, in uniting with them, as the United States proposed to the Spanish Government to do by itself upon that occasion. For, in the draft convention which I have had the honor to transmit to you, it is said: "They engage respectively to prevent and to repress, *so far as may lie in their power* ["], etc., etc. . . . a phrase which does not bind any of the three Governments beyond that which their respective Constitutions will permit them to do.

This passage of the project will, I am emboldened to hope, facilitate its adoption by the Government of the United States, and will enable it, in signing the common declaration proposed to it today by France and England, to assure a future tranquillity to the commerce of the world in these parts, to discourage culpable undertakings against Cuba, and to draw still closer the bonds of friendship which unite the United States to France, as well as to England and Spain.

Accept, Mr. Secretary of State, [etc.].

2631

William C. Rives, United States Minister to France, to Edward Everett, Secretary of State of the United States [1]

[EXTRACT]

No. 183   PARIS, *January 6, 1853.*

SIR: . . . The two occurrences referred to in your Despatch N⁰ 56,[2] to wit, the military operations of Monsieur Raousset Boulbon in Mexico & the supposed occupation by a French Squadron of the Bay & Peninsula of Samana in the Eastern part of the Island of San Domingo, were not known or heard of here 'till a week ago, when rumors of both were brought for the first time by the weekly Steamer from New York to Liverpool. These rumors being of a very vague & uncertain character, & one of them indeed, that of the occupation of Samana, being positively contradicted by several of the Government Journals here, I did not feel that it would be proper for me to make them the subject of a conversation with the Minister of Foreign Affairs, until accounts should reach me of a less questionable character. In this state of things, when I was about to take leave of the Minister in my rather hurried interview of last evening, he himself introduced the subject of the reported occupation of Samana by a French Squadron, & said to me that it was a *fable (une histoire)*, from beginning to end.

He stated that his Colleague the Minister of the Marine had informed him that he had every reason to beleive that not a single French vessel of war was at Samana or in its neighborhood at the time of the reported occupation, & that no orders or instructions, certainly, had issued from his Department authorising such a proceeding—that to promote as far as possible the pacification of the Island, French vessels had been instructed occasionally to show themselves along the coast, but that their movements were solely with a view to that object. I remarked to the Minister of Foreign Affairs

---

[1] Despatches, France, vol. 34. Received January 25.
  The omitted portion relates to the application of Rives for an audience with the Emperor of France, Napoleon III, for the purpose of presenting his new credentials.
[2] Above, this volume, pt. v, December 17, 1852, doc. 2489.

that the rumor of this occupation, touching as it did very important &
vital interests of the United States, had naturally excited the prompt
attention of the American Government & people, & that I should be most
happy to communicate to you the spontaneous & formal contradiction he
had given to it, upon his own sense of what was due to the frank & cordial
relations of the two Governments.

The conversation, then, turned to the adventures of Monsieur Boulbon in
Mexico who, he said was, no doubt, a Frenchman, but like almost every
body else in that unfortunate country, was acting in entire independence of
all national control & responsibility.   He said he hardly deemed it necessary
to assure me that his proceedings were wholly unauthorised by the French
Government, and he treated the mock-heroic annexation of Sonora to France
as Monsieur de Sartiges had done in his conversation with you—as a *mauvaise plaisanterie*.   If any thing else should occur here in regard to either of
these questions, I will not fail to give you the earliest information of it.

I have the honor [etc.].

2632

*William C. Rives, United States Minister to France, to Edward Everett,
Secretary of State of the United States* [1]

[EXTRACTS]

No. 185   PARIS, *January 13, 1853*.

SIR: I was received in public audience by the Emperor on the 10th instant
for the purpose of presenting my new letters of credence.[2] . . .

When the Emperor concluded these remarks, he invited me to take a seat.
The Grand Chambellan [Chamberlain] & the Grand Maitre des cérémonies,
with their attendants, then retired, the Minister of Foreign Affairs remaining.   The Emperor entered into general conversation with me, enquired if I
had good news from America, & spoke particularly of the impression which
the extraordinary activity he had witnessed in all the pursuits of life, during
his short sojournment in the United States, had made upon him, compared
with which, he said, Europe seemed to him at the time to be *asleep*.   After a
few words on the general relations between Europe & the United States, he
adverted to your answer to the notes of the Ministers of France & England
proposing a joint convention with the United States on the subject of Cuba,
& said he regretted it was not more satisfactory.   I ventured to ask His
Majesty in what respect it was not satisfactory.   I understood the Emperor
to say that, while disavowing the intention of making any effort at present to
obtain possession of Cuba, it held out the idea of it's future acquisition

[1] Despatches, France, vol. 34.   Received February 1.
[2] The omitted portion relates to his audience with the Emperor.

by the United States; and he then appealed to the Minister of Foreign Affairs to state the import of it.   The Minister of Foreign Affairs concurred in the same interpretation of it.

I remarked to His Majesty that I had not yet been furnished with a copy of your note & that I could not, therefore, speak of the interpretation to be put upon it, but that in a Government like ours, where the Executive power was temporary & passed into new hands every four years, it would be evident to His Majesty that no Cheif Magistrate could undertake to tie up the hands of succeeding administrations from doing what the exigencies or interests of the nation at any future period might be supposed to require—that the Government of the United States had given evidence of its anxious desire to respect the rights of all other powers, & had acted with scrupulous respect to those of Spain in regard to Cuba—and that in a recent debate in the Senate of the United States, which had, doubtless, attracted the attention of the Minister of Foreign Affairs, distinguished members of that body of all parties had reproved & denounced, in the strongest terms, any attempt by citizens of the United States to disturb the rightful sovereignty of Spain over that Island.   I proceeded to say that, besides this determined opposition to all unlawful attempts on the Island of Cuba, there was one other point which might be considered as equally fixed in the policy of the United States, & that, I was persuaded, His Majesty would fully appreciate—that in consideration of the peculiar geographical relation of that Island to the territory, navigation & commerce of the United States, they never could consent to see it pass into the possession of any other maratime power; and I added that the same consideration naturally made the public mind in the United States very sensitive to the rumor which had, for a short time, recently prevailed of the occupation by a French Squadron of the Bay of Samana in San Domingo, & which had already been the subject of a conversation I had had the honor to hold with the Minister of Foreign Affairs.   The Emperor received these observations with his usual courtesy; and after some expressions of personal civility which he was pleased to add, the audience terminated.

A day or two after my last despatch, the rumor of the occupation of Samana by a French Squadron was revived by a Telegraphic despatch from London which professed to embody the American news brought by the Steamer *Baltic*, about a week ago, in her last arrival at Liverpool.   This Telegraphic intelligence was the subject of comment, the same evening, in two of the Parisian Journals in the interest of the Government, the *Patrie* & the *Constitutionnel*, both of which called it in question & put the public on its guard against similar rumors.—On the following day, the *Patrie* again noticed this revived rumor, & pronounced it to be "completely false"; and it's contradiction was reproduced, in identical terms, in the *Constitutionnel*, the *Journal des Débats*, & probably the greater number of the daily news-papers of Paris.

Notwithstanding these repeated contradictions of the rumor in question, which we have every reason to beleive is, down to the present time, without foundation, an article of a remarkable character appeared, a few days ago, in a publication which is issued from time to time, in successive *cahiers* or *Nos*, by the Department of Agriculture & Commerce, entitled *Annales du Commerce Exterieur*. I enclose herewith the N⁰ of that publication referred to, in which you will find a "*Note sur la presq-ile de Samana*" in which you will see the maritime advantages of that station very studiously set forth, in a military as well as commercial view, more particularly in reference to Steam-Navigation on account of its abundant supply of coal. This article has since been republished in the *Journal des Débats*, & in the *Constitutionnel* with remarks which, brief as they are, seem to merit attention. I enclose extracts from those Journals containing the matter referred to, & also the articles of the *Patrie* & other newspapers alluded to in the preceeding paragraph, all of which I have caused to be arranged in the order of their dates that you may the better appreciate their bearing & connexion. The No. of the "Annales du Commerce Exterieur" sent herewith, tho' bearing as you will perceive at the bottom of the page the date of November 1852, was not published 'till four or five days ago.[1] It may not be amiss to mention that nothing whatever has yet appeared in the *Moniteur*, so far as I have seen, in regard to this subject, while it has been the not unfruitful theme of news-paper paragraphs to the rest of the Parisian Press.

There can be no doubt that the attention of the French Government has, on several occasions, been called to the expediency of obtaining a foot-hold, under some form or other, in the Island of San Domingo. In the "Annuaire des deux Mondes" for 1850 which appeared in September 1851, & of which the different portions were contributed by able & well-informed writers, the subject is presented in the following very pointed & significant terms.

> The direct intervention of a great Power under the form of protectorate, partial occupation or pure & simple annexation is, therefore, no longer, at the present moment, a question of progress merely for the Dominicans; it is a question of life or death, & this question, now as in the outset of the insurrection—in the anguish of a desperate situation as in the intoxication of the first hour of deliverance—after eight years of discouraging refusals as in the first flush of their French hopes—this question is one which they still persist to address to France. No person, no navigator particularly, is ignorant of the magnificent advantages that France would derive from such a solution, which would not cost us a centime or a soldier. We confine ourselves to saying that henceforward Spain has but one interest in its ancient colony, & that is, that it be not occupied either by England or the United States. As to those two Powers, they have legitimated in advance our entire freedom of action, as they have spared no pains, each one for itself, to draw the Dominicans into their own orbit.

[1] None of the extracts from newspapers mentioned in this paragraph, or elsewhere in this despatch, are included in this publication.

In the presence of so strong an invitation as this addressed to the politic intervention of the French Government, & the evidences which have been recently given of the public interest attached here to the great military & commercial advantages of the Bay of Samana, it would seem that the vigilance of the United States could not be too earnestly directed to that important point.   The formal contradiction given by the Minister of Foreign Affairs to the rumors, which have lately prevailed, must be considered conclusive with regard to any present designs of the French Government; but we live in times when new views & new complications are liable to arise with the events of each succeeding day.   The friendly offices which we have performed to the Dominican Republic would undoubtedly justify the strongest representations to be addressed to that Government without delay against any concession or surrender to other Powers which would compromise the interests or safety of the United States; and I should think it by no means an useless precaution, in the present state of things, to add that to other measures for averting a possible, if not impending danger.

An article has recently appeared in the *Courrier du Havre* professing to give from authentic sources an explanation of the nature & objects of Monsieur Raousset-Boulbon's operations in Sonora which I enclose herewith.

I have the honor [etc.].

2633

*William C. Rives, United States Minister to France, to Edward Everett,
Secretary of State of the United States* [1]

No. 188   PARIS, *January 20, 1853.*

SIR: I had a free & informal conversation a day or two ago with Monsieur Drouyn de L'huys [Lhuys] Minister of Foreign Affairs, of the principal points of which I proceed to give you an outline.   Referring to the intimation given by the Emperor in the audience for the presentation of my new letters of credence, which co-incided with an inference I had drawn from some observations of the Minister himself, that your note in answer to the Ministers of France & England on the subject of the proposed convention concerning Cuba[2] was not satisfactory, I remarked to Monsieur Drouyn de L'huys [Lhuys] that, although I had not yet been furnished with a copy of your Note & did not, therefore, know it's contents, I could not see any just ground of dissatisfaction in the circumstance mentioned of it's holding out the idea of the possible future acquisition of the Island of Cuba by the United States—that the President of the United States had not only dis-

---

[1] Despatches, France, vol. 34.   Received February 8.
[2] See Everett's note to the Count de Sartiges, above, this volume, pt. v, December 1, 1852, doc. 2488.   A similar communication went to the British Minister in Washington.

avowed any wish or intention of attempting any change in the existing relations of Cuba, but had formally declared his opinion that it's acquisition by the United States, even by purchase, would at the present time be inexpedient—that it's acquisition in any irregular or unlawful manner was opposed equally by all parties in the United States, as he had seen from the recent debate in the Senate—that if, in the unknown & possibly remote future, an occasion should present itself for it's honorable & peaceable acquisition, with the consent of its rightful sovereign, & the United States should deem it necessary to it's interests to avail itself of such an opportunity, I could not perceive why France should feel herself called on to oppose any obstacle to it—that whatever motives of jealousy another great power might suppose itself to have with regard to the growth of our national importance, France, I thought, as our ancient ally & having so many common & no conflicting interests that I could see with us, ought to view with pleasure, instead of distrust, the steady advance & development of the United States in every legitimate & proper manner—and that it was, therefore, not without surprise that we had seen her, on two recent occasions, acting in formal concert with a power which had been her enemy as well as ours, in the adoption or proposition of measures that seemed to us dictated by an unreasonable spirit of jealousy & distrust.

Monsieur Drouyn de L'huys [Lhuys] replied to these observations at considerable length & with great apparent frankness. He disavowed all jealousy with regard to the natural growth & expansion of the United States. He intimated even that if ever hereafter it should be the policy of Spain voluntarily to cede Cuba to the United States, it would excite no umbrage on the part of France. He said that the unlawful enterprises which had of late been directed against Cuba from the shores of the United-States had naturally excited anxiety in Europe, & that the French Government had desired, in the interest of humanity & of the general peace of the world, to do all it could, by timely & friendly precautions, to guard against the recurrence of attempts which, if renewed, would lead to a sanguinary struggle, & considering the determination of Spain to defend this the last remnant of it's colonial power at every cost & sacrifice, to a not improbable catastrophe which could not be contemplated without horror. As to the form in which those efforts had been employed by the French Government, he said he was not insensible of the unfavorable impressions which might have been produced in the United States by a mode of proceeding which departed from the *traditions* of their ancient relations with England & the United States respectively; but that an appeal had been made to their co-operation by the English Government & it was difficult to decline an invited concert, where a common object seemed to be pursued by both parties. Monsieur Grouyn de L'huys [Lhuys] said, however, if he had been Minister of Foreign Affairs at the time, he would have taken a different course & would have entered directly into communication with the Government of the United States in the frank & cordial spirit of their ancient alliance, independently of England or any other power. He added it was not too late now to adopt the course he would have preferred, as a new subject of interest to both Governments had arisen in the reports respecting Samana, which might furnish the occasion for entering into friendly communication with each other as well with regard to Cuba as San Domingo, & making a mutual renunciation of pretensions to either the basis & bond of a new compact between the two Countries.

For obvious reasons, I gave no encouragement to this suggestion of Monsieur Drouyn de L'huys [Lhuys] which he rather intimated a wish that I should bring formally to your notice; but I excused myself by saying that as the present administration would very soon go out of office, there would be no time for it to act on any new proposition. Monsieur Drouyn de L'huys [Lhuys] said he assented to what he understood to be the policy hitherto professed by the Government of the United States, which he stated very nearly in the terms of your Despatch N° 56,[1] to wit, to avoid, as far as possible, all disturbance of the existing political relations of the West-Indies. But, he added, that to make this policy either just or practical, it must be reciprocally observed by all the great maritime powers; and that if France was, on this principle to abstain from advantages which might be offered to her in San Domingo, the United States ought, by the same rule, to forbear acquisitions in Cuba.

From the disposition shewn to connect these two questions, I cannot avoid the conclusion that the views of the French Government with regard to Samana are held in *Abeyance* to await the progress of events & of public opinion in the United States in relation to Cuba. This impression is confirmed by the obvious reserve with which the Minister of Foreign Affairs spoke of the future in regard to Samana. He repeated his contradiction of the report which had prevailed of it's actual occupation by a French naval force, saying that no such fact had occurred & that no such instruction had been given, and that he had nothing to add to what he had already said to me on that subject. I enclose herewith a very remarkable article[2] which may merit your attention in this connection, & which appeared in the Constitutionnel two days ago. It bears the signature of a writer, Monsieur Granier de Cassagnac, who has been known on more than one occasion to have expressed the personal opinions & intentions of the Head of the Government. In developing what he calls the *politique nouvelle* of France, you will see that he insists particularly on the necessity of directing the energies & attention of the nation to *exterior* objects, presenting a new field of enterprise & *expansion*, & makes it a special reproach to the Government of Louis Philippe

[1] Above, this volume, pt. v, December 17, 1852, doc. 2489.
[2] Not included in this publication.

that it declined the offer which was made it of the *admirable* peninsula of Samana & indeed of the whole Dominican Republic, as well as other advantageous opportunities of acquiring territory & influence in America.

I have the honor [etc.].

2634

William C. Rives, United States Minister to France, to Edward Everett, Secretary of State of the United States [1]

[EXTRACT]

No. 190   PARIS, *February 2, 1853.*

SIR: I received some time ago, a despatch from the Department of State, Nº 52,[2] addressed to me while the Honble Mᴿ Conrad was acting Secretary, requesting me to endeavor, indirectly & without any formal enquiry to ascertain, as far as practicable, the actual position of the relations between this Government & the Republic of Ecuador as connected with the differences which had arisen between that Republic & the late Chargé d'Affaires of France. Keeping in view the caution prescribed by Mᴿ Conrad, I have availed myself of every occasion which has fallen in my way to endeavor to obtain incidentally the information desired, but the result of the enquiries thus pursued has not been very explicit or satisfactory. The occurrences referred to have excited so little attention here, that hardly any thing is known about them except in official quarters, & in those quarters great reserve is shown in speaking of them.

I am inclined to think from all I have been able to learn that the conduct of Monsieur Montholon, without being formally disapproved, has not met the entire approbation of his Government. Considering, however, the national dignity to have been wounded in the disorderly & violent manifestations of which he was the object, orders have been sent, I have heard within a few days past from a person who appears to have means of information, to the Commander of the French Naval forces in that latitude to repair to Guyaquil [Guayaquil], & to demand explanations & satisfaction of the Government of Ecuador. What is the nature of the satisfaction to be demanded my informant did not know.— I learn from General Santa Cruz, Minister of the Republic of Bolivia, who informs me that he is in correspondence with the Minister of Foreign Affairs of Ecuador, that the Ecuadorean Government is disposed to give explanations & *reasonable* satisfaction. Whatever may be the sympathies of this Government with regard to the designs of General Flores, I have heard nothing that would

[1] Despatches, France, vol. 34.   Received February 22.
[2] Above, this volume, pt. v, October 14, 1852, doc. 2487.

lead me to beleive that his late enterprise had been instigated by France.[1] . . .

I have the honor [etc.].

P. S.

I send herewith a copy just published in the *Annales du Commerce Exterieur* of a Treaty of commerce & navigation between France & the Dominican Republic [2] which appears to have been concluded at San Domingo on the 8th May last & of which the ratifications were exchanged at Paris in the month of August.

2635

William C. Rives, United States Minister to France, to William L. Marcy, Secretary of State of the United States [3]

[EXTRACT]

No. 198   PARIS, *March 31, 1853.*

SIR: . . . The Emperor also received yesterday another deputation from England—that of the English Company formed for effecting a junction of the Atlantic & Pacific Oceans by the Isthmus of Darien. I enclose the semi-official account of this audience [4] as relating to a subject which will, doubt-

[1] The omitted portion relates to the marriage of Emperor Napoleon III.
[2] Not included in this publication.
[3] Despatches, France, vol. 34. Received April 18.
The omitted portion relates to European political affairs.
[4] The following account has been translated from the official journal *Le Moniteur Universel*, dated March 30, 1853, except the speeches, given in English by Sir Charles Fox and the Emperor, which were copied from the London *Times*, dated March 29, 1853:

PARIS, *March 29, [1853].*

The Emperor to-day granted an audience, at the Tuileries Palace to a deputation from the English company for the junction of the two oceans, the Atlantic and the Pacific. The deputation was composed of the following members, the first three of whom are concessionaires of the enterprise: Sir Charles Fox, Bart., head of the firm, Fox, Henderson & Co; Mr. Thomas Brassey, entrepreneur, to whom the contract for the work has been awarded; Dr. Cullen, who discovered the route adopted; Mr. Gisborne, chief engineer of the company; Mr. Forde, assistant engineer; Mr. Brownell, merchant of Liverpool; Mr. W. Hamilton, former member of Parliament, member of the Royal Geographic Society; Mr. Mackinnon, captain of the Royal British Navy; Señor de Rivero, Chargé d'Affaires of Peru in France; Señor Rojas, Chargé d'Affaires of New Granada in France; Mr. J. R. Crampton, engineer, submarine telegraph constructor; Mr. C. S. Stokes, administrator concessionaire of the Western Railway of France (chemin de fer de l'Ouest en France); Mr. Melvil-Wilson, merchant of London; Dr. Black, secretary of the company.

Sir Charles Fox, president of the deputation, delivered the following address in English,

"Sire:—In approaching your august throne my first duty is to tender to your Imperial Majesty the cordial expression of the respectful gratitude of the Directors of the Atlantic and Pacific Junction Company for the prompt kindness with which your Majesty has condescended to grant an audience to their deputation.

"The rapid increase of commercial navigation round Cape Horn has now, for some

less, be felt to be one of particular interest to the United States, as well [as] of common concern to all commercial nations.

I have the honor [etc.].

---

years, attracted the practical attention of men of business to that which had previously been considered a merely speculative object of scientific inquiry. I mean the necessity for a direct passage for ships between the Atlantic and Pacific Oceans, across the isthmus which unites North and South America.

"In the year 1851 my attention was directed by Dr. Cullen, who had himself traversed the isthmus, to the route across Darien, between Porte Escoses and San Miguel, which his experience had led him to consider the best.

"On examining the Admiralty charts, which, as your Imperial Majesty is well aware, are very detailed and accurate, I was able to ascertain that the line proposed to me was the only one which could enjoy the advantage of a sufficient natural harbour at each end; that the length of the passage would not accede [exceed] 60 kilometres; and that the only question to be decided was, whether the engineering difficulties of the ground were such as to prevent within a reasonable expenditure the construction of a channel of sufficient width and depth to satisfy the requirements of all nations. In conjunction, therefore, with Mr. Brassey and several friends, I commissioned Mr. Gisborne and Mr. Forde, civil engineers, to examine the isthmus, and I have had the satisfaction to ascertain from their report that it is perfectly possible to cut a channel 160 feet wide and 30 feet deep, without locks, between the two harbours which I have mentioned, at an expense by no means out of proportion to the objects to be attained and to the revenue which may reasonably be expected. We have accordingly formed a company to carry out this object.

"At the outset of our investigations, and as soon as we had obtained the necessary concession from the local authority of New Granada, we deemed it right, as a matter of courtesy, to offer to the United States a share in the undertaking. We have throughout received the cordial approbation of Her Britannic Majesty's Government.

"Our next step is, with the full consent of that Government, to solicit the patronage and support of your Imperial Majesty. France, as one of the great maritime Powers, has an evident interest in this great question of a junction between the two oceans. France, who owes so much to your Imperial Majesty, will, we believe, be grateful to you, Sire, for granting your Imperial countenance and support to our undertaking—and in the name of this deputation and of the company whom we have the honour to represent, I venture to hope for this support with perfect confidence, because we know that your Imperial Majesty, not only as the chief of this great nation, but also by your personal knowledge of the subject, is pre-eminently qualified to appreciate the object which we have in view and the means which we have adopted."

The Emperor replied in English as follows:—

"Gentlemen, I received with the liveliest interest the intelligence of the formation of a great company for the junction of the two oceans. I have no doubt that you will succeed in an undertaking which must render so important a service to the commerce of the whole world, since such eminent men are placed at the head of your company. I have long appreciated all the advantages of a junction between the two seas, and when I was in England I endeavoured to draw the attention of scientific men to this subject. You may, therefore, rest assured, gentlemen, that you will meet with all the support from me which such noble efforts deserve."

The company's report, plans, and maps were then laid before the Emperor, who examined them with particular attention. Sir Charles Fox presented the members of the deputation, and His Majesty addressed to each of them the most gracious expressions. When the deputation withdrew the Emperor said:—

"I am happy to have seen your honourable deputation the very day after having received the one which, on the part of the merchants of London, expressed to me the most friendly sentiments in favour of peace—sentiments with which my own feelings have always been in complete accord."

2636

John Y. Mason, United States Minister to France, to William L. Marcy,
Secretary of State of the United States [1]

No. 16   PARIS, *April 22, 1854.*

SIR: By appointment I had an interview with M. Drouyn de Lhuys at the
department of Foreign Affairs to day and made the enquiry directed in your
despatch No. 5 [2] in regard to the supposed interference of the French Government in the affairs of St. Domingo. When I stated the object of my inquiry and the information contained in Mr. Elliott's report on which it
was founded, he promptly replied that the French Government had no desire
to interfere with the internal affairs of the Dominican Republic—much less
to acquire any right of control over it—that recognising the existence of that
Republic, they looked only to the de facto Government without any desire
that this person or that should be the President, and, that the instructions
to the French agents were all based on this sound general principle and that
no conduct of any such agent inconsistent with these instructions was authorized or would be approved by the Imperial Government—said he would go
further and inform me, but asked that it might be regarded as *confidential*
with my Government, that apprehending that there had probably been
some indiscretion, on the part of the French agent at St. Domingo, which
had given rise to the suggestions made by Mr. Elliott, and, as he had received
information to that effect from other sources, orders had already been given
for his removal from San Domingo.

Expressing cordial feelings towards me personally and to my country the
minister declared his wish, that, on all occasions I would use the same direct-
ness in my enquiries and avowed his readiness on all subjects to answer
frankly and unhesitatingly. I am satisfied, that this Government has no
desire to do anything in San Domingo, in an unfriendly spirit towards the
United States—or with a view to recover the rights of sovereignty over
the Island—

I am [etc.].

2637

John Y. Mason, United States Minister to France, to William L. Marcy,
Secretary of State of the United States [3]

No. 28   PARIS, *July 20, 1854.*

SIR: I have the honor to acknowledge the receipt of your despatch No.
20.[4] marked confidential and have read it and the accompanying papers

---

[1] Despatches, France, vol. 36. Received May 14.
[2] See above, this volume, pt. v, December 22, 1853, doc. 2492.
[3] Despatches, France, vol. 36. Received August 7.
[4] See above, this volume, pt. v, June 27, 1854, doc. 2494.

with the deepest interest. I am happy to beleive that however misunderstood abroad, the course of my government has been characterised
in its whole management of the affair of the Black Warrior by dignity,
moderation and justice. The demands for reparation of the private injury,
and for redress of the national insult offered to the United States by the
Cuban authorities will be regarded as by no means exaggerated, and the
vindication contained in your reply to Mr. Calderon [1] appears to me to be
most complete. That response is one of the most powerful and conclusive
papers which you have ever written, and, this is no light commendation.
I hope to be able to make known its contents to Mr. Drouyn de Lhuys.—
But it is a task of some delicacy, because I do not wish to recognise any
jurisdiction in France over the subject; and while I desire that correct
knowledge should be had by the Imperial Government on a question which
may involve very grave consequences, I do not desire to manifest any great
anxiety to propitiate France in regard to a national dispute between two
independant nations to which she is not a party—I may be embarrassed
too if after reading the dispatch to him, the Minister should ask me for a
copy which I could not give him. He accords to me however so much
freedom of communication, and, I have found him so enlightened and free
from prejudice that I hope to accomplish your wishes in an unexceptionable
manner: You may rely on my doing so discreetly or not at all—The solution
of the difficulties with Spain by the sale of Cuba to the United States is of
very doubtful result. That it is the interest of Spain to accede to the Liberal offers which will be made, I have no doubt. The impoverished condition of her treasury, the total prostration of her credit, and her being at this
moment embroiled by a most formidable insurrection headed by men of
character and long, and honorable service would impress an enlightened
ministry, one would suppose with the importance of divesting herself of a
remote insular possession which adds nothing to her physical strength and
requires, to keep it in subjection, a large portion of her military force while
its nett revenues accruing to the mother country—under a system of Government weak, oppressive and corrupting in its tendencies—bears no proportion
to the annual interest of the price which the United States would pay her
for the cession. The obstinate pride which Spain has exhibited in regard
to all her former Americen Possessions by which they have been lost to her
without equivalent, with the single exception of Florida, is supposed still to
exist. Experience has taught no lesson of wisdom and it is said that no
ministry would dare to cede Cuba. There are some persons here of high
rank and influence in France, who think that it is better for Spain, and for
Europe, that the sale should be made; but how far they can exert an influence

[1] Apparently he refers to Marcy's despatch to Soulé, No. 16, June 22, 1854, which is
below, in the volume and part containing Communications to Spain, wherein he comments
at length upon Calderon's note.

on Spain, I cannot say: the influence if exerted at all would be indirectly from Paris, and, those who may be inclined to favor the cession, would probably look to their own personal advantage. The practicability of such an arrangement, depends first on the policy and disposition of Spain herself, secondly on the influence which might be brought to bear on her by other powers, to defeat it. First that Spain is averse to the cession I have no doubt. But she is in no condition unaided to make war with the United States. Her treasury is exhausted and she is without credit—her internal condition is in the last degree deplorable.— The accounts of the insurrection headed by Generals Dulce and ODonnuell heretofore published, are not to be relied on. The telegraph is in the hands of the Government and the espionage on the mails so complete, that no intelligence, unacceptable to the Government, can cross the frontiers through that channel. After repeated assurances that order was restored, and the rebel forces demoralised, and in full retreat—it is now admitted in the "Moniteur" that Barcelona has joined them and that regiment after regiment has gone over to the insurgents.— It is said that the Marquis de Turgot having hurried back to Madrid from the baths to which he had gone for his health, had advised the Queen to change her Ministers—and in the "Constitution" of yesterday it is plainly indicated that while France would not interfere in the internal troubles of Spain, the Queen had not been without good advice in regard to measures which might have averted the peril which surrounds her. It is not probable that the insurgents will if successful, be satisfied with the concessions which they had first demanded. An increase of demand may be anticipated if we look to the lessons taught by history, and, the accompanying extract from a published letter of General Dulce [1] will show that the queen herself is aimed at, by the movement which has been undertaken. This condition of things would justify the conclusion, that the civil war will still further exhaust her strength and resources and warrant the proposed renewal of the offer to buy Cuba so far as Spain herself is concerned.

The second inquiry involves very grave considerations, and, diffident as I would be in giving an opinion or speculative views which should influence great measures of my government I will venture to state the grounds on which the opinions, I entertain, are founded.

I have no doubt that both France and England will use all the influence which they can bring to bear, to prevent a sale of the Island to the United States. It is because its possession will so strengthen the United States that they would not desire it; No one questions that as a portion of the United States Cuba would be better governed—her inhabitants more happy —and her productions vastly increased—and, that it would be, in a corresponding degree, more valuable to the commercial interests of the world— as Louisana is unquestionably more profitable to France, as a state of the

[1] Not found.

Union, than it would have been as her colony.— But its possession would so strengthen the military defenses of the United States especially of the gulf coast and the valley of the Mississippi, and, weaken the security of the British and French Possessions in the West Indies—it would so swell the commerce and political Power of the United States, that, these two Governments would not willingly see such an acquisition. But notwithstanding these views of policy, and, notwithstanding Spain may from whatever considerations, refuse the renewed offer of purchase, the question remains will France and England, or either of them, engage in war as allies of Spain if the United States shall resort to the declaration of war in vindication of its national rights and honor. My opinion is that they will not.

In regard to England whose commercial communications with the United States is but little short of two hundred millions in value whose operations depend on the great staples of the United States for employment—whose manufactories enjoy there so profitable a market and whose people may depend on us for bread it is not conceivable that she would shut off this essential intercourse and turn loose on her commerce the privateers which the United States would be compelled to put into commission, to resist such a combination against them.

But with France, it may be, that there are considerations which would make it more desireable to maintain a closer political connection with Spain than is the case with England. If the Queen shall lose her throne, and, her child whose claims are deeply affected by circumstances connected with its paternity shall share her fate, as is most probable, it would—the competitors for the crown of Spain would be Don Carlos a legitimist Bourbon and the Duchess of Monpensier [Montpensier] the wife of Louis Phillip's son—the accession of either would not be favorable to the present dinasty of France. But this possibility would induce France to interfere in the internal troubles now agitating Spain if she attached any great importance to it.— And I have reason to beleive that France will not interfere.—

But is there motive sufficient to induce France to take part in a war against the United States?

It is a favorite saying with M. Drouyn de Lhuys, that if he knows, in any given state of things, what the interest of a nation is, he can anticipate the course which her Government will pursue.— On this theory he has founded his unchanging hope that all Europe will favor the Western Allies against Russia.— What is the interest of France in such a conjuncture as we are considering?

First.—It is well known that success in the war with Russia is regarded as essential, perhaps, to the continuence of the Imperial Power.— Consummate as has been the ability, with which the Emperor has maintained and strengthened himself on the throne, adverse fortune in this war would impair if not distroy his prestige, and endanger his throne itself—and no one yet sees a prospect of peace.— In sending the French troops from Calais—in British ships a few days since—under Baraguay d'Hilliers to a destination unknown as yet, the Emperor issued an address to his army and spoke of his taking the command in person as a future event not impossible.—

The power of the western allies, is very great, but they obviously have their hands full, and the necessity of directing undivided energies to the prosecution of the war with Russia, and, maintaining quiet at home—with the elements of opposition to the Imperial Government not so much to its measures as to its existence—as are known to exist in France, and, the revolutionary feeling which exists in a greater or less degree in every country in Europe adverse to royalty and in favor of freedom, render it scarcely possible that there shall be a disposition to engage in war with a new enemy whose power in war, though latent, is appreciated to its full extent, and whose friendly intercourse is of incalculable importance to France.

$2^{\underline{d}}$ As a financial measure France cannot offord to go to war with the United States on mere grounds of calculation. The estimated receipts into the Treasury for the current year according to the Budget prepared before the commencement of the war, exceeded the probable disbursements, by about four millions of francs—this estimate of receipts assumed an increase on those of the last year. The Corps Legislative [Législatif] determined to provide for the extraordinary expenses of the war, by loan.— One of two hundred and fifty millions of francs has already been made—the interest of which will more than absorb the supposed excess of receipts.— The results of the first six months of this year have been found by actual experience instead of exceeding as was anticipated to have fallen short of the receipts of the same period of the preceding year by more than six millions of francs, and further loans will be necessary to meet enormous outlays for the war. These loans must be offered under the disadvantages of increasing and indefinite demands on the Treasury, with revenues already insufficient to meet the ordinary expenses. Taxation is already so high and the French people—especially the inhabitants of Paris, are so sensitive on the subject, that, an increase at all commensurate with the increasing expenditures caused by the war, will not probably be attempted. If in connection with this view we consider that in the estimates of revenue presented in the Budget, calculation is made on the imports on American productions to an amount of from six to eight hundred millions of francs, it will be seen that the suspension of commercial intercourse with the United States, and, the necessary loss of revenue with means, already deficient must prove disasterous to the financial condition of France.— And when to this certain positive loss, is added the increased expenditures of a new war—it would appear to be impossible, that the project could be entertained in the absence of any implication of French honor. The disposition to aid the weak on one hand, or to restrain the growing strength of the other party—cannot in my judgment stimulate the enlightened Government of France to such an act of infatuation as a war with the United States.

3. Such a course, besides its influence in the particulars already alluded to, would affect the manufacturing interests of France to an enormous extent—and with a fatal influence. In Lyons alone, it is estimated, that thirty thousand persons are engaged in manufacturing goods, for the Markets of the United States—for the manufacturers of Paris a market of great value would be closed by the war—the opening demand for the cheap wines of France, under the proposed modified tariff would be lost, and the supply of cotton for their Manufactories cannot be procured except from the United States—and, above all, in the existing state of things in Europe, the dificient crops of France must be supplied with the bread stuffs of America.

It is incredible under these circumstances that France will take part with Spain in war with the United States if the latter power shall resort to the alternative of war as a measure which indipendant Nations have a right, on their own responsibility, to adopt in vindication of National honor—or interest. I do not intend to carry the idea that there is no circumstance which will induce this proud and powerful nation to aid the Spaniards in their occupation of Cuba; still less that France would be restrained by these powerful considerations, from engaging in war with the United States. I have but little doubt that if an armed expidition, not only without authority from the United States but in violation of the Law, shall attempt to invade Cuba—the English and French squadrons in the West Indies, will aid the Spanish authorities in repelling the invaders: because in doing so—the two Governments would not expect the United States to sustain the lawless expidition. Still less do I suppose that France would hesitate to maintain by arms its National honor when wounded, whatever might be the prudential considerations to restrain her.

In maintaining Spain in the occupation of Cuba, no such controlling consideration can exist.

These views lead me to the conclusions which I have already indicated.

There is still much uncertainty on the subject of the actual co-operation of the German states against Russia. The answer of the Emperor Nicholas has not yet been made public and doubts are obviously felt both here and in England as to the future course of the German States. You will remember that in his speech at the opening of the Corps Ligislatif [Législatif] the Emperor mentioned Austria and Prussia as States, who would follow France and England to the war, to maintain the integrity of Turkey. In his proclamation to his armies on the recent occasion of the embarkation of the French troops at Calais, no mention is made of their co-operation.— Austria has not marched her armies into the principalities as soon as has been expected—but I was informed yesterday of a fact which indicates that she will take part in the war. The Bey of Tunis being about to send troops to aid the Sultan, chartered Austrian vessels, for their transportation. The Austrian Consul at Tunis applied to Mr. Hübener the Minister at Paris for instructions, whether the transports, in performing the service, should wear the Austrian flag, and the reply was—that they should. This of itself will be an act of war—but whatever may be the present attitude of the German states or of those lying North of Germany the war with Russia fully occupies the Western Allies. For indipendently of the Power of Russia, there is no security that the flame, which has broken out in Spain, may not be kindled, on any serious reverse befalling the allies, throughout Europe; adding to the complications of the war and increasing the necessity of both France and England giving all their energies and devoting all their resources to the contest in Europe.

In regard to the information given by the United States Consul at Havanna that the Marquis Villuma has sent out a treaty between France and Spain for the protection of Cuba, I have the strongest conviction that he has been misenformed if not deceived. The policy of endeavoring to produce a belief of the existance of such a treaty is obvious.— But I have good reason to believe that no treaty exists.— Nor do I believe that one will be made. There have been some negociations to unite Spain with France and England in the war in Europe, Spain engaging to send troops to Italy and France and probably England becoming her allies—but they were not consummated and Spain is in no condition to fulfill the stipulations expected of her. The efforts made when the annexation of Texas was pending to defeat the measure by diplomacy, and even by menaces and intimidation, will probably be repeated and with the same result. For the considerations which influenced the great Maritime Powers of Europe then to bear their disappointments—have now infinitely more force.

If any thing shall occur to modify my opinion I will hasten to communicate it.—

I have the honor [etc.].

2638

John Y. Mason, United States Minister to France, to William L. Marcy,
Secretary of State of the United States [1]

[EXTRACT]

Unofficial.   PARIS, *October 5, 1854.*

MY DEAR SIR: . . . Mr. Soulé is still here, but will leave to-day. He has after consulting Mr. Buchanan, decided on Ostend as the place, and,

[1] Despatches, France, vol. 36. Received October 21.
    The omitted portions of this despatch relate to the difficulties which arose between the authorities at San Francisco and the French consul at that port. It also relates to European political affairs.

Monday next, as the time of meeting.[1] I expect to leave Paris, on the day after to-morrow. . . .

I am very truly [etc.].

2639

John Y. Mason, United States Minister to France, to William L. Marcy, Secretary of State of the United States [2]

No. 36 PARIS, *October 25, 1854.*

SIR: On my return to Paris on the 20th Inst, I availed myself of the earliest opportunity to see the Minister of Foreign Affairs. For some time he has resided in the Country and received at the Department only twice a week. Failing in my efforts to see him on the 21st, I succeeded on Tuesday the 24th and held with him a conversation which was somewhat significant.— After some preliminary communications his Excellency observed that he had wished to see me, and had been about writing to me, to apprize me, that Mr. Soule's [Soulé's] presence in France was not agreeable and as the most friendly mode of accomplishing what was deemed necessary the prevention of his entering the Territory of France, he wished me to inform Mr. Soulé. I did not feel inclined to be the medium of a verbal communication on so grave a subject, and answered, that I did not know how I could undertake the task, but wished to know the reasons of so unusual a proceeding. He enumerated some circumstances, evincing unfriendliness to the Imperial Government, as he alledged, embracing Mr. Soule's [Soulé's] rencontre with the French Ambassador at Madrid, and, giving grounds of suspicions of his being in communication with the enemies of the Government. I expressed to him a strong disbelief in the justice of these suspicions, and, not being informed of all the particulars of the *personal* misunderstanding occurring in Spain—which, of course, I regretted, told him I was not prepared to discuss it—but protested that it ought not to be deemed sufficient cause for so grave a proceeding affecting him in his public character and thereby the country which he represented. He said that the minister of the Interior to whose Department such matters belonged, had some information on the subject the nature or effect of which he did not explain—he said, that, he could not under the Law of Nations, question the right of the Emperor's Government, to prohibit Mr. Soulé, though accredited as a public minister to another Country, the privilege of passage through France.

[1] See Marcy's No. 26, to Mason, above, this volume, pt. v, August 16, 1854, doc. 2495, instructing him to confer with Soulé and Buchanan, United States Ministers to Spain and Great Britain, respectively, on the difficulties over Cuba between the United States and Spain; and concerning this meeting, see, also, below, in the volume and part containing Communications from Spain, the despatches, dated October 15 and 20, 1854, from Soulé, and below, vol. VII, pt. II, Buchanan's despatch dated October 18, 1854, doc. 3026.

[2] Despatches, France, vol. 36. Received November 13.

This communication was made to me about 4 o'clock on Tuesday the 24th and subsequent information induces me to believe, that, Mr. Soulé was actually arrested in his journey, at Calais before that hour. Under your orders he had been in Paris for at least two weeks, but a short time before, and this was the first intimation, which I had received, of objections on the part of this Government, to his visiting or travelling through France—nor do I believe that he had received any such notice.

The minister proceeded to express his regret that there were evidences of an unfriendly feeling on the part of the United States towards France which were exhibited by no other Nation or people. He enumerated "the Dillon Affair"[1] the publication of a letter to the people of France by Mr. George N. Sanders, who had been Consul of the United States at London, and, the ungracious and insulting Treatment of the officers of some French Ships of War, while on shore in New York. I replied that I had received two despatches from my Government showing the careful collection and elaborate examination of the facts of the Dillon case, which I would communicate to him as soon as some copies were completed, and, that I desired that he would carefully examine them, and, I was persuaded that neither in the occurrences, nor in the conclusions, would he find any proofs of an unfriendly feeling towards France—that I was sure that his Excellency knew too well, the nature of our institutions, gravely to complain of a letter published in England, by a private individual although he had been formerly in the official employment of the United States; that, having adopted their own form of Government, and denying all right of interference by other nations in their affairs, the people of the United States recognized the same right, as appertaining to every other people, and that neither the Government or people of my country, would approve any attempt, on the part of any of our citizens to disturb the peace or interfere with the Institutions of other Countries, in an illegal or offensive manner, and, that in the present enlightened age, it was not to be expected, that the minds of men would concur in approving any particular form of government;—that I had seen some account, in the Newspapers, of the occurrence at New York, to which he alluded, and, I inferred, that the parties concerned were Frenchmen, who may have had their own reasons for disatisfaction, and, this uncourteous conduct was no evidence of the feeling of the community—that French Naval Officers, would I felt assured, readily acknowledge, that in all the ports of the United States they had received hospitality, and kind offices from our people generally, and I regretted, that, one so enlightened as his Excellency had permitted an insulated and exceptional case, of a disagreeable deportment, on the part of a few individuals, so to occupy his mind as to induce him to mention it. On the whole the conversation was not an agreeable one, and, I was surprised,

---

[1] This affair related to the arrest of the French consul at San Francisco, for refusing to appear in court to give testimony in a criminal case.

and said to him, that I had never before found him in so complaining a mood towards my country.

I could not but suspect that the late conferences held by Mr. Soulé, Mr. Buchanan and myself,[1] about which there has been much speculation, had exerted some influence in producing the feeling, which I have not before observed and possibly, the reported treaty with the Government of the Sandwich Islands to which he made a passing, but, not a distinct allusion, may have had its share of influence.

At 5 o'clock this morning I learned by a note from Mr. Soulé, that on his way from London to Madrid, intending to pass through France, he was arrested at Calais, and compelled to return to Dover.— As soon as I am correctly informed of the facts I will address the French Government on the subject.

I have the honor [etc.].

2640

John Y. Mason, United States Minister to France, to Drouyn de Lhuys, Minister of Foreign Affairs of France [2]

PARIS, *October 27, 1854.*

SIR: I have received information that on the 24th Inst. Mr. Soulé on his arrival at Calais, from the shores of England was notified by a police officer that orders had been given by the Imperial Government, that, he should not be permitted to enter France, and, by these orders he was compelled to return to England where he remains.

Mr. Soulé is a citizen of the United States accredited as Envoy Extraordinary and Minister Plenipotentiary of his Country, to the court of Spain.— He had in the execution of orders of his Government visited Paris and London and was returning to his post at Madrid by the most usual and convenient route, through the Territory of France, when he was thus arrested in his journey. He had received no notice of the determination of the Emperor's Government to deny to him the privilege, accorded by all nations to citizens or subjects of friendly powers travelling under their protection, and, especially to those who are clothed with the sacred character of Public Ministers; for he was actually arrested in his journey some hours before I received the intimations in regard to him, which you did me the honor to give me in the afternoon of the 24th Inst.

If authorised by the Emperor's Government it cannot but be regarded by the Government and people of the United States not only as a most unusual and humiliating act towards the Minister personally, but as a national in-

---

[1] See above, this part, p. 659, note 1.
[2] Despatches, France, vol. 36; enclosed with Mason to the Secretary of State, No. 37, October 30, 1854, below, this part, doc. 2641.

dignity of a very grave character, only to be extenuated by facts established by conclusive proofs.

Without waiting for special instructions to that effect, I regard it, as my imperitive duty to hasten to ask for what reasons one of my fellow citizens chosen by my country as her Representative to a foreign power has been so treated, while relations of amity and peace exist and are cherished by the United States with France.

My Government will be filled with painful anxiety until satisfactory information in reply to this enquiry can be communicated.

I cannot but hope that Your Excellency will furnish me with such explanations as may releive the Minister from the position in which he has thus been placed and which will enable me to allay the unpleasant feeling which the intelligence of this occurance will occasion in the U. S.

I avail myself of the opportunity [etc.]

2641

John Y. Mason, United States Minister to France, to William L. Marcy, Secretary of State of the United States [1]

No. 37   PARIS, *October 30, 1854.*

SIR: An incident of very grave import has transpired. In my number 36,[2] I communicated the intelligence that the minister of the United States to Spain had been prohibited by alleged orders of the Emperor's Government from entering France.—That I might without delay ascertain the facts, of this extraordinary and unusual proceeding, I sent Mr. Piatt, secretary of this Legation, to Dover, to communicate with Mr. Soulé.—He left Paris in the evening of the 25th and, on his arrival, finding, that Mr. Soulé had left Dover he proceeded to London where he had an interview with that gentleman. The forbidding his entering France, was wholly unknown to Mr. Soulé, and he assures me that "neither by deed, nor by words uttered or written, has he afforded, the shadow of a pretence for the wanton measure, which in violation of his rights as a citizen of the North American Republic and of his privileges as one of its accredited Ministers, has interdicted to him, a passage through France on his way back to Madrid."

I lost no time, after the return of Mr. Piatt, to address to the Minister of Foreign Affairs, under date of the 27th Inst. a communication, of which I send you a copy.[3] It was sent to the Foreign Office on the 28th and I have not yet received an answer.

It is impossible not to regard this humiliating indignity, as deeply in-

---

[1] Despatches, France, vol. 36. Received November 13.
[2] Above, this part, October 25, 1854, doc. 2639.   [3] Above, this part, doc. 2640.

jurious, when it is remembered that Mr. Soulé, acting under your orders, has recently spent more than two weeks in Paris, and, while sojourning here, neither he nor I received any intimation that his presence was objected to by the French Government.

Seeing no adequate cause, to justify an unfriendly feeling towards the United States, I cannot but hope that the French Government finding that they have acted on erroneous information, will at once redress the grievous wrong.

If in this I am disappointed earnest as I have been since I have represented my country at this Court, to cultivate the most cordial relations of amity, between the two Countries, I must consider the incident as of such grave importance, that it is not impossible, I shall regard it to be my duty, to terminate my mission by demanding my passports.

I will not lose a moment in keeping you advised of the reply to my note, and of the progress of events, in connection with this most extraordinary affair.—

I have the honor [etc.].

2642

Drouyn de Lhuys, Minister of Foreign Affairs of France, to John Y. Mason, United States Minister to France [1]

[TRANSLATION]

PARIS, *November 1, 1854.*

SIR: I have received the letter you did me the honor to write to me, under date of the 27th of last month,[2] in which you ask me for some explanations, as to the motives of the determination taken with regard to Mr Soulé.   I must, in the first place, state the manner in which matters came to pass.

The Minister of the Interior had to give directions that Mr. Soulé should not be allowed to enter France, without the knowledge of the government of the Emperor.   The instructions of Mr. Billaut [Billault] were strictly followed and carried out with the utmost propriety by the Commissary of police at Calais.   Accordingly, that functionary did not invite Mr. Soulé to embark again for England; he left him perfectly free to remain at Calais, until he should receive orders from Paris which he was about to request.   It was simply a question of waiting patiently for one day, at the utmost; but Mr. Soulé, after saying "that he did not expect any regard on the part of the french government, and that, besides, he did not care for it," preferred to go back to England immediately.   The Minister of the Interior did, nevertheless, forward his definitive instructions to Calais by telegraph, and I can do nothing better than to transcribe them here.   "If Mr. Soulé presents

[1] Despatches, France, vol. 36; enclosed with Mason to the Secretary of State, No. 41, November 11, 1854, below, this part, doc. 2643.   [2] Above, this part, doc. 2640.

himself for the purpose of re-entering France, you will give him to understand that the government does not authorize him to sojourn there, but that it makes no opposition to his passing through in order to go to Spain, and you will offer to him to *viser* his passport for that destination.''

You perceive, Sir, that the Government of the Emperor has not sought, as you seem to believe, to prevent an Envoy of the United States from traversing the french territory, in order to repair to his post, and acquit himself of the commission with which he was charged by his Government. But, between that simple passage and the stay of a foreigner, whose antecedents, I regret to say it, have awakened the attention of the authorities whose duty it is to preserve public order amongst us, there is a difference which the Minister of the Interior was bound to appreciate. If Mr. Soulé had been going directly to Madrid, the route by France was open to him; if it was his intention to come to Paris, with a view of remaining here, that privilege was not accorded to him. It was, therefore, necessary to consult him, as to his intentions, and it was himself who would not allow time to do so.

Our laws are strict with respect to foreigners. The Minister of the Interior causes their rigorous provisions to be executed, when it is shown to him that there is any necessity for such action; and then, he makes use of a discretionary power which the government of the Emperor has never allowed to be discussed. The quality of foreigner, on the part of Mr. Soulé, placed him within the scope of the measure of which he was the object; all that remained was, to reconcile this measure with the public character with which he is invested. You will acknowledge, Sir, that this is what we have done, and that the Government of the United States, with which the Government of H. M. the Emperor has at heart to cultivate relations of friendship and esteem, has in no ways been assailed in the person of one of its representatives. The Minister of the United States in Spain is free, I repeat, to pass through France; Mr. Soulé who has no mission to fulfil near the Emperor, and who, conformably with a doctrine sanctioned by the law of nations, would need, on account of his origin a special agreement, to enable him to represent, in his native land, the country of his adoption, Mr. Soulé, as a simple private individual, comes within the pale of the common law, which has been applied to him, and he cannot lay claim to any privilege.

Accept, Sir, [etc.].

2643

*John Y. Mason, United States Minister to France, to William L. Marcy,
Secretary of State of the United States* [1]

No. 41   PARIS, *November 11, 1854.*

SIR: In my Despatch No. 37,[2] I informed you of the occurrences at Calais by which Mr. Soulé was interrupted in the prosecution of his journey to Spain and with that Despatch, I sent you, a copy of my letter to M. Drouyn de Lhuys, Minister of Foreign Affairs, of the 27th of October last.[3]

On the 1st of November,[4] I received, from his excellency, a note in reply, of that date, and I send the original, retaining a copy for the files of the Legation.

Until the receipt of this note, I had understood the prohibition of Mr. Soule's entering France to be unqualified, and such too was the understanding of that Gentleman, for by reason of its execution he had returned to England.

On the 6th Inst. I addressed to the Minister of Foreign Affairs a communication of which I send you, here-with, a copy.[5]

I have received no reply, and, presume, that it will conclude the correspondence, which, I felt it to be my duty to open, without waiting for special instructions from the President.

The result I am happy to say is that no impediment exists to the passage of the American Minister, accredited to the Spanish Government, through France, to his place of official duty—this is recognized beyond doubt, a principle of the Law of Nations, interesting to every country, because its denial would seriously embarrass the maintenance of Diplomatic Missions, whose influence in promoting peace and in preserving good relations in the family of Nations, is universally acknowledged.

I communicated to Mr. Soulé, at London my correspondence with the Emperor's Government, and, on the morning of the 9th Inst. he arrived in Paris, and, left on the 11th for Bordeaux, where he expects to find the U. S. Steam-frigate San Jancinto [Jacinto], in which he will take passage for Spain.

I have the honor [etc.].

[1] Despatches, France, vol. 36. Received November 27.
[2] Above, this part, October 30, 1854, doc. 2641.   [3] Above, this part, doc. 2640.
[4] Above, this part, doc. 2642.
[5] Not included in this publication. In this note he stated that he would communicate to his Government the intelligence received in the Foreign Minister's note of the 1st instant, above, this part, doc. 2642, and that he regretted that the "precise telegraphic order" incorporated in the latter note, "did not precede Mr. Soulé's arrival at Calais." He also stated that he was gratified to learn that Mr. Soulé would be allowed to pass through France to his post in Spain.

2644

John Y. Mason, United States Minister to France, to William L. Marcy, Secretary of State of the United States [1]

[EXTRACT]

No. 116   PARIS, *February 13, 1856.*

SIR: . . . The Spanish Minister, Mr: Olozaga [Olózaga], told me, last night, that some uneasiness had been created at Madrid, by suggestions, probably coming from England, that the Walker and Kinney expeditions to Central America, were intended ultimately for Cuba. He asked me, to furnish him with any information in my possession, to show that such suspicions were not wellfounded.—I told him, that when I received the President's message with the accompanying documents, I would show them to him, and I thought he would be satisfied by them, that the intimations were insidious, and that my Government had acted in good faith, in withholding its favor from those expeditions, whatever might be their objects.

I am [etc.].

2645

John Y. Mason, United States Minister to France, to William L. Marcy, Secretary of State of the United States [2]

No. 118   PARIS, *February 18, 1856.*

SIR: I have received your Despatch No: 75, of the 1ˢᵗ of February, instant.[3] I have not found occasion to speak to the Minister of Foreign Affairs on the subject of the affairs of the Argentine Confederation and Buenos Ayres; and am gratified at the views taken in your despatch, now acknowledged.

Mr: Alberdi sent to me three days since, his secretary, to inform me, that he was indisposed, and to communicate the fact, that the Imperial Government had decided to withdraw the Chevalier de Moyne [Le Moyne], the French Minister resident at Buenos Ayres, and has appointed Monsieur Lefevre [Lèfebre] de Becour [Bécourt], as Envoy Extraordinary and Minister Plenipotentiary to the Argentine Confederation, to reside at Parana. I perceive no occasion, to confer with the French Government, on my part, and will not do so, unless you find it desireable in some contingency, to instruct me to do so. I do not foresee that it will occur.

I am, very respectfully [etc.].

¹ Despatches, France, vol. 38.   Received March 4.
The omitted portion relates to European political affairs.
² Despatches, France, vol. 38.   Received March 11.
³ Above, this volume, pt. v, doc. 2497.

2646

John Y. Mason, United States Minister to France, to William L. Marcy, Secretary of State of the United States [1]

[EXTRACTS]

No. 147   PARIS, *June 8, 1856.*

SIR: In the conversation to which I referred in my Nº 146,[2] matters transpired, which it may not be uninteresting to mention.

The Paris correspondent of the London Post had expressed the opinion, that France would exert her good offices to bring the complications of the United States and England to a friendly solution, but that if such a result could not be attained, and actual collision should ensue, he was confident, England might reckon on the "active alliance of France." I took occasion, in the interview with the Minister of Foreign Affairs, without referring to such an opinion, to enquire if Count Sartiges had done anything at Washington, in regard to the differences unhappily existing between England and the United States. He replied, that he had;—that France regarded with great regret, the misunderstandings between two countries, with both of which she is in friendly relations,—and that the Emperor's Government would hail with satisfaction the restoration of good relations between the two countries.—That the French Government was ready to exert its good offices, in producing this result;—that as to England and the United States, this disposition was founded in perfect equality towards the two countries. That M. de Sartiges' efforts to promote a reconciliation, were characterized by this spirit. I said, that I felt authorized by the friendly sentiments so frankly expressed, to enquire, if in the deplorable event of a failure to secure a friendly settlement of conflicting views, and actual hostilities occurring between the United States and England,—my country should anticipate any change of the existing sentiments of equal regard on the part of France? He replied emphatically, no; such was not the purpose or policy of France. I stated, that if anything should occur, bearing on these questions, especially if any orders were given to the French Ships of war in the Gulf of Mexico, which might produce or endanger collision in that sea, that I would rely on his frankness, to notify me,—that my Government might be informed. He assured me that my wish would be gratified. In the course of the conversation, I referred to the great interests which American citizens, who did not participate in military operations in Nicaragua, had in that country, which required protection, and explained the considerations which had induced the President of the United States, to recognize the de facto Government of

[1] Despatches, France, vol. 38. Received June 24.
[2] Not included in this publication. His No. 146 alludes to a conversation with the Minister of Foreign Affairs, in which the latter convinces Mason that the French Minister of War had no intention of insulting the American officers who had recently applied to him for information in regard to the war in Crimea.

President Rivas. He said, that without the desire to discuss the subject, he must in frankness tell me, that the Emperor's Government had seen that measure with regret. I replied, that I felt quite sure, that the measure could be justified on the most honorable principles, and on the most rigid interpretation of the Law of Nations and the usages of Governments.

The friendly purposes and pacific policy, towards us, indicated by the remarks of the Minister of Foreign Affairs, I believe exist, and there are circumstances, which go very far to confirm that policy. . . .[1]

I am, therefore, impressed with the irresistible and undoubting conviction, that no consideration growing out of the affairs of England, or of friendship for England, will induce the enlightened Government of France, devoted above all other things, to the interests and welfare of France and her people, to interrupt the friendly relations of France and the United States. I express these opinions with strong confidence, and submit to your better judgment, giving sincerely the reasons which have led me to form them. The assurances are strong,—but they have not a tythe of the strength, without any distrust of their sincerity, which the circumstances which I have briefly stated, have in my view. A Government, so considerate of the interests of the country, so deferential to the public opinion of France, so anxious to conciliate the favor of the masses, as the Emperor's Government manifestly is, cannot, when there is no implication of French honor, be so mad, as to engage in war with the United States. Instead of fleets and armies, France will send to the United States, enormous orders for Bread. This I confidently predict.

I am [etc.].

2647

John Y. Mason, United States Minister to France, to William L. Marcy, Secretary of State of the United States [2]

No. 148   PARIS, *June 9, 1856.*

SIR: Mr: Balcarce, Chargé d'Affaires from the State of Buenos Ayres, has done me the honor to call on me, to explain the relations at present subsisting between the State which he represents, and the confederated States, whose capital is Parana,—and to show the actual strength and condition of Buenos Ayres. As the views presented by Mr: Balcarce, are intended for the Government of the United States, I yield to his request, and send herewith his original letter and the printed matter which accompanied it.[3]

I am [etc.].

[1] The omitted portion relates to internal affairs in France.
[2] Despatches, France, vol. 38.   Received June 24.
[3] The printed matter is not included in this publication. It contained the two enclosures, mentioned in the following translation of Balcarce's letter, dated June 2, 1856:

Footnote 3, p. 668—*Continued*

Juan R. Balcarce, Chargé d'Affaires of Buenos Aires at Paris, to John Y. Mason, United States Minister to France

PARIS, *June 2, 1856.*

Mr. MINISTER: I have the honor to send to Your Excellency the following series of observations regarding the State of Buenos Ayres, begging you to be so good as to inform His Excellency the Minister of Foreign Affairs of the Government of the United States thereof and call them to his illustrious attention.

Having indirectly learned that the French Government intended to make a change in the existing diplomatic relations by recalling its Minister to Buenos Ayres, Mr. Lemoine [Le Moyne?], my Government, unable to account for a step which nothing in the friendly attitude of the two Countries had given reason for, instructed me to talk with His Excellency the Minister of Foreign Affairs of France in this regard, who was so kind as to receive my explanations but who, while assuring me that no unfavorable sentiment had dictated that step, confirmed its accuracy, adding that it was one in common with the Government of the United States.

This circumstance, Mr. Minister, was a very profound surprise to me. I know, as a matter of fact, the good relations which, for a number of years, have not ceased to exist between the Government of the United States and the State of Buenos Ayres, where an American Minister Resident has been accredited since January 19, 1855 and where not the slightest cause for a disturbance in our reciprocal relations has arisen. My Government further knows that the Cabinet at Washington, in its lofty spirit of fair dealing, has continually professed the policy of neutrality and non-intervention in the domestic affairs of States.

I took the liberty of stating this feeling of astonishment to Your Excellency in person, and although your reception was most kind, I could not help but keep the impression, after the conversation with which you favored me, that perhaps the Government of the United States does not have entirely accurate information regarding the liberal character of all the measures originating with the present Government of Buenos Ayres, regarding its most enterprising action with respect to the free navigation of rivers in its interior, and finally on the great and valuable facilities which its new customs jurisprudence assures foreign commercial interests.

I venture to believe that this justifies me in enclosing to Your Excellency:

1. The Customs Law for 1856, with the request that you give your attention to the conditions, eminently favorable to foreign commerce, which it sanctions.

2. The Treaty concluded in December 1854 with General Urquiza; which treaty recognized the *statu[s] quo* and hence the legal and regular existence of the established Government.

General Urquiza has just recently denounced it and it is unfortunately legitimate to connect this step with the official news of the change in diplomatic relations between the Governments of the United States and France, and the State of Buenos Ayres.

As regards the free navigation of the rivers of the interior, the Government of Buenos Ayres, far from trying to obstruct it, as malevolent insinuations tend to make it appear, was the first to recognize, on October 18, 1852, as a principle of general expediency, the opening of the Plata River to traffic and to the commercial navigation of all countries. It had permitted it and proclaimed it.

If there was any later protest, it did not apply at all to the *recognized, sanctioned* and *practised* principle of the free navigation of rivers, but only to the Treaty signed by General Urquiza with the Governments of the United States, France and Great Britain and in which this fugitive and conquered General unduly encroached, with regard to a matter connected with the navigation of rivers, on rights which are for the State of Buenos Ayres alone to exercise.

The political situation of the country was never seen under such normal conditions and in a more favorable light. In 1853 Buenos Ayres adopted a most liberal Constitution, protecting interests in general and particularly advantageous for foreigners. May 27, 1854, the Chambers elected their first constitutional Governor, Dr. Obligado, whom public confidence had already of its own accord invested for a year with the power which he still holds at the present time. Two Treaties later concluded on December 20, 1854 and January 8, 1855, between General Urquiza and the Government of Buenos Ayres, Treaties which sanctioned the recognition of the *statu[s] quo*, rendered valid for all concerned the separate, constitutional position of that State. Finally, all foreign nations having relations with it, except England and Chile, have maintained Representatives there.

Footnote 3, p. 668—*Continued*

Under this new Constitution, with a Government separate from the other Confederated Provinces, as it had been once before from 1820 to 1825, Buenos Ayres has made the most remarkable progress, commercially and governmentally, in a few years. The European population in the State is approximately: 15,000 British subjects; 18,000 French subjects; more than 30,000 Sardinians and a considerable number of various other nationalities.

In 1853, the total amount of exports from Buenos Ayres, under all flags, was 47,000,-000 francs, 8,500,000 francs of which was for the United States. (Annals of French Commerce, February issue.) According to this publication, the general value of the merchandise exported in 1854 amounted to 51,300,000 francs. That of the first six months of 1855 shows a still greater increase; in fact, that half year alone gives a figure of more than 42,000,000 francs, which is almost within four millions of the total exports of the year 1853. But these figures are lower than the actual amounts, for the Statistical Register of the State of Buenos Ayres for 1854 shows the value of the exports for the same year to be more than 76,500,000 francs, 14,000,000 francs of which were for the United States.

In 1854, the general port traffic included 1536 vessels from overseas, with a capacity of 342,000 tons, 140 of which were American vessels with a total capacity of 43,101 tons. In coastwise traffic, 5960 vessels were employed. The public revenues followed the law of this general increase, and to such an extent that the Government was able to set aside a sum of 50,000 francs a month for the payment of the interest on the loan of 5 million piastres which was contracted at London in 1824, and which served to cover the needs of the war which Buenos Ayres was carrying on against Brazil at that time. These revenues amounted to 70,000,000 paper piastres in 1855, a relatively high proportion and the more worthy of note in that the Confederated Provinces, in spite of the fact that they are enjoying peace and order, lack the resources to meet their ordinary expenses and even under most onerous conditions for them, they could not negotiate a loan. These Provinces still owe Brazil 2,000,000 francs. So improved was the condition of receipts of Buenos Ayres in January and February last that it enabled the Government to make such advantageous proposals to the holders of Buenos Ayres bonds (of the English loan) that these bonds immediately rose 30 per cent on the London Exchange.

With regard to public instruction, the efforts of the Government of Buenos Ayres have not been less great or less fruitful.

From a material point of view, the city of Buenos Ayres has made important improvements in its seat. The number of new buildings has doubled in three years. The provisions preparatory to its illumination by gas are being completed; a railroad has been started; the result of it will be to expedite the transportation of products to the city from the country; a customhouse is being built; seventeen warehouses have been completed and can now hold up to 12,000 tons of packages. Finally, to facilitate the disembarkation of persons arriving and the unloading of merchandise in the port of Buenos Ayres, the Administration had a pier 400 meters long erected, which is now in use, and a permit to construct a second pier, this latter of iron, has been granted to a company.

It has already been said that the State of Buenos Ayres was the first to allow and proclaim the free navigation of the Plata River and of its tributaries, in the part which belongs to that State. But that does not mark the limit of its international spirit of liberalism. Foreign flags have been placed by it on the same footing as the national flag. It has abolished pilotage, lighthouse and port dues for vessels carrying more than 50 emigrants. It has perceptibly restricted the conditions of the customs tariff. Foreign trade has secured valuable transit and transhipment facilities. By liberal concessions of land and of rights of settlement, protective decrees have assured immigration of a whole system of guaranties, so that no complaint has arisen from immigrants since they have settled.

It is pertinent to add that, on account of its geographical location, its numerous population and an industrial richness which the future cannot but increase, the State of Buenos Ayres has always been and has become more than ever the true center of foreign interests in this part of America. If there was need of new evidence of this fact, it would be found both in the statistical data of the Register of the State of Buenos Ayres for the second half of 1854 and in the French annals of foreign commerce (February issue). It would suffice to draw a comparison in this regard by the aid of these data between Buenos Ayres and the Confederated Provinces. The Government of Buenos Ayres, moved by a consideration of intelligent patriotism, has, moreover, no desire but

2648

John Y. Mason, United States Minister to France, to William L. Marcy,
Secretary of State of the United States [1]

Private & Confidential.   PARIS, *June 12, 1856.*

SIR: Since writing and sending off my Despatch,[2] a communication has
been made, by a person who has opportunities of knowledge, which may
justify a distrust, that the French Government is adopting measures to send
a very imposing naval force to the stations of South America and the Antilles. The person who made this communication, represents the measures
as taken at the request of England, and in concert with that power. As this
person violates confidence, in making the communication, I have not seen
him, nor does he know that I am aware of his intelligence. His communica-

---

to see the Confederation peaceful, happy and prosperous: it has endeavored and still
endeavors, without in any way meddling in the domestic affairs of the Confederation, to
offer it all facilities which might, on its part, aid in achieving this result, asking nothing
in exchange but a fraternal reciprocity.

After this succinct exposition of the situation of the country, would it be right, to
remove the interests which America and Europe have in the Plata, seeking for them
elsewhere than in the place where they are, in fact, concentrated? Would it be right
to believe that the State of Buenos Ayres might oppose the free navigation of rivers
when it was the first to proclaim it and when, since this declaration and the putting into
practice of this freedom of the rivers, its prosperity has done nothing but increase?
Would it be right and logical to be apprehensive on its account of the ambition of
Brazil, when, on the one hand, it is protected therefrom geographically, and on the
other it has always victoriously restrained that ambition by force of arms? Finally,
would it be right, would it be advantageous to favor a system of attack, the obvious
purpose of which is to attract to the Provinces of the present Confederation a commercial traffic which has its established traditions in the State of Buenos Ayres? Let
us assume a disturbance in the diplomatic relations between the United States or
Europe and the State of Buenos Ayres; a disturbance which would not be occasioned
by any grievance, to which, on the contrary, all the measures taken by the latter State
are opposed and should have rendered impossible; what happens? Profound uneasiness on the part of the foreign population; the halting of commercial maritime traffic,
and on the other hand, strong encouragement is offered to various ill-intentioned men in
the country who may still nourish hopes of anarchy, and dreams of attempts to overthrow [the Government].

When once it is fully shown that the State of Buenos Ayres is materially prosperous,
that its policy is enlightened and liberal and that all its efforts tend to favor the growth
of foreign interests and their identification with indigenous interests, it would not be
understood why anyone should wish to break or change the existing diplomatic relations, to the advantage of the Confederated Provinces. In any case, would it not be
fairer and more advantageous for the United States and Europe to keep their missions
in the two countries than to loosen or break their connections with Buenos Ayres in the
maintenance of which the prosperity and development of foreign trade are directly
involved in this section?

Such, Mr. Minister, is the brief but absolutely accurate exposition of the general
situation of the country. Brought to Your Excellency's attention and, through your
kind mediation to that of the Government of the United States, I do not doubt that,
with the awakening of a natural spirit of just cordiality, it will seek to tighten international bonds with Buenos Ayres, instead of loosening them.

Please accept, Mr. Minister, [etc.].

[1] Despatches, France, vol. 38. Received June 28.
[2] He evidently refers to his No. 147, above, this part, June 8, 1856, doc. 2646.

tions were entirely voluntary, obviously dictated by the hope of reward. He has made them to Mr: Wilbor, who is very discreet. If I find corroborative circumstances, I may send Mr: Wilbor to Washington next week, to explain to you, in such way that the author of the disclosure may not be betrayed.

It is not impossible, that France may be disposed to act in concert with England, in regard to the independence of the Central American States, under the mistaken idea, that the United States Government is tacitly permitting, if not conniving at, the immigration of our citizens in Nicaragua, with the ultimate purpose of annexation. I consider it proper, to give you this information now, lest my opinions expressed in my late Despatch,[1] may be regarded as too strongly expressed, if events shall verify the accuracy of the information given.—I will see the Minister of Foreign Affairs tomorrow, *Friday*, and read to him that part of my Despatch, which purports to give our conversation, to test its accuracy, without indicating that any doubt exists on my mind, of the sincerity of the assurance given, I will endeavor to learn, whether any change has arisen in the views of the Emperor's Government, since my last conversation with him. Mr: Wilbor's informant represents that the communication from England was received on Saturday last; my conversation took place on the day before; but I saw Count Walewski on Saturday night, and I saw nothing to justify a suspicion that any change had occurred, which he intended to make known to me.

The number of *Galignani's Messenger* of this morning, will give you some idea of the views of our affairs which are presented to the public here. The Herald and the Tribune, of New York, are the papers most freely quoted from, and, if credited, are of course very unfavorable to the Government of the United States. This I constantly endeavor to neutralize and counteract;—but I cannot succeed, without means which I have not at my command,—and without measures which it would be very distasteful to me, to adopt.

I cannot persuade myself that the conclusion which I had reached, as announced in my despatch, is incorrect,—yet I am very sensible, that as this Government is directed by one will, and the personage with this great power, distinguished for his reserve, it is difficult to rely absolutely on conclusions founded only on general reasoning. Yet, where there is no French interest to be subserved, and so many real interests endangered, I cannot believe, that the Government can contemplate any measure, which may involve war with a country, whose friendly intercourse is so vastly beneficial to France.

I will add, that I hear today, from a good source, that the French army is about to be reduced by the discharge of about one hundred thousand men.

I make this private and confidential. I cannot do otherwise than write it,

---

[1] Evidently his despatch of June 8, 1856, doc. 2646.

and yet I regret, that the information which I communicate, is so meagre—
and may or may not be worthy of consideration.

I am [etc.].

2649

*John Y. Mason, United States Minister to France, to Lewis Cass, Secretary of
State of the United States* [1]

No. 233   PARIS, *June 8, 1857.*

SIR: Your despatch No. 109 of the 16th of May ult⁰ [2] was received at the
Legation on the 2ᵈ instant, and I availed myself of the first opportunity
presenting itself to execute the instruction which it conveyed to me.

On Friday last I was received by Count Walewski at the Ministry of Foreign Affairs, and making known to him your wish that for his information
he should read the copy of your letter to Lord Napier, the British Minister
at Washington,[3] placed it in his hands. He courteously received it, read it
carefully and returned it. He made no observation on the subject of the
affair of which the letter treated—but enquired if I had received any official
intelligence in regard to the present condition and probable result of the questions between England and the United States, on Central American Affairs.
I informed him that I had not, but from what I [had?] heard, I inclined to the
opinion that as the British Government had declined to accept the Dallas-
Clarendon Treaty in it's amended form, no further step would be taken by
the President until the meeting of the Senate in December next. He mentioned that M. de Sartiges had written that you had doubts, whether an
agreement would be arrived at, and Count Walewski, seemed to be of opinion, that the difficulty consisted in the fact that the United States insisted
on an acknowledgement or admission by Great Britain that she had no
right to the Bay Islands. I remarked that I did not know precisely the
position of the question—that it was in my opinion quite certain that Great
Britain had no well founded claim of title to the Islands, and that as she had
professed to be willing to relinquish her possession and restore the Islands to
their rightful owners—the Republic of Honduras, any mere form of words
ought not to defeat this purpose—and that I hoped the affair would be adjusted—but that I did not believe that my Government would be content
with; much less co-operate in a form of surrender to Honduras which
imposed conditions inconsistent with that Republic's dignity as a Sovreign
State or with her rights of Jurisdiction over her territory and it's inhabitants. Count Walewski's manner was courteous and he seemed to
desire very much to see the affair adjusted. Indeed I feel quite satisfied

---

[1] Despatches, France, vol. 41. Received June 24.
[2] Above, this volume, pt. v, doc. 2499.
[3] Below, vol. VII, pt. I, doc. 2776, April 22, 1857.

that the Imperial Gov.ᵗ would deeply regret any interruption of good relations between the United States and Great Britain.— Bound to the latter
by the bonds of Alliance, and to the former by ties of interest and friendship,
I am quite sure that all it's influence will be exerted by the Imperial
Government to produce an amicable Solution of any question which may
arise.

With highest esteem [etc.].

2650

John Y. Mason, United States Minister to France, to Lewis Cass, Secretary of
State of the United States [1]

No. 283   PARIS, *December 12, 1857.*

SIR: I have the honor to acknowledge the receipt of your Despatches,
Nos. 130. and 131.[2]— I regret to inform you, that your No. 129,[3] has not
reached the Legation, and therefore I will be obliged if you will have the
goodness to send me a Duplicate. Before receiving your 131, I had some
conversation with Count Walewski on the subject.[4] He had heard of the
negotiation of the Treaty, and mentioned the fact to me. I confidently assured him that it would be found that the United States had sought no selfish advantage by its Treaty, but to secure to the world a transit across the
Isthmus from the Atlantic to the Pacific—that, as in the case of Honduras,
I was confident that my country would see with no feeling of dissatisfaction
seperate Treaties made by France and England to receive the same advantages which are accorded to us. The policy of the Imperial Government,
at this moment, is decidedly to extend the French Commercial Marine as
much as possible— The Colonial possessions in the Pacific, and the whale
fisheries in that Ocean combined with the general policy referred to give
much interest to every means of transit across one Continent which shortens
the long voyage around the Cape. Count Walewski informed me, that
the Imperial Government would propose a Treaty with Nicaragua. Nothing occurred in our interview, which indicated dissatisfaction with what had
been done. The escape of Walker, on another expedition has excited much
remark in general circles here—but I doubt not, that the measures of the
Government of the United States, and especially your Treaty with Mr:

---

[1] Despatches, France, vol. 42. Received January 1.
[2] No. 130 is not included in this publication. It enclosed a letter to the Persian Ambassador at Paris. No. 131, however, is above, this volume, pt. v, November 23, 1857, doc.
2501.
[3] No. 129 forwarded a box of books.
[4] The subject was the Cass-Irisarri Treaty, signed on November 16, 1857. For the few
differences between this treaty, which never became effective, and a later treaty between the
United States and Nicaragua, concluded June 21, 1867, which is published in Malloy,
Treaties, Conventions, etc., between the United States and Other Powers, see above, vol. IV,
doc. 1409, note 2, p. 629.

Iyissarri [Irisarri?] will as soon as known, put a stop to all ill-natured suspicions that he has the sympathies of the Government.

I will take an early opportunity to explain to Count Walewski, how completely the facts warrant the opinions which I expressed to him.

I am, Very Respectfully [etc.].

2651

John Y. Mason, United States Minister to France, to Lewis Cass, Secretary of State of the United States [1]

[EXTRACTS]

No. 284   PARIS, *December 12, 1857.*

SIR: The pending misunderstanding between Spain and Mexico has for some time excited much interest in Europe.

About two weeks since Mr Olaguibel the Mexican Minister to France, introduced to me a most interesting conversation which he requested me to regard as confidential.— I asked if he was unwilling that I should communicate to you it's substance— He said, by no means, but he would wish that it might be regarded at Washington as well as here, as confidential. I assured him that it would be so treated.

It is now some months since Mr Lafraga arrived in Paris en route for Madrid with his credentials as Minister Plenipotentiary of Mexico to Spain. He opened a communication with Marshal Serrano the Ambassador of Spain at the French Court, with a view to ascertain if he would be received in his official character at Madrid. After a lapse of two months and a half, he proceeded to Madrid encouraged by the Spanish Ambassador to expect recognition, but not assured.— On his arrival he was delayed, and his reception postponed under various pretexts for two months and a half more, until his patience being exhausted, he notified the Spanish Ministry, that unless he could be permitted at once to present his letters of credence to Her Majesty, he had no course left but to withdraw himself from Madrid. He was permitted to retire from Spain and has been since residing in Paris.

England and France had submitted to Spain and Mexico a proposition that their Governments would with the consent of the Governments of the disagreeing States take into friendly consideration the dispute existing with the hope of producing a friendly solution. Spain accepted the offered mediation unconditionally. Mexico also accepted but with a reservation that Spain should in advance receive the Mexican Diplomatic Representative.— When the British Government was informed of this qualified acceptance on the part of Mexico, Lord Clarendon in writing informed General Almonte that he saw no objection to the Mexican condition, but subsequently no

[1] Despatches, France, vol. 42. Received January 1.

doubt after communication with Paris made known his disapproval of it. The French Government through Count Walewski has informed M. Olaguibel, that the condition is inadmissable on the ground, that the usual relations of amity being suspended and the two Countries of Spain and Mexico in a state of quasi war, the Emperor's Government does not consider it proper to exact of Spain such a concession before the removal of the causes of dispute by amicable adjustment.

M. Olaguibel is decidedly of opinion that the Spanish Government will not accede to the Mexican condition, and two weeks since was equally confident that Mexico would not recede, and that the affair would not be amicably adjusted. In the mean time the condition of affairs in Mexico has materially changed and anxiety as well as uncertainty is felt as to the effects of the existing condition of things.— I saw yesterday, Mr. Olaguibel, and Genl Almonte the Mexican Minister at London now casually here. Mr O. assured me that his conviction that the affair would not be satisfactorily settled, by mediation is stronger than before. He said that he had discovered, that an intrigue was on foot to restore Santa Anna to power, countenanced by Spain: that on information transmitted by him, a General Cortez had been arrested at Vera Cruz, and was now a prisoner at Mexico: that in his possession were found papers, of grave importance, and that there was a strong desire in Mexico for war with Spain.— A significant incident recently occurred here.— When the Duke of Rivas, on assuming his functions as Ambassador of Spain to France agreeable to usage, sent his cards to the members of the Diplomatic Corps, below his rank, indicating the day and the hour, when he would receive them, a card was sent to the Mexican Plenipotentiary, but he declined to attend as the Minister of his Country had not been received at Madrid. He sent, however through a friend, a message to the Duke, expressing his regret that existing circumstances had deprived him of the pleasure of paying his respects, which he yet hoped to do under more favourable auspices. He received no answer. Yesterday, in the anti-chamber of the Minister of Foreign Affairs, where the several members of the Diplomatic Corps were waiting to see the Minister, I was conversing with Genl Almonte and Mr. Olaguibel, when the Duke of Rivas entered. He addressed me with much cordiality, but no interchange of salutation or civility occurred between him and the Mexicans. Mr O. expects war, and in that event, he relies largely on expected aid from citizens of the United States. I cautioned him, that while it may happen thus, in the event of war, adventurous men will be found ready to expatriate themselves, and enter the Mexican service, but it must not be expected, that the President of the United States, with the most friendly feelings towards Mexico, and the most earnest desire to see her maintain her dignity, and illustrate the wisdom and efficiency of the Republican System of Government, could countenance any acts violative of our neutrality laws. He expressed a confident belief, that the French and British Governments would not interfere in case of war, and that if Spain persisted to the extremity of war, she would lose Cuba.   I expressed my satisfaction, that he seemed so confident, that the allied Governments of Europe would not interfere by force of arms, because in the event of such intervention, it would present a very grave question for consideration of my Government, which I would prefer should not arise.   My own opinion founded on general reasoning, is that Spain will not make war on Mexico.

The Ministry of Narvaez is overthrown, and a new Ministry formed whose power cannot last.   It is the general opinion in Europe that the condition of Spain is deplorable.   Financial distress prevails, there, as well as throughout Europe.   Queen Isabella's Government grows weaker, and intestine troubles must be the result.   I feel quite confident, that the time approaches, when the combined influence of political and financial weakness will give to the United States, improved chances of acquiring the Island of Cuba by fair and honourable purchase.   To such an arrangement, in spite of obstinate pride, the necessities of Spain, and danger of its capture, if it shall arise, must soon incline her, unless the effects of existing causes, shall disappoint all reasonable expectation.—   It may furnish the counterpart of the history of the acquisition of Louisiana. . . .[1]

No one can doubt that these questions, and their complication, may contain the elements of an European quarrel, of a very grave character—and the actual condition of things appear to justify the opinion, that neither England nor France, will be disposed to engage in hostilities or encourage angry feeling with the United States, on account of Spain, whose corrupt and ill conducted Government is constantly committing gross blunders, and whose intestine dissentions have no strength to enable that fine Country to perform its appropriate part in the family of European Nations.   I think there is good reason to entertain strong hopes that the President will have it in his power to add to the territory of the United States, the Island of Cuba, and thus illustrate his administration by a natural solution of the disturbing questions which agitate us, and add to the moral and physical strength of the Country—and that this great acquisition may be effected without any implication of the Honor and good faith of our Country.

Presuming that the subject of this Despatch will interest you, as it does me, I will not fail to obtain all accessible information from authentic sources and communicate it.   The large dimensions which have been given to our Country, by its wonderful progress, make it more important to the rest of the world, and impart to us increased interest in passing European events.— I will watch these events, in all their aspects, but especially so far as they may affect this momentous question.

Very Respectfully [etc.].

[1]The omitted portion relates to political affairs in Europe.

2652

John Y. Mason, United States Minister to France, to Lewis Cass, Secretary of State of the United States [1]

[EXTRACTS]

No. 285   PARIS, *December 24, 1857.*

SIR: Mr. Olaguibel has been recalled as the Minister of Mexico to the Imperial Court, and Genl Almonte has been received as his successor. It will be my desire to cultivate with him, the best relations of courtesy and civility. I doubt not he will reciprocate the feeling. He has promptly called at this Legation, after presenting his credentials. I send herewith these copies of a printed publication on the subject of the disputed questions between Mexico and Spain, which at this moment possess much interest.[2] . . .

In my last interview with Count Walewski, I read to him your despatch No. 131[3] on the subject of the Treaty lately negotiated with Nicaragua, and explained to him, the objects of the United States Government, in that regard. He declared it a very good thing, reiterated the expression of the interest which France felt in all the routes of transit across the Isthmus— and said that Nicaragua had invited France to make a Treaty for the guaranty of the route, and left me to infer, that it would probably be done, but without the slightest intimation, that there was any unpleasant feeling here, in consequence of what has been done by the United States.

I am [etc.].

2653

John Y. Mason, United States Minister to France, to Lewis Cass, Secretary of State of the United States [4]

[EXTRACTS]

No. 323   PARIS, *June 27, 1858.*

SIR: I have received your No. 146,[5] with its accompanying papers. I am gratified to have in my possession, a copy of the Convention which you signed with the Representative of Nicaragua.[6]

I have had no reason to suppose, that its provisions were unacceptable to the Imperial Government.

[1] Despatches, France, vol. 42.   Received February 1.
[2] Not found.
   In the omitted portion he comments upon the Message of the President of the United States.   [3] Above, this volume, pt. v, November 23, 1857, doc. 2501.
   [4] Despatches, France, vol. 43.   Received July 15.
   [5] Above, this volume, pt. v, June 9, 1858, doc. 2502.
   [6] Apparently he refers to the Cass-Irisarri Treaty.   For a comment upon this treaty, see above, this part, p. 674, note 4.

I have not heard from the Minister of Foreign Affairs, an expression of opinion on the subject, but I have more than once conversed with him in regard to routes of Transit across the Isthmus—and have never perceived any indication of a desire on the part of France, to control them—all that appeared to be desired, was that such means of passing from Ocean to Ocean, should be open to the commerce and people of all nations.

Soon after M. Felix Belly left France, the object of his visit was spoken of here, in consequence of views presented in some of the newspapers of the United States. I do not know M. Belly, and I had not then and have not now, any authoritative information in regard to his purposes or employment. I was however induced to believe, that he had no official character in Central America, from the French Government—but was an agent of a business firm here, probably backed by the Credit Mobilier Company, and his object was a purely speculative adventure. . . .[1]

. . . There has been a general decline of business and of prices—and no stock has declined more than that of the Credit Mobilier. Within a few months it has fallen more than one half of the price which it had commanded. I do not believe, that this concern can furnish the Capital for any important undertaking in Central America.

In the London Times of the 24th Inst: is published a letter from the intelligent Paris correspondent of that paper, in which he gives the results of his information in regard to M. Felix Belly and his operations in Central America. I am inclined to believe, that it will be found to be substantially correct. I enclose a slip which contains it.[2] Besides this, I send a copy of a letter, which I received a few days since from Mr. Marcoletta[3] [Marcoleta]

[1] In the omitted portion he states that the general opinion is that the Crédit Mobilier has no connection with the French Government.

[2] Not included in this publication. The correspondent states that he has "excellent authority for affirming" that M. Belly is neither the official nor unofficial agent of the French Government.

[3] In the following translation of a letter from Marcoleta, the name of the American Company mentioned herein is spelled two different ways in the French copy in the manuscript volume; and in a document not included in this publication, it is referred to as the Stephens Company:

José de Marcoleta, Nicaraguan Minister to Great Britain and France, to John Y. Mason, United States Minister to France

[TRANSLATION]

AUX LOGES EN JOSAS, NEAR VERSAILLES (SAÔNE ET OISE), *June 10, 1858.*

SIR: The London "Times" of the 2d and the 5th instant published a convention signed at Rivas, Nicaragua, May 1, last, with the representative of a French firm for the canalization of the isthmus of Nicaragua. But that newspaper refrained from publishing the additional article which states that "the said concession will have no effect if the Steebing [Steebins?] Company of New York fulfills the engagements previously contracted with the Government of Nicaragua, in the current month of June, the last period given the Steebing Company to open the transit route.

I believe it advantageous to the interests of both countries to make the preceding declaration.

Mr. Belly, the representative of the French Company above mentioned, has already

which refers to the same subject.   He once resided at Washington in a Diplomatic capacity, but is not accredited here in any such character.   I have had no previous correspondence with—and have not seen him for many months.— As he has volunteered his letter to me, I will now ask him to give me explicit information on the subject of the additional article of which he speaks.   I will, without delay, endeavor with the necessary caution, to obtain information from the Minister of Foreign Affairs, and other persons and write you again more fully on the subject.   My belief is, that unless combined with the schemes of other private persons and aided by Capital in London and the United States, M. Felix Belly's effort to establish a transit route across the Isthmus will be an utter failure.

The business and money market of France are in a very unsatisfactory state, and it is not possible in my opinion, to sell shares in any such enterprise, with advantage at the Paris Bourse.   I have no belief, that it is any part of the policy of the Emperor, to involve his Government, in probable or possible collision with the United States, by inaugurating here a system of protection or political affinity with the Central American States.   At no period, since my residence in Europe, has there been a more grave necessity for his giving his undivided attention to European Affairs.

As I anticipated, the appointment of a Military man as Minister of the Interior, and of the Public Safety was but temporary—   General Espinassi has retired and M. D' Lanza, the first President of the Imperial Court, has been appointed as Minister of the Interior.   The concluding words which formed part of the title of his predecessor, are now discontinued.[1] . . .

I am, Very Respectfully [etc.].

---

gone to New York to unite the interests of the new Company with the Steebins [Steebing?] Company, or any other [company] composed of American citizens: later he will go to London with the aim of putting those same interests in touch with English capital. Thus the convention in question in no way bears the stamp of exclusiveness; quite the contrary, the enterprise, if it materializes, will have the triple advantage of combining the interests of all under the auspices of the United States, France and England, whose citizens will mutually make up the general company which, in the case, will be formed for the construction of a canal or a railway across the isthmus of Nicaragua.   The Commerce of the World cannot fail to profit thereby.

Kindly accept, Mr. Minister, the assurance of my distinguished consideration.

[1] The omitted portion relates to a newspaper comment upon the massacre of part of the crew of a French vessel, off the coast of Africa.

2654

John Y. Mason, United States Minister to France, to Lewis Cass, Secretary of State of the United States [1]

Private and Confidential.   PARIS, *July 10, 1858.*

DEAR SIR: Recent events have indicated the wise forecast, of the Ministers who composed the Ostend and Aix La Chapelle Conference.[2]

They declared the opinion, that Spanish Occupation of Cuba is dangerous to the Peace of the United States, and it is signally illustrated by these events.—I have seen the incidents occur with great satisfaction.— They have elicited proofs of the devotion of the United States to the true exposition of the Laws of Nations, to the fundamental principle of the equal right of all nations to the free and unrestricted use of the Sea, and to their own dignity.

There can be no doubt, that the extraordinary fact of a blockade of the Island by an armed force, in time of profound peace, was of itself calculated to convince every one, that the Sovereignty of Spain over the Island, was dangerous to the interests of Commerce, and to the public peace. When in the practical execution of the plan of blockade, British Cruizers claimed and exercised the right to visit, delay and search our vessels, it could not be otherwise, than that a spirit of indignation should be excited. The prompt and dignified manner in which these pretensions were met by the United States, has commanded general approval, and I think, the result will be a definitive settlement of a dangerous question, for the benefit of all nations.— The right of visit as of search, except in times of War, to determine the question of contraband, will be acknowledged to have no foundation in the Laws of Nations, but to depend exclusively on Treaty agreement. Thus, four great questions of right, Belligerent and Neutral, will have been settled within five years. The principle that the Flag protects the Cargo, that a friend's goods in an enemy's bottom are not liable to confiscation, that legal Blockade can only be maintained by an adequate force present, to prevent access to the coast are acknowledged, and now the irriting [irritating?] question of the right of visit in time of Peace, will I trust be definitively settled, by the acknowledgement that it can exist only by Treaty. A source of injury, irritation and war will be thus closed—all these principles, just and wise, have always been maintained by the United States.—I am happy to observe, that the long cherished policy and principles of France are yet prevalent, and that the opinion of France on the question of visit, is in complete accord with ours.

[1] Despatches, France, vol. 44. Received July 30.
[2] Reference is made, presumably, to the conferences held in October, 1854, composed of Soulé, Buchanan, and Mason, the United States ministers, respectively, at Madrid, London, and Paris. For documents relating to these conferences, see in the volume and part containing Communications from Spain, under date of October 15 and 20, 1854, and below in vol. VII, pt. II, under date of October 18, 1854, doc. 3026.

Recent events have also produced important effects in Europe.   British measures on the coasts of Cuba, have excited much attention to the condition of the Island, and to the question of the Slave Trade.   The French Government explicitly declares that from motives of humanity negro slavery has been abolished, and there is no purpose to recede from that measure.   Labor is required, where the slaves were emancipated.   It is asserted that the Africans or Indians who may be sent to those Islands to supply the want will be free, and this view, however fallacious others may regard it, seems to to satisfy the French public.

For some time, there have been evidences of a very excited feeling between England and France.   The attempt to ass[ass]inate the Emperor on the 14th January, the origin of the preparations for that act of murder at London, the abortive effort to strengthen the Criminal Law of England, and the failure to convict in prosecutions, when the accessory acts of encouragement or aid, were clearly proved, made a grave impression in France.   The denunciations of the French scheme of African Emigration have not contributed to restore good feeling.

On the question raised with us, by the British cruizers on the coast of Cuba, there exits [exists?] on the part of France, no approval of British acts, and a new phase has been given to the subject, which is not without its interest to us.   The language used in the British House of Lords, especially by the British Minister of Foreign Affairs, is considered here, as tantamount to a declaration that England will not sustain Spain in the possession and Sovereignty of Cuba.   In the number of the Constitutionnel, of the 26th June which I send herewith,[1] you will observe a very significant article, on this subject.   It is understood here, that this Journal speaks by the inspiration of the Count Walewski—and there is now, much discussion, of the probable movements of the United States, towards the acquisition of the Island, the abandonment of Spain by England in the event of collision, and the course which France will pursue in that event.

One of my Diplomatic Colleagues said to me a few days since, when the relations of England and the United States, wore a threatening aspect, that the best and wisest course for Spain, was to cede Cuba to the United States. I replied simply, that the policy of the United States is Peace, and that to secure that great object, I had no doubt, that my Government would purchase Cuba, at a price far more advantageous to Spain, than the possession of the Island.   But I asked, would Spain sell? he thought not, that she was proud and obstinate and considered the Island more valuable, than I seemed to regard it.   She seems as much disinclined to sell as ever.   There are many who believe that France will sustain Spain by Force, if her possession of the Island shall be in danger.   The circumstances of the Emperor's position may produce such a result.   If his popularity shall decline, and the

---

[1] Not found.

necessity shall arise to employ the Army and Navy, it is certainly not impossible, that he would engage in war. But with whom is a question to be considered.— It is true that the colonies of France, are regarded with increased interest, and Cuba being considered the Key of the Gulf of Mexico, the French would not desire to see Cuba under the Laws of the United States. But I yet entertain the opinion which I have heretofore expressed to the Department, that neither France or England would engage in war with the United States, on account of Cuba. The reasons stated in my No. 310.[1] still exist,—in regard to England with increased force, in regard to France with controlling influence, if wisdom shall govern her Counsels.— Yet there are considerations not to be disregarded. The Alliance between England and France is greatly weakened—bad feeling in the masses of the two Countries is more aggravated, and even the Governments have given manifest evidences of irritation.

The Conferences of the Congress of Paris, are protracted, and altho: the proceedings are secret, it is understood, that the sole questions considered, relate to the organization of the principalities. Fuad Pacha [Pasha?], the Turkish Plenipotentiary is sick, but in Diplomatic circles, it is believed that serious diversity of opinion prevails—and the course of things is not agreeable to Austria.

The Conferences will not close before the end of July, but I believe they will end in accord. That there is an uneasiness in regard to European relations is well known, and no one can foresee at what moment, there may arise grave complications. The indications are that the relations of Russia and France will become more friendly, while those of Austria and England will take the same direction. Between Austria and Russia, there is deep hostility.—And England and France are not such close friends as they have been. Sardinia under all circumstances will go against Austria. You will have observed the manifestations exhibited in England of apprehensions of hostility from France. They have not been disguised in the Press or Parliament.—I do not see any proofs of the augmentation of the land or naval forces of France. The approaching naval display at Cherbourg will be very imposing, and will exhibit a very efficient naval force at the command of the Emperor. But I do not believe, that there is any immediate purpose of placing it in active service against any Foreign power. Still it is held in readiness, and it is not impossible that it may be so held, with a view to operations in our Hemisphere if occasion shall arise. But I repeat, that I do not believe, that there can be such madness as to employ it.— While I

[1] Not included in this publication. In that despatch Mason stated that he believed that if the unsettled questions with England were satisfactorily adjusted, and a new treaty of commerce made with France, all pretext for animosity towards the United States would be put aside and would, referring to Spain, "increase the probability of non-interference in any condition of our relations with that country which a regard to our National Honor, may require us to adopt."

have this opinion confirmed by all that I see, and the best consideration which I can give to the subject, I have felt it to be my duty to communicate the fact, that there are those who believe, with confidence that France will oppose any transfer of Cuba to the United States, by force of arms, if nothing short of this resort will defeat the transfer.   But, I do not believe it.   I do not doubt, that there are strong Spanish influences near the Imperial Government.   The plain indications that the British Government, is abandoning Spain, will appeal to the strong desire of the Emperor to be regarded by the world, as the protector of the weak against the strong— and he will desire to maintain an influence with Spain, so that she may be a friendly neighbor to France, and will never be inclined to take part in favor of Louis Philippe's family, against his Dynasty.—   The recent change of Ministry, and restoration of O'Donnell to power is considered a triumph of the French over the English interests at Madrid.   Yet, I repeat, I do not believe, that any other means, than those of persuasion or remonstrance will be used on the part of France, as between Spain and the United States.

The reasons assigned in the Despatch to which I have referred, for this opinion, as founded on the interests of France, exists with full force.   Indeed, at no former period, has there been a greater necessity to cherish the monied and business interests of France, than to-day.—Business is languishing. By the last report of the Bank of France, it appears, that the Institution has specie in its vaults, which would justify an issue of notes equal to fifteen hundred million of francs,—while its actual circulation does not exceed six hundred millions.   The trade and business of the Empire, does not justify loans on good security, for three fifths of the Bank's available means. Nothing could show more clearly, the stagnation of business.   The expense of a Foreign War cannot be incurred, without madness, under such circumstances. The Bourse shows the general decline of securities, and confirms the conclusion.   Cuba as a Spanish dependancy is dangerous to our peace, and the present is a favorable moment, to urge the adjustment of all questions with Spain—and once more to attempt a transfer of the Island by purchase.   The spanish authorities will not close her ports to the African slave trade, and the trade cannot be suppressed while they are open.   The opinion is entertained by many, that we obtain Africans as slaves, through Cuba, altho: it is well known as a fact, that not a single African as a slave, has been imported into the United States, since 1808.—If Cuba shall come under our jurisdiction, no market can exist there, for Africans as slaves, and our military defences will be infinitely strengthened, while commercially, the Island will be more valuable to the world, than it has ever been before or ever will be under any foreign Rule—such has been the experience in regard to every acquisition of territory by the United States.—   Our measures will of course be fair and honorable, but I would not hesitate to take them, in consequence of the possible or probable opposition of any Foreign power.—

It is announced this morning in the *Moniteur*, that the Queen of England and the Prince Consort, will arrive at Cherbourg on the 4th of August, as the guests of the Emperor and Empress. The grand naval Fète [Fête], is to take place on the 7th when Her Majesty will be present. This arrangement is but another evidence of the anxiety of the two Governments to allay apprehension. Nothing can show more clearly the apprehension of collision in Europe, than the fact, that the Island of Perim, is occupied and being fortified by the English, and that it is probable, that no one of the Plenipotentiaries, will bring forward the question, in the pending conferences.

All the nations of Europe, desire, if it be possible to avoid war, but it cannot be disguised, that there is danger of such a contingency. Neither of the leading powers of Western Europe, under existing circumstances can afford to engage in war with us, unless their own national honor or interests are gravely implicated—such is my confident opinion. There are some, whose opinions are entitled to much respect, who think, that a question of the acquisition of Cuba by the United States, will excite a collision with France.

In view of the interests of France, of the character of the Emperor, of the principles and policy of his Government, and of the mutual relations of France and the United States, I cannot anticipate such a result, if our measures, be those which are founded in honor and good-faith, adopted as every independent nation, in the assertion of her rights and dignity, has the right to resort to. But the necessity of considering the question in this aspect, shows most decisively, how largely the peace of the United States, is involved in the continued spanish ownership and occupation of this Island, which lies at the gateway, of the outlet to the valley of the Mississippi, and in sight of our shores.

I am, Very Respectfully [etc.].

2655

John Y. Mason, United States Minister to France, to Lewis Cass, Secretary of State of the United States [1]

No. 328   PARIS, *July 30, 1858.*

SIR: I received your No. 146,[2] with its enclosures, and after carefully examining them, I availed myself of the first occasion to converse with His Excellency, Count Walewski, on the subject. I remarked that M. Felix Belly, a Frenchman, had recently visited Central America, and by his conduct had attracted much notice, and by his acts, manifested a very unfriendly feeling towards the United States—that there was reason to believe, that he had exercised an influence, with the Executive of Nicaragua, to withold its ratification of a recent Treaty, with the United States, after

[1] Despatches, France, vol. 44. Received August 21.
[2] Above, this volume, pt. v, June 9, 1858, doc. 2502.

the Treaty had met the concurrence of the Constituent Assembly.—And that it would be very gratifying, if his Excellency would have the goodness to inform me, whether M. Belly, held any official character or represented in any sense, the authority of the Imperial Government while in Central America. Count Walewski replied emphatically, that as he was informed, M. Felix Belly was the agent of a private commercial firm of Paris,—Messrs. Milhaud & Company, and was engaged in his visit to Central America, in a private enterprise, solely—that he had no official character conferred by the Government, and that the Emperor's Government had no knowledge of his intention to go to Central America, and had given him no instructions, and no authority for his proceedings.—

I thanked the Minister for the information given, and asked him, if he had seen a draft of the Treaty, signed at Washington by Mr. Yrisarri [Irisarri], and General Cass,[1] and I offered to show it to him. He said he believed he had a copy. I said, that one object of that Treaty, was to guarranty a transit route for the use and benefit of all nations, across the Isthmus— and that my Government tho: making it alone, had no desire to secure commercial advantages to the exclusion of other nations—that it was already known that the policy of the United States, did not justify joint Treaties in regard to American Affairs—but that the guarranties of the neutrality of routes of transit, useful to commerce and travel, were intended for the benefit of all who might desire to use them. No remark was made by the Minister, indicative of any hostility or dissatisfaction with the measures of the United States in this regard. Finding that M. Belly was not in any sense an agent of the Imperial Government, I forbore to allude to the false and indecent paper purporting to have been signed by Messrs. Martinez & Mora,[2] as a declaration, which has been published in the news-papers in juxta-position with M. Belly's agreement, with the Executive Governments of Costa Rica and Nicaragua.

No enquiry was made, and no intimation was given of the purpose of the Imperial Government in regard to the proposed protectorate of France, England, and Sardinia over the Central American Republics.— But I venture to express the opinion, that if suggested by M. Belly, the Presidents of the two Republics will not find their offer, favorably received, whenever it, shall be made, otherwise, than through the newspapers.— Mr. Marcoletta [Marcoleta] has addressed to me a second letter in answer to a note which I addressed to him. I send to you copies herewith.[3] He signs his

[1] This treaty, signed on November 16, 1857, never became effective. For the few differences between it and a later treaty between the United States and Nicaragua concluded June 21, 1867, published in Malloy, *Treaties, Conventions, etc., between the United States and Other Powers*, see above, vol. IV, doc. 1409, note 2, p. 629.

[2] It refers presumably to the document dated May 1, 1858, above, vol. IV, doc. 1449, note 2, p. 692.

[3] Mason's letter to Marcoleta was not found, but Marcoleta's second letter to Mason (his first was dated June 10, 1858, above, this part, p. 679, note 3) follows:

note as you will observe, as named Minister &c to France and England. If he has delivered his letters of credence, and been received in his official character, I am not aware of the fact. The additional article of which he has furnished me a copy, I also send.[1] Altho: not published, I presume, it forms a part of M. Belly's contract.

It seems to be understood here, that to execute the ship canal, which he has undertaken, a capital of not less than £15000.000 sterling will be required. I am informed, that it is not expected by the projectors, that this large sum can be raised for such a purpose, without contributions in England and the United States. I feel quite confident, that it cannot be effected in France alone. Messrs. Milhaud & Company, from what I hear of their commercial standing cannot afford to contribute so large a sum. It is probable a mere speculation, founded on the hope of selling the scrip. Independently of the state of the Paris Bourse, and the difficulty of raising large sums of money, by paper securities depending for value on results of operations in Foreign Countries, it is not probable, that in view of the intrinsic difficulties of a canal of such enormous dimensions, that M. Belly and his friends will find capitalists ready to employ sufficient funds in his enterprise. The policy of the Imperial Government, has been manifested, for some years, to discourage heavy outlays of French Capital in Foreign Countries. I have no idea, that the Government will itself engage in such an undertaking— but this is only my decided opinion founded on no authoritative assurance.

I have endeavored to observe your wise injunction of discretion in propounding my enquiries and eliciting the information which you desired me to obtain.—I have read to Count Walewski, so much of this Despatch as relates to his observations in our conversation, and he confirmed my understanding of their purport. I feel satisfied, that if any purpose of the Imperial Government, had been matured or conceived, for a measure in regard to the Central American states, which would necessarily interest the United

---

José de Marcoleta, Nicaraguan Minister to Great Britain and France, to John Y. Mason, United States Minister to France

LOGES-EN-JOSAS (SEINE-ET-OISE), *July 10, 1858.*

SIR: In reply to the letter which you did me the honor to address to me under date of yesterday [Not found.—Ed.], relative to the construction of a canal through the Isthmus of Nicaragua, to the convention signed at Rivas with the representative of a French firm, on the 1st of May last, and to the additional article which forms the principal subject of your letter, I can only, *for the present,* confirm the correctness of the contents of my letter of June 10th last [Above, this part, p. 679, note 3.—Ed.]. As I have at hand at the place in the country where I now am, only an excerpt, hastily made, of the said convention, and as I intend to go to Paris in a few days, I am counting on the pleasure of going myself to confer with you on the subject and of handing to you personally the *literal certified* copy which you desire to obtain. I shall endeavor to do so promptly enough to enable you to send the document in question to Washington by the next steamer.

I remain with the greatest consideration [etc.].

[1] This article is quoted, fully, in the first paragraph of Marcoleta's note to Mason dated June 10, 1858, above, this part, p. 679, note 3.

States, the Minister, who is always frank and friendly in his communications with me, would have informed me.— I certainly drew no inference of such a purpose, from his remarks in my conversation, with His Excellency.

I am, Very Respectfully [etc.]

2656

John Y. Mason, United States Minister to France, to Lewis Cass, Secretary of State of the United States [1]

[EXTRACT]

No. 353—Confidential.   PARIS, *October 12, 1858.*

SIR: An American Lady of great intelligence, temporarily residing in Paris, but mixing more in French society than American, called some days since, to ask me to send a letter addressed to the President, which she desired to reach him safely.   She is very grateful to the President for acts of kindness which she has heretofore received at his hands.—In the interview she mentioned that she had formed the acquaintance of M. Felix Belly, who seemed to have impressed her with favorable opinions of his enterprise in Central America.   I told her, that I would send her letter, and I begged that she would not be duped by any artifice of M. Belly, that he was bitterly hostile to the United States, that it was believed, that he, tho: a mere adventurer, had induced the Government of Nicaragua, to reject an important Treaty, negotiated by President Buchanan's Administration, the stipulations of which would prove eminently beneficial to the whole commercial world, and that his probable object was speculation, for the advantage of himself and his associate to be developed on the Bourse, while his feelings are entirely malignant towards her country.   She seemed surprised, thanked me for information which would place her on her guard, and volunteered to say, that she would advise me of any thing which it was material for my Government to know,—and yesterday I received from her a note, of which I enclose, confidentially a copy.[2]   At the date of our conversation, it was understood, that Messieurs Belly and Milhaud had quarrelled, and that as M. Milhaud had stopped the supplies in money, M. Belly was about resorting to the Courts, against him.   Miss W's letter is the reflex of what M. Belly wished to impress on her mind, possibly in the hope, that it would reach me.   I have not and do not intend to write or visit my correspondent.   But I took occasion of a visit to the Ministry of Foreign Affairs, to enquire of M. de Billing, the Minister's Chef de Cabinet, what progress, M. Belly

---

[1] Despatches, France, vol. 44.   No receipt date appeared on the file copy.
[2] Not included in this publication.   It stated that Belly was the sole negotiator of the enterprise, having quarrelled with his associate, Milhaud, and that the former boasted that all the European powers combined could not impede the accomplishment of his desires; he also stated that France had consented to accord him protection.

makes in his enterprise, taking occasion to suggest, that it was rumored that he spoke largely of the co-operation of the Governments of England and France.   M. de Billing replied, that he knew nothing of M. Belly's affairs, that, that person had endeavored to see himself and the Minister, and no interview had been accorded.   In two numbers of the *Patrie*, which I send herewith,[1] you will find, published articles, on the subject, which seem to be significant that M. Belly's bubble is on the point of bursting, and that he is conscious of his condition, he has grown quite desperate.   If the note imputed to Lord Malmesbury be authentic, you will observe, that his Lordship holds out no hope of patronage until Belly's canal shall be completed—that I think, is a contingency not soon to occur.   I have no reason at all satisfactory to myself for suspecting that the French Government gives to M. Belly any countenance.   Yet, I have thought it proper, to make this communication.   If you will pardon the suggestion, it would be well, to show the inflamatory article in the *Patrie* to M. de Sartiges—after his positive disclaimer which I communicated to the Department, I doubt whether it is prudent again to speak directly to Count Walewski on the subject, unless something should transpire, which has not yet been developed.

The *Patrie* is distinguished for malignant hostility to the United States, but these articles are undoubtedly conceived by inspiration of M. Belly.

You will find in the *Patrie* of yesterday's date, an article on the Filibusters, as condemned by M. Buchanan.—Its style is different from its predecessors.—

I think M. Felix Belly is exploded.[2] . . . .

I am, Very Respectfully [etc.].

2657

John Y. Mason, United States Minister to France, to Lewis Cass, Secretary of State of the United States [3]

No. 358   PARIS, *November 1, 1858.*

SIR: In my number 284, of the 12th December 1857,[4] I communicated some information which the Mexican Minister had kindly given me, on subjects which were not without interest to the public, and especially to our country.   At that time, Mexico had agreed to accept the profered mediation of England and France, for the arbitration of the disputed question between Spain and Mexico, on the condition, that Spain would in advance receive the Minister sent out by Mexico.

Spain would not agree to the condition.   Mr. Olaguibel thought that Mex-

[1] Not found.
[2] The omitted portion states that the Minister of Foreign Affairs had not replied to his proposition for a new commercial treaty.
[3] Despatches, France, vol. 44.   Received November 29.   [4] Above, this part, doc. 2651

ico would not secede. Rumors have again obtained circulation through the Journals of Europe, that Spain is preparing for the invasion of Mexico— it is even stated that twelve thousand Troops is the number to be sent. I cannot believe that Spain will resort to such serious measures of aggression. Nothing can be more deplorable than the condition of Mexico, according to the recent accounts, which have been received from that Country— and it is not impossible that Spain may suppose it a favorable moment, for a demonstration.—Mr. Olaguibel is still here, tho: superseded by General Almonte, and called yesterday, to tell me, that he believed, that Spanish troops are about to be sent to Cuba with the ostensible purpose of attacking Mexico. He believes that the intention is seriously entertained, and re-joices, because he is persuaded that if any-thing can heal the unhappy divisions amongst his countrymen, it will be effected by a Spanish invasion. He expects to return to America in a few weeks and will visit Washington, on his way to Mexico.

I have uniformly endeavored to impress on him, the policy of the United States, in reference to wars between countries with whom we are at peace; but he manifestly counts on aid from the United States in the event of war.

On Tuesday last, I met General Almonte at the Ministry of Foreign Affairs, and he communicated some information of interest—speaking of the rumors referred to he expressed his disbelief in their authenticity.

I learned from him, that since the date of my Despatch No. 284, Mexico has abandoned her condition and accepted the mediation, unreservedly; that he had been instructed and empowered by his Government to effect an adjustment of the disputed questions, with Spain, under the mediation of the two Powers, France and England: that he had addressed himself to the Queen's Government at Madrid to this effect, declaring his readiness to enter without delay on the duty assigned him, but had received no reply.

Differing with Mr. Olaguibel, he expressed the confident opinion, that, under the circumstances existing, Spain will not ignore the reference to the mediating powers, and commence hostilities against Mexico, before a serious attempt at adjustment shall fail of success. In that opinion, I am inclined, to concur, and yet the United States cannot be indifferent to the concentration of large land and naval forces, in the Gulf of Mexico.—I cultivate the relations with Gen¹ Almonte and his predecessor, which will enable me to obtain authentic information on questions which interest us, but take care to commit the United States to nothing. Mʳ Mon, a new Spanish Ambassador, in place of the Duke of Rivas has arrived in Paris but has not yet received the Diplomatic Corps. He will be the fifth Ambassador of that Country to this Court, whom I have seen during my short residence here.

I am, Very Respectfully [etc.].

2658

John Y. Mason, United States Minister to France, to Lewis Cass, Secretary of State of the United States [1]

[EXTRACT]

Private and Confidential.   PARIS, *November 8, 1858.*

MY DEAR SIR: . . . I see nothing and hear nothing to induce me to change my opinion about M. Belly's prospects. I have not seen him, and have had no communication directly or indirectly from him.—Yet I have heard occasionally of his vaulting hopes—and he appears to increase in bitterness towards the United States in proportion as his own affairs become more desperate.— I have refused to hold communication with him, and do not expect again to hear anything concerning him. Nothing can surpass the ignorance and folly of his views, but his excessive impudence. I write you in this form, my dear Sir, because I am unwilling to introduce anything into my official despatches, which could not prudently at any future time be made public.

I am, Very Respectfully [etc.]

2659

John Y. Mason, United States Minister to France, to Lewis Cass, Secretary of State of the United States [2]

[EXTRACT]

No. 362   PARIS, *November 18, 1858.*

SIR: . . . In *Galignani's Messenger*, of this day's date, it is announced by telegraph, that the "Europa" brings intelligence, that "the French and English Governments had written to Mr. Buchanan, a note, announcing the intention of the two Western Powers to insist on the provisional maintenance of the Clayton-Bulwer Treaty, in order to give every facility to the transport of the Mails between the two Oceans." This is the text of the announcement as published in the *Messenger*—and in the *Patrie*, of this date, is an article, obviously coming from M. F. Belly, on Central America and the Law of Nations—which you will find in the slip, enclosed.[3]

I have heard nothing, which would indicate that any disposition had been manifested by the Government of the United States inconsistent with the purpose attributed to the Western Allies, as the motive of their notice.—

---

[1] Despatches, France, vol. 44. Received November 29.
The omitted portion relates to European political affairs.
[2] Despatches, France, vol. 44. Received December 3.
The omitted portion relates chiefly to commercial affairs.
[3] Not included in this publication.

Nor have I received any intimation of the purpose of the French Government to give us notice of any kind.—

The society for the construction of the Suez Canal is organised, and the subscriptions opened, headed by the Prince Jerome.

The projet for the Nicaragua Ship Canal of M. Belly, has not proceeded so far. I have heard of no subscription to that enterprise. It is said, that M. Belly is disposed to suppress that portion of his Treaty which authorizes the French Government to keep two ships of war in the waters of Nicaragua.— In a letter written recently, by the Paris correspondent of the London *Times*, a statement is made of cost of construction and probable receipts, which show the character of the scheme.

M. Belly declares that he is not an engineer, but has made notes, and on them a person in Paris, who claims to be an Engineer, makes his estimates, without ever having been in the Country, through which the Canal is to pass. With these feeble lights, he estimates the whole cost, at 90.000.000 francs, and the annual income from tolls, when the canal shall be complete at 50.000.000 francs. What a magnificent project for the Bourse. There seems to be no recollection, of careful topographical surveys and estimates, which give quite a different view of the affair, in all its bearings.

I am, Very Respectfully [etc.].

2660

John Y. Mason, United States Minister to France, to Lewis Cass, Secretary of State of the United States [1]

Private and Confidential. PARIS, *December 11, 1858.*

MY DEAR SIR: I have the honor to acknowledge receipt of your No. 167 of the 10th Nov: last,[2] with its enclosure.— I am greatly obliged by the care which you have taken to communicate to me, such interesting information. As a defence of the honor of our Country, against the indecent assaults of the Presidents of Nicaraugua and Costa Rica it is complete.— Wisdom, patriotism, a regard for the independence and safety of the States of the American Continent justify the Resolution avowed in regard to European political intervention in their affairs. But depend on it, there will not be wanting manifestations of unwillingness on the part of some European states, not to recognise it.—I have good reason to believe, that the recall of the British Minister at Washington has proceeded from some suggestion made by him to you, that England acquiesced in the Monroe Doctrine.—As I received this information, confidentially, I therefore beg that you will so regard this communication.—I receive from the Imperial Government, the most earnest assurances of a cordial desire to maintain

[1] Despatches, France, vol. 44. Received January 5. [2] See above, pt. v, doc. 2504.

relations of friendship with us.   But I am not without anxiety.   The threatened invasion of Nicaraugua by the filibusterrs has produced much sensation, and if Walker's expedition shall elude our officers and despite the
earnest efforts of the Government to frustrate their plans, proceed on the
illegal expedition, I am compelled to say, that there will be much danger
of collision between them and the French Cruizers.—This Government,
has directed that a Treaty shall be negotiated at Washington between France
and the two Central American Governments, and pending these negotiations,
the French Squadron in the West Indies has orders to resist the attempts of
the unauthorized Invaders of the two Republics.

Today Count Walewski had a conversation with me, on this subject, and
requested me to communicate its purport, to you.—   Impressed with its
gravity, and the mischief which may result, I will ask another interview
with the Minister, that I may incur no risk of mistake or misapprehension,
in communicating the substance of his remarks.—   They were deeply
interesting, emphatic in expression of an earnest desire to preserve most
cordial relations with the United States, and earnest in the wish, that the
purposes and policy of the Imperial Government, shall be clearly understood and appreciated by the President, and Government of the United
States.   The conversation was so brief, that I cannot undertake to detail it
until I have seen the Minister again, and when I will have my memorandum
of the conversation verified by him and will send it to you, by the steamer
which leaves Liverpool on Saturday next.—

I cannot believe, that such madness will rule the hour, as to permit the
interruption of peaceful relations with the United States.   At no period
since I have lived in Europe, have the motives for the preservation of peace,
on the part of France, been stronger than at this moment.—   Yet I apprehend that there is danger in the execution of the orders, which I am sure have
been given, and I will tell Count Walewski so candidlly and firmly.—

If the Fillibusters do not leave the United States, all will probably end
well—but if the French Officers by mistake or design, interrupt a vessel
on the High seas, with our flag or attack or interfere with a passenger
steamer having no illegal purpose, the consequences must be very serious.—

The tone of the French press on the subject of Central American affairs,
has much moderated.—   But I have a suspicion that Lord Palmerston's
visit to Paris and Compiègne have not been with friendly views to us.   The
liberal members of Parliament who drove him from power, and have kept
Lord Derby in, will at once withdraw their support from a Ministry which
shall threaten war with the United States, and the issue of the Monroe Doctrine may be artfully raised by schemes for political power to embarrass the
Derby Ministry.   The Emperor is not with out a weakness of desiring to be
the protector of the weak.—   But, at the same time, it is but just to say,
that the most emphatic assurances are voluntarily given, of earnest and

sincere friendship to the United States.— I will give you some proofs of this in my next. I write this to go by the "Fulton" from Havre, which will reach New York before the next Liverpool Steamer.

Very Respectfully [etc.].

Postscript   *Sunday, December 12, 1858.*

I addressed to Count Walewski, this morning a note—and this evening have his reply. I enclose copies.[1] The promised interview cannot take place, until after the sailing of the "Fulton."

I will not fail to send to you the result of the interview of Tuesday, by the Liverpool steamer of Saturday next.

2661

John Y. Mason, United States Minister to France, to Count Walewski, Minister of Foreign Affairs of France [2]

Paris, *December 12, 1858.*

Mʳ Mason Envoy Extraordinary and Minister Plenipotentiary of the United States gravely impressed with the importance of the observations which His Excellency Count Walewski, Minister of Foreign Affairs, addressed to him on Friday last with a request that they would be communicated to his Government at Washington, finds it important to precise accuracy in making the desired communication, to request an interview with the Count Walewski.

Mʳ Mason's next despatches to Washington ought to leave Paris on Thursday the 16ᵗʰ instant.— He therefore requests His Excellency to grant him an interview at as early a day as may suit Count Walewski's convenience.

If not asking too much Mʳ Mason will be very much obliged if Count Walewski will have the goodness to make a written memorandum of his observations on the second point, concerning the Isthmus of Central America, which he did Mʳ Mason the honor to address to him.

Mʳ Mason renews to Count Walewski assurances of his high consideration.

[1] This correspondence immediately follows this despatch.
[2] Despatches, France, vol. 44; enclosed with Mason to the Secretary of State, unnumbered, dated December 11, 1858, but not sent before the 12th, above, this part, doc. 2660.

2662

Count Walewski, Minister of Foreign Affairs of France, to John Y. Mason, United States Minister to France [1]

PARIS, *December 12, 1858.*

The Minister of Foreign Affairs presents his compliments to the Minister of the United States and takes pleasure in advising him that he will have the honor to receive him on Tuesday at 1 o'clock.

2663

Minute of a conversation between John Y. Mason, United States Minister to France, and Count Walewski, Minister of Foreign Affairs of France— begun on December 10, 1858, and continued on the 14th of the same month [2]

[EXTRACTS]

PARIS, *December 16, 1858.*

When the conversation reported in my Despatch of the 11th inst: to the Secretary of State [3] had ended, I rose to withdraw.—

The Minister said, that he wished to speak to me, on two subjects, adding that we often interchanged opinions in a friendly manner, and that he now desired to speak to me in that spirit.— I acknowledged in suitable terms my sense of the honor, which his Excellency was pleased to show me.[4] . . .

II. The second point related to Central America.

The conversation was necessarily brief, as many members of the Diplomatic Corps were in attendance, and unwilling to incur a risk of mistake, in regard to a subject which appeared to me of the gravest importance and probably involving very serious consequences, I addressed a note to the Minister asking an interview, to which I received a prompt answer, inviting me to come to the Ministry on Tuesday the 14th Inst.[5]

I regarded it as fortunate, that I received Gen[1]: Cass's Despatch No. 169,[6] on the morning of Tuesday, a short time before I left my house, to meet the engagement.— I was in attendance, at the hour named, and was promptly admitted by His Excellency,—I remarked, that the information which he had communicated to me, on Friday, had filled me with anxiety—that my

[1] Despatches, France, vol. 44; enclosed with Mason to the Secretary of State, unnumbered, dated December 11, 1858, but not sent before the 12th, above, this part, doc. 2660.

[2] Despatches, France, vol. 44; enclosed with Mason to the Secretary of State, No. 368, December 16, 1858, below, this part, doc. 2664.

[3] Above, this part, doc. 2660.

[4] The omitted portion related to the first subject discussed, which was the position of the French government regarding "the right of search" on the high seas.

[5] For these two notes of the same date, see above, this part, December 12, 1858, docs. 2661 and 2662.   [6] Above, this volume, pt. v, November 26, 1858, doc. 2505.

Government far from justifying the hostile invasion of the territory of a
country in amity with the United States, by unauthorized individuals, had
exerted its power to prevent it, and the intervention of Foreign Governments,
against such expeditions, threatened very serious dangers to the peace
which happily existed. But that as his Excellency had been so good as to
request me to be the medium of conveying some kind words to my Government, I had an anxious wish to communicate them exactly as he wished to
be understood, and I asked if he had thought it worth while to comply with
my request, that he should make a memorandum in writing.— He said
that it was not necessary—That the Emperor's Government had determined to negotiate a Treaty with the two Republics of Nicaragua and
Costa Rica, guarrantying the neutrality of transit routes across the Isthmus,
which were and ever would be interesting to the commerce of the world—
that in this, France only pursued the course already taken by the United
States and England.— That as a proof of his friendly feeling towards the
United States, the Emperor had directed the negotiation to take place
at Washington—that these two Republics had represented, that they
were threatened with invasion by Fillibusters, which if it should occur,
would be disastrous in many respects, but especially in embarrassing negotiations of the character in which France was about to engage—and had
requested that orders might be given to the squadron in the West Indies to
render them aid in suppressing any such invasion: that the Emperor's
Government had yielded its assent, and given the orders—and that M. de
Sartiges had communicated the fact to the Secretary of State—that on
receiving the report of his interview with Genl: Cass, he had addressed to
M. de Sartiges a despatch covering the ground of our conversation—which
would be made known to the Secretary of State, and supersede the necessity
of his making any memorandum, in pursuance of my request. The Minister
read to me his last instructions to the French Minister at Washington.

I remarked, that I deeply regretted the issue of the orders, as in my
judgment they threatened much mischief—that passenger steamers were
passing from Ports of the United States, to the Isthmus en route for the
Pacific, and if by mistake or design one of them should be fired into or
molested, the consequences would be most serious.—

He promptly replied that was impossible of occurrence, for nothing would
be done under the orders, except in Costa Rica or Nicaragua, at the request
of their Governments, and only in the event of an actual hostile invasion—
and that the orders were limited to the pendency of negotiations of the proposed Treaty. He added, that what he desired to make known at Washington through me, was the assurance of the earnest and sincere friendship of
the Emperor's Government towards the United States, and that in what
had been done, nothing had been done inconsistent with that feeling.

I then took occasion, to say to His Excellency, that I had opportunely received a despatch from my Government which made it my duty, to give to him certain information which I could not better impart than by giving him the Despatch to read— He took Gen[1]: Cass's No. 169,[1] and read it carefully, and aloud. When he read the sentence "The position we have taken, we shall adhere to, that this country will not consent to the re-subjugation of those States or to the assumption and maintenance of any European authority over them", Count Walewski remarked, nothing of the kind is contemplated by France, in its measures towards Central America. The Minister did not say, that "the French Government will abstain from all forcible interference in the affairs of Central America."— But I understood him to state distinctly that no political protectorate was contemplated, that the orders to the French Cruizers, were only against actual hostile invasion, by Fillibusters, and limited to the pendency of negotiations of the contemplated Treaty—and that it was earnestly hoped, that the efforts of the Government of the United States, to prevent the sailing of the Expedition would be successful. I cannot pretend to give the entire conversation— I have endeavored to give its substance.— In conclusion, I remarked, that it would be a subject of deep regret, if the peaceful relations of the two countries, should be interrupted when there were such grave material interests involved in their preservation, and so little occasion or necessity for their interruption.

His Excellency replied that such a result was not possible.

The manner and bearing of the Minister throughout the interview was kind and earnestly conciliatory.— I endeavored to follow his example.

2664

John Y. Mason, United States Minister to France, to Lewis Cass, Secretary of State of the United States [2]

No. 368   PARIS, *December 16, 1858.*

SIR: I send herewith the Minute[3] which I have prepared of the substance of my conversation with the Minister of Foreign Affairs, of which I gave you notice, in private letter [4] sent by the "Fulton". I regret that I have not the advantage of submitting it again to the examination of the Minister. I will however do so, tomorrow. I cannot wait to do so as my mail must leave here immediately to reach Liverpool for the steamer. I content myself with saying, that in my opinion, no desire or purpose exists with this Government to interrupt the friendly relations of the two countries.— And I sincerely hope

[1] Above, this volume, pt. v, November 26, 1858, doc. 2505.
[2] Despatches, France, vol. 44. Received January 6.
[3] Above, this part, December 16, 1858, doc. 2663.
[4] *Ibid.*, December 11, 1858, doc. 2660.

that no untoward incident may occur, which will force consequences so much to be deprecated.— I received your No. 169 [1] a few moments before I went to the Minister on Tuesday.   Its arrival was very opportune.   At a suitable moment in our interview, I informed him of the nature of my instruction and observing that I could not better fulfil my duty, than to give him the opportunity of reading your Despatch which was dignified, comprehensive and conciliatory.— He asked if the Despatch was for him, I replied that it was not, but he would perceive, that it stated the substance of what I was to say to him in better terms than I could employ.   I would be gratified if you would authorize me to give him a copy if he desires one.

I am satisfied that it will serve a good purpose, by indicating the perfect frankness, which we wish to observe on the delicate subject to which it refers.

I forbear, saying more, as I am very desirous to secure the transmission of my Despatch by the next steamer.

I am, With Respect [etc.].

2665

John Y. Mason, United States Minister to France, to Lewis Cass, Secretary of State of the United States [2]

Confidential.   PARIS, *December 18, 1858.*

Dear SIR: On the 17th Inst:, I received your letter of the 1st Dec. Inst: marked confidential.[3]   Your Despatch No. 169 of the 26th Nov: ult:,[4] reached me on the 14th of this month.   Agreeably to your request, I enclose an exact copy of the Despatch.   There is no mark or indication on it, that it was to be treated as Confidential.— I read it with great care, and my anxieties already excited by information received from the Minister of Foreign Affairs, of the orders given to the French Cruizers in the West Indies, were not abated, when I read in your despatch that the subject to which your conversation with M. de Sartiges related, had assumed "a very grave aspect".

Impressed, with the most earnest conviction, that in regard to the Central American States, and on every question connected with them, the course of my Government had been and always would be, just, magnanimous and forbearing, and on the other hand, convinced, that the true interests of France forbade, any interruption of peaceful relations with the United States, and that as no sufficient reason existed, the Imperial Government, would not hazard such a consequence, I took your Despatch No. 169, with

---

[1] Above, this volume, pt. v, November 26, 1858, doc. 2505.
[2] Despatches, France, vol. 44.   Received January 13.
[3] Not found.   [4] Above, this volume, pt. v, doc. 2505.

me, and at the conclusion of my conversation with Count Walewski, I handed it to him for perusal, as I have already informed you. I repeat, that I had read it with the greatest care—that in my judgment it was manly, dignified, comprehensive yet clear, firm yet conciliatory. I would regret very much, the failure to mark it confidential, if it had been regarded, by the French Minister in a different light, than that in which it appeared to me.— Such was not the result, and firmly impressed with the belief, that its frank submission to the perusal of the Minister, has done much good, I rejoice, that the Minister saw my instruction in your own admirable language. I consider all danger of collision passed, and not likely to recur. I believe that the frankness, and firmness, with which the affair has been discussed, has contributed largely to this happy result.

I am extremely gratified at the very kind tone of your letter of the 1st Inst: and especially grateful for your considerate expression of confidence in my discretion in communicating the information placed in my possession.

I saw Count Walewski, again on Friday, yesterday, and said to him that the Despatch which I had given to him to read, was, I had some reason to believe intended to be marked confidential, but by inadvertence of the copying clerk, it was not so marked, I had therefore to ask his Excellency, not to expect a copy as I could not give one—that I had always found that frankness on my part, representing my Government was met by the Emperor's Government in a corresponding spirit, and that as my Government honored me, with confidence in my discretion, the act of showing him my instruction on a most delicate affair, was mine which I would regret, if any mischief had been the result. I was happy to believe, that none had. He concurred and concluded with a renewed expression of the opinion, that hostilities between the United States and France were impossible.

I took the occasion to say, that these questions concerning Central America were dangerous and ought to be settled. That as [to?] the neutrality of Transit Routes, there could be no disagreement, for even in the case of the Cass-Yrissarri Treaty, which had probably failed of ratification by the unauthorized interference of M. Belly, the leading object was to give equal benefits of Transit routes across the Isthmus to the whole world—that as to the Mosquito protectorate and the Bay Islands, the Emperor's Government, would show its love of peace, civilization and Justice, by using its influence with the British Government, to abandon its claim of a protectorate and to restore the Bay Islands to Honduras, to which Republic they belonged. That we do not want them. There was no definite reply, but the suggestion was not received with any marks of dissatisfaction or disapproval.— I will not be surprised to witness that in the future, the adoption of the course suggested.

M. de Lesseps announces that the funds for the construction of the Suez Canal, are already subscribed, 220,000 shares in France and the rest in European States—made under circumstances which show remarkable enthusiasm, not in France alone, but in other continental states, and a passenger from India reports, that the British are actually fortifying the Island of Perim.— If the British have sought to involve France with us on the subject of transit routes by land or water, across one Isthmus, the Suez Canal to which they are opposed and which they [1] favored by France, Austria, Piedmont, Russia, and the Italian States generally, and enthusiastically supported by Egypt, presents a question on which France may discover the motive of British advice, and find, that there is a disposition to use France, when her interests are not so largely involved, and to oppose her when they are.

I will look with anxiety for your answer, to this and my late communications. If in what I have done, I shall be so fortunate as to receive the approval of the President and yourself, I will be happy.

I believe, that the results have been good, and, that the moment is auspicious to press our proposed Treaty of Commerce and Navigation, and I will be misstaken, if there be not manifested, extraordinary proof of friendship towards the United States by France in that affair.

Most respectfully [etc.].

2666

Count de Sartiges, French Minister to the United States, to Lewis Cass, Secretary of State of the United States [2]

[TRANSLATION]

GEORGETOWN [D. C.], *March 12, 1859.*

SIR: Contradictory reports having reached Paris in regard to the relative position of the Governments of Nicaragua and Costa Rica and of various companies, one of which a French company, with which those two Governments, separately or by common agreement, have concluded contracts for turning to advantage the transit across the isthmus of Nicaragua, Count Walewski has asked me to let him know what is correct in the various assertions which have been made to him on this subject. I venture to hope, sir, that you will be so good as to excuse the liberty I take in addressing myself directly to you, officiously, [The French word, in the original, was, undoubtedly, "officieusement"—meaning "semi-officially" as well as "officiously."—Ed.] to inquire the opinion of the Government of the United States in regard to the position in which, according to its point of view, the various American companies, each claiming to be in exclusive possession of the grant of the privilege of turning to advantage the transit way from Greytown to San Juan del Sur, stand towards the Governments of Nicaragua and Costa Rica.

[1] It is thus in the original in the manuscript volume.
[2] Notes from France, vol. 17. The receipt date was not indicated.

It is only in a point of view of commercial interest that I have the honor to ask you for this information.

Accept, Sir, [etc.]

2667

John Y. Mason, United States Minister to France, to Lewis Cass, Secretary of State of the United States [1]

No. 394   PARIS, *May 16, 1859.*

SIR: I availed myself of the opportunity presented on Friday, by the weekly reception of the Ministry of Foreign Affairs, to converse with Count Walewski, on the several matters, which I desired to bring to His Excellency's notice.

I. I read to him, your instruction to myself, contained in your No. 179.[2]

I stated, that the course pursued by Sir William Gore Ousley, had not met the justification of the United States—and had not removed, the misunderstandings between the British and United States Governments on the subject of the Clayton-Bulwer Treaty. That these disagreements related to the Mosquito protectorate, and the British occupation of the Bay Islands. That what the Government of the United States insisted on, and expected was, that the Mosquito Indians, would be treated, as all the European Colonizing Nations had without exception, acted towards them, on the American Continent—that the aborigines had been regarded by none, as possessing the right of eminent Domain, or invested with the attributes of Independent Governments, with power to negotiate, Treaties, with extraterritorial nations. That as the Mosquito Territory is within the legitimate limits of Nicaragua, the United States expected Great Britain to relinquish the protectorate, and thus place the Mosquito Indians and their territory under the jurisdiction of that Republic, with such conditions as would secure the Indians remaining, from injustice.—

There seemed to be no reason to doubt, that these terms could be arranged, so as to obviate all just complaint, and remove a dangerous relation between the Indians, England and Nicaragua. I also alluded to the cession of the Bay Islands to Honduras, as a measure which the Government of the United States expected the British Government to effect.—That in urging these measures, my Government had been influenced by a disinterested regard for the welfare of the two sister Republics—and that there was yet reason to believe that the British Government would in good time, meet the expectations of the United States—And thus have the Treaty stipulations for the neutrality of transit routes across the Isthmus of Central America, in full force.

[1] Despatches, France, vol. 45. Received June 6.
[2] Above, this volume, pt. v, the second document dated April 12, 1859, doc. 2508.

That in regard to this principle of equal privilege and rights in the use to transit routes, open to all nations, by whomsoever executed, the policy of the United States was unchanged and unchangeable—That governed by no ungenerous or selfish motives, the Government of the United States, desired to see the physical advantages of the Isthmus, improved so as to give to the commerce of all Nations an open, neutral transit between the Atlantic and Pacific Ocean, with equal charge—that in obtaining this great end all that the United States would insist on with the Nicaraguan Government, is, that rights invested in Citizens of the United States, by that Government should be respected—that this duty to our citizens would be performed, and it was expected that all other nations would do the same, towards their citizens or subjects.   That a correspondence had recently taken place between the Count de Sartiges and Genl. Cass, on this part of the subject, and the Secretary of State, had frankly furnished the Emperor's Minister with an exposition of the views of his Government, on the question—which I presumed was already in His Excellency's hands.

That the precise object of my request, for an interview with His Excellency, was to communicate to the Imperial Government the facts, that the President had earnestly desired, in the most amicable and honorable manner to effect a Treaty, with Nicaragua—that the Cass-Irrisari [Irisarri] Treaty was negotiated with this object, and although signed more than eighteen months since, that Treaty had not yet been ratified, and the President could not regard the conduct of the Nicaraguan Government, but as insulting to the United States, as its acts had been oppressive and unjust to our citizens, that steam vessels placed in the waters of Nicaragua by Americans, to whom the right of navigation had been conceded, while engaged in the peaceful exercise of the granted right, had been seized, their officers and crews made prisoners, and the flag of the United States, ignominiously hauled down and that of Nicaragua hoisted in its place.   As a necessary consequence, grave complications had arisen, and I was instructed in a spirit of friendship and candor, to communicate to His Excellency, the copy of an instruction to the Minister of the United States at Managua, which would explain, the present condition of things, and the course, which the President felt compelled to adopt towards Nicaragua, if satisfactory reparation shall not be made.

I placed in His Excellency's hands, a copy of your letter addressed to Genl. Lamar, dated the 1st of april 1859,[1] and remarked, that after he had the opportunity to read it, I would be happy to converse more fully on the subject, when he had more leisure, if it should be his wish that I should do so. Count Walewski's manner was very kind and cordial, but he made few observations, and I preferred that receiving my general summary, he should carefully read the paper, which I left with him, before he replied.   I impressed on him, that my only object was to place in his possession facts and

[1] Above, vol. IV, doc. 1113.

purposes of my Government, which a high respect for the Imperial Government induced the President to desire to be communicated.

II. I then passed to the subject of the arrest of the French Consul at New Orleans. The Minister had received a report of the incident, and was entirely satisfied with the purport of your note to Count de Sartiges. I told him, that for reasons which I had stated to his predecessor, M. Drouyn de L'Huys [Lhuys], I had expected some such affair, resulting from the use, as synonimus, of words in the English and French texts of the Treaty, which did not mean the same thing—that the English word crime and the French word crime did not convey the same meaning, and that, while I always regretted anything which was unpleasant to France or the United States, in their intercourse, I really was gratified, that an affair, so harmless, had occurred, since it had led promptly to an agreed interpretation of the 2nd Article of the Treaty of 1853. That in future that Article would exempt French Consuls in the United States, from persecution for misdemeanors, and American Consuls in France would not be amenable for délits—that "Crime," in the French text would be regarded as synonimous with felonies, in the English. And that if Consuls of either country shall be guilty of misdemeanors or délits, tho: not subject to criminal persecution such measures may be taken, as might with propriety be taken by either Government, if such offence were committed by Diplomatic Agents.

His Excellency declared his entire satisfaction, with the answer given to the French Minister at Washington, and I feel confident, that no unpleasant consequences will follow. The enclosed slip taken from the Patrie of the 16th of May,[1] will show the moderate views of the French Press. On the subject of Nicaraguan affairs, the Minister will probably speak to me again. I will studiously impress on him, that it is only in a spirit of candid friendship, that the subject is mentioned; that we recognize no right in France, or any Foreign Government to supervise our proceedings with that Republic, and, observing justice and moderation we will maintain our rights and dignity, if the course of our neighbor shall make the vindication necessary. While we feel quite assured, that there will be no effort on the part of the Imperial Government to exercise a political protectorate, or controlling influence in Nicaragua, unfriendly, to us.

I have the honor [etc.].

[1] Not included in this publication.

2668

W. R. Calhoun, United States Chargé d'Affaires ad interim at Paris, to Lewis Cass, Secretary of State of the United States [1]

No. 5   PARIS, *November 7, 1859.*

SIR: The Minister of Foreign Affairs held his first fall reception on Friday last. I attended by invitation of His Excellency with the other members of the Diplomatic Corps now in Paris.

His Excellency's manner was particularly kind, and his allusions to the position here of the late Minister of the United States to France were in the most gratifying terms. In the course of conversation on Mexican Affairs, I alluded to the matter referred to in your Nº 194.[2] I related in as brief a manner as possible, some of the circumstances attending the change of direction of the Conducta which arrived at Vera Cruz in June last, and mentioned that it was stated that the course adopted by General Miramon was determined in concurrence with the Foreign Ministers at the City of Mexico—including necessarily the Minister of France. I remarked that I was sure if the facts are correctly stated, His Excellency will manifest his displeasure at this interference of His Majesty's Minister in Mexico. His Excellency received the remark with interest, and very frankly said he had not before received, any information on the subject.

I have the honor [etc.].

2669

W. R. Calhoun, United States Chargé d'Affaires ad interim at Paris, to Lewis Cass, Secretary of State of the United States [3]

[EXTRACT]

No. 24   PARIS, *February 28, 1860.*

SIR: . . . In your Despatch Nº 194 [4] you directed the late Mʳ Mason to refer incidentally in conversation with the Minister of Foreign Affairs, to the alledged conduct of the Minister of His Majesty the Emperor of France to Mexico in interfering with the internal affairs of that distracted republic. I have referred to the subject in two seperate conversations

[1] Despatches, France, vol. 46.   Received November 26.
W. R. Calhoun, the writer of this despatch, of South Carolina, was commissioned secretary of legation to France, September 15, 1857.   He acted as chargé d'affaires *ad interim* from October 3, 1859 to February 28, 1860.   He resigned November 15, 1860.
[2] Above, this volume, pt. v, September 19, 1859, doc. 2509.
[3] Despatches, France, vol. 46.   Received March 17.
The omitted portion refers to enclosed correspondence, from the French Admiral of Marine, regarding the forwarding of two collections of French nautical charts and instructions, one to be sent to the Naval Observatory at Washington, and the other to Commander Maury of the United States Navy.
[4] Above, this volume, pt. v, September 19, 1859, doc. 2509.

and the Count Walewski replied that he had no information on the subject.

Copies of communications were forwarded to me and in the accompanying despatch reference is made to a copy of a communication from the Minister of Mexico at Washington to the Hon. Secretary of State.[1] This copy was no doubt inadvertently left out of the envelope.

I did not feel authorised to furnished the information, contained in the communications further than was necessary to allude to the matter.

Mʳ Thouvenel, Minister of Foreign Affairs, has partially recovered from his indisposition and has been able to receive the Hon. Mʳ Faulkner.

His Majesty the Emperor has appointed Sunday next to receive His Excellency's letters of credence.

I have the honor [etc.].

2670

Charles J. Faulkner, United States Minister to France, to Lewis Cass, Secretary of State of the United States [2]

No. 24   PARIS, *May 28, 1860.*

SIR: Señor Herran, Minister Plenipotentiary for the States of Honduras and San Salvador, and Dʳ G. Holland, of New-York, recently paid me a visit in relation to the Honduras Inter Oceanic Railway Company, the latter with a letter of introduction from the American Consul at Liverpool. They made a very full and interesting exposition of the advantages of that Inter Oceanic route, and requested my cooperation in securing for it the favorable consideration of the Imperial Government of France. I informed them that I could take no official action on the subject, but they might rest well assured that the Government of the United States would look with the greatest favor upon every enterprise that was designed to multiply channels of communication, and to facilitate intercourse between the Pacific and Atlantic States of the Confederacy. They left expressing gratification at this assurance.

I have not yet seen the treaty which is said to have been concluded between the United States and Honduras on the 28ᵗʰ of March 1860, and in which a reference is alledged to have been made to this Inter Oceanic route. The last which has been received at this Legation, is the treaty with Paraguay concluded March 12ᵗʰ 1860.

Since my visit from Señor Herran and Dʳ Holland, they, and others interested with them, in this enterprise, have had an interview with the Emperor an account of which, taken from the London *Times,* I herewith send you.[3] It is more full in its details, and more accurate in its statements,

[1] See above, this volume, pt. v, p. 498, note 3.
[2] Despatches, France, vol. 47.   Received June 22.   [3] Not included in this publication.

as I have been assured by Señor Herran, than any account which has appeared in the Paris papers.

I am, very respectfully [etc.].

2671

Charles J. Faulkner, United States Minister to France, to Lewis Cass, Secretary of State of the United States [1]

No. 39   PARIS, *July 30, 1860.*

SIR: I was engaged to-day in preparing my Despatch No. 38 touching recent events in Southern Italy, and the proposed intervention by France on behalf of the Christians in Syria with a view to be forwarded this evening by the Adriatic, when I observed in the London *Times*, just received, a paragraph announcing that England and France had come to some understanding to interfere in the affairs of Mexico. I immediately left my Despatch unfinished, and called to see Mʳ Thouvenel, at the Ministry of Foreign Affairs, and inviting his attention to the paragraph which I had seen, I inquired of him as to the truth of the statement therein contained. He very promptly gave me the following explanation. He said the paragraph had reference to the action of the British and French Governments taken some months ago, and not to anything very recent; that England, France and Spain, perceiving that the commercial interests of their respective countries, as well as the rights of their citizens, were injuriously affected by the lawless and disorderly condition of affairs in Mexico, had proposed to unite in a common effort by the single exercise of their moral influence, to arrest the unfortunate state of things in that Republic, and if possible to restore a return to tranquillity and order. He declared that these Governments, in the movement referred to, had not the slightest idea of resorting to force or to material pressure of any kind in the accomplishment of the object sought. In making this Declaration, however, he said that, should all moral influence fail in restoring order in that Republic, those Governments reserved the right separately to protect the interests of their citizens in such manner as they might deem proper, should any emergency hereafter require it. He further stated that all the purposes of France in connexion with that proposed action in Mexico had been freely and frankly communicated to you through the French Chargé d'Affaires at Washington.[2]

I have the honor [etc.].

[1] Despatches, France, vol. 47.   Received August 13.
[2] See the reply of Cass to this despatch, above, this volume, pt. v, August 31, 1860, doc. 2510.

INDEX

INDEX

307–10; favorable impression left by him in Ecuador, 318.

Cyane, U. S. sloop of war, mentioned, 484–90.

Dallas-Clarendon Convention (1856) between U. S. and Great Britain, failure of ratification, 673–4.

Dalmatia, Duke of. *See* Soult.

Daniels [Danels?], John D., U. S. citizen, claim against Ecuador, mentioned, 274.

Darasse, P., French consul in Dominican Republic, opposes Dominican Republic granting U. S. coal depot on Samana Bay, 132–3, 143–6, 173; U. S. commissioner protests against his conduct, 142–3 and note, 157; Spain rewards him for his conduct, 178; informs Dominican Republic of conditions for continuing mediation in dispute with Haiti, 160 and note.

Daru, M., member, French National Assembly, mentioned, 603.

Davis, F. O., owner, U. S. merchant vessel *Lyons*, mentioned, 281.

Debrin, J., secretary, Dominican plenipotentiaries negotiating treaty with U. S., mentioned, 158 note.

Dacotah, American schooner, mentioned, 72.

Deffaudis, Baron, French Minister to Argentina and Mexico, mentioned, 437, 509; France dissatisfied with his conduct in Mexico, 518; his responsibility for failure of Hood's mission to Buenos Aires, 574, and France's disapproval of his conduct, 575.

Degalo, Dominican merchant vessel, mentioned, 217.

Delmonte, Manuel T., Dominican Minister of Foreign Affairs, correspondence, 57 note, 188; mentioned, 85; requests French protectorate over Dominican Republic, 52, 55–6 and note, 58 note; abandons idea of French protection, 63; seeks U. S. view of protection or annexation of Dominican Republic, 53; desires U. S. mediation in hostilities with Haiti, 72–5.

Democracia, La, Ecuadoran newspaper, mentioned, 235–6, 307, 359–60, 364–5.

Denison, William, head of band of American citizens colonizing on shore of Santiago River, mentioned, 323–5, 331–2.

Denmark, refuses to recognize U. S. consul at St. Thomas, 15; recognizes independence of Dominican Republic, 121; threatens blockade of Dominican ports, 195.

Devastation, British war vessel, mentioned, 131, 143–4.

Devoize, A., French chargé d'affaires at Montevideo, mentioned, 595 note, 598 note, 599–600.

Domicile in a foreign country, rights and duties attached to, 485–8.

Dominican Republic

African equality with American citizens in U. S. sought by, 22.

Aliens in. *See* Aliens.

Altavela Islet dispute with U. S. *See* Altavela *and* Guano.

American citizens and. *See* American citizens.

Asiatic immigration to, 209–10.

Baez, President of. *See* Baez.

Canary Islands emigration to, 212–13.

Carenero Chico harbor suggested as coal depot for U. S., 129.

Colonization of, by whites desired by Dominican Republic, 51; by blacks desired by Great Britain, 58–9.

Commercial conditions in, 120–1, 195.

Constitution sought to be revised by Baez to make him President for life, 181–2.

Courts of, 51.

Cuba and. *See* Cuba.

Denmark and. *See* Denmark.

European Powers, Dominican dependence upon, 120; loan sought by Dominican Republic, 194–5; consulates closed in Dominican Republic because of its failure to reunite with Haiti, 202–4, 206; suspected European domination of, 213–14.

Filibustering expeditions from U. S. to. *See* Filibustering expeditions.

France, suggested protection of Dominican Republic, 10, 42–3, 47 and note, 52–3, 55, 56 and note, 57, 63–4, 182–3; opposed by U. S., 48, 50, 52, 55–6, by Great Britain, 43, 57–8 and note; France seeks control over, and alliance with, 39, 115–18; Dominican dependence upon France, 120; U. S. seeks information as to agreements between, 32–4; commercial treaty (1852) concluded, 41; not ratified by France, 67; ratified by Dominican Republic, 117; analysis of treaty, 124; France considered unfriendly to Dominican Republic, 71; relations between, 121–2; Monroe Doctrine's effect upon these relations, 122; France desires Dominican Republic to assume part of Haitian debt to France, 78–9; Dominican Republic refuses, 78–9; French citizens deported as spies, 117; alleged French interference in domestic affairs of, 117–19, 188, 479; interference denied by France, 652; contract of French company to work mines of, 192–5; France presses claims against, 200–1, 206–7; Dominican Republic suggested as French colony, 209. *See also* Haiti, Independence, Spain *and* United States *under this title*.

Dominican Republic (*continued*)
Government of, described, 27–9.
Great Britain, suggested protection of Dominican Republic, 43, 182–3; protection refused by Great Britain, 49; Dominican dependence upon Great Britain, 120; commercial treaty (1849) concluded, 5–7, 41, 49–50, 67–8; treaty rejected by Dominican Republic and negotiations renewed, 67–8, 76; ratified by Dominican Republic, 87, 89; analysis of treaty, 124; its effect upon U. S. trade with Dominican Republic, 87, 89–90; Great Britain seeks control over, 39, 44; considered unfriendly to, 71; contract of British company to work mines of, 192–5; Great Britain presses claims against, 200–1, 206–7. *See also* France, Haiti, Independence, Spain and United States *under this title*.
Guano deposits on Altavela Islet. *See* Altavela *and* Guano.
Haiti, war of independence of Dominican Republic between, 3, 27, 30–1, 38, 42, 85, 155; reasons for separation of the two countries, 27–9; relations between, 16, 119; Haitian claims to Dominican territory, 84–5, sustained by Great Britain and France, 155; Dominican ability to maintain itself against Haiti, 87, 89, 155; Haitian invasions of Dominican Republic, 42, 46–8, 54–5, 59, 61, 78, 88–91, 110, 110–11 note, 126–7, 194, 212, 214, opposed by U. S., 10, 59, 70, 77, 79, countenanced by France, 44; Haiti's reasons for invasions, 59; effect of invasions upon U. S. commerce, 60–1, upon Haitian commerce, 123; British, French and U. S. proposals for peace, 11–14, 45, 57, 59–60, 61–4, 69–75, 82, 83–4 note, 87–91, 93–4, 96–7, 96 note, 97–101, 99–100 note, 101–4, 101–3 note, 104–5 and note, 108 note, 114–15, 127, 129, 133, 143–4, 160 and note, 198, 457–9, 477, 618–19; Haitian appreciation of proposals, 109; Haiti's official actions on, and rejection of, proposals, 105–9, 107–9 and note, 111–13, 143–4; Spain suggested as mediator, 71; Spanish proposals for peace, 168, rejected by Dominican Republic, 168; Haitian proposals for peace, 83–4, 114 note, 171–2, rejected by Dominican Republic, 112, 114–15 note; advantages of U. S. intercession, 86–7; message of President Fillmore regarding peace between, cited, 111–15; union between, urged by France, 22–3, 44, 66–7, 189–90 and note, 201–2, 208, 218–19, by Spain, 201–2, by Great Britain, 66–7, 79, 80 and note, 81, 201–2, opposed by U. S., 14, 59, forced by Haiti, 28, 29–31; effect of union upon U. S., 59–60;

British proposals for union rejected by Dominican Republic, 81–2 note; failure of union, 203–4, 206; U. S. suggests treaty between, 208; boundary settlement between, 218. *See also* Baez, France, Great Britain, Independence, Spain *and* United States *under this title*.
Independence of, declared by Dominican Republic, 27, 38; Dominican attempts to establish, 29–31, 94–6; maintenance of, considered improbable, 203–4; suggested recognition by U. S., 3, 27–9, 31–2, 45, 53, 76–7, 79, 117, 129, 199, 204–5 note, 207–8, 214, refused by U. S., 3, 10, 23–4, 48, 117; suggested recognition by Haiti, 94–6, 194–5, refused by Haiti, 3, 30–1; recognition by France, 45, 121, by Great Britain, 45, 121, by Denmark, 121, by the Netherlands, 121. *See also* Haiti *under this title*.
Indians, proposed immigration to, 209–10.
Military conditions in, 121.
Netherlands, treaty of peace, friendship, commerce and navigation with, analyzed, 124; recognizes independence of, 121.
Political conditions in, 43–8, 50, 66, 75–6, 115, 120, 163–4, 181–4, 187–9, 194, 199–200, 204–6, 205 note, 216. *See also* Baez, Santana, Segovia.
Population of, 50.
Progress of, since separation from Haiti, 85, 204–5 note; dependent upon Spanish decision on protectorate, 210.
Puerto Rico, suspected union between, 213–14.
Racial conditions in, 38–9, 58–9, 86, 122–3.
Religious toleration in, suggested in treaties with, 67–8.
Samana Bay, proposed cession. *See* Samana Bay.
Spain, Dominican separation from, 28, 29; suggested Spanish protectorate, 119, 125, 168, 182–3, 210, 212, 214, 215; Spain accepts protectorate, 209, 214, 216, 219 note; Dominican opposition to protectorate, 168, 215–16; suggested alliance between, 115–17; Spanish interference in Dominican internal affairs, 168–71, 173–5, 180, 182–3, 188, 200; treaty (1855) concluded preventing aliens from obtaining concessions in Dominican Republic, 163; difficulties as to meaning of treaty, 167, 169; Spain offers citizenship to all who ask for it in Dominican Republic, 167–8, 172, 175; Spanish claims against, 200–1, 206–7; Dominican Republic suggested as Spanish colony, 209; Spanish emigration to, 212–13; Spanish loan obtained, 215, 216; U. S. seeks information as to relations between, 32–4, 64–6. *See*

Nicaraguan ship canal and transit route
(*continued*)
Construction contracts for, 494; U. S.
views on, 496–8.
France's cooperation in guaranteeing protection of, sought by U. S., 454–6,
604–16, 678–9, 694–5; alleged treaty
between France and Nicaragua regarding, 693, 696. *See also* Belly,
Clayton-Bulwer Treaty.
United States policy toward, 493–4, 602,
700–2. *See also* France *under this title*.
Nicolson, Commodore, commanding U. S.
squadron off Buenos Aires, 523, 534.
Nuñez de Caseres, José, Haitian Lieut.
Governor and Auditor of War, mentioned, 29–31.

Obligado, L', French brig, mentioned, 303.
Ocoa bay [Dominican Republic], mentioned
as possible coal depot for U. S., 196.
Olaguibel, Mexican Minister to France,
mentioned, 675–6, 678–90.
Olivier, French citizen, claim against U. S.
for its treatment of him in taking
possession of California, 453–4, 578–9.
Orejuela, Ramón María, Colombian consul
general in Ecuador, mentioned, 419,
422.
Oribe, Gen. Manuel, claimant to presidency
of Uruguay, mentioned, 571–2, 593.
Orleans, Duchess of, mentioned, 508.
Ouseley, Sir William Gore, British Minister
to Central America, mentioned, 495–6.

Paez, Gen. José Antonio, President of
Venezuela, Flores relations with, 266.
Pageot, Alphonse Joseph Yver, French
Minister to U. S., correspondence,
453–4, 578–9.
Pakenham, Richard, British Minister to
U. S., mentioned, 443–4.
Palmer, Aaron H., Ecuadoran consul general in U. S., correspondence, 296–7,
429.
Palmerston, Lord, British Secretary of
State for Foreign Affairs, mentioned,
43, 49, 67–8, 88, 91, 272 note, 458,
508–9, 582, 602.
Pampero, steamship used in expedition
from U. S. to Cuba, 460.
Panama ship canal and transit route, U. S.
seeks France's cooperation in securing
protection of, 454–6, 490, 604–9;
French support for construction of,
sought by Atlantic and Pacific Junction
Company, 650–1 and note.
Pandour, French brig of war, mentioned,
583–9.
Paraná River, treaty between U. S. and
Argentina for free navigation of, cited,
360–1.
Paris Declaration of 1856, U. S. instructions
and objections to Ecuador's adhesion

to, 236, 382–7, *see also* vol. I, pt. I,
docs. 32 and 34, pp. 46 and 50; U. S.
proposes amendment of declaration to
Ecuador, 387–9, 387 note, 395–6;
Ecuador's attitude toward U. S. proposed amendment, 390–1, 397–8, 403;
Ecuador adheres to declaration without
amendment, 391–4; U. S. abandons
attempt to have Ecuador amend
declaration, 403–4, and suggests amendment as additional article to neutral
rights at sea convention (1856) between
U. S. and Ecuador, 403–5; U. S. proposed amendment of declaration recognized in treaty (1856) between Colombia and Costa Rica, 391, and accepted
by France, Great Britain and Russia,
396.
Parish, Robert A., Jr., American citizen,
mentioned, 22.
Parker, Commodore Foxhall A., U. S. N.
mentioned, 76, 79.
Pasto province, dispute between Colombia
and Ecuador for possession of, 269.
Patrie, French newspaper, mentioned, 644,
689, 691.
Patriota, Spanish brig, mentioned, 65.
Paulding, Capt. Hiram, U. S. N., mentioned,
174–5.
Paz, De, Spanish chargé d'affaires in Ecuador, protests against guano treaty between U. S. and Ecuador, 339–40,
342, 354–5, 380–1.
Pedro I, Emperor of Brazil, abdication,
503–4 and note, 506; Spain opposes his
return to Portugal, 503 note; seeks to
return to throne of Portugal, 503–4 and
note; Brazil opposes his return to
Brazilian throne, 504 note.
Pedro II, Emperor of Brazil, succeeds to
Brazilian throne, 503–4 and note.
Pelaez, General, Spanish military representative in Dominican Republic, 215.
Pellion, Commodore Alphonse, commander,
French naval forces on western coasts
of America, correspondence, 295 note.
Penelope, French frigate, mentioned, 286,
296, 302, 306 note.
Perdomo, Mateo, member, Dominican
Congress, mentioned, 157 note.
Pereira, Jacob, acting U. S. commercial
agent to Dominican Republic, correspondence, 170–2, 175–85.
Periodico Oficial, Ecuadoran newspaper,
mentioned, 313–14.
Perle, French sloop of war, mentioned, 524,
526.
Pernetti, member, British Academy of
Sciences, historiographer on Bougainville's expedition to Falkland Islands,
mentioned, 506.
Perry, U. S. brig, mentioned, 590 note.
Persian, British brig of war, mentioned, 64,
80.